WITH MY FACE
TO THE ENEMY

✦

ESSAYS BY
David Herbert Donald, Gary W. Gallagher,
James M. McPherson, Stephen W. Sears,
and Others

EDITED BY
Robert Cowley

WITH MY FACE TO THE ENEMY

PERSPECTIVES ON THE CIVIL WAR

G. P. PUTNAM'S SONS
NEW YORK

G. P. Putnam's Sons
Publishers Since 1838
a member of
Penguin Putnam Inc.
375 Hudson Street
New York, NY 10014

All essays were previously published in *MHQ: The Quarterly Journal of
Military History*. The following were excerpted from books and are reprinted
by permission of the publishers: "Lincoln Takes Charge" from David
Herbert Donald, *Lincoln,* Simon & Schuster. "Packs Down—Charge!"
from Paddy Griffith, *Battle Tactics of the Civil War,* Yale University Press.
"Lord High Admiral of the U.S. Navy" from Joseph T. Glatthaar, *Partners
in Command: The Relationships Between Leaders in the Civil War,* Free Press.
All other essays are reprinted by permission of the authors.

Maps by MapQuest.com, Inc.

Library of Congress Cataloging-in-Publication Data

With my face to the enemy : perspectives on the Civil War : essays /
David Herbert Donald . . . [et al.]; edited by Robert Cowley.
p.   cm.
ISBN 0-399-14737-3
1. United States—History—Civil War, 1861–1865.
I. Donald, David Herbert, date.   II. Cowley, Robert.
E468.W76   2001   00-053358
973.7—dc21

Printed in the United States of America

1   3   5   7   9   10   8   4   2

This book is printed on acid-free paper. ♾

BOOK DESIGN BY DEBORAH KERNER/DANCING BEARS DESIGN

ACKNOWLEDGMENTS

I wish to express my special thanks to Byron Hollinshead and Sabine Russ at American Historical Publications for their assistance in all aspects of the development of this book. I also want to thank those who, during the ten years I edited *MHQ: The Quarterly Journal of Military History,* contributed so much: Marleen Adlerblum, Barbara Benton, Catherine Burnett, Susan Chitwood, Tamara Glenny, Douglas Hill, Tania Inowlocki, Michele Mancuso, Elihu Rose, Edna Shalev, Richard Slovak, Edward M. Strauss III, and John Tarkov—as well as the present staff of *MHQ,* Rod Paschall, Roger L. Vance, and Christopher Anderson.

R.C.

CONTENTS

LIST OF MAPS   xi

INTRODUCTION · ROBERT COWLEY   xiii

I. FIRST SHOTS

    Lincoln Takes Charge · David Herbert Donald   3

    Band of Brothers: The West Point Corps · Thomas Fleming   27

    The Ordeal of General Stone · Stephen W. Sears   41

II. THE STRATEGIC VIEW

    What Took the North So Long? · Williamson Murray   59

    Failed Southern Strategies · James M. McPherson   72

    How Lincoln Won the War with Metaphor · James M. McPherson   87

III. 1862 AND 1863: BLOODY YEARS

    Grant's Tennessee Gamble · Geoffrey Perret   105

    Malvern Hill · Stephen W. Sears   122

    The Last Word on the Lost Order · Stephen W. Sears   145

    Defending Marye's Heights · Joseph H. Alexander   160

    A Hellish Start to the Year:

        The Battle of Stones River · Tom Wicker   177

    Stonewall Jackson's Last March · Stephen W. Sears   190

    The Antagonists of Little Round Top:

        The Victor · Gideon Rose   218

        The Other Man · Glenn W. LaFantasie   227

    Packs Down—Charge!

        The Frontal Attack · Paddy Griffith   238

IV. LEADERS AND THEIR BATTLES

When Lee Was Mortal · Gary W. Gallagher   245

The Stonewall Enigma · John Bowers   261

Lord High Admiral of the U.S. Navy:
    David Dixon Porter on the Mississippi · Joseph T. Glatthaar   273

Grant at Vicksburg:
    A Lesson in Operational Art · Joseph T. Glatthaar   298

Hawk in the Fowlyard: Jeb Stuart · John M. Taylor   307

The Rock of Chickamauga: George H. Thomas · John Bowers   320

Considering Longstreet's Legacy · Glenn W. LaFantasie   332

Paladin of the Republic:
    Philip H. Sheridan · Paul Andrew Hutton   348

V. THE LAST ACT

The Andersonvilles of the North · Philip Burnham   367

"Kill the Last Damn One of Them":
    The Fort Pillow Massacre · Noah Andre Trudeau   382

The Boys of New Market · Geoffrey Norman   395

The Walls of 1864 · Noah Andre Trudeau   412

The Fiery Trail of the *Alabama* · John M. Taylor   429

Jubal Early's Raid on Washington · Charles C. Osborne   443

The Crater · John M. Taylor   459

The Battle of Westport · Noah Andre Trudeau   472

The Second Surrender:
    Bennitt's Farm, North Carolina · John M. Taylor   486

Rebel Without a War: The *Shenandoah* · Robert F. Jones   498

Ulysses S. Grant's Final Victory · James M. McPherson   511

LIST OF MAPS

Northern Strategy   63

Grant's Campaign   111

The Battle of Malvern Hill   133

The Battle of Fredericksburg   164

The Confederates' Natural Defense   165

The Battle of Stones River   185

Jackson's March at Chancellorsville   199

Grant's Vicksburg Campaign   282

The Battle of New Market   400

The Shenandoah Valley—1864   401

The Overland Campaign   415

The Wilderness   418

The Battle of Spotsylvania   422

North Anna River   423

The Battle of Cold Harbor   427

Early's Raid on Washington   447

The Battle of the Crater   463

The Battle of Westport   478

The Confederacy's Last Days   491

The Cruise of the CSS *Shenandoah*   504

INTRODUCTION

ROBERT COWLEY

THE CYCLE OF INTEREST IN THE CIVIL WAR HAS COME AROUND again, as inevitable as a wheel turning, and the indications are that it won't soon go away. It's easy enough to point to the harbingers. James M. McPherson's best-selling *Battle Cry of Freedom* has become the standard history for our generation; Shelby Foote's three-volume narrative, *The Civil War,* has enjoyed a well-deserved resurgence and is now accorded classic status. The novel *Cold Mountain* by Charles Frazier, an account of a Confederate deserter's attempt to reach home in the last winter of the war, remained on bestseller lists for months. Nothing, perhaps, left an impression on the public more vivid than Ken Burns's PBS television series on the war. There are now hundreds of Civil War websites. Battlefields are thronged with tourists and weekend reenactors. (Recently, driving home from the commuter train, I noted a sign advertising a Civil War encampment—in Connecticut.) A grand new museum of the Civil War has just opened in Harrisburg, Pennsylvania. Notable sites, once threatened by developers' bulldozers, have been preserved. The toppling of the observation tower at Gettysburg, long regarded as an eyesore, became national news, as was the accidental unearthing of a Union soldier's bones at the same battlefield. He was reburied with full military honors.

Meanwhile, in what amounts to an historical stock exchange, reputations soar or plummet: the current re-examination of Robert E. Lee's generalship, not all of it complimentary, is a case in point, and something that would have been unthinkable in an earlier era. Issues such as the considerable roles of women or African-Americans receive attention previously denied them; overlooked battles are no longer forgotten. Scarcely a week passes without a new work on some aspect or personality of the war, both great and trivial. I would hazard a guess that if you examine the estimated 70,000 titles on the subject that have appeared since 1865, you will find clusters that rise to a peak every thirty years or so. (The Vietnam War, in which all things military fell into disrepute, may have stretched out the most recent interval; but in general the rule holds.) The Civil War is an event so big that each generation can find a new way to look at it.

Should we wonder at such renewed enthusiasm? It is, the lawyer-historian Alan T. Nolan writes, "a folk epic told over and over again." No event on this continent, not even the American Revolution, was quite so important or had so many future repercussions. The Civil War finally brought us together as a nation, made us truly a "union"—though, alas, it did not resolve the issue that caused it, race. "The Civil War," Robert Penn Warren observed, "is our only 'felt' history—history lived in the national imagination."

I confess to being a Civil War addict, even if the affliction has not seized me as violently as it has some. I've always disliked the dismissive term "Civil War buff," which seems unfairly to separate the historian from the enthusiast. Historians should be enthusiasts and enthusiasts historians: They have much to teach one another.

I came on the war when I was nine or ten, probably through the historical novels for boys of Joseph A. Altsheler, a name little remembered these days: Although his cliff-hangers dangle over a lyrically evoked early American landscape, the attitudes of his characters would never pass current political correctness tests. Altsheler produced a series on the Civil War, in which the alternating heroes were a Southern teenager and his Northern cousin. The novel that I remember best was called *The Guns of Bull Run,* but the fact that the wrong side came out on top gave me diminished pleasure. I grew up in what was once rural Connecticut, a part of the world where many towns seem to be built around Civil War memorials; a predisposition to the Union is almost genetic.

My father was a more reasonable mentor. He was a writer, and when I returned from school in the afternoon and he had finished work, we'd take long walks, a daily ritual. A man reserved and formidably inscrutable, he seemed most comfortable when telling me how to identify an oak from the five points of its leaf or what Lee had done wrong at Gettysburg. I could almost picture the cannons wheel by wheel at the wooded verges of those New England fields and tiers of muskets poking from behind stone walls. I think my father enjoyed my curiosity about the war. History sometimes seemed the one thing that cemented our too-often distant relationship.

With his encouragement, Ulysses S. Grant became my hero, though as far as I was concerned, the life of the Union commander could have ended the evening following the famous Palm Sunday afternoon meeting with Lee at Appomattox. Boys are seldom interested in aftermaths. Grant, as I would learn much later, disproved F. Scott Fitzgerald's adage that there are no second acts in American lives. (My father had *his* father's two-volume leather-bound set of Grant's *Personal Memoirs;* I still own it.) Other candidates for my pantheon were Philip Sheridan, who was too nasty to deify, and William Tecumseh Sherman, who was too enigmatic—the very quality that intrigues me so much about him now. My father's favorite was George H. Thomas, "The Rock of Chickamauga," the Virginian who remained with the Union and destroyed two Confederate armies in Tennessee—which now strikes me as a locus of contention nearly as important as Virginia. Thomas became a hero too, and it should come as no surprise that you'll find an article about him in this anthology. Lee and his lieutenants? I could never warm to them—except, perhaps, to that strange, difficult, military genius, Stonewall Jackson. Don't worry: I've tried not to allow my pro-Union prejudices to influence my choice of articles.

In the mid-1950s my father and I toured the eastern Civil War battlefields. I should explain how the trip came about. He had a novelist friend named Hamilton Basso, who came from New Orleans—one of his first books was a biography of the Confederate general P. T. Beauregard—but had settled in Connecticut. His novel *The View from Pompey's Head* was a bestseller at the time. Ham was a person I admired, and I can still play back from memory his softly positive drawl, with just the hint of a lisp in it. Every year the Bassos would invite me to spend a couple of days at their place. During one of those stays, just before my senior year at college, Ham and I got into an intense discussion of the Civil War: It was time, he said, for me to look at the event as Southerners experienced it. Just before I left, he took me into his study and wrote me a check for a hundred dollars—which would have approached five hundred today. "I want you to use this to look at battlefields," he said.

I did. My father kicked in more money, and the two of us went off for a week. We spent two days at Gettysburg. (Other people I've met over the years also went with *their* parents: I've begun to think that a visit to Gettysburg is a specially American rite of passage.) At midweek in early September forty-six years ago, there were few people in evidence; the earth at the summit of Little Round Top—a spot that receives much attention in these pages—was not trampled bare then, the price of the newfound notoriety bestowed on it by Michael Shaara's novel *The Killer Angels,* in which the rocky eminence plays a central part. We continued on to Antietam, magical in its emptiness; it still was, and to this day remains, one of the purest military sites in America. (Stephen W. Sears's "The Last Word on the Lost Order" is a fine accounting of the accident that led to the battle's being fought there.)

One afternoon near the end of our trip we stopped along the edge of the national park road that ran through the Wilderness in northern Virginia. Following old trenches, we wandered deep into what was still a jungle of second- and third-growth timber, ominously claustrophobic. The imprints of ancient violence had not disappeared. We had a sense of what men on both sides must have felt in one of the worst, and most confusing, battles of the war, when the enemy was everywhere and nowhere, and even the woods caught fire. (Noah Andre Trudeau covers this story in "The Walls of 1864.") Today you can look into those same recesses and see merely new subdivisions. The trenches, perceptibly shallower now, stop at the edge of the backyards, and the only monuments in sight are playsets.

The following year I applied for a job at *American Heritage.* One of the people who interviewed me was Bruce Catton, who at that time had established himself as the preeminent popular historian of the Civil War. Bruce, a baldish man with a graying mustache and rimless glasses, spoke in a wry Midwestern voice. We discussed, mercifully, not my ambitions but the battlefields I'd recently visited. We talked about The Bloody Angle of Spotsylvania, where hand-to-hand combat had gone on for a day and a night. The savagery of the war, he said, was something that continually amazed him. Catton repeated a story told him by an aged veteran when he was growing up. It seemed that a hungry Confederate marauder had been stealing food from the Union encampment. One day he was caught.

"So what did you do?" young Catton asked.

"We cut his nuts off and let him go."

I did get the job at *American Heritage,* and worked with Bruce, though I was never as close to him as Stephen W. Sears was. Sears and I were separated by a partition. It was Bruce, Steve told me not long ago, who got him interested in Civil War history and who later encouraged him to write about the war. The books Sears has produced over the years—on the Peninsula campaign, Antietam, Chancellorsville, as well as his biography of George McClellan—add up to one of the most complete pictures of the war in the East yet limned. We are fortunate to include a number of Sears's narratives, including the dolorous tale of Charles P. Stone, a decent commander undone by enemies on his own side; the Battle of Malvern Hill, where Lee ordered what might be thought of as his first Pickett's Charge; and an account of Stonewall Jackson's left hook out of nowhere at Chancellorsville, the classic American battle maneuver.

It was that conversation with Sears that led me, out of curiosity, to ask other contributors to this anthology how they first became attracted to the Civil War. For some, like Noah Andre Trudeau, it was the accident of place. Trudeau, who has worked almost twenty-five years for National Public Radio in Washington, D.C., started to wander nearby battlefields. He sought out spots where commanders had directed actions or soldier memoirists had fought, always asking himself the question "What did he feel like?" That is easier to do in some battlefields than in others. At Petersburg, he points out, the trenches and the famous crater "look like speed bumps." But in places like North Anna or Cold Harbor, where what he calls "the walls of 1864" run through wooded areas not yet threatened by suburbanization, it's still possible to have a sense of the landscape where armies collided.

For people like John Bowers, the author of articles on Jackson and Thomas, tradition plays a major role. Bowers grew up in Tennessee and had a grandfather and great-uncle who fought on opposite sides: The war, he says, "was an event that happened just down the road. It was part of the oral lore of my family, handed down through generations." Where tradition did not exist—not all the contributors to this book can boast of Civil War ancestors—there were always books: Few events in history have been picked over so exhaustively. Many of the writers represented here came to the Civil War through reading. When John M. Taylor was sixteen, for example, he had to spend a week in bed recovering from an operation. He devoured—that's the best word for it—all three volumes of Douglas Southall Freeman's *Lee's Lieutenants*. His father, Maxwell D. Taylor, was superintendent of West Point at the time, and Jack went to the Academy library, where he started to read all he could find on the war. He remembers the original Appomattox surrender correspondence between Lee and Grant, both West Pointers, on swinging glass panels, which you could read on both sides. The panels were next to a sunny window, "something that would make curators blanch today," he says. The documents have long since been removed from public view—and the fatal sun. Taylor writes here not about that surrender, but a less well-known but even bigger one that occurred more than two weeks later at the Bennitt farm in North Carolina, where the Confederate commander Joseph E. Johnston made terms with Sherman and began a friendship that would last the rest of their lives.

Gary W. Gallagher, whose article "When Lee Was Mortal" appears in the section "Leaders and Their Battles," teaches Civil War history at the University of Virginia and is one of our most esteemed authorities on the subject. He grew up on a farm in southern Colorado, far from any battlefield. He'd seen articles in *National Geographic* on Vicksburg and Gettysburg, and at age ten started to save money for *The American Heritage Picture History of the Civil War*, with text by Bruce Catton. The book appeared in 1960, and was crammed with color illustrations and specially drawn maps: It cost what now seems an unbelievably modest $19.95. But for a young boy, the price represented months of saving. At that point Gallagher began to buy, borrow, and cadge everything he could find on the war. A lawyer in his small town learned of his interest and lent him books. A few years later, during a summer interval between growing seasons, Gallagher's father said that he could go with his mother and grandmother to visit Civil War sites—if he promised to be back in twelve days. The boy and the two women made it all the way to Virginia and Gettysburg, and got back in time.

James M. McPherson's discovery of the Civil War came about the same time as Gallagher's. "Curiously enough," McPherson says, "my interest began during the Centennial in 1961 but was not because of it." The civil rights movement was his impetus. A graduate student in American history at Johns Hopkins University, he was struck by the parallels between the racial conflicts of the 1960s and those a hundred years earlier. (McPherson was involved in local demonstrations in Maryland—but, as he says, "I was just a foot soldier in the ranks.") His research focused on the Abolitionists, those civil rights activists of the 1850s. "That led me like an arrow to the Civil War." You will find three contributions by McPherson in this anthology, including a moving account—that's a worsened word but one that is quite fitting here—of my old hero Grant's race with death to finish his memoirs, and an extraordinary essay, "How Lincoln Won the War with Metaphor." Language, as McPherson points out, can have a strategic effect, and great war leaders like Lincoln, FDR, and Winston Churchill shared a sure instinct for words that not just inspired but literally guided their side to victory.

When I was editor of *MHQ: The Quarterly Journal of Military History*, I learned early on to expect howls of protests from my readers if I did not include at least one article per issue on some aspect of the Civil War. My able successor, Rod Paschall, has kept to that policy. This book is the result. I could point to other articles here that sum up some of my criteria of choice. I was constantly on the lookout for viewpoints unjustifiably ignored. Joseph H. Alexander's account of the Battle of Fredericksburg as the Confederates experienced it is a perfect example—as is Philip Burnham's essay on the lethal Union prison camps, "The Andersonvilles of the North." It is a truism that no two people bear the same witness to an event, and there is a *Rashomon*-like quality to the paired articles by Gideon Rose and Glenn W. LaFantasie on the antagonists of Little Round Top, the fight on the second day of Gettysburg that may have determined the outcome of the battle as much as Pickett's Charge. Can this be the same encounter we're reading about? Too, certain battles deserve more attention. Take the New Year's 1863 barroom brawl at Stones River—or Murfreesboro, as it is sometimes known—that Tom Wicker describes. This hungover holiday confrontation in the freezing Tennessee mist cost both sides nearly as many men as the more famous Shiloh. I also felt that the naval war deserves more attention than it usually receives. There were dazzling encounters, like that of the Confederate raider *Alabama* and the USS *Kearsarge* off Cherbourg described in Taylor's "The Fiery Trail of the *Alabama*." But more often it was a matter of gunboats patrolling, and controlling, rivers and the necessary boredom of a blockade that contributed as much as land battles to the defeat of the Confederacy. That is a facet of the war that Williamson Murray takes up in "What Took the North So Long?"—as good a piece on the strategy of the war as you'll ever find.

No doubt future generations will revise our revisions. The Civil War is the turning point in our history that will never cease turning. That is the way it should be.

✦

*Major, tell my father that I died
with my face to the enemy.*

✦

COLONEL I. E. AVERY, C.S.A.,

ATTRIBUTED,

JULY 2, 1863

Gettysburg, Pennsylvania

✦

I

FIRST SHOTS

LINCOLN TAKES CHARGE

DAVID HERBERT DONALD

Eighteen sixty-one began as the year of indecision. It was a year of inept-ness, of groping for solutions, of opportunities missed. It was also one of the most important years in American history. By the time Abraham Lin-coln, the victorious presidential candidate of the young Republican Party, took office on March 4, seven Deep South states had already seceded and four more would shortly follow; key border states were up for grabs. For months, the outgoing administration of James Buchanan dithered and did nothing. Then, on January 9, when the *Star of the West,* carrying supplies and troops, attempted to reach Fort Sumter in Charleston Harbor, South Carolinian batteries fired on the ship and forced it to turn back. Even these first real shots of what would soon be-come a civil war hardly seemed to jolt Washington out of its torpor. But the new incumbent, a fifty-two-year-old Midwestern lawyer with little administrative, legislative, or military experience, gave scant promise of more effective leadership. There were army sharpshooters on the roofs as the outgoing and incoming presidents drove in a carriage up Pennsyl-vania Avenue to the still domeless capital where Lincoln would deliver his inaugural address. "If you are as happy, my dear sir," Buchanan re-marked, "on entering this house as I am in leaving it and returning home, you are the happiest man in this country."

Happy Lincoln was not; the tensions of office brought on insomnia and fainting spells. Indeed, he would bungle the first crisis of his ad-ministration—Fort Sumter. As the distinguished historian David Her-bert Donald points out, he may even have made it worse—though by this time there was probably no preventing the final breakup of the union. At 4:30 A.M. on Friday, April 12, artillerymen of the newly pro-claimed Confederacy commenced firing on Sumter, which officially ca-pitulated three days later. Lincoln promptly called on the loyal states to supply him with 75,000 militiamen. (There was no formal declaration of war: in his mind this was not a war but a rebellion.) Increasingly, Lincoln would take charge, and that is the story, surely one of the great American stories, that Professor Donald has to tell.

David Herbert Donald is the Charles Warren Professor Emeritus of American History and Civilization at Harvard University. "Lincoln Takes Charge" was excerpted from his biography, *Lincoln*. He is a two-time winner of the Pulitzer Prize for biography, for *Charles Sumner and the Coming of the Civil War* and for *Look Homeward: A Life of Thomas Wolfe*. He is also the author of *Lincoln's Herndon, Lincoln Reconsidered,* and editor of *Why the North Won the Civil War.*

AT THE NEWS OF ABRAHAM LINCOLN'S ELECTION IN 1860, disunion erupted in the South. South Carolina promptly moved to secede, and the other states of the Lower South began to take initial steps toward secession. A few Northerners thought the dissatisfied states should be allowed— even encouraged—to go in peace. A much larger number favored a new agreement, in the spirit of the Missouri Compromise and the Compromise of 1850, that would keep the Southern states in the Union. At least as many others opposed any concessions to the South.

President James Buchanan was torn between his belief that secession was unconstitutional and his conviction that nothing could be done to prevent it. The lame-duck Congress was controlled by the recently formed Republican Party, a still imperfect fusion of former Whigs, former Democrats, and former members of the American Party. With experience only as an opposition party, Republicans had never before been called on to offer constructive leadership. All eyes now turned to Springfield, Illinois, where an inexperienced leader with a limited personal acquaintance among members of his own party groped his way, on the basis of inadequate information, to formulate a policy for his new administration.

Over the next three months, Lincoln issued no public statements and made no formal addresses. At most he could be cajoled only into offering bland observations: "Let us at all times remember that all American citizens are brothers of a common country, and should dwell together in the bonds of fraternal feeling." Behind his silence lay a recognition of his own weakness: the presidential electors did not meet until December 5, and their ballots would not be officially counted until February 13. Until then, he had no legal standing as a public official.

He was also following the advice of most leaders of his party. Any indication that he was frightened by Southern bluster might inadvertently cause demoralization and panic in the North. In addition, Lincoln believed that Unionists were in a large majority throughout the South and that, given time for tempers to cool, they would be able to defeat the secessionist conspirators. He did not believe that any sizable number of rational citizens could contemplate disrupting the best government the world had ever seen. In the past, Southerners had threatened to dissolve the Union in order to extract concessions from the North. That must be what was happening now.

While Lincoln was constructing his cabinet—trying to balance it both politically and geographically to maintain peace among the competing interest groups that constituted the Republican Party—the country was falling to pieces. On December 6, South Carolinians elected an overwhelmingly secessionist state convention, which on December 20 declared that state was no longer a part of the Union. By the end of January, Florida, Mississippi, Alabama, Georgia, and Louisiana all followed, and secession was under way in Texas. In February, representatives of six states met at Montgomery, Alabama, and drew up a constitution for the new Confederate States of America. As the Southern states seceded, they seized federal arsenals and forts within their borders. Of the major installations, only Fort Pickens at Pensacola, Florida, and the fortifications at Charleston, South Carolina, remained under the control of the U.S. government. Late in December, Major Robert Anderson, in command at Fort Moultrie on the shoreline at Charleston, transferred his small garrison to the more defensible Fort Sumter, erected on a rock shoal in the harbor. On January 9, when the *Star of the West,* bearing supplies and 200 additional troops, tried to reinforce the Sumter garrison, South Carolinians fired on the ship and forced her to retreat.

Buchanan and many other conservatives favored calling a national convention to amend the Constitution so as to redress Southern grievances. The House of Representatives created the Committee of Thirty-Three, with one congressman from each state, to deal with the crisis. After much debate, the committee proposed admission of New Mexico as a state, allowing its people to decide for or against slavery; more stringent enforcement of the Fugitive Slave Act, which required that slaves who escaped to the North must be returned to their masters; repeal of the personal-liberty laws enacted by Northern states to prevent the reclamation of fugitives; and adoption of a constitutional amendment prohibiting future interference with slavery. The Senate set up a similar Committee of Thirteen, which was unable to agree on a program, but one of its members, John J. Crittenden of Kentucky, long a leader of the Whig Party and more recently a supporter of the Unionist ticket headed by John Bell of Tennessee, came up with a broad proposal to extend the Missouri Compromise line through the national territories, with slavery prohibited north of that line but established and maintained with federal protection south of it. Crittenden's plan also called for vigorous enforcement of the Fugitive Slave Act and for repeal of the personal-liberty laws.

However, the chances for a compromise in 1860–61 were never great. The Crittenden Compromise, the most promising of the suggested agreements, was opposed by influential Southerners and Northerners alike. Only intervention by the president-elect might have changed the attitude of Republicans in Congress and, in so doing, conceivably could have induced the Southerners to reconsider their position. But Lincoln considered these compromise schemes bribes to the secessionists. Grimly he told a visitor: "I will suffer death before I will consent . . . to any concession or compromise which looks like buying the privilege to take possession of this government to which we have a constitutional right."

His commitment to maintaining the Union was absolute. "The right of a State to secede is not an open or debatable question," he said. The concept of the Union—older than the Constitution, deriving from the Declaration of Independence with its promise of liberty for all—was the premise on which all his other political beliefs rested.

Pressured by members of his party in Congress, who were better informed and more alarmed about the South, Lincoln reluctantly agreed to accept minor concessions that would yield nothing of substance but might give some support to Southern Unionists. He had always accepted the constitutionality of the Fugitive Slave Act, because the Constitution provided for the rendition of runaway slaves to their owners, and now he said he was willing to see it more efficiently enforced, provided that it contained "the usual safeguards to liberty, securing free men against being surrendered as slaves." The personal-liberty laws were enacted by the state legislatures, not the Congress, but if such laws were "really, or apparently, in conflict with such law of Congress," they should be repealed. He indicated that he cared little about the abolition of slavery in the District of Columbia or interference with the interstate slave trade. He was even willing for New Mexico to be admitted without prohibition of slavery, "if further extension were hedged against." But on one point he was immovable: the extension of slavery into the national territories. Like most Republicans, he believed that if slavery could be contained within its present boundaries it would inevitably die out, but if the South's "peculiar institution" was allowed to expand it would take on a new and virulent life.

✦

ON FEBRUARY 11, Lincoln bade an emotional final farewell to his neighbors and left Springfield. For the next twelve days, the presidential train slowly moved across the country, in a journey of 1,904 miles over eighteen railroads. Special precautions were taken to prevent sabotage or accident along the route. The stated object of this roundabout journey was to give the people an opportunity to become acquainted with the first American president born west of the Appalachian Mountains, and Lincoln made frequent appearances at the rear of the train. The trip offered superb opportunities for a politician, and Lincoln played the crowds with consummate skill. There were also constant calls on Lincoln to speak at stops along the way—to welcoming committees, at receptions, and to state legislatures in Indiana, Ohio, New York, New Jersey, and Pennsylvania. The president-elect repeatedly asked Northerners to stand firm in the crisis. Over and over he stressed that he had been elected to uphold the Constitution and enforce the laws.

Meanwhile, Jefferson Davis was inaugurated provisional president of the Confederate States of America on February 18; Alexander H. Stephens—Lincoln's friend and colleague in the House of Representatives in the 1840s, from whom he had expected strong support of the Union—became provisional vice president. On that same day, General David E. Twiggs surrendered all the U.S. military outposts in Texas to the secessionists. In response, Lincoln made it clearer than ever that he intended to preserve the Union. In New York City he told the audience, "Nothing . . . can ever bring me willingly to consent to the destruction of this Union."

After Lincoln addressed the Pennsylvania legislature, he and his most trusted advisers met to discuss rumors of a conspiracy to assassinate him in pro-Southern Baltimore; Senator William H. Seward of New York, his former rival for the Republican presidential nomination, and others believed the report to be genuine. Lincoln was not entirely convinced, and he recognized that he might appear ridiculous fleeing from a nonexistent danger. On the other hand, he respected the judgment of Allan Pinkerton, head of the Pinkerton National Detective Agency. That evening, wearing a soft felt hat instead of his usual stovepipe, and with his long overcoat thrown loosely over his shoulders to help conceal his height, Lincoln slipped out of his hotel in Harrisburg and boarded a special train. At Philadelphia, accompanied only by Pinkerton and a bodyguard, he entered a sleeping car of the train to Baltimore and occupied a berth Pinkerton had reserved for an "invalid passenger." At

Baltimore, without being observed, Lincoln transferred to the Camden Station across town and went on to Washington. Inevitably, Lincoln's secret night ride attracted unfavorable comment and some ridicule. Lincoln came to regret that he had allowed himself to be persuaded to undertake the night trip. It was a sound and reasonable decision—but it did nothing to sustain the reputation for firmness that he had been so carefully building on his long journey from Springfield.

The ten days between Lincoln's arrival in Washington and his inauguration were among the busiest in his life, filled with endless calls and receptions. No words were more welcome than those of his Democratic opponent for the presidency, Stephen A. Douglas, who urged Lincoln to persuade Republicans to compromise but pledged that he and his Democratic followers would not try to gain political advantage from the crisis. "Our Union must be preserved," he told Lincoln solemnly. "Partisan feeling must yield to patriotism. I am with you, Mr. President, and God bless you." When the Illinois senator left, Lincoln exclaimed to another visitor: "What a noble man Douglas is!"

Lincoln also made his final cabinet selections. Seward, who had already been offered the post of secretary of state, had increasingly come to think of himself as the premier of the incoming administration. In his mind, the brilliant policy he had pursued as a senator had saved the country during the months since the election. By conciliating the South with such proposals as extension of the Missouri Compromise line, he believed that he had stopped the hemorrhage of secession. Unionists were still in control of Virginia, North Carolina, Tennessee, and Arkansas, and he was convinced that they would remain loyal so long as peace was preserved. Seward was confident he could persuade Lincoln to agree that the fever of secession should be allowed to run its course in the Deep South while Unionism should be fostered in the Upper South by avoiding all provocations.

Lincoln's selection of Salmon P. Chase of Ohio, a rival for the presidential nomination who bluntly denounced secession, as secretary of the treasury was a signal that Lincoln was not going to follow Seward's cautious and conciliatory approach toward the South. Frustrated and despondent, Seward drafted a letter of withdrawal; but Lincoln made it clear to Seward's followers that he would not get rid of Chase. On the morning of the inauguration, while the procession was forming, Lincoln sent Seward a brief note asking him to reconsider. Genuinely worried about the fate of the nation, the New Yorker felt that he did "not dare to go home, or to England, and leave the country to chance"—in other words, to Abraham Lincoln. He continued to doubt Lincoln's plan for what he termed "a compound Cabinet," but on the day after the inauguration he agreed to serve.

✦

AT NOON on March 4, Buchanan—who had given his successor no help or advice—and Lincoln entered an open barouche at Willard's Hotel to begin the drive down Pennsylvania Avenue to the Capitol. Determined to prevent any attempt on Lincoln's life, General Winfield Scott had placed sharpshooters on the roofs of buildings along the avenue, and companies of soldiers blocked off the cross streets. He stationed himself with one battery of light artillery on Capitol Hill; General John E. Wool, commander of the army's Department of the East, was with another. The presidential procession was short and businesslike, more like a military operation than a political parade.

Entering the Capitol from the north through a passageway boarded so as to prevent any possible assassination attempt, Buchanan and Lincoln emerged to a smattering of applause on the platform erected at the east portico. Lincoln read his inaugural address, an eyewitness recalled, in a voice "though not very strong or full-toned" that "rang out over the acres of people before him with surprising distinctness, and was heard in the remotest parts of his audience." When he finished, the cadaverous Chief Justice Roger B. Taney, now nearly eighty-four years old, tottered forth to administer the oath of office to the sixteenth president of the United States.

The audience could not be quite sure what the new president's policy toward secession would be, because his inaugural address, like his cabinet, was an imperfectly blended mixture of opposites. The draft he had completed before leaving Springfield was a no-nonsense document: it declared that the Union was indestructible, that secession was illegal, and that he intended to enforce the laws. "All the power at my disposal will be used to reclaim the public property and places which have fallen," he had originally pledged, "to hold, occupy, and possess these, and all other property and places belonging to the government, and to collect the duties on imports." Promising that "there needs to be no bloodshed or violence; and there shall be none unless forced upon the national authority," Lincoln had urged secessionists to pause for reflection: "In *your* hands, my dissatisfied fellow countrymen, and not in *mine,* is the momentous issue of civil war. . . . With *you,* and not with *me,* is the solemn question of 'Shall it be peace, or a sword?'"

Lincoln showed this warlike draft to several of his associates. Francis P. Blair Sr. (the Maryland Unionist who had advised a generation of presidents), remembering his glory days when Andrew Jackson stared down the South

Carolina nullifiers, approved it and urged that no change be made. But Seward thought the speech much too provocative. If Lincoln delivered it without alterations, he warned, Virginia and Maryland would secede and within sixty days the Union would be obliged to fight the Confederacy for possession of the capital at Washington. Dozens of verbal changes should be made, deleting words and phrases that could appear to threaten "the defeated, irritated, angered, frenzied" people of the South. Something more than argument was needed "to meet and remove *prejudice* and *passion* in the South, and *despondency* and *fear* in the East."

Lincoln made many of the changes Seward proposed. Seward's suggested final paragraph was too ornate for his taste, but he incorporated its ideas in language distinctively his own:

> I am loth to close. We are not enemies, but friends. We must not be enemies. . . . The mystic chords of memory, stretching from every battlefield and patriot grave, to every living heart and hearthstone, all over this broad land, will yet swell the chorus of the Union, when again touched, as surely they will be, by the better angels of our nature.

Reaction to the address was largely predictable. In the Confederacy, it was generally taken to mean that war was inevitable. A correspondent of the *Charleston Mercury* viewed this pronouncement from "the Ourang-Outang at the White House" as "the tocsin of battle" that was also "the signal of our freedom." In the Upper South, the *Richmond Enquirer* said it meant that Virginia must choose between invasion by Lincoln's army or Jefferson Davis's. In the North, Republican papers generally praised the address. The most thoughtful verdict was offered by the *Providence Daily Post,* a Democratic paper: "If the President selected his words with the view of making clear his views, he was, partially at least, unsuccessful. There is some plain talk in the address; but . . . it is immediately followed by obscurely stated qualifications."

✦

ON THE MORNING AFTER THE INAUGURATION, Lincoln found on his desk a report from Major Anderson that the provisions for Fort Sumter would be exhausted in about six weeks. Unless Anderson was resupplied within that time, he would have to surrender. He warned that it would take a force of 20,000 well-disciplined men to make the fort secure.

Lincoln was not prepared for this emergency. There was no executive branch of the government; the Senate had yet to confirm even his private secretary, John G. Nicolay. None of his cabinet officers had been approved, though he was already meeting with them.

Lincoln needed all the help he could get because, as he freely admitted later, when he became president "he was entirely ignorant not only of the duties, but of the manner of doing the business" in the executive office. He tried to do everything himself. There was no one to teach him rules and procedures, and he made egregious mistakes. For example, he thought he could issue orders directly to officers in the navy without even informing Secretary of the Navy Gideon Welles, and he attempted, without congressional authorization, to create a new Bureau of Militia in the War Department.

The new president allowed office seekers to take up most of his time. From nine o'clock in the morning until late at night, his White House office was open to all comers; sometimes the petitioners were so numerous that it was impossible to climb the stairs. But Lincoln was incorrigible. With a sad smile he explained to Senator Henry Wilson of Massachusetts that these people "dont want much and dont get but little, and I must see them."

The news from Fort Sumter forced Lincoln to make a hard choice: he must either reinforce Anderson's garrison or evacuate it. Lincoln wrestled with the problem. He was temperamentally averse to making bold moves; it was his style to react to decisions made by others rather than to take the initiative himself. In these troubled days, he made no public pronouncements and did not even discuss the Sumter crisis at the first formal meeting of the cabinet, on March 6. In subsequent informal conversations, the president told Welles that he wanted to avoid hasty action so as to gain "time for the Administration to get in working order and its policy to be understood." Lincoln asked General Scott to evaluate the situation, and he received the disheartening response that it would require a naval expedition, 5,000 regular army troops, and 20,000 volunteer soldiers to reinforce the fort. Since these could not be produced, surrender was "merely a question of time."

The Sumter crisis was the principal topic of discussion at a cabinet meeting on March 9, when the secretaries learned for the first time how grave the situation was. If relieving Anderson required an expeditionary force of at least 25,000 men—at a time when the entire U.S. Army numbered only 16,000, mostly scattered in outposts along the Indian frontier—the inescapable conclusion was that the fort must be surrendered.

Lincoln learned that not all military experts were as pessimistic as Scott. Former navy lieutenant Gustavus Vasa Fox, who was knowledgeable about coastal defenses, had been advocating a plan to reinforce or resupply Sumter from the sea, using powerful light-draft New York tugboats under the cover of night to run men and supplies from an offshore naval expedition to the fort. His plan had gotten nowhere under the Buchanan administration, and Scott, with the traditional scorn that army men showed for navy planners, thought it was impracticable. Now Postmaster General Montgomery Blair, who was a West Point graduate, endorsed it, and Lincoln began to give it serious consideration.

On March 15, he asked each member of his cabinet whether Sumter should be provisioned. Seward took the lead in opposing any such attempt. An expedition to relieve Sumter would "provoke combat, and probably initiate a civil war." Welles, Secretary of War Simon Cameron, and Secretary of the Interior Caleb B. Smith echoed Seward's views. Chase admitted having some doubts, and he did not advise reinforcing Sumter if it would precipitate a war; but on the whole, he thought this unlikely and therefore voted in favor of resupplying Anderson. Blair strongly urged an expedition, saying that only prompt reinforcement of Anderson's garrison could demonstrate "the hardy courage of the North and the determination of the people and their President to maintain the authority of the Government."

With his advisers divided, Lincoln was unable to reach a decision. He knew that evacuation "would be utterly ruinous" politically. "By many," he explained to Congress a few months later, "it would be construed as a part of a *voluntary* policy—that, at home, . . . would discourage the friends of the Union, embolden its adversaries, and go far to insure to the latter, a recognition abroad . . . in fact, it would be our national destruction consummated.

"This could not be allowed," he concluded—but he did not know how to avoid it. Like any other administrator facing impossible choices, he postponed action by calling for more information. After several conversations with Fox, to whom he took a great liking, he sent the former lieutenant to Charleston, ostensibly to bring Anderson messages about possible evacuation but in reality to get a firsthand look at the fort and the Confederate fortifications that threatened it. In a separate move, the president asked Stephen A. Hurlbut, an old friend from Illinois who had been born in Charleston, to go to South Carolina and ascertain the state of public opinion.

Fox returned to Washington more confident than ever that it was possible to resupply Fort Sumter by sea at night. But on March 27, Hurlbut offered a bleak picture of public opinion in South Carolina. "Separate Nationality is a fixed fact," he reported; "there is no attachment to the Union . . . positively nothing to appeal to." He judged that any attempt to reinforce Sumter would be received as an act of war; even "a ship known to contain *only provisions* for Sumpter would be stopped and refused admittance."

The next day, Lincoln received shocking advice from Scott: evacuation of Fort Sumter would not be enough to retain the loyalty of the Upper South, including Virginia, Scott's native state; it was necessary also to surrender Fort Pickens, on the Florida coast, even though that fort was securely in Union hands and could be reinforced at will. Only such liberality would "soothe and give confidence to the eight remaining slave-holding States, and render their cordial adherence to this Union perpetual." That night Lincoln did not sleep at all, aware that the time had come for decision.

In the morning he got up deeply depressed. The cabinet met at noon. Each member—except Cameron, who was absent—gave a written opinion. Seward remained obdurately opposed to sending an expedition to Sumter; but sensing that the president was determined to take some action, he favored holding Fort Pickens "at every cost." But now Chase and Welles came out unequivocally for reinforcing Sumter, and Blair threatened to resign if the president followed Scott's advice.

The advice of the majority of the cabinet reinforced Lincoln's own view. He directed Welles and Cameron to have an expedition ready to sail from New York by April 6. The strain under which Lincoln labored in arriving at this decision was immense. His wife, Mary, reported that he "keeled over" and had to be put to bed with one of his rare migraine headaches.

Over the next week, Seward tried, with a growing sense of desperation, to reverse Lincoln's course. In the hope of avoiding hostilities, he had, through intermediaries, been in touch with the official commissioners whom the Confederate government sent to Washington in order to negotiate terms of separation, and he had given his word that the troops would be withdrawn from Fort Sumter. He was still confident he could negotiate a settlement of the crisis if Anderson's garrison was evacuated. Now he was trapped between his pledge and Lincoln's determination to proceed with a relief expedition.

One of Seward's schemes was to deflect the Sumter expedition by reinforcing Fort Pickens. Seward proposed calling on Captain Montgomery C. Meigs, the army engineer in charge of construction at the Capitol, to organize an expedition. President Buchanan had sent 200 soldiers to the fort on the warship *Brooklyn,* but the Confederates surrounding the fort threatened to fire if they were landed. Unwilling to start a war on his own initiative, the Union commander agreed to an informal truce: he would keep his men aboard ship, and the Confederates would not attack the fort if it was not reinforced. After becoming president, Lincoln had ordered that the troops be landed, but he still did not know what had happened; however, he guessed his order "had fizzled

out." Now he asked Meigs, who was familiar with the Florida forts, to organize a relief expedition.

Thus, two projects got under way at the same time. The Sumter mission,
pressed chiefly by Welles and Blair, was largely a naval expedition commanded by Fox; the Pickens expedition, sponsored by Seward, was an army affair led by Meigs. The task forces preparing these fleets worked in secrecy and,
partly because of interservice rivalries, partly because of antagonisms among
cabinet members, each was kept largely in the dark about what its rival was
doing. Inevitably there were contests for the limited resources available for
these projects.

On April 4, Lincoln notified Major Anderson by a private messenger that
Fox's expedition would attempt to provision Fort Sumter and, in case it met
resistance, to reinforce it. Then, two days later, he learned that his earlier order to reinforce Fort Pickens had not been carried out. And Meigs's expedition
could not possibly reach Fort Pickens before Fort Sumter was either reinforced
or compelled to surrender.

Making one more attempt to avert hostilities, Seward wrung from the
president a promise to warn South Carolina officials before sending a relief expedition. On April 6, Lincoln sent a State Department clerk to Charleston to
inform Governor Francis Pickens that "an attempt will be made to supply
Fort-Sumpter with provisions only; and that, if such attempt be not resisted,
no effort to throw in men, arms, or ammunition, will be made, without further notice." Intended to avoid provoking South Carolina authorities, this
message instead only destroyed the slight possibility that Anderson could be
secretly reinforced.

The president knew from Hurlbut's report that the South Carolinians
would attack any Union ship—even one known to contain only provisions—
from the other forts in the harbor, all of which were now in Confederate
hands. But in addition to giving Seward's schemes a last chance, he was building a historical record to prove his peaceable intent throughout the crisis. By
this point he was fairly sure that the Sumter expedition would lead to bloodshed.

On April 12, while the Union fleet lay helpless offshore, the Confederates
began bombarding Fort Sumter, and after thirty-four hours Anderson and his
garrison were forced to surrender. There were no casualties on either side during the firing, but during the surrender ceremony an accidental explosion of a
pile of cartridges killed one Union private, mortally wounded another, and injured four others. The war had begun.

Three months later, Lincoln's old friend Orville H. Browning visited the

White House. According to Browning's diary, Lincoln did not denounce the Confederates, who after all fired the first shots, nor did he express any feeling of regret, much less of guilt, over his own role in bringing on the war. He mentioned the terrible stress of the weeks between his inauguration and the attack on Fort Sumter and spoke of his physical exhaustion, but he did not acknowledge that his ineffectual leadership had contributed to the crisis and made no mention of divided counsels in the administration, inadequate preparation of the relief expeditions, or bureaucratic snarls and interservice rivalries.

Lincoln probably remembered an instructive letter that Browning wrote him before his inauguration: "In any conflict . . . between the government and the seceding States, it is very important that the traitors shall be the aggressors, and that they be kept constantly and palpably in the wrong. The first attempt . . . to furnish supplies or reinforcements to Sumter will induce aggression by South Carolina, and then the government will stand justified, before the entire country, in repelling that aggression, and retaking the forts." That was the scenario Lincoln had followed in sending the Sumter expedition. "The plan succeeded," he told Browning. "They attacked Sumter—it fell, and thus, did more service than it otherwise could."

This does not mean that Lincoln sought to provoke war. His repeated efforts to avoid collision in the months between his inauguration and the firing on Fort Sumter showed that he had adhered to his vow not to be the first to shed fraternal blood. But he had also vowed not to surrender the forts. That, he was convinced, would lead to the "actual, and immediate dissolution" of the Union. The only resolution of these contradictory positions was for the Confederates to fire the first shot. The attempt to relieve Fort Sumter got them to do just that. After the attack, Lincoln told Congress, "No choice was left but to call out the war power of the Government; and so to resist force, employed for its destruction, by force, for its preservation."

✦

THE ATTACK ON FORT SUMTER revived the Lincoln administration, which had appeared indecisive and almost comatose, and gave it a clear objective: preserving the Union by putting down the rebellion. Many Northerners were euphoric, confident that the Union, with its vast natural resources, its enormous superiority in manufactures, and its 300 percent advantage in railroad mileage, was bound to prevail. Surely its 20 million inhabitants could easily defeat the 5 million in the Confederacy (though this changed to 16 million versus 9 million after the states of the Upper South seceded). Seward thought the war would be over in ninety days. The *New York Times* predicted victory in thirty days, and the *New York Tribune* assured its readers "that Jeff. Davis & Co. will be swinging from the battlements at Washington . . . by the 4th of July."

The president was not so optimistic. Overhearing boastful contrasts of Northern enterprise and endurance with Southern laziness and fickleness, Lincoln warned against overconfidence. Northerners and Southerners came from the same stock and had "essentially the same characteristics and powers," he said. "Man for man," he predicted, "the soldier from the South will be a match for the soldier from the North and *vice versa.*"

On April 15, the day after Fort Sumter surrendered, Lincoln issued a proclamation announcing that the execution of the laws in the seven states of the Deep South was obstructed "by combinations too powerful to be suppressed by the ordinary course of judicial proceedings," and he called for the states to supply 75,000 militiamen "in order to suppress said combinations, and to cause the laws to be duly executed." At the same time he summoned a special session of Congress, to meet on July 4.

A tidal wave of approval greeted his proclamation. Large Union demonstrations assembled in nearly every Northern city. Democrats as well as Republicans rallied behind the president. Senator Douglas announced that while he "was unalterably opposed to the administration on all its political issues, he was prepared to sustain the president in the exercise of all his constitutional functions to preserve the Union, and maintain the government, and defend the Federal Capital." Returning to Illinois, Douglas worked heroically to convince Democrats in the West to support the president, because "the shortest way to peace is the most stupendous and unanimous preparation for war."

The only criticism of Lincoln's proclamation was that it called for too few men. Douglas told Lincoln that he should have asked for 200,000 men, and Browning thought he needed 300,000. But in calling for only 75,000 men, Lincoln was acting on Scott's advice. Lincoln also recognized that the government was unprepared to arm, feed, transport, and train hundreds of thousands of new recruits.

He called for troops to serve only ninety days not because he believed that the war would be over quickly but because a 1795 law limited a call-up of militia to not more than thirty days after the assembling of Congress. With Congress called into session on July 4, the volunteer force would have to be disbanded by August 4. He could have convened Congress earlier, but that would have meant an even shorter term of service for the volunteers.

The Northern states promptly began to fill their quotas with eager volunteers. But the states of the Upper South, still in the Union, gave a very different response. "I can be no party to this wicked violation of the laws of the country, and to this war upon the liberties of a free people. You can get no troops from North Carolina," Governor John W. Ellis responded to Lincoln's call. The governors of Virginia, Tennessee, and Arkansas echoed his words. All four states promptly seceded from the Union. Within weeks all joined the Confederacy, which moved its capital to Richmond.

In the border slave states, initial reactions to Lincoln's proclamation were also unfavorable. "Kentucky will furnish no troops for the wicked purpose of subduing her sister Southern States," Governor Beriah Magoffin responded, and Governor Claiborne Jackson of Missouri denounced the call for troops as "illegal, unconstitutional, and revolutionary in its object, inhuman and dia-bolical." In Delaware, where slavery was a minor factor, the governor refused to comply with Lincoln's requisition but permitted volunteer companies to offer their services for the support of the Constitution and laws of the country.

More important was Maryland, a state that nearly surrounded the national capital and controlled the only railroad access to the District of Columbia. "The excitement is fearful," Governor Thomas Hicks and Baltimore Mayor George W. Brown telegraphed the president on April 18. "Send no troops here." The next day the 6th Massachusetts Regiment, on its way to defend Washington, was attacked by a secessionist mob as it attempted to cross Bal-timore, and four soldiers, along with some civilians, were killed. Wanting to shore up the governor, a wavering Unionist who tended to collapse under se-cessionist pressure, Lincoln agreed for the time that reinforcements would be marched around, rather than through, Baltimore.

Doubting that this arrangement would last, he said to the Marylanders half-playfully: "If I grant you this concession, that no troops shall pass through the city, you will be back here tomorrow demanding that none shall be marched around it." He was right. Shortly afterward, Governor Hicks asked him to stop sending any troops through Maryland and suggested ask-ing Lord Lyons, the British minister plenipotentiary at Washington, to medi-ate the sectional conflict.

That was too much for Lincoln. When a Baltimore committee descended on his office on April 22 and demanded that he bring no more troops across Maryland and make peace with the Confederacy on any terms, he had had enough. "You would have me break my oath and surrender the Government without a blow," he exploded. "There is no Washington in that—no Jackson in that—no manhood nor honor in that." He had to have troops to defend the capital, and they could only come across Maryland. "Our men are not moles, and can't dig under the earth; they are not birds, and can't fly through the air," he reminded the committee. "Go home and tell your people that if they will not attack us, we will not attack them; but if they do attack us, we will return it, and that severely."

The threat was an empty one, because Lincoln did not have enough troops to defend Washington, much less to reduce Baltimore. After the firing on Fort Sumter, the capital seemed almost deserted because of a steady exodus of pro-Confederate officials, including high-ranking army and navy officers. The most notable of these was Robert E. Lee, who declined an offer to head the Union armies because he felt he must go with his state, Virginia. To preserve some semblance of order in the national capital, the abolitionist Cassius M. Clay, wearing three pistols and an "Arkansas toothpick" (the large-bladed bowie knife), organized the Clay Guards, and Senator-elect James H. Lane of Kansas recruited the Frontier Guards from among fellow Kansans who were in Washington looking for jobs.

For nearly a week, Washington was virtually under siege. Marylanders destroyed the railroad bridges linking Baltimore with the North and cut the telegraph lines. A Confederate assault from Virginia was expected daily, and everyone predicted that it would be aided by the thousands of secessionist sympathizers in the city. In the lonely hours, Lincoln paced the floor of the White House, gazing wistfully down the Potomac for the sight of ships bringing reinforcements and breaking out eventually in anguish: "Why don't they come! Why don't they come!"

On April 25, the arrival of the 7th New York Regiment changed the picture. General Benjamin F. Butler had discovered an ingenious way of circumventing Baltimore by ferrying men down the Chesapeake Bay to Annapolis, where they could be entrained for Washington. Within days, thousands of troops began pouring into Washington. There was still a danger that when the Maryland legislature met in Frederick on April 26, it would vote to secede. Scott was ready to arrest secessionist politicians in advance of this meeting, but the president directed him to hold off, observe the proceedings, and, only if it became necessary, resort "to the bombardment of their cities—and of course the suspension of the writ of habeas corpus." Neither of these extreme measures proved necessary, but to make certain that Maryland remained loyal, Butler occupied Federal Hill, overlooking Baltimore Harbor, on May 13.

Meanwhile, on April 27, Lincoln did authorize the suspension of habeas corpus along the route between Washington and Philadelphia. This meant that the military authorities could make summary arrests of persons thought to be aiding the Confederacy or attempting to overthrow the government. Such persons could be detained indefinitely without judicial hearing and without indictment, and the arresting officer was not obliged to release them when a judge issued a writ of habeas corpus. The president's action at this time was of limited scope and did not attract great attention until the arrest of one John Merryman, lieutenant of a secessionist drill company, at Cockeysville, Maryland. Imprisoned at Fort McHenry in Baltimore Harbor, Merryman secured a writ of habeas corpus from Chief Justice Taney, which ordered that he be tried before a regular court or released. When the arresting officer, under Lincoln's orders, refused to accept the writ, Taney felt he had no alternative but to rule that the chief executive had acted unlawfully. He reminded Lincoln of his oath to "take care that the laws be faithfully executed" and warned that if such usurpation continued "the people of the United States are no longer living under a government of laws." Unprepared at this time to make a general argument for broad presidential war powers, Lincoln ignored Taney's ruling.

The situation in Kentucky was as critical as that in Maryland. Lincoln could not let his native state, which controlled the south bank of the vital Ohio River, fall under Confederate control. Ties of kinship and commerce, along with the institution of slavery, linked Kentucky to the South, but a long tradition, personified by Henry Clay and John J. Crittenden, bound the state to the Union. Lincoln's call for troops aroused the pro-Southern elements in the state to bitter opposition. Fortunately, he had sober and responsible friends in Kentucky, like Joshua Speed and his brother James, a prominent attorney in Louisville, on whose advice he could implicitly rely. When Kentucky adopted a policy of neutrality, "taking sides not with the Administration nor with the seceding States, but with the Union against them both," the president shrewdly avoided a confrontation. He had "the unquestioned right at all times to march the United States troops into and over any and every State," Lincoln told former Kentucky congressman Garrett Davis, but he promised that if Kentucky made no demonstration of force against the United States, he would not molest her.

Ostensibly respecting Kentucky's neutrality, both Union and Confederate authorities worked surreptitiously to strengthen their supporters in the state. Lincoln named Robert Anderson, the hero of Fort Sumter and a native of Kentucky, commander of the newly created Military Department of Kentucky, which embraced all of the state within 100 miles of the Ohio River, and he authorized William Nelson, another Kentucky native, to distribute arms secretly to the Unionists. But he avoided hostilities during the uneasy neutrality, recognizing that Unionism was growing faster in Kentucky than secessionist sentiment.

Less successful was Lincoln's handling of Missouri, a border slave state of enormous strategic importance because it controlled traffic on the Ohio, Mississippi, and Missouri river network so vital to the Northwest. Not familiar with the politics of the state, Lincoln had to rely on the Blair family, whose primary interest was in promoting the political fortunes of Francis Preston Blair Jr. The pro-Southern faction in eastern Missouri rallied at Camp Jackson (named after the pro-secession governor), just outside St. Louis, while pro-Union forces organized inside that city under the command of the aggressive Nathaniel Lyon. When Lyon forced the men at Camp Jackson to surrender, fighting broke out in the streets of the city, and twenty-eight deaths resulted. The governor then formed a military force and put it under the control of former governor Sterling Price. General William S. Harney, who commanded the Military Department of the West, worked out a truce with Price roughly comparable to the neutrality established in Kentucky. But Lyon, backed by the Blairs, undermined Harney's support in Washington, and Lincoln failed to support the truce. Internecine war resulted.

In Virginia, meanwhile, delegates from the strongly Unionist western counties, outraged when the state convention voted to secede, returned to their homes resolved to secede from secession. A Unionist convention held at Wheeling in effect set up a rival government to the Confederate government of Virginia in Richmond and elected Francis B. Pierpont governor. The convention also called for the creation of a new state out of the western counties of Virginia. Since the Constitution provides that no state shall be divided without its own permission, the Pierpont regime was set up as a kind of puppet government that would consent to this proposed partition. Pierpont fulfilled his function. Ostensibly speaking for the entire state of Virginia, he approved the secession of the western counties, which then applied for admission to the Union as the state of West Virginia. The Pierpont administration left Wheeling and spent the rest of the war under the shelter of Federal guns at Alexandria.

While maintaining a tenuous hold on the border states, Lincoln took steps to increase Northern preparedness. On April 19, he proclaimed a blockade of the ports of the seven Confederate states, subsequently extended to include those of North Carolina and Virginia. Beginning to realize that way left little time for legal niceties, on May 3, without congressional authorization, he called up additional volunteers, this time for three years. At the same time he expanded the regular U.S. Army by adding eight regiments of infantry, one of cavalry, and one of artillery and ordered the enlistment of 18,000 seamen in the navy.

In the weeks after the firing on Fort Sumter, the demands on the president's time were incessant and exhausting, but now that he could clearly see what had to be done he bore up well under the strain. When the writer Bayard Taylor visited Washington, he was delighted to discover, contrary to rumor, that Lincoln was not exhausted or sick but instead appeared "very fresh and vigorous . . . thoroughly calm and collected." Even Seward was impressed. "Executive skill and vigor are rare qualities," he wrote his wife in June. "The President is the best of us; but he needs constant and assiduous coöperation."

✦

LINCOLN'S JULY 4, 1861, message to the special session of Congress offered a full explanation of the course he had pursued in the Sumter crisis, blamed the Southerners for beginning the conflict, and defended the subsequent actions he had taken to sustain the Union. Valuable as history, the message was more significant as prediction. Taken together with his proclamation of April 15, it clearly defined Lincoln's view of the war and explained how he intended to prosecute it.

The conflict, he consistently maintained, was not a war between the government of the United States and that of the Confederate States of America. To define it as such would acknowledge that the Union was not a perpetual one and that secession was constitutional. This Lincoln could not even tacitly admit. Throughout the next four years, he sustained the legal fiction that the war was an "insurrection" of individuals in the Southern states who joined in "combinations too powerful to be suppressed by the ordinary course of judicial proceedings." Though he sometimes referred to the conflict as a civil war, he usually called it a "rebellion"—a term he employed more than 400 times in his messages and letters.

With some exceptions, such as his practical decision not to treat captured Confederate soldiers as common criminals (which, Jefferson Davis bluntly warned him, would have led to retaliation), Lincoln adhered to his definition of the war. The implications of his decision were far-reaching. Because, in his eyes, the Confederacy did not exist, there could never be any negotiations leading to recognition or a peace treaty. The states of the South remained in the Union, fully entitled to all the protections guaranteed by the Constitution—including slavery. When victory came, the Southern states would be, as they always had been, equal to all others in the United States.

Lincoln also made it clear that he considered the prosecution of the war pri-

marily a function of the chief executive as commander in chief, to be carried
out with minimal interference from the other branches of the government and
without excessive respect to constitutional niceties protecting individual
rights. On such matters as suspension of the writ of habeas corpus, he claimed
that in a dangerous emergency when Congress was not in session, the chief executive was obliged to act. The next years would see greater infringements on
individual liberties than in any other period in American history. The writ of
habeas corpus was repeatedly suspended in localities where secession seemed
dangerous; on September 24, 1862, and again on September 15, 1863, Lincoln suspended the privilege of the writ throughout the country. By the best
count, 864 persons were imprisoned and held without trial in the first nine
months of the war. After February 1862, when such arrests became the
province of the secretary of war, the number of cases greatly increased. Most of
the people so arrested were spies, smugglers, blockade runners, carriers of contraband goods, and foreign nationals; only a few were truly political prisoners,
jailed for expressing their beliefs. It was nevertheless clear from Lincoln's first
message to Congress that devotion to civil liberties was not the primary concern of his administration.

The Congress that heard Lincoln's message on July 5, when a clerk read it
in a dull monotone, was controlled by members of his own party. After the
withdrawal of Southern senators and representatives, Republicans held large
majorities in both chambers—32 out of 48 members of the Senate, 106 out of
176 members of the House of Representatives. Congressmen from the border
slave states who called themselves Unionists generally cooperated with the
Republicans during this session. Only about one out of four members of either chamber belonged to the Democratic Party—which was decimated by
secession and demoralized by the unexpected death, on June 3, of Stephen A.
Douglas, who might have led a loyal opposition to the Lincoln administration.

The reception of the president's message indicated that party lines were, for
the moment, unimportant. Few had the heart to engage in partisan bickering,
and "irrepressible applause" greeted Lincoln's recommendation that Congress
appropriate $400 million to sustain an army of 400,000 men. Converting it-
self, as one member said, into "a giant committee of ways and means," the
Congress promptly went beyond the president's requests and appropriated
$500 million to field an army of 500,000 men.

In the country, too, the message was greeted with enthusiasm. Most commended the president's seemingly straightforward account of the events leading up to the attack on Fort Sumter. Several editors noted with pleasure that

Lincoln made no mention of slavery but put the issue before the country simply as one of Union versus Disunion. It was no surprise that a Republican paper like Greeley's *New York Tribune* praised the message, but it was a sign of the times when the Democratic *New York World* commended "this excellent and manly Message," which contained "more unborrowed and vigorous thought" than any presidential utterance since the days of Andrew Jackson.

Congress promptly moved to pass bills retroactively approving most of Lincoln's extraconstitutional actions. There was dissent only on the suspension of the writ of habeas corpus, which made many Republicans, as well as nearly all the Democrats, unhappy. But such discord was muted, because the Union army was preparing to advance while Congress debated.

Pressure for an offensive had been building ever since Lincoln's initial call for troops, though nobody had a clear idea of what strategy should be followed. Initially Lincoln, who made no pretense of having military know-how, thought the troops should be used to repossess Fort Sumter and other captured federal installations among the Southern coast, but this thoroughly impracticable scheme would have required large amphibious operations far beyond the competence of either the army or the navy in 1861. General Scott, the most revered military expert in the country, offered what was described as an "Anaconda Plan," which called for cordoning off the Confederacy with a tight naval blockade while advancing with an army of perhaps 85,000 down the Mississippi River from southern Illinois. The plan had some merit—but it rested on the remarkable assumption that the Confederate army in Virginia, which even Scott granted might total more than 100,000 men, would remain idle while the Union forces were advancing in the West.

Despite the absence of clear strategic plans, the demand for a Union advance became explosive after Federal troops suffered several minor setbacks during the early months of the war. Since Scott was too old and infirm to take the field, Lincoln put General Irvin McDowell, a forty-two-year-old West Point graduate who had served with distinction in the Mexican War, in charge of the advance. On June 29, Lincoln met with his cabinet and military advisers in the White House to discuss McDowell's plans, which were simple and direct. Believing that General P. G. T. Beauregard had about 35,000 Confederate soldiers at Manassas, Virginia, he proposed to attack them before they could be reinforced. Scott demurred because he believed in "a war of large bodies," not "a little war by piecemeal," but the president and the cabinet overruled him, and McDowell was authorized to begin his campaign on July 9.

It was not until a week later that McDowell was ready to move—a very costly week's delay that allowed the Confederates to learn the Union strategy and to reinforce Beauregard's army with Joseph E. Johnston's troops from the Shenandoah Valley. Slowly McDowell's army began to march out to meet the Confederate army at Manassas. (That is what the Southerners called the place; Yankees found that one undistinguished Southern crossroads looked much like another, and they called the field of engagement Bull Run, after the creek that meandered near it.) McDowell's plans were widely known in Washington, and his invading army was accompanied by six U.S. senators, at least ten representatives, scores of newspapermen, and many of what a reporter called "the fairer, if not gentler sex," who often brought picnic baskets in their buggies.

Assured by Scott that McDowell would be successful, Lincoln quietly went to church on July 21. In mid-afternoon he went to Scott's office, only to find the general in chief taking his afternoon nap. When the president woke him up, the general said that early reports from the battlefield signified nothing and, before dropping off to sleep again, predicted McDowell's victory. But by six o'clock that evening, Seward came to the White House with the news that McDowell's army was in full retreat. At the War Department, the president read the dispatch of an army captain of engineers: "The day is lost. Save Washington and the remnants of this army. . . . The routed troops will not reform." All evening the president and the cabinet members clustered in Scott's office, hearing more and more alarming news. That night, stretched out on a couch in the cabinet room of the White House, the president listened to firsthand reports from terrified eyewitnesses. He did not go to bed that night.

The next day Lincoln began to assess the damage. He learned that many of McDowell's troops had fought bravely and well. The Union army would have won the battle except for the unanticipated arrival of Johnston's forces from the Shenandoah Valley. Even then, facing overwhelming odds, most of the Volunteer Union regiments had retreated in good order; the demoralized mob described by so many witnesses was largely composed of teamsters, onlookers, and ninety-day troops whose terms of enlistment were about to expire. The army was defeated but not crushed, and McDowell's troops were fed into the substantial fortifications on the south side of the Potomac. By nightfall Cameron wired back to some worried New Yorkers: "The capital is safe."

The immediate political reaction to the defeat was to rally behind the president. In order to make that support clear, both houses of Congress voted almost unanimously for John J. Crittenden's resolution declaring "that this war is not waged . . . for any purpose of conquest or subjugation, nor purpose of

overthrowing . . . established institutions [meaning slavery] . . . but to defend . . . the Constitution and to preserve the Union."

But such unity was only a facade. Bull Run was a severe Union defeat, and
finger-pointing and recriminations inevitably followed. McDowell unfairly
received a good share of the blame. Scott, too, was condemned for allowing
such an ill-prepared campaign to get under way. Restive under criticism, the
old general made an apology that was more like a defense when he talked with
several Illinois congressmen in Lincoln's presence two days after the battle. "I
am the greatest coward in America," he announced. "I will prove it; I have
fought this battle, sir, against my judgment; I think the President of the
United States ought to remove me today for doing it; as God is my judge, after my superiors had determined to fight it, I did all in my power to make the
Army efficient. I deserve removal because I did not stand up, when my army
was not in condition for fighting, and resist it to the last."

The president interjected: "Your conversation seems to imply that I forced
you to fight this battle."

Scott avoided a direct response by saying: "I have never served a president
who has been kinder to me than you have been."

Unlike the general, Lincoln was willing to assume the blame for the defeat.
Coolly reviewing the evidence, he concluded that the Manassas campaign,
though unsuccessful, had not been ill-advised. He knew that Union soldiers
were raw recruits, but so were their Confederate opponents. On neither side
did commanding officers have experience in conducting large-scale engagements.

The president moved immediately to remedy the causes of the Union defeat. To boost morale, he visited the fortifications around Washington and assured the troops that as commander in chief he would make sure they had all
needed supplies. But he also recognized the need for better discipline. Clearly
a new commanding general was needed, and on the day after the battle Lincoln summoned George B. McClellan, the hero of small engagements in western Virginia, to take charge of the forces around Washington and build a new
army out of the three-year volunteer regiments that were just beginning to arrive in the capital.

✦

DURING THE NEXT SEVERAL MONTHS, while McClellan was organizing
and training the new soldiers, Lincoln had a breathing spell from political
pressure, because everybody recognized that it would take time to build a real
army. Meanwhile, Lincoln worked harder than almost any other American

president; relaxed times with his family were rare. In addition to his regular schedule visitors still thronged the business rooms of the White House from early morning until dusk.

Stories of Lincoln's accessibility to even the humblest petitioner, his patience, and his humanity spread throughout the North. For the first time in American history, citizens began to feel that the occupant of the White House was their representative. They referred to him as Father Abraham, and they showered him with homely gifts: a firkin of butter, a crate of Bartlett pears, New England salmon. With special appropriateness, a man from Johnsburgh, New York, sent the president "a live American Eagle[,] the bird of our land," which had lost one foot in a trap. "But," the New Yorker continued, "he is yet an Eagle and perhaps no more cripled [*sic*] than the Nation whose banner he represented, his wings are sound and will extend seven feet."

BAND OF BROTHERS:
THE WEST POINT CORPS

THOMAS FLEMING

No institution more poignantly mirrored the split of a nation than the U.S. Military Academy at West Point. In the single building that served as the cadet barracks, Northerners tended to live in the east wing while Southerners occupied the south and west wings, with the central sally port acting as a kind of Mason-Dixon line. Sectional differences led to constant brawls. Not long after Lincoln's election, resignations began. (The first man to go, Henry Farley of South Carolina, would fire the signal gun that opened the bombardment of Fort Sumter.) No one was immune. The newly appointed superintendent, Major Pierre G. T. Beauregard of Louisiana, would arrive on January 23, 1861, just as his state was about to secede; five days later the secretary of war relieved him of his post. Beauregard headed south and would lead the Confederate army at Bull Run. But for many at West Point the crisis of confidence would go on for months. Comradeship ran almost as deep as sectional loyalties and, as Thomas Fleming relates, partings of friends, often forever, could be genuinely affecting. (The same partings of West Point graduates were taking place at military bases all over the country: About a third of the thousand-odd officers on the active list would go south.) Soon many of these same men would be busy killing one another.

Sometimes past performances at the academy could offer a clue to the way leaders would behave in action. Before the Battle of Atlanta in the summer of 1864, William T. Sherman asked three of his generals what their classmate, the Confederate commander John Bell Hood, had been like as an underclassman. Impetuous, they replied, and Sherman set about preparing for an immediate Confederate attack—which came, and which he handily beat back. "The battlefield," Fleming writes, "was the grisly graduate school in which West Point men learned the ultimate lessons in the art of modern war."

Thomas Fleming is a historian whose many books include *West Point: The Men and the Times of the U.S. Military Academy; 1776: Year of Illusions; Liberty! The American Revolution;* and most recently, *Duel: Alexander Hamilton, Aaron Burr, and The Future of America.* Fleming is a former president of the American center of P.E.N., the international writers' organization.

DURING THE CLOSING WEEKS OF HIS TERM IN OFFICE, President James Buchanan sent an order to the United States Military Academy at West Point. He wanted the cadet corps to march to the chapel on Washington's birthday and hear "the friendly counsel and almost prophetic warnings" contained in George Washington's farewell address.

Accordingly, on February 22, 1861, the corps assembled in the small pillared chapel with the painting of the Republic's eagle above the altar, flanked by a pleading female Peace and a brooding Roman soldier symbolizing war. They listened to one of the professors read the first president's advice to "properly estimate the immense value of your national union to your collective and individual happiness."

The West Point marching band had awakened the cadets that morning with "The Star-Spangled Banner." Since classes had been suspended for the holiday, after chapel the young men spent the rest of the day discussing politics and impending war. At tattoo, the band turned out again and marched across the Plain (the academy drill field) to the strains of "Washington's March" until the front ranks reached the sally port that led into the inner courtyard formed by the barracks. At that point they again swung into "The Star-Spangled Banner."

Cadets filled every window on both sides of the area. George Armstrong Custer, who had spent the previous twelve months defending Southerners and the Southern cause, gave a cheer for the flag. At a nearby window, his close friend Tom Rosser replied with another for Southern rights. The entire corps instantly took sides, and shouts echoed back and forth above the music until every throat was hoarse—and there was no longer any doubt that West Point was as tragically divided as the nation.

This was not a complete surprise to either the cadet corps or the faculty. Throughout the 1850s, altercations between Northern and Southern cadets were commonplace. When Secretary of War Jefferson Davis, class of 1828, visited his alma mater in 1854, he was "surprised to see so many gray hairs" on the head of the superintendent, Colonel Robert E. Lee. One of the reasons for Lee's strain was the growing animosity between Northern and Southern cadets. Again and again, Lee reminded the cadets that they were a "band of brothers," urging them to live together in peace and harmony. Once when he said this, after a fistfight between two cadets, one of them responded, "If we were all like you, it would be an easy thing to do."

Not all Lee's efforts were in vain. The cadet corps was still unified on some issues. When the superintendent's ebullient nephew, Fitzhugh Lee, was caught going over the wall once too often and was listed for dismissal, the entire corps pledged themselves to stay in bounds for the rest of the year if the charges against Fitz were dropped. The elder Lee asked the secretary of war to accept the terms, and Fitz graduated in 1856.

Lee also succeeded, after a fashion, with his favorite cadet, J. E. B. Stuart. The feisty young Virginian was constantly in trouble, putting his fist into the teeth of anyone who cast a slur on the South. Lee exhorted with a lecture on "the evil tendencies" of such behavior and an appeal to Stuart's intelligence, and Jeb's response suggested there was already something magical in Lee's leadership. Cadet Oliver O. Howard was an outspoken abolitionist, and at this point in the 1850s it was not difficult for the Southerners to persuade almost everyone else in the school to join them in ostracizing him. But after Howard fought back, blackening a few eyes and loosening some teeth among his tormentors, Jeb Stuart was the first to step forward and declare the ordeal ended. "He spoke to me, he visited me, and we became warm friends," Howard later said.

Lee was reassigned in 1855 and spent the next six years as a cavalry commander in Texas. At West Point the band of brothers continued to quarrel. In 1855, when First Captain Edward L. Hartz of Pennsylvania put a Southern classmate on report for breaking a regulation, he called Hartz an insulting name and the first captain bloodied his nose. The Southerner challenged Hartz to a duel but was contemptuously refused.

Morris Schaff of Ohio got into a shouting match with a Southerner who had made insulting remarks about one of the Ohio senators, Ben Wade. The Southerner towered over the diminutive Schaff, who expected a bad beating before the end of the day; but as the cadets returned from class, Custer and a gigantic Iowan fell in step beside Schaff, and Custer said, "If he lays a hand on you, Morris, we'll maul the earth with him." Thereafter, the Southerner left Schaff alone.

A kind of crisis was reached after John Brown's raid on Harpers Ferry in

October 1859, which infuriated Southern cadets on general principles and, on a more personal level, because one of the whites Brown had seized, Colonel Lewis Washington (great-grandnephew of the first president), was the father of cadet James B. Washington. Among the people Brown killed during his raid was George W. Turner, class of 1831, who had resigned from the army in 1836 and became a prosperous farmer near Harpers Ferry; Turner had foolishly exchanged fire with Brown's riflemen.

Inflamed Southern cadets aimed a lot of their remarks at Emory Upton of Massachusetts, another outspoken abolitionist. Wade Hampton Gibbes of South Carolina noted that Upton had previously attended Oberlin College, the only racially and sexually integrated school in the nation, and suggested Upton had no doubt enjoyed the Negro coeds there. Upton demanded an apology, Gibbes declined, and the young Northerner challenged him to a fight.

They slugged it out in a room cleared of furniture, while half the corps packed the nearby halls and stairs. It was a miracle that a riot did not break out. The bigger, stronger Gibbes gave Upton a terrific beating. But the real climax of the fight, according to Morris Schaff, came when Upton's roommate, John Rodgers of Pennsylvania, strode to the head of the stairs and, with eyes "glaring like a panther's," said, "If there are any more of you down there who want anything, come right up." Schaff recalls that moment as when the South saw "what iron and steel there was in the Northern blood when once it was up."

After Lincoln's election in November 1860, as Southern states decided on secession, cadets from those states began to withdraw from the Academy. Red-haired Henry Farley of South Carolina was the first to go, on November 19, 1860, and four days later another South Carolinian, James Hamilton, joined him; friends and family had obviously notified them that the Palmetto State was expected to secede on December 20.

For most of the Southerners, the decision to go home or stay with the Union was intensely painful. Schaff later described how he parted with his roommate, John A. West. After a meeting of the Georgia cadets, West returned to his room with tears in his eyes to tell Schaff he had resigned. Schaff helped him pack and walked him to the cadet limits near the library. There, fighting back tears, they threw arms around each other and said good-bye.

Charles Ball of Alabama had an equally emotional and more public sendoff. He was a first sergeant in the corps, which meant he was the leading candidate for the first captaincy. Schaff said he was "one of those rare young men who carry with them the fascinating mystery of promise." When Ball said good-bye to his battalion, in an outburst of pure feeling they hoisted him to their shoulders and carried him down to the wharf where a steamboat awaited him.

Elsewhere, graduates of West Point also wrestled with their consciences. No one exemplified the dilemma better than Major Robert Anderson, commander of Fort Sumter, who had been at the Academy with Jefferson Davis and fought beside him in Mexico. Born in Kentucky, Anderson was married to a Georgian, and he had once owned a plantation and slaves in that state. But the major felt he was duty-bound to defend the fort until the government ordered its evacuation.

At 4:30 A.M. on April 12, former cadets Wade Hampton Gibbes and Henry Farley, both now with the provisional forces of South Carolina, sent the first shells arching over the bay to explode above Fort Sumter. The war had begun. (After the fort's surrender, Anderson returned to the North and was promoted to brigadier general. He served in the field and at other posts until ill health forced him to retire in late 1863.)

At West Point, there were more poignant farewell scenes. One of the most touching was the departure in May 1861 of Lieutenant Fitzhugh Lee, who had returned to the Academy as a tactical officer. Lee went to every room and shook hands with each cadet. The night before he left, his fellow officers gathered under his window and serenaded him. When Lee departed in an omnibus, the entire corps came out to the front of their barracks and doffed their hats.

The first (senior) class was graduated a few weeks ahead of schedule. No sooner had the graduates departed than the members of the new first class, who had been at West Point four years, asked to be graduated. The government was delighted to oblige. Led by its top student, Patrick O'Rorke of New York, the class left for Washington at the end of June. True to form, its favorite bad boy, George Armstrong Custer, was left behind in the guardhouse. While he was officer of the day at the summer encampment, a fight had broken out; instead of breaking it up, he had organized a circle around the combatants and acted as referee.

Of the 278 cadets at West Point on the day Lincoln was elected, 86 were from Southern states. Of these, 65 went South. Southerners also departed—en masse—from Harvard, Yale, Columbia, and Princeton. There is no record of a single Southern man at these colleges staying with the Union.

Beyond West Point's walls, other graduates were making fateful decisions. Robert E. Lee's agonizings are well known: his conference with Winfield Scott; the offer from Lincoln to command the Union armies; his refusal—and

Scott's warning him, "Lee, you have made the greatest mistake of your life. . . ."

Others unburdened themselves to friends of their West Point youth. Few were more frank than Braxton Bragg, class of 1837, who wrote to William Tecumseh Sherman, class of 1840, that "a few old political hacks and barroom bullies are leading public opinion. . . . I shall continue to hope, though without reason, that Providence will yet avert the great evil. But should the worst come we shall still be personal friends." Years later, Sherman said, "I think I knew Bragg as well as any living man. His heart was never in the Rebel cause." This may be at least a partial explanation for Bragg's poor performance as a general.

Sherman's agony was no less intense. He was superintendent of the Louisiana Military School when South Carolina seceded. He poured out his emotion to one of the faculty members, calling the South's plunge to war "folly, madness, a crime against civilization" that would make him fight "against your people whom I love best."

George H. Thomas, Sherman's closest friend from West Point days, refused a request from the governor of Virginia that he resign from the army and become the state's chief of ordnance. His two sisters addressed impassioned pleas to him to stand by old Virginia. But Thomas had spent less than eighteen months in Virginia since his graduation in 1840, and his wife was from Troy, New York. He stayed with the North, soon replacing Lee as colonel of the 2nd Cavalry.

In the fear-ridden Washington of 1861, Thomas's loyalties remained suspect, and he watched other men with far fewer qualifications become generals before him. He was rescued by Sherman, whose brother was a senator from Ohio, and whose stepbrothers, sons of former senator Thomas Ewing, were also influential. Sherman said he would stake his reputation on his friend's loyalty, and Lincoln finally made Thomas a brigadier general.

Sherman brought Thomas the good news personally. Thomas, whose middle name should have been Imperturbable, did not even smile. For a moment, even Sherman had doubts about his friend. He watched as Thomas mounted his horse. "Where are you going?" he asked. "I'm going south," Thomas replied. "My God, Tom," Sherman exclaimed, "you've put me in a hell of a spot. . . ." "Give yourself no trouble, Billy," Thomas said. "I'm going south at the head of my troops."

The West Point soldier who ultimately personified Midwestern solidarity with the Union had no hesitation whatever about which way to go. When a friend with Southern sympathies burst into his father's leather-goods store in Galena, Ohio, to announce that Jefferson Davis had just been elected president of the Confederacy, Sam (Ulysses S.) Grant, class of 1843, looked down on him from a shelf ladder and then snapped, "Davis and the whole gang of them ought to be hung."

At army posts around the nation, the news of Fort Sumter was heard with shock and dismay. One of the most dramatic reactions took place in Los Angeles. Tall, soldierly Captain Winfield Scott Hancock, class of 1844, and his wife, Almira, invited their Southern friends to a farewell party. The guests included George Pickett and Dick Garnett, friends from Mexican days as well as West Point, and Lewis Armistead of Virginia, who had failed to graduate with the class of 1837 but had joined the army two years later and won three promotions for bravery in Mexico.

The evening was full of suppressed emotion. Around midnight, the wife of one of the officers began playing some of their favorite songs. She struck up "Kathleen Mavourneen," with its mournful words of parting: "It may be for years, it may be forever." Armistead put his hands on Hancock's shoulders and said, "Hancock, good-bye. You can never know what this has cost me, and I hope God will strike me dead if I am ever induced to leave my native soil should worst come to worst." He gave Mrs. Hancock a small satchel of personal mementos, asking her not to open it unless he was killed. In that case, he wanted her to keep his prayer book for herself.

Powell (A. P.) Hill of Virginia, class of 1847, debated with his Northern friend George McClellan, class of 1846. In earlier days, they had both sought the hand of blonde-haired Nellie Marcy, one of the capital's reigning belles of the 1850s. Nellie had been inclined to Hill, but her father, Captain Randolph Marcy (class of 1832), persuaded her to marry McClellan, who was prospering as a railroad executive. There were rumors (apparently untrue) that the rivalry had soured the men's friendship, but now they parted with regret. "Hill, I am truly sorry you are going to leave us," McClellan told him. "But to be frank, I cannot blame you. . . . I am an Ohioan and I am standing by my state, too." (Note the difference between McClellan's mild words to Hill and Sherman's passionate outburst about loyalty to George Thomas. It is illustrative of the difference in the two soldiers' future conduct of the war.)

All told, 286 West Point graduates opted for the Confederacy. Over 100 other Regular Army officers appointed from civil life chose the Stars and Bars—totaling about a third of the more than 1,000 officers on the active list. The total was not overwhelming—but Southerners had dominated the higher reaches of the army for a long time, partly because they tended to stay in the service and partly because for the previous eight years the secretary of war had been a Southerner.

The loss of so many prominent officers panicked the politicians, and Simon Cameron, Lincoln's secretary of war, turned their resignations into a ferocious attack on West Point, wondering aloud whether the Southerners' "extraordinary treachery" might not be due to "a radical defect in the system of education itself." Lincoln did not help matters when he echoed Cameron and publicly deplored the defections, noting that not one common soldier or sailor had deserted the flag. The president apparently forgot that an officer could resign, but an enlisted man deserted at the risk of being shot. (James Longstreet, class of 1842, en route south to volunteer for the Confederacy, was asked by a sergeant if he could join Longstreet. The future lieutenant general sternly told the man to serve out his hitch.) Radical Republicans called for the abolition of the Academy. Supporters pointed out that of the graduates, forty-seven Virginians, seven Tennesseans, eight North Carolinians, and six sons of South Carolina had remained loyal.

If a prize had been given to the most conflicted West Pointer, it might have gone to Philip St. George Cooke, class of 1827, of Virginia. The elder Cooke stayed with the Union, while his son, John Rogers Cooke (not a West Pointer), joined the Confederacy to fight beside Philip's son-in-law, Jeb Stuart, class of 1854.

In the South, where a West Pointer was president, graduates were appointed to commands as fast as they volunteered. In the North, with hostility to the academy rampant, the pace was slower. Grant wrote the government a letter volunteering his services and did not even get a reply. A friend wangled him a colonel's commission from the governor of Illinois.

Some graduates were analyzing the strategic situation with remarkable accuracy, even if they were not in high command. Senator John Sherman wrote in his memoirs of riding out in 1861 with his brother, "Cump," to have dinner with George Thomas in Maryland, where Thomas's regiment was on duty. Spreading a map on the floor, the two soldiers put a dot on Richmond as a primary target, but they spent far more time tracing lines of march to Knoxville, Chattanooga, Nashville, and Vicksburg. Senator Sherman was later amazed not only at their prescience, but by the fact that they became "leading actors" in the battles for these Western cities.

Exactly what West Point contributed to the success of its graduates in the Civil War is a thorny subject. The academy's military philosopher in the antebellum years was Dennis Hart Mahan. One can find in his generalizations not a little of the offensive strategy of Robert E. Lee, class of 1829, and Stonewall Jackson, class of 1846. Mahan urged operations that "if carried out to their legitimate ends may change the entire aspect of the war." He said a general with daring should "abandon [a] portion of [his] territory" and maneuver so that his "entire moveable army strikes at the enemy in the heart of his own country." In another Mahan maxim, "Celerity is the secret of success," one can conjure the vision of Jackson's foot cavalry baffling four Union armies in the Shenandoah Valley in 1862.

Both sides paid Mahan the compliment of reprinting and widely distributing the weirdly titled book in which he condensed his military wisdom: *Advance Guard, Outpost and Detachment Service of Troops with the Essential Principles of Strategy.* But like many similar books, a lot depended on the man who read it. Braxton Bragg certainly never got much out of it. Nor did George Meade, class of 1835, as demonstrated by his lackadaisical pursuit of Lee's army after Gettysburg. In justice to Mahan, he remarked in his discussion of pursuit: "This is a part of generalship no theory can teach to one to whom nature has not given the faculties of a general."

Although the West Point officer was admirably equipped to command a battalion or a regiment, beyond that level, as was perhaps best described by Jacob Cox (a citizen soldier from Ohio who rose to the rank of major general), "the mental furnishing of the West Point man was not superior to that of any other liberally educated man." He admitted, however, that the citizen soldier lacked the professional's "habit of mind" and familiarity with danger and violent death. Cox was not opposed to West Point. But he remarked that the experience of the West Pointer after graduation was "confined to company duty," and a graduate had no more opportunity for enlarging his strategic and tactical thinking than any other officer in the army.

Cox's conclusions were supported by the performance of West Point officers in the early years of the war. Irvin McDowell, class of 1838, the luckless Union commander at the First Battle of Bull Run, lamented to a congressional committee that he had had "no opportunity to test my machinery. . . . There was not a man [in the army] who had ever maneuvered troops in large bodies."

The battlefield was the grisly graduate school in which West Point men learned the ultimate lessons in the art of modern war. Certainly nothing else explained the emergence of Grant as a great general—nor the partnership of this inarticulate, instinctive man with the voluble, philosophical Sherman. Once, in a moment of typical candor, Sherman told a fellow officer why he became Grant's loyal lieutenant:

I'm a damn sight smarter than Grant; I know more about organization, supply, and administration and about everything else than he does; but I'll tell you
where he beats me and where he beats the world. He don't care a damn for what
the enemy does out of his sight, but it scares me like hell.

But we can identify another reason for Grant's success—the group of young
West Point graduates who came to be known as "Grant men." Among the
best was James Harrison Wilson, class of 1860, who was never hesitant about
advising generals. Serving as an aide-de-camp during the Battle of Antietam,
he found Joseph Hooker, class of 1837, leaving the field with a foot wound.
Wilson told him he should return to the firing line even if he had to be carried on a stretcher.

When McClellan was relieved as commander of the Army of the Potomac,
Wilson listened while another general advised him to seek a command in the
West. Little Mac haughtily replied that he did not feel he could take a "lower"
command. Wilson told him he should take anything that was offered to him,
and if nothing was offered he should shoulder a musket in the ranks.

Not every general would put up with this kind of subordinate. But Grant
saw that Wilson combined brains and gall. He played a key role in the Vicksburg campaign, being the first to propose the plan of running the city's batteries with the gunboats and transports, then meeting the troops south of the
city to ferry them to the other side of the river for an attack from the rear.

West Point connections played another role in Sherman's army. When John
Bell Hood, class of 1853, replaced Joseph Johnston, class of 1829, as the commander of the Southern force defending Atlanta, Sherman asked three of his
generals who had been at the academy with Hood what they thought he
would do. All agreed that the impetuous Southerner would attack immediately. Hood had graduated at the bottom of his class and was known for his
fixed belief that courage and spirit were all that an army needed to win battles. Hood attacked exactly as predicted, and he was beaten back with ruinous
casualties.

When Sherman marched to the sea, he left behind him George H. Thomas
in Nashville to defend his rear and the ramparts of the Midwest against
Hood's army. "Never before since the world began did such absolute confidence exist between the commander and commanded," Sherman later wrote.
"We recited together four years in the same section, served as lieutenants in
the same regiment for ten years." The only telegram Sherman sent as he
marched off from Atlanta was to Thomas, telling him he was confident that if

Hood attacked him, "you will whip him out of his boots." Which is exactly what Imperturbable Tom proceeded to do at the Battle of Nashville.

Even as the Union fought a losing war in the East, the West Pointers persisted where amateurs might have despaired. They not only kept an army in being; they displayed superiority in a crucial arm of the Army of the Potomac, the artillery. In 1862, at Gaines' Mill and even more decisively at Malvern Hill, Fitz John Porter, class of 1845, stood alone with his single corps against Lee's assaults, smashing attack after attack with his massed artillery until he finally had to withdraw.

After Malvern Hill, a story circulated through the Confederate army about Major General John Bankhead Magruder, class of 1830, who had spent thirty years in the 1st U.S. Artillery. He reportedly saw his old battery on the crest of the hill and ordered his division to capture it. With that disregard for death that made them legendary, the Confederate infantry charged—to be met by a rain of canister and grape from the guns, now commanded by twenty-two-year-old Edmund Kirby, class of 1861. After three tries, the earth was carpeted with bodies. Magruder supposedly shook his head and exclaimed, "Ah boys, I knew you couldn't take old E Company!"

There were many other encounters across the battle lines. As Custer vaulted from lieutenant to brigadier general, he frequently found himself charging cavalry commanded by his old friend Tom Rosser. Once, while reconnoitering the Union lines in full view of Northern sharpshooters, Rosser threw back his gray, red-lined cape. Custer hastily ordered everyone along the line to hold his fire. The next day he sent a message under a flag of truce: "Tam, do not expose yourself so. Yesterday I could have killed you."

Custer's impudent rivalry with Rosser came to a head in the Shenandoah Valley in 1864. Beside a stream appropriately known as Tom's Brook, Rosser awaited the Union attack. Riding forward, Custer swept his hat from his head, bowed, and then led his division in a headlong charge. Rosser's line broke, and Custer chased him for ten miles in what Union men called the "Woodstock races." Custer captured Rosser's supply train and wagons containing his official papers and trunks of clothes. The next day, he pranced out of his headquarters wearing Rosser's gray uniform, which was several sizes too big for him. Under a flag of truce, he sent "Tam" another note, asking him to be sure his tailor made the tails shorter the next time.

Meanwhile, Powell Hill, McClellan's onetime rival in love, had become a Confederate major general, and his division was soon famed for the ferocity of his attacks. He seemed to take special pleasure in frustrating McClellan's battle plans. As one story goes, some Union soldiers became convinced that more than a little of Hill's pugnacity could be traced to his romantic grievance over Nellie Marcy. Once, after beating off a series of Hill's assaults, the bluecoats were trying to get some rest when blaring bugles and rattling musketry announced another Hill attack. "My God, Nellie," one veteran groaned while pulling on his boots, "why didn't you marry him?"

The Battle of Gettysburg was, in many ways, a climactic West Point confrontation. Commanding the Union lines on Cemetery Ridge was Major General Winfield Scott Hancock. Among the brigadiers under George Pickett were Richard Garnett and Lewis Armistead. One wonders if Armistead remembered his solemn words at their farewell party in Los Angeles about never leaving his native soil.

Garnett, too sick with fever to walk, rode his horse, while Armistead strode at the head of his brigade, his black slouch hat on the point of his sword, so his men could keep track of him. In the first blast of fire from the men on the ridge, Garnett went down, riddled by a dozen bullets. But Armistead reached the stone wall where another West Point graduate, Alonzo Cushing, class of 1861, ignored mortal wounds to fire one last blast of canister with his only remaining gun. At almost the same moment, Hancock, on his horse behind the line, went down with a minié ball in the groin. Only when Armistead turned to summon his men did he realize he was almost alone. Seconds later he was cut down, along with the few men who had kept up with him. As Union soldiers carried him to the rear, he asked for his friend Hancock and wept when informed that he, too, had suffered what looked like a mortal wound. (Hancock recovered, however.) A few days later, Almira Hancock opened the satchel Armistead had given her in Los Angeles. In the prayer book was inscribed a soldier's motto: "Trust in God and fear nothing."

Not all encounters among the West Point men in the war were so tragic. One night during the drive on Richmond in 1864, Grant noticed that bonfires had suddenly sprouted all along the Confederate line. Scouts informed him that the Southerners were celebrating because George Pickett's wife had given birth to a son. "Haven't we some kindling on this side of the line?" Grant asked. "Why don't we strike a light for young Pickett?" Soon, answering bonfires were glowing along the Union lines. A few days later, under a flag of truce, Federal soldiers delivered a baby's silver service, engraved: "To George Pickett Jr. From his father's friends, U. S. Grant, Rufus Ingalls, George Suckley."

The meeting of Grant and Lee at Appomattox provided the final confrontation between West Point graduates. The story is too well known to be repeated in detail here. But there are a few sidelights that are pertinent to the role of the U.S. Military Academy. As Lee debated whether to surrender, Edward Porter Alexander, class of 1857, the Confederate artillery commander, urged him to order the men to "scatter like rabbits and partridges in the bushes." Lee shook his head. "The men would have no rations, be under no discipline. They'd have to rob and plunder," he said.

Later, Alexander said he felt Lee was speaking from a moral plan so far above him that he was almost ashamed to say another word. But he could not resist one more passionate plea. "A little more blood or less now makes no difference. Spare the men who have fought under you for four years the mortification of having to ask Grant for terms and have him say unconditional surrender. . . ." Quietly, Lee replied, "General Grant will not demand unconditional surrender. He will give us as honorable terms as we have a right to ask or expect."

In the white clapboard farmhouse, Grant offered Lee and his men the best terms he could devise. Within the hour, three days' rations—fresh beef, salt, hard bread, coffee, and sugar—flowed into the lines of the starving Confederates. When Northern bands began playing and batteries fired victory salutes, Grant sternly ordered a stop to the celebrations. "The Rebels are our countrymen again," he said. Later that night, when someone told Grant he should have held Lee and his generals for trial instead of paroling them, the Union commander said, "I'll keep the terms no matter who's opposed."

Within minutes of the surrender, Custer rode into the Confederate camp in search of old friends. Among the first he found was Fitzhugh Lee, who had won a reputation as a cavalry commander under Jeb Stuart. With a shout these two birds of a feather embraced each other and rolled on the ground, laughing like schoolboys.

The next day Lieutenant General George Meade rode over to visit Robert E. Lee. Doffing his cap as officers did in the old army, he said, "Good morning, General."

"What are you doing with all that gray in your beard?" Lee asked.

"You have to answer for most of it," Meade replied.

On a train from Montgomery to Atlanta one night a few months later, Morris Schaff encountered Charles Ball, the former first sergeant of the corps, who had fought hard and long as a cavalry colonel. "As soon as he recognized me," Schaff recalled, "he quickened his step and met me with such unaffected cordiality that the car seemed to glow with new lamps." Schaff wondered if "I could have shown so much magnanimity had the South conquered the North and had I come home in rags to find the old farm desolate."

Thirty-seven years later, on June 9, 1902, the surviving veterans of both sides came to West Point to celebrate the academy's 100th anniversary. Among the chief speakers was Edward Porter Alexander. Looking back, he declared that "it was best for the South that the cause was lost. . . . Whose vision is not so dull that he does not recognize the blessing it is to himself and to his children to live in an undivided country?" Closing, Alexander paid tribute to West Point for teaching them "not the skill to unravel conflicting political creeds . . . but rather to illustrate by our lives manly courage and loyalty to convictions." The band struck up "The Star-Spangled Banner," as it had done on a night long ago, and with a heartfelt cheer the gray-haired veterans threw their arms around each other and then wept.

THE ORDEAL
OF GENERAL STONE

STEPHEN W. SEARS

Behind the lines in the North, 1861 saw the beginning of what Bruce Catton called "The Era of Suspicion." Much of the hysteria centered on Washington, a city that felt itself under siege—which indeed it was in the first month or so of the war until Union troops were able to cow secessionist militants in Baltimore and prevent the national capital from being surrounded. There have been few similar periods in American history. You have to look ahead to the Red Scares that followed the two World Wars to find a time of equal paranoia. Eighteen sixty-one might be called the year of the "Reb" Scare.

Setbacks on the battlefield only made matters worse. On July 21, the perceived calamity of Bull Run (which was actually a rather evenly fought encounter) had dashed Union hopes of an early victory. Then, in October, exactly three months later, came another disaster, Ball's Bluff. In an encounter by the Potomac that should never have been fought, the Union took some 900 casualties. Many were drowned in the panic of trying to retreat across the river, or were isolated on the Virginia side and captured. A search began for a scapegoat, and as so often happens in these cases, the chief victim was mostly innocent. He was a West Pointer named Charles P. Stone. (The person who should have been blamed had been conveniently killed, and was now hailed as a martyr. It helped, too, that he was a senator who had raised his own regiment.) Stone became trapped in a Washington power struggle, betrayed by the perjured evidence of the very men he had accused of fraud and cowardice, and ultimately destroyed.

Stephen W. Sears is one of the foremost historians of the Civil War. His books include *Landscape Turned Red: The Battle of Antietam; George B. McClellan: The Young Napoleon; Chancellorsville;* and *Controversies & Commanders: Dispatches from the Army of the Potomac.*

SHORTLY BEFORE MIDNIGHT ON SATURDAY, FEBRUARY 8, 1862, eighteen men of Company B, 3rd United States Infantry, were mustered for special duty at their barracks on Franklin Square in Washington. To their surprise, they were taken in charge by a full-fledged brigadier general, George Sykes, commander of the City Guard, which was responsible for keeping order in the capital. Shouldering their rifles and falling into step behind General Sykes, the regulars set off through the quiet, dimly lit streets.

Their first stop was on H Street, at the home of Lord Lyons, the British ambassador, where a reception was taking place. Sykes went inside but soon returned empty-handed; whoever he was looking for was not socializing with Lord Lyons. Resuming its march, the detail turned onto Seventeenth Street. Halfway down the block, Sykes halted the men again and entered a second house. Again he came out alone, but this time he remained in front of the house, pacing expectantly.

In a few minutes a second officer, also wearing the one-star shoulder straps of a brigadier general, came down Seventeenth Street and turned in where Sykes was waiting. The two men greeted each other as friends; they had served together in the same regiment in the old army before the war. Then Sykes drew himself up and said, "Stone, I have now the most disagreeable duty to perform that I ever had—it is to arrest you."

"Arrest me!" said the newcomer. "For what?" Sykes said he did not know—could not even conceive the reason—except that it was by order of Major General George B. McClellan, general in chief of the army. He added, "I may as well tell you that you are to be sent to Fort Lafayette." Looking back on the moment, Stone remembered his reaction as utter astonishment—"Why, Fort Lafayette is where they send secessionists!"—and he exclaimed (perhaps embroidering the recollection somewhat), "They are now sending there one who has been as true a soldier to the Government as any in service."

The guardsmen, waiting at a respectful distance, took all this in and whispered among themselves: That explains it—it must take one brigadier general to arrest another. Flanking the prisoner, they fell into step once more, this time following H Street past Lafayette Park across from the White House. After half a mile they reached the Chain Building, where officers of the City Guard were quartered. The prisoner was locked in a small room on the top floor, with an armed sentry posted at the door. Early the next morning, permitted pen and paper, he wrote McClellan's adjutant general for a copy of "whatever charges may have been preferred against me, and the opportunity of promptly meeting them." He signed himself Charles P. Stone, brigadier general of volunteers. "I supposed there was some strange misunderstanding," he later remembered thinking, "which all connected with the Government & Army would be happy to have cleared up." He received neither answer nor acknowledgment.

That evening, under escort of a lieutenant and two detectives, he was put aboard the night train to New York. At Philadelphia there was some mix-up about the railroad passes, and General Stone ended up paying his own fare for transport to prison. In the small hours of February 10, twenty-four hours after his arrest, Stone was placed in solitary confinement in Fort Lafayette, the military prison at the Narrows of New York Bay.

✦

SO BEGAN THE ORDEAL OF CHARLES POMEROY STONE, an ordeal that is unique in American military history. When he was finally released from confinement six months later, his reputation both as a soldier and as a patriot was in shreds. In a congressional hearing room and in the nation's newspapers he had been charged, tried, judged, and convicted of disgracing his uniform and betraying his country. He was called the Benedict Arnold of the Civil War.

Yet Charles Stone was guilty of nothing whatever. He had not been, and never would be, charged with a single violation of either military or civil law. Caught up in a power struggle involving the army, the Congress, and the Lincoln administration, General Stone was convicted by innuendo and the secret testimony of conspirators.

The Stone case is rich in ironies. The first of these is that at the time of his arrest, no Northern officer had displayed his loyalty more conspicuously and with more dedication than Charles Stone. Indeed, he was the very first soldier to answer his country's call during the secession crisis. On January 2, 1861, he was commissioned by the then general in chief, Winfield Scott, to take command of the District of Columbia volunteers and organize them for the defense of the capital. On Inauguration Day, amid reports of secessionist plots to assassinate President-elect Lincoln and overturn the government, Stone and his troops steadfastly stood guard over the change of administrations.

With the coming of war, Stone's solid military credentials gained him rapid promotion to high command. An 1845 graduate of West Point, he had served with the artillery in the Mexican War, winning two brevets for gallantry. In the peacetime army he was posted on the Pacific Coast as an ordnance officer. After Fort Sumter he was named colonel of a regiment of regulars, then brigadier general of volunteers. When George McClellan was called in to organize the Army of the Potomac after the Bull Run debacle, he chose his old friend Stone to command a division. "He was a most charming and amiable gentleman," McClellan later wrote of Stone. "Honest, brave, a good soldier, though occasionally carried away by his chivalrous ideas."

What McClellan termed Stone's devotion to chivalrous ideas is better described as a stiff-necked rectitude toward his soldierly duties. Like most regular officers of the old army (including his chief, General McClellan), Charles Stone displayed a conservative turn of mind, especially toward politics, the institution of slavery, and the volunteers under his command. These ingredients, combined with his particular assignment in the Army of the Potomac, made a recipe for serious trouble.

In August 1861, McClellan posted Stone's division along the upper Potomac, making it the extreme right of the Union line guarding Washington. Division headquarters was at Poolesville, Maryland, across the river from Leesburg, Virginia, where the extreme left of the Confederate line was based. It was an assignment that bred problems, for Maryland was a slave state being held in the Union by the iron grip of the Lincoln administration. Runaway slaves frequently appeared in the Federal camps seeking sanctuary, but by the policy then in effect they were to be returned to their Maryland owners, who were (officially at least) loyal citizens of the United States.

Not content with simply following the rules, General Stone went out of his way to settle the whole issue. In a general order to his troops, he warned them "not to incite and encourage insubordination among the colored servants in the neighborhood of the camps." They must not disgrace their government by acting the part of "incendiaries." His gratuitous edict was not welcomed by all his soldiers, particularly those in New England regiments where abolitionist sentiment was strong. (Stone himself was from Massachusetts, but he took pride in having entirely escaped any taint of abolitionism.) There was much grumbling in the ranks about having to play the role of slave-catching Simon Legrees.

Stone had little enough popularity with his men to begin with. There was a streak of old-army martinet in him, an affinity for unbending, by-the-book discipline that did not sit well with volunteers. An officer who stood by him during his coming trials admitted that Stone was "not a man that gets a particular hold on the hearts and enthusiasm of volunteer soldiers." One regiment in particular raised Stone's hackles: the 2nd New York, a militia unit that in his eyes lacked discipline and most other soldierly attributes. He repeatedly came down hard on the regiment's officers, which as a group he re-

garded as poor command material. In due course the 2nd New York would
have its revenge on the general.

It was the Battle of Ball's Bluff, on October 21, 1861, that set loose the
forces that would destroy Charles Stone. By later Civil War standards, Ball's
Bluff was a minor action, with total casualties of less than 1,100. By the standards of 1861, however, it was a serious enough affair, and for the Federals,
who suffered 85 percent of the casualties, it was a humiliating one as well.
Coming three months to the day after Bull Run, it roused the insistent demand, in Congress and across the North, for answers to why it had happened
and who was responsible. Ball's Bluff roused in the army an equal insistence
that these answers not be revealed.

In mid-October, General McClellan had received word that the Confederates were reducing their Leesburg garrison. He decided to see if a threatening
move on his part might bluff them into abandoning Leesburg entirely, thus
giving up the anchor of their line on the upper Potomac. To be sure, he had
no intention of inviting a battle for Leesburg; McClellan believed his Army of
the Potomac still too weak in manpower, arms, and training to meet the enemy in open combat. Yet any gain won by maneuver alone would suit him
very well. On October 19, he advanced Brigadier General George McCall's division along the Virginia side of the Potomac to within a dozen miles of Leesburg. On the Maryland side of the river, General Stone was instructed to
"keep a good lookout upon Leesburg" to see if McCall's movement might
drive the Confederates away. "Perhaps a slight demonstration on your part
would have the effect to move them," McClellan added.

In truth, McClellan was engaging in wishful thinking, waiting hopefully
like Mr. Micawber (as he liked to say) "in case anything turned up." He credited the Rebels with an army three times its actual size and substantially
larger than his own, and he cannot seriously have expected them to give up
Leesburg so obligingly. He must have finally come to that conclusion himself
for, on October 20, he ordered McCall and his division back to Washington.
He told Stone nothing of this, however. Indeed, he seems to have forgotten
about Stone and his "slight demonstration."

On that day, October 20, Stone dutifully moved his troops up to the Potomac opposite Leesburg and made threatening motions at crossing over to
Virginia. During the night, a detachment of the 15th Massachusetts did cross
the river, at a place called Ball's Bluff, and made a reconnaissance toward Leesburg. On the morning of October 21, the 15th's colonel reported that the enemy had spotted him.

Stone, who was at Edwards Ferry, another crossing point four miles downstream, sent Colonel Edward D. Baker to take command at Ball's Bluff. He gave Baker the discretion to withdraw the men from the Virginia shore or to reinforce them, as the situation might dictate. Stone would meanwhile add weight to the demonstration by crossing a brigade at Edwards Ferry. Assuming McCall's division was then advancing upriver toward Leesburg, he expected that these Federal threats to Leesburg from three directions ought to achieve McClellan's purpose very nicely.

Edward Baker was one of the better-known officers in the Army of the Potomac. An old Illinois friend of Abraham Lincoln's—the Lincolns named their second son for him—Baker had moved west and in 1860 was elected senator from Oregon. After Fort Sumter he raised a regiment and was commissioned its colonel, and in these early months of the war he was partial to appearing in the Senate in full uniform to declaim against secessionists and all their works. Baker was much admired for his oratorical skills, but (as events were to prove) he was sadly lacking in comparable military skills. Apparently all he recalled from his Mexican War experience was reckless dash.

When Colonel Baker reached the Ball's Bluff crossing, heavy fire could be heard from across the river. Without going to the scene to investigate, and with only the sketchiest information, he determined to make a battle of it. He ordered three additional regiments to Ball's Bluff, but for some time remained behind to speed the crossing in the few available boats. Finally he crossed and took command. "I congratulate you, sir, on the prospect of a battle," he told one of his officers.

Baker's tactical dispositions were as rash as his decision to give battle. Soon the Federals were driven into a meadow at the edge of the bluff, facing a deadly converging fire from the enemy posted in good cover on higher ground. Baker went out front to rally his men by personal example and in an instant was cut down by four bullets. He was dead before he hit the ground.

None of these Yankee troops had been under fire before, all of them could see the trap closing, and Colonel Baker's death was an unnerving blow. Organization began to unravel and then was gone altogether. There was a desperate scramble down the steep bluff to the water's edge. The fugitives found nowhere near enough boats to carry them to safety, and then the largest of the craft was swamped by panicked men and capsized in the swift current, drowning almost everyone in it. Others tried to swim for it, and from the rim of the bluff above the Rebels poured down a murderous fire until the surface of the river was lashed into white water by the torrent of bullets. Of the 1,700 Federals who had crossed over to Ball's Bluff, less than 800 made it back to Maryland. Hundreds were captured, and scores were drowned.

Had he lived, Colonel Baker would certainly have borne primary responsibility for the disaster. He had committed to battle without appraising the situation, failed to take the shortage of boats into account, and on the battlefield handled his troops badly. Stone could be faulted for giving the inexperienced Baker discretionary rather than positive orders, yet he had no reason to think Baker would so mishandle his part of the demonstration. As McClellan explained to his wife, "the man *directly* to blame for the affair was Colonel Baker who was killed—he was in command, disregarded entirely the instructions he had received from Stone, and violated all military rules and precautions." McClellan officially cleared Stone of culpability: "The disaster was caused by errors committed by the immediate Commander—*not* Genl Stone."

But if Colonel Baker was the immediate cause of the defeat, General McClellan was also culpable. The entire operation had been without point or purpose. His telegraphed orders during the fighting were misleading and confusing. He later insisted he never intended that Stone send a single man across the river, but there was no such stricture in his dispatches. Most serious was his failure to tell Stone that he had withdrawn McCall's division. Everything Stone did was based on the assumption that he was acting in concert with McCall. He never suspected the Confederates were free to concentrate entirely against him. The whole business, a Federal officer wrote home, was "plainly an unpremeditated and unprepared effort, and failed, as nine out of ten such hasty affairs will."

Yet these truths about Ball's Bluff were not easily seen at the time. General McClellan's role was carefully concealed behind a veil of government censorship. Colonel Baker was transmuted into a dead hero, killed in the heat of battle as he rallied his men, his brave sacrifice a bright spot in an otherwise grim story. The first authentic account of Ball's Bluff to penetrate the censorship was Stone's official report, which appeared in the *New York Tribune* on October 30. (Its publication was unauthorized, the *Tribune* reporter having clandestinely made or stolen a copy at Stone's headquarters.) While commending Baker's courage, Stone was unsparing of Baker's failings. Baker's friends in the army, the Congress, and the press rushed to his defense, aiming their shafts at the one visible target, General Stone. "I was bound not to care for the barking of newspaper correspondents and editors," Stone said. He responded with a supplemental report that was even harder on Baker. It was made necessary, he said stiffly, by the "persistent attacks made upon me by the friends (so called), of the lamented late Colonel Baker, through the newspaper press. . . ."

Soon more than Stone's military competence was being questioned. A Massachusetts soldier wrote his governor, John A. Andrew, to complain that his regiment was forced by Stone's orders to capture fugitive Negroes and send them back into slavery. Governor Andrew publicly protested "such dirty and despotic work. Massachusetts does not send her citizens forth to become hunters of men. . . ." Charles Sumner, the Bay State's celebrated abolitionist senator, was also aroused. "Brigadier General Stone has seen fit to impose this vile and unconstitutional duty upon Massachusetts troops," Sumner announced to the Senate, and he termed it an outrage. Outraged himself, Stone wrote Sumner a letter that all but challenged the senator to a duel. Stone raised tempers even higher by reissuing his order that cautioned his troops against "encouraging insubordination" among Maryland's slaves. Charles Stone was certainly treated unjustly, a journalist later remarked, but he had a manner that "provoked injustice."

Congress acted as a forum for debate on the Ball's Bluff disaster. In the House the noisy Roscoe Conkling of New York termed it "the most atrocious military murder ever committed in our history as a people." When McClellan rejected Congress's call for an investigation, Conkling called it a cover-up. Suppose that General Stone "is a martinet and not a soldier; suppose he turns out to be halfway, either in his soldiership or his loyalty," he said, "is that a reason why investigation should be muzzled or throttled?" Stone sought a court of inquiry and a chance to rebut "the extraordinary batch of misstatements made by Mr. Conkling." He was warned off by McClellan's staff. "Don't write or say anything now," he was told. "Keep quiet. Your military superiors are attacked."

By the time this exchange took place, early in January 1862, a major new player had entered the Stone case. Congress had established the Joint Committee on the Conduct of the War to investigate every aspect of military policy and, as one senator explained it, to "teach men in civil and in military authority that the people expect that they will not make mistakes, and that we shall not be easy with their errors." It was destined to become one of the most notorious investigative committees in congressional history.

Beyond its commendable oversight functions of ferreting out waste and corruption in government contracts and inefficiency in military administration, the committee sought to stamp its particularly vehement attitude toward war-making on the army's high command. Under the chairmanship of Senator "Bluff Ben" Wade, a case-hardened Radical Republican from Ohio, it pressed for the promotion of generals with proper (i.e., Republican) attitudes and for dismissal of generals exhibiting Democratic leanings. It intruded on military policy-making and pushed the administration to adopt radical measures. Its methods of taking testimony in closed session and browbeating witnesses led opponents to call it a star chamber. Such became the notoriety of the Wade committee that during World War II Senator Harry Truman, heading a similar investigation, was at pains not to model his committee on its predecessor.

Bluff Ben Wade set as his first task to get to the bottom of the Ball's Bluff affair, and a variety of witnesses were called to testify in closed session. Stone testified on January 5, 1862, repeating what he had said in his report that earlier was leaked to the press. He was forbidden by McClellan's express orders to reveal anything of the plans or orders of the high command. McClellan, aware that the committee was making a case against him for the continued inactivity of the Army of the Potomac, was determined to give it no further ammunition by having his own role in the Ball's Bluff disaster revealed. "They want a victim," he remarked in discussing the committee with one of his officers. "Yes—and when they have once tasted blood, got one victim," the officer warned him, "no one can tell who will be the next victim!" With that McClellan colored and said nothing more. No doubt the general in chief believed Stone innocent "of all improper motives" (as he later put it), yet he had no intention of taking Stone's place on the block.

To this point, despite the restrictions McClellan had placed on his testimony, Stone seemed safe enough in his defense. He might have been slandered in the newspapers and in Congress, as he claimed, but thus far nothing really very damaging to him had come out of the Wade committee's investigation. Then the case took a startling new turn with the testimony of Colonel George W. B. Tompkins, of the 2nd New York militia.

His regiment had not even been at Ball's Bluff, but Colonel Tompkins had a tale to tell anyway. He said that General Stone was not the loyal Union man he claimed to be, that he communicated with the enemy under flags of truce, and that sealed packages were exchanged on these occasions. Stone allowed civilians to pass back and forth across the Potomac. Tompkins claimed that secessionist-minded Marylanders had "a good opinion generally" of Stone. He said that not a man in his regiment was willing to fight under the general. Chairman Wade asked if they doubted his ability or his loyalty. They doubted both, Tompkins replied.

Colonel Tompkins was followed by a parade of other 2nd New York informants—no fewer than ten of the thirty-six witnesses in the Ball's Bluff inquiry were from this one regiment—who painted similar pictures. To be sure, not a single witness could give any actual, direct evidence of General Stone's disloyalty, but all had heard stories of suspicious goings-on with the enemy. They understood, they said, that Stone had even permitted the Rebels to erect a fort guarding Leesburg without interference. These assorted lieutenants and captains, paymasters and quartermasters, enlightened the committee on how Ball's Bluff should have been fought and won.

It is the striking uniformity of this 2nd New York testimony that first suggests a conspiracy, which becomes readily apparent when the witnesses are examined more closely. The ringleader was certainly Tompkins, who, the committee staff reported, came unbidden to the case and "rendered efficient service" in collecting evidence against Stone. His motive is equally clear. Stone had brought serious charges against Tompkins, first for filing a false muster, a fraud to gain the pay of nonexistent soldiers, and second for "misbehavior before the enemy" at the Battle of Bull Run. Headquarters had affirmed to Stone that the misbehavior was cowardice and that Tompkins ought to be cashiered, but to avoid further public "embarrassment" about Bull Run it suggested that he threaten the colonel with court-martial to pressure him into resigning "for the good of the service." Two other 2nd New York witnesses had also been brought up on charges by Stone, one for filing a false muster and the other, a quartermaster, for fraud in falsifying his accounts.

McClellan later claimed he brought these "disgraceful charges" to the attention of the committee, but if so it went unnoted in the committee's records. The committee also shrugged off the sworn testimony of other witnesses who explained (for example) that flags of truce were perfectly normal between opposing forces, and that what had been exchanged at these meetings was nothing more sinister than packages of letters from prisoners of war. Wade and his colleagues had their teeth into something and would not be deterred. Clearly, General Charles Stone was soft on secessionism as well as slavery, and the disaster at Ball's Bluff had been no accident. Colonel Baker was the victim not of his own rashness but of a betrayal by his superior officer.

The committee promptly took its evidence impeaching Stone's loyalty to the new secretary of war, Edwin M. Stanton. When Stanton entered the scene, the Stone case had its grand inquisitor. The war secretary, an acquaintance wrote, was a man of grim determination and strong suspicions, "a sleuth-hound sort of man who never lost his scent or slackened his purpose." Stanton immediately formed an alliance with the Wade committee, which urged him at least to have General Stone investigated. Stanton went further than that. On January 28, he ordered McClellan to relieve Stone of his command, arrest him, and hold him "in close custody until further orders." McClellan did not carry out the order, but instead went to the committee to argue that Stone be given the chance to answer the charges made against him. The committee agreed to the request and, on January 31, Stone testified for a second time.

However, he was not permitted to read any testimony or confront any witnesses; it was said that if he knew their identities he might take reprisals. Instead, Wade summarized the case against him. He said witnesses blamed Stone for the Ball's Bluff defeat, especially for failing to reinforce Colonel Baker from the position at Edwards Ferry. Stone could only repeat that the fight at Ball's Bluff had been made on Baker's responsibility. It would have been "false soldiership" for him to try to break through from Edwards Ferry, even had he known of Baker's crisis; militarily it simply could not be done, since he had lacked both the force and the time. "We are not military men, any of us," Wade told him. "But you judge military men," Stone replied. That was true, Wade said, "but not finally. We only state what, in our opinion, tends to impeach them . . . and leave it to better judges to determine."

As for his alleged disloyalty, Stone said with rising emotions "that is one humiliation I had hoped I never should be subjected to." The charge "utterly astounded" him. Were he a traitor, he pointed out, he could easily have turned Washington over to the secessionists during the crisis a year earlier. "And now I will swear that this government has not a more faithful soldier." He insisted that any dealings he had with the enemy were perfectly proper under the usages of war, done only for the benefit of his captured men. As for permitting the Rebels to build fortifications within range of his guns, he said, "That is simply false—it is simply false." (Later, when he read his testimony in the committee's report, Stone remarked, "A few strong expressions which I used I notice are not there.") They were not military men, Wade repeated; they only gathered the evidence and let others decide.

There for a time the matter rested. However biased the committee might be and however injudicial its methods, it lacked any actual powers to carry the inquiry farther. As Wade pointed out, it only gathered evidence; it would be up to the president or secretary of war to act. Wade reported the supposedly conflicting points in Stone's testimony to Stanton, who in turn pressed McClellan on the arrest order. McClellan cast about for some way to dispose of the explosive situation without further damage to himself or the army. Then, a week after Stone testified, Allan Pinkerton provided him with the solution.

Pinkerton, the Chicago private detective who directed McClellan's military intelligence gathering, spent much of his time interrogating those who reached Federal lines "from the other side"—refugees, fugitive slaves, Rebel deserters. One of those he questioned was a Jacob Shorb, a refugee from Confederate-held Leesburg who claimed to be a good Unionist at heart. Shorb told of overhearing one Confederate officer call Stone "a very fine man," and another one comment on the frequency of flags of truce. Someone else told him that the Confederate commander, Brigadier General Nathan G. Evans, was overheard to say "that *General Stone was a brave man and a gentleman.*"

Although even Pinkerton admitted that Shorb, and the thinness of his testimony, "did not impress me very favorably," McClellan was impressed enough to question the man personally. On February 8, satisfying himself that Shorb's story "tended to corroborate some of the charges against General Stone," he showed the report to Stanton. The secretary of war repeated the arrest order, and this time McClellan obeyed promptly. That night, General Sykes and the detail of guardsmen arrested Stone. The Pinkerton report went into the army files marked "Full account of Gen. Stone's treachery."

✦

THE STORY OF STONE'S ARREST MADE HEADLINES. Stanton released enough details to leave no doubt that the case involved disloyalty. "Everybody was astounded by the news that General Stone had been arrested," a New York diarist wrote. "He is now in Fort Lafayette, charged, it is said, with treasonable correspondence. . . . That there has been treason somewhere in high quarters is certain, and if Stone is guilty, I hope he may be speedily hanged." A diarist in Washington learned that the arrest was "entirely the act of McClellan & Stanton," and that Senator Wade and his committee "claim to have developed the facts." The *New York Tribune* warned in an editorial, "The knell of traitors within already tolls."

The Articles of War required an officer ordering an arrest to file charges within eight days. That date came and went, and Stone and the counsel he employed dutifully requested copies of the charges from McClellan's headquarters, from the army's adjutant general, from the secretary of war. They met a blank wall. McClellan's staff replied that the case was "still under investigation." Stanton said that charges were being framed and would be filed in good season. The adjutant general did not reply. "Then I began to see that malice and not mistaken justice was at work," Stone said.

The Committee on the Conduct of the War did hear nine more witnesses after Stone's arrest, but they added little that was new. Indeed, more of this testimony supported Stone than condemned him, and the committee ended its inquiry. Pinkerton continued to collect what he labeled "further information concerning Gen. Stone's treachery." There was a remarkable consistency to his reports. Virtually every refugee and fugitive slave interviewed hit on the same phrase to describe how Virginians thought of General Stone—as "a very nice man"—which suggests that each was asked the leading question, "Have you ever heard General Stone called a very nice man?" Several were kept close at hand should their testimony be needed against Stone. Jacob Shorb, Pinkerton's main catch from across the river, remained on the secret service's witness payroll at $3 a day throughout Stone's imprisonment.

As the weeks passed, it became increasingly obvious that no one in Washington wanted General Stone actually charged and brought to trial. So long as those empowered with enforcing the Articles of War chose to ignore them, Stone was helpless. The Committee on the Conduct of the War was satisfied that it had found the truth about Ball's Bluff and demonstrated Congress's power to investigate the military. General McClellan was exceedingly anxious not to expose himself or the army to the public scrutiny of court-martial proceedings. McClellan may well have believed in Stone's loyalty, as he later claimed, yet he paid only lip service to getting him his day in court.

For Edwin Stanton, the grand inquisitor, General Stone was merely a pawn to be cynically manipulated in a larger game. Possessing one of the best legal minds in the country, Stanton was certainly aware that the case against Stone would never stand up in court-martial. There was not a scrap of direct evidence of his disloyalty. All the testimony was hearsay; the story of every witness would collapse under cross-examination. Yet keeping Stone where he was, uncharged but guilty in the court of public opinion, suited the war secretary's purposes. To Stanton, Charles Stone's real guilt was his lack of heart for the kind of unsparing war needed to destroy the South and slavery. So long as Stone was shut away in military prison, incommunicado but for all to see, he was an object lesson to others of his kind (others like General McClellan), a warning that generals must be subservient to the policies and politics of the administration that employed them.

Stone did not lack for defenders during his ordeal. Winfield Scott, his superior in Washington at the outbreak of the war, now retired, was outraged by the arrest: "Why if he is a traitor I am a traitor, and we are all traitors." Without Charles Stone, he insisted, the capital would have been lost. A month after the arrest a petition calling for justice and an immediate trial arrived at the White House from Massachusetts, Stone's home state, signed by first families of the Commonwealth, the mayor and aldermen of Boston, major figures of business and the bar, the Harvard faculty, and hundreds of others. Stone had enough supporters in the Senate to pass a resolution calling on the president for a report on the arrest.

In this debate, Senator James A. McDougall of California termed General Stone's patriotism above reproach, yet it was said he was a traitor. "Who says it?" McDougall asked. "Rumor says it—the great manufacturer of falsehoods. . . ." Lincoln replied that the general had been arrested under his "general authority," but it was not now in the public interest "to make a more particular statement of the evidence." The president was keeping his distance, leaving the matter to Stanton. Not for the first time, the secretary of war would be the administration's lightning rod.

Senator McDougall went on to call for a court of inquiry in the matter, and he took the Committee on the Conduct of the War to task for its responsibility in the imprisonment of Stone. Chairman Wade leaped to the committee's defense. "There was, and is, probable cause for the arrest of General Stone," he said. Wade was scornful of the notion that Stone's constitutional rights had been violated, and he offered a novel defense of the committee's efforts: It should be obvious, he said, "that if people are shut up in dungeons, and restrained of their liberties, it is that the Constitution may live."

After seven weeks in grim Fort Lafayette, Stone was transferred to the less confining Fort Hamilton, but there was no reply to his request for a suspension of arrest so that he might serve in the spring campaign then beginning in Virginia. In late June he wrote wearily to a friend, "For one hundred and thirty odd days I have been hoping what you have hoped—a trial and acquittal—but up to this time have not advanced so far as to receive any word of charges . . . , so I am in a complete muddle."

The break in Stone's case finally came after five long months of captivity. At Senator McDougall's instigation, a section was inserted in a pending military "pay and emoluments" bill that spoke to the matter of officers under arrest. The accused, it said, must be told the charges against him within eight days of arrest, and was entitled to trial within thirty days. No names were mentioned, of course, but the section contained the key language that it applied to "all persons now under arrest and waiting trial." The bill passed both houses of Congress on July 8, and it was signed into law by the president on July 17.

Vindictive to the last, Secretary Stanton waited until the thirtieth day to acknowledge the new law. Only on August 16, 1862, did General Charles Stone walk out of Fort Hamilton a free man.

He still had to liberate his reputation. In Washington he renewed his call for the charges against him and for a forum in which to refute them. He went to the White House to appeal to the president. Lincoln told him, Stone related, "that if he told me all he knew about the matter he should not tell me much." Henry W. Halleck, the new general in chief, said he knew nothing of the case and could find out nothing, nor did he have orders assigning Stone to duty. In September, with the Confederates invading Maryland and the military scene in crisis, McClellan sought Stone to command a division to meet the invaders. Secretary Stanton denied the request. Early in 1863, a new commander of the Army of the Potomac, General Joseph Hooker, applied for Stone to be his chief of staff. Stanton turned aside that request as "not considered in the interests of the service." The grand inquisitor would not recant.

Finally, late in February 1863, more than a year after his arrest, Charles Stone gained the hearing he sought. The Committee on the Conduct of the War allowed him to read the testimony taken in the Ball's Bluff inquiry and to testify for the third time. Stone went down the list of allegations, thoroughly demolishing each one and discrediting witness after witness. With McClellan gone from the high command and his gag order lifted, Stone could finally detail the orders under which he had acted on that day of battle sixteen months before. Chairman Wade expressed astonishment at his testimony. Stone reminded him that against the earlier generalized charges he could make only generalized denials. Six weeks later, the committee published—without comment—the entire Ball's Bluff inquiry, including Stone's most recent testimony. The utter falsity of the case against General Stone, and the injustice of it all, was at last publicly revealed.

In due course Stone was given a command in the Western theater, but in the spring of 1864, on Stanton's order, he was mustered out of the volunteer service, his rank reverting to colonel in the regular army. In August of that year he returned to the Army of the Potomac as commander of a brigade, but after less than a month, still dogged by the rumors of disloyalty and certain he was under surveillance, he resigned his commission. In recounting his ordeal to an early historian of the war, in 1866, Stone remarked, "If you can make out the *reason* it is more than I have ever been able to do."

Charles Stone would return to military service, albeit foreign, after the war, acting as chief of staff for thirteen years in the army of the khedive of Egypt. He afterward pursued an engineering career, and in a final irony his last project before his death in 1887 was supervising work, within sight of his wartime prison, on the foundation for the Statue of Liberty.

In writing about the first year of the Civil War, the historian Bruce Catton has called it an Era of Suspicion. More than anything else, it was suspicion—combined with conspiracy—that trapped Stone and imprisoned him and destroyed his career. Against the unholy conjunction of an unprincipled congressional committee, an inquisitorial secretary of war, and a weak-willed army administration, General Stone had no defense.

"The whole chapter, from beginning to end, has been as impenetrable as the veil of Isis," the *New York Times* had editorialized when the Committee on the Conduct of the War finally published its Ball's Bluff report. "There was *something* behind, but that was all that could be made out. . . . As it is, General Stone has sustained a most flagrant wrong—a wrong which will probably stand as the very worst blot on the National side in the history of the war." This was written in 1863 and proved to be prophetic. No doubt that judgment was the only satisfaction Charles Stone ever gained from the affair.

II

THE
STRATEGIC VIEW

WHAT TOOK
THE NORTH SO LONG?

WILLIAMSON MURRAY

To begin to answer the question posed in Williamson Murray's title, first look at a map. The distance between New Orleans and Washington is just over 1,000 miles, and that, as the saying goes, is as the crow flies. In the last year of peace, 1860, a train trip between the two cities would take about five days. But think in Napoleonic terms, as everyone did in that era. The conqueror of Europe, Murray points out, needed eight years of campaigning, from 1799 until 1807, to extend his domination from the Franco-German border to the boundary with Czarist Russia, or about the same thousand miles. Add to that another geographic presence that Napoleon did not have to contend with. Wilderness covered much of the American distance, especially west of the Appalachians, a mountain barrier that mostly resisted the movement of armies. For the South, terrain and distance were great equalizers.

But geography was just a beginning. There were many other questions involved, which Murray examines here. Were Confederate soldiers, inured to outdoor life, better suited to war than their Union counterparts? Was there a "natural superiority of Southern officers and generals," as another popular explanation would have it? Have we fixated too long on events in the East, at the expense of the Western theater, where the war may really have been won? How strong were ideological considerations? How did citizen armies master the "real" conditions of war, ones that made the old Napoleonic set-piece battles increasingly obsolete? How did the leaders of the North, who had no background in war of this magnitude and intensity, come to evolve a coherent, and ultimately effective, strategy? Was the wonder, finally, not that it took the North so long, but that it didn't take even longer?

Williamson Murray is a professor of history emeritus at Ohio State University and, with Allen R. Millett, the author of the recently published *A War to Be Won: Fighting the Second World War.*

THE CIVIL WAR DEVASTATED THE SOUTH AND SAVAGED THE armies of both sides, exacting a casualty toll that made it one of the costliest wars in modern times and the worst in American history. At the heart of the bloody struggle lay the grand strategy of the North. As so often has happened in history, Northern strategy emerged only gradually. The path to victory was not clear on either side in 1861. Nor was the outcome of the war preordained. Political and military leaders on both sides enjoyed few of the prerequisites in education, inclination, and background to wage a war of this magnitude and intensity.

The North was eventually victorious because its leadership learned from its mistakes and adapted to the "real" conditions of war. In particular, Abraham Lincoln, a backwoods Illinois lawyer with only ninety days of militia experience in the Black Hawk War of 1832, and Ulysses S. Grant, perhaps the clearest-thinking general in American history, solidified Northern strategy and grasped victory from the wreckage of the early days.

The North, of course, relied on its great superiority in population, industrial resources, financial reserves, and agricultural production. Why, then, did it take so long for the federal government to achieve victory? We might begin by examining several popular explanations for the length of the war. The most persistent is that Southern soldiers, largely drawn from a yeoman class of farmers, had spent their lives shooting game and inuring themselves to hardship in a healthy outdoor environment. The Northern population, on the other hand, condemned to work in dark, dank factories, supposedly had developed few of the attributes that an army requires. Such a view, however, flies in the face of social evidence and the testimony of those who fought. One Southern officer, writing to a Northern friend immediately after the war, put the case differently. "Our officers were good," he commented, "but considering that our rank and file were just white trash and they had to fight regiments of New England Yankee volunteers, with all their best blood in the ranks, and Western sharpshooters together, it is only wonderful that we weren't whipped sooner." The fact is that nearly 80 percent of the Northern

population lived in rural areas, like their Southern counterparts, and it is hard
to see much difference in the social composition of the armies.

A corollary argument holds that the crucial factor in the war's length lay in
the natural superiority of Southern officers and generals, an aristocratic group
of West Point cavaliers who had been raised in the antebellum South to appreciate warrior values. The legends surrounding Robert E. Lee, Stonewall
Jackson, and Jeb Stuart lend a certain plausibility to the argument, and the
dismal record of the Union Army of the Potomac in the eastern theater of operations supports it. With two victories (Gettysburg and Five Forks), twelve
defeats, and one draw (Antietam), the Army of the Potomac had a record of
unambiguous failure matched by no other unit of equivalent size in the history of the United States Army. But historians have for too long overempha-
sized the war on the Eastern front.

In fact, in the West, the reverse was true: There, Confederate forces fared
just as badly as their counterparts in the Army of the Potomac and as a result
of the same kind of wooden-headed leadership. Floyd, Pemberton, Bragg, and
Hood on the Confederate side in the West fully matched the incompetence of
McDowell, McClellan, Hooker, and Burnside in the Army of the Potomac. In
his memoirs, Ulysses S. Grant recounts one anecdote from the pre-war army
that captures the nature of Bragg's leadership:

> On one occasion, when stationed at a post of several companies commanded
> by a field officer, [Bragg] was himself commanding one of the companies and
> at the same time acting as post quartermaster and commissary. He was first
> lieutenant at the time, but his captain was detached on other duty. As a com-
> mander of the company he made a requisition upon the quartermaster—him-
> self—for something he wanted. As quartermaster he declined to fill the
> requisition, and endorsed on the back of it his reasons for doing so. As company
> commander he responded to this, urging that his requisition called for nothing
> but what he was entitled to, and that it was the duty of the quartermaster to fill
> it. As quartermaster he still persisted that he was right. In this condition of af-
> fairs Bragg referred the whole matter to the commanding officer of the post.
> The latter, when he saw the nature of the matter referred, exclaimed, "My God,
> Mr. Bragg, you have quarrelled with every officer in the army, and now you are
> quarrelling with yourself."

One of the soldiers in the Army of Tennessee reflected a perfect understanding of Bragg's leadership when asked whether he was in the general's

army. "Bragg's army? Bragg's got no army. He shot half of them himself up in Kentucky, and the other half got killed at Murfreesboro!" The superior command skills of the Confederate generals in the East were more than counterbalanced by the quality of Union leadership in the West.

As for the romantic image that clings to Eastern Confederate generals, one might well remember Jackson's and Lee's ruthless brand of leadership. The former's marches up and down northern Virginia were frequently punctuated by summary executions of deserters; under his cold-eyed Presbyterian command, there was nothing cavalier about serving in his army. As for Lee, he was as ferocious a combat leader as the American army has produced. At Malvern Hill he brashly threw his men against a Union artillery concentration deadlier than any in the war. He won the day, but only at tremendous cost. War is a nasty business, and the Confederate generals in the East were extremely good at it.

The length of the war has far more to do with the immensity of the geographic arena and the complexities of modern war than with the supposed superiority of Southern manhood and the competence of Southern generals. Geography offers a major clue as to why the North found it so difficult to project its industrial and military power into the Southern states and end the rebellion. Taken together, Mississippi and Alabama are slightly larger than what once was West Germany. The distance from central Georgia to northern Virginia is approximately the distance from East Prussia to Moscow. The distance from Baton Rouge to Richmond exceeds the distance from the Franco-German border to the current Soviet-Polish frontier. Considering that it took Napoleon from 1799 to 1807 to reach the frontiers of czarist Russia, one should not be surprised that it took the North so long to conquer the South. Exacerbating the challenge was the fact that primeval wilderness covered substantial portions of the South, particularly in the Western theater of operations. While the Eastern theater was relatively close to the centers of Northern industrial power, the starting point for the Western armies—Cairo, Illinois—was nearly a thousand miles from the North's industrial center. Without railroads and steamships, the North would not have been able to bring its power to bear and probably would have lost the war.

The first formidable problem confronting the North in the Civil War lay in mobilizing its industrial strength and population and then deploying that power into the Confederacy. The problems of mobilization were daunting. The regular army was little more than a constabulary designed to overawe Indians on the frontier; it was certainly not prepared for large-scale military operations. Nowhere was there a body of experience from which to draw in solving the issues that now arose; the armies and their support structure had

The North's strategy for defeating the Confederacy had three features: blockading the coast, securing the Mississippi, and capturing the capital at Richmond. But tactical setbacks—most notably in the East, where Union commanders engaged in little more than stopgap maneuvers—forced a new operational feature: Sherman's March, which ended close to the Virginia border.

to come from nothing. The politicians knew nothing about war. The military leaders may have read a little of Baron de Jomini's works on the Napoleonic Wars, but the knowledge they derived was probably more harmful than helpful. Certainly no one had read Clausewitz; and though by 1864 Lincoln and Grant were to evolve an approach resembling Clausewitz's, their success resulted more from trial and error and common sense than from military history or theory.

The South did possess one significant advantage at the beginning of the war. Since it had no regular army, officers who resigned their commissions in the federal army to return home and serve the Confederacy found themselves spread throughout the newly formed state regiments, where their experience could at least provide an example to others.

But in the North, since regular units continued to exist, the experience of those within the professional officer corps was not used to best advantage in creating the Northern volunteer armies. Grant records the value of just one experienced officer—himself—in training the Twenty-first Illinois. "I found it very hard work for a few days to bring all the men into anything like subordination; but the great majority favored discipline and by the application of a little regular army punishment all were reduced to as good discipline as one could want." The Twentieth Maine, trained by another lone regular officer, Adelbert Ames, also suggests the importance of experience in the training process. Not only did Ames turn out one of the best regiments in the Army of the Potomac, but Joshua Chamberlain, second-in-command of the regiment and up to July 1862, a professor of Greek at Bowdoin College, arguably became the best combat commander in the Army of the Potomac by the end of the war. All too often Union regiments did not have that one officer and therefore had to learn on the battlefield—which was an expensive process.

The armies themselves, whichever side one describes, retained a fundamentally civilian character. Photographs of even the units of the Army of the Potomac, supposedly the most spit-and-polish of all the Civil War armies, suggest a casualness that perhaps only the Israelis have exemplified in the twentieth century. When properly led, however, these troops were capable of sacrifices that few units in American military history have equaled. The performance of the First Minnesota at Gettysburg is only one case among hundreds. Although it sustained 80 percent casualties on the second day, it was back in the line receiving Pickett's charge on the third.

The whole first year of the war largely revolved around the complex task of raising, equipping, training, and deploying the forces that the strategic and political requirements of the war demanded. These problems presented themselves concurrently, not sequentially. Nor could Civil War military leaders depend on former certainties of war. The rifled musket had drastically altered combat. With killing ranges extended by 300 to 400 yards, Napoleonic set-piece tactics were no longer valid. Through a process of learning on the battlefield, Civil War armies substantially changed the manner in which they deployed and defended themselves as the war proceeded. How to wage offen-

sive warfare against modern long-range firepower, however, remained an un-
solved problem. Ultimately it would require the four long years of the First
World War before answers to this question began to appear.

The initial strategic moves of the war turned out entirely in favor of the
Federal government. Above all, Lincoln's political acuity brought the all-
important border states over to the Union camp. Ruthless action secured
Maryland and Missouri, while cautious maneuvering led the South to mistakes that tipped Kentucky to the North. Gaining Maryland secured Washington; Missouri represented the first step down the Mississippi; and the
securing of Kentucky would in early 1862 allow an obscure Union brigadier
general to move against Forts Donelson and Henry. The latter success may
have been among the most decisive in the war; the Tennessee and Cumberland
rivers were now open to Federal naval power as far as they were navigable. In
effect Grant not only captured an entire Southern army but also made Tennessee indefensible by the South, while affording the Union the opportunity
to cut the only east-west railroad that the Confederacy possessed.

However, the North's grand strategy took considerable time to emerge, at
least in its fullest, winning form. The federal government's senior commander
at the start of the war, General Winfield Scott, had a three-point strategic
framework, the famous Anaconda Plan: (1) to blockade the South, (2) to capture its capital, and (3) to open up the Mississippi. It was a start, but only a
start; the North would have to add a number of elements to achieve victory.
The Battle of Shiloh in April 1862, which underlined how drastically the tactical game had changed, should have warned how difficult this war would
prove to be. The federal government was going to have to break the will of a
population—a population, moreover, inflamed by nationalism and possessing
both a huge territory on which to draw and a Confederate government willing to take drastic measures to keep shirkers in line. Little of that was clear in
April 1862; thus Grant was widely criticized in the North when Shiloh's casualties became known. But Grant at least sensed the depth of Southern hostility and its implications after the slaughter of Shiloh:

> Up to the battle of Shiloh, I, as well as thousands of other citizens, believed
> that the rebellion against the Government would collapse suddenly and soon,
> if a decisive victory could be gained over any of its armies. Donelson and Henry
> were such victories. An army of more than 21,000 men was captured or de-
> stroyed. Bowling Green, Columbus, and Hickman, Kentucky, fell in conse-
> quence, and Clarksville and Nashville, Tennessee, the last two with an
> immense amount of stores, also fell into our hands. The Tennessee and Cum-

berland rivers, from their mouths to the head of navigation, were secured. But when Confederate armies were collected which not only attempted to hold a line farther South, from Memphis to Chattanooga, Knoxville and on to the Atlantic, but assumed the offensive and made such a gallant effort to regain what had been lost, then, indeed, I gave up all idea of saving the Union except by complete conquest.

Grant's emergence in 1862 was seemingly one of the great surprises of the war; certainly the vicious backbiting that characterized Major General Henry Halleck's reports on the future Northern commander did little to speed the process. Nevertheless, one should not assume that Grant was entirely an unknown quantity. Confederate General Richard S. Ewell wrote in spring 1861: "There is one West Pointer, I think in Missouri, little known, and whom I hope the Northern people will not find out. I mean Sam Grant. I knew him in the Academy and in Mexico. I should fear him more than any of their officers I have yet heard of. . . ."

Grant, of course, exercised little influence over Union grand strategy at the beginning; that was left to supposed prodigies such as George McClellan, whose sense of personal importance came close to losing the war in the East. Grant's conquest of the Mississippi in 1862 and 1863 opened up the great inland waterway, split the Confederacy, and cemented the alliance of the Eastern and Western states that would ultimately crush the Confederacy. His opening move at Forts Donelson and Henry exposed the one crucial geographic weakness of the Confederacy: the fact that its rivers in the West allowed Northern armies to penetrate into the very heartland of the Confederate nation. Tennessee, northern Alabama, and northern Georgia were all now within reach of invading Union troops. But under the constraints of Halleck's insipid leadership and Brigadier General William Rosecrans's tardy drive, the Union push took a considerable length of time to develop. There were some in the Confederacy who recognized how dangerous this threat might become, but Jefferson Davis continued to emphasize the Eastern theater at the expense of the West and to support the inflexible and incompetent leadership of Braxton Bragg.

Unfortunately, Grant's second great victory—and his second battle of annihilation—at Vicksburg never realized its full potential. Once the Mississippi had been opened, his victorious army dispersed and the Union high command wasted Grant during the summer of 1863. The humiliating September defeat at Chickamauga, however, forced the high command to reorganize the Western theater under Grant's control, sending him considerable reinforcements from the East. Lincoln and Secretary of War Edwin Stanton redeployed two corps from the Army of the Potomac, moving 25,000 men, along with their artillery and horses, over 1,200 miles in less than two weeks. This awesome logistic accomplishment underlines how far the North had advanced in its ability to mobilize and utilize its resources. Grant more than repaid the trust of the Lincoln administration with his smashing victory at Chattanooga in late November. His devastating defeat of Bragg's army solidified the Northern hold over Tennessee and established a solid base from which the Union's Western armies could break the South apart at its very heart: Georgia. None of this had been imaginable at the onset of war. By now the North could logistically deploy, maintain, and put into battle an army of 100,000 men in the very center of the Confederacy.

Chattanooga set the stage for the Lincoln-Grant partnership—and the full evolution of Northern grand strategy—that saw the war through to its victorious conclusion in spring 1865. By the beginning of 1864, the Anaconda Plan had for the most part been realized: The Mississippi was open; the blockade was largely effective; and only Richmond remained untaken. Northern strategy moved in new directions. Lincoln had seen early in the war that a concerted, concurrent Union effort in all theaters would be required to break the outer ring of Confederate resistance. But George McClellan had babbled about the foolishness of such an approach and had contemptuously dismissed Lincoln's proposal. McClellan, as a disciple of Jomini, could think only in terms of capturing the enemy's capital or seizing some central position that would lead to a decisive battle. Lincoln thought in far broader terms. He would learn, while McClellan, like the Bourbons who briefly regained power between Napoleon's two reigns, learned nothing.

Both Lincoln and Grant looked beyond the Eastern theater. Grant's grand strategy for 1864, after he was made commander of all the U.S. armies, aimed to crush the Confederacy with thrusts from a number of different directions. His instructions to General William Sherman (similar orders were given to General George Meade) made his intentions clear.

> It is my design, if the enemy keep quiet and allow me to take the initiative in the spring campaign, to work all parts of the army together and somewhat toward a common center. For your information I now write you my programme as at present determined upon.
>
> I have sent orders to [Major General Nathaniel P.] Banks by private messen-

ger to finish up his present expedition against Shreveport with all despatch. . . .
With [his] force he is to commence operations against Mobile as soon as he can.
It will be impossible for him to commence too early.

[Major General Quincy] Gillmore joins [Major General Benjamin F.] Butler
with 10,000 men, and the two operate against Richmond from the South side
of the James River. . . . I will stay with the Army of the Potomac, increased by
[Major General Ambrose E.] Burnside's corps of not less than 25,000 effective
men, and operate directly against Lee's army wherever it may be found.

[Major General Franz] Sigel collects all his available force in two
columns . . . to move against the Virginia and Tennessee. . . .

You I propose, to move against [Joseph E.] Johnston's army, to break it up
and to get into the interior of the enemy's country as far as you can, inflicting
all the damage you can against their war resources.

I do not propose to lay down for you a plan of campaign, but simply to lay
down the work it is desirable to have done, and leave you free to execute in your
own way.

Grant concluded by telling Sherman that Sigel probably had the smallest
chance of achieving his objective, but, as Lincoln had suggested during the
strategy briefing, "If Sigel can't skin himself, he can hold a leg whilst someone else skins." There is no clearer, more concise strategic conception in
American military history. It spelled the end of the Confederacy by 1865.

Why it did not spell defeat for the Confederacy in 1864 is worth examining. Failure to achieve victory before 1865 reflected the extraordinary difficulty in planning, coordinating, and executing military operations, as well as
the inevitable impact of political reality on the world of military operations.
Unfortunately, two key elements in Grant's strategy—Banks's move against
Mobile, and Butler's move from Bermuda Hundred to cut the Petersburg-
Richmond railroad—failed to materialize. Banks remained tied to the disastrously inept Red River campaign; consequently his move against Mobile,
which would have tied one corps of the Army of Tennessee to Alabama, did
not occur and that unit reinforced Johnston's defense of Atlanta. Butler's attack from Bermuda Hundred collapsed in a welter of incompetence rarely
seen this late in the Civil War. As Grant noted in his memoirs, Butler
"corked" himself and his army into a position where he could exercise no influence on the unfolding campaign. Had he succeeded, Lee would have been
forced to divide his forces against two foes. As it was, Butler's army was simply subsumed into the Army of the Potomac. The results of these failures prevented victory in 1864. Sherman faced far more effective resistance in his

offensive against Atlanta, while the Army of the Potomac confronted an Army of Northern Virginia that was able to devote full attention to the defense of northern Virginia.

Significantly, Grant did not complain in his memoirs that the great spring offensive failed because of the incompetent leadership of "political" generals. He was well aware that Lincoln needed the support of "war Democrats" in the upcoming presidential campaign and that keeping Butler and Banks in positions of high responsibility was therefore essential for political reasons; both were "war Democrats." Good strategy, as with all things in war, is a fine balance of choices. As the British commander James Wolfe commented before Quebec in 1757: "War is an option of difficulties." The delicate coalition that Lincoln was holding together in the North was essential to the successful settlement of a war that had opened wounds not only between the North and the South but also within the North itself. To risk damaging that coalition by removing Banks and Butler was to risk losing the presidential election, and defeat in November might well have eviscerated whatever battlefield successes the Union army would achieve in 1864.

In assuming his position as commander of all Union forces, Grant was initially inclined to remain in the West. But his justified trust in Sherman's competence led him to change his mind: He would accompany the Army of the Potomac. Meade's competent but hardly driving brand of leadership in the last half of 1863 suggests that the Army of the Potomac's commander required the support of a more senior officer upon whom he could rely in moments of crisis. Grant would provide that support. He understood, however, that as an outsider he was not in a position to replace that army's senior leadership. He therefore was compelled to fight the coming battles of spring 1864 with a fundamentally flawed instrument—a military organization whose cohesion, willingness to sacrifice, and dogged determination were second to none in American military history, but whose repeated failures to seize the initiative, incapacity to take risks, and sheer bad luck resulted in a long record of defeat and reversal.

Thus, the Army of the Potomac fought the spring and summer battles in Virginia at appalling cost to itself and the nation. As a brigadier in the Army of the Potomac wrote his wife after Spotsylvania Court House: "For thirty days it has been one funeral procession past me and it has been too much." However, while Grant pinned Lee and the Army of Northern Virginia to Richmond, Sherman battled General Johnston back in Atlanta. The pressure on Lee prevented the Confederate government from reinforcing Johnston. Jefferson Davis then made the fatal mistake of replacing Johnston with General

John B. Hood. Hood's slashing attacks from Atlanta wrecked his army, lost Atlanta, and opened the way for Sherman's March to the Sea. The march again allowed Union forces to bisect the Confederacy and further fragment the span of Southern control, while opening up the last undamaged areas of the South to attack.

It also opened the way for the final chapter in the evolution of the war's strategy: a straight-out Union policy aimed at breaking the will of the Southern population by destroying the property, homes, and sustenance on which the survival of the South rested. In May 1864 Sherman had already confided to his wife his perplexity that the Southern population had not yet given up: "No amount of poverty or adversity seems to shake their faith. . . . [N]iggers gone, wealth and luxury gone, money worthless, starvation in view, yet I see no sign of let up—some few deserters, plenty tired of war, but the masses determined to fight it out." Sherman's frustration in front of Atlanta had led to bombardment of the city irrespective of the danger to civilians or to its military usefulness. The March to the Sea had taken place soon afterward, and while Sherman's progress through Georgia was not aimed directly at civilian lives, its "collateral" effects—the ruthless destruction of homes and foodstuffs and the starvation and disease that followed in its wake—indicated how far the North was willing to go in this war. As Sherman warned in a letter to the citizens of northern Alabama in 1864:

> The government of the United States has in North Alabama any and all rights which they choose to enforce in war, to take their lives, their houses, their land, their everything, because they can not deny that war exists there, and war is simply power unconstrained by constitution or compact. If they want eternal warfare, well and good. We will accept the issue and dispossess them and put our friends in possession. To those who submit, to the rightful law and authority all gentleness and forbearance, but to the petulant and persistent secessionists, why, death is mercy and the quicker he or she is disposed of the better. Satan and the rebellious saint[s] of heaven were allowed a continuance of existence in hell merely to swell their just punishment.

Sherman then noted that the American Civil War, unlike traditional European warfare, was "between peoples," and the invading army was entitled to all it could get from the people. He cited as a like instance the dispossession of the people of North Ireland during the reign of William and Mary.

General Philip Sheridan's conduct of the Shenandoah campaign suggests that Sherman's treatment of Georgia, Alabama, and South Carolina was not a matter of idiosyncratic choice but rather represented a larger strategic and policy design of the authorities in Washington and the Union high command. Clearly indicating these were Grant's instructions to Sheridan to turn the Shenandoah into "a barren waste . . . so that crows flying over it for the balance of this season will have to carry their provender with them." Sheridan followed his orders. His remark to the Prussians during the Franco-Prussian War of 1870–71 that they were "too humanitarian" in their treatment of the French population suggests how far the Union's strategy had descended into a relentless crushing of popular resistance. As he added to his European listeners, "Nothing should be left to the people but eyes, to lament the war!" Admittedly, neither Sherman nor Sheridan reached the level of Bomber Command's "dehousing" campaign of World War II. But Northern military forces were on the ground; they could spare the inhabitants their wretched lives while destroying the economic infrastructure, homes, foodstuffs, and farm animals far more effectively than "Bomber" Harris's force could ever dream of in World War II.

The Civil War was the first modern war, one in which military power, built on popular support and industrialization, and projected by the railroad and steamships over hundreds of miles, approached the boundary of Clausewitz's "absolute" war. Neither the strategic vision nor the military capacity to win the war existed at the onset. The mere creation of armies and their requisite support structure created problems that were neither readily apparent nor easily solved. The Union leadership did evolve a strategy that at last brought victory, but the cost was appalling: somewhere around 625,000 dead on both sides, equaling the total losses of all our other conflicts up to the Vietnam War. A comparable death toll in World War I would have been about 2.1 million American lives. Given what we now know of the cost of war in the modern world, we should not be surprised at the cost of this terrible conflict. We should, rather, wonder how the leaders of the Union—unversed in strategy at the beginning of the war, masters by its end—were able to see it through to its successful conclusion.

FAILED SOUTHERN STRATEGIES

JAMES M. McPHERSON

Soon after the outbreak of the war, the new president of the Confederacy, Jefferson Davis, set forth his national strategy. "We seek no conquest," he proclaimed in a message to his congress, "no aggrandizement, no concession of any kind from the State with which we were lately confederated; all we ask is to be left alone." It was a remarkably succinct, if somewhat ingenuous, statement. Unfortunately his military strategy, as James M. McPherson points out, lacked the same coherence of purpose. That is perhaps surprising in a man who, unlike Lincoln, had as solid military credentials as almost anyone in the now divided nation. A West Pointer—a connection that looms so large in the Civil War—Davis had fought with distinction against Mexico and had been Franklin Pierce's secretary of war.

Davis and his generals did face special problems. Because of the nature of the Confederacy, an association of sovereign entities, the needs of the individual states could take precedence over those of the new nation as a whole. To what extent could the Confederate leaders concentrate their forces? To what extent should they spread them around the outer perimeter of the Confederacy, thus giving the states equal protection? Should they trade space for time in the hope, as McPherson writes, that "a defensive strategy of attrition might wear out the will or capacity of the enemy to continue fighting"? And if a survival-oriented strategy didn't work, when and where should the Confederacy go on the offensive? How best to gain the recognition from the powers of Europe that the South so badly needed? Faulty strategic choices, McPherson argues, as much as or more than the internal divisions of the Confederacy, may have made its downfall inevitable.

James M. McPherson is one of the finest historians writing today. He
is professor of history at Princeton University and the author of ten
books, including *Battle Cry of Freedom,* which won the Pulitzer Prize in
History.

IN NARRATIVES OF THEIR CAMPAIGNS WRITTEN YEARS AFTER
the Civil War, Generals Joseph E. Johnston and Pierre G. T. Beauregard agreed
that the Confederacy should have won the war. The Southern people, wrote
Johnston, were "not guilty of the high crime of undertaking a war without the
means of waging it successfully." And Beauregard insisted that "no people ever
warred for independence with more relative advantages than the Confederates."

The thinly veiled charge contained in such statements was that the Confederacy's failure lay on the shoulders of its commander in chief, Jefferson
Davis. To such accusations, leveled in private as well as in public, during the
war as well as after it, Davis did not deign to reply directly in the 1,200 pages
of his own postwar account, *The Rise and Fall of the Confederate Government.* Instead, he declared loftily, he would tell the truth in full confidence "that error
and misrepresentations have, in their inconsistencies and improbabilities, the
elements of self-destruction, while truth is in its nature consistent and therefore self-sustaining."

In the spirit of this indirect exchange, Davis's relationships with his generals have framed much of the analysis of the reasons for Confederate defeat. His
feuds with Johnston and Beauregard, his supposed favoritism toward Generals Braxton Bragg and John Bell Hood—or, alternatively, according to historian Steven E. Woodworth, his failure to sustain Bragg and his fatal refusal to
jettison Lieutenant General Leonidas Polk—are often portrayed as major
causes of disasters in the Western theater, where the Confederacy lost the war.
At the same time, Davis's personal rapport with General Robert E. Lee, for
which most historians give Lee the principal credit, helps explain the Confederacy's relative success in the Eastern theater. Davis and Johnston's relationship overlapped both theaters. This "dysfunctional partnership," maintains
Johnston's biographer Craig L. Symonds, "was an unalloyed disaster for the
cause they served" and responsible in large measure "for the failure of the Confederate war effort." In the end, this and other rifts between Davis and his
Western generals more than outweighed the victories secured by the powerful
team of Lee and Davis.

The focus on the interpersonal relations between Davis and his generals in much historical writing reflects another facet of a larger tendency in scholarly literature to emphasize internal divisions as the principal causes of Confederate defeat—divisions of race, class, gender, and region. Such internal explanations overlook the truth that the North experienced equal if not greater internal divisions during the war that at times came close to crippling the Union war effort. The same point can be made about Abraham Lincoln and his generals. Davis had Joe Johnston, but Lincoln had Major Generals George McClellan and George Meade. Davis had Beauregard, but Lincoln had Major General John Frémont. If Davis looked bad by sticking too long with Bragg—or, if we go along with Woodworth, by sticking too long with Polk and other corps commanders in the Army of Tennessee—Lincoln looked bad by successively appointing and then dismissing Major Generals John Pope, Ambrose Burnside, and Joseph Hooker over the course of a year during which the morale of the Army of the Potomac sank to a point perilously close to collapse.

Although the personalities and the relationships among the commanders in chief and their principal Union and Confederate army commanders had an important impact on the outcome of the war, a focus on strategy rather than personalities might yield a better understanding of the South's failure.

A review of the larger context of Confederate military strategy will prove helpful. During the last two millennia, studies of military leadership have usually concentrated on victorious generals and their strategies. One thinks of Hannibal, Julius Caesar, Alexander the Great, Marlborough, Frederick the Great, Napoleon Bonaparte, Wellington, and Helmuth von Moltke. In the case of the American Civil War, much professional study of strategy and leadership, particularly by British military historians but also by some Americans, has focused on Lieutenant General Ulysses S. Grant, Major General William T. Sherman, and Lincoln. One thinks of J. F. C. Fuller and John Keegan on Grant, Basil H. Liddell Hart on Sherman, Colin Ballard on Lincoln, and also of T. Harry Williams, Kenneth P. Williams, Herman Hattaway, and Archer Jones. The purpose of such studies has often been to derive some positive lessons, some formula for success from their campaigns.

Two exceptions to this emphasis on the victors are the numerous studies of German generals and their strategies in both world wars and studies of Confederate generals, especially Robert E. Lee and Thomas J. "Stonewall" Jackson. These exceptions, however, at least partially prove the rule; that is, even though the Germans and the Confederates lost their wars in the end, they won a good many victories along the way and exhibited a strategic or tactical brilliance that has made their campaigns fit studies to divine the secrets of their success—and perhaps also their failures.

Karl von Clausewitz's dictum that war is the continuation of politics by other means is so often cited that it has become almost a cliché. Because of its familiarity, however, historians sometimes gloss over the distinction that Clausewitz drew between politics and other means while blurring the continuity between them. To unpack the meaning of Clausewitz's aphorism, it is necessary to distinguish between two kinds of strategy: national strategy, the shaping and defining of a nation's political goals in time of war; and military strategy, the ways in which armed forces are used to achieve those goals.

In the United States the first is defined by the president and Congress; the second is conducted by military commanders. The president plays a key role in formulating both kinds of strategy as head of state and commander in chief. He serves as the intermediary between the government and the armed forces, conveying the national strategy to his generals while communicating to Congress and the public the ability of the armies to achieve those goals.

In theory there should be a congruity between national and military strategy. That seems an obvious common-sense observation. But in practice, military strategy in many wars has diverted from national strategy. Wars have a tendency to assume a character and momentum that become increasingly incompatible with the original national strategy. And in many wars, sharp disagreements about war aims develop within the polity, giving military commanders mixed and confusing signals about national strategy, which inhibits their ability to devise the correct military strategy. That is what happened to the United States in Vietnam. During other wars, conflict between national strategy, as defined by civilian leadership, and military strategy, as defined by generals, can cause a nation to fight at cross-purposes. President Harry Truman insisted on a limited war in Korea, while General Douglas MacArthur wanted to fight an unlimited one. Truman finally had to fire MacArthur, producing a sense of frustration among many Americans who, like MacArthur, desired to overthrow Communism in North Korea and perhaps in China as well.

The experience of Vietnam as well as the military intervention in Lebanon during the 1980s and Somalia during the 1990s led then Chairman of the Joint Chiefs of Staff Colin Powell to develop the "Powell Doctrine," which is essentially a formula for clarifying national strategy and harmonizing it with military strategy. According to the Powell Doctrine, before the United States undertakes a military action abroad, there must be a clearly defined national purpose supported by the polity and a precise military strategy to accomplish that purpose, no more and no less. America's decisions to enter the Gulf War, the intervention in Haiti, and, more debatably, in Bosnia resulted from the Powell Doctrine.

✦

THE MOST SUCCESSFUL WARS IN AMERICAN HISTORY have been those with a close congruity between national and military strategy. The national strategy in the American Revolution was independence; the military strategy achieved this goal, no more and no less. The national strategy in the Mexican War was the Rio Grande border for Texas and the acquisition of New Mexico and California; when these were assured, the United States stopped fighting. In World War II the national strategy was not merely the liberation of Europe and Asia from Fascist conquest but the overthrow of Fascist governments in the Axis nations themselves. This required a military strategy of total war and unconditional surrender; that was precisely the type of war that the Allies conducted. During the Persian Gulf War the national strategy was to drive Iraq's army out of Kuwait; when that was done, the coalition forces stopped fighting.

During the Civil War the Northern national strategy changed as the conflict expanded from a limited war to restore the antebellum status quo to an unlimited one to destroy slavery and the social order it sustained, in order to give the United States that "new birth of freedom" Lincoln invoked during his Gettysburg Address. Lincoln's genius as commander in chief was his ability to shape and define this expanding national strategy and eventually to put in place, after three rocky years, a military strategy and military leaders to carry it out.

Jefferson Davis as commander in chief suffers by comparison, in part because the Confederacy lost the war and in part because of his personality and leadership flaws. Davis was thin-skinned and lacked Lincoln's ability to work with critics for a common cause. Lincoln was reported to have said of McClellan in the fall of 1861, "I will hold McClellan's horse if he will only bring us success." It is hard to imagine Jefferson Davis saying the same of Joseph E. Johnston. Because of dyspepsia and neuralgia that worsened under wartime pressures and left him virtually blind in one eye, Davis was wracked by pain that exacerbated his waspish temper. Even his wife, Varina, noted that "if anyone disagrees with Mr. Davis he resents it and ascribes the difference to the perversity of his opponent." Lincoln was more eloquent than Davis in expressing his country's war aims, more successful in communicating them to his people. Nothing that Davis wrote or spoke during the war has resonated down through the years like the conclusion of Lincoln's first inaugural address, his annual message to Congress on December 1, 1862, the Conkling letter of August 26, 1863, the Gettysburg Address, or his second inaugural speech.

In his first message to the Confederate Congress after the outbreak of the war, however, Davis did define clearly and concisely the Confederate national strategy: "We seek no conquest, no aggrandizement, no concession of any kind from the State with which we were lately confederated; all we ask is to be let alone." This was a thoroughly defensive national strategy. It was grounded in an important fact, so obvious that its importance is often overlooked: The Confederacy began the war in firm control of nearly all the territory it claimed. This is rarely the case in civil wars or revolutions, which typically require rebels or revolutionaries to fight to gain control of land or government or both.

With a functioning government and a strong army already mobilized or mobilizing in May 1861, the Confederacy embraced 750,000 square miles in which not a single enemy soldier was to be found, save at Fort Monroe, Virginia, at the mouth of the James River, and Fort Pickens, on an island off Pensacola, Florida. All the Confederacy had to do to win the war was to defend what it already had.

The nearest comparison to the Confederacy's initial situation was that of the United States on July 4, 1776. And Davis, like the leaders of that first American war of secession, seems initially to have envisaged a "thorough defensive, survival-oriented" military strategy, in the words of Steven Woodworth, that would be consistent with his thoroughly defensive national strategy. Like Roman General Quintus Fabius in the Second Punic War, George Washington in the American Revolution, or Russian General Mikhail Kutuzov in 1812, such a survival-oriented strategy would trade space for time, keep the army concentrated and ready to strike enemy detachments dangling deep into Confederate territory, and above all avoid the destruction or crippling of the main Southern armies. Such a defensive strategy of attrition might wear out the will or capacity of the enemy to continue fighting, as the Americans and Russians had done in 1781 and 1812.

Did it matter if this Fabian strategy yielded important cities and territory? During the Revolution, America lost New York, Philadelphia, Charleston, Savannah, Williamsburg, and Richmond yet won its independence. On one occasion during the Civil War, Jefferson Davis articulated such a strategy:

> There are no vital points on the preservation of which the continued existence of the Confederacy depends. Not the fall of Richmond, nor Wilmington,

nor Charleston, nor Savannah, nor of all combined, can save the enemy from the constant and exhaustive drain of blood and treasure which must continue until he shall discover that no peace is attainable unless based on the recognition of our indefeasible rights.

But Davis said this in November 1864, after the crucible of war had forged a fierce Confederate nationalism that had sustained the will to fight despite the loss of territory and cities—though not for long after the subsequent loss of the cities named by Davis. In 1861, however, Confederate nationalism was still fragile. The Southern states had seceded individually on the principle that the sovereignty of each state was superior to that of any other entity. The very name of the new nation, the Confederate States of America, implied an association of still-sovereign states. This principle was recognized in the Confederate Constitution, which was ratified by "each State acting in its sovereign and independent character."

An example of Davis's respect for the concept of state sovereignty was his policy of trying to brigade Confederate troops by states—something much less frequently done in the Union Army. Given the existence of this initial provincialism, if Davis had tried to pursue a purely defensive strategy in 1861 by concentrating Confederate troops in Virginia and Tennessee, for example, and leaving other areas to fend for themselves, the Confederacy might have fallen to pieces of its own accord. Popular and political pressures compelled Davis to scatter small armies around the perimeter of the Confederacy at a couple of dozen points in 1861.

The danger of such a dispersal, labeled by T. Harry Williams as a "cordon defense" and by Craig Symonds as an "extended defense," was that an enemy superior in numbers and resources might break through this thin, gray line, cutting off and perhaps capturing one or more of these small armies and penetrating far into Confederate territory, as if the South had been left undefended. That is precisely what happened in late 1861 and early 1862 in western Virginia, Missouri and Arkansas, Kentucky and Tennessee, coastal North and South Carolina, southern Louisiana, and even northern Mississippi and Alabama. In a rare confession (made, to be sure, in a private letter), Davis wrote in March 1862, "I acknowledge the error of my attempt to defend all of the frontier."

He need not have been so hard on himself. Under the circumstances of 1861 he had little choice. The governors of North and South Carolina, or Mississippi, Arkansas, and Alabama, not to mention the citizen soldiers from those states who had sprung to arms to defend home and family, would not have allowed him to totally deplete their states of troops to fight in Virginia or Tennessee. Such parochialism would remain a problem for Davis and the commanders of his principal armies during most of the war. But the experiences of 1861 and early 1862 did drive home the need for some degree of concentration to meet the main enemy threats.

UNDERLYING THIS PRINCIPLE OF CONCENTRATION was the advantage of interior lines. From 1861 to 1864 the Confederates repeatedly used their interior lines in both the Eastern and Western theaters to achieve at least a partial concentration of force to strike at invading Federal armies. The first, and one of the most famous, examples was the transfer by rail of most of Joseph Johnston's small army from the Shenandoah Valley to Manassas, Virginia, in July 1861 to repel Brigadier General Irvin McDowell's attackers at the First Battle of Manassas and drive them in a rout back to Washington.

Nine months later, when confronted with a buildup of McClellan's forces on the Peninsula, the Confederates again used interior lines to transfer most of Johnston's army from Centreville to Yorktown. As Craig Symonds points out, this campaign revealed a difference between Davis and Johnston concerning the relationship between interior lines and concentration. Davis desired to leave a substantial force along the Rappahannock River to protect that region against Union forces south of Washington and thus retained part of his concept of an extended defense. Johnston wanted to concentrate nearly all Confederate units in Virginia against McClellan, as near to Richmond as possible, even at the risk of temporarily yielding northern Virginia, the Shenandoah Valley, and the Peninsula to the enemy. After disposing of McClellan, Johnston said, the main Confederate army could then recapture these other regions.

That is what eventually happened in the summer of 1862, but the army was not under the command of Johnston, who was wounded at the Battle of Seven Pines and replaced by Robert E. Lee on June 1. Part of the army of 90,000 men that Lee concentrated in front of Richmond by the last week of June 1862—the largest single Confederate army of the war—was drawn from the Shenandoah Valley. During the previous two months Stonewall Jackson had brilliantly executed another operation that emulated a successful American strategy of the Revolution: the concentration of superior numbers in a mobile force to strike separated enemy outposts or detachments. George Washington had done this at Trenton and Princeton, and other American commanders had done the same in the Carolinas. Stonewall borrowed a page from their book and struck smaller Union detachments at McDowell, Front

Royal, and Winchester and then turned on his pursuers to check them at Cross Keys and Port Republic.

Jackson then joined Lee's concentrated army that drove McClellan away from Richmond in the Seven Days' campaign—though Jackson himself did not perform up to expectations during the campaign. Soon, however, he exceeded expectations. At Lee's request, Jackson exploited interior lines to concentrate against Pope along the Rappahannock River as McClellan was withdrawing from the Peninsula. Using a favorite strategic operation of Napoleon's—*les manœuvres sur la derrière,* wide flanking movement to get into the enemy's rear—Jackson marched around Pope's flank, destroyed his supply base at Manassas, and held out against superior numbers of attacking Federals until Lee could reconcentrate his entire army to win the Second Battle of Manassas.

Confederates in the Western theater also practiced the strategy of concentration in 1862. After the Federals had broken through the cordon defense of the other Johnston—General Albert Sidney—at several points in Kentucky and Tennessee and had captured 20 percent of his troops at Fort Donelson, Johnston retreated all the way to Corinth, Mississippi. There he concentrated his scattered forces for a counterthrust at Shiloh. Although this effort did not produce a Confederate victory and it cost Johnston his life, Shiloh nevertheless set the Federals back on their heels for a time. The Confederate Army of Mississippi, now commanded by Beauregard, was finally forced to evacuate Corinth at the end of May 1862, just as Joseph Johnston's army in Virginia had evacuated Yorktown several weeks earlier. But these retreats set the stage for offensive operations later in the summer under new commanders (Lee in Virginia and Maryland and Bragg in Kentucky) that by September took the armies across the Potomac River and almost to the Ohio River.

These September campaigns accomplished a startling reversal of momentum. They also represented a new phase in Confederate strategy, which has been variously labeled as offensive-defensive, offensive defense, or defensive-offensive. Davis himself described it as offensive-defensive and contrasted it with what he called "purely defensive operations." This confusion of nomenclature perhaps reflects confusion about the precise nature of this strategy and about whether Davis favored it, opposed it, or both favored and opposed it with varying emphasis according to circumstances on the offensive or defensive element.

The effort to sort out these variables is hindered by the failure of the principals—Davis, Lee, Beauregard, Bragg, and others—to define systematically what they meant by offensive-defensive or purely defensive. Historians must tease out the meaning by a study of what they said and did in particular campaigns. One way to approach this matter is by way of an analogy from football, in which any coach would agree that the best defense is a good offense. Of course Lee knew nothing about modern American football, but he would have understood the slogan. Indeed, he could almost have invented it. "There is nothing to be gained by this army remaining quietly on the defensive," he wrote on the eve of the Gettysburg campaign. "We cannot afford to keep our troops awaiting possible movements of the enemy. . . . Our true policy . . . so to employ our own forces, as to give occupation to his at points of our selection." (In other words, we can win only if we keep our opponent off balance with an imaginative offensive.) A year later Lee told Major General Jubal Early that "we must destroy this army of Grant's before he gets to the James River. If he gets there, it will become a siege and then it will be a mere question of time."

✦

IN WARFARE, another source of confusion about the meaning of an offensive-defensive strategy sometimes results from a failure to distinguish between strategy and tactics. When Davis or Lee or any other commander spoke of the offensive-defensive—or words to that effect—were they referring to strategy, tactics, or both? They did not always offer a clear answer. Several combinations of offensive or defensive tactics and strategy are possible; Lee's campaigns demonstrate this. The Seven Days' and Gettysburg campaigns illustrate the offensive in both strategy and tactics, but the Seven Days' campaign served the defensive purpose of relieving the threat to Richmond. Fredericksburg was a defensive battle in both strategy and tactics. Antietam culminated an offensive campaign, but the Confederates fought there mainly on the tactical defensive. Second Manassas was part of a strategic offensive and was both defensive and offensive in tactics. From Spotsylvania to the end of the war, Lee's army fought almost entirely on the defensive, both strategically and tactically, though Jubal Early's raid down the Shenandoah Valley and into Maryland was an offensive strategic diversion to aid an essentially defensive strategy in Virginia.

The same variables characterized Western campaigns and battles. The first day at Shiloh was a Confederate offensive, both strategically and tactically, as was the second day at Chickamauga. Every battle during the Vicksburg campaign was defensive both in strategy and tactics for the Confederates, as was each of Johnston's fights during the Atlanta campaign. After Hood succeeded Johnston, he promptly launched three tactical offensives to serve the strategic defense of Atlanta. Hood's later invasion of Tennessee was a strategic offensive that came to grief both in the tactical offensive at Franklin and the tactical defensive at Nashville.

What determined these variables was the strategic and tactical situation at a given time and place. When Davis contrasted the offensive-defensive with the purely defensive, he was probably speaking of both strategy and tactics in different combinations according to circumstances. Failure to sort out these circumstances and the resultant variables accounts for much of the confusion and ambiguity about Confederate strategy.

Lee biographers Emory Thomas and Steven Woodworth have both clarified and muddied these waters in their writings on Confederate strategy. Both authors detect a significant difference of emphasis between Davis and Lee, neatly spelled out by Woodworth in his book with the double-entendre title *Davis and Lee at War:* "For Davis, the war could be won simply by not losing, for Lee . . . it could be lost simply by not winning." That is why Davis seemed at times to favor what he called "purely defensive operations," a Fabian strategy that would conserve the Confederacy's resources by compelling the enemy to consume his resources by repeatedly attacking, thereby suffering heavy casualties and eroding the will of the Northern people to sustain an increasingly costly effort to destroy the Confederacy.

Yet from the time Lee took command of what he renamed the Army of Northern Virginia, Davis apparently approved all of the general's operations that have come to be known as offensive-defensive: the attacks against McClellan during the Seven Days' campaign, the shift of operations to northern Virginia culminating in the Second Battle of Manassas, the invasion of Maryland, the counterthrust against Hooker at Chancellorsville followed by the invasion of Pennsylvania, and even the detachment of Early in 1864 to raid down the Shenandoah Valley to the very outskirts of Washington. This strategy was also applied in the West, where Albert Johnston and Beauregard launched an offensive at Shiloh, Bragg and Brigadier General E. Kirby Smith invaded Kentucky, and Bragg subsequently counterattacked Major General William Rosecrans at Murfreesboro and Chickamauga. In addition, Hood counterattacked Sherman around Atlanta and then launched raids against Sherman's communications in north Georgia preparatory to an invasion of Tennessee, while Major General Sterling Price moved north in an extraordinarily ambitious invasion of Missouri.

If Davis opposed these offensives, we have little record of it. On the contrary, we have plenty of evidence of his approval, especially of Lee's and Hood's operations. With respect to Davis's cordial relations with Lee, both Thomas and Woodworth have suggested that Lee charmed and smooth-talked Davis into such support so skillfully that, as Thomas expresses it in his biography of Lee, "Davis was unaware of the difference between himself and Lee." Indeed, the "difference was not apparent during the war" and has also escaped most historians. Thomas finds the dissonance between Davis and Lee most salient in Lee's two most ambitious offensive efforts to conquer a peace: the invasion of Maryland in September 1862, and the invasion of Pennsylvania nine months later. Yet curiously, Thomas also notes that Davis "was delighted with Lee's invasion of Maryland." If so, that helps explain why their dissonance was not apparent to Davis at the time or to most historians since. In any event, it is quite true that during the Gettysburg campaign Davis held some troops in the Richmond area, instead of combining them with brigades in North Carolina commanded by Beauregard, to conduct a diversionary action near Culpeper and draw Federal forces away from Pennsylvania, as Lee had requested. Davis did so for the very good reason that, as Lee headed north, 16,000 Union troops on the Peninsula commanded by Major General John A. Dix were threatening Richmond from the east in a brief campaign that has been all but ignored, while Beauregard had his hands full dealing with a major Federal effort against Charleston.

✦

ALTHOUGH DAVIS AND LEE appeared to be in accord on most matters of strategy, Thomas and Woodworth are nevertheless onto something in their focus on areas of disagreement. As Thomas explains, the difference in strategic outlook was a subtle matter of which word should receive the greater emphasis in the concept of an offensive-defensive strategy. But there is an unacknowledged irony here if Woodworth is correct that Davis really preferred a "thoroughly defensive, survival-oriented grand strategy." These words describe Joseph Johnston's strategy almost perfectly. But of course it was with Johnston that Davis quarreled most bitterly. So thoroughly defensive and survival-oriented was Johnston's strategy during the Atlanta campaign that historian Richard McMurry was not being altogether facetious when he said that Johnston would have fought the crucial battle of that campaign on Key West. If Davis's choice of Hood to replace Johnston is any clue to his strategic leaning, it was more to the offensive than the defensive, for Hood was one of the most offensive-minded of the generals who came up under Lee's tutelage.

A related issue in a discussion of Confederate strategy concerns the East vs. West debate. In May 1863 the top Confederate leadership confronted a crucial decision about allocation of resources and effort between the Eastern and Western theaters. Lee had recently won a just renowned victory at Chancellorsville. But the Confederacy faced a dangerous situation at Vicksburg and in

middle Tennessee. Lieutenant General James Longstreet and some others proposed the detachment of two divisions from Lee's army to reinforce Bragg for
an offensive-defensive campaign against Rosecrans, which might also relieve
the pressure against Vicksburg. In such a scenario, Lee would clearly have to
remain entirely on the defensive in Virginia, a prospect he did not relish. Instead he counseled Davis to turn him loose on an offensive into Pennsylvania
while the Western armies remained on the defensive. The result of Davis's decision to support Lee's plan was the loss of Vicksburg and middle Tennessee
while the Army of Northern Virginia limped home after suffering a crippling
25,000 or more casualties at Gettysburg.

Was this a strategic blunder or bad luck? Was Lee's preoccupation with
Virginia a consequence of parochialism that limited his vision to the East
while the war was being lost in the West? Did his preference for both an offensive strategy and offensive tactics, especially at Gettysburg, bleed his army
to death? Did Lee gain too much influence over Davis on these matters to the
detriment of a sound strategic vision for all theaters, which would have con-
served Confederate manpower and eroded the Northern will through a defensive strategy of attrition?

These are important questions, and several influential historians have answered them in the affirmative. But ultimately these questions are unanswer-
able. We just do not know what would have happened if Longstreet had taken
two divisions to Tennessee in May 1863, if Lee had not invaded Pennsylvania,
or if Lee himself had gone west to take command in that troubled theater as
Davis asked him to do in August 1863 and again after the debacle at Chattanooga in November.

What we do know is that Lee was far from alone in perceiving Virginia as
the most important theater. Most people in the North and South, as well as
European observers, shared that view. While it may be true that the Confederacy lost the war in the West, it is also clear that Lee's victories in the East
came close on several occasions to winning the war, or at least to staving off
defeat. The Confederacy was tottering on the edge of disaster when Lee took
command on June 1, 1862, with the enemy six miles from Richmond and a
huge amount of the Western Confederacy under Union control after a long
string of Northern victories in that theater. Within a month Lee's offensive-
defensive strategy during the Seven Days' battles had dramatically reversed
the equation in the eyes of most observers, whose view was focused on Virginia. This almost universal fixation on the Eastern theater was what
prompted Lincoln's lament on August 4, 1862, to Count Agénor-Etienne de
Gasparin, a pro-Union French aristocrat: "It seems unreasonable that a series

of successes, extending through half a year, and clearing more than a hundred thousand square miles of country, should help us so little, while a single half-defeat [the Seven Days' battles] should hurt us so much."

During the next two months Lee and Jackson's offensive-defensive strategy came close to winning European diplomatic recognition. Antietam prevented that, but Confederate successes during the next nine months, again mainly in the East, reopened this possibility and so discouraged many Northern voters about the prospect of winning the war that the Copperheads made great gains and threatened the Lincoln administration's ability to continue the war.

Lee and his offensive strategy appeared invincible. Gettysburg proved that it was not, but the lingering legacy of invincibility made Meade so cautious that the Army of the Potomac accomplished little for the next ten months.

Again in the summer of 1864 it was principally Lee and his army that almost caused the North to throw in the towel and forced Lincoln to conclude in August that he would not be re-elected and the Union might not be preserved. To be sure, Lee's strategy as well as tactics were now defensive, but the event that did more than anything else to convince many Northerners of the war's hopelessness was an offensive stroke—Early's raid toward Washington. As late as February 1865, Secretary of War Edwin M. Stanton and Senator Charles Sumner agreed that "peace can be had only when Lee's army is beaten, captured, or dispersed." So long as that army remained "in fighting condition, there is still a hope for the rebels," but "when Lee's army is out of the way, the whole Rebellion will disappear." And so it proved; Appomattox was the actual, if not literal, end of the war.

There is an inevitable tendency to get so wrapped up in the subject at hand as to neglect part of the context. In the discussion of whether Davis's relations with his generals helped or hurt the Confederate cause, whether more emphasis on the West or a more Fabian defensive strategy might have won the war, it is easy to forget that such matters did not occur in a vacuum. The Federal Army's command relationships and strategies both shaped and responded to Confederate command relationships and strategy.

Two anecdotes illustrate this point. In the Wilderness on the evening of May 6, 1864, a Confederate attack on the Union right rolled up that flank and routed two brigades. A Union brigadier rode up to Grant's headquarters and told the general in chief in a panic-stricken voice that all was lost, Lee was in his rear and the Army of the Potomac was doomed. Grant replied in disgust: "Oh, I am heartily tired of hearing what Lee is going to do. Some of you always seem to think he is suddenly going to turn a double somersault and land in our rear and on both of our flanks at the same time. Go back to your command, and try to think what we are going to do ourselves, instead of what Lee is going to do."

The second anecdote concerns Gettysburg. Several million words, or so it sometimes seems, have been written about which Confederate general was responsible for losing the battle: Lee because of overconfidence, aggressive tactics, or mismanagement; Stuart because of his absence; Ewell because of his failure to attack Cemetery Hill on July 1; or Longstreet for his lack of enthusiasm and promptness in the attacks on July 2 and 3. It was left to George Pickett to fill the void left by these various interpretations. When someone thought to ask Pickett after the war who he thought was responsible for the Confederate defeat at Gettysburg, he reflected for a moment before replying, "I always thought the Yankees had something to do with it."

HOW LINCOLN WON
THE WAR WITH METAPHOR

JAMES M. McPHERSON

"Communication and inspiration," James M. McPherson writes, "are two of the most important functions of a president in time of crisis." Words, too, are weapons, and because they can both arouse and support a people's will to fight, they are a vital part of any successful war strategy. In this respect, we have to compare Abraham Lincoln to Franklin D. Roosevelt or Winston Churchill: all three happen to have been both great war leaders and expert practitioners of the language of persuasion. By contrast, Jefferson Davis, Lincoln's Confederate opposite, spoke and wrote with an unimaginative stiffness. McPherson calls him "relentlessly literal," a man who lacked "Lincoln's concern for reaching the common people or his knack for doing so."

Lincoln's skill in the use of figurative speech and his talent for metaphor makes him one of the true masters of the American language. It was a time when such mastery was necessary, as never before. Take Lincoln's telegram to the then commander of the Army of the Potomac, Joseph Hooker, when Lee's invasion force began the march out of Virginia that would end at Gettysburg: "If the head of Lee's army is at Martinsburg {Maryland} and the tail of it on Plank road between Fredericksburg and Chancellorsville, the animal must be very slim somewhere. Could you not break him." Hooker chose not to, and within days Lincoln replaced him with George G. Meade, who became the victor of Gettysburg. Or could there be a better summation of the Union strategy at the end of 1864 than Lincoln's remark that "Grant has the bear by the hind leg while Sherman takes off the hide"? But there were also passages in the president's writing that, McPherson writes, come "as close to a lyrical expression of Northern purpose as anything short of poetry could." Such eloquence captured the popular imagination and defined "the meaning of Union and why it was worth fighting for."

Could Jefferson Davis have written a Gettysburg Address?

James M. McPherson is one of the finest historians writing today. He is professor of history at Princeton University and the author of ten books, including *Battle Cry of Freedom,* which won the Pulitzer Prize in History.

IN AN ESSAY ON THE REASONS FOR CONFEDERATE DEFEAT IN the Civil War, the Southern historian David M. Potter made a striking assertion: "If the Union and Confederacy had exchanged presidents with one another, the Confederacy might have won its independence." Is this rather dramatic conclusion justified? Most historians would probably agree with Potter's general point that Jefferson Davis's shortcomings as a leader played a role in the Confederate defeat. They would also agree that one of Davis's principal failures was an inability to communicate effectively with other Confederate leaders and with the Southern people. As Potter put it, Davis "seemed to think in abstractions and to speak in platitudes."

Abraham Lincoln, by contrast, most emphatically did not think in abstractions and rarely spoke in platitudes. We have not had another president—except perhaps Franklin D. Roosevelt—who expressed himself in such a clear, forceful, logical manner. It is no coincidence that Lincoln and Roosevelt were great war presidents who led the United States to its most decisive victories in its most important wars. Their preeminent quality as leaders was an ability to communicate the meanings and purposes of these wars in an intelligible, inspiring manner that helped energize and mobilize their people to make the sacrifices necessary for victory. By contrast, Jefferson Davis, as another historian, Paul D. Escott, has concluded, failed to do a good job "in eliciting the enthusiasm and energies of the people."

Wherein lay Lincoln's advantage over Davis in this matter? It certainly did not derive from a better education. Davis had received one of the best educations that money could buy in his day: He attended one "college" in Kentucky and another in Mississippi (actually secondary schools or academies); he went to Transylvania University in Kentucky, which was one of the best genuine colleges west of the Appalachians at that time; and he graduated from the

military academy at West Point, the best American school for engineering as
well as for military science in that era. From his education Davis acquired
excellent training in the classics, rhetoric, logic, literature, and science. He
should have been a superb communicator, and in many respects he was, by the
standards of the time. He could write with vigorous logic, turn a classical
phrase, quote the leading authorities on many a subject, and close with a
rhetorical flourish.

Lincoln had only a year or so of formal schooling in the typical rote-learning
"blab schools" of the day, schooling that he obtained, as he later put it, "by lit-
tles"—a month here, a couple of months there, spread out over a period of a
few years. Lincoln was basically a self-taught man. Of course he later read law,
which along with the practice of that profession helped to give him an ability
to write and speak with clarity, a skill in logical analysis, and a knack for finding exactly the right word or phrase to express his meaning. But Davis also
had most of these skills of expository writing and speaking. So we are still left
with the question: Wherein lay Lincoln's superiority?

The answer may be found in a paradox: Perhaps the defects of Lincoln's education proved a benefit. Instead of spending years inside the four walls of a
classroom, Lincoln worked on frontier dirt farms most of his youth, he split
rails, he rafted down the Mississippi on a flatboat, he surveyed land, he
worked in a store, where he learned to communicate with the farmers and
other residents of a rural community. Lincoln grew up close to the rhythms of
nature—of wild beasts and farm animals, of forest and running water, of seasons and crops, and of people who got their meager living from the land.

These things, more than books, furnished Lincoln's earliest education.
They infused his speech with the images of nature. And when he turned to
books, his favorites were the King James Bible, *Aesop's Fables, Pilgrim's
Progress,* and Shakespeare's plays. All are rich in figurative language—allegory,
parable, fable, metaphor—in words and stories that seem to say one thing but
mean another, in images that illustrate something more profound than their
surface appearance.

Here lies one of the secrets of Lincoln's success as a communicator: his skill
in the use of figurative language, of which metaphor is the most common example. We all use metaphors every day. We tell someone to stop beating
around the bush; we say that we have too many irons in the fire; we express a
desire to get to the heart of the matter; we worry about fitting square pegs
into round holes; we see light at the end of the tunnel; and so on. Most of
these examples are "dead" metaphors—that is, they are so commonplace that
we often do not realize that they are metaphors, and they thus lose their power

to evoke a vivid image in our minds. The best "live" metaphors are those that use a simple, concrete figure to illustrate a complex and perhaps abstract concept, thereby giving life and tangible meaning to something that might otherwise escape comprehension.

One of the first things that strike a student of Lincoln's speeches and writings is his frequent use of images and figurative language. His speeches and letters abound with metaphors. Many of them are extraordinarily well chosen and apt; they have the persuasive power of concreteness and clarity. By contrast, Jefferson Davis's prose contains few metaphors or images of any kind. It is relentlessly literal. It is formal, precise, logical, but also stiff, cold, and abstract. Davis's wartime letters and speeches bristle with anger and bitterness toward Yankees and toward his critics and adversaries within the Confederacy. But the few metaphors he used to illustrate his points are quite dead—references to sowing the seeds of discontent and thereby harvesting defeat, and the like.

To be sure, a number of Lincoln's metaphors were dead on arrival. He complained of dealing with people who had axes to grind; he said more than once that he wanted everyone to have a fair start in the race of life; he referred to the ship of state and its navigational problems during his presidency. But Lincoln could neatly turn a seemingly dead metaphor into a live one. In his first message to a special session of Congress that met three months after the war began, he critically reviewed the long and, as he put it, sophistic attempt by Southern leaders to legitimize their actions with arguments for state sovereignty and the constitutional right of secession. "With rebellion thus sugar-coated," said the president, "they have been drugging the public mind of their section for more than thirty years," and this war was the result.

Here Lincoln injected life into a rather tired metaphor, "sugar-coated," and used it to clinch his point in a luminous manner. This occasion also gave Lincoln an opportunity to define his philosophy of communication with the public. The government printer who set the message in type objected to the phrase about sugar-coating the rebellion. "You have used an undignified expression in the message," the printer told the president. "A message to Congress [is] a different affair from a speech at a mass-meeting in Illinois. . . . The messages [become] a part of history, and should be written accordingly. . . . I would alter the structure of that, if I were you."

Lincoln replied with a twinkle in his eye: "That word expresses precisely my idea, and I am not going to change it. The time will never come in this country when the people won't know exactly what *sugar-coated* means!"

Lincoln was right: People knew exactly what he meant then, and his metaphor retains its pithiness today.

Lincoln used a different but equally expressive metaphor to describe the threat of secession on another important occasion, his speech at Cooper Institute in New York in February 1860, a speech that gave him great visibility among Eastern Republicans and helped launch him toward the presidential nomination three months later. This time he discussed Southern warnings of the dire consequences if a Republican president was elected. "In that supposed event," said Lincoln, directing his words to the South, "you say, you will destroy the Union; and then, you say, the great crime of having destroyed it will be upon us! That is cool. A highwayman holds a pistol to my ear, and mutters through his teeth, 'Stand and deliver, or I shall kill you, and then you will be a murderer!'"

No one could fail to understand Lincoln's point. And through his whole life, one of his main concerns was that everyone understand precisely what he was saying. A colleague who praised this quality once asked Lincoln where his concern with exact clarity came from.

"Among my earliest recollections," replied Lincoln, "I remember how, when a mere child, I used to get irritated when anybody talked to me in a way I could not understand. I don't think I ever got angry at anything else in my life. . . . I can remember going to my little bedroom, after hearing the neighbors talk of an evening with my father, and spending the night walking up and down, and trying to make out what was the exact meaning of some of their, to me, dark sayings. I could not sleep . . . when I got on such a hunt after an idea, until I had caught it; and when I thought I had got it, I was not satisfied . . . until I had put it in language plain enough, as I thought, for any boy I knew to comprehend. This was a kind of passion with me, and it has stuck by me."

Many contemporaries testified to this Lincolnian passion, and to his genius for using everyday metaphors to achieve it. Francis Carpenter, the artist who spent six months at the White House during 1864 painting a picture of Lincoln and his Cabinet, noted that the president's "lightest as well as his most powerful thought almost invariably took on the form of a figure of speech, which drove the point home, and clinched it, as few abstract reasoners are able to do." Lincoln was also famous for telling stories. Many of them were parables intended to make or illustrate a point, and a parable is an extended metaphor. "It is not the story itself," Lincoln once said, "but its purpose, or effect, that interests me."

When Lincoln said "Now that reminds me of a story," his listeners knew that they could expect a parable. Take for example this story that Lincoln told soon after he had gotten rid of his controversial secretary of war Simon Cameron. Since some other Cabinet members had also made enemies among one faction or another, a delegation of politicians called on the president and advised him that this might be a good time to make a wholesale change in the Cabinet. Lincoln shook his head and replied, "This reminds me of a story. When I was a boy I knew a farmer named Joe Wilson who was proud of his prize chickens. But he started to lose some of them to raids by skunks on the henhouse. One night he heard a loud cackling from the chickens and crept out with his shotgun to find a half-dozen of the black and white critters running in and out of the shed. Thinking to clean out the whole tribe, he put a double charge in the gun and fired away. Somehow he hit only one, and the rest scampered off."

At this point in the story, Lincoln would act it out by holding his nose and screwing up his face in a pained expression while he continued. "The neighbors asked Joe why he didn't follow up the skunks and kill the rest. 'Blast it,' said Joe, 'it was eleven weeks before I got over killin' one. If you want any more skirmishing in that line you can just do it yourselves!' "

The moral of the story was clear to all. But not everyone approved of Lincoln's habit of telling stories—a few of which were a good bit earthier than this one. Some people considered it undignified for the president of the United States to carry on in such a fashion. But Lincoln had a reply for them, as related by Chauncey Depew, a prominent lawyer, railroad president, and New York Republican leader. Said Depew:

> I heard him tell a great many stories, many of which would not do exactly for the drawing room, but for the person he wished to reach, and the object he desired to accomplish with the individual, the story did more than any argument could have done. He once said to me, in reference to some sharp criticism which had been made upon his story-telling: . . . "I have found in the course of a long experience that common people"—and, repeating it—"common people, take them as they run, are more easily influenced and informed through the medium of a broad illustration than in any other way, and as to what the hypercritical few may think, I don't care."

This was something that Jefferson Davis never understood. He would never have been caught telling a story about skunks to make the point that solutions are sometimes worse than problems. He did not have Lincoln's concern for reaching the common people or his knack for doing so. Lincoln was especially fond of animal metaphors and parables, as in the case of the skunk story. This derived in part from his own rural background and also undoubtedly from the many boyhood hours he spent with *Aesop's Fables*. During one of those hours his cousin Dennis Hanks said to him, "Abe, them yarns is all lies." Lincoln looked up for a moment, and replied, "Mighty darn good lies, Denny." And as an adult Lincoln was aware that these "lies," these fables about animals, provided an excellent way to communicate with a people who were still close to their rural roots and understood the idioms of the forest and barnyard.

Some of Lincoln's most piquant animal metaphors occurred in his comments about or communications with commanding generals during the war. General George B. McClellan clamored repeatedly for reinforcements and understated his own strength while overstating that of the enemy. On one of these occasions Lincoln, who had already reinforced McClellan and knew that Union forces outnumbered the Confederates, said in exasperation that sending troops to McClellan was like shoveling flies across the barnyard—most of them never seemed to get there.

Later on, when Joseph Hooker had become commander of the Army of the Potomac, Lincoln visited him at the front. Hooker boasted that he had built this force into "the finest army on the planet." He added that he hoped God Almighty would have mercy on Bobby Lee because he, Joe Hooker, would have none.

Lincoln listened to this and commented that the "hen is the wisest of all the animal creation, because she never cackles until the egg is laid." And to be sure, it was Lee who could cackle when he beat Hooker decisively at Chancellorsville. Lee then invaded the North in the campaign that led to Gettysburg. As Lee began to move north, Hooker proposed to cross the Rappahannock River and attack his rear guard. Lincoln disapproved with these words in a telegram to Hooker: "I would not take any risk of being entangled upon the river, like an ox jumped half over a fence, and liable to be torn by dogs, front and rear, without a fair chance to gore one way or kick the other." Napoleon himself could not have given better tactical advice or phrased it half so well.

A week later, when the Confederate invasion force was strung out over nearly a hundred miles of Virginia roads, Lincoln telegraphed this message to Hooker: "If the head of Lee's army is at Martinsburg and the tail of it on the Plank Road between Fredericksburg and Chancellorsville, the animal must be very slim somewhere. Could you not break him?" But Hooker seemed reluctant to fight Lee again. The president therefore replaced Hooker with George G.

Meade, who won the Battle of Gettysburg, though he proved to be cautious and defensive afterward.

Thus in 1864 Lincoln brought to the East his most successful commander, Ulysses S. Grant, to become general in chief. In a private conference with Grant soon after the general arrived in Washington, Lincoln referred to the military situation and said that he could best illustrate what he wanted to say with a story.

There was once a great war among the animals, said the president, and one side had great difficulty finding a commander who had enough confidence in himself to fight. Finally they found a monkey, by the name of Jocko, who said he could command the army if his tail could be made a little longer. So the other animals found more tail and spliced it onto Jocko's. He looked at it admiringly, but said he thought he needed just a little more. So they found some more and spliced it on. This process was repeated many times until Jocko's tail was so long that when coiled it filled the whole room. Still he called for more tail, and they kept adding by coiling it around his shoulders and then around his whole body—until he suffocated.

Grant understood the point; unlike McClellan and other generals, he would not keep calling for more troops as an excuse for not fighting. Instead, he worked out a plan for the two main Union armies, in Virginia and Georgia, to advance simultaneously against the two principal Confederate armies while smaller Union forces elsewhere pinned down Confederate detachments to prevent their reinforcing the main Southern armies. This was the kind of coordinated offensive that Lincoln had been urging on his generals for two years, and he was delighted finally to have a commander who would do it. Lincoln's expressive description of the auxiliary role of the smaller armies on the periphery was "Those not skinning can hold a leg." Grant liked this phrase so much that he used it in his own dispatches.

Later on, when Grant had Lee's army under siege at Petersburg while Sherman was marching through Georgia and South Carolina destroying everything in his path, Lincoln described Union strategy this way: "Grant has the bear by the hind leg while Sherman takes off the hide." On another occasion Lincoln changed the metaphor in an official telegram to Grant: "I have seen your despatch expressing your unwillingness to break your hold where you are. Neither am I willing. Hold on with a bull-dog grip, and chew & choke, as much as possible." In the end Grant's chewing and choking while Sherman took off the hide were what won the war.

The principal cause of this war was slavery, and one of its main consequences was the abolition of slavery. This peculiar institution gave rise to many Lincolnian metaphors, animal and otherwise. One of them was a metaphor of snakes and children that Lincoln used in several speeches during his tour of New England in the late winter of 1860. The central tenet of the Republican party's policy was to restrict the spread of slavery into new territories while pledging not to interfere with it in states where it already existed and was therefore protected by the Constitution. Lincoln considered slavery a moral wrong and a social evil. He hoped that the South would eventually take steps to end it voluntarily and peacefully. In the meantime, he said, we must not introduce this evil where it does not now exist.

"If I saw a venomous snake crawling in the road," said Lincoln in illustration of his point, "any man would say I might seize the nearest stick and kill it; but if I found that snake in bed with my children, that would be another question. I might hurt the children more than the snake, and it might bite them. . . . But if there was a bed newly made up, to which the children were to be taken, and it was proposed to take a batch of young snakes and put them there with them, I take it no man would say there was any question how I ought to decide. . . . The new Territories are the newly made bed to which our children are to go, and it lies with the nation to say whether they shall have snakes mixed up with them or not."

In our day of thirty-second political spot commercials on television, this metaphor seems long and involved. But Lincoln's audiences understood it perfectly and appreciated it boisterously. The stenographic report of this speech at New Haven indicates prolonged applause, laughter, and cheering as he spun out the metaphor. A professor of rhetoric at Yale was so taken with Lincoln's speech that he followed him to another town to hear him speak again and then gave a lecture on Lincoln's techniques to his class.

The day after Lincoln spoke at Norwich, Connecticut, the town's leading clergyman happened to travel on the same train with him and talked with him, praising Lincoln's style, "especially your illustrations, which were romance and pathos, and fun and logic all welded together. That story about the snakes, for example, . . . was at once queer and comical, and tragic and argumentative. It broke through all the barriers of a man's previous opinions and prejudices at a crash, and blew up the citadel of his false theories before he could know what had hurt him."

Lincoln used a number of other metaphors to describe slavery, including that of a cancer that must be prevented from spreading lest it kill the body politic. His best-known slavery metaphor formed the central theme of the most famous speech he gave before the Civil War, the House Divided address in 1858. Here the house was a metaphor for the Union, which had been divided against itself by slavery and could not continue to be so divided forever without collapsing. Therefore the Republicans wanted to stop the further spread of slavery, as a first step toward what Lincoln called its "ultimate extinction."

This metaphor of a house divided became probably the single most important image of the relationship between slavery and the Union, and remains so today. It provided an instant mental picture of what Republicans stood for. It also helped provoke the South into secession when Lincoln was elected president, because no matter how much he professed his intention to tolerate slavery where it already existed, had not this Black Republican Yankee also called slavery a moral wrong and looked forward to its ultimate extinction?

In that same speech, Lincoln elaborated the house metaphor to illustrate another of the Republican party's favorite themes—that the Democrats were dominated by a "slave power conspiracy" to expand the institution of bondage over the whole country. "When we see a lot of framed timbers," said Lincoln, "different portions of which we know have been gotten out at different times and places by different workmen—Stephen, Franklin, Roger, and James, for instance—and when we see these timbers joined together, and see they exactly make the frame of a house . . . we find it impossible not to believe that Stephen and Franklin and Roger and James all understood one another from the beginning, and all worked upon a common plan, or draft."

The point of this rather elaborate metaphor seems obscure today, but Lincoln's audience knew exactly what he was talking about. The four men he named were Stephen Douglas, leader of the Democratic party; Franklin Pierce and James Buchanan, the previous and current presidents of the United States, both Democrats; and Roger Taney, chief justice of the United States, also a Democrat. The house for which each of them separately framed timbers, but with a secret understanding to make everything fit together, was a conspiracy to expand slavery. The timbers were the Kansas-Nebraska Act, which repealed the Missouri Compromise and made possible the expansion of slavery north of latitude 36° 30', where it had previously been prohibited; the Dred Scott decision, which included the legalization of slavery in all the territories; the Democratic pledge to acquire Cuba as a new slave territory; and other items.

After the Civil War broke out, Lincoln's main problem—next to winning the war—was what to do about slavery. And by the second year of the war, the slavery issue had become bound up with the fate of the Union itself as Lincoln gradually came to the conclusion that he could not win the war without striking down slavery.

In his public and private communications concerning slavery during the war, Lincoln used a number of telling metaphors and similes. His first effort was to persuade the loyal border states to accept a policy of gradual, compensated emancipation. This proposal, he said in an appeal to the people of the border states in May 1862, "makes common cause for a common object, casting no reproaches on any. It acts not the pharisee. The change it contemplates would come gently as the dews of heaven, not rending or wrecking anything. Will you not embrace it?"

When the border states did not respond, Lincoln shifted from soft blandishment to blunt warning. In July 1862 he called border-state congressmen to the White House. By then the war had taken a harder turn. Republican congressmen had passed a bill to confiscate the property of those who rebelled against the government, including their slave property. Lincoln himself had just about decided to issue an emancipation proclamation to apply to the Confederate states. The impact of these measures was bound to spill over into the Unionist border states. Slaves there were already emancipating themselves by running away to Union army lines.

In these circumstances Lincoln now told border-state congressmen that his plan of gradual emancipation with compensation from the Federal government was the best they could get. Otherwise, as the war continued to escalate in intensity, "the institution in your states will be extinguished by mere friction and abrasion." The image of friction and abrasion was a most appropriate one, but it left the border-state congressmen unmoved. Most of them voted against Lincoln's offer—and three more years of war did extinguish slavery by friction and abrasion, in the border states as well as in the Confederate states.

After his unsuccessful appeal to the border states, Lincoln made up his mind to issue an emancipation proclamation. He used a variety of metaphors to explain his reasons for doing so. "It had got to midsummer 1862," the president later summarized. "Things had gone on from bad to worse, until I felt that we had reached the end of our rope on the plan of operations we had been pursuing; that we had about played our last card, and must change our tactics, or lose the game!" Both of the metaphors here—"the end of our rope" and "played our last card"—are rather tired, almost dead, but the context and the importance of the issue bring them alive and make them effective.

Lincoln liked the cardplaying metaphor; in letters to conservatives who objected to the government's total-war policy of confiscation and emancipation, he wrote with some asperity that "this government cannot much longer play a game in which it stakes all, and its enemies stake nothing. . . . It may as well be understood, once and for all, that I shall not surrender this game leaving any available card unplayed."

Lincoln used other, more original and expressive metaphors at the same time, asking one conservative if he expected the government to wage this war "with elder-stalk squirts, charged with rose water." To a Southern Unionist who had complained that emancipation of slaves owned by rebels would inevitably expand into emancipation of slaves owned by loyal Unionists as well, Lincoln replied with an angry letter denouncing those Unionists who did nothing to help the North win but expected the government to take time out to protect their property while it was struggling for its very survival.

The president spun out a metaphor of a ship in a storm to clinch the point. Do Southern Unionists expect, he asked, "to touch neither a sail nor a pump, but to be merely passengers—deadheads at that—to be carried snug and dry, throughout the storm, and safely landed right side up? Nay, more; even a mutineer is to go untouched lest these sacred passengers receive an accidental wound."

When the constitutionality of the Emancipation Proclamation was questioned, Lincoln defended it by citing his military powers as commander in chief in time of war to seize enemy property. He also used an apt metaphor to illustrate how a lesser constitutional right—of property in slaves—might have to be sacrificed in the interests of a greater constitutional duty, that of preserving the nation's life. "Often a limb must be amputated to save a life," Lincoln pointed out in this age without antibiotics when everyone knew of wounded soldiers who had lost an arm or leg to stop the spread of fatal infection. "The surgeon," Lincoln continued, "is solemnly bound to try to save both life and limb; but when the crisis comes, and the limb must be sacrificed as the only chance of saving the life, no honest man will hesitate. . . . In our case, the moment came when I felt that slavery must die that the nation might live!"

Yet another metaphor that Lincoln used to illustrate a point about slavery is particularly striking. This one concerned the definition of *liberty*. The South professed to have seceded and gone to war in defense of its rights and liberties. The chief liberty that Southerners believed to be threatened by the election of Lincoln was their right to own slaves. In a public speech in 1864 at Baltimore, in a border state where the frictions and abrasions of war had by then just about ground up slavery, Lincoln illustrated the paradox of conflicting definitions of *liberty* with an Aesopian fable: "The shepherd drives the wolf from the sheep's throat, for which the sheep thanks the shepherd as a liberator, while the wolf denounces him for the same act as a destroyer of liberty, especially as the sheep was a black one."

This image leaves no doubt which definition of *liberty* Lincoln subscribed to, or whose cause in this war—the Northern shepherd's or the Southern wolf's—was the nobler one. The passage comes as close to a lyrical expression of Northern purpose as anything short of poetry could.

And at times Lincoln's words became poetic. He liked to read poetry. His favorites were Burns, Byron, and above all Shakespeare. He knew much of Burns and Shakespeare by heart. As president, Lincoln liked to relax by going to the theater—as we know to our sorrow. He went to every play of Shakespeare's that came to Washington. He especially enjoyed reading the tragedies and historical plays with a political theme. The quintessence of poetry is imagery, particularly metaphor, and this is true most of all in Shakespeare's plays. Lincoln's fondness for this medium undoubtedly helped shape his use of figurative and symbolic language. As a youth he had tried his hand at writing poetry, but the way in which we best know him as a poet is through several famous passages from his wartime speeches and state papers. In these he achieved unrivaled eloquence through the use of poetic language.

A rather modest example of this occurs in a public letter that Lincoln wrote in August 1863 to be read at a Union rally in Illinois—and of course to be published in the newspapers. This letter came at a major turning point in the war. Union armies had recently captured Vicksburg and won the Battle of Gettysburg, reversing a year of defeats that had created vitiating doubt and dissent. But even after these victories, the antiwar Copperhead movement remained strong and threatening. Its animus focused mainly on the government's policy of emancipation and the enlistment of black troops. By the time of Lincoln's letter, several black regiments had already demonstrated their mettle in combat.

Lincoln addressed all of these issues. In delightful and easily understood imagery he noted the importance of the capture of Vicksburg in opening the Mississippi River and credited soldiers and sailors of all regions, including black soldiers and loyal Southern whites, in accomplishing this result:

> The signs look better. The Father of Waters again goes unvexed to the sea. Thanks to the great North-West for it. Nor yet wholly to them. Three hundred miles up, they met New-England, Empire, Key-Stone, and Jersey, hewing their way right and left. The Sunny South too, in more colors than one, also lent a hand. On the spot, their part of the history was jotted down in black and

white. . . . Nor must Uncle Sam's Web-feet be forgotten. Not only on the deep sea, the broad bay, and the rapid river, but also up the narrow muddy bayou, wherever the ground was a little damp, they have been, and made their tracks.

Shifting from these cheerful, almost playful images, the president turned to the Copperheads, who had been denigrating emancipation and calling the whole war effort a useless and wicked failure. It was not a failure, said Lincoln; the Union had turned the corner toward victory. And when that victory comes, he said,

there will be some black men who can remember that, with silent tongue, and clenched teeth, and steady eye, and well-poised bayonet, they have helped mankind on to this great consummation; while, I fear, there will be some white ones, unable to forget that, with malignant heart, and deceitful speech, they have strove to hinder it.

Here Lincoln was writing primarily about a process—about the means of victory in the way for the Union. It was when he defined the *purpose* of that war—the meaning of Union and why it was worth fighting for—that he soared to his greatest poetic eloquence. "Union" was something of an abstraction that required concrete symbols to make its meaning clear to the people who would have to risk their lives for it. The flag was the most important such symbol. But Lincoln wanted to go beyond the flag and strike deeper symbolic chords of patriotism. And in so doing he furnished some of the finest examples of poetic metaphor in our national literature.

In the peroration of his first inaugural address, Lincoln appealed to the South with an evocation of the symbols of a common history and shared memories as metaphors for the Union. "We are not enemies," he declared. "Though passion may have strained, it must not break our bonds of affection. The mystic chords of memory, stretching from every battlefield, and patriot grave, to every living heart and hearthstone, all over this broad land, will yet swell the chorus of the Union, when again touched, as surely they will be, by the better angels of our nature."

Having summoned forth the past as a metaphor for Union, Lincoln invoked the future in the peroration of his message to Congress in December 1862. Now he added emancipation to Union as the legacy that the people of that generation would leave to their children's children. "Fellow-citizens, we cannot escape history. . . . The fiery trial through which we pass, will light us down, in honor or dishonor, to the latest generation. . . . We shall nobly save, or meanly lose, the last, best hope of earth. . . . In giving freedom to the slave, we assure freedom to the free."

Lincoln put these symbolic themes of past, present, and future together in his most famous poem, the Gettysburg Address. This elegy uses no metaphors in a conventional sense; rather, there are what two literary scholars have called "concealed" or "structural" metaphors—that is, metaphors built into the structure of the address in such a way that they are not visible but are essential to its meaning. The Gettysburg Address contains three parallel sets of three images each that are intricately interwoven: past, present, future; continent, nation, battlefield; and birth, death, rebirth. Let us disaggregate these metaphors for purposes of analysis, even though in the process we destroy their poetic qualities.

Eighty-seven years in the *past* our fathers *conceived* and *brought forth* on this *continent* a *nation* that stood for something important: the proposition that all men are created equal. *Now* our generation faces a great war testing whether a nation standing for such an ideal can survive. In dedicating the cemetery on this *battlefield,* the living must take inspiration to finish the task that those who lie buried here nobly advanced by giving the last full measure of their devotion.

Life and death in this passage have a paradoxical but metaphorical relationship: Men died that the nation might live, yet metaphorically the old Union also died, and with it died the institution of slavery. After these *deaths,* the nation must have a *"new birth* of freedom" so that the government of, by, and for the people that our fathers conceived and brought forth in the past "shall not perish from the earth" but be preserved as a legacy for the *future.*

Contrary to common impression, Lincoln's Gettysburg Address was not ignored or unappreciated at the time. Lincoln himself may have contributed to this legend, for he reportedly told his friend and bodyguard Ward Hill Lamon that the speech was "a flat failure." Mixing a live metaphor with a dead simile (as Lamon remembered it a quarter century later), Lincoln said that the address "won't scour"; it "fell upon the audience like a wet blanket." It is true that admiration for the Gettysburg Address grew over the years, but many listeners and readers immediately recognized its greatness. One of them was Edward Everett, the main orator of the day, who wrote to Lincoln the next day: "I should be glad, if I could flatter myself, that I came as near to the central idea of the occasion, in two hours, as you did in two minutes."

Jefferson Davis did not—and probably could not—write anything like the

Gettysburg Address, or like anything else in the way of images and metaphors that Lincoln used to illustrate his points both great and small. Communication and inspiration are two of the most important functions of a president in times of crisis. Thus perhaps David Potter's suggestion that if the Union and Confederacy had exchanged presidents the South might have won the Civil War does not seem so far-fetched after all.

III

1862 AND 1863: BLOODY YEARS

GRANT'S
TENNESSEE GAMBLE

GEOFFREY PERRET

U. S. Grant would never happen today. Even for nineteenth-century America, his rise from obscurity was extraordinary, not just meteoric but, in its permanence, comet-like. The Civil War could do that to reputations—and it could, as easily, undo them. (The explorer turned politician John Charles Frémont, under whom Grant briefly served in the fall of 1861, was one of those shooting stars who burned out early.) And yet Grant's emergence was not totally unforeseen. In the spring of 1861, the Confederate general Richard S. Ewell wrote: "There is one West Pointer, I think in Missouri, little known, and whom I hope the Northern people will not find out. I mean Sam Grant. I knew him in the Academy and in Mexico. I should fear him more than any of their officers I have yet heard of . . ."

Well he might. At the beginning of February 1861, Grant was clerking at his father's leather-goods store in Galena, Illinois. A year later, he was a brigadier general who had, with considerable daring, stripped his Cairo, Illinois, home base of men and munitions and was heading up the Tennessee River for the rampart that controlled it, Fort Henry. Fort Henry would actually surrender to U.S. Navy gunboats while Grant's men were still trying to reach it. (Most of the Confederate garrison escaped in full view of a volunteer division.) Fort Donelson on the Cumberland, just twelve miles away, was another matter. Grant had learned his lesson, as Geoffrey Perret tells us here, and the North would have its first great victory. More important, Donelson's capture would open the way to Nashville, which was not just one of the key rail hubs of the South but an important center for iron foundries. Too often generals would win on the battlefield but fail to translate their victories into campaigns with meaningful outcomes. Grant, that winter, would take a

strategic leap, the kind of follow-up that most victorious leaders in the
Civil War neglected.

Geoffrey Perret is the author of a number of well-regarded works on
American military history, including biographies of U. S. Grant, Douglas
MacArthur, Dwight D. Eisenhower, and a forthcoming life of John F.
Kennedy.

THE BIGGEST SURPRISE OF THE CIVIL WAR WAS ULYSSES S.
Grant, who had left the army in 1854 dogged by rumors that his undoing was
drink. The bottle was only part of the story. Grant drank because he was a
highly intelligent man bored by peacetime service in California and profoundly depressed at being separated from his wife and children for nearly two
years. The very day in 1854 he received his commission as a captain in the
regulars, he submitted his resignation. Few of his fellow West Point graduates
from the class of 1843 had made permanent captain by 1854. In quitting
when he did, Grant was making the point that it was the army that had failed
him, not he who had failed the army.

After "studying the poverty question," as he wryly put it, first as a farmer,
then as a rent collector in St. Louis, he went to work in his father's leather
store in Galena, Illinois. Grant returned to active duty in June 1861, when he
received the colonel's commission that he had sought in the Union army, the
volunteer force that Lincoln raised to fight the Civil War. Two months later
Grant became a brigadier general, at the age of thirty-nine. His rapid ascent
in the Union army owed nothing to battles won—he had not yet fought one.
He had a powerful patron in Congress, Representative Elihu B. Washburne of
Illinois. With a general's star on his shoulder stripes, he had overtaken not
only his 1843 U.S. Military Academy classmates but many officers in the regular army, such as the highly admired Colonel Charles F. Smith, who had
served as commandant at West Point when Grant was a cadet.

In the fall of 1861, Grant, with headquarters at Cairo, Illinois, commanded
an area that from a Southern perspective resembled a dagger's point poised to
strike the Confederate defensive line that ran for 150 miles from Columbus,
Kentucky, to Bowling Green, Kentucky. The highly regarded Lieutenant
General Albert Sydney Johnston, commanding Confederate forces from
Arkansas to the Cumberland Gap, could block the Federals from using three

great rivers—the Mississippi, the Tennessee, and the Cumberland—as highways into the South so long as he held this front intact.

Columbus, only twenty miles south of Cairo, was high on a bluff on the
Mississippi and crammed with cannon. It was simply impregnable. Despite
that, in November 1861, Grant, itching for a fight, took 3,000 men down the
Mississippi and attacked the steamboat landing at Belmont, Missouri, just
across the river from Columbus and well within range of its heavy guns. He
swiftly captured the rebel encampment at Belmont on November 7, only to
be brought to the brink of annihilation several hours later when Confederate
regiments from Columbus crossed the river and landed in his rear. Showing
remarkable skill under fire, he extricated his force intact.

During the Belmont operation, Major General Henry Wager Halleck was
installed in St. Louis as commander of the Department of Missouri. He became, that is, Grant's superior. The highly intellectual Halleck disliked Grant
intensely, although they had never met. Grant's reputation as a drunkard was
enough to make Halleck consider him unfit for a major command.

He turned his capacious mind to removing Grant from combat command.
Grant did not know it, but Halleck intended to replace him with a retired
major general named Ethan Allen Hitchcock, whom the war department was
urging to return to active duty. If Halleck's plan worked, Grant would find
himself occupying a headquarters far from the front, where he would spend
the rest of the war counting blankets and forwarding supplies.

Grant, meanwhile, was urging Halleck to allow him to attack Fort Henry,
the Confederate rampart on the Tennessee. Named after a Confederate senator
named Gustavus Henry, the fort was so badly sited it was in danger of being
flooded when the winter rains arrived. Halleck, however, refused to sanction
an attack. Then, in late January 1862, intelligence reports reached Halleck
that fifteen regiments were moving from Virginia to Kentucky to bolster the
line from Columbus to Bowling Green. Halleck immediately authorized
Grant's proposed attack.

It took only a few days to assemble an army at Paducah for an advance on
Fort Henry, fifty miles away. Grant was taking twenty-three regiments, totaling nearly 17,000 men, supported by ironclad gunboats and a large flotilla of
steamers to carry his troops. Grant wired Halleck on February 3: "Will be off
up the Tennessee at six (6) o'clock [A.M.]."

The steamboats could not carry the entire army south in a single lift. They
took John McClernand's 1st Division in the initial phase, and halfway to Fort
Henry a small cavalry force was dropped off to reconnoiter the enemy's position. McClernand was Grant's cross. A former congressman and Springfield

neighbor of Lincoln, McClernand had too much political influence to be ignored, and had been given a brigadier general's commission. Vain and bom-
bastic ("born a warrior" was how McClernand described himself), and nursing
presidential ambitions, he had been given a general's star early in the war.
Grant considered McClernand incompetent and insubordinate but had no
way of getting rid of him. Many a Union army division was commanded by
someone with all too obvious political connections and all too imperceptible
military skills.

Five miles north of Fort Henry the steamers disembarked McClernand and
the approximately 3,000 men of the 1st Division on February 4. McClernand's troops were going to make the direct attack on the fort, while two
other divisions seized the high ground around it.

The next day, Grant decided to take a good look at the defenses of Fort
Henry for himself and boarded one of the ironclads, the gunboat *Essex.* There
was a broad stream, known as Panther Creek, only two and a half miles north
of the fort. Grant wanted to see whether he could land McClernand's division
closer to its objective, sparing the troops from having to cross the stream under enemy fire.

The *Essex* moved south until it was slightly below Panther Creek. A
twenty-four-pound shell whistled past and crashed into the riverbank nearby.
The next shot screamed toward the *Essex,* smashed through the officers' cabins
on the stern deck—fortunately missing Grant and the gunboat commander,
William D. Porter—before going out at the stern and splashing into the
brown waters of the Tennessee. The gunboat promptly withdrew.

McClernand's men were re-embarked and brought closer to the fort but
were landed just north of Panther Creek. They would have to advance on foot
from there. Despite this disappointment Grant had, he informed his wife, Julia, "a confidant [*sic*] feeling of success." And so, in his own way, had the
Union naval commander, Flag Officer Andrew H. Foote, who taunted Grant
and his staff, "I shall take it [Fort Henry] before you get there with your
forces."

As dusk gathered along the river, creating mists and fogs, a torpedo—or
mine—that had been fished out of the Tennessee a few hours before was carried up to the fantail of the gunboat *Cincinnati.* A naval armorer began to dis-
arm the mine for the edification of a handful of curious brass, including
Grant, Foote, McClernand, and C. F. Smith, commanding Grant's 2nd Division. The black and ugly object began fizzing loudly.

While the enlisted men remained rooted to the spot, their officers made a
dash for the ladder leading to the deck above, Grant in the lead. When they

reached the gun deck safely, Foote teasingly asked Grant, "General, why this haste?"

"Oh, for no particular reason," said Grant, making fun of Foote's boast, "except that the navy may not get ahead of us!" Fortunately for the enlisted men on the deck below, the mine was a dud.

Late at night on February 5, Grant wrote "Field Orders No. 1" for the assault the next day. McClernand was to set his division in motion at 11:00 A.M., the time that the gunboat flotilla would begin steaming toward the fort. McClernand's troops were to cut the roads near Fort Henry—preventing reinforcements from getting in, the defenders from getting out.

Foote was unhappy. He objected that Grant was not allowing enough time for the troops to slog their way through the muddy countryside and still to be certain of launching a ground assault that coincided with the naval attack. Grant ignored Foote's protest. "Field Orders No. 1" remained as written.

In the morning, four ironclads set off shortly before 11:00, and by 12:30, they were in line abreast, ready to duel with the gunners of low-lying Fort Henry. Heavy rains had raised the Tennessee almost to record levels. The raging river was already swamping the fort, making it untenable. If the gunboats did not force the defenders out, the water soon would. The battle began at a distance of little less than a mile.

Despite Foote's poor health—at fifty-five, he was dying of renal failure—he remained a combative sailor. He pushed his gunboats forward until they had closed to 300 yards. Foote's gunners found themselves firing point-blank into the tormented earthen heaps that had passed for a fort only an hour or so earlier. Confederate gun crews were remorselessly driven from their pieces by intense and accurate fire. To fight on was to die. A little before 2:00 P.M., Fort Henry's commander, Brigadier General Lloyd Tilghman, hoisted a white flag. The fort would surrender to the Union Navy.

All of the gunboats had survived the encounter, but several had suffered serious damage. Worse, though, from Foote's point of view, was the loss of veteran sailors to death or crippling wounds. It was going to be hard to find fully trained and experienced replacements for them this far from the coast. The boats could be patched up in a few weeks, but it might be months before the vessels were as well manned again.

Meanwhile, McClernand's troops were floundering in the mud more than a mile from Fort Henry. The 1st Division had not even cut the roads leading east. This failure allowed some 2,500 of the fort's 2,600 defenders to escape under McClernand's splendid Roman nose. McClernand looked like a conqueror, but wasn't.

Having played no role in the battle, McClernand's command found itself little more than the tardy, mud-spattered witness to Fort Henry's surrender. Foote had made good his boast, while Grant's badly conceived order showed he still had much to learn about combined-arms operations.

Not that arriving second dampened the spirits of his volunteers. When they reached Fort Henry around 3:00 P.M., they looted the tents, wrote jubilant letters of triumph on captured stationery, fired the enemy's muskets, smoked the enemy's pipes, and threw an impromptu victory party in celebration of their lucky, victorious selves. There was no sense of chagrin at having been beaten to the objective by Foote's sailors. "We had enough of fighting ere the war was over," wrote one of them, "and after [Belmont] we never begrudged other forces the honor of gaining victory without our help."

Most of the ninety-two Confederates captured were wounded men. Those who got away departed in good order, carrying their arms and equipment right past the slackly led and unenterprising 1st Division. Vain, boastful, and almost comically ambitious, McClernand seemed oblivious to the importance of the mission spelled out in Grant's orders. The Confederates who paraded across McClernand's front would fight another day, at nearby Fort Donelson.

Grant tried to cover up this failure in his official report on the battle by asserting that because McClernand's troops were asleep at 11:00 P.M. the previous night, when he had written out his field orders, "I did not deem it practicable to set an earlier hour than 11 O'clock today to commence the investment."

The feebleness of this excuse reflects something Grant never discussed, hardly even dared hint at—his lack of confidence in his volunteers and their officers (McClernand especially) at this stage of the war. Military history is hardly short of examples of commanders being told late at night that they would advance on the enemy at dawn. Winfield Scott had done it in Mexico. Grant tried to confuse the issue by claiming, "The garrison I think must have commenced their retreat last night or early this morning," which he would have known was simply untrue from conversations with the fort's captured officers, as well as from McClernand.

Believing that Fort Donelson, only twelve miles to the east, was a mere outpost, lightly manned and now ripe for the taking, Grant penned a telegram to Halleck that was a trumpet blast: "Fort Henry is ours. . . . I shall take and destroy Fort Donaldson [sic] on the eighth and return to Fort Henry."

Even though the report of reinforcements heading west proved false, victory worried Halleck. Fort Henry captured was another place to defend. And

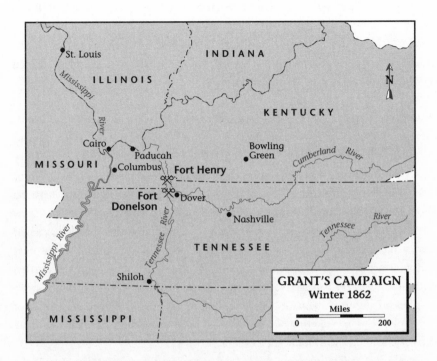

In the early months of 1862, Union forces in Tennessee achieved not only their first victories of the war but ones that had genuine strategic consequences. The campaign began when U. S. Grant, accompanied by gunboats, moved south from Paducah, Kentucky, along the Tennessee River. His objectives were Forts Henry and Donelson, Confederate strongholds that, like stays on a girdle, cinched the narrow midriff between the Tennessee and Cumberland rivers. Once they were captured, Union forces could sweep on to the industrial and rail center of Nashville and compel the Confederates to retire from their two threatening Kentucky outposts, Columbus, where their batteries blocked the Mississippi, and Bowling Green; gunboats could range down the Tennessee and into the very heart of the South.

suppose the Confederates hit back? What if they launched an attack on Cairo from Columbus? An army in the flush of victory is always likely to be overextended and vulnerable on its flanks or in the rear. And there was no doubt about it, Cairo was virtually undefended. Grant had stripped the place of men and munitions when he set off for Fort Henry.

✦

HE HAD RUN HUGE RISKS, probably never gave them more than a moment's thought, and won, while the vaunted Albert Sidney Johnston was proving to be a vacillating commander. If Fort Henry was Grant's opportunity to strike, Cairo was his. One strong thrust at Cairo and chances are that Grant would have been forced to scramble back from Fort Henry. At the least he would have abandoned all thought of pressing on to Fort Donelson.

Such recklessness only reinforced Halleck's conviction that Grant was a bad investment, bound to go bust one day. After Fort Henry, Halleck was almost desperate to get rid of him, but he still hadn't heard whether Ethan Allen Hitchcock was returning to active duty. The advance to Fort Henry had been a splendid, albeit hair-raising, success. Union forces had cracked the center of the Columbus to Bowling Green front, but by all accounts it was the navy that had won at Fort Henry, not Grant.

Halleck sent Grant a message: "Hold on to Fort Henry at all hazards. Picks and shovels are sent and large reinforcements will be sent immediately." Along with entrenching equipment, Halleck also dispatched his own chief of staff, Brigadier General George W. Cullum, to Fort Henry. On arriving there, Cullum told Grant he had come "to facilitate your very important operations," but Grant wouldn't have been fooled for a moment. He surely saw Cullum for what he was—Halleck's spy.

Four days after Fort Henry fell, Hitchcock reluctantly got back into uniform. There was no chance of getting Hitchcock sent west from Washington before Grant made his twelve-mile advance on Fort Donelson, but the first part of Halleck's plan was working. At least the old warhorse was back in harness. Halleck promptly urged George McClellan, the general in chief, to have Hitchcock assigned to his department.

The morning of February 12, Grant informed Halleck: "We start this morning for Fort Donelson in heavy force." Then he rode out from Fort Henry at the head of 15,000 troops, chatting animatedly with his staff, excited as only movement and the thrilling phenomenology of war could excite him. Suddenly the spirited stallion ridden by surgeon John H. Brinton broke into a fast walk. "Doctor," called Grant, "I believe I command this army, and I think I'll go first." The staff burst out laughing while a chagrined Brinton reined in his horse and fell in behind Grant.

It was a magnificent day—blue skies, balmy temperatures—a heady taste of spring in the middle of winter. Grant's innocent volunteers threw their overcoats and blankets aside, and their volunteer officers, no wiser than they, made no attempt to stop them. When Grant first told Halleck he intended to seize Fort Donelson, his confidence bordered on complacency. He seemed to imagine it would be no harder to take than Fort Henry and, if he could, he would have gladly seized it without the help of the self-satisfied sailors. "The Army is rather chop fallen," a gloating Flag Officer Foote had informed his wife after Fort Henry fell, and Grant came to proffer congratulations through gritted teeth.

By the time Grant set off for Fort Donelson, carrying no more baggage than a toothbrush in a waistcoat pocket, he had revised his earlier opinion. He now believed there might be as many as 10,000 Confederates at the fort. It was a bad guess. There were closer to 20,000. Albert Sidney Johnston had allowed two of the officers there—Brigadier Generals Gideon Pillow and Bushrod Johnson—to talk him into making a do-or-die stand.

For one thing, defeating Grant on the Cumberland would redeem the loss of Fort Henry. For another, the position was strategically placed, surmounting a 120-foot bluff overlooking a bend in the river. It was, in effect, the rampart that blocked a Union advance on Nashville, seventy miles to the southeast. Nashville was one of the most important railheads in all of North America.

Fort Donelson was protected by a multilayered defensive system. There were entrenchments, an impressive abatis, and thousands of rifle pits. As Grant's leading units approached the outer entrenchments three miles west of the fort, brisk firefights erupted. A Confederate cavalry force under the brilliant Nathan Bedford Forrest harried Grant's overly confident troops.

The moment was ideal for a spoiling attack against Grant's army as it picked its way along two narrow roads winding through heavily wooded and hilly terrain. Yet apart from this sporadic skirmishing, no attempt was made to block Grant's advance. Confederate commanders in the West were too embroiled in heated arguments over strategy to pay attention to tactics.

The night of February 12, Grant and his staff bedded down at the Widow Crisp's small log farmhouse, four miles from the fort. The general was snug in a double feather bed set up in the kitchen, which also boasted a large fireplace. For Grant, who was suffering from a severe and lingering cold, it could hardly have seemed more welcoming.

However, his soldiers, out in the open, were incredulous at the fickleness of Tennessee weather. When the sun went down on a springlike day, it was followed by a bitter, midwinter night that fell like a hammer blow, stunning Grant's young volunteers. They suffered for want of the heavy brown blankets and warm blue overcoats they had so gleefully thrown away only that morning. Their only comfort was provided by the pigs.

The woods between Henry and Donelson were dotted with farms, and most of them seemed to have at least one large pig herd roaming the February woods, gorging on acorns. Throughout the fight for Fort Donelson, the evening air was spiced with the aroma of roasted pork rising from huge bonfires in the Federal camp.

Grant's plan for taking Fort Donelson was a reprise of his plan at Fort Henry. He would place a cordon around it, and the gunboats would wreck the fort's artillery. An infantry assault would crush the demoralized survivors.

Fort Donelson was commanded by Brigadier General John Floyd, who had served as secretary of war under Lincoln's predecessor, President James Buchanan. His principal subordinates were two other brigadiers, Gideon Pillow and Grant's old friend Simon Bolivar Buckner, a fellow cadet at the academy. Buckner had helped Grant out when he was in New York in 1854 on his return from California, desperately short of money. Floyd had never been a professional soldier; nor had Pillow. Although he had commanded a volunteer division in the Mexican War, Pillow had no military talent. The sole professional, Buckner, carried less weight than either of the two politicians.

As scouts reported in and prisoners were interrogated, it became obvious to Grant as he sat at Mrs. Crisp's kitchen table the morning of February 13 that Fort Donelson was much more strongly held than he had imagined. He sent a cable to Halleck demanding reinforcements and gave his division commanders, John McClernand and C. F. Smith, firm instructions. They could probe the enemy's position, but they were not to bring on a battle.

As Smith's troops deployed on the Union left and McClernand's advanced toward high ground on the right, both got involved in heavy fighting that had no purpose at all. For a couple of hours Grant's army was at risk of being drawn into what is known as "a soldier's battle"—one where men fight simply because they are fighting. There is no objective to be seized, no victory to be won.

While volleys of musketry erupted and cannon roared back at cannon, Grant—almost gray from head to foot after galloping down muddy roads—was boarding Foote's flagship, the *St. Louis*. Over the next hour or so he insisted that Foote had to send his gunboats against the fort. Halleck had already demanded as much in a message to the Navy Department, and here was Grant applying the pressure in person. Normally an aggressive old salt, Foote was reluctant to attack. The fighting at Fort Henry had left him in need of replacements for his injured sailors, and two of his ironclads were still being repaired.

He had four mortar boats ready to be launched, and he begged Grant to wait a little longer, so he could get them into action. Their high-angle, plunging fire was the best way of battering down the fort's ramparts and knocking out its artillery. Grant refused to wait: Every hour's delay only worked to the defenders' advantage. In the end, rather than risk being blamed for any failure to take Fort Donelson, Foote had little choice but to do as Grant and Halleck demanded. A confident Grant left the flagship in a jaunty mood. Swinging himself up onto his horse, he couldn't resist telling a knot of curious bystanders that with the help of the gunboats he could take Fort Donelson and capture every one of its defenders. Then he galloped away like a man heading for a party.

Next day, February 14, Foote's gunboat flotilla—four ironclads in the lead, followed by two timberclads—steamed toward Fort Donelson. Foote unwisely repeated the tactics that had paid off at Fort Henry. He had his flotilla get in close. It was a mistake. Fort Donelson's artillery consisted largely of medium calibers. The heavy ordnance aboard the ironclads had nearly every gun in Fort Donelson outranged. They could have given the defenses a leisurely pounding. Instead, the gunboats pressed steadily on, increasing the effectiveness of Fort Donelson's artillery with every yard they advanced. Two of the ironclads were knocked out of action. They drifted away down the Cumberland, their steering shot away.

Defeating the gunboats ought to have provided whatever encouragement the defenders of Fort Donelson needed to mount a strong counterattack. Foote's failure was a serious rebuff, an opportunity to be exploited. But no, Floyd and Pillow were as inert as ever.

Grant's position was far from brilliant at this point. Even after receiving reinforcements, he had only 20,000 men at Fort Donelson, while another 5,000 guarded the two roads over which his supplies traveled. The two sides had a roughly equal number of troops to put into battle. Yet it is an axiom of war that the attacker nearly always needs an advantage of at least three-to-one to be sure of defeating a well-entrenched enemy. Had Grant made a frontal assault on Fort Donelson, he would have run up a casualty list longer than his blue-clad arm—and might still not have won a victory, as he was well aware.

The alternative, a prolonged siege, was not without its own risks. The fort might eventually fall, but not before Halleck had found a way of getting Grant out and someone Halleck respected, such as Hitchcock, in. Grant, however, was still completely unaware of the machinations in St. Louis. He did not realize until after the war that Halleck had been trying hard to replace him. The reason for his burning impatience now was not the knife threatening his back but something even more compelling: A siege was simply not in Grant's nature. The very thought made him squirm. War was movement, battles, the clash of arms, the decisive result. He wrote gloomily to Julia late that night, "The taking of Donelson bids fair to be a long job."

Grant was lucky once again, luckier than most generals can ever hope to be. But he had his own way of generating luck—press the enemy hard, press him often, and he is almost sure to make a major mistake. With a Federal army camped at his door and Foote's gunboats controlling the river, the volatile Pillow grew panicky. Having earlier insisted that the fort absolutely had to be held, he now began arguing it would have to be abandoned. He wanted the defenders to launch a surprise attack early next morning, punch a hole in the Union lines, and make a break for it—but not before coming back and collecting all their supplies and artillery.

After an early breakfast in the Widow Crisp's kitchen the morning of February 15, Grant dictated some messages, including one to Halleck—"Appearances now indicate we will have a protracted siege." Then he rode off to see Foote, who had suffered a leg injury during the previous day's engagement and was in no condition to travel. It was a bitterly cold morning, and sleet blew across the battlefield. Grant and Foote had a brief, inconclusive discussion aboard the *St. Louis,* anchored out in the Cumberland.

The gunboats were too damaged to mount another attack, said Foote. He would not be able to do much before the mortar boats were available. Grant returned to the landing in a somber frame of mind, just as his aide, Captain William Hillyer, galloped up ashen-faced. A ferocious battle had erupted, Hillyer panted. The rebels were making an all-out assault, and McClernand's division was in full retreat. Grant galloped back to the farmhouse.

At dawn on February 15, intense artillery fire had poured down on McClernand's 1st Division, on the right of Grant's line. For the next few hours, Confederate troops led by Buckner attacked repeatedly, driving McClernand's men back, never giving them time to consolidate in a new position. C. F. Smith and the 2nd Division were too far to the left to offer support, but help was at hand.

Only the previous day Grant had organized the fresh regiments Halleck had sent him into a provisional division and entrusted it to Brigadier General

Lewis Wallace, a man destined to be far less famous for anything he did in the Civil War than for his best-selling novel *Ben-Hur.* Wallace's bright green division was hurriedly wedged into the center of the Union line. When the pressure on McClernand's division became overwhelming, Wallace moved one of his three brigades to the right. McClernand's survivors retreated through it, taking shelter behind.

The Confederates had succeeded in punching a hole in the encircling Union line. A road south was wide open. Floyd and Pillow could now make a fighting retreat toward Nashville. There was nothing to stop them getting most of their army out by nightfall.

Grant galloped up to his headquarters at the farmhouse, and his staff quickly briefed him. He scribbled a note to Foote, urging him to have his gunboats open fire. Grant's note said he needed to raise the morale of his troops and depress that of the foe. "If all the Gun Boats that can, will immediately make their appearance to the enemy, it may secure us a Victory. Otherwise all may be defeated . . . I must order a charge to save appearances. I do not expect the Gun Boats to go into action but to make their appearance and throw shells at long range." The navy obliged.

Riding on to inspect the situation, Grant arrived on the battlefield at the left of the line. C. F. Smith's 2nd Division was well posted on the frozen ground and intact. As Grant rode through Wallace's division, everything at first seemed under control. But at the right-center of the line there was confusion, and when he reached the right wing he found a mood close to panic. Men were milling around complaining they were out of ammunition, yet there were hundreds of ammunition boxes piled up nearby.

Volunteer officers sometimes had to be led by the hand, even in the middle of battle, and problems of ammunition supply in close combat persisted throughout the way. Grant pointed to the nearby ammo crates and told the soldiers bluntly, "Fill your cartridge boxes quick and get into line. The enemy is trying to escape and must not be permitted to do so."

Wallace and McClernand were conferring when Grant galloped up holding a sheaf of what looked like telegrams in his left hand. McClernand grumbled, "This army wants a head"—an implied rebuke for Grant's absence during the crisis.

Grant ignored that, blandly responding, "It seems so." He told Wallace and McClernand to pull their men back onto higher ground, dig in and hold until reinforcements arrived. McClernand replied that it was too late for that—the enemy had a clear road out.

Grant's face flushed, and he crushed the papers in his left hand. Then, in a voice so calm it sounded almost strange, he said in a matter-of-fact way, "Gentlemen, the position on the right must be retaken."

Shortly after this, the pressure slackened abruptly. Instead of making a fighting withdrawal, the Confederates were returning to their own lines to collect supplies and artillery. This was war à la Pillow, and a weird godsend it was to the Federals. Grant turned to his chief of staff, Colonel Joseph D. Webster. "Some of our men are pretty demoralized," he said, "but the enemy must be more so. He has attempted to force his way out but has fallen back. The one who attacks first now will be victorious, and the enemy will have to be in a hurry if he gets ahead of me."

It was obvious to Grant that if the Confederates had put nearly all their weight into an attack against his right, they must be wide open to a powerful counterstroke over on the left. Grant cantered up to C. F. Smith's command post. He found Smith, the awe-inspiring West Point commandant of his cadet years, sitting under a tree. "General Smith," said Grant, "all has failed on the right. You must take Fort Donelson."

Smith, a tall, handsome, and slender sixty-year-old, got to his feet, pulled himself erect, brushed his flowing white moustache, and responded, "I will do it."

When Smith's division charged, it found the Confederate position as lightly manned as Grant had foreseen, but a huge abatis blocked any direct assault on the fort. Smith rode among his men, shouting, "Damn you, gentlemen. I see skulkers! I'll have none here. . . . You volunteered to be killed for the love of your country, and now you can be. . . . I'm only a [professional] soldier and I don't want to be killed, but you came to be killed. . . ." His men scrambled over the abatis and fell on the defenders behind it. Many a Confederate fled rather than fight. Night and a light snowfall descended on a Confederate army that was hunkering down, and on thousands of Smith's men who were now inside the last line of Donelson's defenses.

Grant and Webster rode over the battlefield at dusk. Icy temperatures were freezing the dead into grotesque attitudes that only accentuated the violence that killed them. The wounded, suffering from pain, thirst, and terror of dying, groaned, sobbed, and called out for help. He felt suddenly depressed. "Let's get away from this dreadful place," he said to Webster. "I suppose this work is part of the devil that is in us all."

Riding away, words came to him, a few lines of poetry. Grant had remembered a poem of Byron's during his first battle in Mexico. Now a poem by Robert Burns flashed through his mind. To any sensitive soul, there is steel in great verse, and the downcast Grant recited to himself Burns's "Man Is Made to Mourn," like a secular prayer.

Man's inhumanity to man
Makes countless thousands mourn . . .

In the middle of the night a Confederate officer approached Smith's lines with a message from General Buckner: The defenders were asking for an armistice. When Smith was informed, he burst out hotly, "I make no terms with rebels with arms in their hands—my terms are immediate and unconditional surrender!" Smith took the letter the Confederate officer was carrying and rode off with it to the Widow Crisp's house. He handed the letter to Grant while Grant, roused from sleep, was still struggling to get dressed. *"There's* something for you to read, General," Smith announced.

"What answer should I send to this, General?" asked Grant when he had finished it.

"No terms to the damned rebels!" Smith replied. Grant, amused, laughed quietly and sat down at the kitchen table to write a reply to Buckner:

Yours of this date proposing Armistice and appointment of Commissioners to settle terms of Capitulation is just received. No terms except unconditional and immediate surrender can be accepted. I propose to move immediately upon your works.

Your obt. svt.
U. S. Grant
Brig. Gen.

When he finished writing, he read the letter aloud. Smith harrumphed. No orotund courtesies for him. A soldier didn't waste his time on folderol. "It's the same thing in smoother words," he said bluntly, then stalked out of the room carrying Grant's letter.

During the night Floyd and Pillow made their escape by boat, leaving Buckner to endure the obloquy of surrender alone. Forrest escaped with his cavalry, riding through water that reached their saddles. Buckner considered Grant's terms unduly harsh, but he had no choice. And when the two men came face to face later that day, they chatted and joked, plainly delighted to be meeting up again. Grant, eager to repay an old kindness, drew Buckner aside and told him that now that he was a prisoner he might find himself in need of money. If so, Grant's purse was available. Buckner's time as a prisoner turned out to be comparatively short. He was later exchanged for a Union officer in Confederate hands and ended the war as a lieutenant general. In 1885, he marched in Grant's funeral procession.

Capturing an entire army intact is a rare and spectacular moment in any general's career. Washington had done it at Yorktown. Scott had done it at Vera Cruz. Surgeon John Brinton was looking forward to seeing the enemy paraded and to Buckner formally handing over his sword. Like victory, capitulation too had its rituals. He asked Grant just when the surrender ceremony would be held.

"There will be nothing of the kind," Grant replied. "The surrender is now a fact. We have the fort, the men, the guns. Why should we go through vain forms and mortify and injure the spirit of brave men, who after all are our own countrymen and brothers?" It was, thought Brinton, a strange note to end on, but the modern always seems strange at first.

That night, Grant wrote to Julia and couldn't resist boasting, ". . . after the greatest victory of the season. . . . Some 12 or 15 thousand prisoners have fallen into our possession. . . . This is the largest capture I believe ever made on the continent."

The surrender of Fort Donelson set the entire North rejoicing. Since Fort Sumter, there had been ten galling months of defeats, retreats, setbacks, frustrations. Here, at last, was a beacon as bright as a gas flare, a coruscating promise that the North could and would defeat the Confederacy, for all its famous martial virtues.

Halleck, McClellan, even McClernand, each claimed that he was really the one who had brought the fall of Fort Donelson. Grant was at most the tool they had used. The man himself was nothing much. Even so, Grant could be forgiven for believing that now, finally, his hold on command was secure. But he would have been wrong. Halleck still intended to shelve him, maybe even dump him.

To Halleck's dismay, Ethan Allen Hitchcock insisted he was no longer up to the rigors of a field command. He demanded, and got, a desk in the War Department. Halleck, however, did not give up. Two weeks after Fort Donelson, he informed McClellan that Grant was being difficult, uncommunicative, and flouting army regulations.

McClellan gave him authority to put Grant under arrest. Halleck did not do that but felt emboldened to give C. F. Smith command of Grant's combat units. Distraught and bewildered, Grant unwittingly called Halleck's bluff.

He threatened to resign and said he would demand an official inquiry into his conduct.

As Halleck was well aware, Lincoln had been so thrilled by Fort Donelson that within hours of the news reaching Washington he asked Congress to approve Grant's promotion to major general. Although Halleck did not give up trying to shelve Grant, the president was obviously in Grant's corner. Halleck was aware of something else, too. An inquiry would soon reveal his ignoble attempts to ruin the career of the Union's most successful general.

Suddenly terrified that Grant might resign in a blaze of publicity, Halleck wasted no time restoring Grant to full command. A month after the fall of Fort Donelson, Grant was leading his army toward Corinth, Mississippi, by way of Shiloh, bloody Shiloh.

MALVERN HILL

STEPHEN W. SEARS

The Eastern theater of the Civil War obsessed Americans, much the way the Western Front in Europe would preoccupy the world half a century later. In the North especially, leaders and public alike became fixated on events in the Washington-Richmond corridor. They tended to overlook, for example, the stranglehold the Federal navy kept on the Confederate coastline or its increasing control of the river system beyond the Appalachians. Nor did they immediately give the campaigns in the West, with their fluid maneuvers and frequently impressive generalship, the credit they deserved. But you can argue that those few Virginia miles were the critical area of the war, and that a disproportionate amount of the Confederacy's political, moral, and economic vitality was concentrated in them. If they fell, so would the Confederacy.

In May and June of 1862, when Union forces reached the outskirts of Richmond they seemed on the verge of a genuine strategic victory in the East, and one that might have ended the entire war. The South's war effort was sagging. In the West it had just sustained a defeat at Shiloh that was costly not just in lives but in transportation systems surrendered. The Federal army commander, George B. McClellan, landed 122,000 men on the peninsula between the York and James Rivers, a daring maneuver that he squandered with a curiously lethargic advance toward the Confederate capital. Already, though, the South was beginning to regain the upper hand. In a series of lightning moves that would become the stuff of military textbooks, Stonewall Jackson drove Union forces out of Virginia's breadbasket, the Shenandoah Valley. Meanwhile, in a confused melee called Seven Pines, on May 31, wounds knocked the Confederate commander Joseph E. Johnston out of action. His replacement, Robert E. Lee, was a general whose reputation until then was greater than his accomplishments. All that would change in a series of battles known as the Seven Days, which lasted from June 25 until July 1, 1862.

Lee attacked and attacked; McClellan withdrew, convinced against the evidence that he was fatally outnumbered. He cracked; his army did not, and it exacted hideous casualties before he ordered it back to its ships. Lee was also misled by illusions. Believing that he was on the verge of destroying "those people" (as he called his opponents), he ordered a final assault at a place called Malvern Hill. The "hill" was really a plateau no more than 150 feet high, with open fields sloping up to a gentle crest, which the Union army had packed with artillery. Malvern Hill would be, in fact, the only Civil War battle in which cannon, firing over open sights at the advancing Confederates, caused more casualties than rifles. (By way of historical reference, Malvern Hill was only a few feet lower than the ridge of Passchendaele in Belgium, where an Allied offensive stalled in 1917: How many grand military hopes have floundered on such puny obstacles?) Stephen W. Sears describes a battle that was for Lee a tactical disaster—and a preview of Pickett's charge at Gettysburg—but, paradoxically, a strategic triumph.

Stephen W. Sears is one of the foremost historians of the Civil War. This article was adapted from his book *To the Gates of Richmond: The Peninsula Campaign.* His books include *Landscape Turned Red: The Battle of Antietam; George B. McClellan: The Young Napoleon; Chancellorsville;* and *Controversies & Commanders: Dispatches from the Army of the Potomac.* He is currently at work on a book about Gettysburg.

IT WAS MORNING ON TUESDAY, JULY 1, 1862, HIS ARMY HAD been fighting and marching for six straight days, and General Robert E. Lee was frustrated and angry. He had succeeded in putting the Yankees to flight, but he had failed to put them to rout. When one of his officers expressed concern that the enemy might escape, Lee responded bitterly, "Yes, he will get away because I cannot have my orders carried out!"

What would become celebrated in Civil War annals as the Seven Days' Battles was clearly approaching some sort of climax. The struggle for Richmond—indeed the entire Peninsula campaign that spring—was rushing toward a decision, and Lee's frustration would color all his actions on this Day Seven. Lee was still smoldering eight months later when he wrote his report of the fighting. "Under ordinary circumstances the Federal Army should have been destroyed," he said.

The Federal army's commander, George B. McClellan, had opened the Seven Days' Battles on June 25 with a sharp probe at Oak Grove, six miles due east of Richmond. The next day Lee seized the initiative, assaulting McClellan's flank at Mechanicsville, north of Richmond. Checked at Mechanicsville, Lee renewed his offensive on Day Three, June 27, at Gaines' Mill, and this time he broke the Yankee line with a bloody, costly frontal attack. Persuaded that he was about to lose his entire army, McClellan took flight across the Chickahominy swamps, seeking haven on the James River to the south. Three days of maneuvering culminated on Day Six, June 30, at Glendale crossroads, where everything about Lee's battle plan went wrong and the Federal army escaped being cut in two.

Now it was Day Seven, and the Yankee army was at the James, on some high ground called Malvern Hill. Lee determined to deliver one more blow lest McClellan escape him finally.

Under the pressure of the repeated Confederate attacks, McClellan had utterly lost his nerve and abdicated his role as field commander. During the Glendale fighting on June 30 he was miles away, aboard the gunboat *Galena* on the James, entirely out of touch with his army. On the morning of July 1, while Lee was venting his anger at the Yankees' escape, McClellan came back from the river to inspect the Army of the Potomac's new line on Malvern Hill. As the troops recognized him, his course was marked by cheering. The general was greatly heartened by the display. He wrote his wife that "the dear fellows cheer me as of old as they march to certain death & I feel prouder of them than ever." He was himself very tired, he told her: "—no sleep for days—my mind almost worn out yet I *must* go through it. I still trust that God will give me success . . ."

McClellan announced to a fellow general that his army was "in no condition to fight without 24 hours rest—I pray that the enemy may not be in condition to disturb us today." Despite his concern, he then made haste to take himself far from the day's probable battlefield. At 9:15 A.M. he was back at Haxall's Landing on the James and on board the *Galena,* and forty-five minutes later the gunboat cast off. His journey was downstream, an hour and a half's steaming time to Harrison's Landing on the north bank of the river. The general went ashore there to inspect what he had determined would be the army's next haven. He made no provision for command of the army in his absence. Simply by being in command at the point of attack, General Fitz-John Porter would become de facto Union commander at Malvern Hill. Porter had performed the same role at Mechanicsville on Day Two and at Gaines' Mill on Day Three.

On July 1, for the first time in the Seven Days, the entire Army of the Potomac was united on the same ground. There was scarcely a man in the army who doubted that the fighting would soon resume; these Rebels, it was agreed, were relentless in their attacks. There was also a sense of the last ditch about this place. The river was at their backs and the enemy would soon enough be in front. Veterans looked around them and remarked that at least this Malvern Hill looked like a good place to fight. Andrew A. Humphreys, the army's chief topographical engineer, posted many of the troops that morning, and he wrote his wife, "There was a splendid field of battle on the high plateau where the greater part of the troops, artillery, etc. were placed. It was a magnificent sight."

For Yankees who had suffered for six weeks in the fetid Chickahominy swamps, this place was by comparison a paradise. "It was as beautiful a country as my eyes ever beheld," Lieutenant Charles Haydon of the 2nd Michigan wrote in his diary. "The cultivated fields, interspersed with belts & clusters of timber & dotted with delightful residences, extended several miles. The hills were quite high, but the slopes gradual & free of abruptness. Wheat was in the shock, oats were ready for the harvest, & corn was waist high. All were of most luxuriant growth." The day had dawned hot and promised to get hotter, but at least on the higher ground there was the chance of a breeze. Still, many men in both armies would fall victim to sunstroke this day.

Malvern Hill was not so much a hill as an elevated, open plateau, about a mile and a quarter north-to-south and three-quarters of a mile wide, just under a mile north of the James and some 130 feet higher than the river. Turkey Island Creek, emptying into the James behind Malvern Hill, had two tributaries, called Turkey Run and Western Run, that framed the sides of the plateau. Western Run, perversely enough, ran along the eastern side of the plateau, then slanted across the Quaker Road to the north, the direction from which the Rebels would be coming. The valley of Western Run was sixty feet below Malvern Hill, but the slope up to the crest of the heights was nearly half a mile long and very gradual.

As Lieutenant Haydon noted, this was good farming country. To the north, along the Quaker Road, the landscape was about the same elevation as Malvern Hill, only dipping lower into the valley of Western Run and then slanting upward again to the plateau. East of the Quaker Road and some 1,200 yards north of Malvern Hill was the Poindexter farm; opposite it, on the west, was the Carter farm. These two farms displayed open ground, but

Western Run, between them and Malvern Hill, was heavily wooded and swampy—a barrier to troop movements.

From the valley of Western Run, the ground up to the crest of Malvern Hill was entirely open. The Crew farm was the largest property in the area, with the Crew house sitting in a pleasant grove on the western side of the Malvern plateau. A quarter of a mile due east along the crest was the West house. Between the two houses the Quaker Road crossed the crest of the hill and ran past the redbrick Malvern House, sited on the southern edge of the plateau with a panoramic view of the James. Malvern House dated from the seventeenth century, when it had been the seat of Malvern Hills manor, but over the decades the manor had lost much of its eminence and its plural form, surviving into the 1860s as simply Malvern Hill. Reaching Malvern Hill on the morning of June 30, Fitz-John Porter had quickly posted defenses. Using Colonel Henry J. Hunt's artillery reserve, he laid out a daunting line of big guns facing west, bracing it with the regulars of General George Sykes's division. As more of his V Corps arrived, Porter extended the line around to the northern front of the plateau, assigning General George Morell's division to the ground between the Crew and West houses. Extending the line from there, completing the northern front, was General Darius Couch's division of the IV Corps, as yet unbloodied in the Seven Days' fighting.

By this arrangement the divisions of Morell and Couch, 17,800 infantrymen, were posted on the north facing the Quaker Road over which the Rebels were expected to approach from Glendale. As important as the infantry in this line, there were eight batteries of field artillery, with thirty-seven guns, thirty-one of which were rifled pieces. Colonel Hunt had laid out much of this gun line, and he was skilled at such work. In reserve were additional field artillery and three batteries of heavy artillery from Hunt's command and from the army's siege train; this array included five 4.5-inch Rodman and five 20-pounder Parrott rifles and six 32-pounder howitzers. Porter would regard Malvern Hill as the Army of the Potomac's best defensive position of any, with all the open ground and the artillery making it stronger even than his posting at Gaines' Mill.

McClellan's primary concern when he inspected the position was for his right or eastern flank, running back two and a half miles from Couch's division on the north front to the James. This flank was behind the difficult ground of Western Run the whole distance; but having already decided to continue the retreat to Harrison's Landing, McClellan felt the risk of an attack, here cutting him off from that point. He had "most cause to feel anxious about the right," he said, and so he posted most of the army there—the two divisions of Samuel Heintzelman's III Corps, the two of Edwin Sumner's II Corps, the two of William Franklin's VI Corps, and one of Erasmus Keyes's IV Corps, with the V Corps division of George McCall—who had been captured at Glendale the day before—in reserve. The entire line was thus in the shape of a U, the open end on the James and the closed end facing north.

The strength of the Malvern Hill position was at the same time its potential weakness. The northern end of the plateau, guarded by the ranked artillery and the divisions of Morell and Couch, was only some 1,200 yards wide, and only so many men and guns could be pressed into this space. If this relatively narrow front should be stormed in major force, just as Gaines' Mill had been on June 27, it would be overwhelmed and broken before reinforcements could take effect. On Day Seven, Malvern Hill looked daunting to the Confederates, and it was; yet there was the example, fresh in everyone's mind, of how one final and finally coordinated assault had won Day Three.

Lee met early with his generals to plan the pursuit of the enemy. In addition to James Longstreet and A. P. Hill, John Magruder joined him on the Long Bridge Road west of Glendale for consultation, and finally Stonewall Jackson arrived. This meeting of Confederate generals on the Long Bridge Road had symbolic significance. In common with the Army of the Potomac, Day Seven marked the first time in the Seven Days that the entire Army of Northern Virginia was united on the same field.

Conspicuously absent from the meeting of Lee's lieutenants was General Benjamin Huger, a division commander. The cautious Huger was as usual waiting for someone to tell him what to do next. Two of Huger's brigadiers, Lewis Armistead and Ambrose Wright, found themselves without orders and reported to General Lee. In the absence of their commander, Lee sent them on ahead toward the enemy. Huger was one to take offense at the thought of anyone else, even the commanding general, issuing orders to his men. He was thus not in the best temper for whatever the day might bring. It was Lee's thought that any fighting on July 1 should be borne by the commands of Jackson, Magruder, and Huger, none of whom had done any fighting the day before. Longstreet and A. P. Hill, who had done all the fighting at Glendale, would be held in reserve.

Lee and Longstreet were riding south on the Quaker Road when they encountered D. H. Hill. That general said he had been talking to a chaplain in his division who was from the area and who had explained that directly ahead of them on the Quaker Road was Malvern Hill, which the chaplain had described as a very imposing position militarily. Harvey Hill, who was not easily impressed by Yankees or their works, was impressed by this. "If General

McClellan is there in strength," he said, "we had better let him alone." Longstreet laughed and said, "Don't get scared, now that we have got him whipped."

Longstreet's attitude was more prevalent in the Confederate high command that day than Hill's; as one of Longstreet's brigadiers put it, "We were on a hot trail." It was obvious the Yankee army was on the run, and from the evidence left behind, from commissary stores and wagons and arms to stragglers by the hundreds, it was demoralized. One more hard push and it might disintegrate. Lee shared that view, and it influenced his decisions on July 1. Each day for five days, starting at Mechanicsville, his designs had been frustrated to one extent or another, from one cause or another. His lieutenants had been late, or become lost, or failed to attack as ordered. The day before, at Glendale, when hardly a quarter of his army got into action, his frustration had peaked. Now the opportunity to destroy McClellan's army was diminishing with each passing hour, and today might be the last chance.

Jackson's command of four divisions was to lead the way from Glendale along the Quaker Road, with Magruder's three following Jackson on the same road. Huger's two brigades under Armistead and Wright had utilized a lane leading off the Long Bridge Road into the Carter farm, west of the Quaker Road; Huger's other two brigades, when they appeared, would make the best way they could. Finally, the commands of Longstreet and A. P. Hill, in reserve, would move off the Long Bridge Road onto the Carter farm.

An unkind fate conspired to lead Magruder astray. Although he was shown Lee's map as they discussed the day's plans, he apparently did not look closely at it. Back with his command on the Long Bridge Road, Magruder told his guides to take him to the Quaker Road. This they proceeded to do. But the guides' Quaker Road was not the Quaker Road on which Stonewall Jackson was just then marching.

It seemed that at some time past there had been a Quaker meetinghouse down along the James River, to which several roads led, and by common usage they came to be known, severally, as the Quaker Road. One of these, the road due south from Glendale to Malvern Hill, was now the site of the Willis Methodist Church, and some of the local people called it the Willis Church Road, but others (including General Lee's mapmaker) still referred to it as the Quaker Road. A second road, turning off the Long Bridge Road, ran southwesterly to the River Road along the James, and some of the local people—including Magruder's guides—called *that* the Quaker Road.

At the moment, Magruder's guides were in the majority, so his three divisions proceeded to march obliquely away from the day's battlefield. The farther they marched the more suspicious Magruder became—he "seemed much put out," his aide Major Joseph Brent recalled. He interrogated his guides, but they insisted this was the only Quaker Road they knew anything about.

Longstreet, who had watched in growing puzzlement as Magruder and his command marched away, finally decided to ride after them and try to persuade Magruder that he had to be on the wrong road. Would he order him to turn back? Magruder asked. He had no authority to do that, Longstreet said, but this surely could not be the right road, whatever its name might be. Magruder had by now come to agree there must be a mistake somewhere, and he ordered the column to reverse course. They returned to the Long Bridge Road and then turned down the same lane to the Carter farm that Armistead's and Wright's brigades had used earlier. But the Quaker Road mistake had consumed more than three hours and thrown Lee's deployment plan into a tangle.

As Magruder's men retraced their steps, Major Brent rode on ahead to reconnoiter the ground where they might have to fight. On a knoll facing Malvern Hill he climbed a tree for a better view. The vista that opened out to him was at once beautiful and menacing. The gentle rise up to the crest of Malvern Hill was yellow with ripe wheat, part of which was already harvested and tied in shocks. Along the crest, visible right and left as far as he could see, were the black muzzles of cannon. Through his glasses he could see blue-clad infantry as well. "The Union soldiers were resting in position," Brent recalled, "some sitting or lying down, and others moving at ease or disappearing behind the ridge." He concluded that this part of the field "seemed almost impregnable." When he climbed down out of the tree, a soldier on picket duty nearby remarked that he was surprised to see the major unhurt; Yankee sharpshooters were very active on this front. "I would have preferred his warning before I climbed," Brent wrote, "to his expression of surprise that I had escaped."

Stonewall Jackson's command arrived on the field, and as he had done throughout the Seven Days, Jackson took the left. His division commanders also positioned themselves. Chase Whiting's two brigades turned eastward off the Quaker Road onto the Poindexter farm. Behind them, in immediate or more distant support, came Charles Winder's four brigades and Dick Ewell's three. D. H. Hill positioned his five brigades to Jackson's right, astride the Quaker Road, making up the center of the Confederate position.

Lee had intended Magruder, marching behind Jackson on the Quaker Road, to take a posting to Hill's right, west of the road. Magruder and his six brigades were nowhere in sight, however, so the place went instead to two brigades already on the scene, Armistead's and Wright's from Huger's divi-

sion. Huger himself, and his other two brigades, were also among the missing. It was close to noon now, and the problem that had plagued Lee repeatedly in this week of battle—communication between units, and between Lee
and his units—was already a problem again. It was a problem that would
grow worse.

Lee took the blacksmith shop of C. W. Smith, on the Quaker Road opposite the Willis Church parsonage, for his field headquarters. From there he
reconnoitered the left himself. He had assigned Longstreet the task of reconnoitering the right. At the Carter farm, half a mile west of the Quaker Road,
Longstreet saw a low, open ridgeline that was within artillery range of the
crest of Malvern Hill and that, he thought, would hold as many as sixty guns
in a kind of "grand battery." On the left, on Jackson's front in the Poindexter
wheat field off the Quaker Road, Lee found similar ground for a second grand
battery. Both sites were at nearly the same elevation as Malvern Hill. And
guns posted there would take the Malvern Hill guns in a cross fire.

Lee and Longstreet compared their findings and quickly agreed on a tactic
for the battle. They would establish two grand batteries, left and right, to
pound Malvern Hill and its defenders in a converging fire and open the way
for the infantry to storm the position. It seemed probable that the fire of two
such grand batteries ought to be enough to beat down the ranks of Federal
guns; if not, there would be opportunity to develop another tactic. But the
guns should be enough. Their cross fire, Longstreet later wrote, ought to "dis-
comfit them as to warrant an assault by infantry."

Having determined his battle plan, Lee announced it to his lieutenants in
an order drafted by his chief of staff, Colonel Robert H. Chilton. This order
demonstrated Chilton's lack of skill at drafting them. "Batteries have been established to act upon the enemy's line," it read. "If it is broken as is probable,
Armistead, who can witness effect of the fire, has been ordered to charge with
a yell. Do the same."

By this it was left entirely to the discretion of a brigade commander, Lewis
Armistead, commanding in his first battle, to judge the effect of an artillery
bombardment and then to decide if the army should attack. Furthermore, the
only signal for a simultaneous charge by fifteen brigades—the Rebel yell of a
single charging brigade—was likely to generate as much confusion as cooperation. To complete his failings, Colonel Chilton did not mark the time it was
sent on any copy of his dispatch, which in the case of one recipient would
make an already ambiguous order even more unclear.

It is unlikely that an order so poorly drawn could have been seen and approved by Lee before it was sent; he cannot have intended to turn over direc-

tion of the Battle of Malvern Hill to a brigade commander. Indeed, why he did not write so important an order himself is puzzling. Perhaps extreme fatigue was affecting his judgment. General Lafayette McLaws, commanding one of Magruder's divisions, testified that when he sought out Lee to deliver a report that day, he found him sleeping under a tree, with no less than President Jefferson Davis at hand to see that Lee was not disturbed. The general, the president explained, had been up all night. However that may be, on July 1 Lee's control over his subordinates was not what it should have been.

The artillery arm of the Army of Northern Virginia had not distinguished itself in the Seven Days' Battles. Seldom had it been employed to good effect, and its employment at Malvern Hill proved to be dismal beyond all previous reckoning. Sharp-tongued D. H. Hill termed the part the artillery played "most farcical," and after the experiences of the day there were few who would have disagreed.

The problems in the left grand battery came down to a matter of numbers. With only ten batteries Stonewall Jackson's command was short of artillery to begin with, and these were divided among three separate commands and scattered widely along the crowded line of march; there seemed no way to get them all together in one place—the Poindexter farm—at one time.

The solution ought to have been found in General William N. Pendleton's artillery reserve, established for just this purpose. Pendleton had thought deeply about the theory and organization of artillery, but actually directing guns on the battlefield did not seem to be one of his ambitions. If anyone from Lee's headquarters located Pendleton and his guns on July 1, there is no record of it. Pendleton himself said the day "was spent by me in seeking for some time the commanding general, that I might get orders," but he admitted this pursuit was unsuccessful. As a consequence, of his four battalions of reserve artillery, containing fourteen batteries, just one battery would be employed that day.

Virginian Carter Berkeley, of the Staunton Artillery, would never forget his experience in the left grand battery in Poindexter's wheat field. With another Virginia battery, William Poague's Rockbridge Artillery, and James Reilly's Rowan Battery of North Carolina, the Staunton Artillery was standing waiting in the Quaker Road. Sergeant Berkeley watched Jackson ride by himself far into the Poindexter wheat field, into which enemy shells were falling with some regularity. After a time Jackson returned and told Chase Whiting, in command of that part of the field, to order the guns forward. Whiting protested. There were supposed to be fifty guns in this grand battery; these three batteries mounted only sixteen. "They won't live in there five minutes," he said. "Obey your orders, General Whiting, promptly and willingly," Jackson snapped. Whiting snapped back, "I always obey my orders promptly, but not willingly under such circumstances." He told his staff to make witness of his protest, then ordered the battery commanders into the field.

Jackson rode ahead, pointing them to some high ground in the wheat a thousand yards from the Federals on the hill. "Forward, Sir," Old Jack called out. As soon as they unlimbered, Sergeant Berkeley recalled, "all the Yankee batteries on the hill beyond stopped firing into the woods and poured into us the most deadly fire that I ever witnessed during the war." There were no Confederate guns firing yet from the other grand battery, and no cross fire; these sixteen guns, in these moments, constituted the largest concentration of artillery fire Lee's army was able to achieve on July 1.

It was not without effect. Matthew Marrin of the 1st Minnesota noted in his diary that the Rebel shelling "tried our pluck to the core . . . General Sumner ordered his II Corps men back out of range and under cover." But the long odds soon told: eight batteries against three, thirty-seven guns against sixteen. Confederate gun carriages were shattered and men and horses killed and wounded. Finally, of the three batteries, only the Staunton Artillery was still firing. Its captain, William Balthis, hit seven times by shell fragments, kept urging his men to stand to their guns. Finally, out of ammunition, they too had to withdraw. There were barely enough horses left to drag the guns off. Eventually, one at a time, three other batteries would try to establish a presence in the left grand battery, only to be beaten down by the Yankee guns.

The Federal shelling took its toll among others on the Poindexter farm as well. The men of the Stonewall Brigade always remembered the volume of fire from Malvern Hill as enough to shock even the famously profane colonel of the 27th Virginia, Andrew Grigsby, into silence. As Stonewall Jackson rode along with Dick Ewell, wrote Ewell's aide Campbell Brown, a shell "pitched viciously down just at the head of Genl. J.'s horse, which kept on at its shambling gait. Jackson talking earnestly to Genl. Ewell, took no notice, but the latter quickly stooping caught his horse by the bridle & stopped him, a second or two before the shell exploded."

D. H. Hill had a similar narrow escape. He was seated at the trunk of a tree writing orders when one of the Yankee shells struck close by, tumbling him over in the dirt and ripping his uniform coat. Hill stood up, brushed off the dirt, and then seated himself and resumed writing, this time behind the tree. "I am not going to be killed until my time comes," he observed.

The failure in the right grand battery that afternoon was, if anything, more dismal. Of Huger's six batteries, only two got to the front and into action. Of

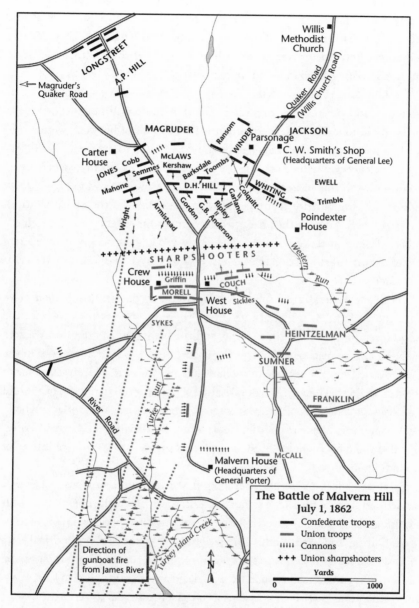

Willis Methodist Church

LONGSTREET

A.P. HILL

Magruder's Quaker Road

Quaker Road (Willis Church Road)

MAGRUDER

Ransom

WINDER

Parsonage

JACKSON

C. W. Smith's Shop
(Headquarters of General Lee)

Carter House

JONES   Cobb

McLAWS
Semmes Kershaw
Barksdale
Toombs

D.H. HILL

Garland
Colquitt

WHITING

EWELL

Mahone

Armistead

Wright

Gordon

Ripley
G.B. Anderson

Trimble

Poindexter House

Western Run

SHARPSHOOTERS

Crew House   Griffin

COUCH

MORELL

West House   Sickles

SYKES

HEINTZELMAN

SUMNER

FRANKLIN

River Road

Turkey Run

McCALL

Malvern House
(Headquarters of General Porter)

The Battle of Malvern Hill
July 1, 1862

▬▬▬ Confederate troops
▬▬▬ Union troops
ⱵⱵⱵ Cannons
+++ Union sharpshooters

Direction of gunboat fire from James River

Turkey Island Creek

N

Yards
0   1000

On a low ridge known as Malvern Hill, the Army of the Potomac laid out a
daunting defensive line. Nonetheless, Lee's entire Army of Northern Virginia
was for the first time united on the field. But for wrong directions and misunderstood orders, the Confederates might well have overrun their opponents.
Stormed repeatedly, the Union army never lost its nerve—which is more than
can be said of its commander, George B. McClellan.

sixteen batteries under Magruder's command, just two opened fire. Of the fourteen in Pendleton's reserve, one was engaged. Seeing the need, A. P. Hill sent his best battery, under Willie Pegram, to join the fight. As they came up and turned into the Carter farm, each battery was thrown into action separately, and each was pounded in its turn by the guns on Malvern Hill.

Captain Cary Grimes's Virginia battery had one man killed and three wounded, and three horses hit, even before they could unlimber. Robert Stiles of the Richmond Howitzers complained that several of his guns were set off by shell fragments before the lanyards could be pulled to fire them. Willie Pegram's battery was reduced to a single gun still firing. The only way Greenlee Davidson's Virginia battery could remain in action was to roll the guns down behind the ridgeline for loading and then push them to the crest for firing. Georgian A. S. Cutts of the artillery reserve, without orders, had to watch the debacle from a distance in frustration. His was one of thirty-five Confederate batteries available for action at Malvern Hill on July 1 that failed to fire a single round.

Of all the Federal guns fired that day, the only ones to prove ineffective were those of the navy's gunboats. From their anchorages in the James the Rebels were out of their direct sight, and the boats had to fire blindly across Malvern Hill to reach them. Their big shells tended to land at random in the Confederate lines. When one of them crashed down near an ambulance far to the rear, the Rebel driver shook his fist and shouted, "You damn son of a bitch! You haint got no eyes, & would as soon hit a ambulance driver as anybody else!" A number of their shells fell short, onto the Union lines. General Porter signaled the navy by flag, "For God's sake stop your firing, you are killing & wounding our men."

By three o'clock or so that afternoon, it was becoming obvious to Lee that his artillery bombardment was not going to beat down the enemy's guns. If anything, the result was exactly the opposite. Another tactic would have to be tried. Calling Longstreet to his side, Lee rode off to the left, beyond Jackson's front, to see if the Federals' eastern flank might be turned. From their observations it seemed feasible, and it was decided to shift the army's reserve, Longstreet's and A. P. Hill's divisions, to the left to make the effort.

Lee had no expectation that McClellan would go any farther in his retreat than Malvern Hill; his position was strong and his gunboats were at hand. Considering the hour and the time required to get the two divisions into their new positions, Lee now had to think of renewing the battle on July 2.

Earlier, Armistead's brigade, the advance of Huger's division, had taken position opposite the center of the Federal line. When Yankee skirmishers

crept forward threateningly, Armistead felt obliged to drive them off. He gave
the task to three of his Virginia regiments. They chased the skirmishers back
easily enough, but in doing so advanced into a withering fire from the hill. Instead of retreating, they rushed forward "in their ardor" (as Armistead put it)
to the cover of a shallow ravine slanting up toward the Crew house. There
were too few of them to advance any farther, and to withdraw would mean
running the gauntlet a second time, so they stayed where they were, huddled
in their precarious lodgment.

John Magruder now arrived in advance of his troops, who were dragging
along behind after their misdirected march. Magruder was very late on the
field—it was four o'clock by now—and he knew nothing of Lee's plan or the
situation except that he was told to take position on Huger's right: to become,
that is, the extreme right of the Confederate line. He made a quick survey of
the field and then sent his aide, Captain A. G. Dickinson, to find Lee and report both his arrival and Armistead's "success" in advancing three regiments
partway up Malvern Hill.

At about the same time, on the other flank, Chase Whiting reported seeing
Yankee troops pulling back across Malvern Hill (this was Sumner's men taking cover from the Confederate shells) and the enemy's artillery fire slacken-
ing on his front (this was its shift to the new targets on the other flank). Lee
was on his reconnaissance when the two reports reached him. Their exact content is not known, but both must have been assertive and positive, for he
changed his plan once again.

From the evidence of these reports—Armistead's advance and the Yankee
withdrawal—perhaps McClellan was taking up his retreat again; perhaps he
was getting away. Lee gave Captain Dickinson new orders for Magruder.
Dickinson made note of them: "General Lee expects you to advance rapidly.
He says it is reported the enemy is getting off. Press forward your whole line
and follow up Armistead's successes . . ."

On the face of it, this was a peremptory order to attack immediately. Yet
that night Lee would seek out Magruder and demand of him, "General Magruder, why did you attack?" From this it would seem that Lee intended his
orders to be softened with discretion—to be taken by Magruder as an order to
attack only if the situation at that time and at that place favored an attack. If
this was in fact the case, it argued once again for Lee to write his own orders
instead of relying on staff officers to interpret them for him.

However that may be, Dickinson returned to find Magruder in a particular
condition of mind. His surgeon was treating him for acute indigestion with a
medication containing morphine, and he was in a morphine-induced state of

agitation and excitement. Just before Dickinson reached him, Magruder had been handed the order written some three hours earlier by Colonel Chilton—and now quite defunct—which to Magruder seemed to outline Lee's plan of attack and which, as it bore no time of sending, he assumed to be a current order. Now came Dickinson's message from Lee, which, on the heels of Chilton's message, had the sound not only of an attack order but of a reiterated attack order. Magruder had no doubt now about what was expected of him: He must launch a full-blooded attack with the least possible delay.

Thus from an unlikely combination of circumstances—a march down the wrong Quaker Road, misunderstood observations, Armistead's ardent Virginians, a medication laced with morphine, and Robert E. Lee's inability to make his orders clear—would spring the bloody battle for Malvern Hill.

Magruder's immediate problems were pulling together enough men for an assault and puzzling out the curious command situation in which he found himself. The only troops at hand were the brigades of Armistead and Wright, both from Huger's command. Those next closest to the front were also Huger's—William Mahone's brigade and Robert Ransom's. Magruder's three divisions—one under his personal command, and those of David R. Jones and Lafayette McLaws—were coming up but were not yet ready for deployment. In any event, it was Magruder who was ordered to make the attack, and he could hardly launch it without employing Huger's troops, who were the first in line.

Huger had a different outlook. Sometime earlier Magruder had sent Major Brent to find Huger. The South Carolinian was as courteous and gentlemanly as ever, Brent recalled, yet it was clear this had become for him a matter of amour propre. He had not been at the front, Huger said, and he did not know where his brigades were, but he understood that "some of them have been moved without my knowledge by orders independent of me, and I have no further information enabling me to answer your inquiries." Clearly Huger was not marching himself or his men to the sound of the guns.

Brent observed that his report of the conversation left Magruder "much perplexed." The general decided his only chance was to bypass Huger entirely and appeal directly to Huger's brigadiers. Brent was hurried to Ransom and Mahone, only to be told that Huger had just sent them strict instructions to ignore any order not issued through him. Ransom said apologetically that therefore he could not go to Magruder's assistance. But Mahone, who regarded his superior with less reverence, cheerfully volunteered his brigade to Magruder.

At 5:30 P.M. Magruder opened the battle as well as he could with the bri-

gades of Wright and Mahone and the half of Armistead's already on the field—
something over 5,000 men, none of them his own. Magruder thought he
ought to have three times that number, but with "the hour growing late," as
he put it, and his orders imperative, he felt he had no choice.

The experience of Ambrose Wright's brigade—3rd, 4th, and 22nd Georgia
and 1st Louisiana—would prove all too typical of the Confederate brigades
that attacked on July 1. Raising the Rebel yell, Wright's men charged out of
the woods and into the open toward the hill. The 22nd Georgia went astray
and only a small part of it joined the assault. Then Wright's remaining force
got too far out ahead of Mahone's, Armistead's regiments were pinned down
off to the left, and Wright's 1,500 men found themselves quite alone on the
slopes of Malvern Hill.

David Winn of the 4th Georgia wrote to his wife afterward: "It is astonishing that every man did not fall; bullet after bullet too rapid in succession
to be counted . . . shell after shell illuminating the whole atmosphere, burst
over our heads, under our feet, and in our faces . . ." The true measure of a
man's courage, Winn said, was simply answering the call "for the desperate
charge."

The first line of General Morell's defense on this part of the hill was the var-
iegated brigade of General Charles Griffin—14th New York, 4th Michigan,
9th Massachusetts, and 62nd Pennsylvania—as well as four artillery batteries;
Fitz-John Porter had Griffin, a veteran artillerist, commanding the guns as
well as the infantry. Wright's charge carried to within 300 yards of this line,
losing men at every step, and then it could go no farther. The artillery fire,
canister at this range, was deadly. Lieutenant Adelbert Ames's Battery A, 5th
U.S. Artillery, would fire the remarkable total of 1,392 rounds on July 1, an
average of 232 rounds for each of his six Napoleons. Ames laconically termed
the canister "effective." There was a slight depression in the ground here, and
Wright's men lay down and took what cover it provided. They kept up a fire
but remained there, awaiting help.

In its turn Mahone's brigade made its charge, met the same incessant fire as
Wright's, and was driven back. Just then, off to the left toward the Quaker
Road, other Confederate troops could be seen emerging from the woods and
advancing on Malvern Hill. D. H. Hill's division was in the fight now.

Harvey Hill had received Colonel Chilton's version of the plan of battle—
he was to move forward when he heard Armistead advance "with a yell"—
about 2:00 P.M. and called together his brigadiers to prepare for action. The
hours passed and nothing was heard from Armistead's direction, and Hill and
his lieutenants began to prepare bivouacs for the night. Abruptly, off to the

right where Armistead was supposed to be (but where Ambrose Wright in fact was) came the unmistakable sound of the Rebel yell, followed by the equally unmistakable sounds of battle. "That must be the general advance!" Hill exclaimed. "Bring up your brigades as soon as possible and join in it."

In his report on the Battle of Malvern Hill, Federal general Darius Couch observed that "the enemy continually re-enforced their column of attack . . ." What Couch saw as continual reinforcement was in truth stark evidence of the Confederates' failure to coordinate their assaults. D. H. Hill had something over 8,200 men in his five brigades, but rather than one unified sweep forward to overwhelm the Federal line, the reality of the day was five separate attacks. To make the charge his brigades had to flounder through thick woods along the Quaker Road and Western Run, and this played havoc with their organization.

William Calder of the 2nd North Carolina, part of General George B. Anderson's brigade, described the charge for his people at home. "Soon the word was passed, 'Up, Second, and at them,' and our Brigade . . . sprang through the woods with a shout," Calder wrote. "We crossed one fence, went through another piece of woods, then over another fence, into an open field on the other side of which was a long line of Yankees . . ." One regiment lost its way in the woods and later went into action with a neighboring brigade. It seemed to Anderson's men that in this open field they were entirely alone, the object of every Yankee gun on the hill. "Our men charged gallantly at them," Calder wrote. "The enemy mowed us down by fifties." Some of the ground here was planted in oats and some of it was freshly plowed, and all of it was without cover.

Colonel John B. Gordon clawed his way to within 200 yards of the Federal guns before his men wavered under the fire and Gordon ordered them to lie down to carry on the fight. Gordon survived unhurt, although he counted the rents of seven bullets in his uniform. His 3rd Alabama lost six color-bearers in succession in the charge and saw the regiment's flag literally torn to pieces. The 3rd Alabama would lose 37 dead and 163 wounded on this day, the highest loss in any Confederate regiment on the field and 56 percent of those who went into battle.

The brigades of General Samuel Garland Jr., Colonel Alfred Colquitt, and General Roswell Ripley attacked in their turn and were buried back in their turn, with a loss of 962 men among them.

The 10th Massachusetts was in General Couch's first line facing D. H. Hill's assaults. In his diary Lieutenant George Hagar wrote that "the rebs poured out of the woods & charged on us . . . They came within yards of us when they turned & ran, what was left of them." There was a respite and they waited, and then the Rebels came on again: "Pretty soon they poured out in 4 lines & charging our batterys posted on the brow of the hill . . . We murdered them by the hundreds but they again formed & came up to be slaughtered . . ."

Couch, rallying his three brigades to hold their lines, had his horse killed under him. He warned Porter that if the assaults continued he must have help. Porter sent a call to Bull Sumner for two brigades from the II Corps. Sumner responded with General John Caldwell's brigade but hesitated to do more. Sam Heintzelman, who was there when Porter's request came, exclaimed, "By Jove! If Porter asks for help, I know he needs it and I will send it." He dispatched a battery and General Dan Sickles's brigade of infantry from the III Corps. From his artillery reserve Sumner sent along a strong eight-gun battery of Parrott rifles.

With his assault faltering and increasing numbers of his men streaming toward the rear, D. H. Hill called for reinforcements and went in search of them himself. He came first on a part of General Robert Toombs's Georgia brigade, from Magruder's command on the right. A political general, Toombs was having a bad day—he had lost control of his brigade and was somewhere else on the field—and Hill rallied the leaderless Georgians himself and led them forward into the battle. They could not brave the torrent of gunfire, however, and collapsed to the rear in disorder. The furious Hill would later happen on Toombs in the dusk and rage at him, "For shame! Rally your troops! Where were you when I was riding up and down your line, rallying your troops?"

Hill did not restrict his fury to the unfortunate Toombs. Considering how close to the enemy's line his own division had come on July 1, he asked, "What might have been done had the other nine cooperated with it?" D. H. Hill suffered 1,756 casualties in this series of fruitless charges, and he had absolutely nothing to show for it.

At Gaines' Mill, Lee won the day by finally getting his forces assembled and under firm, unified control and then advancing in mass and overwhelming the Federal defenders. He could not quite manage that same tactic at Malvern Hill. Better than 23,000 men under Magruder, Huger, and D. H. Hill would go on the attack this day, more than enough to overwhelm Porter's line, yet each assault was piecemeal, hardly a brigade at a time.

All the same, it was a close-run thing. "The battle was desperately contested," the Federal artillerist Henry Hunt testified, "and frequently trembled in the balance." At one point Colonel Hunt positioned several of his reserve batteries far back on the plateau, to play on the enemy's new line of advance should Porter's battle line be broken. Before leading his last reserves into the fight, Porter would take the precaution of destroying his diary and dispatch book lest they, and he, fall into the hands of the victorious Rebels.

In midafternoon the gunboat *Galena* had steamed back from Harrison's Landing with General McClellan aboard, and about 3:30 he appeared once again on Malvern Hill. At the time the Federal gunners had gained the best of the artillery duel and Magruder was yet to launch his infantry attack, and the battle was in abeyance. After consulting for a time with Porter at his Malvern House headquarters, McClellan made a rapid tour of the defensive positions. Then general and staff rode to the extreme right of the line, over-looking the James, and remained there. After a time, his aide William Biddle wrote, "we heard artillery firing away off to the left; we were too far away to hear the musketry distinctly . . ."

When seeking the presidency in 1864, McClellan would suffer the charge, from editorial writers and cartoonists, of dereliction of duty at Malvern Hill, of taking safe haven aboard the *Galena* while his army fought for its life. William Brickham of the *Cincinnati Commercial,* for example, wrote that "Mc-Clellan on gunboats during the battle of Malvern Hill was the meanest pic-ture that this bloody rebellion has painted." The charge, though valid, was misdirected. While McClellan did board the *Galena* on the morning of July 1 with the all-but-certain knowledge that his army would be attacked that day and then steamed away ten miles downriver, at the time the attack finally came he was back on the field—though far distant from the scene of combat.

Yet McClellan was reluctant to correct the record, for in doing so he risked having his excursion on board the *Galena* during the Glendale battle on June 30 revealed, an excursion that by any definition was a true dereliction of duty. Testifying before a congressional committee, McClellan said he simply could not remember whether or not he was on a gunboat. There remained, however, the verdict rendered by such fighting men as Colonel Francis Barlow of the 61st New York. "I think the whole army feel," Barlow wrote three days after Malvern Hill, "that it was left to take care of itself and was saved only by its own brave fighting."

Lee was also on the battlefield, but at the very center of it, trying to sort out and salvage a fight that had burst out of his control. Longstreet, who was with the commanding general when the battle erupted, wrote afterward that it opened "in some way unknown to me . . ." Lee had as little understanding of what had triggered the fighting, but now that it had spread to the commands of Magruder, Huger, and D. H. Hill and was beyond stopping, he was deter-

mined to make the best of it. He was with Lafayette McLaws's division west
of the Quaker Road when a call for help from Magruder reached him. He advanced McLaws personally and sent word to Magruder to redirect his assault
more toward the right, against the enemy's flank. He also pressed Benjamin
Huger, and that general finally released Robert Ransom's big brigade to Magruder's support.

Magruder tried frantically to rush his own three divisions into action in
support of Huger's men, but it was a task that frustrated his best efforts. One
difficulty was a serious shortage of manpower. On June 30, Day Six, Magruder
had some 12,500 infantry under command. Now, as dusk fell on Day Seven,
neither Magruder nor his lieutenants had any idea how many of those infantry
were still on the scene. Every road and every grove behind Magruder's front
was filled with his stragglers. All told, he brought hardly 7,100 infantrymen
into battle on July 1, and only two of his sixteen batteries.

Magruder's own division, the brigades of Howell Cobb and William Barksdale, was first to arrive and first to go in. Like Hill's brigades then fighting on
their left, they attacked piecemeal. Barksdale's Mississippians charged into
what their commander called "a terrible fire" of every type of artillery missile
imaginable, and they lost one-third of their numbers. Cobb's brigade passed
through the wreckage of Armistead's Virginians and met the same terrible
fire. The 2nd Louisiana lost three color-bearers and then the regimental commander. His second-in-command took up the flag and he too was killed.
These Louisianians lost 182 dead and wounded, second only to the 3rd Alabama that day.

Ransom's North Carolina brigade of Huger's division, when it belatedly
reached the field, was marched at the double-quick almost half a mile behind
the battle line so as to come up on the extreme right of the formation. Ransom personally led the brigade to within forty yards of a Yankee battery before the wave of charging men broke and fell back down the slope. The charge
cost Ransom 499 men, the highest number in any Confederate brigade on
July 1.

Virtually every Southerner who stormed Malvern Hill and left a record of
his experience spoke in awe of the Federal guns. The ground shook under their
cannonade. Brigadier General David R. Jones, commanding one of Magruder's divisions, summed it up for his family by saying, "The fire from the
enemy's artillery was truly terrific." D. H. Hill, looking back on Malvern Hill
after four years of war, believed more than half the Confederate casualties that
day were a result of artillery fire, a circumstance that he called "unprecedented." The Federals were awestruck as well. A gunner in a battery of big

thirty-two-pounders that Hunt unleashed on the attackers admitted to a friend that it had made him heartsick to see his shells "cut roads through them some places ten feet wide. . . . They would close up & come ahead . . ."

Behind the Confederate lines it was chaos. Walking wounded and wrecked batteries and stragglers by the thousands—what Major Brent called "the bashful men"—filled every road and byway and every clearing. Units that Stonewall Jackson ordered forward in response to D. H. Hill's appeal for help were held to a virtual standstill by this tide washing back from the battlefield. General Winder and his staff went in among the throngs of stragglers and tried to drive them back to the front, with limited results. Lieutenant McHenry Howard came on a dozen men lined up behind a single tree, and saw only "a shiver pass up the file when the hindmost was struck with the flat of a sword . . ." None of Jackson's men would reach the front in time to affect the course of the battle.

It was fast growing dark now, and the battle rushed to its climax. Private Oliver Norton of Morell's division watched as "rebels swarmed out of the woods, seemingly without end . . ." Artillerist Henry Hunt, pushing fresh batteries to the front to replace those that had exhausted their ammunition, had a second horse killed under him. To Captain Richard Auchmuty of Morell's staff, it seemed "that the men stood like heroes." Morell's casualty list reflected that stubborn stand. Charles Griffin's brigade in the first line lost 534 men and three of its four regimental commanders. The 62nd Pennsylvania had five color-bearers shot down. Morell's other two brigades in support had 566 more casualties between them.

A final desperate charge was made by McLaws's two thinned brigades, under Paul Semmes and Joseph Kershaw, along with remnants of brigades from earlier attacks—including Armistead's and Wright's men, who had been clinging to the hill below the Crew house for three or more hours. McLaws called the scene "a slaughter pen." Irishmen of the 69th New York struggled with Irishmen of the 10th Louisiana. For its full length the crest of Malvern Hill was wreathed in battle smoke, with only angry red flashes to mark the positions of the guns and waving flags to mark the lines of battle.

At almost the center of the line, near the Quaker Road, the spear point of the Confederate thrust reached into the line of guns, forcing Captain John Edwards's battery of Parrott rifles, 3rd U.S. Artillery, to limber up and fall back to avoid being taken. But with that effort the final charge spent its force and slowly receded. Light of day on July 2 would reveal this high-water mark precisely outlined in a line of bodies in gray and butternut.

In the darkness the Federal guns continued firing, bathing the smoky crest of the hill in a pulsating dull red light, so that it looked like a depiction of the maw of hell. Along the Quaker Road below the hill, staunch old Isaac Trimble of Ewell's division doggedly pushed his brigade toward the front. Stonewall Jackson rode up and asked Trimble what he was doing. "I am going to charge those batteries, sir," Trimble said. "I guess you had better not try it," Jackson told him. "General D. H. Hill has just tried it with his whole division and been repulsed; I guess you had better not try it, sir." Old Jack rode on, and finally the Federal guns stopped firing. Night closed on Malvern Hill.

✦

THIS LAST DAY OF THE SEVEN DAYS had proved fruitless and expensive for the Army of Northern Virginia. The cost came to 866 dead, 4,235 wounded, and 535 missing (most of whom had to be counted among the dead), a total of 5,636. In the weeklong battle only Gaines' Mill had cost more, and at least that could be counted a victory. Malvern Hill could only be counted a defeat. Federal losses were something over half as great—314 killed, 1,875 wounded, and 818 missing, a total of 3,007. In the harsh verdict of D. H. Hill, the attacking forces "did not move together, and were beaten in detail . . . It was not war—it was murder."

Malvern Hill was clearly a battle Lee did not intend to be fought the way it was fought, and it demonstrated a lack of effective control over his lieutenants. Never again would he exercise so slack a rein. When he asked Magruder that night, "Why did you attack?" Magruder answered promptly, "In obedience to your orders, twice repeated." There was nothing Lee could say to that.

It was Magruder's misfortune to arrive on the battlefield three hours late, and then to open the battle on the strength of a misunderstanding. Huger's feeble performance did not actually contribute greatly to the defeat, yet neither would he have contributed anything to another outcome. Neither man ever again commanded in the Army of Northern Virginia.

For all the failings of planning and preparation, this was a battle Lee might well have won, in the same way he won Gaines' Mill, with disastrous consequences to the Army of the Potomac. Better management of their forces by his field commanders—even average management by Magruder and Huger—would have driven the Federals off the hill in disorder and gained for Lee the final victory he had sought all week.

However serious the day's results, Lee lost the battle but won the larger contest. At 9:30 that night Fitz-John Porter signaled McClellan that "against immense odds, we have driven the enemy beyond the battlefield and the firing ended at 8:30." He went on to say that if he could be resupplied, "we will hold our own and advance if you wish." Here was Porter, the soul of military caution, proposing to follow up the Malvern Hill victory with a counteroffensive. The next morning he said to a fellow general that he had spent the night "urging McClellan to move forward on Richmond at daylight."

McClellan, however, had long since made up his mind. His only thought was safe haven at Harrison's Landing. Without even waiting for Porter's verdict on the day's events, in contradiction to all of Porter's later arguments, he ordered the retreat continued.

Malvern Hill is customarily considered, along with Pickett's Charge, to be one of Robert E. Lee's great mistakes of the war. Simply judged on the tactical level it was indeed a mistake, yet unlike Pickett's Charge it sealed a larger victory. The Army of the Potomac would be rendered impotent, penned up at Harrison's Landing until it was evacuated from the Peninsula six weeks later. The Seven Days proved to be Richmond's deliverance, and the Battle of Malvern Hill, for all its bloody fumbling, was vital to that result. Lee failed to break the Yankees' army, but he most assuredly broke the Yankees' commanding general.

THE LAST WORD
ON THE LOST ORDER

STEPHEN W. SEARS

Is there an episode in the Civil War that plays better into a counterfactual scenario than the finding of the Lost Order of Antietam? As the capitalization indicates, the document—Robert E. Lee's Special Orders No. 191—has long since slipped into American legend. On September 9, 1862, a Confederate messenger riding out of Lee's Maryland invasion headquarters presumably dropped a sealed envelope wrapped around a gift of cigars in a clover field near Frederick, Maryland. Four days later, after an overaged Indiana corporal named Barton W. Mitchell spotted the package, the Civil War hung in the balance. George B. McClellan, who was once again commander of the Union Army of the Potomac, now knew his opponent's most secret plans and had the opportunity to destroy him. Here the questions begin. How was SO 191 actually lost? And why wasn't that loss discovered? What if McClellan had moved sooner and had been able to gobble up in turn each of Lee's divided divisions—taking them in detail, as the military expression goes? Would that have brought the Civil War to an abrupt end? But then what if SO 191 hadn't been lost in the first place? What if Lee had continued on into the broad, rich valleys of Pennsylvania and had engaged McClellan on his own terms? Would a Confederate victory on Northern soil have brought, Saratoga-like, recognition from Great Britain and France, followed by military assistance and intervention, guaranteeing that the United States would be permanently split into two nations? What is certain is that Corporal Mitchell's discovery produced the bloodiest single day of the whole war.

Stephen W. Sears is one of the foremost historians of the Civil War. His books include *To the Gates of Richmond: The Peninsula Campaign; Landscape Turned Red: The Battle of Antietam; George B. McClellan:*

The Young Napoleon; Chancellorsville; and *Controversies & Commanders: Dispatches from the Army of the Potomac.* He is currently at work on a book about Gettysburg.

IN THE ANNALS OF MILITARY INTELLIGENCE, THERE IS NOTHing quite like the Lost Order. Even the most spectacular code-breaking accomplishments of World War II never handed one general's army to another "on a silver platter," as one chronicler of the Lost Order puts it. Civil War historians grope for superlatives to describe this opportunity of a lifetime, this hit on "the all-time military jackpot."

At the time, however, there was an astonishing lack of interest in how the Lost Order was lost, in how it was found, even in what it meant in the larger scheme of things. Resulting in the Battle of Antietam, it was one of the pivots on which the course of the Civil War turned, yet considerable time passed before that notion sank in. Even today, tellings of the story of the Lost Order have been marked by mystery and misunderstanding.

Special Orders No. 191—the Lost Order's official designation—was key to Robert E. Lee's strategic plan for the fall campaign of 1862. He composed SO 191 on Tuesday, September 9, at his headquarters at Frederick in western Maryland, where he was resting his army and contemplating nothing less than gaining independence for the Confederacy. General Lee was on a winning streak and had no intention of letting his opponent up. In June he had beaten George McClellan outside Richmond; in August he had beaten John Pope at Manassas outside Washington; and now, learning that McClellan was again opposing him, he intended to deliver a knockout blow on Northern soil.

This instinct for the kill was a key element of Lee's genius, as was his intuitive reading of the man he was fighting. Only the day before, he had been heard to describe McClellan as "an able general but a very cautious one." (He repeated that characterization another time, except then he labeled McClellan "timid," not "cautious.") Lee's entire design, as he spelled it out that Tuesday, was calculated with McClellan's shortcomings in mind.

It was Lee's intention, in crossing the Potomac into Maryland, to draw the Federal army after him and away from its Washington base. In due course, somewhere off to the north and west in the Cumberland Valley of Pennsylvania, he would maneuver McClellan into a finish fight. He was very clear on that point: "I went into Maryland to give battle," he said in discussing the campaign after the war, and had it all gone as planned, "I would have fought and crushed him."

To clear the way for this march westward, he had to establish a new line of communications to Virginia through the Shenandoah Valley, and to do that he had to dispose of the Federal garrisons guarding the Shenandoah at Harpers Ferry and Martinsburg. SO 191 was designed for that purpose. He assigned six of his nine divisions to the operation, under the overall command of Stonewall Jackson.

In dividing his army in the face of a superior foe, Lee was violating a military canon, but it gave him no concern. He had done it twice before, against McClellan in June and against Pope in August, and twice it had brought him victory. The Federals were reported to be advancing from Washington with great caution and were several days' march away. Jackson would be back and the army reunited before McClellan caught on to what was happening; in ten days they would be in Pennsylvania, Lee said, with "a very good army, and one that I think will be able to give a good account of itself."

During the afternoon of September 9, his headquarters' staff busied itself making copies of SO 191 for the generals involved and dispatching them by courier. Each copy was on a single sheet, written front and back, and listed in detail the assignment of every major command in the Army of Northern Virginia. Each was marked "Confidential" and signed "By command of Gen. R. E. Lee" with the name of R. H. Chilton, Lee's chief of staff. Each was delivered in an envelope that was to be signed by the recipient and returned by the courier as proof of delivery.

All the deliveries but one were made without event. The exception was the copy addressed to General D. H. Hill, which someone at headquarters had wrapped around three cigars, for Hill was known to enjoy a good smoke. The packet with Chilton's copy of SO 191 never reached Hill or anyone at his headquarters authorized to sign for it.

What General Hill received instead that day was a copy of SO 191 in the handwriting of Stonewall Jackson himself. To this point in the campaign, Hill had been under Jackson's orders, but now he was reassigned as the army's rear guard. Consequently, when Jackson received the copy of SO 191 addressed to him, he made a copy of it to inform his former subordinate of the change. Hill thus received his new orders from the same source he had been receiving orders from for the past week, and thought nothing of it.

For some reason that no one at Lee's headquarters could ever explain, no alarm was raised on September 9 over the lack of a delivery receipt for the copy of SO 191 that Chilton had addressed to D. H. Hill. No one in the chain of command that Tuesday suspected, as Hill later phrased it, "that there was something wrong in the manner of transmitting it. . . ."

The next morning, September 10, at his customary starting time of first light, Stonewall Jackson led the way westward on the National Road out of Frederick and across South Mountain. Through the day the rest of the army followed, division by division, until only a cavalry picket remained at Frederick. Over the next three days, three of Jackson's divisions, varying their route from what was specified in SO 191, crossed the Potomac at Williamsport and, pushing the Yankee garrison from Martinsburg ahead of them, closed in on Harpers Ferry from the west. Jackson's two other columns, under Lafayette McLaws and John Walker, adhering exactly to the plan, marched by separate routes to complete the encirclement of Harpers Ferry.

Meanwhile, in a second deviation from SO 191's order of march, Lee took James Longstreet's two divisions with him to wait at Hagerstown, near the Pennsylvania border. D. H. Hill's one division remained at Boonsboro, on the National Road beyond South Mountain, to act as rear guard. Jeb Stuart's cavalry patrols, continuing their watch on Federal movements, reported nothing untoward. Except that it was running twenty-four hours behind schedule, the Harpers Ferry operation was proceeding smoothly.

"As soon as I find out where to strike, I will be after them without an hour's delay," General McClellan promised Washington when he moved into Maryland on the trail of the enemy. But finding out where to strike was proving uncommonly difficult. His cavalry, under Alfred Pleasonton, was unable to break through Jeb Stuart's troopers for a firsthand look at Lee's Army of Northern Virginia. Pleasonton's intelligence-gathering was therefore limited to interrogating Rebel prisoners and deserters and questioning civilians who had picked up bits of information from Confederate soldiers passing through their towns or stopping at their farms.

The result was an intelligence Babel. Reports handed to McClellan had enemy columns marching toward every point of the compass, even eastward straight at him, which caused him to halt for a time and prepare to meet an attack. The Confederates planted stories wherever they went, so that Stonewall Jackson was "reliably reported" to be where he was and where he wasn't in about equal measure.

Mixed in with these tales from talkative clergymen and boastful prisoners and credulous country folk was some highly accurate intelligence. But all of it arrived at headquarters in an indiscriminate jumble, so McClellan could make little sense of it. As late as September 12, it was his best guess, he told his wife, that "secesh is skedadelling & I don't think I can catch him. . . . I begin to think that he is making off to get out of the scrape by recrossing the river at Williamsport. . . . He evidently don't want to fight me—for some reason or other." On that day, as on previous days, the average march in his Army of the Potomac was six miles.

McClellan was especially befuddled about the size of Lee's army. It was an article of faith with George McClellan that he was fated to be the underdog in any contest against Lee, and the intelligence reaching him in Maryland reinforced that delusion. He finally settled on a count for "the gigantic rebel army before us" of 120,000 men, "numerically superior to ours by at least twenty-five per cent." That this calculation multiplied every Confederate soldier facing him by three was a truth quite beyond his imagining. On Saturday morning, September 13, when McClellan arrived in Frederick with the Potomac army's headquarters, he was acting every inch the cautious captain that General Lee believed him to be.

The Federal Twelfth Corps also advanced to Frederick that morning, with the Twenty-seventh Indiana Regiment in the lead. The column splashed across the Monocacy River at Crum's Ford and went on two miles along a back road to the outskirts of town. There the order came back to halt and make camp. Company F of the Twenty-seventh appropriated a clover field alongside the road for its bivouac. Later it would be said that this field was where D. H. Hill's division had camped during the Confederate occupation of Frederick, but that was simply speculation. Hill's division had been posted several miles away on the Monocacy. There is no certain evidence that any Confederate troops had camped in this particular clover field.

Company F had the odd distinction of having the largest contingent of tall men in the regiment—two-thirds of the company stood six feet or more—and the unique distinction of having the tallest man in the entire Union army, Captain David Van Buskirk, who was half an inch shy of being seven feet tall. Corporal Barton W. Mitchell was about to give Company F another mark of distinction.

Mitchell was himself unusual in that he was much older than almost all his fellow soldiers. He was a man in his forties, a farmer in civilian life, who had volunteered in 1861 despite having a wife and four children to support. Patriotism ran strongly in his family: His oldest son had recently enlisted in another Indiana regiment.

Company F stacked arms, and Mitchell was relaxing and chatting with Private John Campbell when he noticed a bulky envelope in the clover nearby. Curious, he picked it up—and found it contained a document of some sort wrapped around three cigars. The cigars were a find, but Corporal Mitchell had the intelligence and the maturity to investigate as well the document they were wrapped in. While he read it through, Private Campbell (as Campbell later testified) "looked over his shoulder and read it with him."

The paper was marked "Confidential" and was headed "Hd Qrs Army of Northern Va Sept 9th 1862 Special Orders No 191." It was studded with names and places that Mitchell immediately recognized: Jackson, Longstreet, Stuart, Lee, Harpers Ferry, Martinsburg, Boonsboro, Hagerstown. It was signed by R. H. Chilton and labeled "For Maj Gen D. H. Hill, Comdg Division." By sheer chance, by fantastic good fortune, Corporal Mitchell had in his hand the missing copy of SO 191, and furthermore he recognized it as something important.

Mitchell took his find to his first sergeant, John M. Bloss, and together they went to the company commander, Captain Peter Kopp. Kopp took one look at the paper and told them to find the regimental commander, Colonel Silas Colgrove. Colgrove read it and, as he later said, "was at once satisfied that it was genuine." He sent Mitchell and Bloss back to their company (presumably with thanks, but apparently not with the cigars; Colgrove's recollection of the cigars is the last mention of them, and who finally smoked them will probably never be known). Then he set off for higher command.

Colgrove skipped brigade and division, the next links in the chain of command, and rode straight to Twelfth Corps headquarters and Brigadier General Alpheus S. Williams. Williams and his adjutant, Colonel Samuel E. Pittman, scanned the paper. As Colgrove remembered their conversation, Pittman said he had served with R.H. Chilton in the old army in Michigan before the war and recognized his handwriting. But Colgrove's recollection was faulty; Pittman had not entered the army until September 1861, five months after Chilton resigned his U.S. commission to join the Confederacy. By Pittman's own postwar recollection, he simply recognized Chilton's name as that of the army paymaster stationed in Detroit when he lived there.

In any event, Williams was persuaded the order was authentic. He sent Pittman with it to army headquarters, along with a brief note for General McClellan: "I enclose a Special Order of Gen. Lee commanding Rebel forces which was found on the field where my corps is encamped. It is a document of interest & is also thought genuine." In a footnote he added, "The Document was found by a corporal of 27 Ind. Reg, Col. Colgrove, Gordon's Brigade."

Colonel Pittman delivered the envelope containing the Lost Order, along with General Williams's covering note, to McClellan's adjutant, Seth Williams. McClellan was in his headquarters tent discussing details of the army's occupation of Frederick with a delegation of local citizens when adjutant Williams interrupted to hand him the find. McClellan scanned the paper and the note with it and suddenly, according to one of his visitors, threw up his hands and exclaimed, "Now I know what to do!"

This description of his reaction is entirely credible in light of the telegram he sent a few minutes later, at noon, to President Lincoln. No doubt he first ushered his visitors out with the explanation that he had urgent army business to attend to. Most of McClellan's dispatches to the president were stiff and militarily formal, for usually the two men were at odds over one thing or another. But this dispatch was like none he had sent before. The general boasted:

> I think Lee has made a gross mistake and that he will be severely punished for it. . . . I hope for a great success if the plans of the Rebels remain unchanged. . . . I have all the plans of the Rebels and will catch them in their own trap if my men are equal to the emergency.

In his elation he became almost giddy, presenting his respects to Mrs. Lincoln and exclaiming over the enthusiastic welcome he had received from the ladies of Frederick that morning. "Will send you trophies," he promised.

What so excited McClellan about the Lost Order was its revelation that General Lee had divided his army into four widely separated segments, at least two of them so isolated from the others as to be fair game for total destruction. (In fact, the Rebel army was even better game than he thought, for Longstreet's move to Hagerstown had divided it into five segments, the largest of which were twenty-five miles and a river crossing apart.) No general could hope to know more about his opponent's most secret plans: McClellan knew Lee's objective; his dispositions for taking that objective; his routes of march; his timetable; and most important, how vulnerable he was to the tactic of divide and conquer.

There is no doubt that McClellan grasped his unique good fortune. That evening he would take the Lost Order from his pocket and tell the brigade commander, General John Gibbon, "Here is a paper with which if I cannot whip Bobbie Lee, I will be willing to go home. . . . Castiglione will be nothing to it." Castiglione was the 1796 military classic in which Napoleon crushed Field Marshal D. S. von Wurmser's divided and overextended Austrian army. To act on this opportunity, however, required General McClellan for once in his life to throw caution to the winds. Time was critical; the Harpers Ferry operation outlined in SO 191 was already in its fourth day.

His time clock of opportunity began ticking at noon on September 13, when he sent his exuberant telegram to President Lincoln. Sounds of gunfire could be heard from Harpers Ferry, indicating that the garrison there still held out. The Lost Order told McClellan that John Walker's Rebel division had crossed the Potomac to invest Harpers Ferry on the south and east. Two more divisions, under the command of Lafayette McLaws, were still in Maryland, holding Maryland Heights, which overlooked the town on the north. According to SO 191, Jackson's "command," its forces unspecified, was at Martinsburg, eight miles beyond the Potomac, to prevent the Yankee garrison's escaping to the west. At Boonsboro, across South Mountain from Frederick, the Lost Order placed D. H. Hill's division and Longstreet's "command," his forces also unspecified.

Just then at Frederick, McClellan had four army corps—thirteen divisions—with which to cross South Mountain and attack Hill at Boonsboro, fifteen miles distant. A half-dozen miles south of Frederick, the army's left wing, three divisions under William B. Franklin, was also fifteen miles distant from its quarry: McLaws's two divisions at Maryland Heights.

It might be supposed that any general presented with such an opportunity would put his troops on the march without a moment's delay, taking advantage of the seven hours of daylight remaining that Saturday to close up to the base of South Mountain and be ready to force the passes in the range at dawn the next morning. General McClellan marched to a different drum: He could never act until all plans were complete, all details perfected, all potential surprises disarmed before they occurred—and the more he studied the Lost Order, the more uneasy he became. He later testified that he gave no thought to its being a *ruse de guerre*—it explained too much to be a plant, and General Williams's note suggested it was found by accident rather than by the enemy's design. Yet he began having worrisome second thoughts about it. He would have to ponder the whole matter before acting.

The Lost Order confirmed some of the intelligence received over the past few days but seemed to contradict other reports. McClellan had been told of a substantial Rebel force at Hagerstown, and of a major crossing of the Potomac at Williamsport, yet neither place was on the routes of march prescribed in SO 191. He told the president he hoped for success "if the plans of the Rebels remain unchanged," but now it looked as if they had been changed. McClellan worried that question for three hours, then at 3 P.M. sent a copy of SO 191 to his cavalry chief, General Pleasonton, with instructions to find out if the routes of march it contained had actually been followed.

Pleasonton knew little about the matter but said he thought Lee's instructions had been followed. That was the wrong answer, but it reassured Mc-

Clellan; thereafter he regarded everything in the Lost Order as revealed truth. With that settled, he decided to begin his movements the next morning, September 14. "My general idea," he told General Franklin, "is to cut the enemy in two & beat him in detail." Reaching that decision cost him eighteen hours of his golden opportunity.

The other factor giving McClellan pause on September 13 was the enemy's numbers. In a dispatch to Washington that night, he listed eight generals in Lee's army, commanding a total of "120,000 men or more . . . & they outnumber me when united." From the Lost Order and other sources, he knew that six of these generals led single divisions, and that gave him a problem with his arithmetic. To make his figures come out, McClellan gave the two "commands" of Jackson and Longstreet a kind of "grand corps" rating, so that in advancing across South Mountain to do battle with (so he thought) Longstreet and Hill at Boonsboro, he anticipated meeting a very substantial force.

That prospect instilled in him further caution. With two days' hard marching, he told General Gibbon that evening, "I will put Lee in a position he will find hard to get out of." By that timetable he budgeted an additional forty-eight hours to gain his reward from the Lost Order. If the loss of SO 191 "was a shabby trick for fate to play us," as a Confederate officer said, fate contrived to even the balance by handing the find to General McClellan.

It might also be supposed that army headquarters, with General Williams's note as a guide, would have made an effort to identify the discoverer of the Lost Order and reward him a field promotion, a mention in dispatches, perhaps nomination for the newly authorized Medal of Honor. Instead the discovery went entirely unremarked; literally no one gave it another thought. When he was asked about it after the war, General McClellan confessed he knew next to nothing about how the Lost Order reached him.

Only in 1886, twenty-four years after the event, was an account of the discovery published in *Century* magazine, whose editors had sought the details from Colonel Colgrove for their "Battles and Leaders" series. There Barton Mitchell was first identified as the finder of SO 191—and in Colgrove's account demoted to private. In 1892 Sergeant Bloss, to whom Mitchell had taken the find, further diminished the corporal's role by manufacturing an account in which he was the actual discoverer, having simply asked Mitchell to pick up the envelope and hand it to him. Bloss had risen in the world to be a school superintendent, and his self-importance had risen as well.

This credit, imperfect as it was, came too late for poor Corporal Mitchell. For him the Lost Order was simply a jinx. The fruit of his discovery, the Battle of Antietam, was fought four days later, and in it he suffered a severe leg wound from which he never really recovered. (Antietam cut a terrible swath through the Twenty-seventh Indiana and especially through Company F. Of those linked to the Lost Order, Corporal Mitchell, his friend Private Campbell, and Sergeant Bloss were all wounded, and Captain Kopp, to whom they took the find, was killed. In all, Company F took 40 percent casualties at Antietam.)

Mitchell spent eight months in the hospital, then was forced by disability to transfer to the ambulance corps. After his discharge his disability grew progressively worse, until he was bedridden. He died early in 1868, not yet fifty. His widow did not succeed in obtaining a survivor's pension until 1890. The army's Pension Office was not moved to act sooner by the claim that it was her husband who had found the famous Lost Order.

✦

IT IS CLEAR ENOUGH how the Lost Order was found, but it is still not clear how it was lost. The best hope is to narrow the possibilities. One certainty is that D. H. Hill was entirely innocent in the matter. Hill spent a quarter of a century vigorously defending himself against those who would make him the guilty party. In 1867 a Richmond editor, E. A. Pollard, charged him with tossing the order away in a fit of petulance at its contents. In 1876 the count of Paris, pretender to the French throne, wrote in his history of the Civil War that Hill carelessly left his copy of SO 191 on a table in his headquarters. In 1884 former Confederate general Bradley T. Johnson retailed a story that the paper was seen to fall from Hill's pocket as he rode through Frederick.

Where Pollard and Johnson and the count heard these tales is anyone's guess. All of them were refuted by the *Century* article and by Hill's repeated declaration that he never saw the copy of SO 191 that the Federals found; he had instead the copy Jackson sent him.

What these theories (and others like them) fail to account for is that although the courier was supposed to take back the envelope with Hill's signature as a delivery receipt, the copy of SO 191 addressed to Hill was found still in its envelope. When Hill learned from McClellan after the war that he had preserved in his private papers both the Lost Order and the envelope in which it left Lee's headquarters that September 9, he put the case with perfect clarity: "If the envelope was with it, the paper was never received." That the order was found not in Hill's former encampment but some miles away is further evidence that it never reached its destination.

Before the account of Corporal Mitchell's discovery appeared, Hill suggested treachery as the cause of the loss. He was supported in this by his adjutant, Major J. W. Ratchford, who noted in a memoir of his service with the general that not long afterward, during the Harpers Ferry operation, a head-quarters courier was unmasked as a Yankee spy and summarily hanged.

The problem with the treachery theory is the place where the Lost Order was found. Surely a traitor to the Southern cause would have found a better way to make certain so important a piece of stolen intelligence reached General McClellan than to drop it in a meadow alongside a back road—not even along one of the major highways in the region—in the hope that at some future time the Federals just might come that way, discover the packet, recognize its importance, and get it to the high command in time to do some good. It is impossible to imagine so naive a spy, or (as it turned out) one so lucky.

The likeliest explanation for the loss of SO 191 is the simplest one: It was accidentally dropped by Lee's courier—whose identity remains unknown—on his way to deliver it to Hill. At some point he would have discovered his loss and probably backtracked in search of it. Perhaps he continued his search as far as Hill's command and found they already had their orders (unbeknownst to the courier, from Stonewall Jackson); perhaps he assumed the order he lost had been found and delivered. Back at army headquarters, he must have contrived some excuse for lacking the signed envelope that was to have served as a delivery receipt. Perhaps he even forged a receipt.

However it happened, it must have happened something like this, and the careless courier, thinking or hoping no real harm had been done, covered his tracks well enough to escape detection and punishment. Remarkably, Lee's headquarters would never investigate the matter at all, even after learning that a copy of SO 191 had been found by the enemy.

Nothing in the tangled story of the Lost Order is more misunderstood than just when General Lee discovered that his opponent had a copy of SO 191. Following the lead of Lee's biographer Douglas Southall Freeman, many historians have assumed that within some twelve hours of the time McClellan was handed the Lost Order, Lee learned that McClellan had it. That is a false assumption. One of the highest trump cards that fate dealt General McClellan that day was the advantage of surprise, for at no time during the Maryland campaign did Lee (or any other Confederate) know about the Lost Order. Not until January 1863, at the earliest, and probably several months after that, did he become aware of the loss, and the finding, of SO 191.

When he did learn of it, it was through the Northern press. The order was first printed (from a copy made by General McClellan himself) in the *New York Journal of Commerce* on January 1, 1863. In March, McClellan testified to a congressional committee that "at Frederick we found the original order issued to General D. H. Hill by direction of General Lee, which gave the orders of march for their whole army, and developed their intentions." A month later his testimony was put into print by the committee and by the newspapers. General Lee, always a careful reader of Northern papers that had been passed through the lines, thus learned for the first time about the loss of SO 191.

The misunderstanding on this point stems from a misreading of what Lee himself said about the Lost Order after the war. In 1868, in reviewing the Maryland campaign, Lee recalled that on the night of September 13–14, he received a dispatch from Jeb Stuart with information from a civilian who had been at General McClellan's headquarters in Frederick that morning. The civilian, a Confederate sympathizer, said that during their meeting McClellan was handed a paper by an aide, seemed excited by it, and exclaimed, "Now I know what to do!"

The civilian had hurried off to tell Stuart of McClellan's response and to report that something—he could not say exactly what—had energized the Federals. On his way, he had seen Yankee troops advancing beyond Frederick toward South Mountain. (In fact this was only a routine movement, ordered some hours earlier, but the civilian tied it to what he had seen at McClellan's headquarters.) Stuart reported this development to Lee at Hagerstown.

In recounting the story, Lee phrased it as McClellan's reaction on being handed the Lost Order, which was true enough but was a fact supplied by Lee from hindsight knowledge. The amateur spy did not know—could not have known—that the paper McClellan read in his presence was a copy of Lee's plans. Neither McClellan nor his staff would have been so careless as to reveal that fact to a civilian, particularly in Maryland, where loyalties were known to be divided. In his report, Stuart made no mention of any Confederate plan, lost or found; Lee said nothing of it to Longstreet that night when they discussed their next move.

Most telling is the testimony of Lee's aide Charles Marshall, who was explicit about the matter. "I remember perfectly," he told D. H. Hill, "that until we saw that report"—McClellan's 1863 account of the finding of the Lost Order—"Gen. Lee frequently expressed his inability to understand the sudden change in McClellan's tactics which took place after we left Frederick. He regarded the finding of that order by McClellan as a complete and satisfactory explanation of the change."

As important as anything else, Lee's actions over the next several days were hardly those of a general who knew his opponent had all his plans. Rather than ordering Jackson to give up the siege of Harpers Ferry and find safer ground, he allowed him to continue it. Instead of instantly marching from

Hagerstown to block the South Mountain passes, he waited until morning to move. Rather than prudently withdrawing across the Potomac to reunite his scattered forces, he ran an immense bluff by standing at Sharpsburg, on Antietam Creek, and then challenging McClellan to fight there. His actions were simply those of a general reacting to an opponent who was now advancing (as he told Jefferson Davis) "more rapidly than was convenient. . . ."

To be sure, the Army of Northern Virginia survived these various perils to fight again on other fields, but it survived only because McClellan squandered his golden opportunity. However little General Lee thought of McClellan's abilities, not even he would have dared to count on that happening.

On Sunday, September 14, Hill had time enough to cobble together a defense of Turner's Gap in South Mountain, with assistance late in the day from Longstreet's column from Hagerstown, against McClellan's belated offensive. To the south at Crampton's Gap, Franklin's equally sluggish advance got no farther that day than the crest of South Mountain. McClellan proclaimed a great victory, but his dream of cutting the enemy in two and beating him in detail—of winning another Castiglione—was fading rapidly.

The next day, September 15, Lee with Hill and Longstreet fell back behind Antietam Creek at Sharpsburg. Lee took his stand that day with hardly 15,000 men of all arms. Nevertheless, McClellan's pursuit was slow and cautious. According to the headquarters journal kept by his brother, Captain Arthur McClellan, the general believed he was facing 50,000 Rebels beyond Antietam Creek. Meanwhile, Franklin's feeble effort to advance toward beleaguered Harpers Ferry was blocked by McLaws. On September 15, too, General McClellan put the Lost Order aside. Whatever advantage he thought he had gained from it, he now decided that its usefulness was at an end.

The narrator of this final twist in the story is Captain William J. Palmer, who visited McClellan's field headquarters a mile or so from Antietam Creek the night of the fifteenth. Palmer, a scout for Pennsylvania's forces and easily the best intelligence gatherer on the Federal side, had an inside look at the view from headquarters. General McClellan, he reported to Pennsylvania's governor, believed that the Harpers Ferry garrison had surrendered to the Rebels that morning, and by nightfall "Jackson re-enforced Lee at Sharpsburg. . . . Rebels appear encouraged at arrival of their re-enforcements." By McClellan's train of thought, the scattered elements of the Army of Northern Virginia were now reunited, he was once more outnumbered, and the Lost Order was no longer of any use as a blueprint of his opponent's operations.

This final twist presents another irony, for it was thanks to the Lost Order that General Lee was granted the reprieve that saved his army. Despite conflicting evidence, McClellan seems to have concluded that Stonewall Jackson spent the siege of Harpers Ferry on guard duty at Martinsburg, where SO 191 placed him; and that on learning of the garrison's surrender that morning, he made the easy march to Sharpsburg to join Lee. To be sure, McClellan had not a scrap of evidence to confirm this—he had none because there was none; even the cheering he had supposed greeted Jackson's arrival was merely Lee's men reacting to the news of the capture of Harpers Ferry. He simply deduced it from his blind faith in the Lost Order.

The first of Jackson's footsore troops did not reach Sharpsburg until noon on September 16, and they continued to trail into the lines throughout the afternoon. Even then just three of his divisions were at hand; fully a third of Lee's army was still absent. Two more divisions reached the field at dawn on September 17, the day McClellan finally chose to offer battle, and the last division arrived only at the last moment during the battle. McClellan spent September 16 pondering his fate and "the gigantic rebel army" facing him.

In the end, the Battle of Antietam represented his final opportunity to profit from the Lost Order. For four days he had wasted glittering chances to divide and conquer his foe, yet at Antietam the odds were still greatly in his favor. Lee, by his own testimony, fought there with fewer than 40,000 men, leaving him outnumbered two-to-one. And although his position was a good one, his back was to the Potomac, inviting certain destruction if his line was breached and he had to fall back. But at this climactic moment, McClellan could not rid himself of his fears and delusions: On September 17 he could not force himself to seek victory, for fear of courting defeat. And so it ended. In the bloodiest single day of the war, he did not gain victory, although he was not defeated, either.

After defiantly holding his position for another day, Lee returned with his battered army to Virginia. At Antietam he had inflicted one-fifth more casualties than he suffered, and in the campaign as a whole he showed a profit— 27,000 Federals (including the Harpers Ferry garrison) and substantial captures of arms and supplies against a loss of 14,000. Nevertheless, he failed in the task he had set for himself. He might claim Antietam as a narrow tactical victory, but he did not win a campaign that was decisive for the war.

And in the end that is how the impact of the Lost Order is measured. Lee termed the loss of SO 191 "a great calamity"; to his mind it was of crucial importance to the Maryland campaign because it enabled McClellan "to discover my whereabouts . . . and caused him so to act as to force a battle on me before I was ready for it."

It is permissible to speculate (as General Lee speculated) that had the Lost

Order never been lost, then sometime during the latter half of September 1862 a great battle would have been fought in the Cumberland Valley of Pennsylvania—the Battle of Greencastle, perhaps, or the Battle of Chambersburg, or even the Battle of Gettysburg—in which "I would have had all my troops reconcentrated, . . . stragglers up, men rested, and *intended then to attack McClellan. . . .*" Lee admitted it was "impossible to say that victory would have certainly resulted," but on one point he was very clear: "The loss of the dispatch changed the character of the campaign."

DEFENDING MARYE'S HEIGHTS

JOSEPH H. ALEXANDER

The futility of the frontal attack was most famously demonstrated at Fredericksburg, a Virginia town fifty miles north of Richmond. If it had served badly a general as resourceful as Lee at Malvern Hill, the frontal attack proved an unparalleled disaster for Ambrose Burnside, another of the serial commanders of the Army of the Potomac, and one of the most inept generals of the Civil War. Having taken over from McClellan after the slugfest at Antietam in September 1862—a tactical tie but this time a Northern strategic victory—Lincoln urged his new head man to push south, while Lee was still recovering. That November, Burnside marched a 110,000-man force, the largest yet assembled on the North American continent, with promising dispatch; but by the time his force reached the heights that overlooked Fredericksburg across the Rappahannock River, it had bogged down in a morass of command and logistical problems. There it sat for three crucial weeks while Lee's Confederates entrenched on the opposite ridge. By the time Burnside began to push his pontoon bridges across the river in December, the Southern positions were impregnable.

Burnside persisted anyway. His main attack centered on the Confederate positions atop Marye's Heights, one of the low hills that rose from the open terrain behind Fredericksburg. But what no one on the Northern side reckoned with was a natural trench at the foot of the heights: a sunken road with an earth-covered stone wall that acted as a parapet behind which as many as 5,000 riflemen crouched. All through a December day, the attackers came, only to melt away in front of the sunken road. As Joseph H. Alexander observes, "Not a single Yankee survived to come within pistol shot of the Southern infantry positions." (The biggest threat to the mostly Georgian force at the foot of Marye's Heights was not the Union human waves but a shortage of ammunition.)

In an earlier day close-order assaults of the sort Burnside presided over might have worked. As recently as the Mexican War, the offense, sensibly conducted, still held the upper hand. The principal infantry weapon was the single-shot smoothbore musket, which was accurate only to about eighty yards. But the rifled musket, which was accurate to about a thousand feet, gave the advantage to the defense. Commanders on both sides did not appreciate its killing power—although a sizable share of the execution at Marye's Heights was actually performed by smoothbores. Presumably many Confederates made up for that deficiency by picking up Union rifles scattered over the battlefield. Overcoats scavenged from the dead were less satisfactory. The ill-equipped victors of Fredericksburg claimed that they had too many bullet holes in them.

Joseph H. Alexander served in the Marine Corps for twenty-eight years, including two combat tours in Vietnam, and retired as a colonel. His books of military history include *Utmost Savagery: The Three Days of Tarawa, Storm Landings: Epic Amphibious Battles in the Central Pacific,* and *Edson's Raiders: The 1st Marine Raider Battalion in World War II.*

The finest army that ever trod the earth has suffered a decided repulse at the hand of a half-naked, half-starved, half-armed foe.

James Gordon Bennett,
New York Herald, December 16, 1862

UNION GENERAL NATHAN KIMBALL LED HIS BRIGADE IN THE first assault against the Confederate positions along Marye's Heights, a ridge just behind Fredericksburg, Virginia, on Saturday, December 13, 1862, an uncommonly warm day in a cold campaign. Kimball's veteran regiments spearheaded the seemingly endless, blue-coated, brass-buttoned river of men flowing across the Rappahannock, through the burning town, into the line of battle.

Emerging from the town, which had been set ablaze by Union artillery, the brigade had to sweep 400 yards uphill in open terrain to seize the Confederate batteries on the crest of Marye's Heights. Kimball chafed as his men lost momentum crossing a drainage canal, queued up dangerously behind the few plank "bridges," then halted again to dismantle rail fences blocking their advance.

Confederate artillerymen opened up a hellish cross fire. None of Kimball's veterans had experienced such deadly cannonading. Kimball reported "a most murderous fire . . . several shells bursting in the ranks and destroying a company at a time." His officers urged the brigade forward, and the men leaned into the fire, scrambling uphill.

Suddenly, the heads and shoulders of a line of Confederate infantry appeared out of nowhere along the base of the heights. A sharp command rang out. A thousand muskets leveled downslope. Heads bent to forestocks, eyes aligning notched gunsights to human targets. Kimball's men flinched involuntarily; an eternity seemed to pass. Another command was drowned by the roar and flame of close-range musketry. The Union front ranks collapsed. The rear echelons stopped to unleash a ragged volley of their own. There were few targets. The enemy ducked down into their concealed ditch to reload, then popped up again on command to deliver another sweeping firestorm. Kimball's brigade recoiled, stumbled back, and went to ground, stunned and fragmented. Kimball fell wounded; so did three of his regimental commanders. In the twenty-minute assault, the brigade suffered 520 casualties, one-sixth of its strength.

Kimball's was the first of many separate Union assaults that day—each spirited but piecemeal and doomed—against some of the strongest defensive positions the Army of Northern Virginia would occupy throughout the war. In every case the blue waves broke against the earth-covered rock parapet later known as the Stone Wall, defended by Southern riflemen clustered along its protected, equally infamous Sunken Road. So thoroughly had Confederate lieutenant general James Longstreet prepared the killing ground on the slopes of Marye's Heights that not a single Yankee survived to come within pistol shot of the infantry positions. The repeated Union assaults against this sector of the Fredericksburg battlefield produced the worst sustained slaughter of the war for the North.

Longstreet's First Army Corps defended the Confederate left at Fredericksburg. His 40,000 troops covered a six-mile span of broken terrain but were concentrated to protect the obvious avenue of approach: Marye's Heights. When General Robert E. Lee expressed concern that yet another Yankee force was massing for an assault on the heights, Longstreet snorted, "General, if you put every man now on the other side of the Potomac on that field to approach me over the same line and give me plenty of ammunition, I will kill them all before they reach my line."

Longstreet excelled on the tactical defensive; Fredericksburg would represent his finest hour of the war. But the point-blank execution of Longstreet's plans would be up to Brigadier General Joseph B. Kershaw's brigade of South Carolinians and Brigadier General Robert Ransom's division of North Carolinians—and a small brigade of Georgians at the epicenter of the storm along the Sunken Road commanded by Brigadier General Thomas R. R. Cobb. One of the newest brigadiers in the Army of Northern Virginia, Cobb would die in the Sunken Road not long after repelling Kimball's assault. His riflemen would wreak a terrible vengeance.

Few romantic illusions were still held by either side by the end of the second year of the American Civil War. From Shiloh to Second Manassas, in 1862 the war had turned uglier, bloodier. While some of the Southern troops still held hopes for an armistice, most of their officers realized the war had moved beyond compromise and would have to be fought to its bitter conclusion.

The intensely savage battle of Antietam on September 17, 1862, gave President Abraham Lincoln his first major victory over the Army of Northern Virginia, albeit a costly one. Lincoln then sensed that Lee's army, sorely depleted and uncharacteristically disorganized after Antietam, was vulnerable to a crunching counterattack or a new thrust against Richmond. With Lee mainly hoping for the respite of winter quarters, Lincoln gambled that a surprise autumn campaign to seize lightly held Fredericksburg and advance toward Richmond, just fifty miles beyond, might prompt Lee to fight on unfavorable ground or forfeit the Confederate capital.

Against this backdrop, during the first week of November 1862, Lincoln ran out of patience with Major General George B. McClellan's overcautiousness, sacked him (for the second and last time), and appointed Major General Ambrose E. Burnside to command the newly refurbished Army of the Potomac. Burnside moved with initial celerity, consolidating his forces just north of Fredericksburg and threatening both Richmond and Lee's scattered army. By November 17, Burnside had major forces occupying Stafford Heights, the high ground dominating the northeast bank of the Rappahannock across from Fredericksburg. The two wings of Lee's army were still widely separated, Longstreet near Culpeper Court House, Stonewall Jackson in the northern Shenandoah Valley near Winchester.

Yet Lee retained the operational edge. He knew the ground, knew his enemy, and remained confident of his ability to converge his forces at the point of attack. He ordered Longstreet immediately to Fredericksburg; Jackson was to pull south down the valley in readiness for Burnside's next move.

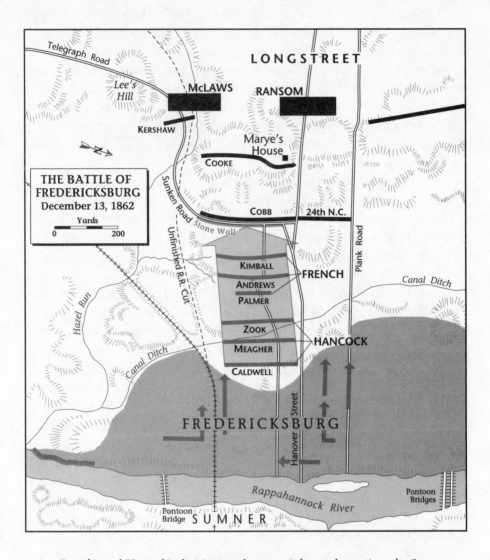

*French's and Hancock's divisions made sequential assaults against the Con-
federate left flank at Fredericksburg. Longstreet anticipated the Union thrust
against Marye's Heights and fortified the high ground accordingly. The dia-
gram on page 165 shows why Fredericksburg was, for the Federals, literally
an uphill battle. The topography forced Union general Edwin V. Sumner to
resort to brigade-level assaults on a narrow front. His men were slowed by the
canal ditch, then decimated by Confederate artillery on the heights and riflemen perfectly positioned behind the stone wall on Sunken Road.*

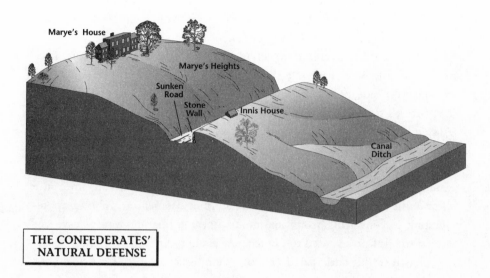

Marye's House

Marye's Heights

Sunken
Road

Stone
Wall

Innis House

Canal
Ditch

**THE CONFEDERATES'
NATURAL DEFENSE**

But Burnside's early acceleration bogged down. With 116,000 men, he now commanded the largest army ever assembled on the North American continent, and neither he nor his staff nor his corps commanders had the experience or fiery vigor to make it function with efficient lethality. Ironically, Burnside could have seized Fredericksburg and all the high ground to the southwest with ease during the first five days of the campaign (November 16–21), when Confederate resistance consisted of barely more than a corporal's guard. The opportunity had not escaped Burnside's attention. He had requested pontoon units with which to cross the Rappahannock as early as November 6. The convoluted staff and command morass that engulfed the movement of these critical units for the next three weeks is one of the classic nightmares in American military history. Commenting on just one of many frustrations for the Northerners, Major General Darius N. Couch said after the battle, "If the pontoons had been there, we might have crossed at once. Yet we lay there nearly a month, while they were fortifying before our eyes."

Burnside's delay in proceeding south proved fatal to the Army of the Potomac. Within two days of Union general Edwin V. Sumner's seizure of Stafford Heights, Longstreet's lead division, commanded by Major General Lafayette McLaws, arrived below Fredericksburg and began developing defensive positions. A week later, Burnside realized with a shock that he now faced the entire Army of Northern Virginia across the river. For his part, Lee then sent half of Jackson's corps farther downstream in case Burnside chose to make his main crossing near Port Royal, under protection of Union Navy gunboats. To Lee, crossing at Fredericksburg no longer made tactical sense.

McLaws and Longstreet, however, prepared to resist a frontal assault. They took a good look at the broken ground rising to a series of hills and ridges on the west side of the Rappahannock and liked what they saw. So did Longstreet's newest artillery commander, Lieutenant Colonel Edward Porter Alexander, who relished the opportunity to develop a comprehensive fire plan along all approaches leading out of town. Fredericksburg's buildings would block fire and observation of the river from the heights, but the Yankees would pay hell moving troops in column into any coherent assault lines once clear of the built-up areas. The time-consuming, momentum-robbing choreography of converting from column to linear formation would leave the Union troops fully exposed to Confederate artillery fire.

Longstreet fully anticipated a major Union thrust against Marye's Heights. He assessed the topography this way: "Taylor's Hill, on our left, was unassailable; Marye's Hill was more advanced toward the town, was of a gradual ascent and of less height than the others, and we considered it the point most assailable, and guarded it accordingly."

The Rappahannock bends sharply to the southeast just above Fredericksburg, and this provided the advantage of shorter interior lines to the defending Confederates. Longstreet deployed his five divisions along the arc from north to south in this fashion: Major General Richard H. Anderson from the river above Beck's Island to the Plank Road; McLaws in the center; Major General George E. Pickett and then Major General John B. Hood aligned to the right, tied in with Jackson's Corps. Upon further study of the lay of the land, Longstreet assigned Ransom's small division, originally his corps reserve, to reinforce the critical segment between the Plank Road and Hazel Run, backing up McLaws's men in the Sunken Road. This arrangement—two divisions overlapping a geographic boundary—had the seeds of disunited command (and led to postwar controversy between Ransom and Kershaw), but it worked during the battle. Both McLaws and Ransom reinforced and resupplied the riflemen posted along the Sunken Road without disruption.

General McLaws, with Longstreet's approval, selected Brigadier General William Barksdale's brigade of Mississippians to dispute the Union crossings of the river in the town, and he chose Cobb's Brigade to man the first fixed line of defense on that flank, the 480-yard length of Telegraph Road that ran parallel to the river along the face of Marye's Heights. The road was "sunken," carved out of the shoulder of the hill in 1831 and bolstered by a shoulder-

height stone wall on the downhill side. The wall itself was further reinforced
by the excavated dirt shoveled from the cut and compacted level with the outside of the wall. It would withstand all the furies of hell. Moreover, it was
nearly indiscernible by an enemy force approaching from downslope. McLaws
described the wall as "invisible from the front." General Kershaw, who would
take command of the sector when Cobb went down, likewise described the
wall as "not visible above the surface of the ground."

The relative invisibility of the defensive positions occupied by Cobb's
Brigade throughout the battle was a major factor in the outcome. Today's visitors to the Fredericksburg battlefield see in many places a reconstructed, free-
standing stone wall and wonder why Union artillery failed to pulverize it
during routine preliminary bombardment. In 1862, however, the wall was almost completely covered by earth; the only "targets" were the occasional rows
of gray caps and butternut slouch hats, immediately obscured by sheets of
flame and gray smoke.

Moreover, Longstreet had chosen the ground with great care. A series of
obstacles between the town and the Sunken Road—especially a lateral
drainage canal—would serve to channel Union assault formations into a narrow funnel across the open fields sloping directly up toward the defensive position. Longstreet directed the construction of a series of rifle pits to extend
the line to the north, past the protection of the wall. He also noted with relish the care with which his artillery battalions placed and fortified their guns
to cover the approaches. This all represented a golden opportunity for the
Confederate gunners, so accustomed to frantic deployments to exposed positions under heavy fire. For once, time and topography seemed on their side.
Burnside's continued delays even enabled Lee to redeploy two huge thirty-
pounder Parrott guns from the Richmond defenses for the first time. Brash
Porter Alexander boasted to Longstreet that "a chicken could not live on that
field below when we open on it." Longstreet surveyed the gun positions and
saw that it was so. Thomas Cobb examined his assigned sector and nodded
grimly. "I believe my brigade can whip ten thousand of them attacking us in
front," he wrote his wife.

Cobb would prove his words, but first he would have to prove himself to
the high-spirited Georgia mountaineers in his brigade, some of whom initially disparaged him as "a damned politician." Cobb, a former attorney, was
indeed a member of the Confederate Congress and younger brother to the influential Howell Cobb, past governor of Georgia. But Tom Cobb, thirty-nine
and combat-seasoned, had commanded his own legion with valor through the
Peninsula campaign: His fighting spirit impressed Lee, who nominated him

for brigadier to the secretary of war in late October. Cobb assumed that rank, somewhat to his own surprise, effective November 1. Lee assigned him command of a five-regiment brigade: the 16th, 18th, and 24th Georgia, plus the infantry components of his own legion and the Phillips Georgia Legion (named after Colonel William Phillips, who founded it and was now out of the war after being badly wounded earlier in the year).

The Confederacy began the war with several legions, combined-arms forces modeled somewhat after the Roman legions of antiquity. A typical Southern legion of 1861 consisted of six companies of infantry, four of cavalry, and a battery of artillery. While effective in the initial, smaller operations, the legions soon placed inordinate logistical and operational restrictions on army commanders. The Confederate War Department dissolved most legions by mid-1862, but Cobb's and Phillips's Legions retained their distinctive identities, the infantry components serving Longstreet, the cavalry under Brigadier General Wade Hampton.

Cobb's Legion, still shattered from the bloody delaying action at Crampton's Gap during the Antietam campaign ten weeks earlier, would fill only a reserve role at Fredericksburg. The Phillips Legion, ineptly deployed at Second Manassas and Antietam by Brigadier General Thomas F. Drayton earlier in the year, would find its validation under Cobb in the Sunken Road. There the men from the hardscrabble farms and crossroads villages of northern Georgia would perform legendary feats of marksmanship with antiquated weapons before the eyes of half an army. Cobb's draconian discipline may have irked the Georgians, but at Marye's Heights they came to respect his combat savvy. The few hours that Cobb and the Phillips Legion shared together defending the heights would show both parties rock-steady and ferocious in battle.

The standoff between the two armies ended early on the morning of December 11, when Burnside finally began to force the crossing of the Rappahannock at Fredericksburg. Two guns on the heights, alerted by Barksdale's pickets, boomed the prearranged signal, and Longstreet's corps hurried into its fighting positions. General Cobb deployed only three regiments into the Sunken Road—the Phillips Legion occupying the left half, the 18th and 24th Georgia the right. With the understrength Cobb's Legion in reserve and the 16th Georgia guarding the ravine along Hazel Run, Cobb had barely a thousand rifles on his main line. Seeing this, General Ransom moved the 24th North Carolina down to extend Cobb's line farther left, between Hanover Street and the Plank Road, although the Tar Heels (and the Phillips Legion's

Company C) lost the protection of the Sunken Road at that stretch, resorting to crude rifle pits, and would suffer higher casualties in the fighting to come.

As Barksdale's Mississippians took a toll of the Union engineers assembling the pontoon bridges, Lee watched the activities intently, still not convinced that this was the main effort. Yet his cavalry patrols reported scant Union activity downriver. Burnside bulled ahead, finally bludgeoning Barksdale and the town of Fredericksburg with heavy artillery from Stafford Heights. The Mississippians did their job well, disrupting the Union army's efforts all day on December 11. But throughout that night and the night of December 12, the hills resounded with the sound of marching men crossing the pontoons and entering the town. Lee ordered Jackson to dispatch the divisions of Jubal Early and D. H. Hill by forced march back to Fredericksburg from the lower crossings.

Burnside's unimaginative attack orders still held the possibility of success at daybreak on December 13. His first assault would concentrate on Lee's right flank, guarded by Jackson's corps, still adjusting its lines to accommodate the late arrivals from downriver. The topography here was less steep and the approach more shielded by vegetation. The brunt of the attack would involve emerging Union division and corps commanders who in seven months would significantly influence the battle of Gettysburg: George G. Meade, John F. Reynolds, John Gibbon, and David B. Birney.

Meade's division attacked with vigor, penetrated Major General Ambrose P. Hill's lines, inflicted heavy casualties, and threatened Lee's entire flank. But neither Burnside nor Major General William B. Franklin, commanding the "Left Grand Division," proved adept at capitalizing on the advantage. Meade and Gibbon attacked virtually alone, neither supporting the other. Confederate reinforcements swarmed savagely around the penetrators and drove them back in disarray, while more than half of Franklin's wing remained in position, unengaged, awaiting orders. Lee's right flank, bloodied but restored, would hold. Both he and Longstreet now looked to the threat to their left.

Lee and Longstreet enjoyed spectacular views of the unfolding main events of the battle from their observation post atop Telegraph Hill (thereafter "Lee's Hill"). It was from this promontory that Lee observed, "It is well that war is so terrible—we should grow too fond of it." On nearby Marye's Heights, Adjutant William M. Owen of the Washington Artillery admired the spectacle below: "How beautifully they came on! Their bright bayonets glistening in the sunlight made the line look like a huge serpent of blue and steel."

The Georgia troops posted along the Sunken Road viewed the approaching blue hosts of Kimball's brigade as something other than spectacular. "It would have made your blood run cold to have seen their great numbers coming over to oppose our little handful," observed Sergeant William R. Montgomery of the Phillips Legion, who was posted near the center of the line.

"Get ready, boys," yelled Cobb and his officers. "Here they come."

The Georgians scrunched down behind the wall, maintaining their concealment to the last. At Cobb's command they sprang up, leveled their muskets, and picked their targets. A thousand fingers carefully took up the trigger slack and waited. The Yankees seemed huge, breathless, closing fast. "Fire!" There was no opportunity to observe the effect. "Down! Reload!" Ramrods twirled, nervous fingers fumbled with percussion caps. The second volley, not as simultaneous as the first, was still thunderous. Through the smoke it seemed that few Yankees were still upright.

Artillerist Owens reported on the action from his higher vantage point on the heights: "A few more paces onward and the Georgians in the road below us rose up, and, glancing an instant along their rifle barrels, let loose a storm of lead into the faces of the advance brigade."

"We waited [until] they got within about 200 yards of us & rose to our feet & poured volley after volley into their ranks which told a most deadening effect," recorded Sergeant Montgomery. "They soon began to waver & at last broke for the rear, but the shouts of our brave soldiers had scarcely died away when we saw coming another column more powerful & seemingly more determined than the first . . ."

✦

SO KIMBALL'S BRIGADE GAVE WAY to that of Andrews, then to Palmer's, then to Winfield Scott Hancock's veterans. The sloping fields became strewn with clumps of blue-clad bodies. Confederate artillery, firing from three quadrants, never stopped shooting the Northerners down. But time and again it was the massed musketry of the Georgians and Carolinians along the Sunken Road that truly stopped each successive assault as if it were poleaxed.

Even so, Cobb was now on borrowed time. For each Union brigade that came to grief in the killing fields below the Sunken Road there were literally thousands of survivors, veteran troops who sought shelter among the houses and outbuildings along Hanover Street or in the unfinished railroad cut on the opposite flank. These ad hoc sharpshooters, armed with the superior rifles of the Union army, opened an increasingly deadly fire against anything that moved above the top of the Confederate embankment. The Georgia infantrymen, for the most part hugging their side of the wall while reloading, escaped the brunt of this fire. But the Telegraph Road within the cut along the foot of Marye's Heights was a good twenty-five feet wide. The field grade officers took their posts in the middle of the road in order to control the fire and discipline of their men. They paid a terrible price for their greater exposure.

Lieutenant Colonel Robert T. "Tom" Cook, the popular commanding officer of the Phillips Legion, went down early, drilled through the head, dying instantly. Two senior captains who succeeded Cook fell wounded almost immediately. Abruptly, Lieutenant John S. Norris found himself commanding the legion, a daunting task at which he would acquit himself well.

Longstreet ordered Ransom to reinforce Cobb. In short order, Brigadier General John R. Cooke led the 27th and 46th North Carolina regiments down the fireswept foreslope past the Marye House into the road and hurried to the center of the line to coordinate with Cobb. Both officers had become brigadiers the same day, and they greeted each other affably amid the great clamor. Then disaster struck. Both generals went down, Cooke severely wounded by a minié ball in the head, Cobb mortally so. Accounts vary as to the cause of Cobb's puncture. Sergeant Montgomery of the Phillips Legion was probably as close to the scene as anyone else at that hectic moment. He would write: "A shot from the enemy's cannon gave him [Cobb] his mortal wound. He was on the right of our Co, only a few feet from me when wounded." Others insist a Yankee sharpshooter knocked him down. Regardless, a lethal piece of lead or steel sliced the femoral artery in Cobb's thigh. Private Payson Ardie of the Phillips Legion helped carry his fallen brigadier to an aid station, but surgeons could not staunch the bleeding, and Cobb soon turned ashen and died.

If ever the Confederate position along the Sunken Road was vulnerable during the multiple Union assaults of December 13, it was during the confused half hour following the loss of Cobb and Cooke. The troops were demoralized at the havoc, ammunition was getting low, and the Yankees never stopped launching fresh brigades up the bloody slope toward them. McLaws, slow to learn of Cobb's mortal wounding, took time to move General Kershaw's brigade of South Carolinians to bolster the Georgians, now threatened by yet another Union advance.

Into the crucial void stepped Colonel Robert McMillan. Commanding the 24th Georgia, and one of the last field grade officers in Cobb's brigade still on his feet, he assumed Cobb's place. McMillan ignored the sniper fire to walk the line between Union assaults, praising and encouraging each company. It seems the transplanted Irishman lost his cool demeanor only once, at the charge of Brigadier General Thomas F. Meagher's "Irish Brigade," preceded by its storied green battle flag. At that sight, McMillan joined Captain Patrick McGovern's Lochrane Guards of the Phillips Legion, screaming Gaelic battle cries and obscenities at their onrushing Irish counterparts. ("Thus, Greek met Greek," recounted the mixed metaphor of one Southern newspaper.) And despite their bravery, the men of Meagher's brigade crumpled and bled and fell back in disorder before that winnowing fire from the Sunken Road.

McMillan, concerned about the concentration of Union stragglers in the nearby railroad cut, called for the 16th Georgia, one of the better regiments in the brigade, to reinforce the right flank of the Sunken Road on the double-quick. Colonel Goode Bryan's men responded immediately, but it had become extremely dangerous to cross the exposed upper slopes and proceed down to the Sunken Road. Two of Cobb's couriers and two of McLaws's had already fallen to the heavy fire beating through the grass.

Suddenly, General Kershaw appeared on the summit on horseback. The combative South Carolinian took a deep breath and spurred his horse in a breakneck gallop through the gauntlet of fire and into the road below, bowling over several surprised infantrymen. Sergeant Montgomery showed more interest in what Kershaw hoped to deliver. The legion was nearly out of ammunition. "I thought we would have to come to charge bayonetts on them," he recounted, "but just in the nick of time here came the old 2d S.C. Vols. like so many wild Indians. I tell you I felt good, for we had shot away 70 rounds of cartridges & the Yankees were still coming." The 2nd South Carolina fell in behind the Phillips Legion, the 8th South Carolina behind the other Georgians of Cobb's Brigade. At the same time, Ransom advanced the 25th North Carolina down the slope and into the lines. Each of these regiments paid heavily for their exposed transit. Each, in fact, would suffer higher casualties than the rank and file of Cobb's Brigade, protected from the start by the bulwark. But now the interior wall was downright crowded. According to Kershaw's report:

> I found, on my arrival, that Cobb's Brigade, Colonel McMillan commanding, occupied our entire front, and my troops could only get into position by doubling on them. This was accordingly done, and the formation along most of the line during the engagement was consequently four deep. As an evidence of the coolness of the command, I may mention here that, notwithstanding that their fire was the most rapid and continuous I have ever witnessed, not a man was injured by the fire of his comrades.

Kershaw did not have all the facts. While the massed troops in the road seemed to have handled the crowded choreography without inadvertently shooting one another, Cobb's brigade sustained "friendly fire" casualties from the South Carolinians posted along the slopes behind them. Private J. S. Wood of the Phillips Legion later stated: "I think our greatest loss was caused by the guns of our own men stationed on the hill to our rear. [We] told them they were killing our own men at the foot of the hill." Adjutant Byrd reported that "several [companies] suffered from the fire of two South Carolina regiments who were behind us, higher up the hill, and did not shoot high enough for the balls to pass over." One survivor of the 7th South Carolina admitted, "When the battle was raging hottest, Colonel Bland saw with his straight eagle eye that some of his men were shooting at Cobb's men . . . He ran up the line to our front, hollering at the top of his voice . . . 'Raise your guns higher!'"

Such incidents were inevitable. Exposed troops under heavy fire in the open, hastily firing nine-pound muskets downhill from a kneeling position (it was impossible to reload a musket rapidly from the prone position), could hardly be expected to hold an accurate sight picture. Likewise, Union troops hugging the folds of the slope after each failed assault suffered as much from wild firing from their rear as they did from the Confederates.

More Southern reinforcements filtered into the Sunken Road, until the ranks along the stone wall grew to six deep. Kershaw and McMillan carefully orchestrated their firing sequence. With more than 5,000 muskets concentrated into that 500-yard stretch, the Confederates were now capable of delivering murderous thousand-round volleys every ten to fifteen seconds.

No armed force in the world could withstand such fire. The Yankee regiments that dutifully churned up that muddy, bloody slope were undeniably brave, heartbreakingly courageous. But General Burnside, a mile away and totally misinformed about the great strength of the Confederate positions, kept feeding new brigades into the slaughter—one at a time, all afternoon.

The men of the Phillips Legion would serve Longstreet and Lee in every subsequent campaign of the war, but they would never again have such a favorable battle position as here in the Sunken Road. Not only could they rest their heavy muzzles on the top of the wall, allowing them to steady their sights and lean into the recoil, but the winter sun hovered over their shoulders, blinding their foe, illuminating their targets. "Our Company was armed with muskets which used a cartridge consisting of a ball and three buckshot," recalled Private E. H. Sutton. These "ball and buck" loads were notably inaccurate at any great distance, but at point-blank range, firing against the massed Union formations, they created great slaughter. Victorious troops scavenging for prized Federal overcoats among the piles of the slain after the battle complained because so many of the garments had been shredded by multiple hits of "ball and buck."

✦

ON THE RECEIVING END, the Northern journalist Murat Halstead described "the wild charge on the stone wall." He wrote, "It was not war; it was madness . . . [as] the blue column moved forward there was the crackle of rifles like a thousand packs of Chinese crackers, and from that ghastly gulf of flame but few of the boys in blue reappeared." Brigadier General Andrew A. Humphreys, whose division of untested Pennsylvanians came as close to the wall as any of the veteran outfits, added a close-range observation: "The stone wall was a sheet of flame that enveloped the head and flanks of the column."

Nor were the Yankees any slouches as marksmen. The interior walls of the Innis House, which stood in the midst of the Phillips Legion during the battle, still bear the scars of hundreds of bullets; their entry/exit paths reflect firing origins from a sector fully 150 degrees in breadth. One of Lee's couriers counted thirteen minié balls in a single telegraph pole on Marye's Heights. Adjutant Owens described the whitewashed brick house near his battery as "so battered with bullets it was transformed to a bright brick-dust red." An abandoned cast-iron stove lying outside the house rang like a bell from the bullet strikes. In the Sunken Road, Private Payton W. Fuller, the Phillips Legion's impetuous young color-bearer, waved his flag like a matador's cape from behind the wall all afternoon. On three occasions Yankee sharpshooters shot the flagstaff out of his hands. At length, the staff beyond repair, he nailed the tattered colors to a board and stood up to wave the awkward flag high overhead. The next shot grazed his forehead, knocking him and his flag into the muddy road. Fuller, chastened, continued to wave the colors, but thereafter from deep cover. By day's end the fabric had fifty-eight bullet holes.

At dusk Burnside finally called a halt to the madness. The lingering smoke and the winter darkness cloaked the ungodly battlefield. Longstreet reported the loss of 1,893 battle casualties from the ranks of his corps, most occurring in those regiments of Ransom's division and Kershaw's brigade that never benefited from the shelter of the Sunken Road. Union losses in only that *sector* were staggering: 7,817 dead, wounded, and missing. Of these, Longstreet later claimed "our musketry alone killed and wounded at least 5,000." These figures could well be higher. Longstreet's artillery officers estimated without undue hyperbole that their cross fires accounted for 20 percent of the Federal casualties, one of the best days of the war for that arm of the Confederate service. Taking this into account still leaves the conclusion that the rebel riflemen defending Marye's Heights may have shot down as many as 6,000 Yankees. The Phillips Legion, accomplished marksmen occupying premier firing positions along at least half of the Sunken Road from start to finish, contributed the major share of this slaughter. The sheer weight of lead and volume of fire delivered by the legion alone is difficult to imagine: 400 riflemen, each shooting an average of sixty "ball and buck" cartridges, equates to 24,000 rounds (each with multiple projectiles) fired at troops advancing upright across an open field in broad daylight at a distance rarely greater than 200 yards. Exclaimed one survivor of the 118th Pennsylvania, "It was simply murder!"

Longstreet's postwar account gave credit to both sides:

> No troops could have displayed greater courage and resolution than was shown by those brought against Marye's Hill. But they miscalculated the wonderful strength of the line behind the stone fence. The position held by Cobb surpassed courage and resolution, and was occupied by those who knew well how to hold a comfortable defense.

Yet as the exhilaration of the battle subsided, the Confederates experienced horror at the sounds and sights of the battlefield to their immediate front that night, the next day, and the following night. Few even attempted to describe the ungodly butchery they had wrought. Sergeant Montgomery, who had seen more combat than any other man in the Phillips Legion, admitted, "I never saw in my life such a slaughter." The temperature plummeted; many of the wounded Federals froze to death. The humanitarian efforts of Sergeant Richard R. Kirkland of the 2nd South Carolina and others to succor their wounded enemies lying in droves below the Stone Wall helped only marginally. No man could view that grotesque field without realizing that the war was beginning to generate its own mindless momentum.

Fredericksburg was an unmitigated tactical disaster for the North but not a strategic catastrophe. Lee, sensing a greater victory over the battered Union army with its back to the river, sought to take the offensive, but his lieutenants pointed to the Federal artillery bristling along Stafford Heights, reminded him how the Union guns at Malvern Hill had riddled his infantry assaults the previous summer, and cooled his ardor. The battle thus served little more than to preserve the Confederacy for another season of war. The Army of Northern Virginia would be allowed five months of winter quarters in which to rebuild its shattered ranks from the heavy fighting of 1862. The men of the Phillips Georgia Legion, replacing their muskets with Union rifles taken from the slopes of Marye's Heights, would follow Lee and Longstreet till the bitter end at Appomattox Court House. Union troops of Major General John Sedgwick's VI Corps would gain temporary redemption by carrying Marye's Heights the following May during the Chancellorsville campaign. But it would take Abraham Lincoln another year and a half to find a fighting general—under whose leadership the Army of the Potomac would recross the Rappahannock in force, for keeps.

Blood-red aurora borealis appeared in the northern sky over Fredericksburg the second night after the slaughter. A fearsome spectacle to the Southern boys, it seemed to portend even greater bloodshed to come.

A HELLISH START
TO THE YEAR:
THE BATTLE OF
STONES RIVER

TOM WICKER

The Battle of Stones River (or Murfreesboro, as it is sometimes known) receives scant notice, but it was about as costly as that more famous Western engagement, Shiloh. Like Shiloh, Stones River, which took place south of Nashville, began with a Confederate surprise in the rain and mist of New Year's Eve, December 31, 1862, that led to a near-rout of Union forces. Like Shiloh, too, a second day of fighting ended with a Confederate retreat that left the Union army masters of the field. So thorough did the Confederate advantage seem by the evening of December 31 that the Confederate commander, Braxton Bragg, telegraphed his good friend Jefferson Davis on New Year's Day to inform him of his victory. He should have waited. Bragg was an unpleasant and difficult man whom nobody (except the Confederate president) liked, whether it was the officers who tried to have him removed or the men whose lives he unimaginatively squandered. It's perhaps a bit unfair to call him the Confederate Burnside, although he belongs in the same exalted circle of ineptitude. If the Union suffered from bad generals in the East, so did the Confederates in the West. By the same token, some of the best Union generals got their start in the West: two of the emerging stars of the North, George H. Thomas and Philip H. Sheridan, fought with distinction at Stones River.

Battles are rarely uplifting, and there is a particularly down quality to Stones River. It was not just the dismal cold and the wet or the huge losses, many of them (especially in the second day of fighting) unnecessary. Apparently troops also fought hungover from too much holiday-week cheer. Stones River can be seen as a drawn battle: Certainly the losses on the two sides were about equal. But draws, like Antietam or Gettysburg, have a way of turning into strategic victories. So it was with Stones River, which left the Union in control of Tennessee and protected the Northern flank in the Vicksburg campaign.

Tom Wicker is the former *New York Times* Washington bureau chief and a columnist for the newspaper. He has written frequently on the Civil War, in, among other works, the novel *Unto This Hour.*

THE NIGHT OF DECEMBER 30–31, 1862, WAS BITTERLY COLD in the vicinity of Murfreesboro, Tennessee. As a freezing rain fell, Union and Confederate soldiers crouched in bivouacs on ground dotted with cedar thickets and limestone outcroppings. A naturally shallow but now rain-swollen stream known as Stones River traversed the soggy landscape.

Early that evening, military bands on both sides had begun a sort of musical duel audible to the shivering troops of both armies—Confederate musicians answering "Yankee Doodle" with "Dixie," the Federals then blaring out "Hail Columbia." Eventually, though, the Union band struck up "Home, Sweet Home," and the Southerners immediately joined in, the familiar refrain sounding mournfully over the river, dark fields, parked cannons, and armed men of North and South huddled around inadequate fires—a melancholy prelude to the death and destruction the morning would bring.

In the preceding weeks, Confederate President Jefferson Davis had personally inspected the Confederate Army of Tennessee at Murfreesboro. Overrating his military capability as usual, Davis made two moves that were to prove disastrous. He detached one of the army's seven divisions to reinforce the defenders of Vicksburg, and retained his old Mexican War comrade, Lieutenant General Braxton Bragg, to command his principal Western army.

Bragg was deeply distrusted by his officers—in particular, by two corps commanders, Lieutenant Generals Leonidas Polk (an Episcopal bishop) and William J. Hardee, as well as Lieutenant General Edmund Kirby Smith, the Confederate commander in East Tennessee. Davis overruled them, however, and left Polk and Hardee as Bragg's principal subordinates, despite the potential for further discord.

The generals' lack of confidence in Bragg stemmed from his uncertain conduct of what they had considered to be a promising invasion of Kentucky in autumn 1862. A Confederate army under Smith had seized Lexington, while Bragg—commanding what was then known as the Army of Mississippi—had interposed his force between Louisville and a Federal army in Nashville. The outlook was promising for an advance to the Ohio River, and perhaps beyond. But Bragg inexplicably abandoned his strategic position, fought the Federals inconclusively at Perryville, then returned to Tennessee, leaving Kentucky in Union control for the remainder of the war.

Believing that Perryville should have been a Confederate victory and the invasion of Kentucky successful, Smith, Polk, and Hardee protested Bragg's subsequent retreat—the latter two generals even journeying to Richmond to complain about Bragg's actions directly to Davis, and to urge his removal. Even then, Davis refused their pleas, foreshadowing their later rebuff at Murfreesboro.

The failed invasion of Kentucky also had produced another conflict that was to bear unhappy consequences for the Confederacy. When the march began, Major General John C. Breckinridge of Kentucky, who had served as vice president in the prewar Buchanan administration, was commanding a Confederate division in Mississippi under Major General Earl Van Dorn. Bragg believed that to have Breckinridge with him in the Kentuckian's home state would be "equal to an extra division." Van Dorn did not, however, want to release the general and his troops, so he resisted their transfer for a month.

Consequently, Breckinridge's men had managed only to reach Knoxville when Bragg turned back from Perryville. Bragg thereafter publicly expressed the opinion that his Kentucky campaign had failed largely because of the absence of Breckinridge and his troops. Breckinridge resented the charge, and animosity grew between the two men. At Murfreesboro, however, when Bragg reorganized his forces into the Army of Tennessee, Breckinridge was assigned to command a division under Bishop Polk, with the so-called "Orphan Brigade" of Kentuckians a vital part of it. Here, buried none too deep, lay obvious roots of trouble.

Meanwhile, Major General Don Carlos Buell, who had commanded Federal forces at Perryville, had been sacked for allowing Bragg to escape and then ignoring President Abraham Lincoln's urgings that he mount a new campaign against the Confederates in Tennessee. Buell had been replaced by Major General William S. "Old Rosey" Rosecrans—a rarity among Civil War commanders in that he was a Roman Catholic and, though a professional soldier, had seen no service in the Mexican War. Beaten on the first day of fighting at Corinth in 1862, the tenacious Rosecrans recovered the next day to defeat combined Southern forces under Major Generals Van Dorn and Sterling Price. Lincoln was to learn, however, that the stubborn Rosecrans could be pushed into action no more easily than Buell had been—though the president never stopped trying.

Another problem for Lincoln was that Rosecrans's appointment risked the displeasure of his best corps commander, Major General George H. Thomas, a Virginian who had remained loyal to the Union and who had believed himself in line for the command. Fortunately, the sort of dissension among commanders that plagued Bragg's army did not develop among Federal forces. Acceding to Lincoln's choice, Thomas continued to serve ably.

Rosecrans took command of the Army of the Cumberland on October 24 and made his headquarters at Nashville, about thirty miles northwest of Murfreesboro. On paper, he had nearly 80,000 men, but about half were detached for guard duty along the supply line that ran from the river port of Louisville through Kentucky to Nashville. He faced both supply and manpower problems. Unusually low water levels on the Cumberland River had been hampering navigation, which multiplied his supply concerns. He also badly needed to reorganize an army that featured five new division commanders and that had been reduced in size to provide reinforcements needed elsewhere. More than thirty regiments bloodied at Perryville, for instance, were not available to Rosecrans at Nashville.

After relentless prodding from Washington to attack Bragg, General in Chief Henry Halleck warned Rosecrans that "I cannot prevent your removal" if he stayed longer in Nashville. Old Rosey replied to such threats, "I am insensible," and refused to budge until he had received—among other needed supplies—at least two million rations for his troops. But by Christmas, the Cumberland had risen, the rail line was open, ample stores were on hand, and the reorganization of the Army of the Cumberland into three corps was complete. He had intelligence reports, moreover, that Davis had weakened Bragg's army with the dispatch of that division to Vicksburg.

For his part, Bragg was convinced that Rosecrans had settled into winter quarters. Therefore, the Confederate general took advantage of Davis's confidence in him by further weakening his army. He sent Major General Nathan Bedford Forrest and Brigadier General John Hunt Morgan with their cavalry forces to undertake independent operations in western Tennessee and Kentucky. At this distance, they could be of no immediate assistance to him if they were needed. Watching from Nashville, Rosecrans concluded that the time to move had arrived. On December 26, his wagon-encumbered army—

three corps marching on three different routes along muddy winter roads—moved south toward Murfreesboro.

In that small city astride the strategic Nashville & Chattanooga Railroad, the Confederates had been enjoying a festive holiday season, enlivened by a Christmas Eve ball in the Rutherford County courthouse and by the dashing Morgan's marriage to a local belle (in a ceremony performed by Polk). But the festivities were not so consuming that Bragg's remaining cavalry, commanded by Brigadier General Joseph Wheeler, failed to discover Rosecrans's advance or to harass the slow Federal march southward.

Skirmishing and Southern raiders, along with miserable weather and roads deep in mire, slowed the Army of the Cumberland. But by December 30, the two armies were confronting each other outside Murfreesboro, both straddling the railroad, the Nashville Pike, and the winding Stones River. The few roads that ran through the area were too narrow and too muddy for quick troop movements in the battle that had become inevitable.

Oddly enough, on the eve of the fight, as their drenched and chilled troops listened across the lines to the sad strains of "Home, Sweet Home," each commander had roughly the same battle plan—an attack by his left on his adversary's right flank. Had both attacks succeeded, the two armies would have been locked in something like a giant pinwheel.

The commander of the Federal right-flank division, Brigadier General Philip Sheridan, and Brigadier General Joshua Sill, who led one of Sheridan's brigades, observed and heard threatening Confederate movements that night. Alarmed, they tried to warn their corps commander, Major General Alexander McCook, but he was unimpressed—until, just after 6 A.M., when Confederate attackers, swarming eerily out of the fog and rain, silently charged toward the Federals.

The lead attackers were from Hardee's corps—Major General J. P. McCown's division—with Major General Patrick Cleburne's division following 500 yards behind. The surprise was complete, the terrifying Rebel yell soon rang out, and Union forces dissolved in confusion, many of their coffeepots still on the fire.

Rolling on like an ocean wave, the Confederates routed two Federal brigades, while their cavalry swept into the rear of panicked and fleeing Union troops. The Confederates shattered what little resistance the Federals were able to offer, pushed on, hit additional enemy lines, and swarmed over those, too, pushing back the Union right nearly two miles. Both sides suffered heavy casualties before the Federals finally formed another line along a major road, the Wilkinson Pike. This stand, a desperate effort to keep Confederate troops from cutting the Nashville Pike and blocking Rosecrans's line of retreat, was aided by a loss of cohesion among the attackers, many of whom were nearing exhaustion after their rapid advance.

Meanwhile, Sheridan, unfazed by the fierce fighting, had brought forward two reserve regiments and had his artillery ready, just south of the Wilkinson Pike. When Polk's supporting corps launched a new but ill-coordinated attack, Sheridan resisted mightily and a desperate fight ensued, the Federals in that sector giving as good as they got. Sill even led a counterattack that appeared to be succeeding, until he was killed by a shot through the head. Confederate Brigadier General Alexander P. Stuart had resisted earlier orders to send in his regiments separately, but finally a concerted attack by his Tennessee brigade drove Sheridan from his strong position in a thick clump of cedars.

The Confederates savagely attacked one artillery emplacement "like a whirl-a-gust of woodpeckers in a hailstorm," wrote one of the attackers. "I cannot remember . . . ever seeing more dead men and horses and captured cannon, all jumbled together." After Sheridan was forced to withdraw, most of the Union right collapsed, and Braxton Bragg and the Army of Tennessee appeared on the verge of a tremendous victory.

Appearances, however, were deceiving. Neither the Nashville Pike nor the railroad was in Confederate hands, so Rosecrans was not cut off from his base as Bragg had intended. Sheridan's stubborn fighting retreat had slowed the Southern advance. Confederate momentum was fizzling out. The reserves of the attacking force had been committed, and Bragg had made no move to strengthen his tired assault columns west of Stones River with troops waiting unengaged east of the river.

It is possible, too, that among these demonstrable problems, all that Christmas celebrating among the Confederate commanders in Murfreesboro might have gone on too long and too cheerily. That day, "John Barleycorn was general in chief," the Confederate memoirist Sam Watkins later wrote, and "our generals, and colonels, and captains had kissed John a little too often."

On the Federal side, Rosecrans, who at first had not realized that his right was broken or that disaster threatened, now rose to the occasion in probably the greatest performance of his military career. Those who saw him that day thought he seemed to be everywhere, making snap but generally correct decisions, showing not the slightest fear or awareness of danger, and generally inspiring his nearly beaten forces by his demeanor as well as by his actions. The correspondent Whitelaw Reid wrote that the general was magnificent as he directed the formation of a new line in an arc anchored against the river, but still guarding the crucial Nashville Pike and the railroad.

"This battle must be won!" Rosecrans shouted again and again to whoever would listen. At one point, as the general and his aides rode furiously along the new Federal line, a Confederate shell decapitated Colonel Julius P. Garesche, Rosecrans' chief of staff and a close friend who had persuaded him to convert to Catholicism. Spattered with Garesche's blood, the general rode on to continue rallying his troops.

Still the furious fighting raged across the woods and fields to the west of Stones River, the roar of the guns reminding a Union colonel of a "continuous pounding on a thousand anvils." Sheridan remained in the thick of it, though three of his brigade commanders had been killed and a third of his men were lost. Miles of ground were strewn with dead and wounded men and horses, littered with broken and abandoned equipment, and in some particularly gruesome spots, slick with blood and entrails.

By noon, the final Union position, constricted but strong, formed a rough angle bending back to the river on each side of its central point—a wooded knoll on both sides of the railroad and slightly northeast of the Nashville Pike, known locally as the "Round Forest." On the last day of 1862, the Round Forest was exposed to Confederate cross fire, but Rosecrans and Thomas collected about fifty artillery pieces behind it, ready to fire over the Union line and into the advancing Southerners. This grand battery was to make the crucial difference as the Confederates repeatedly attacked the Round Forest—and just as repeatedly were thrown back. The fighting there was so ferocious the soldiers dubbed the woods "Hell's Half-Acre."

First a brigade of Mississippians, veterans of the Battle of Shiloh, tried it. Then a brigade of Tennesseans came close, before a counterattack drove them back. Of 425 men in the Eighth Tennessee making the second attack, 306 became casualties. Other regiments suffered almost as badly.

Bragg then called for reinforcements from General Breckinridge's fresh division, which had been doing little on the east side of Stones River. The brigades of Brigadier Generals Daniel Adams and John Jackson were the first to cross and arrive before the Round Forest—but only after Rosecrans and Thomas had been given an hour's respite to strengthen and resupply their position.

Adams's Louisianans and Alabamans were ordered to charge across ground already littered with the corpses of Mississippi and Tennessee men. The fresh troops marched smartly to the attack. Some Federals gave way, but most held, firing incessantly. Rifle and cannon shots tore ghastly holes in the Confederate ranks until Adams's shattered brigade at last fled back across the killing ground.

Jackson's Georgia-Mississippi brigade was next. These men charged, fell back, re-formed, and charged a second time. This attack, too, was repulsed, with a third of Jackson's men and all of his regimental commanders killed or wounded. But incredibly, Bragg, aided and abetted by Polk, ordered the two late-arriving brigades of Breckinridge's troops to try again to take the Round Forest. This time, the units attacked together, instead of one after the other.

"The dreadful splendor of this advance can only be conceived, as all description must fall vastly short," wrote Union Colonel W. B. Hazen. But at the same time, one of the charging Confederates observed, "the sheets of fire from the enemy's cannon looked hideous and dazzling." Inexorably, the two brigades' splendid advance met the fate of those that had gone before—slaughter, near destruction, flight, failure.

Bragg at last had had enough. The day's fighting was over. But though the Southern general exultantly wired President Davis in Richmond claiming victory, the Battle of Stones River was far from finished. On New Year's Day 1863—the very day that Abraham Lincoln's Emancipation Proclamation, issued the previous September, went into effect and freed the slaves in all states in rebellion—William S. Rosecrans displayed his tenacity. With Sheridan urging him on, he prepared to renew the fight.

On that rainy and freezing first day of a new year, Braxton Bragg was wrongly convinced that his forces had so mauled the Army of the Cumberland that Rosecrans would have no choice but to withdraw to Nashville, so the Confederate commander took little or no action. While Bragg dallied, Old Rosey consolidated and improved his position. The Federals had occupied strategic high ground east of Stones River that dominated part of the Confederate line. In his conviction that Rosecrans would retreat, Bragg had not bothered to occupy that same ground, from which he could have threatened Union forces, because he had not expected to remain on the field.

Old Rosey had moved first. Bragg therefore realized on January 2 to his consternation that he now had either to retreat after a battle he thought he had won or drive the Federals off that crucial height. For a man as vain as Bragg who was already stung by criticism of his withdrawal at Perryville, retreat was not an option. He immediately looked for troops to use against the Federal position, and the force best situated to make the attack, he quickly decided, was the division of John C. Breckinridge.

Numerous accounts by Confederates present at Stones River and by historians later studying records of the battle ascribe Bragg's attack order to per-

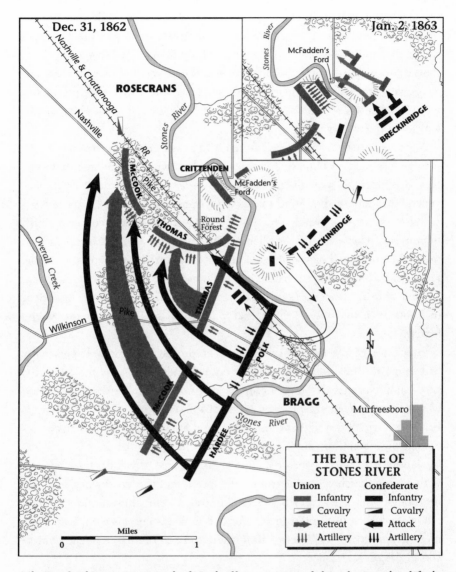

The Battle of Stones River south of Nashville was a tactical draw but one that left the Union forces under Major General William S. Rosecrans in possession of the field. It began on New Year's Eve 1862, when Braxton Bragg's Army of Tennessee drove the Union right wing back across the Wilkinson Pike to a four-acre wood on a railroad line called the Round Forest, or (as Union soldiers dubbed it) "Hell's Half-Acre." The battle resumed two days later (inset). Major General John C. Breckinridge attacked the Union left, drove it back over Stones River at McFadden's Ford—and was in turn driven back to his starting point. The next day Bragg retired.

sonal animus against Breckinridge and his fellow Kentuckians. Bad blood between the two men, as previously mentioned, dated to the failure of Bragg's invasion of Kentucky. Later, at the Murfreesboro encampment, Breckinridge, then a division commander in the Army of Tennessee, intervened to protest the execution of a Kentucky soldier who had deserted and been caught, but Bragg, a renowned disciplinarian, coldly refused the former vice president's plea. The deserter was shot by a firing squad while the rest of the Kentuckians looked on resentfully.

Whether personal animosity entered into Bragg's decision to order Breckinridge to attack on January 2 is debatable. It is well documented, however, that Breckinridge strongly protested the order. The Kentucky politician-general may have had in mind that two days previously Bragg had ordered— one after the other—five bloody frontal attacks on the Round Forest in which hundreds of Confederates had died, including many of Breckinridge's own men. He might well have considered their deaths needless, even inexcusable. He may also have believed that he had the prestige to get the order rescinded. He had, after all, been the South's favored Democratic candidate for president in 1860, in a four-way election that put Abraham Lincoln in the White House.

Breckinridge also had a tactical reason to protest the order. He personally had seen a formidable Union artillery emplacement being assembled on the west bank of Stones River, on a bluff at least ten feet higher than the ground he was being ordered to capture on the east bank. His scout, Captain William P. Bramlette, had observed that those guns could fire virtually point-blank across the narrow stream into any Confederate force on the east bank.

Confronting Bragg beneath a large sycamore tree, Breckinridge knelt and with a stick sketched on the ground the location of this enemy position that he thought made the attack suicidal. It was a compelling argument by a renowned leader, but unfortunately for Breckinridge and his men, even a former vice president was inferior in military rank to the irascible and controversial Bragg.

"Sir, my information is different," the army commander replied to Breckinridge's description of the Union gun position (though Bragg had not himself reconnoitered the area). "I have given the order to attack the enemy in your front and expect it to be obeyed."

Breckinridge's son Clifton, who was on the field at Stones River, recalled later that Brigadier General Roger Hanson of the Orphan Brigade, known as "Benchleg" because of a limp, was so incensed when Breckinridge relayed the attack order that he threatened to "go at once to headquarters and kill Bragg."

Hanson was restrained but remarked, in an apparent premonition of his own death, "I believe this will be my last."

Bragg's order proved to be non-negotiable. He ordered the attack for late afternoon in hopes of preempting a counterattack. So, to the sound of a signal gun fired at 4 P.M. on that grim and freezing January 2, 5,000 Confederates surged forward. The Southern troops, including the Orphan Brigade, marched off in good order and spirits, though a body of water in their front split their ranks. At the first upward slope of the ground, they paused and fired a single volley, then rushed up the incline toward the defending Federals.

The Union right flank was quickly turned. As the weight of the spirited Confederate charge dislodged the Union troops on the high ground, the Federals began to withdraw downhill toward McFadden's Ford, a shallow crossing of Stones River. The Confederates followed with a yell, pursuing troops whose sporadic resistance managed only to slow their attackers. But as the Confederates passed over the crest of the targeted high ground, they were exposed—as Breckinridge and Captain Bramlette had feared and predicted—to the massed and waiting Union artillery beyond McFadden's Ford on the west bank.

Union Captain John Mendenhall, the artillery chief for Major General Thomas L. Crittenden's corps, gave the order to fire. Roger Hanson was one of the first Kentuckians to fall, but as the cannons roared, the carnage was general and immediate. Even so, the yelling Confederates poured down the hill toward the river, some of them—believing victory was in their grasp—getting across to the uphill bank. But additional Federal infantry formed an effective defense beside Mendenhall's well-placed artillery, which continued to tear great gaps in the Confederate ranks.

Edward P. Thompson of the Orphan Brigade recalled, "[T]he very earth trembled as with an exploding mine, and a mass of iron hail was hurled upon them. The artillery bellowed forth . . . [T]here were falling timbers, crashing arms, and whirring of missiles . . . the bursting of the dreadful shell, the groans of the wounded, the shouts of the officers . . . [O]ne horrid din that beggars description."

The terrible concentrated fire from Union artillery and infantry quickly routed the attackers. The Confederates now lost all semblance of organization. Federal pursuers, at first surprised by the Confederates' disintegration, soon splashed across McFadden's Ford. Firing at will, they chased the fleeing Southerners back to the point from which, barely forty minutes earlier, they had bravely set off on the fatal charge that Bragg had ordered so incautiously—or perhaps callously, as many of his critics believed then and later.

About a third of Breckinridge's attacking division, some 1,700, were shot down. Color-bearers fell like leaves in autumn. Colonel Joe Nuckols, badly wounded himself, brought out the flag of the Fourth Kentucky, but only after three standard-bearers had been shot while carrying it. Thirteen of that regiment's twenty-three officers were killed or wounded. A quarter of the Orphan Brigade's personnel—more than 400 men—were dead, wounded, or missing; more than 27 percent of all Kentuckians engaged fell before enemy fire.

"My poor orphans! My poor Orphan Brigade!" Breckinridge cried out over the strewn corpses of his men. "They have cut it to pieces!"

That night and the next day, the torn and exhausted armies lay facing each other across a river that "ran red" and threatened to rise under a cold, persistent winter rainfall. With more than half of his troops on the west bank, the remainder on the east, Bragg feared that floodwaters would divide his army irredeemably. He knew, moreover, that he was outnumbered, as he had believed he had been at Perryville, and his cavalry had informed him that the Army of the Cumberland was being reinforced from Nashville. That high ground he had at first neglected was still in Federal hands and still threatened the Army of Tennessee.

So, on the night of January 3, Braxton Bragg gave another order to retreat. As after Perryville, not all of his officers agreed with the decision or approved of Bragg's conduct of the just-concluded battle. But there was no one to whom an appeal could be immediately directed.

That night and the next day the Army of Tennessee trudged, largely unchallenged, forty miles south to a new defensive line around Tullahoma—foreshadowing a decisive Union advance that ultimately would engulf Chattanooga and Atlanta and effectively bring the war to an end.

The Army of Tennessee's retreat also brought to an ignominious conclusion a battle that had begun December 31 with a Confederate surprise attack—and what Bragg thought he could report to Richmond that night as a sweeping triumph. But after the bloody repulse at McFadden's Ford, Stones River had become a strategic Union victory—and for North and South alike one of the worst bloodlettings of the war.

The winter struggle at Stones River resulted in casualties on both sides roughly equivalent to those incurred in 1862 at Shiloh—about 23,000 killed, wounded, and missing Federals and Confederates in each battle—and Stones River had greater strategic consequences. The Union victory, however limited, made possible the long, slow advance past Chattanooga and Lookout Mountain to Atlanta and the heart of the Confederacy, and therefore its final spasmodic collapse.

Coming only days after the shocking Federal defeat at Fredericksburg, moreover, Stones River was fought at just the right time to foreclose what was perhaps the most favorable moment for British recognition of the Confederacy. It was a victory that counterbalanced Fredericksburg and combined with the moral dimension that the emancipation of slaves lent to the Federal cause, it could hardly have come at a more propitious time for Abraham Lincoln.

It is no wonder that in the summer of 1863 Lincoln wrote Rosecrans that he could never forget "whilst I remember anything, that about the end of last year and the beginning of this, you gave us a hard-earned victory, which, had there been a defeat instead, the nation could scarcely have lived over."

Gratitude, however, is fleeting. On October 20, 1863, after the inconclusive Confederate victory at Chickamauga, William S. Rosecrans was relieved as commanding general of the Army of the Cumberland. He never again received a combat assignment.

STONEWALL JACKSON'S LAST MARCH

STEPHEN W. SEARS

Stonewall Jackson's left hook out of nowhere at Chancellorsville on May 2, 1863, may be the classic American battle maneuver. (It was reenacted most recently by Norman Schwarzkopf in the Gulf War.) Thanks to the vigorous scouting by J. E. B. Stuart's cavalry, Jackson and Lee learned that the Union right flank was "in the air," and they looked for, and found, a hidden way to reach it. They were abetted in their plan by the nature of the landscape in that area of Virginia, a maze of second-growth timber known as the Wilderness, with dirt lanes meandering through the woods, mostly out of sight of Union eyes. It seems incredible that the Northern commanders did not prepare themselves for some sort of flanking operation by Jackson. The flank attack was his military trademark. As the South Carolinian diarist Mary Boykin Chesnut wrote, "Down here, we sleep securely, with the serenest faith that Stonewall is to flank everybody and never be flanked himself." Surprisingly, at the one spot where the woods opened to reveal Jackson's marching columns, the southward direction they were then following on their circuitous twelve-mile route convinced Union observers that they were in retreat.

Stephen W. Sears relates here a story that is, like Jackson's maneuver, one of the classics of American military history—from Lee and Jackson's pre-dawn conference, seated in a clearing on hardtack boxes, to Jackson's dying words: "Let us cross over the river, and rest under the shade of the trees."

Stephen W. Sears is one of the foremost historians of the Civil War. His books include *Landscape Turned Red: The Battle of Antietam; George B. McClellan: The Young Napoleon; To the Gates of Richmond: The Peninsula Campaign; Chancellorsville;* and *Controversies & Commanders: Dispatches from the Army of the Potomac.* He is currently at work on a book about Gettysburg.

ON MAY DAY IN 1863, STONEWALL JACKSON, LIEUTENANT general, was at the peak of his fame. Readers of the Southern press were accustomed to seeing him referred to as the "hero of the war." His nickname—it was said at First Bull Run in 1861 that he stood "like a stone wall"—seemed to fit him perfectly and had spread through the newspapers to make him instantly identifiable. Rather than Thomas J., he was "Stonewall" to everyone across the Confederacy—everyone except his men, who called him "Old Jack."

Jackson's particular fame was as a flanker. Armies in this war, said his fellow general James Longstreet indelicately, were as sensitive about their flanks as a virgin. It seemed that Stonewall Jackson was forever either attacking a Yankee flank or turning one. He did so first in his celebrated Shenandoah Valley campaign in the spring of 1862. Soon afterward, in the Seven Days at Richmond, he attempted (less successfully) a turning movement by the left flank. Later that summer his eminently successful left hook at Second Bull Run put him in the military textbooks. Even at Antietam that fall he found an opportunity in his defensive role to smash into an exposed enemy flank. "Down here," wrote Charleston diarist Mary Chesnut, "we sleep securely, with the serenest faith that Stonewall is to flank everybody and never be flanked himself."

Now, at dusk on this May Day evening, near the intersection of the Orange Plank Road and the Catharine Furnace Road in the Wilderness of Virginia, Stonewall Jackson and Robert E. Lee sat together on a fallen log in a little clearing and plotted out the last and greatest of Jackson's flank marches.

The spring campaign of 1863 in Virginia was now in its fifth day, and General Lee had concluded that only a high-stakes gamble could put him back into this battle. "Fighting Joe" Hooker (his nickname, like Jackson's, was a press creation) had all the best of it so far. Through the winter, Hooker's Army of the Potomac had confronted Lee's Army of Northern Virginia across the Rappahannock River at Fredericksburg. Now, in a brilliant stroke, marching by the right flank, Hooker had swiftly and secretly established the bulk of his army at the Chancellorsville crossroads, in the Wilderness south of the river and west of Fredericksburg. The enemy, Hooker announced to his troops, "must either ingloriously fly, or come out from behind his defenses and give us battle on our own ground, where certain destruction awaits him."

Hooker would later be derided for his boastfulness, yet he told a simple truth. Lee's choices were few and grim. He had underestimated his opponent and now stood to pay for it. When he saw in the papers that this latest Yan-kee general to challenge him was called Fighting Joe Hooker, he began refer-ring to him as "Mr. F. J. Hooker." In his overconfidence he let Longstreet and half his I Corps linger in an abortive campaign at Suffolk, below Richmond, while Hooker stole a long march on him. As a consequence, one-quarter of the Army of Northern Virginia was absent from this campaign on the Rappahan-nock.

Hooker's stolen march covered four days, April 27–30—a long sweep up-river from opposite Fredericksburg, an unopposed crossing of the Rappahan-nock, then a long sweep back downriver and across the Rapidan, the Rappahannock's tributary, to reach Chancellorsville, ten miles due west of Fredericksburg. By May 1, Hooker had five army corps established there. While all this was going on, he held Lee at Fredericksburg by crossing below the town and establishing two corps in the bridgehead. Porter Alexander, the Confederate soldier and historian, paid Hooker the compliment of calling this "decidedly the best strategy conceived in any of the campaigns ever set on foot against us."

On April 30, with Hooker's movements at last clear to him, Lee made his first major decision of the campaign: to give battle rather than retreat from the Rappahannock line. He marched west from Fredericksburg to accept Hooker's challenge, leaving just five brigades to hold the Fredericksburg lines. The next day, May Day, the spearheads of the two armies clashed along the Orange Plank Road and the Orange Turnpike in front of Chancellorsville.

From the way the Federals pulled back at almost the first contact, and from the way they strongly entrenched themselves around Chancellorsville, it was obvious that Hooker wanted to fight his battle defensively. He was inviting attack; he was daring Lee to attack. But in so doing he had to give up the ini-tiative, and on the battlefields of this civil war the initiative was something that had always served Robert E. Lee very well.

Several years later, when shown an account by a Stonewall Jackson disciple giving Jackson the dominant role at Chancellorsville, Lee made a point of set-ting the record straight. "I am misrepresented at the battle of Chancellorsville in proposing an attack in front, the first evening of our arrival," he wrote in reference to the events of May 1. "On the contrary, I decided against it, and stated to Gen. Jackson, we must attack on our left as soon as practicable . . ." Thus, their discussion in the clearing in the Wilderness on the evening of May 1 was not about what to do, but only about how to do it.

Earlier, Lee himself had reconnoitered on the right, toward the Rappahan-nock. An obvious tactic would be to turn Hooker's left to cut him off from his base across the river. But the enclosing Wilderness argued against it. Lee stated it simply: He found "no place fit for attack . . ." It would have to be a left hook.

Lee's decision to "attack on our left" required two vital pieces of intelligence: the location of Hooker's right flank and a hidden way to reach that flank. The answers lay in the terrain of this Wilderness landscape, and the roads through it.

It was called the Wilderness of Spotsylvania, or simply the Wilderness—a distinctive tract of Virginia woodland some seventy miles square. Since colonial times the Wilderness had been the site of a nascent iron industry, but all that remained of it now was Catharine Furnace, a mile and a half southwest of Chancellorsville. Abandoned in the 1840s, the furnace had recently been reactivated to produce iron for the Confederate war machine. It was this iron industry that gave the Wilderness its distinctive character. Most of the first-growth timber had been cut to make charcoal to feed the furnaces and foundries, to be replaced by a second-growth tangle of dwarf pine, cedar, hickory, and a scrub oak known locally as blackjack. Undergrowth in this warped and pinched forest grew dense and brambly. Men who fought in the Wilderness would remember it with fear and hatred—a dark, eerie, impenetrable maze.

Back in 1816, to cater to traffic on the newly built Orange Turnpike between Fredericksburg and Orange Court House, George Chancellor opened a tavern ten miles from Fredericksburg. It was a substantial building of brick, two and a half stories, with accommodations for travelers. Chancellor ambitiously named his tavern and its outbuildings Chancellorsville. While his settlement never grew into its name, it was at least the most prominent landmark in the Wilderness of Spotsylvania.

In the 1850s the Orange Turnpike was taken over by new owners, who proceeded to construct a plank-covered all-weather road to Orange Court House that only in part followed the Turnpike right-of-way. For the first half-dozen miles out of Fredericksburg, the two ran as one; then the Plank Road looped off to the south before rejoining the Turnpike at Chancellorsville. Two miles farther west, at Wilderness Church, they divided again and ran separately to Orange Court House.

There were as well numerous little country roads and byways and forest tracks crisscrossing the Wilderness, many of them known only to the local people. What cleared ground there was mostly bordered the Turnpike and the Plank Road. The largest clearing, some seventy acres, was at Chancellorsville, but there were other clearings to the west at Fairview, Hazel Grove, Dowdall's Tavern, and Wilderness Church.

To locate the Federals' right flank, Lee called on his cavalryman J. E. B. Stuart. Hooker had sent most of his cavalry off to the south to raid Confederate communications, and Jeb Stuart's troopers quickly established domination over what cavalry remained with Hooker's army. The brigade of Stuart's lieutenant Fitzhugh Lee owned every road south and west of the Chancellor house. In late afternoon Fitz Lee had skirmished with Yankee infantry a mile or so south of Wilderness Church, on the Carpenter homestead. There, Fitz Lee reported, was the Federals' right flank.

In his search for information, Stuart remembered that Beverly Tucker Lacy, Jackson's "chaplain general," knew the Wilderness well. Lacy explained that by marching by way of Catharine Furnace, it was possible for a column to swing around south by west by north in an arc to reach the Orange Plank Road or the Orange Turnpike behind the enemy. Furthermore, with Stuart's cavalry in firm control of the roads, the march could be made secretly.

Lee was aware that the three Federal corps Stuart had identified the day before were at Chancellorsville. He was not aware that two other corps had joined Hooker, but even had he known of them it is unlikely it would have altered his determination to fight here. He stated the case to President Jefferson Davis: "It is plain that if the enemy is too strong for me here, I shall have to fall back, and Fredericksburg must be abandoned. If successful here, Fredericksburg will be saved and our communications retained." To test if the Federals were too strong, he would fight.

That night Generals Lee and Jackson and their staffs made a simple bivouac in a nearby clearing in a pine thicket. The chill of the spring morning awakened Lieutenant James Power Smith before first light on May 2, and looking around the bivouac he saw that everyone was asleep except the two generals. They were warming themselves over a small fire, deep in conversation. When Smith fell back asleep they were still talking.

Jackson had risen that morning even before Lee, to set the plan in motion. He called first for Lacy, to mark the roads on a map, and the chaplain obliged him: south by west on the Catharine Furnace Road, west on what he called a "blind road" across to the Brock Road, then north on that to the Orange Plank Road and then the Orange Turnpike. When laid down on a map, however, the route appeared to Jackson to pass too close to the enemy's force as seen by Fitz Lee's cavalry the day before. Was there not some other route with a longer arc? Lacy could not say for sure, but he knew someone who could—Charles C. Wellford, the proprietor of Catharine Furnace. Jackson seized on that. He roused his mapmaker, Jed Hotchkiss, and sent him with Lacy to seek out Wellford.

Hotchkiss and Lacy rode with all speed the two miles to Wellford's house, roused him from his bed, and explained what they wanted. By the light of a candle in his parlor, Wellford marked on Hotchkiss's map exactly what they needed. From the Furnace, Wellford explained, he had recently cut a new road through the Wilderness to the Brock Road in order to haul cordwood and ore for his iron-making operations. He also knew of a byway paralleling the Brock Road, a brief detour that would shield them from the Yankees' view. Wellford's son could act as a guide. Exclaiming their thanks, Hotchkiss and Lacy raced back to camp.

They found the two generals together, and Hotchkiss offered his report. Lee and Jackson were seated at their fire on empty hardtack boxes discarded by the Yankees the day before. Hotchkiss set out another hardtack box as a table, spread his map, and pointed to the route Wellford had outlined. After a few questions their agreement was obvious: Here was the hidden route to the enemy's rear.

The exchange that followed, Hotchkiss wrote, impressed itself "on my mind very forcibly." As he recalled it, "Gen. Lee began by saying, 'Well, General Jackson, what do you propose to do?' Gen. Jackson, moving his finger over the route indicated on the map, said, 'I propose to go right around there.' Gen. L. replied, 'What do you propose to do it with?' Gen. J. said, 'With my whole command.' Gen. Lee then said, 'What will you leave me here to hold the Federal army with?' Gen. J. replied, 'The two divisions that you have here.' After a pause Gen. Lee said, 'Well, go ahead.'"

With no more drama than that in this dawning hour of May 2, the matter was settled. Lee made notes for the necessary orders, and when he was done Jackson rose and saluted and said, "My troops will move at once, sir."

✦

THAT NIGHT AT THE CHANCELLOR HOUSE, Captain William Candler of Joe Hooker's staff was on duty, and in the small hours of the morning he found time to write a letter home. The Federals had been attacked the day before by Johnny Reb, he began. "Fell back at first to draw him on, then took a position and gave him 'fits.'" Candler expected the battle to resume as soon as it was light. "They must come out of their works and attack us in our own position. Today will tell a big tale. God grant we may be successful."

During these hours there was no pause in preparations to meet the expected Rebel attack. The pioneers worked through the night, felling trees for barricades and clearing fields of fire for the guns. The line, roughly convex in shape, was just over six miles long, guarded by thirty-one batteries and manned by nearly two-thirds of the infantry of the Army of the Potomac.

The left was anchored solidly on the Rappahannock to shield the army's communications with the north bank. Running south by west, it then formed a shallow salient around the Chancellorsville crossroads. From there it ran due west along the Orange Plank Road, where it was manned, on the extreme right flank, by Oliver Otis Howard's XI Corps—three divisions, fewer than 11,000 men, extending the line a mile and a half from Dowdall's Tavern, past Wilderness Church and the point where the Orange Turnpike branched off, to the farmstead of James Talley on the Turnpike.

Some 500 yards beyond Talley's the line simply ended, where Howard ran out of men. There was no natural feature here on which to anchor a defense, nor any formidable force with which to make a defense, only two regiments and two guns pointing to the west down the narrow road through the dark, silent forest. Fighting Joe Hooker's right flank, in the phrase of the military textbooks, was "in the air."

In the five corps on this Chancellorsville line there were thirteen divisions, thirty-six brigades—all told, 72,300 troops and 184 pieces of artillery. The strength of this force was multiplied by field fortifications. Hooker had prayed for the chance to fight his battle defensively, and at every hand was evidence that his prayer was about to be answered. By far the weakest link in Hooker's defensive chain—as he well knew—was Howard's XI Corps. It was not only the smallest in the army but also the poorest in quality, and Hooker had his doubts about its commander. He had posted Howard on the far right simply to keep him out of the most likely line of fire. Hooker ordered John Reynolds's I Corps up from the bridgehead below Fredericksburg to secure this "in the air" flank, but due to a communications lapse Reynolds would not reach the scene before nightfall.

That morning Hooker rose early to ride his lines. His first priority was his first concern, the right. He rode his favorite warhorse, a white charger, and according to a witness "made a fine appearance." At every position he was cheered to the echo. It is said that this morning, May 2, 1863, was the last time the Army of the Potomac would ever raise a spontaneous battlefield cheer for its commanding general.

Some fortifying had been done on Howard's line, but it was not extensive. It was clear that Howard was relying on the Wilderness itself as his first line of defense. Where his line ended there were two of the guns of Captain Julius Dieckmann's battery and two infantry regiments, some 700 men, posted behind a flimsy barricade of saplings and brush. They faced west. Everything else on the line of the XI Corps faced south.

✦

CALLED OUT AT FIRST LIGHT, the 1st South Carolina Regiment was forming up when Stonewall Jackson rode past to the front. "We rose, on the point, I felt, of breaking into the old cheer," J. F. J. Caldwell wrote, "but reading battle in his haste and stern look, we contented ourselves with gazing at him and giving expression to our foolish speculations." When in due course Jackson took up his line of march, "breaking off square to the left," veterans began to speculate with more confidence. "I knew old Jack was going to the rear of old Joe," John Brooks of the 20th North Carolina would insist.

Jackson's powerful flanking column included the infantry of three of his II Corps divisions, under Robert Rodes, Raleigh Colston, and A. P. Hill—a total of fifteen brigades, 29,400 men. The artillery complement was twenty-seven batteries, 108 guns. With artillerymen and cavalrymen, the total in the column came to 33,000. Lee was left with seven brigades from the divisions of Lafayette McLaws and Richard Anderson, a total of 14,900 men of all arms, to hold the lines in front of Chancellorsville. Jubal Early with five brigades was guarding Fredericksburg.

Such a move as this was hardly unprecedented for Robert E. Lee: He had ignored military convention and divided his army in the presence of a superior foe during every previous campaign he had fought, except Fredericksburg in December. But dividing his army and then dividing it again within twenty-four hours, literally under the guns of an army twice the size of his own, was unprecedented. Yet as Lee appraised the situation and measured his opponent, the risk became acceptable.

The major risk, of course, was to that segment of the army commanded by Lee himself. He accepted it because of his confident reading of his opponent's mind. The suspiciously easy victory of the day before, the reports of the enemy fortifying so strenuously, made it apparent that Fighting Joe Hooker was anxious to do his fighting defensively. Consequently, so long as Jackson did not tip his hand too soon that day, that ought to give Lee's little force security from attack. By seizing the initiative—by realizing the initiative was his for the taking—Lee went a long way toward lowering the odds against himself.

The other factor in lowering the odds was Stonewall Jackson. Lee had perfect confidence in his lieutenant. He knew him to be a master of concealment and a genius at exploiting surprise. With three divisions at his command, Jackson was certain to overwhelm initially whatever part of Hooker's army he struck. After that, in the fluid heat of battle in the entangling Wilderness, there was no telling what results might follow.

It was a Stonewall Jackson tradition for his "foot cavalry" to set out on a march at first light, but on this day, May 2, 1863, his greatest march, there was delay. Too much had been left for morning. Rodes's division was to head the column, and when his lead brigade stepped off it was already close to seven o'clock.

Not long afterward, at the intersection of the Plank Road and the Catharine Furnace Road, Lee stood quietly by the roadside watching Rodes's men march past and turn down the Furnace Road. Jackson rode up, mounted on his rawboned warhorse, Little Sorrel. He paused for a brief conversation with the commanding general. Their words—their last words—went unrecorded. Jackson's forage cap was pulled low over his eyes, and his expression was intense. He gestured, pointing toward the enemy. Lee nodded, and then Jackson rode on.

The order of march had Rodes's division leading, followed by Colston's and then Hill's. The column carried only its fighting trains—ammunition wagons and ambulances—marching with the artillery behind their assigned divisions. Cavalry advanced on the right to secure all roads and byways in the direction of the enemy. The march regimen was standard: one mile in twenty-five minutes, ten minutes' rest each hour, a rate of two miles per hour. There would be only a fifteen-minute midday break. Old Jack was balancing his need for speed with his need to have troops fresh enough for an attack when they reached the target.

Jackson set out on his celebrated flank march that morning with, as it turned out, an imperfect idea of where the enemy's flank was located. His last intelligence put it at about the Carpenter farm, on a byway that ran south from Wilderness Church to the Brock Road. The first half of the march would follow the extended Furnace Road to the Brock Road. Turning right to head north on the Brock Road, however, would have soon brought the column within a thousand yards of Carpenter's and revealed it to any Yankees who might be there.

It was at this point that Wellford made his second contribution of the day. A turn left on the Brock Road instead of right, he explained, would in a short distance bring the marchers to the entrance of a private road that ran west of and parallel to the Brock Road. Following this byway northward, the column would be quite out of sight of Carpenter's. Once past that point, the soldiers would return to the Brock Road and take it to its crossing of the Orange Plank Road. By turning back eastward on the Plank Road, they would be just over two miles from Wilderness Church—and, by all accounts, the rear of Hooker's army.

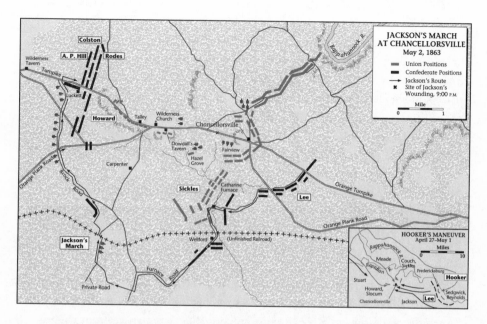

Hooker's initial advance on Chancellorsville is shown in the small inset map. Above are the Union and Confederate positions on May 2, as well as the path of Jackson's risky march. His shock attack on Howard's unprotected flank sent the Federals reeling back along the Orange Turnpike.

Jackson stayed back for a time to prod the marchers along. "Press forward, press forward," he said to the passing ranks. "See that the column is kept closed and that there is no straggling," he told the officers repeatedly. "Press on, press on. . . ."

There was to be no music and no calls, nor any cheering. A North Carolina soldier recalled Jackson riding past his regiment "at a long gallop," his cap held aloft, and the men, all mute, raising their caps in a return salute. Jackson pushed on to the head of the long column, riding with Rodes just behind the troopers of the advance. The staff stopped at Wellford's and brought along Charles B. Wellford, son of Catharine Furnace's proprietor, to act as guide. A civilian volunteer, young Wellford fairly burst with pride at the invitation to ride with Jeb Stuart's cavaliers.

Veterans among the foot cavalry would rank this Chancellorsville flank march considerably less demanding than some of their marches under Old

Jack in the Shenandoah the spring before, or during the Second Bull Run campaign in the summer of 1862. This May day was breezy and pleasant and not too hot. The roads were soft and damp from the rains, and there was no choking dust. (This was a double blessing: The enemy could not track the movement by the dust the marchers raised.) "For hours our silent columns swept along the roads at the quick step, now turning to the right, and now to the left . . . ," a man in the 14th South Carolina recalled. "We lost the points of the compass and became about as much bewildered in regard to course or directions, as we already were in regard to the object of the expedition."

✦

FOR A MILE OR SO after it left the Orange Plank Road, the Catharine Furnace Road ran westerly through dense, concealing forest. Nearing the furnace, the road crossed a stretch of high, open ground, then dropped down and turned due south for three-quarters of a mile before turning west again into the concealing forest. That first opening, near the furnace, was visible to any Yankee observers posted in the Hazel Grove clearing to the north. Beginning at eight o'clock that morning, observers perched in tall trees began reporting a steady procession of Rebel troops crossing that open space from the east "toward the right."

The III Corps commander, Dan Sickles, got Hooker's approval to bring up a battery of rifled guns to shell the enemy column. The Rebels were seen to double-quick across the opening under the fire. Sickles, never shy in reporting results, claimed the enemy's trains and artillery "hurried past in great confusion, vainly endeavoring to escape our well-directed and destructive fire."

Back at the Chancellor house, Hooker was dictating a dispatch to Howard. He began by noting that "the disposition you have made of your Corps has been with a view to a *front* attack by the enemy. If he should throw himself upon your flank," Howard was cautioned, ". . . examine the ground and determine upon the position you will take in that event, in order that you may be prepared for him in whatever direction he advances." Then, after examining the sighting reports from Hazel Grove, he added a postscript: "We have good reason to suppose that the enemy is moving to our right. Please advance your pickets . . . to obtain timely information of their approach." The dispatch was timed 9:30 A.M. and sent to Howard by courier. Hooker believed this was warning enough to "wake up a dead man to his true condition."

Howard replied, "I am taking measures to resist an attack from the west." That was no doubt reassuring to Hooker, but the sum total of Howard's measures was posting a Signal Corps officer to relay messages to his headquarters.

No pickets were advanced; no troops or guns were repositioned. Howard continued to trust to the densely tangled Wilderness to protect his position.

Sickles was not content with simply shelling the enemy sighted near Catharine Furnace. He kept petitioning Hooker to let him attack, and Hooker finally agreed. At 1:30 P.M. Sickles reported his progress. Only as they approached the furnace could he finally see that the Rebel column, instead of continuing to move west, was in fact turning southward. That discovery offered a whole new perspective on events. Sickles leaped to a conclusion: "I think it is a retreat."

✦

WHILE THE TAIL of Jackson's flanking column was evading its tormentors, the head was moving forward swiftly and silently and secretly. At 1:30 that afternoon, about the time Sickles signaled Hooker that the Rebel army was in retreat, Stonewall Jackson was searching out the right flank of Hooker's army.

Jackson's column had been guided by young Wellford along the back roads that took it out of sight of the Carpenter farm. Each byway that came in from the right, toward the Federals, was sealed off by Jeb Stuart's cavalry. Now, reentering the Brock Road, the marchers reached its crossing of the Orange Plank Road. As the plan was formulated early that morning, an advance eastward on the Plank Road for some two miles ought to turn the enemy's right.

The cavalry turned into the Plank Road to reconnoiter. On the left was a high open knoll, and Fitz Lee climbed it for an observation. He would never forget the moment: "What a sight presented itself before me!" Back he went at a gallop for Stonewall Jackson. Accompanied only by a courier, Jackson followed the cavalryman up the track to the knoll. There, spread out before them not 700 yards distant, was the Yankee army.

Jackson could see straight along the Plank Road to where it was joined by the Orange Turnpike at Wilderness Church. "There were the lines of defence, with abatis in front, and long lines of stacked arms in the rear," Fitz Lee remembered. "Two cannon were visible in the part of the line seen. The soldiers were in groups in the rear, laughing, chatting, smoking, probably engaged, here and there, in games of cards, and other amusements . . ."

At the left of this vista was the Talley homestead, and at the right Dowdall's Tavern, residence of Melzi Chancellor, a son of the founder of Chancellorsville. What Jackson was seeing, although he could not know it, was the better part of Howard's XI Corps. He had to assume that since yesterday the enemy had withdrawn from Carpenter's to this new line. It was also clear that any attack by way of the Plank Road against this position would be little better than a frontal assault. To carry out the plan, Jackson would have to alter it so as to strike from beyond the flank.

Old Jack studied the scene through his binoculars for perhaps five minutes, responding to Fitz Lee's remarks with complete silence. Finally he turned to his courier and said tersely, "Tell General Rodes to move across the old Plank Road, halt when he gets to the old Turnpike, and I will join him there." The courier turned his horse and was gone; then, still without a word to Fitz Lee, Jackson followed him. Rodes moved his soldiers north to the Turnpike, swung east for half a mile to the farm of John Luckett, and halted. No Federals blocked his way or were in his sight. His men had marched just under twelve miles.

Jackson paused to scribble a brief dispatch to General Lee, which he marked "Near 3 P.M." He wrote, "The enemy has made a stand at Chancellor's which is about 2 miles from Chancellorsville. I hope as soon as practicable to attack. I trust that an ever kind Providence will bless us with great success."

In the 14th South Carolina, far back in the flanking column, there was little notion of what the Confederates were doing that day or where they were going. They were toiling along the Brock Road when a cavalryman came tearing down toward them on some urgent errand. Infantry never missed an opportunity to gibe cavalry. "We're going to have a fight, boys, for the cavalry's going to the rear!" was the call. The trooper grinned and called back as he passed, "You're right this time. Our men are advancing on them now!"

Jackson's column was so long and so roadbound that deploying from marching formation to fighting formation was exasperatingly slow. As soon as they were placed, the men sank down gratefully. Many slept. Others chewed on their corn bread and speculated and waited, with the certainty of Old Jack's veterans, for the fight to start. The first line as deployed over the next few hours was entirely Rodes's troops. Straddling the Orange Turnpike, his line of battle extended some three-quarters of a mile to each side and contained some 7,800 men in a double rank. A skirmish line was pushed out 400 yards ahead in the dense woods. Two hundred yards back was a second line, comprising one brigade of Rodes's division and two from Colston's. A third line contained one brigade of Colston's division and two of Hill's. About a third of the column could not be fitted into this attack formation. Nor could most of the guns.

This force with which Jackson intended to make his attack consisted of some 21,500 infantry and eight guns, and it took half the afternoon to arrange everything to Jackson's satisfaction. He was determined to attack on the broadest possible front, taking the maximum advantage of his numbers against what was sure to be a very narrow-front enemy defense.

In no previous battle had Jackson ever had the time and opportunity to plan an assault with such care. A half mile ahead beyond the forest lay the foe, unsuspecting. It was like some long-ago tactical lesson learned in a classroom at West Point, now miraculously made real, on a real battlefield. Captain Marcellus Moorman, commanding one of the horse batteries in the advance, sought out Jackson to clarify his orders. As they talked they could hear artillery rumbling off to the east. Jackson asked the artilleryman how distant it was. Moorman said he thought five or six miles. "I suppose it is General Lee," Jackson said, adding matter-of-factly, "Time we were moving."

Howard's XI Corps was manning its lines with fewer than 11,000 men. About two-thirds of these were German or of recent German descent—to the rest of the army, "Dutchmen" who spoke comical English if they spoke English at all and who had never shared in this army's trials. The army's attitude ranged from one man's irritation that the Germans "were allowed their lager beer & ale when no other part of the army could get any" to unthinking contempt for anyone foreign, an outgrowth of the anti-immigrant Know Nothing politics of the 1850s. To be sure, the Army of the Potomac had peculiar notions of "foreignness"—Thomas Meagher's Irish Brigade was no less foreign than Leopold von Gilsa's German Brigade, but no comparable stigma attached to the Irish—and there was no accounting for it. The best solution to all this, for the Dutchmen, would be a strong showing here, in their first battle with the Army of the Potomac.

It was a simple fact that nothing really good had ever happened to this corps. Certainly the men had entered on this campaign willingly enough, as a way of proving their mettle and earning their place in the army, but what they needed was the best sort of leadership the army had to offer. They got instead the poorest sort.

In diaries and letters a good many XI Corps men would remember the calm of that Saturday afternoon, with arms stacked and bands playing and the "sweet and tantalizing scent of boiling meat" in every encampment. In mid-afternoon, wrote Thomas Evans of the 25th Ohio, "there was a feint made on our right after which the band played us a national air. Thus, as we supposed, we were secure from danger, such was the nearsightedness of our commander."

Unimaginative, unenterprising, uninspiring, a stiflingly Christian soldier, Otis Howard was the wrong general in the wrong place with the wrong troops that day. In the face of uncertainty—and May 2 was a day of many uncertainties—his way was to close his mind to everything but word from his superiors. Further, the general commanding under Howard on the army's far right flank, Charles Devens Jr., was another of the poorest sort. Devens, out of the Harvard Law School and the Massachusetts militia establishment, was a harsh disciplinarian with a lofty Bostonian's view of non–New Englanders, an attitude that did not sit well with the Germans who made up two-thirds of his division.

Devens shared with Howard the belief that information of military importance flowed only down the chain of command, not up it. In any case, May 2 was not a good day for Devens to begin with. His horse had carried him into a tree, badly bruising his leg, and he was easing the pain with brandy, which improved neither his temperament nor his judgment.

✦

AFTERWARD, a number of officers from the XI Corps would come forward to insist they had detected Stonewall Jackson's flanking column in plenty of time to meet and halt it. But when they reported these sightings to their generals, they were ignored or laughed at or called coward. They described the sightings in books and articles and interviews, and declared themselves prophets without honor; history would be different, and men would be alive today, if only they had been listened to.

It is quite true that the secret of Jackson's flank march was not perfectly kept—with 33,000 men and 108 guns, it could not be perfectly kept—and it is quite true that warnings that should have been heeded were shamefully ignored. Yet it is also true that among those witnesses were those who larded their testimony with what they learned and understood only after the fact. What was actually seen of Jackson's forces by the Federals on May 2 was a good deal less, and a good deal more ambiguous, than hindsight claimed.

In their march between the Catharine Furnace clearing and the Turnpike, Jackson's men were concealed every step of the way by at least a mile and a half of Wilderness—and for good measure tightly screened by Stuart's cavalry—from any observers in Howard's command. As Major Norvell Cobb, 44th Virginia, expressed it at the time, "The country being wooded & thick, and his troops masked by a cavalry force which skirmished with the enemy, all got by, undetected."

At the time, before hindsight and the humiliation of their wrenching experience later that day warped their view, what these various officers actually reported to their superiors was what their pickets had been reporting ever since they took up this line two days earlier—sightings of parties of Rebels, pickets and scouts, mostly Stuart's men, sealing the byways and probing the Federals' positions. A threatening enemy was indeed being seen out there in the deep woods and on the narrow tracks, but at that time and place what was seen did not include any marching infantry or artillery.

Beginning at three o'clock or so, however, there was a series of actual sightings of Jackson's forces that by any measure ought to have jolted the high command into action. But these had the misfortune to arrive in the midst of or after the welter of vague picketline sightings so annoying to Howard and Devens. They interpreted the new sightings as just more of the same; as in Aesop's fable, the cry of "Wolf!" was being heard at every hand.

But more than anything else, all these sightings could now be explained by the belief in an enemy in retreat. The maps showed the Orange Plank Road and the Orange Turnpike running west to Orange Court House. Lee in retreat must be detouring to the south and west around the Federal army to reach these roads; any Rebels seen to the west of Howard must be merely a rear guard posted by the army that Fighting Joe Hooker had predicted would ingloriously fly. As Devens told one of his alarmed officers, since he had received no warnings from corps or army headquarters, there was nothing alarming about these various sightings. Headquarters, to generals like Devens and Howard, was the font of all knowledge.

Yet the general belief at the Chancellor house that Lee was retreating in no way repealed Hooker's 9:30 A.M. warning to Howard or Howard's duty to act on it. The warning was in force for a full five hours before word reached Howard that the enemy might be retreating, and he did nothing in all that time. A bitter Joe Hooker would charge that "my instructions were utterly and criminally disregarded."

However that may be, beyond any doubt Dame Fortune was smiling on the South that day. For the Federals it was pure mischance that Reynolds's 16,900 I Corps men were not dug in on the army's right flank. Then the Federals misinterpreted the sighting at Catharine Furnace as a retreat. But most of all, it was surely good fortune for the Confederacy that when Stonewall Jackson finally signaled the charge, he was aiming squarely at the ineptly led XI Corps of the Army of the Potomac.

It was about 5:45 P.M., the sun was low in the west, and many of the Yankees were cooking supper when Von Gilsa's regiments on the far west of the line heard a bewildering commotion in the woods in front of them. Suddenly quail in numbers came beating through the treetops, and then there was a rush of frantic deer and rabbits straight toward them out of the woods; one man claimed he saw a bear among the fleeing game.

The men whooped and pointed at the sight, and then they heard the crackle of gunfire and the bloodcurdling banshee screech of the Rebel yell coming from in front and from left and right to the limits of their hearing. Then they knew. Years afterward, thinking back on it, Ohioan Thomas Evans wrote, "Jackson was on us and fear was on us."

✦

AT 5:30 THAT AFTERNOON, on the Orange Turnpike, Stonewall Jackson sat his horse alongside Robert Rodes. He turned and asked, "Are you ready, General Rodes?" Rodes's "Yes, sir!" was prompt. Without pose or gesture Jackson said quietly, "You can go forward then."

The men advanced quickly, shouldering their way through the matted vines and briars and tangled underbrush, through the Wilderness that Howard thought was impenetrable by an army. "The command was given forward march, guide right," wrote North Carolinian John Brooks. "In less than ten minutes our pickets commenced firing on the enemy and five minutes more our line of Battle gave them a volley that will last them untill peace is made."

George Doles's Georgia brigade smashed head-on against the outlying Yankee defenses. Two of Von Gilsa's German regiments, the 41st and 45th New York, posted along the Turnpike facing south, were turned so quickly that they ran without firing a shot. The section of Captain Dieckmann's battery that pointed west down the road managed to fire two rounds, but then the charging Georgians were on them and shot down the battery horses, and the gunners left their pieces and ran.

In the woods north of the road, Von Gilsa's only regiments facing west, the 700 men of the 54th New York and 153rd Pennsylvania, managed to stand a few minutes longer. Doles quickly shifted the 21st Georgia to flank them. "We were ordered forward and the boys all gave a few keen yells and said they intended to have some Yankee crackers before they slept that night," Lieutenant Thomas Hightower of the 21st Georgia wrote home. The New Yorkers on the threatened flank broke and ran. The 153rd Pennsylvania was a nine-month regiment that had never been in battle before, and now the troops on both sides of it were gone, and the order was passed for the Pennsylvanians to save themselves. "It was futile now," wrote Private Francis Stofflet, "and my anxiety was how to escape capture and where to find my company and regiment." In just ten minutes Von Gilsa lost 264 men, half of whom were captured, including two of his four regimental commanders.

Colonel John C. Lee of the 55th Ohio, the next regiment in line, galloped back to the Talley house for help. He found General Devens stubbornly unwilling to act without instructions from higher authority; Howard was absent, and no word reached him from corps headquarters. Lee pleaded for permission to change front to meet the attack. His brigade commander, Nathaniel McLean, looked inquiringly at Devens, who said nothing. Finally McLean told Lee, "Not yet."

Back at his regiment, Colonel Lee found a full-blown crisis. The Rebel battle line had crashed out of the forest into the Talley clearing, and McLean's Ohio brigade was hopelessly out of position. Again Lee spurred back to the Talley house, and again Devens was silent. McLean resignedly waved the colonel back to his command. Lee would be one of several to insist Devens was too befuddled by drink to know what he was doing.

Doles's Georgians and, on their left, Edward O'Neal's Alabamians came on at the double-quick, greatly overlapping the ragged line of Ohioans. The remains of McLean's brigade fell back 500 yards and rallied around divisional headquarters at the Talley house. Devens had finally stirred himself to action, and he and McLean were trying frantically to stem the tide. Devens was soon wounded in the foot and helped from the field, and the line was outflanked and it broke apart. Four of McLean's five colonels were dead, wounded, or captured, along with 688 of his men. Luther Mesnard of the 55th Ohio could hardly believe what he was seeing. "To the right or left or in front as far as I could see, everything was fleeing in panic," he wrote. "It seemed to me that the whole army had gone to pieces."

✦

LIKE RUSHING WATERS FROM A BURST DAM, Jackson's massive assault came boiling out of the woods into the next open ground to the east along the Turnpike. This was the clearing surrounding Wilderness Church and the intersection of the Plank Road and the Turnpike. The two brigades of Carl Schurz's division held this ground, supported on the east by the last of the corps's units, Colonel Adolphus Buschbeck's brigade of Adolph von Steinwehr's division. Beyond Buschbeck there were no Federal troops anywhere in sight for more than a mile.

Howard, just returning to his headquarters, would remember the moment in the metaphor of a great storm: "It was a terrible gale! The rush, the rattle, the quick lightning from a hundred points at once; the roar, redoubled by echoes through the forest . . ." Fugitives from Devens's division spread panic like a contagion. Devens's men, Howard wrote his wife, "immediately gave way, broke up & ran upon the other troops with such momentum that they gave way too. Such a mass of fugitives I hav'nt seen since the first battle of Bull Run." (Howard, who had commanded a brigade in that battle, recognized a rout when he saw one.)

Around Wilderness Church the scene was utter chaos. Officers trying to pivot their regiments to meet the assault had neither time nor space to do so. Masses of men and pack mules and horses and wagons from Howard's trains bowled over what formations there were and broke them up. In desperate flight, Dieckmann's remaining four guns took to the fields to escape, became tangled in a wattle fence, and were captured.

Meanwhile, around Dowdall's Tavern, the XI Corps was making its last stand. Howard and his staff rushed into the stream of fugitives, trying to arrest it. Howard took up an abandoned stand of the national colors and rode with it recklessly toward the fight, hoping by example to inspire a rally. His horse, he wrote his wife, became panicked by the firing "and stood so straight on his hind legs, that I had to come down—but I was soon up again." However derelict he was in his command duties, Howard lacked nothing in personal courage.

His last stand was with the last of his troops, Buschbeck's brigade. Its position covered a thousand yards end to end, but soon enough Rodes easily outflanked it on the north. In twenty minutes this last line was turned like all the others. The 495 casualties in Buschbeck's brigade included three of the four regimental commanders, down with wounds.

Jackson's men were exultant. They had seen their enemies retreat before, but never was it like this. "You never saw such a grand sight in your life," Robert Garnett of the 21st Virginia wrote home. "We came up in rear of the yankeys late on Saturday evening. You never saw such a charge as we made upon them, we soon got them routed and then it was a perfect foot race . . ." The Federals attempted to stand behind some rifle pits, Louisianian William Clegg wrote, "but they were soon routed from them and we pressed on driving them from three successive lines. They were flying in great disorder . . ." The historian of the 1st North Carolina remarked how "the thick woods through which we were passing was like a strainer, letting the lean and lesser Dutchmen escape, while we secured the fat ones."

Driving forward, Rodes's division soon became disordered by the stretches of woodland in its path, by the spurts of resistance it met, and simply by the sweet taste of victory. Artillerist Porter Alexander watched "men singly & in groups, firing, stopping to load, & then pressing forward again." Colonels and captains took over direction of the assault when it outdistanced higher commands. Colston's second line closed up on Rodes's and in many places the two lines became intermixed, causing further confusion. Hill's third line, in the rear, seldom found targets.

As he rode close behind his swiftly advancing forces, Jackson called to every officer he encountered, "Press forward! Press forward!" By the account of Captain Robert E. Wilbourn, the general's signal officer, "All the orders I heard him give were simply a repetition of this order." When he came up to Major Robert Beckham, whose horse battery was blazing away with canister right up alongside the infantry, Jackson leaned down to shake the hand of the startled Beckham and tell him, "Young man, I congratulate you!" To Rodes, too, he offered congratulations for gallantly conducting the drive. "I had never seen General Jackson so well pleased with his success as that evening," Wilbourn wrote. "He was in unusually fine spirits and every time he heard the cheering of ourselves which was the signal of victory he raised his right hand a few seconds as if in acknowledgment of the blessing and to return thanks to God for the victory."

Old Jack might well have given thanks. In just an hour and a half, his surprise attack had flanked and overwhelmed the XI Corps, driven it a mile and a quarter, and routed it from its last feasible defensive position. From Dowdall's Tavern it was less than two miles to the Chancellor house, and there was no knowing if the Confederate drive could be stopped short even of that point. The sun was down now, however, and there were perhaps forty minutes of evening twilight remaining. Just then, as Porter Alexander put it, daylight was worth a million dollars a minute to the fortunes of the Confederacy.

✦

JUST TO THE EAST OF DOWDALL'S TAVERN the Wilderness closed in, leaving the Orange Plank Road as the primary corridor of escape for Howard's wrecked corps. This narrow corridor ran for half a mile before the forest gave back to form ever-larger clearings, first at an old schoolhouse, then at Fairview, finally at the Chancellor house. When Buschbeck's line collapsed, the stream of fugitives here became a torrent.

By some fluke of acoustics, the roar of Jackson's assault did not immediately reach Federal headquarters at the Chancellor house. Hooker was sitting on the front porch with Captains Harry Russell and William Candler of his staff when at about 6:30 a commotion down the Plank Road attracted Russell's attention. He stepped out into the road, focused his glass, and after a moment shouted, "My God, here they come!"

General and staff mounted and rode fast toward the right to identify this rush of men and vehicles. To their astonishment it proved to be the outriders of Devens's routed division. Amidst the clamor and babble of explanations could be heard repeated cries of *"Alles ist verloren!"* ("All is lost!")

A man in the 94th New York who came upon the scene a few minutes later tried to catalog it: "Men on foot on horseback on mules & in teams were rushing & piling back for dear life telling all kinds of yarns & we began to think that there was another Bull Run . . . Some had no caps some not coats all going for dear life, teams & droves of cattle all rushing back to the rear. After a while we found out that the 11th Corps composed of *Dutchmen* . . . had stampeded shamefully . . ."

Rushing into the Chancellorsville clearing, panicked men surged northward over every byway, crying out for directions to the bridges and safety across the river. Many had thrown away their rifles and torn off their corps badges to become anonymous. Old-timers seeing this flight who had served on the frontier were reminded of cattle and buffalo stampedes. To others it seemed like the blind flight of sheep. Amidst this din and confusion the band of the 14th Connecticut blared out "Yankee Doodle" and "The Red, White, and Blue" and "The Star-Spangled Banner" over and over again.

When a final count of the Dutchmen could be made, it was found that of the nearly 11,000 in line when Jackson struck, just over 2,400 were casualties. The assault was so sudden, and so enveloping, that nearly a thousand of these were prisoners. Nine guns were lost. The loss in Jackson's attacking force that day was some 800. Howard would later admit, "I wanted to die. . . . That night I did all in my power to remedy the mistake, and I sought death everywhere I could find an excuse to go on the field."

By now the Confederates were almost as disorganized by victory as the Federals by defeat. Colston's second line continued to pile into Rodes's first, especially during the pause when the Yankees under Buschbeck made their last stand. The battle lines were also becoming compressed, as by a funnel, narrowing from a mile and a half wide at the start to a half mile or so as the attackers drove past Dowdall's Tavern. As the formations entered the darkening woods beyond Dowdall's, it became harder than ever to maintain control.

Finally, at about 7:15 P.M., Rodes ordered a halt to reorganize. "Such was the confusion and darkness that it was not deemed advisable to make a farther advance," he would explain. He sent word to Jackson recommending that Hill's troops in the third line come forward to take over the advance while he re-formed his brigades.

Jackson was not in the least deterred by the disorganization of his command, the fading light, or the Yankee defenses. An enemy on the run must be kept on the run. He sent off staff aides with injunctions to straighten out the disorder. From Dowdall's Tavern he went forward himself, calling out, "Men, get into line! Get into line! Whose command is this? Colonel, get your men instantly into line!" His intent was unchanged—drive straight for Chancellorsville along the axis of the Plank Road to link up with General Lee, while at the same time sweeping into the enemy's rear by the left flank. Only now Hill's division must take the advance. When Brigadier General James Lane applied to him for orders, Jackson told him sharply, "Push right ahead, Lane!"

Lane's brigade now had the lead, with the 37th and 7th North Carolina posted in line south of the Plank Road, the 18th and 28th North Carolina extending the line north of the road, and the 33rd North Carolina in skirmish formation out ahead. Here and there in the deeply shadowed woods in front, there were bursts of firing.

"When I gave my orders," Lane explained later, "I cautioned all of my regimental commanders to keep a bright lookout, as we were in front of everything & would soon be ordered forward to make a night attack." The Yankees in front of them did not seem to be running any longer. And an hour or so earlier, there had been a brush with Yankee cavalry near this spot. Admittedly, as one officer recalled, the prospect of a cavalry attack "in that dense country seemed to be as unlikely as an attack from a gun-boat." Still, Lane's men would be alert for anything.

✦

OLD JACK RODE AHEAD ON THE PLANK ROAD toward the front. At an old schoolhouse he encountered Hill and his staff. How soon would he be ready to advance, Jackson asked. "In a few minutes," Hill replied, "as soon as I can finish relieving General Rodes." Looking intently at Hill, Jackson said, "General Hill, as soon as you are ready push right forward. Allow nothing to stop you."

Leaving Hill to follow, Jackson rode slowly up the Plank Road past Lane's deployed brigade. All that was ahead of him now was Lane's skirmish line and then the enemy. It was always Jackson's way to lead like this from up front, to see the battlefield for himself, and it was a habit that worried his staff. The little party was about halfway between Lane's line of battle and his line of skirmishers when Major Sandie Pendleton nerved himself to ask, "General, don't you think this is the wrong place for you?" Jackson said in his abrupt way, "The danger is over. The enemy is routed. Go back and tell A. P. Hill to press right on."

No one in Lane's brigade—at least no officer—realized that Jackson's party, and then Hill's, were riding out ahead of the lines, and in the darkness—it was after nine o'clock now, and the moonlight had not taken effect yet—they were not easily seen. Apparently Jackson and Hill each assumed the other had given notice of their presence to Lane's battle line. There was no real reason for Jackson to be where he was just then, except his own impatience. Lane's brigade would soon advance and catch up with his party in good season, and they would sweep on to Chancellorsville. A routed enemy must always be pressed so it could not catch its breath and make a stand. That was Old Jack's credo.

Jackson's party, riding slowly, reached a point 150 yards beyond Lane's battle line. Hill's party was fifty or sixty yards behind. When he was asked about it later, Hill said that since his superior officer was riding to the front, he considered it his duty to accompany him. The firing from the earlier clashes had died out. In the darkness the silence was almost eerie, and they sat their horses and listened.

Abruptly, off to the right, there was a single shot. Captain Wilbourn thought it came from the right rear, but he admitted it might have been more to the right or right front—possibly a Yankee skirmisher, but it was hard to tell. Then, in support or in reply, there was a spatter of shots and then a fusillade, as if set off by spontaneous combustion. There was no doubt this fire came from the right rear, where the 37th and 7th North Carolina regiments of Lane's brigade were nerving themselves for action.

The fire tore through Hill's party and then Jackson's, and the Plank Road became a scene of desperate confusion. Men and horses went down; maddened horses bolted, some with riders, many without. In Hill's group four were killed or wounded. It was the same in Jackson's party: one killed, several wounded, horses down or tearing off in every direction.

Jackson was not hit. He and other survivors spurred across the Plank Road away from the fire and into the trees on the northern margin for shelter, then instinctively turned back to their own lines. The noise of their racing horses, wrote Captain Alfred Tolar of Company K, 18th North Carolina, "seemed to the average infantryman like a brigade of cavalry."

At that the murderous fire redoubled. To Wilbourn it seemed to be an extension of the first fire from the right, leaping across the Plank Road and igniting the line of battle on the other side. It was aimed more at sound than sight. In the light of the muzzle flashes, some thirty or forty yards away, Wilbourn saw men kneeling in line and firing, the classic infantry stance for repelling a cavalry charge. The men he saw lit by their own fire were the 18th North Carolina infantry.

Lieutenant Joseph Morrison of Jackson's staff had thrown himself off his wounded and panicked horse and now ran toward the infantry line screaming to cease fire: "You are firing into your own men!" Hill, too, had leaped from his horse to escape the bullets, and he was shouting the same order. Major John Berry commanding this section of the line, suspecting a Yankee trick, called out, "Who gave that order? It's a lie! Pour it into them!" "I tried to stop them," cried an anguished aide of Hill's, "but they would fire . . ."

✦

AT LAST THEIR FIRING WAS HALTED, but not before three bullets had struck Jackson. Once among the trees he had thrown up his right arm to ward off branches, and one bullet hit his right hand. A second struck his left forearm, and a third shattered the bone in his upper left arm near the shoulder. As his left arm fell uselessly at his side he lost the reins, and Little Sorrel, wounded and maddened by the fire, bolted back toward the Plank Road. A low branch nearly knocked Jackson out of the saddle. On the road the horse rushed away from the fire, toward the enemy, but Jackson grasped the reins with his injured right hand and regained control. Wilbourn and signalman W. T. Wynn caught up and helped rein in the frantic animal. They were now at about the point in the road where they had been first fired upon.

The general, Wilbourn wrote, seemed utterly stunned. "Gen. J. looked up the road towards our troops apparently much surprised at being fired at from that direction, but said nothing." Wilbourn told him, "Those certainly must be our troops," and he nodded, still saying nothing. Asked if he was hurt badly, he finally spoke: "I fear my arm is broken." He was bleeding profusely and losing strength, and Wilbourn and Wynn eased him out of the saddle and laid him under a small tree on the margin of the road.

"General, it is remarkable that any of us escaped," Wilbourn said, to which Jackson agreed: "Yes, it is Providential." Now Hill and some of the staff were there. Hill took off Jackson's bloody gauntlets, helped Wilbourn bind the wound and fashion a sling, and sent off for the nearest brigade surgeon. When he arrived, Jackson whispered to Hill, "Is that a skillful surgeon?" Assured that the man was well regarded, Jackson said, "Very good, very good."

Lieutenant Morrison, who had gone ahead to check the road, came rushing back and said, "We must get away from here. The Yankees are placing a battery in the road not a hundred yards from us." Jackson said he thought he could walk with their help, and they got him on his feet and started slowly back. Finally someone came with a litter, and with that they could carry the general at a better pace. Suddenly, from the road behind them, there came a storm of fire. They pressed on until one of the litter bearers was hit, and then they had to put Jackson down until the fire slackened. The canister sparked and flashed as it struck rocks in the roadway.

For better shelter they resumed their awkward march in the woods bordering the road. One of the bearers stumbled over a root or a vine and Jackson was spilled out of the litter, falling directly on his wounded arm. "For the first time he groaned, and groaned piteously," wrote one of the bearers. "He must have suffered excruciating agonies."

At last, after about half a mile, the litter party met Dr. Hunter McGuire, the corps's medical director, with an ambulance. "I am badly injured, Doctor," Jackson said. "I fear I am dying." McGuire administered whiskey and morphine, then supervised placing the general in the ambulance. Torches were procured and the way cleared, and the ambulance proceeded carefully over the rough road westward to the newly established II Corps field hospital at Wilderness Tavern.

One of the casualties of the Federal barrage was A. P. Hill, struck across the back of the legs by a shell fragment. Unable to walk or ride, Hill sent for the only major general now left with the corps, Jeb Stuart, to take over the command. Stuart was at the rear and would be some time arriving; until then Jackson's army was leaderless. The word was quietly passed to stand down. The great Chancellorsville flank attack was over.

✦

SHORTLY AFTER ELEVEN O'CLOCK, some two hours after he was wounded, Stonewall Jackson was gently placed on a cot at the field hospital at Wilderness Tavern. He was in shock and weak from hemorrhaging; the fall from the litter had reopened the wound. Dr. McGuire administered more whiskey as a stimulant and covered the general warmly and let him rest. Gradually his pulse strengthened until by 2:00 A.M. McGuire felt he was strong enough to undergo examination and treatment. The doctor explained to Jackson that his wound appeared serious enough that it might require amputation. "Yes, certainly, Doctor McGuire," the general said. "Do for me whatever you think right."

Chloroform was administered, and after confirming that the humerus in the left arm was shattered, Dr. McGuire performed a standard circular operation to amputate the arm two inches below the shoulder. (The Reverend B. T. Lacy would supervise the burial of the amputated arm in the family graveyard at Ellwood, the nearby home of Lacy's brother.)

Half an hour after the operation, Jackson was awakened and given half a pint of coffee. "Very good; refreshing," he said. An hour later Major Pendleton of his staff arrived, sent by Jeb Stuart to ask the general "what his dispositions and plans were." Jackson seemed to rouse himself to concentrate on the matter. "His eye flashed its old fire," Dr. McGuire wrote—but it was only for a moment. Then Jackson fell back and said to Pendleton, "I don't know, I can't tell. Say to General Stuart that he must do what he thinks best."

Meanwhile, Captain Wilbourn was reporting on events to General Lee. It was 3:00 A.M. on May 3 when he reached Lee's bivouac close by the Orange Plank Road east of Chancellorsville. "After telling of the fight & victory," Wilbourn wrote, "I told him Gen. J. was wounded, describing the wound &c when he said, 'Thank God it is not worse. God be praised that he is yet alive.' He then asked me some questions about the fight & said, 'Captain, any victory is dearly bought that deprives us of the services of Jackson even temporarily.'"

Wilbourn went on to say that A. P. Hill was also wounded and that Jeb Stuart had been sent for to take the command. After questioning the captain closely about the position of Jackson's forces, Lee roused his staff officers for orders. Wilbourn heard him announce, "We must press these people right away."

✦

STONEWALL JACKSON'S FLANK ATTACK DID NOT, of course, by itself decide the Battle of Chancellorsville. Yet it proved the decisive event of that bloody struggle. Fighting Joe Hooker could not—or would not—ever regain the initiative that Jackson's march wrenched from him.

On May 3 there was a savage battle for the Chancellorsville crossroads as Stuart drove Jackson's troops repeatedly against the Yankee lines until finally he broke them and reunited his force with Lee's. Hooker fell back northward and entrenched himself in a salient enclosing his Rappahannock bridges. He had staked much that day on seeing Lee attacked from the rear by John Sedgwick's corps, advancing from the Fredericksburg bridgehead. Sedgwick, however, was halted a few miles short of his target, and by day's end Lee was in firm control of events.

Hooker's grand plan of campaign had now fallen to pieces, but he had bound himself to it and seemed incapable of changing with events. It was as if Jackson's surprise thrust had paralyzed his mental processes. (Hooker's mental processes were not helped by the severe concussion he suffered in the May 3 fighting when a Rebel cannonball splintered a pillar on the Chancellor house and hurled it against him.) He stood stubbornly behind his defenses, waiting for his cavalry raiders under George Stoneman to sever Lee's railroad lifeline, as ordered; surely Lee would break off and retreat once his supplies were cut off. But Stoneman, the most bumbling of any of Hooker's generals, made a dismal failure of his raid.

Lee turned on Sedgwick's corps on May 4 and drove it back across the river. With that, with his plan in shambles, seeing no profit in renewing the battle, and with no new ideas, Hooker ordered a withdrawal. By May 6 the Army of the Potomac was back on the north bank of the Rappahannock, and Lee could declare victory—surely the most hard-won and most unexpected victory of his career.

During the fighting on May 4, Stonewall Jackson was transported by ambulance in a daylong journey from Wilderness Tavern to Guiney's Station, on the railroad below Fredericksburg, so that he might recuperate in a safer environment. He was placed in the estate-office building on the property of Thomas Chandler. In these first days after the surgery he seemed to be progressing normally, but then he began to have symptoms of what Dr. McGuire recognized as pneumonia. Effective treatment of pneumonia was beyond the skills of 1860s medicine.

Slowly, steadily, the general's life ebbed. By May 10 it was certain this would be his last day. It was Sunday, and he expressed his hope of dying on a Sunday. During periods of delirium brought on by the drugs sedating his pain, he spoke of his past battles and battlefields. At the end, in midafternoon, he was heard to say, "Pass the infantry to the front . . ." Then he was silent, and then came the famous last words, spoken clearly and peacefully: "Let us cross over the river, and rest under the shade of the trees."

THE ANTAGONISTS OF LITTLE ROUND TOP

THE VICTOR

GIDEON ROSE

and

THE OTHER MAN

GLENN W. LaFANTASIE

The postmortems of Gettysburg, that central battle of American history, have focused mostly on the events of the final afternoon of July 3, 1863. But had it not been for a lesser, but equally violent, struggle a day earlier at Little Round Top, there might have been no need for Pickett's Charge with its more than 7,000 casualties. Little Round Top, then a bare, boulder-choked eminence about 200 feet high, gave the side that held it a virtually unobstructed view of the entire battlefield and controlled Cemetery Ridge to the North, where the Union army was arrayed. If Confederate batteries had been established on its summit, they could have enfiladed the Union line, forcing a retirement and handing the victory to Lee. But they did not reach that point and the Southern High Water Mark would have to have been reached elsewhere.

The two essays that follow tell the story of Little Round Top from the point of view of the opposing leaders, Joshua Lawrence Chamberlain, the college professor from Maine, and William C. Oates, the former frontier brawler turned respectable lawyer from Alabama. Talk about the *Rashomon* effect: Except for the outcome, their experiences, and those of the men who fought under them, could not have been more different. But taken together these pieces memorably record the stresses men undergo in battle, and the parts delay, fatigue, confusion, and (in the case of the Confederates) thirst can play. Or command decision. The holding of

Little Round Top may have come down to an amateur soldier's desperate but wise gamble when his Down East volunteers ran out of ammunition and his line seemed ready to crumble.

Gideon Rose works for the Council on Foreign Relations in New York City.
Glenn W. LaFantasie, who has taught Civil War history at Gettysburg College, lives in the Blue Ridge Mountains of Virginia. He is working on a book about Little Round Top.

THE VICTOR

GIDEON ROSE

AS BULLETS FLEW through the woods on Little Round Top, Colonel Joshua Lawrence Chamberlain considered his limited options. In front of him the Confederates kept coming—his troops had beaten off several charges already, and bodies lay up and down the rocky slope. To his right the rest of the brigade was also under attack. To his left had been empty ground, but now shots were coming from there, too. He had detached a company to patrol those woods hours earlier, but had not heard from them since. Just a few minutes ago, to protect against a flanking attack, he had extended the left of his line back at an angle. But this exposed his position, and the two-thirds of his men who were left had no ammunition.

The brigade commander's orders had been simple: "This is the left of the Union line. You understand. You are to hold this ground at all costs!" If Chamberlain retreated, the Confederates would roll up Cemetery Ridge, and Gettysburg would be lost. Another charge was brewing down below, and with bayonets alone his troops couldn't resist it. Suddenly he knew what he had to do. When a lieutenant asked permission to rescue some wounded in front of the line, the colonel's answer surprised him: Take position with your troops first—the 20th Maine is attacking!

At the next command, Chamberlain's bent-back left line swung down the slope, men screaming with rifles held high. Then the rest of the regiment joined in, moving together "like a great gate upon a post." The surprised Confederates at the bottom of the hill wavered, then broke when shots rang out from behind them too—the lost company had finally reappeared. The charge turned into a rout, and Cemetery Ridge was secure. Chamberlain became one of the finest infantry commanders of the Civil War, rising to major general by its end, but he won his Congressional Medal of Honor for saving the day at Little Round Top.

✦

ONE YEAR EARLIER, Chamberlain was teaching college freshmen how to write. At thirty-three he seemed successful and content, a licensed preacher living a sober and respectable existence in a small New England town. His faculty colleagues didn't want him to volunteer, because he might hurt himself; besides, his leaving would shift the balance of departmental politics. Other successful Civil War generals may have emerged from prewar obscurity, but none made as strange a journey in as short a time.

Chamberlain was born in 1828 in Brewer, Maine, the eldest son of a middle-class farmer. His father sent Lawrence, as his family called him, to a military academy and wanted him to go on to West Point, but influenced by his mother's religiosity the boy opted instead for the ministry, and chose Bowdoin. At college he won several prizes, taught Sunday school, led a choir, and fell in love with the minister's daughter. He followed college with a seminary. An oration he gave, however, pleased the Bowdoin faculty so much that they offered an instructorship in logic and natural theology, so in 1855 he took his degree from the seminary, married, and began teaching. By 1861 he was a professor of rhetoric and modern languages.

But something inside him gnawed. The would-be missionary soon tired of being a junior faculty member at a small college, especially when the material taught was so dull and the work was such drudgery—in one year alone he had to grade 1,100 written themes. Chamberlain would write to his wife during the war, "I have my cares and vexations, but let me say that no danger and hardship ever makes me wish to get back to that college life again . . . Why I would spend my whole life in campaigning, rather than endure that again."

Reading about the early Union defeats, he chafed at the bit. In 1862, perhaps to deflect his militaristic intentions, the college granted him a two-year leave of absence to study in Europe. He accepted, went straight to the governor's office, and volunteered his services for the war effort. A well-respected professor, he was offered a colonelcy and command of a new regiment; he modestly took the position of lieutenant colonel instead. In early August, within two weeks of the start of his leave, Joshua Lawrence Chamberlain was on his way to a new career.

He found himself second-in-command of the 20th Regiment Infantry, Maine Volunteers—almost 1,000 New England farmers and laborers who had signed up for the Union, adventure, or the bounty. These proud Yankees were unused to military discipline; upbraided for his poor hygiene at a medical inspection, one private shot back that he thought it "cussed mean business to go around and peek in other folks' ears."

Chamberlain's superior was Adelbert Ames, wounded in 1861 at Bull Run (for which he, too, would receive a Medal of Honor). Together they enforced order, but much of Chamberlain's time went into teaching himself soldiering. He wrote to his wife, "I *study*, I tell you, every military work I can find . . . I am bound to understand *every thing*. And I want you to send my 'Jomini, Art of War.' . . . The Col. and I are going to read it."

By September, the 20th Maine had arrived in Washington, where it was assigned to the 3rd Brigade, 1st Division, V Corps of George McClellan's Army of the Potomac. Within days the regiment was moving toward Antietam. Held in reserve during the battle itself, it saw some action afterward, and Chamberlain had the first of many horses shot out from under him.

Early in December the army's new commander, Ambrose Burnside, launched a drive to Richmond, but it was stopped by Robert E. Lee's Army of Northern Virginia on the fortified heights beyond Fredericksburg. Furious but futile Union assaults on December 13 gained nothing but casualties; moving forward in late afternoon, the V Corps passed endless lines of stretcher-bearers going the opposite way. The 20th Maine had time only to make a short rush before darkness fell, then dug in on the front line.

Six months out of academia, Chamberlain spent a cold, gruesome night: "For myself it seemed best to bestow my body between two dead men among the many left there by earlier assaults, and to draw another crosswise for a pillow out of the trampled, blood-soaked sod, pulling the flap of his coat over my face to fend off the chilling winds, and still more chilling, the deep, many-voiced moan that overspread the field . . ." When the Confederates counterattacked in the morning, the Maine troops used corpses as protection, and beat the attackers back.

Two days later the Union forces retreated. On the far side of the river the V Corps commander, Fighting Joe Hooker, rode past Chamberlain and called out, "You've had a hard chance, Colonel; I am glad to see you out of it!" Tired and slightly wounded, he replied, "It was chance, General; not much intelligent design there!" Hooker said, "God knows I did not put you in!" to which Chamberlain shouted, "That was the trouble, General! You should have put us in. We were handed in piecemeal, on toasting forks." Luckily for him, a shocked Hooker ignored this breach of military etiquette and just rode on.

Soon Burnside followed McClellan out the door, and Hooker became the army's new head. In winter quarters the troops faced drill, boredom, and lice. Eventually a late spring campaign began, which would end in another Union disaster, at Chancellorsville. On the eve of the battle, however, the 20th Maine was vaccinated for smallpox. In the primitive medical conditions a hundred men came down with the disease, and the regiment was quarantined in the rear. Ames and Chamberlain both finagled their way into battle anyhow, and for their efforts were promoted, with Chamberlain becoming a full colonel and getting command of the regiment.

One of his first duties was to quell a mutiny. To fill out the 20th Maine's ranks, headquarters had transferred 120 men from a disbanding regiment. These soldiers had inadvertently signed three-year contracts instead of two-year ones; they tried to go home with their fellows, but were marched instead in an ugly mood to the 20th Maine. Chamberlain's orders were to shoot them if they continued to resist, but he was loath to do it. Instead he gave them food and removed their guards. Then, speaking to them as men instead of criminals, he offered a choice: If they would join his ranks, he would see that they were treated well, but like any other soldiers in a top fighting unit. Chamberlain had not been a professor of rhetoric for nothing—all but six of the mutineers accepted the deal.

Within days the soldiers heard a flurry of rumors, and then confirmation: Lee's army was no longer in front of them across the Rappahannock, but invading the North again. The Army of the Potomac followed. At the end of June, Hooker resigned and George Gordon Meade took over the command; by this point the jaded men of the 20th Maine hardly cared.

✦

GETTYSBURG STARTED BY ACCIDENT. Beforehand, both armies were largely blind. J. E. B. Stuart's cavalry, supposed to provide Lee with precise information on the Federals, had broken contact when its impulsive commander decided to ride around the whole Union force. Meade, appointed four days before the two sides met and still trying to learn the details of command, was little better off. When forward elements of the two armies bumped into each other outside a strategic crossroads, reinforcements were called in, and one of the most important battles in history began.

On the morning of July 1, Confederate troops tried to enter the town of Gettysburg, Pennsylvania, to capture a supply of shoes. They were met by two brigades of Union cavalry whose commander had noted the value of the cross-roads, and by early afternoon almost 50,000 troops were involved on both sides. Eventually the Confederates broke the Union right, forcing a retreat through the town to Cemetery Hill on the south. While up to this point the Southerners were triumphant, Lee knew that further progress would be tough if the Union soldiers could fortify their positions. He instructed Richard Ewell to attack with his corps, "if practicable"; Ewell demurred, pleading his troops' weariness, and by nightfall Union reinforcements had arrived and dug in.

By dawn on July 2, the two armies faced each other on parallel ridges south of town. The Confederates occupied Gettysburg itself and Seminary Ridge. The Union position opposite curled around Culp's Hill and Cemetery Hill on top and stretched two miles down Cemetery Ridge. The line ended in a pair of hills separated by a depression. The near one, Little Round Top, was a couple of hundred feet high, while the far one, Big Round Top, was higher, steeper, and thick with timber. As far as Meade knew, his troops were arrayed along the line in good defensive positions, and he awaited the Confederate attack. But in fact, around midday Dan Sickles, the impulsive commander of the III Corps on the Union left, had moved his position about a half mile forward, disconnecting it from the rest of the army and leaving the Round Tops undefended.

Lee had pondered his situation overnight. He wanted to attack, but the Union right seemed strongly defended and the Confederate troops there were tired, so he decided to press forward on the Union left with James Longstreet's fresh corps. By midafternoon these troops ran into Sickles's men. Scouts sent south and east reported nobody there, and Longstreet's divisional commanders argued passionately for a flanking movement like the one Longstreet himself actually favored. But Lee had made his intentions clear, so Longstreet began a frontal attack at about 4:00 P.M.

At first the Confederates gained ground, especially to the south. The 15th Alabama on the right of the Confederate line pushed a battalion of Union sharpshooters back and occupied Big Round Top, where they stopped for a rest and a water break in the sweltering heat. But the water carriers, dispatched earlier, never arrived—they had been captured—and both the delay and the thirst were crucial during the ensuing battle. By the time the Southerners moved against the smaller hill across the way, Union troops had suddenly materialized, and the advance was checked.

What had happened was this: At around 3:00 P.M. Meade had reconnoitered his position, sending General Gouverneur K. Warren to inspect the southern end. Warren reached Little Round Top around 3:30 P.M., only to find it almost deserted. A junior officer thought some Confederate troops might be nearby, so Warren ordered a gunner near the base of the hill to fire a single shot toward a stand of woods in the west. As the round whistled overhead, hundreds of Longstreet's soldiers turned to follow its flight. When they did so, sunlight glinted off their barrels and bayonets, giving away their presence.

Warren realized that the position was about to be overrun and sent aides to get help; word soon reached the V Corps reserves just coming up from the rear. Colonel Strong Vincent, commanding the lead brigade of the column, heard the message and took it upon himself to occupy Little Round Top. Arriving just minutes before the Confederates, he quickly positioned his four regiments on the western and southern slopes of the hill. At the left end of the Union line, he put Joshua Lawrence Chamberlain and the 20th Maine; Chamberlain's first move was to send a company out to patrol the open woods to his left. Almost immediately the Alabama troops attacked, and the battle for Little Round Top began in earnest.

The first Confederate charges stalled under withering fire; but they kept coming, and soon the ground was covered with bodies. At one point a Union regiment on the right broke, and Vincent was mortally wounded trying to rally them. But once again a reserve unit came up at just the right moment, continuing its journey to the line and through it, crashing into the attackers halfway up the slope. Its colonel, Patrick H. O'Rorke, was killed instantly with many of his men, falling a few feet from Vincent, but the position held, and the Southerners shifted their focus to Chamberlain's side of the hill.

When repeated attacks from three Alabama regiments couldn't push the Maine soldiers back permanently, the Confederates decided to move farther east and roll up the Union flank. It was at this point that Chamberlain refused his line-bending back the left side while keeping his front intact. Although the men had marched over 100 miles in five days, going into battle straight from the road with no rest, the 20th Maine fought furiously. Chamberlain ordered everybody—even the sick, the musicians, and the remaining mutineers—into the line. Two of his brothers were fighting as well; earlier, when a shell flew overhead, he had ordered them to disperse, saying, "Boys, I don't like this. Another such shot might make it hard for mother."

By now the Southerners had pressed even farther east and were enfilading the Maine position. At about 6:30 P.M., realizing he had no ammunition and no choices left, Chamberlain gave the famous order for his men to fix bayonets and charge in a "right wheel," sweeping south and west. Just then the company he had detached earlier, together with some of the sharpshooters who had retreated at the start of the battle, joined in, and the Confederates broke. Participants later recalled only fragments from the passionate confusion of the fighting. At one point in the melee, an Alabamian officer fired his revolver point-blank at Chamberlain with one hand, missed, and then handed his sword over with the other hand. (The colonel kept the man's gun as a souvenir, and hung it in his study after the war.) Because Union troops were on two sides of the Confederates, some men were shot from the front, some from the back, and others simultaneously from both directions.

The 20th Maine began the battle with 28 officers and 358 men. It suffered at least 128 casualties, including 38 killed; Chamberlain was wounded twice. They inflicted at least as much damage on their opponents, in addition to capturing several hundred prisoners from various regiments. But even after their charge there was work to do—Big Round Top was still in enemy hands, and the new brigade commander asked Chamberlain to take it. At about 9:00 P.M.—still without ammunition—the Maine troops crept up the steep hillside in the dark, pushing the Confederates back and taking twenty-five more prisoners. The regiment was finally relieved the next morning and sent to a support position behind the Union line. The bombardment preceding Pickett's Charge kept them awake, but they weren't needed, and so sat out Gettysburg's final, futile act.

✦

MALARIA KEPT CHAMBERLAIN FROM FRONTLINE DUTY during the fall and winter. Nevertheless, when Ulysses S. Grant came in as Meade's superior in 1864 and started a summer campaign, Chamberlain begged for orders, and soon he was commanding a new brigade, created when the V Corps was reorganized. This time Grant was determined to finish off Lee, and the two forces circled around Richmond, fighting as they went. Union troops almost broke through at Petersburg on June 15, but the Confederates rallied. By the time reinforcements arrived, the defenses had stiffened. In a last, desperate attempt to stave off trench warfare, Grant attacked early on the eighteenth.

Chamberlain led a successful charge into the heart of the enemy's position, losing another horse, but he ended up in an exposed salient, facing a boggy plain surrounded by bristling defenses. As he dug in, a runner from headquarters told him to attack again. Chamberlain could hardly believe that such an order would be given, and he immediately wrote back a poignant message explaining the situation and arguing that it was a pointless sacrifice of the men under his command.

But Meade overruled his protest. So Chamberlain formed his troops, walked in front, and gave the order to attack. (He explained later, "It was a case where I felt it my duty to lead the charge in person, and on foot.") The enemy fire was as brutal as he had expected, and men dropped around him. When the color-bearer fell, Chamberlain grabbed the flag himself and kept moving forward. Soon he came to a large patch of swampy ground and realized it had to be bypassed. Since his shouts were lost in the roar, he stopped, turned to face his troops, and pointed a way around with the flag and his saber. While he stood there a bullet entered a hip and passed all the way through his abdomen, forcing him to drop the flag. Thrusting his saber into the dirt and resting on that, he continued to direct the troops. When the last man passed, he crumpled to the ground. Needless to say, the attack failed.

In his memoirs Grant would write: "Chamberlain . . . had several times been recommended for a brigadier-generalcy for gallant and meritorious conduct. On this occasion, however, I promoted him on the spot . . ." It appears to have been one of only two battlefield promotions Grant ever gave. Chamberlain's wounds were so bad that doctors gave up hope and released an obituary to the newspapers, but he simply refused to die.

Wounds and illnesses forced him in and out of hospitals during the rest of 1864, but he was determined to take part in the war's last campaigns. Grant started a final encirclement of Lee in late March 1865. In battles around the Quaker Road and the White Oak Road, Chamberlain led his men to striking successes against several times his numbers. At one point, bloody and mud-spattered, he found himself behind Confederate lines. By feigning a Southern accent he duped a crowd of would-be captors, leading them back into Union lines where they were taken instead. At another point he took a bullet through the chest, bleeding so much that once again someone sent a telegram to the newspapers announcing his death. But like a character in a movie, he recovered consciousness soon after and, minutes later, was back on a horse rallying his men, shouting, "Once more! Try the steel! Hell for ten minutes and we are out of it!" Grant later brevetted him to major general for actions during the campaign.

On April 9, Lee finally submitted to the fate he could no longer forestall. Grant insisted on a formal surrender to a section of his army, and he chose Joshua Lawrence Chamberlain as the man to accept it. Surprised and honored, Chamberlain asked only that, for the ceremony, he command his old troops, the 20th Maine and the 3rd Brigade.

On a gray morning three days later, the soldiers formed in ranks near the McLean House at Appomattox. As General John B. Gordon drew abreast, leading the old Stonewall Brigade at the head of the Confederate column,

Chamberlain broke the silence with an order he had thought over carefully: "Carry arms!" At once his troops shouldered their weapons, giving the martial salute. A startled Gordon recognized the significance of the gesture and ordered his troops to match it. Thus ended the American Civil War, with a show of mutual respect and honor from two of its greatest protagonists.

✦

BY HIS MID-THIRTIES, Chamberlain had two careers behind him; in the next five decades he would add several more. He was offered a Regular Army colonelcy after the war—an outstanding honor for a Volunteer—but had to decline for medical reasons, returning instead to Maine and his students at Bowdoin. As a genuine war hero Chamberlain was a natural political candidate, however, and he allowed his name to be submitted for the Republican gubernatorial nomination. He went on to win four one-year terms handily.

Ultimately, though, Chamberlain did not have the spirit of a politician, and in 1870 he and the party bosses agreed to part company. The next year he accepted an offer to become president of Bowdoin, on condition that he have a free hand with curricular and institutional reforms. These soon put him at the forefront of a nationwide revolution in higher education, which created the modern university system out of a handful of provincial colleges for clergymen. But he may have been too radical locally; the reforms were resisted and eventually overturned. He stepped down as president in 1883; when he retired from teaching two years later due to recurring illness, he had taught every course except mathematics and physical science.

In the final years of the century, Chamberlain decided to try his hand as an entrepreneur, although he never managed to do much better than break even. He served on innumerable charitable and corporate boards and was even president of an art academy. In addition to speaking frequently on the veterans' lecture circuit, he kept exploring new interests during his last years. At seventy he gave a lecture series on European political theorists, and in the same year learned Arabic so he could read the Koran in the original. His history of the last campaigns of the war, *The Passing of the Armies*, is still in print.

In early 1914, weakened by an inflammation of his Petersburg wound, the gallant professor succumbed to pneumonia. His death preceded by a few months the reemergence of trench warfare half a world away. Thousands of mourners crowded the Portland City Hall for his funeral, while admirers from across New England and the nation paid their respects.

Not long before, Chamberlain had visited the Gettysburg battlefield one final time. "I went . . . to stand again upon that crest whose one day's crown of fire has passed into the blazoned coronet of fame; to look again upon the rocks whereon were laid as on the altar the lives of Vincent and O'Rorke." Bronze statues of these other Union colonels who fell during the fighting now adorned Little Round Top, along with one of General Gouverneur K. Warren and monuments to all of their troops. The white-haired old man rested on his cane, gazed over the slopes where so many of his friends and comrades had died, and then slowly walked away.

THE OTHER MAN

GLENN W. LAFANTASIE

WHEN COLONEL JOSHUA L. CHAMBERLAIN and his men of the 20th Maine Regiment fixed bayonets and charged headlong down the rocky slopes of Little Round Top at Gettysburg on July 2, 1863, they propelled themselves into fame and glory. Chamberlain received a Congressional Medal of Honor for saving the Union left flank that day, and the reputation of the 20th Maine soared in the aftermath of its brave assault. The same cannot be said of the Confederate troops and their commander, who were driven off the hillside into the dark vale below and, as fate would have it, into undeserved oblivion as well. No laurels were awarded to the 15th Alabama Infantry for its courageous, and costly, attempt to turn Chamberlain's left; no medals were pinned to the breast of Colonel William C. Oates, who commanded the regiment in battle for the first time.

Overshadowed by the victorious Chamberlain, Oates has become a modern casualty of the fight on Little Round Top, a vanquished foe whose name is rarely mentioned in connection with Chamberlain's. It is true, though, that Oates's name has not been entirely forgotten. Students of the Gettysburg battle and the Confederate side of the war know him well as the author of a massive memoir and history of the 15th Alabama entitled *The War Between the Union and the Confederacy and Its Lost Opportunities,* which was published in 1905. But beyond the footnotes of history, and apart from the standard historical accounts that mention his role on Little Round Top, William Oates remains generally unknown—and certainly unappreciated. His story, however, reveals the spirit and nerve of a remarkable man and officer, a fierce warrior who experienced at Gettysburg both his finest hour and his worst.

✦

WILLIAM CALVIN OATES WAS BORN IN 1833 in the wire-grass section of southeastern Alabama, where the frontier was still untamed and uncivil. He ran away from home when he was sixteen—not because he wanted to, but because the local sheriff issued a warrant for his arrest after he had cracked open a man's skull in a no-holds-barred brawl. For the next few years, Oates wandered through the Gulf States and Texas, sometimes making his money as a house painter and sometimes as a gambler, but barely managing to stay one step ahead of the law. Everywhere, he ran into trouble, mostly because of his uncontrollable, hair-trigger temper.

A giant of a man at six feet two inches, Oates took his fighting seriously. He once boasted that he had assaulted an employer for refusing to pay his wages by holding the man with his left hand while hitting him "eight or nine times with my right fist." Anyone foolish enough to challenge him paid a serious price in cuts and bruises, broken bones, and—Oates's specialty—gouged eyes. There was no denying two simple facts about Oates: He liked to fight, and he was very good at it.

But in Waco, Texas, where he got mixed up with artful gamblers and ruthless outlaws, Oates finally met his match. One day, while passing time in a saloon, he inadvertently offended one of the town's most infamous gunmen, a blackguard who, according to Oates, was "very dangerous" and "half crazy all the time with whiskey and morphine." The man challenged him to a gunfight in the street, and Oates went to his hotel to get his pistol. In his room, he realized this duel with a known killer—a man with notches on his gun—was not a particularly good idea. There was only one way out. He quickly gathered his belongings together and got out of town unseen. It was a prudent retreat.

Not long after leaving Waco, Oates ran into his younger brother, John, who had been sent by their parents to find William and bring him home. The two Oates brothers returned to Alabama, stopping only a few times along the way to play cards and brawl with the losers. William successfully avoided the arrest warrant still pending against him by settling down in the adjacent county. He then underwent a remarkable transformation from rapscallion to respectable citizen, a mystifying metamorphosis that set his life on a new course. Oates never explained why this change in his life came about. It was as if he had experienced a personal great awakening, and perhaps to some extent he had. Since childhood, his goal had always been to become a professional man, to rise above the poverty of his father, and as boys he and his brother John would spend sunny summer afternoons beneath the shade trees near the family cabins pretending to be ministers of the Gospel and leading their imaginary parishioners in soulful prayer and rousing hymn. After his romps and adventures, his wild living and undisciplined ways, he was now ready to return to the track he and John had laid for themselves, and his younger brother may have helped Oates regain the direction and ambition he had cast aside in his teens. The brothers gave up the idea of becoming preachers, but they were determined to make something of themselves.

William Oates went about the task of improving himself in great earnest. By the time he was twenty-five, he had taught school, attended an academy, read law with a prominent firm, passed the bar, and opened his own practice in the quiet crossroads town of Abbeville. (Later John also studied law and became an attorney.) Yet it was the experience of being a "preceptor in the common schools of our country," William Oates said, that had really turned his life around. "I have already learned the difficulties [to] be encountered in eradicating vicious and licentious habits contracted in youth," he declared in an unfinished autobiography written in 1857, "and in securing the harmonious action of the moral and intellectual faculties, principally by endeavoring to produce such effects in my own character, and partly from the many efforts to produce such happy effects in my pupils' thinking." For Oates, self-improvement became his religion and the gospel of his personal awakening.

In Abbeville, the Henry County seat, he became a pillar of the community. Although he opposed secession (after the war, he reversed himself and defended the right of secession), when Alabama left the Union in January 1861, he decided nonetheless to support the Confederacy. When fighting began the following spring, Oates raised a company of volunteers, named it the Henry Pioneers, and was proclaimed captain by the enlisted men. By July, after the first battle of Manassas (Bull Run), the Henry Pioneers had been incorporated as Company G into the 15th Alabama Infantry, and Oates and his men were on their way to reinforce the Confederate army in Virginia.

Over the next two years, as the smoke of war rolled thickly over the landscape of Virginia, the 15th Alabama served well in the cause of the Confederacy, first assigned to George B. Crittenden's brigade, later Isaac Trimble's brigade, in Richard S. Ewell's division, which was attached to Stonewall Jackson's army during the Shenandoah campaign in 1862. Later still, the 15th was transferred to General James Longstreet's corps of the Army of Northern Virginia and placed in Evander M. Law's brigade. The regiment, which gained a good reputation for dependability on the battlefield, saw action in several engagements, including Malvern Hill, Cedar Mountain, Second Manassas,

Sharpsburg (Antietam), and Fredericksburg. Having demonstrated his bravery under fire on several occasions, Oates was appointed colonel of the regiment in May 1863 (with rank to date from April 28, 1863), and a few weeks
later he was leading his battle-hardened men on the dusty march that would
take them to Gettysburg, Pennsylvania.

✦

NOW COLONEL OATES, the former frontier brawler turned Confederate
warrior, stood under the hazy sun at the head of his regiment near the Emmitsburg Road on this hot afternoon of July 2, waiting impatiently for orders
to advance. He and his men were covered in dirt and mud after marching
twenty-eight miles since before dawn with Law's brigade as it moved up with
General John B. Hood's division to form the right flank of Longstreet's long
gray lines south of the town. It was now nearly four o'clock, and the 15th had
been on its feet for more than twelve hours. The men were tired, and they
were very thirsty.

Oates could do nothing about their aching bones, but he tried to take care
of their parched throats by sending off a detail of men to fill the regiment's
canteens in a well to the rear of the brigade. Suddenly the terrible roar of the
Confederate artillery shattered the stillness, and the Union cannon replied by
pouring a shower of iron and lead into the lines of Hood's infantry. Within
minutes the order to advance was heard over the screaming shells, and Law's
brigade stepped forward, an uneven wave of butternut brown. As his lines advanced in quick time, Oates looked around desperately for the water patrol,
which had not yet returned. The detail was nowhere in sight, and it never did
catch up with the regiment—instead it got lost and walked into the Union
lines, where it was captured, Oates later reported, "canteens and all." Years after the battle he remarked, "It would have been infinitely better to have
waited five minutes for those twenty-two men and the canteens of water, but
generals never ask a colonel if his regiment is ready to move."

The 15th Alabama tramped ahead toward an open field near the base of Big
Round Top, the highest elevation on the battlefield. But Oates was actually
operating in the dark, having no idea at all where the brigade was headed or
where it would end up. Only later would he learn that Longstreet's attack was
intended to turn the left flank of General George Gordon Meade's Army of the
Potomac while another of Lee's lieutenants, General Ewell, was expected at
the same time to hammer away at the Federal right flank to the north. Not
everything, however, was going according to plan this day, as Oates and his
men would soon discover for themselves. Ewell had failed to get his own attack going, and the Union commander on the left, General Daniel Sickles,

had inexplicably moved his lines forward, bewildering Longstreet's brigades by putting thousands of blue-clad soldiers where they had no business being—and surprising General Meade as well by exposing the left flank and rear of the Union army. Years later Oates remarked wryly: "Rapid change of conditions in all human affairs bring[s] unexpected results."

And so it was with the 15th Alabama. As the regiment surged ahead through the fields and woods toward Big Round Top, the men began to pick up speed and the officers on horseback had to slow them down, telling them not to rush it. Just before the brigade crossed a meandering stream called Plum Run, the Confederate lines were rearranged by the high command, and the two regiments on the far right—the 44th and the 48th Alabama—were swung in a wide arc to the rear and then to the left, leaving the 15th and the 47th Alabama regiments on the extreme right flank of the assaulting column.

Out of nowhere came General Law riding up to Oates. Law looked younger than his twenty-six years, and certainly not old enough to be commanding a brigade, but looks did not matter at all to Oates, who regarded his brigadier as a "brave man and a good fighter." Law ordered seven companies of the 47th Alabama to stay with the 15th; in the event that the two regiments became separated from the brigade, Oates was to assume overall command. The Alabamians' mission, the general explained, was to work their way around the base of Big Round Top until they reached Little Round Top, the smaller of the two hills on the southern edge of the battlefield, where they were to find the Union left, turn the enemy's flank, and "do all the damage" they possibly could.

As Law galloped off, Oates lost no time obeying his orders, but no sooner had the 15th and the 47th crossed Plum Run than an enemy force—two battalions of the 2nd U.S. Sharpshooters—opened fire on the Alabamians from behind a stone fence at the foot of Big Round Top. Knowing he could not advance and leave these Federals in his rear, Oates called out the command, "Change direction to the right." The 15th and the 47th swung obediently—and impressively—around to face their adversaries in such a show of force that the sharpshooters skedaddled up the western slope of Big Round Top, firing sporadically from behind boulders that Oates said were "thicker than grave stones in a city cemetery." Halfway up the hill, the sharpshooters dispersed and melted into woods.

Rather than return to the base of the hill, as Law's orders required him to do, Oates decided to continue the strenuous climb to the summit, hoping he could root out the sharpshooters and any other Federals who might still be lingering in the vicinity of Big Round Top. The ascent, however, was more than he had bargained for. "Some of my men," he later recalled, "fainted from heat, exhaustion, and thirst." On the hilltop, Oates told his men to rest; meanwhile, he tried to figure out what to do next. Through the foliage of the trees, he could see the tiny houses of Gettysburg in the distance. Closer still, he could see the billowing smoke and hear the thunder of battle rising from Devil's Den and Little Round Top.

As Oates was contemplating his options, Captain Leigh R. Terrell, General Law's assistant adjutant general, bounded up on horseback and demanded to know why Oates had halted his troops. Terrell indignantly told Oates that Law—now in command of the division, since Hood had been wounded—wanted the Alabama regiments "to press on, turn the Union left, and capture Little Round Top, if possible, and lose no time," as Oates later put it. Oates replied that it would make more sense for the regiments to remain on Big Round Top and wait for artillery to be deployed on its summit, thus converting the hill into a veritable Gibraltar. Terrell said Law's orders were specific and he had no authority to change them. Oates simply must obey. With that, Terrell wheeled his horse around and loped down the hill.

Oates, who recognized he had little choice in the matter, quickly got his men to their feet and led them down the northern side of Big Round Top, toward the sound of the guns. As he and his men descended the steep slopes, he spied a park of Federal ordnance wagons behind the Round Tops a few hundred yards to the east, and he detached a full company from the 15th and told it to capture the wagon train. Oates the gambler was taking a risk, a bigger risk in fact than any he had ever taken playing cards in Texas, for this time he was needlessly risking the lives of his men by dividing his command in the face of the enemy.

The Alabamians finally reached the level valley floor between the Round Tops, where the rumble of musketry was getting louder with every step. Cautiously, Oates advanced his line under a dark canopy of trees and through a thick cloud of smoke that hung nearly motionless in the air. The men's thirst was now unbearable; yet they moved on.

Oates did not see the thin blue line of Colonel Chamberlain's 20th Maine, which held the extreme left flank of the Union army, until after he heard the spattering cracks of the enemy's muskets. Then, only forty or fifty steps ahead appeared the smoky shadows of the Maine regiment standing behind a protective ledge of rocks—"a splendid line of natural breastworks," Oates called it, "running about parallel with the front of the Forty-seventh regiment and my four left companies, and then sloping back in front of my center and right at an angle of about thirty-five or forty degrees." Surprised by the volley, which Oates described as "the most destructive fire I ever saw," he halted his men where they stood, grateful they had not broken and run. Then, coolly, he ordered the Alabamians to return fire.

Little Round Top was now all ablaze, from the right of the Confederate line on the southern slope, where the 15th Alabama had encountered the 20th Maine, around to the left flank on the western face of the hill, where other regiments from Hood's division were making their own brave dash to dislodge the Federal brigade of Colonel Strong Vincent from its defensive stronghold—men from Alabama and Texas wrestling desperately among the boulders with men from Michigan, New York, and Pennsylvania.

There was pandemonium all across the hill. Years later, when the soldiers put their memories to paper, many participants told the story of Little Round Top to fit their conceptions of Napoleonic military tactics: individual boxlike regiments confronting enemy units in one-on-one struggles. But the fight for Little Round Top was not that simple. The terrain of the steep hillside, strewn with boulders and crags and crevices, meant that no unit could hold its line together for very long. The attacking Confederates were often separated from their companies and even from their regiments; some regiments overlapped in the assault line without realizing it or wanting to.

On the 15th Alabama's left, the 47th Alabama had drifted toward the west, and it soon found itself confronting the right wing of the 20th Maine, the entire front of the 83rd Pennsylvania, and a few companies of the 44th New York. Not surprisingly, the massed fire from these Union regiments was overwhelming. What happened next is hazy, but it would appear that in the melee the 47th became exposed to a bristling cross fire from the 44th New York. Caught in this sheet of flame, Lieutenant Colonel Michael J. Bulger of the 47th fell seriously wounded, and when he went down the regiment broke and retreated in utter confusion.

With the 47th retreating, Oates kept the 15th's left flank as secure as he could while concentrating on his right, where the Union line was the thinnest. He jumped atop a large boulder and ordered the 15th to "change direction to the left, swing around, and drive the Federals from the ledge of rocks." Not everyone could hear the command over the racket of muskets and the screams of men, but finally his right wing figured out what he wanted done, and the line swung out to do it.

The men of the 15th Alabama charged up the rocky ridge of Little Round Top like devils unleashed from hell. Oates was in front of his men, yelling out commands, waving his pistol to urge the Alabamians forward, taking a moment now and then to get a shot off at the enemy. The 15th succeeded in pushing the 20th Maine back a few paces to another ridge of rock. From its new position, Oates's regiment was able to keep up "a constant flank and cross fire upon the enemy" for about five minutes. In response to this threat, Chamberlain extended his front and then refused his left wing, pulling it back almost perpendicular with his right, although Chamberlain himself confessed that his line resembled more a horseshoe than an angle.

The 20th Maine answered the Alabamians with a heavy fire that Oates said made his line waver "like a man trying to walk against a strong wind." Knowing he must either advance or retreat, Oates ordered his men forward again. Passing through the line and waving his sword, he shouted, "Forward, men, to the ledge!" Up and down the hillside, the lines of the 15th Alabama and the 20th Maine moved back and forth for almost an hour in a macabre dance of death. Five times, Oates reported, the Union soldiers "rallied and charged us, twice coming so near that some of my men had to use the bayonet."

While the two regiments were locked in a death grip on Oates's right, the fighting continued on his left, where now his own flank had become exposed to cross fire from the Pennsylvania and New York regiments that had driven off the 47th. According to Oates's published and unpublished accounts, his Alabamians—despite the withering cross fire—pushed so hard up the hill that they turned Chamberlain's right flank just as the Union colonel was changing his front. Years later Chamberlain denied Oates's statement, claiming his right was well covered by the 83rd Pennsylvania, but it is likely Oates and his men bent back the 20th's line into what one historian, Harry W. Pfanz, calls a "hairpin," rather than the horseshoe Chamberlain described.

In any event, Oates knew that the fight on his left was the very worst his regiment endured on Little Round Top; it was there, he said, that the 15th suffered its greatest losses. "The carnage in the ranks," Oates later remarked, "was appalling." In this hornet's nest, the regiment's officers became easy targets. One captain, Henry C. Brainard, was trying to rally his company when he was hit. "O God! that I could see my mother," he was heard to exclaim, and then he was dead. Lieutenant John A. Oates—William's younger brother, who had found him in the wilds of Texas—rushed to take charge of Brainard's company, but suddenly he was struck by eight balls, and the elder Oates watched helplessly as his brother slumped to the ground. He died twenty-three days later in a Union field hospital. For William Oates, the loss of his brother at Gettysburg was a wound that never healed. "No brothers loved each other better," Oates lamented.

As the casualties mounted on the 15th's left, the situation was hardly any better on the right, where the contest for Little Round Top had become a brutal, hand-to-hand fight. In a fierce encounter, Oates saw a Maine soldier reach for the colors of the 15th Alabama just as a Confederate sergeant "stove his bayonet through the head of the Yankee, who fell dead." Hoping to gain a tactical advantage, Oates sent a contingent of forty or fifty men to enfilade Chamberlain's regiment from the right, but the men from Maine would not let their line be turned.

It was now about 6:45 P.M., and the shadows on the hillside of Little Round Top were lengthening. Oates realized that with each passing minute his position was becoming more untenable. He heard a report that Federal infantry was closing in on his right flank and his rear, and he was convinced— although he was probably mistaken—that "some dismounted cavalry were closing the only avenue of escape on my left rear." He began to feel like Captain Nolan at Balaklava. Caught in this tightening vise, Oates ordered his command "to face and fire in both directions," front and rear. "While one man was shot in the face," Oates recalled, "his right-hand or left-hand comrade was shot in the side or back. Some were struck simultaneously with two or three balls from different directions." The blood, he said, "stood in puddles in some places on the rocks." And then he was told that the regiment's ammunition was running low.

Two of his captains ran through the hail of bullets to suggest it was time to withdraw. Oates was determined to hold on. "We will sell out as dearly as possible," he told the officers before sending them back to their companies. But as the bullets whistled in every direction, and as his men kept failing, Oates reconsidered the plight of his suffering command. He decided they must retreat, for they really had no other choice. Quickly he sent word through the ranks that on his signal the men should begin withdrawing. "We would not try to retreat in order," Oates later explained, "but every one should run in the direction from whence we came"—Big Round Top and the relative safety of its summit. It was the right decision, not unlike the time in Texas when he discerned that it would be better to retreat than to face an enemy simply for the sake of pride.

But fate was about to intervene. At precisely the same moment that Oates called out his command to retreat, Chamberlain ordered his men to fix bayonets and charge down the bloody slope into the stunned Alabamians, who were at once thrown off balance by the force and momentum of this astounding assault. Watching this flood tide roll toward them, the men of the 15th Alabama panicked. "We ran like a herd of wild cattle," Oates admitted after the battle, although he never acknowledged in public that it was the force of the 20th Maine's great attack—rather than his own decision to retreat—that swept his regiment off the slopes of Little Round Top. As the 15th Alabama bolted down the hill, the company of soldiers sent to capture the wagon train suddenly showed up from its failed mission and were drawn into the stampede of routed Alabamians. Halfway up the northern side of Big Round Top, the company stopped, formed a firing line, and let loose a volley that effectively halted the 20th Maine in its tracks and sent it back into the valley between the Round Tops.

The rest of Oates's men kept running. He could not hold them back. Many Alabamians scattered into the woods and hid behind boulders. Some stopped to help the wounded and were either shot or captured for their efforts. Overcome by the heat and fatigue, and perhaps a little by shock, Oates collapsed during the retreat, and he was carried to the summit of Big Round Top by two "stalwart, powerful men." At the hilltop, where he was revived, he briefly turned command over to a captain. Around sunset, after the fighting near the Round Tops was over, Oates resumed command and led his regiment down to an open field not far from the spot where the brigade had begun its advance earlier that afternoon.

The battle on the Confederate right had ended. It was dark when the 15th Alabama bivouacked for the night, but Oates called the roll anyway. He was shocked to learn the extent of his losses. Of the nearly 500 electives who had marched into battle four or five hours before, only 223 enlisted men and 19 officers answered the roll (although a good number of men who had dropped from exhaustion, sustained minor wounds, or conveniently become lost later rejoined the regiment). In the end, Oates reported that the 15th Alabama had lost seventeen killed, fifty-four wounded, and ninety missing on July 2. It is not clear, however, whether Oates took into account all the casualties he should have, or even had a fair estimate of the size of his regiment before it went into battle. After the war he complained that veterans of the 20th Maine, including Joshua Chamberlain, had exaggerated the number of Alabamians captured on Little Round Top, but it must also be said that his own figure of ninety missing was probably too low. Nevertheless, by any count, the losses of the 15th Alabama were staggering that day. And the reality of those casualties, of the price his regiment had so dearly paid, taught Oates a bitter lesson about war and its futility. In a private letter written in 1898, he acknowledged reluctantly and very honestly: "Had I succeeded in capturing Little Round Top, isolated as I was, I could not have held it [for] ten minutes."

✦

AFTER THE WAR, after the sound of the guns had faded away, William Oates resumed his career as an attorney, and he later achieved prominence as a seven-term U.S. congressman from Alabama and a one-term governor of the state. But for as long as he lived he could not put out of his mind that ghastly day at Gettysburg, the day the rocks and earth were soaked in blood. Often he tried to make some sense out of it all. He never could.

The best he could do was to conclude that Gettysburg and the attack on Little Round Top were lost opportunities that caused not only Lee's defeat in Pennsylvania, but ultimately the fall of the Confederacy as well. If Longstreet had ordered Hood's division to sweep around to the rear of the Round Tops, if artillery had been rushed to the summit of Big Round Top while Oates was there, if Oates's men had not marched so far before the battle, if the advance of Law's brigade had been delayed long enough for Oates's water detail to return, if he had had another full regiment under his command that afternoon, then the Battle of Gettysburg might have become Robert E. Lee's greatest victory—not to mention William C. Oates's moment of personal glory. "It is remarkable," Oates reflected, "how small an occurrence or omission, trivial in itself, often turns the tide of battle, and changes governments and the maps of nations."

PACKS DOWN–CHARGE!
THE FRONTAL ATTACK

PADDY GRIFFITH

The frontal attack, relying on the charge, is the tactical feature we most associate with the Civil War, but increasingly it was becoming a Napoleonic relic—in the words of the British military historian Paddy Griffith, "a horribly dangerous business." As we have seen in earlier accounts of battles like Malvern Hill or Fredericksburg, attackers never even reached the enemy lines. Rarely did a direct infantry assault have brilliant results. There is no better example of success than the charge of Jackson's troops at Chancellorsville; but that was a case in which the concealing woods allowed them, in effect, to ambush the Union right flank.

What actually happened during a charge? How could momentum be maintained? What was the famous "Rebel yell" and how did such carefully orchestrated cheers reinforce shock tactics and dispel "the loneliness of fear"? What was the optimum pace of advance? And most important of all, how did commanders motivate troops to cross the last few vital yards and actually grapple with the enemy?

More often than not, however, the best offense was a good defense.

Paddy Griffith is the author of *Battle Tactics of the Civil War,* from which this article was adapted, and *Battle Tactics on the Western Front.* Formerly a senior lecturer in war studies at the Royal Military Academy at Sandhurst, in England, he is a freelance writer and publisher, specializing in military history.

A MAJOR INFANTRY ATTACK IN THE CIVIL WAR WAS A HORRIBLY dangerous business, just as it had been in Napoleonic times. Troops were often asked to advance in a closely packed formation, under a dense hail of bullets, right up to bayonet range of the enemy. Sometimes the attackers had enough morale to keep plodding forward despite all dangers and losses; sometimes their mere appearance scared off the enemy. But usually they would have an overriding desire to halt and open fire or take cover; their impetus would melt away, and the battle would turn into a bloody but indecisive firefight, often as close as thirty yards.

The problem for tacticians was to find ways to persuade their men to cross the vital, final few yards separating the opposing battle lines. Some means had to be found to give the troops that added little bit of enthusiasm or some other combat edge that could make all the difference.

One solution for an officer was to have his troops ambush the enemy at close range, exploiting covered terrain and shock—as Wellington's infantry had done in the Peninsular War and as Marshal Bugeaud recommended for the French in Algeria in the 1830s and 1840s. Another solution was to exploit darkness or mist, but this often spread as much confusion as it avoided. Many Civil War officers also followed the Napoleonic doctrine of ordering the troops not to stop to fire in an attack—and sometimes not even to load their muskets—although the soldiers usually disregarded such orders and opened fire anyway.

In the end, however, officers were usually left with only the simple and traditional means of accelerating assaults. It was an article of faith that troops committed to a charge should be fresh and well in hand, preferably having eaten not long before. Failure to observe this principle had brought disaster to the British at New Orleans, and it was to bring equal disaster to many a Civil War regiment thrown carelessly into a fight. At Culp's Hill, on the second day of Gettysburg, George H. Steuart's Confederate brigade had been in action for six hours, and had run out of ammunition at least once, when it was asked to make a difficult uphill attack against superior numbers. The attack was made without support from infantry or artillery but under enfilading cannon fire. We can scarcely attribute its failure to recent improvements in musketry; it was due merely to neglect of the most basic rules of warfare. That some attackers came within twenty yards of the enemy line shows what better planning might have achieved.

Another obvious course of action was for an officer to make maximum use of his vocal cords. As Charles E. Davis, historian of the Thirteenth Massachusetts Volunteers, wrote:

> In Battle the order to charge is not given in the placid tones of a Sunday-school teacher, but with vigorous English, well seasoned with oaths, and a request, frequently repeated, to give them that particular province of his Satanic Majesty most dreaded by persons fond of a cold climate.

Modern studies of combat psychology have shown that constant chatter in a fighting unit helps dispel the loneliness of fear and strengthens cohesion. Civil War officers who shouted themselves hoarse in battle were thus doing the right thing, even though the deafening roar of combat might drown them out—and on at least one occasion a regiment made earplugs for themselves to deaden the din.

Nor was it only the officers who were supposed to shout. Whole regiments were encouraged to do so. Everyone yelled, defenders as well as attackers. Davis continued:

> At the same time you are ordered to yell with all the power of your lungs. It is possible that this idea may be of great advantage in forcing some of the heroic blood of the body into the lower extremities. Whatever may be the reason, it was certainly a very effective means of drowning the disagreeable yell of the enemy.

The above may be termed "defensive" use of yelling, to help one's regiment remember its identity. "Offensive" use could be still more effective, as a weapon to chase off the enemy. John J. Pullen says in *The Twentieth Maine* (one of the best military books ever written) that in the Wilderness battle "the yellers could not be seen, and a company could make itself sound like a regiment if it shouted loud enough. Men spoke later of various units on both sides being 'yelled' out of their positions."

At Malvern Hill the Confederate orders were to "Charge with a yell" if the enemy started to break, and this was fairly standard practice in the assault. The "Rebel yell" became famous and feared, with its ululating wolf-howl "ow-ow-ow-ow" running back and forth along the Confederate battle line. Every other type of yell also created an impression just as shattering as a volley held to close range or a silent onset of determined men. Whether it was a demure New England cheer, a Hoosier yell, an Indian war whoop, a Texas war whoop, a "regular Mississippi yell," or "Three times three for Tennessee" did not matter; the effect was the same. Wellington's men had used carefully timed cheering as a part of their shock tactics fifty years earlier, and it became yet another part of Napoleonic warfare that was carried over into the Civil War.

Another way to speed an attack was simply to lighten the men's load. Infantry on campaign had to carry on their backs everything they needed to live and fight, so it was hardly surprising if they found their loads heavy and cumbersome. On many occasions units were ordered *en masse* to deposit their baggage either before entering battle or, more heroically, before launching into some especially daring venture once battle had been joined. "Packs down—charge!" was almost as stirring a cry to the weary warrior as the more conventional "Fix bayonets—charge!" and certainly signaled an even more serious intention. To throw down one's pack, especially if no arrangements had been made for guarding or recovering it, was equivalent to instant destitution for the soldier. Only the most complete victory could make good the loss, so troops could be expected to fight with the reckless abandon of those who have nothing further to lose. Only the most careful timing of the order to discard packs—neither too wastefully early nor too dangerously late—would leave an officer with his full credibility and authority intact among his soldiers.

Related to this subject is the whole question of plunder. Troops could be motivated in the attack by the hope of adding to their possessions by seizing the packs of the enemy. There was more than a grain of truth in General D. H. Hill's anecdote about the wounded Irish soldier at Chickamauga who urged on his companions by shouting, "Charge them, boys! They have chaase [cheese] in their haversacks!"

The packs-down charge was perhaps less common in Napoleon's time than in the Civil War, since the pace of drill maneuvers back then was intended to be slower. In his tactical manual published immediately after the war, however, General Emory Upton confirmed the value of the double-quick time, or jog, of 165–180 paces per minute, as set forth in Colonel William J. Hardee's 1855 *Tactics,* which trained Civil War armies, Southern and Northern. (Hardee's two-volume treatise was basically a translation of the drill procedures, then considered to be at the forefront of tactical thinking, developed by the French *Chasseurs à Pied* in the 1840s.) Upton also accepted that a unit might jog around the battlefield as much as 4,000 paces in twenty-five minutes. On the other hand, he did put in a word of caution, warning that these fast-moving units would be physically and psychologically fragile, and that colonels should be wary of accelerating the gait until the enemy was close, since cohesion and *esprit de corps* might otherwise be lost.

At Gettysburg, General John Hood's troops found that their attempt to double forward 400 yards on a hot day left them exhausted for the fighting at the far end. At Seven Pines, the Seventeenth Virginia doubled a mile and a half to the battlefield, regrouped to draw breath behind a woodpile, then made a charge. Whether it was because the men were still winded or because fugitives had retired through the ranks, the attack dissolved in confusion. A few weeks later at Frayser's Farm, the same regiment was warned not to double forward until the enemy was in sight, but it did so anyway while there was still almost a mile to cross. The result was once again a shambles. Presumably it was something like this that led Sergeant Hamlin Coe of the Nineteenth Michigan to make a startling comment about an action at Adairsville in 1864: "Although our regiment was broken and in disorder, they charged like tigers." Under the circumstances, one would have expected the men to break and run like frightened rabbits.

The basic contradiction between charging at speed and charging in compact formation was never widely understood in the Civil War, any more than it had been in the *Chasseurs à Pied.* Units that tried to go too fast tended to fall apart, while units that marched forward sedately in closed ranks had all too many opportunities to stop, open fire, and lose their impetus. This had already been a universal problem in Napoleonic times, and was again to be one in the European wars of the mid–nineteenth century—and as late as the Franco-Prussian War. Only a few troops managed to find a reliable solution, and fewer still could make the packs-down, double-quick charge work. In the Civil War there was too little training to acclimatize regiments in the correct use of the enormously demanding *Chasseur* tactics. That would have required going through the motions many times over in the roughest country available, something that was not possible. So the armies either improvised ineffectively or reverted to outmoded tactics. The result, in the event, was that the majority of infantry attacks came to grief.

IV

LEADERS AND
THEIR BATTLES

WHEN LEE WAS MORTAL

GARY W. GALLAGHER

Of the U.S. Army officers who resigned in 1861 to join the Confederacy, Robert E. Lee seemed the South's stellar acquisition. A hero of the Mexican War and the popular former superintendent of the Military Academy at West Point, Lee had been offered the command of the principal United States military force. He turned it down in April and headed back to his home state, Virginia. (What if he had accepted General Winfield Scott's offer? It's one of the genuine might-have-beens of American history. The Union army in the East could have used a man like Lee, and didn't find him until Grant came on the scene.) Lee, as Gary W. Gallagher tells us, turned out to be something of a disappointment at first. To be sure, he handled with great skill the organization of Virginia's troops and the digging of fortifications. But he saw the forces he raised led by other men. His attempt to keep western Virginia, which was predominantly Unionist, in the Confederate fold was a failure. The area seceded from the secessionists, becoming the new state of West Virginia—a loss for which Lee was partly blamed. (Lee, who presided over so many costly battles later on, was derided in the Southern press for "his extreme tenderness of blood.")

The spring of 1862 found Lee acting as the chief military advisor to Jefferson Davis, a futureless desk job. But then, on May 31, at the Battle of Seven Pines, just five miles from Richmond, the Confederate commander, Joseph E. Johnston, was wounded, and the man known as "old-stick-in-the-mud" or "the king of spades" took his place. Three months later Lee's troops were marching into Maryland; Britain and France were seriously considering the recognition of the Confederacy. "The Civil War," Gallagher writes, "witnessed no other strategic reorientation of such magnitude in so short a time." What had happened to bring on the change in Lee? And why would a man who was so recently on a fast track to nowhere soon become idolized, the irreproachably saintlike figure who was the Confederacy's George Washington?

Gary W. Gallagher is the John L. Nau III professor of history at the University of Virginia. His books include *The Confederate War, Lee and His Generals in War and Memory,* and a collection by leading Civil War historians that he edited, *The Richmond Campaign of 1862: The Peninsula and the Seven Days,* and *The Myth of the Lost Cause and Civil War History* (with Alan T. Nolan).

JAMES LONGSTREET'S FIRST CORPS AWAITED AN IMPORTANT review on the afternoon of April 29, 1864. Recently returned to the Army of Northern Virginia after several trying months in north Georgia and east Tennessee, Longstreet's soldiers stood in ranks extending across a broad field partially framed by oak woods. About one o'clock, under a bright spring sun that played off the burnished metal of thousands of muskets, music and an artillery salute announced the appearance of Robert E. Lee. The general guided Traveller between a pair of square gateposts and onto the crest of a knoll opposite the waiting infantry. "As he rode up to the colors, and the men caught sight of his well-known figure," reported a witness two days later, "a wild and prolonged cheer, fraught with a feeling that thrilled all hearts, ran along the lines and rose to the heavens. Hats were thrown high, and many persons became almost frantic with emotion." Longstreet waved his hat enthusiastically, and Lee uncovered his head in restrained acknowledgment of the demonstration. Shouts mingled with tears among the veteran soldiers: "What a noble face and head!" "Our destiny is in his hands!" "He is the best and greatest man on this continent!" An artillerist described a "wave of sentiment . . . [that] seemed to sweep over the field. Each man seemed to feel the bond which held us all to Lee. . . . [T]he effect was that of a military sacrament, in which we pledged anew our lives."

The soldiers at this memorable review—the last ever held by Lee—honored their unspoken pledge during bitter fighting over the next six weeks. They joined the rest of the Army of Northern Virginia to provide Lee with an instrument capable of blocking Ulysses S. Grant's powerful offensive blows. Taking heart from Lee's effective leadership during the Overland campaign, Confederate civilians articulated their own bond with the general. Typical was Catherine Ann Devereux Edmondston, a North Carolinian who followed events in Virginia very closely. "This constant anxiety & watching must tell on our men!" she wrote on June 11, 1864. "How does Gen Lee support it?

God's blessing only & God's strength enables him to bear up under [the strain]. What a position does he occupy—the idol, the point of trust, of confidence & repose of thousands! How nobly has he won the confidence, the admiration of the nation. . . ." Edmondston believed "'Marse Robert' can do any & all things. God grant that he may long be spared to us. He nullifies [Braxton] Bragg, [Robert] Ransom, & a host of other incapables."

The emotional review and Edmondston's comments illuminate Lee's profound impact on the men in his army and on civilians behind the lines. Well before the midpoint of the Civil War, most Confederates looked to him as their greatest hope for winning independence. He and his army came to occupy a position in their fledgling nation much like that of George Washington and the Continental Army during the American Revolution. Repeated disasters in the Western Theater and along the Confederacy's coasts took a toll on Southern morale throughout the war, but news from Virginia provided an effective counterbalance. Thousands of Confederates believed that their struggle for nationhood might succeed so long as Lee and the Army of Northern Virginia remained in the field, an attitude that persisted despite mounting evidence of Northern superiority. As late as mid-March 1865, an astute foreign visitor commented about the degree to which Confederates drew strength from Lee: "*Genl R. E. Lee* . . . [is] the idol of his soldiers & the Hope of His Country," wrote Thomas Conolly, a member of the British parliament: "[T]he prestige which surrounds his person & the almost fanatical belief in his judgement & capacity . . . is the one idea of an entire people. . . ."

How did Lee become such a towering presence in the Confederacy? He had begun the Civil War with a strong reputation. His service in the war with Mexico, as superintendent of West Point, and as a senior cavalry officer in the late 1850s had made him known in many circles. Winfield Scott's lavish praise of Lee's accomplishments in Mexico had been especially noteworthy. When it became known in April 1861 that Lee had resigned his United States commission and would take command of Virginia's state forces, the Richmond *Enquirer* gleefully reported Scott's sorrow at losing Lee's services for the Union cause. Another Virginia newspaper rejoiced that Lee, "the very Flower of the Army," had left his old flag to serve a new one. Confederate citizens emulated their newspapers in noting Scott's discomfort, as when South Carolina diarist Emma Holmes quoted the old general as saying "'that it was better for every officer in the army to die, himself included, than Robert Lee,' on account of his military genius." It would be an exaggeration to say that all Confederates placed Lee first among Southern officers in the spring of 1861, but he was an admired figure from whom much was expected.

This public confidence gave way to doubt and criticism during the initial year of the conflict. Appointed major general in charge of Virginia state forces in late April 1861, Lee spent a feverish six weeks organizing resources to defend the commonwealth's borders. He oversaw mobilization of thousands of volunteers, ordered construction of fortifications at key points, and worked closely with Governor John Letcher in selecting officers to lead Virginia's soldiers. More than 40,000 Virginians were under arms by the end of May, all of whom were transferred to Confederate service on June 8, 1861. A week later, in his last significant action as major general of state forces, Lee submitted to the governor a straightforward document that underscored the impressive results of his labors relating to "the military and naval preparations for the defence of Virginia."

He then embarked on a period of frustration and trial that sent his reputation plummeting to its wartime nadir. He had been appointed a Confederate brigadier general on May 14, and two days later the Confederate Congress had authorized his advancement to the rank of full general (he would not be confirmed in the latter rank until August 31, 1861, at which time he became the third-ranking officer in the Confederate army, behind Samuel Cooper and Albert Sidney Johnston). While Lee completed his work as head of Virginia's state forces, the major Confederate field commands in the state had been given to P. G. T. Beauregard at Manassas Junction and to Joseph E. Johnston in the lower Shenandoah Valley. Lee remained in Richmond, functioning as a military adviser to President Jefferson Davis and chafing at his relative inactivity. "My movements are very uncertain," he confessed to his wife on June 24, "& I wish to take the field as soon as certain arrangements can be made." That wish went unfulfilled for another month. Lee watched from a distance as Confederate soldiers under Beauregard and Johnston—a quarter of whom he had raised and equipped—won the battle of First Manassas on July 21.

On July 28, before public celebration over First Manassas had abated, Davis directed Lee to coordinate the defense of western Virginia. This initial assignment to the field would yield only bitter fruit, a result Lee may have anticipated as he left Richmond for a region of rugged mountains and predominantly Unionist sentiment. Federals had established a menacing presence west of Staunton at Cheat Mountain; farther southwest, they also stood poised to move through the Kanawha Valley, whence they might threaten the vital Virginia & Tennessee Railroad and its connection to lines that ran to Knoxville and Chattanooga. Unfortunately for Lee, three inept officers held the major Confederate commands in this theater. Henry A. Wise and John B. Floyd, former governors of Virginia who loathed each other and bickered openly, stood guard in the Kanawha region, and William W. Loring, who considered Lee an unwelcome interloper, led Confederate troops at Huntersville near Cheat Mountain. Of the three, only Loring, who had fought in the war with Mexico and risen to the rank of colonel in the Mounted Rifles, possessed significant antebellum military experience.

Lee formulated a strategy—undoubtedly too optimistic considering the situation and personalities involved—to push the Federals westward toward, and perhaps beyond, the Ohio River. Following a small Union victory on September 10 at Carnifix Ferry, he sought to overpower Federals at Cheat Mountain through an offensive involving five separate columns. Awful weather and poor subordinate leadership, together with Lee's overly complex plan, contributed to an ignominious failure on September 11–15. Lee next tried to fashion a victory in the Kanawha Valley, shifting Loring's troops to that region and striving to get Wise and Floyd to cooperate. Miserable roads, squabbling generals, and short supplies frustrated his hopes to attack the Federals under William S. Rosecrans, and Rosecrans proved unwilling to be the aggressor when Lee took up a defensive position at Sewell Mountain in late September and early October. Later in October, Lee ordered Loring's troops back to Huntersville and placed the units remaining in the Kanawha Valley in defensive positions. On October 30, he departed from western Virginia, a majority of whose citizens had voted six days earlier to separate from Virginia and create a new state loyal to the Union.

The campaign in western Virginia seriously diminished Lee's military stature. The best that could be said of his effort was that he had prevented further Union advances in the region and protected the railroads. Such meager accomplishment failed to satisfy fellow Confederates who yearned for decisive success on the battlefield. The influential Richmond newspaper editor Edward A. Pollard spoke for many others in terming the Lee of September and October 1861 "a general who had never fought a battle . . . and whose extreme tenderness of blood induced him to depend exclusively upon the resources of strategy, to essay the achievement of victories without the cost of life." The diarist Mary Boykin Chesnut noted tersely that "Floyd and Lee can not yet cope with [Jacob D.] Cox and Rosecrans."

Another difficult assignment quickly came Lee's way. In early November, Davis named him head of a new department encompassing the coastal regions of South Carolina, Georgia, and eastern Florida. Lee arrived in Charleston on November 7, the same day a Union fleet captured the forts protecting the entrance to Port Royal Sound. Aware that the enemy had won a strategic foothold between Charleston and Savannah and possessed the means to land troops at numerous other points, he spent the next four months constructing a viable defensive line along 300 miles of the Atlantic coast. Little applauded at the time, this work showed Lee's engineering and administrative skills and rendered the area much better able to resist Northern military power over the next three years. He focused on improving fortifications at Charleston and Savannah, placing obstructions in navigable rivers that Northern gunboats could use to penetrate inland, and concentrating troops at strategic places along the railroad that ran between Charleston and Savannah.

A telegram from Jefferson Davis on March 2, 1862, ended Lee's stay along the coast. The president wished to see him as soon as possible, and on March 5, Lee departed for Richmond. Eight days later General Orders No. 14 announced Lee's assignment "to duty at the seat of government," where, under Davis's direction, he would manage "the conduct of military operations in the armies of the Confederacy." It was another desk job. This time Lee would serve as principal military adviser to the president, and he informed Mrs. Lee that he saw no "pleasure or advantage in the duties."

Growing Federal threats in Virginia occupied much of Lee's attention. By mid-April, George B. McClellan had placed his 120,000-man Army of the Potomac on the Peninsula below Richmond. Another 60,000 Federals spread in a great arc from Fredericksburg, across the Shenandoah Valley, and into the Alleghenies. At Lee's suggestion, Davis instructed Joseph Johnston, who had abandoned the lines at Manassas in early March, to concentrate his strength opposite McClellan on the Peninsula. Lee then formulated a strategic offensive that would deny McClellan reinforcements from Federal forces north and northwest of Richmond. The execution of this strategy he entrusted to Stonewall Jackson, who responded with his famous Shenandoah Valley campaign of May and June 1862.

✦

MEANWHILE, McClellan's host moved inexorably closer to Richmond. On May 31, Johnston ordered assaults against the Army of the Potomac at Seven Pines, just five miles from the capital, in a battle that continued the next day. Indecisive tactically, this fighting nevertheless ranked with the most important engagements of the war because Johnston received a disabling wound on the first day of battle. Command of the army passed briefly to Gustavus W. Smith, the senior officer on the field, and then, on June 1, to Robert E. Lee.

Davis's choice of Lee to lead the Army of Northern Virginia provoked a mixed reaction. Some Confederates had wondered why Lee was denied a major field command for so long. Typical of this group was J. T. Hubard, one of Stonewall Jackson's soldiers, who had commented in late February 1862 about the "singular manner in which Virginia's favorite general—Robert E. Lee has been kept in the back-ground, and obscure men put forward." Others inside and outside the army, including many who had thrilled at the news of Lee's decision to accept Virginia's major generalcy in April 1861, took a far dimmer view. The campaign in western Virginia and Lee's service along the south Atlantic coast had created an impression that Lee lacked aggressiveness, preferred entrenching to fighting, and otherwise failed to meet popular conceptions of a strong general. Catherine Edmondston, who later would become a staunch admirer, voiced a common attitude about Lee in early June: "I do not much like him," she wrote, "he 'falls back' too much. He failed in Western Va owing, it was said, to the weather, has done little in the eyes of outsiders in SC. His nickname last summer was 'old-stick-in-the-mud.'"

Two members of Lee's staff recalled in postwar memoirs the hostility with which many Confederates viewed Lee at this juncture. Armistead L. Long, Lee's military secretary, described the winter of 1861–62 as a time when the "press and public were clamorous against" his chief. Edward Porter Alexander, who served as chief of ordnance in the Army of Northern Virginia from June through early November 1862, wrote that at the time Lee took command "some of the newspapers—particularly the Richmond *Examiner*—pitched into him with extraordinary virulence, evidently trying to break him down with the troops & to force the president to remove him." The *Examiner,* Alexander recalled, claimed that "henceforth our army would never be allowed to fight" but only to dig, "spades & shovels being the only implements Gen. Lee knew anything about."

Lee confronted a daunting military situation in June 1862. Unremitting defeat had stalked Confederate efforts in the Western Theater earlier that year. Forts Henry and Donelson had fallen, and a failed Southern counteroffensive at Shiloh left Federals in control of much of middle Tennessee. The loss of New Orleans in late April and of Memphis in early June added to an already grim picture. In the East, McClellan's army closed in on Richmond. Although Stonewall Jackson's small victories in the Shenandoah Valley in May and early June lifted Southern spirits, the loss of Richmond, coming on the heels of so much defeat west of the Appalachians, almost certainly would have doomed the Confederacy.

Apart from the purely military dimension of his challenge, Lee had to deal with a restive Confederate populace. No analysis of his generalship should overlook the importance of civilian expectations. He served in a democracy at war, and the key to success lay in providing the type of leadership that would generate continued popular support for the national military effort. Since the victory at First Manassas in July 1861, it seemed to many Confederate citizens that their armies had forged a record dominated by defeat and retreat. The result had been an erosion of public morale and an almost frantic yearning for offensive victories. During the winter of 1861–62, a Richmond newspaper alluded to a "public mind . . . restless, and anxious to be relieved by some decisive action that shall have a positive influence in the progress of the war." In late June 1862, from his vantage point as a clerk who served successive Confederate secretaries of war, John B. Jones observed that whenever combat ceased "our people have fits of gloom and despondency; but when they snuff battle in the breeze, they are animated with confidence."

Lee certainly understood the state of Confederate morale as he prepared to face McClellan outside Richmond. As he would do in all of his subsequent campaigns, Lee sought to take the initiative, to force the enemy to react to his moves rather than waiting to respond to theirs. Aggressive by nature, he must have known that his preference for dictating the action suited his people's temperament. This was not a "new" Lee. Public criticism over the preceding months had not persuaded him that he must alter his strategic and tactical outlook. He had tried to be aggressive in western Virginia; along the south Atlantic coast, he had lacked the resources and opportunities to strike the enemy. His new position and the strategic situation he inherited presented him a chance to fly his true colors as a field commander.

Lee used his first three weeks in charge of the Army of Northern Virginia to plan an offensive against McClellan in the Seven Days' Battles, a decision that saved Richmond and laid the groundwork for his later fame. When Confederates attacked at Mechanicsville on June 26, McClellan lay at Richmond's doorstep with more than 100,000 men, and Irvin McDowell menaced the capital with another 30,000 Federals at Fredericksburg. Additional Union forces lurked in the Shenandoah Valley and northern Virginia. Three months later, Lee's bold strategic and tactical movements had won victories at the Seven Days' and Second Manassas and had pushed the military frontier in the Eastern theater across the Potomac River into western Maryland. The Civil War witnessed no other strategic reorientation of such magnitude in so short a time.

The battle of Antietam ended this spectacular run in mid-September, but Lee already had accomplished immense good in the crucial area of civilian morale. Confederates exulted at the thought of an aggressive posture that took the war to the enemy. A newspaper in Macon, Georgia, struck a familiar note in applauding Lee's decision to march northward toward Maryland: "Having in this war exercised Christian forbearance to its utmost extent, by acting on the defensive, it will now be gratifying to all to see . . . the war carried upon the soil of those barbarians who have so long been robbing and murdering our quiet and unoffending citizens."

Lee's offensive successes swept away doubts about his willingness to take chances and thrust his name to the front rank of Southern generals. The *Richmond Dispatch* commented about how quickly the transformation occurred. "The rise which this officer has suddenly taken in the public confidence is without precedent," noted the paper eight days after the conclusion of the Seven Days': "At the commencement of the war he enjoyed the highest reputation of any officer on the continent. But the fame was considerably damaged by the result of his campaign in the mountains." Formerly among Lee's critics, the *Dispatch* now suggested that Lee had lacked only a proper opportunity to demonstrate his "great abilities." An officer writing as Lee's army prepared to cross the Potomac in September 1862 supported the *Dispatch*'s view. "We have the best leader in the Civilized world," affirmed Colonel Robert H. Jones of the 22nd Georgia Infantry. "Genl Lee stands now above all Genls in Modern History. Our men will follow him to the end."

Shortly after the war, the editor Edward A. Pollard of the *Richmond Examiner* accurately summed up the impact of the Seven Days' on Lee's reputation. Among Southerners hoping for offensive action in late 1861, stated the acerbic journalist, Lee may have been "the most unpopular commander of equal rank in the Confederate service." But his aggressive performance during the Seven Days' set him on a course where he "might have had the Dictatorship of the entire Southern Confederacy, if he had but crooked his finger to accept it."

The stunning victory at Chancellorsville in May 1863 confirmed Lee as the leading military hero of the Confederacy. In the scrub forest of Spotsylvania County he wrested the initiative from Joseph Hooker and sent the far more powerful Federal army reeling back across the Rappahannock River. The manner in which Lee accomplished this latest triumph thrilled the Confederacy. Dividing his army no fewer than three times, he had marched rapidly, attacked furiously, and vanquished a posturing foe. "Thus ends the career of Gen. Hooker, who, a week ago, was at the head of an army of 150,000 men, perfect in drill, discipline, and all the muniments of war," wrote a Richmonder. "He came a confident invader against Gen. Lee at the head of 65,000 'butternuts,' as our honest poor-clad defenders were called, and we see the result! An active campaign of less than a week, and Hooker is hurled back in disgrace and irreparable disaster!" Lee turned north after Chancellorsville and by the anniversary of his initial offensive at Mechanicsville had placed 75,000 Confederates on Pennsylvania soil.

The soldiers who marched toward Pennsylvania in June 1863 possessed an almost breathtaking confidence that Lee would lead them to victory no matter what the odds. The preceding fall, straggling and desertion had plagued the Confederate invading force as it marched into Maryland. At that stage of the conflict, the army had not yet become *Lee's* army. By the summer of 1863 it had. Comments from Lieutenant Lewis Battle on the eve of the Pennsylvania invasion typified feeling toward Lee within the Army of Northern Virginia. Battle's 37th North Carolina Infantry gave three cheers for the general after he reviewed A. P. Hill's Light Division in the wake of Chancellorsville; Lee heard the cheering and turned his attention to the men. "It is impossible for me to describe the emotions of my heart as the old silver-headed hero acknowledged the salute by taking off his hat," wrote the awestruck Lieutenant Battle of the moment when Lee and the Carolinians faced each other. "In fact, I was almost too proud for the occasion for I could not open my mouth to give vent to the emotions that were struggling within."

The Army of Northern Virginia's second campaign across the Potomac ended in bloody defeat at Gettysburg, but that should not obscure the magnitude of what Lee had accomplished during just one year in field command. His fabled string of victories had won the hearts of his soldiers, inspirited the Confederate people, and transformed him and his army into the nascent republic's principal rallying point. As the war dragged on with increasing fury and Confederates inside and outside the army coped with escalating material hardship, Lee and his men functioned as the most important national institution.

Even after the bloody tactical repulse at Gettysburg (which was not perceived as a decisive defeat by most Confederates), faith in Lee among his soldiers and behind the lines remained largely unshaken. The victories of 1862–63, though admittedly won at a horrific price in Southern blood, had created an expectation of success in the Virginia theater that sustained Confederate morale for nearly two more years. Letters and diaries from the period 1864–65 frequently described Lee as invincible and expressed faith in his ability to withstand anything the North could throw against him. Thus could a soldier serving in the Western theater comment in May 1864—nearly a year after Gettysburg—that he had "complete faith in General Lee, who has never been known to suffer defeat, and probably never will."

In early 1864, Brigadier General Clement A. Evans of Georgia penned an evaluation that captured succinctly the relationship between Lee and his soldiers. "General Robt. E. Lee is regarded by his army as nearest approaching the character of the great & good Washington than any man living," recorded Evans in his diary. "He is the only man living in whom they would unreservedly trust all power for the preservation of their independence." Although

Stonewall Jackson had inspired enthusiastic support, the "love and reverence for Lee is a far deeper and more general feeling." Lee had no enemies, believed Evans, adding that "all his actions are so exalted that mirth at his expense is never known."

Lee's widely admired personal qualities supplemented success on the battlefield to nourish his fame and popularity among Confederates. He seemed to embody all the virtues cherished by antebellum white Southerners. His generosity toward others impressed countless observers, as did his modesty. "The General is affable, polite, and unassuming," remarked a man who traveled with Lee on a train in early 1864, "and shares the discomforts of a crowded railroad coach with ordinary travelers." Pronouncing Lee "as unostentatious . . . in dress as he is in manners," this individual noted that the Confederacy's greatest hero wore "a Colonel's coat, (three stars without the wreath) a good deal faded, blue pantaloons, high top boots, blue cloth talma, and a high felt hat without adornment save a small cord around the crown." Surgeon Samuel Merrifield Bemiss had touched on similar qualities in describing Lee to his children in April 1863. "I wish you all could see him—" wrote Bemiss, "he is so noble a specimen of [a man] . . . always polite and agreeable, and thinking less of himself than he ought to, and thinking indeed of nothing, hoping and praying for nothing but the success of our cause and the return of blessed peace."

On the battlefield, Lee exhibited the type of unquestioned courage Confederates demanded from their most popular leaders. Francis Lawley of *The Times* of London remarked about this quality as exhibited during the battle of Fredericksburg on December 13, 1862. Describing how Lee rode slowly along the Southern lines, Lawley told his readers, "It would be presumptuous [of] me to say one word in commendation of the serenity, or, if I may so express it, the unconscious dignity of General Lee's courage, when he is under fire." The Englishman believed Lee's behavior in combat reflected his personality away from the fray: "No one who sees and knows his demeanour in ordinary life would expect anything else from one so calm, so undemonstrative and unassuming." It seemed to Lawley, who borrowed a phrase from a biographer of Britain's Lord Raglan, that Lee possessed an "antique heroism" that bespoke utter disregard for danger.

✦

PERHAPS MOST reassuring to Confederates who believed themselves to be God's chosen people was Lee's deep Christian faith. The *Richmond Dispatch* developed this theme in late April 1861, asserting that a "more heroic Christian, noble soldier and gentleman could not be found." Lee seemed the perfect instrument to translate Confederate desires for independence into reality. "Of him it was said before his appointment, and of him it may well be said," stated the *Dispatch*, "no man is superior in all that constitutes the soldier and the gentleman—no man more worthy to head our forces and lead our army. . . . His reputation, his acknowledged ability, his chivalric character, his probity, honor, and—may we add to his eternal praise—his Christian life and conduct make his very name a 'tower of strength.'"

Lee also looked the part of a general. Mary Chesnut called him "the picture of a soldier." A. J. L. Fremantle, the British officer whose remarkable diary of his journey through the Confederacy has captivated generations of readers, confirmed Mrs. Chesnut's observation in a detailed description of Lee during the Gettysburg campaign. "General Lee is, almost without exception, the handsomest man of his age I ever saw," wrote Fremantle on June 30, 1863. "He is fifty-six years old, tall, broad-shouldered, very well made, well set up—a thorough soldier in appearance; and his manners are most courteous and full of dignity. He is a perfect gentleman in every respect." Fremantle also thought Traveller a handsome mount, and man and horse together cut a striking figure. Beyond appearances, Fremantle noted that Lee had "none of the small vices, such as smoking, drinking, chewing, or swearing, and his bitterest enemy never accused him of any of the greater ones." The Britisher could imagine no man who had so few enemies or enjoyed such universal esteem: "Throughout the South, all agree in pronouncing him to be as near perfection as a man can be."

Lee's gentlemanly demeanor and Christianity—both of which contributed to his Confederate fame—would have counted for little if he had not achieved success on the battlefield. It is important to reiterate that he often pursued the strategic and tactical offensive to fashion his victories in 1862–63. This element of his leadership frequently has been questioned by historians because it led to a high number of Southern casualties. Critics such as J. F. C. Fuller, Russell F. Weigley, Grady McWhiney, Thomas L. Connelly, and Alan T. Nolan have discussed at length how Lee's famous victories (as well as some of his defeats) drained Confederate manpower, suggesting that perhaps the South would have been better off with a less pugnacious officer in charge of the Army of Northern Virginia. In a passage representative of this interpretive tradition, Nolan described Lee's generalship as dominated by "devotion to the offensive, daring, combativeness, audacity, eagerness to attack, taking the initiative." Lee's leadership sometimes resulted in flashy victories, conceded Nolan, but the attendant casualties "unilaterally accomplished the destruction of his force" and thus hurt the Confederacy.

There can be no denying that the Army of Northern Virginia paid a fright-ful butcher's bill. In 1862, more than 20 percent of its soldiers became casu-alties during the Seven Days' Battles, and roughly the same proportion fell at both Second Manassas and Antietam. During the first half of 1863, the army lost 20 percent again at Chancellorsville and suffered even more at Gettys-burg. In all, more than 90,000 Confederates fell between Lee's assumption of command and the end of 1863.

Did the results justify such horrible attrition? In their determination to paint Lee as overly aggressive, the general's critics have focused on counting strengths and losses; they have been much less interested in trying to assess the impact of Lee's operations on civilian morale. Yet the latter question is the more important one, because only persistent popular will enabled the Con-federacy to maintain its resistance for four long years. With the exception of his seemingly effortless repulse of Ambrose E. Burnside's clumsy assaults at Fredericksburg in December 1862, each of Lee's campaigns between June 1862 and June 1863 conveyed to the Confederate people a sense that their most famous army was taking the war to the enemy rather than simply await-ing the next Federal move. Confederates mourned the army's huge losses but directed remarkably little criticism toward Lee as the officer responsible for the effusion of blood. Even during the protracted defensive fighting of 1864–65, Lee inspirited Confederates because he retained a reputation as an audacious commander who would seize any opportunity to smite the enemy.

Joseph E. Johnston presents an interesting contrast to Lee in this regard. Although respected by most of his soldiers and popular in some civilian quar-ters, Johnston's reputation suffered from a widespread belief that he too often adopted a passive defensive strategy and yielded too much ground without a major struggle. Johnston either misread Confederate expectations or ignored them; the result was sharp criticism of his generalship at crucial points in the war. During his retreat up the Peninsula in the spring of 1862, for example, a young Georgian complained that "General Joseph Johnston, from whom we were led to expect so much, has done little else than *evacuate,* until the very mention of the word sickens one. . . ." Two years later, after Johnston had withdrawn from northern Georgia into the works surrounding Atlanta, a sol-dier in the Army of Tennessee guessed that Jefferson Davis removed the gen-eral in favor of John Bell Hood "for not fighting and [for] allowing the Yanks to penetrate so far into Georgia." Initially a supporter of Johnston, this man thought him "too cautious, . . . not willing to risk a battle until he is satisfied he can whip it." Late in the war, when Johnston had returned to command in the Carolinas, a young South Carolina woman bitterly denounced him: "This arch-retreater will probably retreat till perhaps he retreats to Gen. Lee, who may put a stop to his retrograde movement."

Confederates impatient with strictly defensive campaigns could argue that such operations had exposed vast stretches of territory to the Federals while yielding only the most meager long-term results. Albert Sidney Johnston's position-oriented defense of the Kentucky-Tennessee arena in 1861–62 sacrificed much of Tennessee and witnessed the surrender of approximately 15,000 soldiers at Fort Donelson. The capitulation of 30,000 Confederates at Vicksburg in 1863 capped another defensive disaster, and Joseph Johnston's retreat to Atlanta in 1864 set up a siege that culminated in a landmark victory for William Tecumseh Sherman. Indeed, every major siege of the conflict occurred during campaigns marked by Confederate defensive strategies, and each of them ended in Union triumph. That roster included Petersburg, which concluded as Lee predicted it would in June 1864. "We must destroy this army of Grant's before he gets to [the] James River," Lee told Jubal Early just after the battle of Cold Harbor: "If he gets there, it will become a siege, and then it will be a mere question of time."

Nor did defensive campaigns conserve Confederate manpower. Leaving aside surrendered troops (a factor that increased dramatically the defender's losses), strategically defensive campaigns during the Civil War often consumed manpower at a rate roughly equal to that experienced by the side on the offensive. Defenders almost always reached a point where they had to attack in order to avoid a siege, and these tactical counteroffensives often took place amid circumstances unfavorable for the attackers. Joseph Johnston's retreat toward Richmond in May 1862 illustrates this phenomenon. In the delaying action at Williamsburg and at Seven Pines, where he became the aggressor because the Army of the Potomac had nearly reached Richmond, Johnston's casualties approached 8,000 compared to fewer than 7,500 for the Federals. Similarly, during May 1864, as Johnston fell back across north Georgia toward Atlanta, Confederates lost 10,000 men to Sherman's 11,768. Even during Lee's masterful defensive campaign from the Rapidan to the James River, throughout which Confederate soldiers usually fought from behind well-prepared breastworks, the Army of Northern Virginia suffered proportionally heavier losses than Grant's relentlessly aggressive Federals.

Jefferson Davis understood that the Confederacy had received an excellent return on its investment of men and matériel in Lee's generalship. With the celebrated victories of 1862–63 doubtless in mind, the Southern president prophesied just after Gettysburg that Lee's achievements would make him and his army "the subject of history and object of the world's admiration for generations to come." At the time Davis wrote these words, Lee already was the object of his nation's admiration—so much so that his surrender at Appomattox signaled the end of the war to virtually all Confederates (as well as to their Northern opponents). Thousands of Confederate soldiers remained under arms after April 9, 1865, but without Lee and his men in the field there seemed no reason to fight on. "[E]verybody feels ready to give up hope," was a Georgia woman's representative reaction to news of Lee's surrender. "'It is useless to struggle longer,' seems to be the common cry," she noted sadly, "and the poor wounded men go hobbling about the streets with despair on their faces." In Richmond, diarist John R. Jones similarly lamented news from Appomattox. Lee and his army had been "the pride, the hope, the prop of the Confederate cause," remarked an emotional Jones, adding, "All is lost!"

The week after Chancellorsville, the *Lynchburg Virginian* told its readers that "The central figure of this war is, beyond all question, that of Robert E. Lee." Untold thousands of Confederates would have agreed with this statement. They saw in Lee the best qualities of a Christian gentleman, a quiet man who thought first of others and turned his surpassing military gifts to the task of assuring Southern independence. More important, they also saw in him their only reliable source for good news from the battlefield, a daring commander whose strategic and tactical skills wrought splendid offensive victories during his memorable first year in command of the Army of Northern Virginia.

Because they believed in Lee so fervently, the Confederate people resisted long past the point at which they otherwise would have conceded their inability to overcome Northern numbers and power. They evinced an almost mystical faith in their hero's ability to overcome any odds. Interestingly, many Union soldiers took a similar view. As one New Englander wrote just after Appomattox, "To tell the truth, we none of us realize even yet that he has actually surrendered." This officer "had a sort of impression that we should fight him all our lives. He was like a ghost to children, something that haunted us so long that we could not realize that he and his army were really out of existence to us."

More than once Lee wrenched the Confederacy toward its goal of independence. During the heady summer and early autumn of 1862, he crafted victories that impressed Europe and sent ripples of doubt and despair through the North. The following spring his success at Chancellorsville, building on the earlier Confederate victory at Fredericksburg, bolstered Northern antiwar sentiment and set the stage for a potentially crucial clash in Pennsylvania: a Confederate victory at Gettysburg might have vastly complicated Abraham Lincoln's task of maintaining Union civilian morale. As late as the summer of

1864, Lee's skillful parrying of Grant's thrusts during the Overland campaign, which resulted in enormous numbers of Union casualties, sent civilian morale in the North plunging to its wartime nadir. Over the course of thirty-four tumultuous months, Lee and his army created a record of military accomplishment amid difficult circumstances to which white Southerners looked with pride both during and after the war. That scores of thousands of their young men had perished to forge that record scarcely affected Lee's reputation. He had given Confederates hope during the war, and after Appomattox he and his army stood as their primary symbol of honorable striving in a cause that had suffered utter defeat.

Lee's return to Richmond on April 15, 1865, afforded an opportunity for fellow citizens to exhibit their affection and respect for him. The depth of feeling among the men, women, and children who welcomed the vanquished warrior recalled that of the First Corps veterans who had greeted him at the review held almost exactly one year earlier. Under a threatening sky that already had drenched the area with intermittently heavy rains, Lee crossed the James River on a Federal pontoon bridge, made his way past the gutted remains of buildings consumed by raging fires along the riverfront a few days earlier, and slowly approached the house at 707 East Franklin Street where Mrs. Lee had lived since January 1864. A resident of Manchester, a small town opposite Richmond on the right bank of the James, described a somewhat bedraggled figure: "[H]is garments were worn in the service and stained with travel; his hat was slouched and spattered with mud." News of the old hero's arrival swept through the fallen capital. "He came unattended, save by his staff—came without notice; and without parade," wrote one woman, "but he could not come unobserved; as soon as his approach was whispered, a crowd gathered in his path, not boisterously, but respectfully, and increasing rapidly as he advanced to his home on Franklin Street. . . ." Outside the house, noted another witness, "crowds gathered around his door to receive him, and cheered him loudly as he approached."

Upon reaching his destination, Lee reined in Traveller and dismounted into a sea of outstretched arms and searching faces. People crowded toward him to shake his hand, simply to touch him, or to voice their admiration. He moved slowly through the throng before turning, near the front door, to bow in recognition of this emotional demonstration. He then, noted Richmonder Sallie Brock Putnam, "passed into his house, and thus withdrew from public observation." His war was over. Ahead lay an uncertain future for Lee—and canonization by white Southerners whose cause he had so ably defended.

THE STONEWALL ENIGMA

JOHN BOWERS

Robert E. Lee's career may have been predictable; that of his right-hand man was not. Thomas J. Jackson, better known as "Stonewall" for his stand at the Battle of Bull Run, was the outstanding tactical commander of the Civil War. Lee knew that the South could never win a war fought mainly on the defensive, and he needed an offensive specialist. He found one in Jackson. Stonewall, as John Bowers writes here, "was a general who won." His credo was simple, and he rarely deviated from it: "Always mystify, mislead, and surprise." He was a man who seemingly came out of nowhere. Born on what was, in 1824, the western frontier of Virginia—Clarksburg is now part of West Virginia—Jackson had gone to West Point, mainly because it offered a free education. Yet another young officer who performed with distinction in the Mexican War and then disappeared into obscurity, Jackson became a professor of artillery tactics and natural philosophy at the Virginia Military Institute, a man known chiefly for his eccentricity and his indifferent teaching. He was not a natural gentleman like Lee or J. E. B. Stuart. He was devout to a fault, and disliked making war or killing on Sundays, though he was sometimes forced to do the latter. This unlikely man also liked novels and art, and had wandered through Europe.

In times of crisis democracy has a way (at least it once did) of creating unexpected leaders, people who, like characters from popular fiction, emerge to take sudden charge when others, supposedly more competent, have failed. That was particularly true of the Civil War. Except for Lee, whose reputation was already well-established, almost all of its major leaders seemed to have experienced periods of debilitating eclipse. Bowers frames a question that may have no definite answer: "How could Jackson—a valetudinarian in peacetime, a poor excuse for a professor at VMI—have proved to be one of the most daring, brilliant, and tenacious generals on the battlefield?" Had he lived through even one more battle—

which would have been Gettysburg—the rest of the Civil War might have been very different. For the South, Jackson, as much as Lee, was the indispensable man. After Chancellorsville there was only one.

John Bowers, whose grandfather fought on the Confederate side at Chickamauga, is the author of *Stonewall Jackson: Portrait of a Soldier* and *The Battles for Chattanooga.*

IN STENDHAL'S NOVEL *THE CHARTERHOUSE OF PARMA,* THE young hero, Fabrizio, is caught smack-dab in the middle of the Battle of Waterloo. Fabrizio is bright, romantic, fearless, and ready to experience the glories of war to the fullest. He expects to find what he has read in books. Yet when he looks around, through the dust and din, the plundering, the screams and carnage, the sutlers plying their trade amid the slaughter, he can find no rational master plan for it at all. It seems like pure chaos.

So it is with battles. So it appears to most men in combat. The Duke of Wellington himself remarked that battles, indeed history itself, can never be recalled with total accuracy. He compared the past to a grand ball, where everyone in attendance sees small moments only. After a battle, though, when tolls have been taken, when ground has been won or lost, there is the victor and there is the vanquished. If anyone should have an inkling of what is happening in a battle—or what is supposed to be happening—it is the commanding general of each side. We say Napoleon lost Waterloo—not General Ney, nor anyone else.

We say that Stonewall Jackson won at Chancellorsville; Robert E. Lee lost at Gettysburg (for which he more than once took complete blame); Ulysses S. Grant won at Fort Donelson; and so on. It is the commanding general who finally, everlastingly, takes the blame or the credit for how a battle turns out.

Thomas Jonathan ("Stonewall") Jackson was a general who won. He commanded the First Virginia Brigade and then the Army of the Valley, CSA, in the Civil War. He took a ragtag band of Virginia farmers, some of his former students at the Virginia Military Institute, a preacher or two, and some neighbors from Lexington and fought off a superiorly numbered Northern army that intended to invade his home state.

He fought in the snow, on scorching summer days, in a blinding rainstorm, up a mountain and down in valleys, through a cornfield and by split-rail fences. He knew how to win. He had an abundant amount of ambition (which he usually kept out of sight), and the hallmark of his character was his single-mindedness in impressing his will upon and prevailing over whatever task and enemy faced him.

He was not a "parade general" like General George ("Little Mac") McClellan, commander of the Army of the Potomac. Little Mac loved spit and polish, the plumes that bobbed in review, the snapping of bright flags. Jackson, who was at West Point with McClellan, went off to fight the Yankees wearing the frayed blue tunic of a VMI professor and the kepi of a student. He preferred the kepi pulled forward until it nearly covered his eyes and he had to tilt his head upward to see. Jackson never tried to look like a general.

Once, a captured Washington official, his leg broken, lay in agony on a stretcher near some Confederate troops. He noticed a strange figure by a campfire. A surgeon said proudly that this was Stonewall, Old Jack. The official asked to be carried nearer so he might have a look. It was a once-in-a-lifetime chance. He saw an improbable figure in a grimy uniform, enormous mud-caked boots, and tiny, filthy cap. The man was hunkered down over the fire like a lowly private. The official looked in wonder, then disbelief, and finally disenchantment. He moaned, "O my God! Lay me down again!"

Word of his reaction spread, and Jackson's troops picked up on the prisoner's words. From that time on, during long forced marches, extra picket duty, and needless drilling, the cry went out: "O my God! Lay me down again!" But though Jackson might push them beyond their endurance, goad them to superhuman efforts, in the end he saved them from the worst of all fates for a soldier: He saved them from defeat; he saved their blood. They held him in absolute affection.

Jackson's most important characteristic was his taciturnity. He did not believe in divulging secrets. At times this trait—and some others—reached a level of obsession. Rarely did he discuss his military credo, his general military thinking. Early in the war he told John Imboden, a comrade-in-arms:

> There are two things never to be lost sight of by a military commander, always mystify, mislead, and surprise the enemy if possible; and when you strike and overcome him, never let up in your pursuit as long as your men have strength to follow; for an army routed, if hotly pursued, becomes panic stricken, and can then be destroyed by half their number. The other rule is, never fight against heavy odds, if by any possible maneuvering you can hurl

your own force on only a part, and that the weakest part, of your enemy and crush it. Such tactics will win every time, and a small army may thus destroy a large one in detail, and repeated victory will make it invincible.

This straightforward prescription, with its emphasis on action, was vintage Jackson. He never intellectualized the game of war, never thought in terms of a grand design. He simply acted in response to whatever immediately faced him.

✦

JACKSON CAME BY his famous nickname, and his reputation for tenacity, at First Manassas. When the Federal assault there reached its apogee on that hot, dusty afternoon of July 21, 1861, only Jackson and his First Virginia Brigade stood on Henry House Hill to bar a complete breakthrough by the Union soldiers. If Irvin McDowell's Federals had broken through, the path to Richmond would have lain open and a rebel rout surely would have ensued. The rebellion, the whole new Confederacy, stood poised at this moment on the brink of near-annihilation. Rebel troops were falling back and were close to panic when General Barnard Bee called to his South Carolinian troops, "Look! There's Jackson standing like a stone wall! Rally behind the Virginians!"

Jackson and his men stood—then charged with an eerie, high-pitched shrieking and whooping that later came to be known as the Rebel Yell. The hapless Federals under McDowell began moving back, finally breaking into a run. Jackson wanted to chase them all the way to Washington, thirty miles down the pike. At this early moment in the war, he wanted to descend on the now-defenseless U.S. capital and capture it. Make a bold move, do the completely unexpected, risk all when he knew he had the enemy at his mercy, when its ranks were demoralized and fatigued and beaten.

That was typical Jackson. Press your advantage for all it was worth! He thought he could end the war—surely come by a peace settlement, which was the aim of this new Confederacy. But everyone else, from Jefferson Davis on down, said the battle was over, that everyone needed to rest and regroup for tomorrow. A golden opportunity for the Confederacy thus slipped away.

✦

REMEMBER, THOUGH, that Jackson was defending his own soil. He was thinking up ways and means to block the invader. History shows that the one being invaded can be a fierce foe, inspired to come up with unorthodox and imaginative tactics. Jackson was defending Virginia against a horde of "foreigners" from New York, Ohio, and Massachusetts. He did invade Maryland later, and while there took part in what has been called "America's bloodiest day," the battle of Sharpsburg at Antietam Creek. When it was over, he took his battered and weary troops back across the Potomac onto the home soil of Virginia.

Jackson was not a natural leader. He was not a Napoleon who could digest reams of intelligence and carry in his head a political program for settlement after the furor of battle ended. In fact, Jackson probably had what we now call a learning disability. At West Point he could learn only by rote—by memorizing his lessons word for word. He was not intuitive and could never afford to cut corners. He had to try ten times harder than the next cadet just to keep up. But he had in spades what far more gifted students lacked—the discipline to impress his will and to succeed. He lay by the fire at West Point, long after taps, studying by the flickering light while his fellow cadets slept. He was near the bottom of his class his first year, and near the top his last (not far behind George McClellan, who placed second in Jackson's class of 1846).

At VMI Professor Jackson taught artillery tactics and natural philosophy in much the same way as he had studied—by rote. He would memorize wide swatches of text and then lecture his fidgety students with it. If a student broke in with a question, Jackson stopped, rewound his recitation to the preceding paragraph, then continued, word for word. He seemed incapable of answering questions off the cuff or indulging in personal anecdotes to enliven his speeches.

Jackson suffered from a variety of physical complaints. His main source of discomfort was his digestive tract, possibly as a result of a spastic colon. His suffering was genuine, but from all accounts of those close to him, he was also a hypochondriac. When he had time and leisure he tended to suffer a great deal more than when he was under extreme pressure and danger—to wit, in war. In peacetime he sought out doctor after doctor, cure after cure.

Many of Jackson's famed eccentricities stem from his unorthodox schemes to ward off these maladies. He would raise an arm suddenly in the midst of conversation and keep it raised as if he were a schoolboy trying to be called on in class. He once explained this habit to a friend: "One of my legs is bigger than the other—and so is this arm. I raise my arm so the blood will run back in my body and lighten its load. It's a cure I've discovered. Everything has a cure."

He sat bolt upright in chairs, not allowing his spine to touch the back. Only that way, he believed, would his internal organs rest properly one on top of another and his digestion be accomplished. He thought he was losing his hearing; that his eyesight was failing. He used a chloroform liniment and swallowed a concoction containing ammonia. He sought out health spas, "taking the waters" at popular resorts, North and South.

When war came in 1861, his ailments and complaints suddenly vanished. He caught what little sleep he needed outdoors on the ground, his saddle for a headrest. He once rode fifty miles, without stopping, to have an hour's secret meeting with Lee, then fifty miles back to his troops, going over twenty-four hours without sleep. It was not unusual for him to place such demands on his 165-pound body then, and he made equally stringent demands on his men.

Jackson had the stomach, metaphorically speaking, for taking extremely harsh measures to enforce his brand of discipline. He brought court-martial charges against General Richard B. Garnett and relieved him of command because Garnett had ordered his greatly outnumbered brigade to retreat at the Battle of Kernstown. No matter that Garnett's troops probably would have been slaughtered if they had stayed in place; no matter that, by retreating, Garnett could cover other Confederate troops and allow their escape from ambush. They had retreated, Jackson hadn't authorized it, and no one on earth could placate Stonewall's anger. It shone with a fine blue light.

Garnett was a noble and brave officer, scion of landed Tidewater gentry. Still smarting from the humiliation of Jackson's charges even after Jackson's death at Chancellorsville, Garnett volunteered to join a doomed charge at Gettysburg and met his death.

✦

THE QUESTION IS, how could Jackson—a valetudinarian in peacetime, a poor excuse for a professor at VMI—have proved to be one of the most daring, brilliant, and tenacious of generals on the battlefield? In searching for the key to personality it is necessary to consider the beginning. Jackson was not of landed Southern gentry; he was not accustomed to tall, cool drinks on a veranda. Tom Jackson was born in what is now Clarksburg, West Virginia, and grew up on what was then the Western frontier. The last buffalo in his region was killed the year of his birth, 1824.

It was Calvinistic country, hardscrabble, and Jackson's life was made even harder by his being orphaned: His father, a lawyer and a veteran of the War of 1812, died when Tom was two; his mother died when he was seven. The boy was shunted among a collection of relatives and then put under the wing of a bachelor uncle, Cummins Jackson, on Cummins's frontier farm, which featured a gristmill and was known as Jackson's Mill.

Cummins Jackson was well over six feet tall, strong as an ox, and had robust appetites. Legend has it that he could pick up a whiskey barrel by himself and let the amber liquid squirt into his mouth. He was known locally as a man who struck sharp deals but was fiercely loyal to friend and family. Throughout his life Tom Jackson showed a tolerance, if not a weakness, for wild, flamboyant characters. He had a softness of heart for Jeb Stuart, and his quartermaster in the Valley Army, John Harman, was a man who swore a blue streak and couldn't be tamed.

The frontier that nurtured Jackson was cruel toward failure and the weak. Only the strong survived. Jackson showed a survivor's instinct throughout his life; but perhaps because he'd been orphaned and displaced, he also showed surprising kindness at times toward those who needed aid. He would quick-march his men thirty miles and then stand guard over them while they slept. He thought nothing of shooting deserters or bringing down brave enemy soldiers who were trying to escape. Yet at West Point he went out of his way to care for cadets who were sick or homesick, and on the streets of Lexington he doffed his hat to passing blacks—a courtesy unheard of in the antebellum South. Deeply sympathetic to the troubles of slaves, he bought the freedom of two and started a "colored" Sunday school in his Lexington Presbyterian Church.

Jackson married twice, both times to women whose fathers were Christian ministers and college presidents. His first wife, Elinor, was the daughter of the Reverend George Junkin, president of Washington College in Lexington (later Washington and Lee); Jackson had done his shy, stiff courting while he himself was a professor at nearby VMI and, marching to his own drummer, as ever, took Elinor's sister along on their honeymoon to Niagara Falls. When Elinor died delivering a stillborn daughter a year later, Jackson became inconsolable, almost suicidal. Only a solitary trip to Europe finally lifted his depression. He kept on close terms with the Junkins for the rest of his life even though several—including Dr. Junkin—fled to the North and joined the Union side.

Jackson's second wife, Mary Anna (known as Anna), was the daughter of the Reverend Robert Hall Morrison, first president of Davidson College. Jackson settled comfortably again into well-regulated domesticity with an overlay of religion. He demanded punctual morning prayers in his home, and in Lexington he was also in the habit of taking a quick cold bath every morning followed by a three- or four-mile walk.

Yet from Anna Morrison Jackson's memoirs and other accounts, we know that Jackson was not the dour Presbyterian some might think. Anna, who is shown as a bright-eyed, dark-haired woman in the few pictures we have of her, could be mischievous with her husband. There was a teasing, bantering, fun-loving side to their marriage. He affectionately called her his *esposa,* a word he had picked up in the Mexican War. She never remarried after he died in 1863, living on in Charlotte, North Carolina, until her death in 1915, and receiving almost daily visits from Confederate veterans who called to pay their respects.

Jackson was as much an enigma in his private life as on the battlefield. His private persona bore no perceptible relation to his reputation in war as a stern, unmerciful foe. Next to Lexington, New York was his favorite city, and before the war he enjoyed dropping in on publishers there and selecting books. He read Melville. On his trip to Europe, he covered a lot of ground, and he brought back many souvenirs. In his Lexington home, preserved today much as it was when he lived in it, there is a doll he purchased in Germany. At a museum in Chancellorsville, there is a well-thumbed map that he used as he sought out Renaissance art in Florence. In civilian life Jackson was receptive to new ideas, particularly those having to do with science. He owned one of the first iron stoves in Lexington.

Jackson was simple and complex by turns, and so were the battles he faced in the Civil War; he brought his genius to bear on all of them. In the winter following Manassas, he fought the Romney campaign in the western Virginia mountains in bone-chilling weather. Horses slid off the side of icy treacherous roads. Wagons stuck. His men suffered frostbite. Still he pressed on. Supporting generals nearly mutinied, and among troops who were serving for the first time under Jackson the cry went up that the man must be mad. How could human beings march in such weather, in such conditions, and, above all, not knowing where they were going or for what purpose?

True to form, Jackson did not divulge his plans: If his troops didn't know what he was up to, surely the enemy never would. He pressed on, sucking lemons, putting his shoulder behind caissons and wagons to free them from mud and snow. He took the strategic hamlet of Romney before the might of the Federal army could get in place there. Federals could well have used Romney as the springboard into Winchester and the whole of the important Shenandoah Valley. Jackson cut them off and served notice by his presence that they had to be mightily concerned with this fidgety and unpredictable commander. They could never overlook him in their strategy—and thus he occupied thousands of Federals who could have been used in McClellan's push on Richmond.

The Valley campaign began on March 23, 1862, with the Battle of Kerns-town, into which Jackson threw some 2,700 Confederates against perhaps 11,000 Federals. Technically he lost (barely)—one of the few fights he ever lost—but as a result Lincoln sent three whole armies after him, 60,000 Union troops. Jackson fought through the Shenandoah in the summer of '62, using lightninglike tactics and completely befuddling his enemy.

Although he was a brilliant tactician and a master of ambush who could seemingly spring from nowhere, Jackson actually had little knowledge of geography and a poor sense of direction or of the lay of the land. In many ways, like many successful people, he was plain lucky. He was particularly lucky to come by one of the greatest mapmakers the Civil War produced—Jedediah Hotchkiss. Hotchkiss was an ex–New Yorker who had fallen under the spell of the Shenandoah on a summer walking tour. He did not believe in the Southern cause, did not believe in slavery, but he believed in supporting the people and land he had become smitten with and he fought for them. When Jackson found out that Hotchkiss was a master cartographer, he put him to work without a pause. It was Hotchkiss who laid out the maps that Jackson followed to surprise his enemy.

In the Mexican War, particularly in the Battle of Chapultepec, Jackson had learned the value of taking the high ground. As a trained artillerist, he also knew the importance of placing heavy guns on an elevated plateau. If he had lived to fight at Gettysburg, no doubt he would have strongly advised against George Pickett's doomed charge of shoulder-to-shoulder infantry against fortified Cemetery Ridge. He himself probably would have found a way to circle behind George Meade and surprise him mightily from the rear.

But of course he did not live to fight in the most critical battle of the war. He died right after his most stunning victory, at the crowning moment of his military career, at Chancellorsville. There he circled around General Joseph Hooker's right flank and launched a surprise attack from the rear.

Hooker, known for good reason as "Fighting Joe," was certain that his defenses were impregnable and was relaxing in the late afternoon on the veranda of Chancellor Mansion, when suddenly a soldier on the road outside cried, "Here they come!"

First came Hooker's own troops, running at full throttle, among them some German mercenaries shouting in broken English that they needed pontoons to cross the river. Behind the blue-clad Federals came in full stride scrawny soldiers in gray—Jackson's troops. Hooker flung himself onto his white steed and rode into the melee, exhorting his men to stand fast and fight, but he changed not one man's mind. The confusion was so complete, the dust and noise and powder smoke so overpowering, that Hooker got swallowed up. Ignored by the onrushing Confederates, he escaped. Jackson, meanwhile, kept pressing toward the ever-receding front. True to his belief in relentless pursuit of a defeated enemy in disarray, he urged his men and officers to cut off escape routes, to press forward—to punish.

It was around nine at night on May 2, 1863, in growing darkness that some of his frontline troops, North Carolinians, mistook him and his party for a Yankee patrol and shot him. Eight days later, on Sunday, May 10, he died quietly, his wife and daughter and a few of his staff beside his bed. Before the end, delirious, he had called out battlefield commands: "Order A. P. Hill to prepare for action! Pass the infantry to the front!" Then a calmness passed over him and he uttered his final, famous words: "Let us cross over the river and rest under the shade of the trees."

Of all those who missed Jackson's presence in battle, Robert E. Lee undoubtedly led the list. Jackson was his right-hand man, the one soldier who could take a general plan of attack and brilliantly devise a method to execute it. No other general worked anywhere near as closely with Lee as Jackson did. The two of them were a perfect symbiosis: Lee, a tidewater patrician with courtly manners and an engineer's mind; and Jackson, the self-made frontiersman who simply willed himself to make up for natural deficiencies. Lee was the only commanding officer with whom Jackson felt totally in tune, with whom he got along.

As a rule, Lee's orders to Jackson were loosely put and circumspectly offered. Jackson would take Lee's vaguely articulated wishes and carry them out with devices of his own making and with his own personal stamp on them. Lee told Jackson early in the war that he wanted him to hold the Shenandoah Valley and keep the Federals' hands tied there. Lee didn't tell him how. It was Jackson who came up with the lightninglike surprise assaults; it was Jackson who pursued crippled and battered enemy troops, inflicting as much damage as possible to make sure they wouldn't attack him the next day.

At heart Jackson was a loner. Only once, at Winchester, did he call his staff to a war council—and he rued the day. On that occasion he had wanted to attack the Union army under General Nathaniel P. Banks, after dark, even though he would have been outnumbered ten to one. His staff, however, advised him to retreat. As he rode out of Winchester, one of the last to leave, he stopped at the top of a hill and turned to look back at the sleepy little Southern hamlet, pinpoints of light showing in a few homes. Dr. Hunter McGuire, his personal physician, stopped beside him. McGuire, who idolized Jackson, later wrote that at that moment Jackson had a look of unholy ambition on his face, which was enough to frighten McGuire. "That is the last council of war I will ever hold!" Jackson said. And it was.

Jackson was rather like a warrior from the Old Testament, a devout Christian who sought mightily to keep the Sabbath holy and to obey the Ten Commandments. A man who didn't even like to mail a letter on Sunday, he was forced to fight some of his major battles on the Sabbath—the Battle of Kernstown, for one—and, of course, the commandment concerning killing had to be overlooked. But in peace and in war, the general did not like to hear the Lord's name taken in vain, and hardly anything pleased him as much as seeing his troops at revival services in the field. Some of his soldiers later confessed that they attended these services simply because they knew it would please Old Jack, not because they felt religious stirrings.

Jackson's life was relatively short. He had been seasoned in the Mexican War, as had Grant, Sherman, and Lee, but unlike them he never lived to become an elder statesman. Because of his dark, full beard and also because of his deep imprint on the Civil War and his reputation as a leader of men, one tends to think of him as older. But in fact Jackson was only thirty-nine when he died, and he fought a young man's war. His stamina, his daring, his uncompromising stances came in part from a young man's makeup. Old men tend to compromise, to delay, to be prudent rather than rash. Not Jackson.

The quality, though, that made Jackson a great general—perhaps the greatest of the Civil War—is an intangible one that defies definition and can't be taught. He personified the word *indomitable.* He would not accept defeat and had a way of coming back, prevailing no matter what was thrown at him. Many of these setbacks would have caused others to lose heart. He came through—despite an apparent learning disability, despite an undermanned army and inferior arms (when bullets ran out, he cried, "Charge them with the bayonet!"), and despite gargantuan demands on his mind and body. When the Battle of Cedar Mountain was being lost, bluecoats storming over Stonewall's regiments in a clatter of musket fire, Jackson himself galloped into the maelstrom, drew his sword, and rallied his retreating troops back into the fight. "Rally, brave men, and press forward! Your general will lead you. Jackson will lead you! Follow me." The tide turned, and Cedar Mountain was won.

In the Seven Days' Battle he suffered what we now might call a nervous breakdown, or shell shock—but somehow, in a near-trance, carried on, though not as the fearsome Jackson he was before, or would be later. He was assigned by Lee's roundabout orders to cross Grapevine Bridge and pursue the Federals. For once, however, he couldn't act. He stared off into space, mumbling. Without his orders and directions, Stonewall's army stalled and the enemy was able to get away. At a camp table, he fell asleep with a biscuit in his mouth.

Without aid from anyone or anything, Jackson willed himself back into the fray. After the Seven Days' he won again at Manassas, invaded Maryland, and gave the South its crowning glory (and final unmistakable victory) at Chancellorsville. Confederate army general Richard Taylor, son of the former U.S. president Zachary Taylor, said the bullet hadn't been molded that would kill Stonewall Jackson. He felt safe around him, for Jackson seemed protected by Providence from the lead and iron that screamed and whined and buzzed around him. Shells would crash into trees and miss Jackson by inches. He was shot in the finger at First Manassas, was thrown off a horse in Maryland, but suffered no other injury until a round of musket fire found him and brought him down at Chancellorsville. Like the rest of us, Jackson proved in the end to be neither immortal nor invincible. However, when the guns at last became silent and a reckoning took place, Jackson came to be thought of as arguably the most formidable general in the conflict.

Over an archway to the barracks at VMI is a saying found in the commonplace book of Stonewall Jackson. Those who knew and cherished him chose this sentence to personify and honor him. It reads, "You may be whatever you resolve to be."

LORD HIGH ADMIRAL OF THE U.S. NAVY: DAVID DIXON PORTER ON THE MISSISSIPPI

JOSEPH T. GLATTHAAR

The role of the U.S. Navy is often overlooked, but it's hard to imagine an outcome favorable to the Union without the blockade and the gunboats that controlled the major rivers of the South. The navy made the difference in the war, and one of the principal reasons for its effectiveness was commanders like David Dixon Porter—the man his great friend Major General William Tecumseh Sherman referred to, just partly in jest, as the "Lord High Admiral." U. S. Grant believed Porter to be the equal of Lord Nelson. Porter, Sherman, and Grant took one another's measure at the siege of Vicksburg, and the result was a combined arms partnership that allowed Union control of the Mississippi to run "unvexed to the sea" (as Lincoln put it). With the coils of the "Anaconda Plan" now wrapped around the Confederacy, the final slow but steady life-denying crush could begin. What follows is an account of experiments that didn't always succeed, of the triumph of military professionalism over political expediency, of successful actions like the daring passage of Union gunboats past the Vicksburg batteries or another formidable combined arms feat, the taking of Fort Fisher, and of friendships forged from the stress of command.

Joseph T. Glatthaar is a professor of history at the University of Houston, and the author of *Partners in Command: The Relationships Between Leaders in the Civil War,* from which this article was adapted.

IN EARLY DECEMBER 1862, DURING A DINNER PARTY ON AN army quartermaster's riverboat at Cairo, Illinois, Acting Rear Admiral David Dixon Porter was feasting on roast duck and champagne when a stir on deck disrupted the festivities. The host politely exited, then moments later returned with a surprise guest: a slightly built, shabby-looking fellow in a brown civilian coat and gray trousers bearing a fresh coat of dust. The quartermaster introduced the unimpressive visitor: "Admiral Porter, meet General Grant."

As the admiral and the general shifted to a table by themselves, Porter, attired in his military finery, felt a twinge of self-consciousness. A navy man who had continually bucked the system for over three decades, he would have preferred a different atmosphere for his initial encounter with Ulysses S. Grant. He feared that if the army general fell victim to first impressions, he might conclude that Porter was just another naval officer, full of himself and his pomp and ceremony, one who had forgotten along the way that a military man was here to fight. Grant's expressions failed to provide a clue about his inner sentiments. All Porter could detect in that "calm, imperturbable face" was an overpowering sense of "determination." No one could ever read the inscrutable Grant.

Porter's predisposition led him to look unfavorably on Grant. Before this gathering, he had studied the February attacks on Forts Henry and Donelson, and he admired Grant's "bulldog courage." He also had to admit that Grant had demonstrated a capacity to cooperate with the navy during that campaign. But from animosity between the services he inferred that Grant's attitudes toward the navy were no different from those of any other army officer. "I don't trust the Army," Porter had commented to the assistant secretary of the navy just three weeks earlier. "It is very evident that Grant is going to try and take Vicksburg without us, but he can't do it."

But the admiral had mistakenly prejudged the general. The two men spoke in earnest, assessing difficulties honestly and calculating how to overcome them most effectively. There was no hint of superiority, no evidence that Grant perceived the navy as a weaker sister service. Instead, his "bulldog tenacity" convinced Porter that this chap Grant could accomplish great things.

For twenty minutes the two men discussed a plan of campaign against Vicksburg, the critical Confederate stronghold on the Mississippi River. Grant had advanced south toward Grenada along the railroads in northern Mississippi, but a long supply line and repairs to a railroad bridge currently delayed his march. Along the Mississippi River, the Federals had begun to accumulate manpower for a blow at Vicksburg. The problem was that Grant held its proposed commander, Major General John A. McClernand, in low regard and wanted his trusted subordinate, Major General William T. Sherman, to direct the movement. Since McClernand was dawdling in Illinois, Grant elected to seize the opportunity and implement his own plan. He would march along the Mississippi Central Railroad, holding the Confederates in his front, while Sherman slipped downriver and stormed the bluffs overlooking the Yazoo River outside Vicksburg. From the high ground Sherman could either sweep into Vicksburg or drive south to the railroad from Jackson, then march on the city. Grant needed Porter's gunboats to provide fire support for Sherman's landing and assault and to assist in the reduction of Vicksburg. Porter approved the concept, and the meeting adjourned as abruptly as it had begun.

Grant and Sherman could not possibly have done better than David Dixon Porter. Born the son of a famous naval officer, Porter lived only for the sea. He sailed on his first voyage at nearly thirteen. Over the next three years he joined the Mexican navy (commanded at the time by his father), fought in a battle against a Spanish warship, and suffered through six months in a Cuban jail as a prisoner of war. In 1829, the sixteen-year-old Porter joined the U.S. Navy. The bulk of his duty for the next thirty years consisted of coastal and harbor surveys, which paid great dividends along the shifting channels of the Mississippi River in the Civil War. During the conflict with Mexico, Porter exhibited courage and dash, sidestepping the orders of his superior and achieving considerable results. But his audacious performance did little for his career. In the postwar years, the navy lapsed into stagnation. Only a politically charged assignment in New York Harbor, where Porter successfully marked courses through the treacherous Buttermilk Channel and Hell Gate, earned him public acclaim. As the 1860 election took place, Porter was weighing a lucrative offer to leave military service and sail vessels for a commercial firm.

When the war broke out, Porter bypassed the Navy Department and went directly to President Lincoln with a plan to save Fort Pickens, near Pensacola, Florida. It worked. Later, he masterminded a scheme to capture New Orleans, even overseeing the construction of some novel mortar boats for the campaign. Porter's contraptions lobbed huge shells into the forts below the Crescent City, damaged them heavily, and enabled his foster brother, Commodore David Farragut, to sail up the Mississippi River and compel the authorities to surrender the largest city in the Confederacy. Porter fell out of grace for indiscreetly criticizing General George McClellan and his Army of the Potomac—

he had advocated an attack on Norfolk to seize the navy yard back in 1861—but he returned to duty as commander of the Mississippi Squadron in late October 1862, with a rank of acting rear admiral. He had entered the war sixteen months earlier as a lieutenant, his rank for the previous twenty years.

Though only five feet six inches tall (near starvation in prison during his teens may have stunted his growth), Porter projected a strong image. His slicked-down black hair, darting brown eyes, long, sharp nose, and dark, curly beard hardened his appearance. A high-pitched voice belied this imposing presence, unless it engaged in repartee or witticisms. Blessed with a photographic memory and keen analytic powers, Porter thought and reacted quickly, occasionally too quickly. His penchant for speaking his mind, at times rashly, provided immediate gratification but caused him subsequent grief. Often during his career, Porter occupied the seat of honor in the naval doghouse for blunt talk, and this doubtless retarded his progress on the promotion track. A tendency to lapse into exaggeration or sarcasm exacerbated this problem with superiors. Porter's unconventionality and peculiar assortment of qualities led many to undervalue him. Lincoln called him "a busy schemer" and underestimated his ability throughout much of the war. Secretary of War Edwin M. Stanton considered him "a gasbag, who makes a great fuss and claims credit that belongs to others," which some may have thought more true of Stanton than of Porter.

The most influential event in Porter's life occurred in his youth, when his father resigned from the U.S. Navy. The commodore had emerged from the War of 1812 as a national hero, one of a cluster of brilliant naval officers. Like his gifted son, though, he never walked away from a squabble. In a dispute with several congressmen in the mid-1820s, naval officers turned against him and in a court-martial suspended him without pay for six months. He served out the sentence and promptly left the service. His impressionable son never forgot or forgave. Throughout his career, David Dixon Porter challenged authority. He despised the stodgy navy leadership, with its fixation on mindless tradition and lack of progressive reform. In fact, his favorite hobby was poking fun at ranking officers who resisted change, through either indiscreet quips—he openly described them as "fogies"—or burlesque sketches. Porter's stance unquestionably earned him the wrath of certain "superiors." But David Dixon Porter refused to succumb to the dictates of the old guard. He battled the stagnation that so appalled him, and he endured the consequences. Young naval officers adored him for it.

Several days after the Cairo meeting, Grant notified Sherman of his new designs and asked him to visit that evening. Together they hammered out the details of the operation. While Grant organized his forces for an overland advance, Sherman would head back to Memphis to gather troops for the Vicksburg landing. That night, Sherman telegraphed Porter to meet him in Memphis. "Time now is the great object," he noted, and Sherman, a thorough planner, wanted everything arranged in advance.

For over a month, Sherman and Porter had exchanged numerous informative letters that pledged harmony of action and established a positive tone for joint army-navy operations. In mid-November, Porter advised Sherman that Grant ought to use his gunboats in any attack on Vicksburg, and added, "I wish to cooperate with the army in every way where I can be of service, and if you can get any message to or from General Grant on the subject, and give me an idea of what is going on, I shall be much obliged to you."

Sherman responded with maps and other information and a call for unity of command. "My opinion is that a perfect concert of action should exist between all the forces of the United States operating down the valley; and I apprehend some difficulty may arise from the fact that you control on the river, [General Samuel R.] Curtis on the west bank, and Grant on the east bank," Sherman explained. "Were either one of you in absolute command, all, of course, would act in concert."

Porter agreed. "I am ready to cooperate with anybody and everybody," penned the admiral, "and all I ask on the part of the military commanders is their full confidence and a pull together." Naturally, when Porter visited Sherman, he expected a warm reception, and as he entered the general's Memphis headquarters, what he saw reassured him. It reminded him a bit of McClellan's command post—officers waiting, clerks scribbling rapidly, orderlies racing about on horseback, and sentries pacing back and forth—but there was a striking contrast. No one wore lace and feathers, and there were no velvet carpets; it was a working headquarters, not a showroom. "Everything was rough and ready," Porter noted with satisfaction.

Some early confusion daunted the admiral's optimism, however. Staff greeted Porter and seated him in a waiting room, where he stayed for an hour, stewing. Finally Sherman appeared and apologized—no one had told him of the admiral's arrival. But then, when Sherman abruptly broke off the discussion to complete business with a subordinate, Porter nearly erupted in rage. Fortunately, he managed to control himself and, within a few moments after conversation resumed, was reassured by Sherman's directness. "He turned towards me in the most pleasant way," Porter recalled, "poked the fire and talked as if he had known me all his life." Sherman chatted openly about preparations he had completed and what steps he intended to take next, interrupting his monologue periodically to dictate some terse message to a subordinate. Porter marveled at this loquacious general whose mind danced from subject to subject with such facility. This was a working general—attired casually, informal in manner, and immersed in his labors. Within minutes, the two men behaved as if they had known one another for years.

By December 19, 1862, Sherman's troops had climbed aboard transports for the strike against Vicksburg. En route, they picked up another division at Helena, Arkansas. Porter's fleet had gained control of the Yazoo River, just north of Vicksburg, and Sherman hoped to land, drive on to the Vicksburg & Jackson Railroad, and force his way into the city. Porter's gunboats would provide an invaluable shield and soften defensive positions around Vicksburg. If Grant could just detain the Confederates to the northeast near Grenada, Sherman would encounter only token opposition.

But in no time the intricate scheme began to unravel. Rebel cavalry raids severed Grant's supply line and compelled his retreat. Rather than come out to block Grant's movement, the Confederates held tight in Vicksburg. And Sherman, wholly unaware of Grant's fate, attacked directly into the lion's mouth. Bayous so bogged the area that Sherman found just two routes to reach the base of the bluffs, only one offering any promise of success. On December 29, with Federal gunboats and mortars shelling adjacent woods to isolate the target area, he ordered his troops to storm the heights. The Federals charged Chickasaw Bluffs with a will, surmounting obstacles and groping up the slick slopes toward the Confederate line. But the fortified position proved too strong. Dissipated by heavy losses, the attackers never gained a foothold. That night, torrential rains drenched the troops and so slopped the assault route that operations there promised only failure.

The next day, Sherman and Porter gathered to assess their options. From this conference emerged a new plan: Sherman would maintain his current position and feign an attack, while Porter would lead his gunboats and 10,000 soldiers farther upriver. With close fire support from the vessels, these troops would storm the heights there. That night, however, a dense fog blanketed the region and precluded any movement by water. Porter canceled the operation. The attempt to carry Chickasaw Bluffs ended in utter defeat.

From the misery of the Yazoo, where over 1,200 Federals sacrificed their lives or sustained wounds and another 550 fell into Rebel hands, a burgeoning friendship formed between Sherman and Porter. Their respect for one another's military conduct cemented the personal rapport they had established in Memphis. Porter not only directed his naval forces skillfully, he cooperated wholeheartedly. The admiral provided sound advice and proved to be a resourceful leader. For his part, Sherman impressed Porter with his mastery of all aspects of the operation and with the way he drew Porter into his confidence. Sherman accepted Porter as a full partner, a refreshing change of pace for a naval officer. To Secretary of the Navy Gideon Welles on the last day of 1862, Porter expressed his complete confidence in the army commander. "General Sherman is quite equal to the emergency," he insisted, "and nothing daunted by his want of success."

Several days after the assault on Chickasaw Bluffs, General McClernand arrived at the mouth of the Yazoo River to supersede Sherman as army commander. A longtime political friend of Lincoln's, McClernand had served with Sherman as a division commander at Shiloh. He impressed neither Grant nor Sherman with his military talents. Porter, who had met McClernand in Washington a few months earlier, held him in even lower regard, calling him a "hybrid general" and interpreting his appointment as an insult to Grant.

Sherman immediately recommended that McClernand withdraw the army to Milliken's Bend, which the new commander did. He then suggested that McClernand employ the army in conjunction with the navy in a campaign against Arkansas Post, a Confederate bastion on the Arkansas River. During the fight along Chickasaw Bluffs, a Rebel vessel from Arkansas Post had descended the river and captured a steamer towing coal and ammunition barges. Unless the Federals silenced the fortress, it would harass traffic on the river and hinder any Union attempts to capture Vicksburg. At the time, McClernand had no specific plans and only a general one to seek the fall of Vicksburg; yet he hesitated to adopt Sherman's recommendation. Sherman then alerted Porter to the problem. Apparently, the two had discussed this as a possible course of action a few days earlier, and Sherman felt sure that "General McClernand will do anything you ask." When they arrived at Porter's flagship, McClernand presented the operation as his own conception. Porter was outraged. He had disliked McClernand beforehand, and now, because the political general had expropriated his friend's plan, Porter resented the man even more. Only a private conversation with Sherman convinced him to participate in the venture. But Porter insisted on a price: Sherman would command the assault force. McClernand concurred.

A massive convoy of Federal transports and gunboats ascended the Arkansas River. By January 11, the troops had disembarked and assumed positions for an assault. Porter's gunboats opened an impressive barrage, and field artillery and infantry joined the fray. In short order, even before Sherman could order an assault, the Confederates raised the white flag. Nearly 5,000 surrendered. McClernand assumed much of the credit, but according to Sherman it was

Porter's gunboats that won the engagement. Porter merely chalked up the lack of magnanimity to army egoism. "I find that army officers are not willing to give the Navy credit (even in very small matters) they are entitled to," he commented with disgust.

When Grant linked up with the victorious joint command near the mouth of the Arkansas River, Sherman and Porter confirmed what he had already anticipated: McClernand was incompetent to lead an important expedition. Sherman, of course, would obey his superior officer's orders, but to reduce Vicksburg the army needed Porter's cooperation with McClernand as well. Porter looked upon McClernand with "distrust." He felt Sherman was "every inch a soldier," and had "the confidence of his men," but he believed McClernand was "no soldier," and had the confidence of "no one, unless it may be two or three of his staff." He grumbled that, since McClernand's arrival, "I have twice the work to do. . . . Sherman used to help me to think, but now I have to think for McClernand and myself." Both Sherman and Porter urged Grant to assume command. Their pleas were unnecessary; Grant had already decided to direct the operations against Vicksburg.

Over the next two months, Grant employed his forces in a host of projects that would enable him to strike Vicksburg without assaulting the bluffs. Each enterprise, regardless of the likelihood of success, received Porter's complete support. Grant attempted to dig a canal that would bypass Vicksburg. But the Confederates realized that by repositioning some guns they could shell the entire course of the man-made waterway, thus eliminating it as a worthwhile Federal venture. West of the Mississippi River, Grant ordered his forces to clear a passage from Lake Providence, in northern Louisiana, through a series of narrow bayous and waterways into the Red River. Yet slow progress and the length of this circuitous route, approximately 500 miles, limited its utility.

East of the Mississippi River, Grant undertook two difficult schemes to reach the upper Yazoo River and avoid the powerful positions near Vicksburg. By breaking the levee along the Mississippi River across from Helena, Arkansas, he hoped to restore an old channel to Moon Lake. From there, soldiers and sailors would wriggle their way through a series of waterways that form the Yazoo River. Confederates felled trees and prepared other obstructions to discourage the Union advance. After much labor, the army-navy contingent worked its way to the intersection of the Tallahatchie and Yalobusha Rivers, where the Confederates had constructed a fort. Since there was no means of attacking from land, the job of eliminating the position devolved to the navy. Twice gunboats shelled it, and twice the Rebel gunners kept them at bay. An effort to flood the defenders from the fort also failed, and Grant had to seek a means of entering the Yazoo River west of this tiny bastion.

The other scheme called for soldiers and sailors to enter Steele's Bayou from the Mississippi River not far from Milliken's Bend, travel north into Black Bayou, east into Deer Creek, north into Rolling Fork, east to Big Sunflower River, and finally south into the Yazoo River, some ten miles above Haynes' Bluff. Porter personally supervised this March operation, forcing his gunboats along waterways at times barely several dozen yards wide. Limbs stretching over the water chewed up his smokestacks, and tree stumps below the surface scraped his hulls. Aggressively, Porter pushed on, plowing all obstacles from his path. Sherman, in command of ground forces, pursued slowly by land. As the gunboats worked their way along Deer Creek, approaching Rolling Fork and more open travel, the Confederates started cutting down timber to obstruct their passage. Several vessels stuck fast in submerged willow branches. In the distant rear, Porter and his sailors could hear locals chopping down trees behind them. Then Confederate snipers began taking potshots at his sailors. The admiral's mortars blindly tossed shells into the woods, to no avail. His situation had suddenly become critical; the Confederates had them trapped. On tissue paper he scrawled a plea for help and entrusted a freedman with its delivery to Sherman.

As darkness crept over his crafts, Porter loaded all guns, secured the portholes, and huddled his sailors belowdecks. Minute after minute ticked away; Porter agonized over the condition of his ships and crew. In the hours before dawn on March 21, he even prepared detailed plans for the destruction of his vessels rather than let them fall into the hands of the Confederates. Sunrise brought small comfort. His situation was unchanged. The mighty gunboats sat helpless with enemy all around.

Shortly after noon, Porter's men could hear the distant crack of rifles. Straining to detect any clues, the sailors finally deciphered the noise: It was Sherman's advance party, skirmishing with the Confederates. Ninety minutes later, Sherman himself, covered with mud, rode up on an old horse to the huzzahs of the seamen. Once he had received word of Porter's plight the day before, Sherman had immediately pushed forward the few troops at his disposal. That evening three boatloads of soldiers had arrived at Black Bayou, and Sherman had led them twenty miles by candlelight through the dense thickets.

Six weeks earlier, when the press had harangued Sherman for his assault on Chickasaw Bluffs, Porter had come to his rescue, releasing letters he had written to the secretary of the navy during the campaign, absolving Sherman of

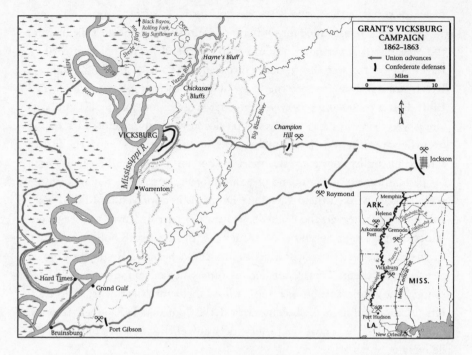

Grant's campaign to capture Vicksburg began in mid-October 1862. His first attempts to breach Confederate defenses north of the town were unsuccessful and Rear Admiral David Dixon Porter's gunboats were unable to reach the Yazoo River via narrow waterways from Milliken's Bend. Finally, in mid-April 1863, Porter ran two supply flotillas past the powerful Vicksburg batteries and was able to transport Grant's men, who had marched south, across the Mississippi, at Bruinsburg. Cutting himself off from his supply lines, Grant raced east to Jackson, fighting as he marched. There, in a victorious engagement, he blocked Joseph E. Johnston's forces from aiding Vicksburg. Grant turned west again and by the last week of May was besieging Vicksburg. The inset map (right) shows the Mississippi River, almost entirely open to the Union after the fall of Vicksburg on July 4. When Port Hudson, Louisiana, surrendered four days later, the Union would have complete control of the river.

blame and even praising his talents as a general officer. Now Sherman was rescuing Porter. "Halloo, Porter," he cried, "what did you get into such an ugly scrape for? So much for you navy fellows getting out of your element; better send for the soldiers always."

Porter took the ribbing good-naturedly. "I never knew what helpless things ironclads could become when they got in a ditch and had no soldiers about," he confessed. The sight of Sherman and the men of the Army of the Tennessee, whom he aptly described as "half horse, half alligator, with a touch of snapping turtle," utterly delighted him.

The failure of the Deer Creek expedition turned Grant back reluctantly to an assault on Haynes' Bluff, north of where Sherman had lost more than 1,500 men the previous December. He had run out of options. Then two trains of thought meshed in Grant's mind. Rear Admiral David Farragut had cruised up the Mississippi River and requested a party to assist in knocking out the batteries at Warrenton, about ten miles below Vicksburg. At the same time, Grant was searching for a means of shipping up to 20,000 men along a route west of the Mississippi River, crossing them over to the east side, and reinforcing Major General Nathaniel P. Banks's command around the Rebel stronghold at Port Hudson, near Baton Rouge. After its fall, Banks could march north on Vicksburg, hugging the river and receiving protection and supplies from the Union gunboats. It suddenly dawned on Grant that his best option might be to move troops, supplies, and transports along the western side of the Mississippi River, shuttle them to the eastern bank below Vicksburg, and then attack that city first, from the south rather than the north. As the winter floods receded and the rains subsided, roadbeds that could carry Grant's men and wagons dried. The only remaining problems were accumulating enough barges and transports and running a few gunboats past the Vicksburg gauntlet to get the soldiers across from the west bank. From despondency bloomed promise.

For Grant's new plan to work, he needed the navy's support. In communications with Porter, he revealed his intentions and requested gunboats. "Will you be good enough, admiral, to give this your early consideration and let me know your determination?" Only a week after his near disaster, Porter did not hesitate. "I am ready to co-operate with you in the matter of landing troops on the other side," the admiral committed, "but you must recollect that, when these gunboats once go below, we give up all hopes of ever getting them up again"—since, moving slowly against the current, his boats would be easy targets for the Confederate guns. If he sent vessels below, he preferred to employ his best craft, "and there will be nothing left to attack Haynes' Bluff, in case it should be deemed necessary to try it." Two days later, Grant, Sherman, and Porter reconnoitered the prospective attack site at Haynes' Bluff. The following day, Grant announced his decision. An attack there "would be attended with an immense sacrifice of life, if not with defeat. This, then, closes out the last hope of turning the enemy by the right."

Porter was lukewarm to the new plan. Yet he not only pledged resources, he consented to supervise the preparation and movement of all vessels that passed the batteries. He agreed simply because Grant had urged it. "So confident was I of the ability of General Grant to carry out his plans when he explained them to me," Porter told the secretary of the navy, "that I never hesitated to change my position from above to below Vicksburg." As Grant accumulated the boats and barges, Porter had them packed with grain sacks, heavy logs, and wet hay for protection and to conceal the fires under the boilers. He also assigned sailors to man several army boats on the hazardous journey.

But before Grant could bring down all the necessary transports and barges, Porter received a blistering rebuke from the secretary of the navy. Dismissing the worthiness of Porter's support for Grant's various schemes around Vicksburg, Welles announced the president's view that patrolling along the river between Vicksburg and Port Hudson "is of far greater importance than the flanking expeditions which thus far have prevented the consummation of this most desirable object."

Porter, who never dodged a fight, responded with clarity and force. "I am sorry the Department is not satisfied with the operations here, but you will please remember, sir, that I was ordered to cooperate with the army, and sagacious officers deem these flanking movements of great importance." Control of the river above and below Vicksburg, he reminded the secretary, would not necessarily lead to the fall of the city. "While it is my desire to carry out the wishes of the Department in relation to all matters connected with operations here, still I must act in accordance with my judgment and a more full knowledge of affairs than the Department could possibly have." Nevertheless, Porter immediately notified Grant that a Navy Department directive "will compel me to go below the batteries with the fleet sooner than I anticipated," with whatever vessels the army had on hand.

On the night of April 16, seven gunboats and several transports, with an assortment of steamers and coal barges lashed to the side, drifted quietly downriver. Detailed instructions that Porter had issued nearly a week earlier carefully outlined the order, fire direction and range, and spacing between boats. He even included contingency plans in the event a vessel sustained a serious hit. Porter personally led the convoy. At 11:16 P.M. the Confederates opened fire on his ironclad, the *Benton,* and within minutes the Rebels ignited huge bonfires on both banks to illuminate the river. For two and a half hours the Vicksburg garrison poured shells into his squadron. Almost miraculously, only one craft, an army transport, sank, although every one sustained some hits.

Just as Porter's gunboat passed out of range, he heard a cry from a small boat: "*Benton,* ahoy!" It was Sherman. He pulled up alongside to check on the condition of Porter and his crew. After receiving the status report, Sherman could not resist a bit of needling. "You are more at home here than you were in the ditches grounding on willow trees," he teased. "Stick to this, old fellow; it suits Jack better." Then off the tireless Sherman went, to examine each vessel as it emerged from the fire.

Throughout the staging process for the movement across the river, Porter regretted Sherman's absence. Everything was chaos; he needed an experienced officer to supervise the loading. "I wish twenty times a day that Sherman was here, or yourself," he complained to Grant, "but I suppose we cannot have all we wish." Within the army, Porter confided to a friend, Sherman "has more brains than all put together." But Grant had other duties in mind for Sherman. While the bulk of the army was embarking for the transfer to the east bank of the river below Vicksburg, Sherman led a feint at Haynes' Bluff to draw away the attention of the city's defenders.

Grant continually had to adapt to overcome problems. A drop in the water level prevented the army from drawing supplies through the swamps, so more vessels, loaded with supplies, had to run the Vicksburg gauntlet to feed the troops. The original landing zone along the east bank of the Mississippi River, Grand Gulf, proved unsuitable as well: Porter's gunboats could not silence the Confederate batteries there, and the secure defensive position on the bluffs precluded a frontal assault. The Federal troops had to trudge farther south. On April 30, 1863, Porter's ships began shuttling Grant's army across the Mississippi River, from Hard Times, Louisiana, to Bruinsburg, Mississippi. After fifteen weeks of toil, Grant finally had positioned his forces to operate against Vicksburg.

While Grant conducted a brilliant campaign against separate Confederate forces to the northeast, Porter slipped down to the mouth of the Red River to relieve Farragut of some of his duties. He returned, however, in time to assist in the fall of the city of Vicksburg. On May 18, Porter could hear the pop of musketry from the area around Chickasaw Bluffs. It was Sherman's XV Corps. Several hours later, he received wonderful reports of a lightning operation that continually kept the Rebel armies off balance. Vicksburg was now completely cut off.

Throughout the siege that followed, the admiral secured the supply line and provided fire support for the army. On May 19 and again three days later, he employed his gunboats and mortars to cover initial, unsuccessful direct assaults on the city and to disrupt the Confederate defenses.

On May 27, Sherman requested a gunboat to attack the water battery that anchored the Rebel left flank. The vessel, the *Cincinnati*, closed on the target and fought aggressively. In the process it sustained numerous hits and in minutes plunged to the bottom of the river, with the loss of forty crewmen. Sherman, who witnessed the entire affair from the bluffs, felt horrible. But Porter chalked it up as one of war's misfortunes. He would agree to lose all his boats, Porter told Sherman, if they would secure Vicksburg. Porter meant it. Back in December, one of his gunboat commanders had struck a mine in the Yazoo River while maneuvering closer in order to fire on the Rebel positions. His vessel sank. When the commander, one of Porter's best, asked about the date of a court of inquiry, the admiral erupted: "Court! I have no time to order courts! I can't blame an officer who seeks to put his ship close to the enemy." Porter then ordered the fleet captain to find the officer another gunboat and chugged away.

When Vicksburg fell on the Fourth of July, 1863, Grant and Porter gathered briefly for some warm congratulations. Two days later, in his after-action report, Grant's acclaim for Porter's aid had not abated. He expressed "thankfulness for my good fortune in being placed in co-operation with an officer of the Navy" such as Porter. The admiral and his subordinates "have ever shown the greatest readiness in their co-operation, no matter what was to be done or what risk to be taken, either by their men or their vessels." Grant then concluded, "Without this prompt and cordial support, my movements would have been much embarrassed, if not wholly defeated."

Sherman, too, heaped praise on the admiral. He regretted that he could not meet Porter on a wharf in Vicksburg to celebrate. "In so magnificent a result," Sherman expounded, "I stop not to count who did it. It is done, and the day of our nation's birth is consecrated and baptized anew in a victory won by the united Navy and Army of our country. God grant that the harmony and mutual respect that exist between our respective commanders, and shared by all true men of the joint service, may continue forever, and serve to elevate our national character, threatened with shipwreck." From a more personal standpoint, Sherman admitted, "Whether success attend my efforts or not, I know that Admiral Porter will ever accord to me the exhibition of a pure and unselfish zeal in the service of our country." On July 18, in the governor's mansion in Jackson, Mississippi, Sherman and a party of generals joined in a hearty chorus of "Army and Navy Forever." The next day, after describing the scene the night before, Sherman pledged eternal support for his navy friend: "To me it will ever be a source of pride that real harmony has always characterized our intercourse, and let what may arise, I will ever call upon Admiral Porter with the same confidence as I have in the past."

✦

EXPOSURE TO OFFICERS of Grant and Sherman's caliber transformed Porter's opinion of professionally trained army officers. Earlier in the war he had confessed to the assistant secretary of the navy, an old friend, "I don't believe in our generals any more than I do in our old fogies of the Navy." Interservice mistrust and rivalry and early war experiences had soured Porter's assessment of high-ranking army personnel. But Grant and Sherman won him over through their cooperation, professional conduct, and sensitivity to Porter's rank and position. "Grant and Sherman are on board almost every day," the admiral noted with pleasure in early March 1863. "Dine and tea with me often; we agree in everything, and they are disposed to do everything for us they can." More than anything, Porter feared "for the sake of the Union that nothing may occur to make a change here."

Porter accorded full credit for the Vicksburg campaign to Grant. In his report to the secretary of the navy, the admiral asserted that

> the late investment and capture of Vicksburg will be characterized as one of the greatest military achievements ever known. The conception of the idea originated solely with General Grant, who adopted a course in which great labor was performed, great battles were fought, and great risks were run; a single mistake would have involved us in difficulty, but so well were all the plans matured, so well were all the movements timed, and so rapid were the evolutions performed that not a mistake has occurred from the passage of the fleet by Vicksburg and the passage of the army across the river up to the present time.

To be sure, Porter liked this pleasant-looking man with an unobtrusive disposition, but his fondness for Grant derived predominantly from his enormous respect for the general's military talents. Grant's quiet confidence, aggressive approach to warfare, and doggedness earned Porter's deepest admiration. No one Porter had ever met could focus on a problem, such as the conquest of Vicksburg, and labor at it as relentlessly. Grant had attempted scheme after scheme just to gain a position from which to launch an attack. Clearly, behind his unaltering countenance worked an adaptable, resourceful, creative mind.

Grant, like Porter, refused to bind himself to conventional methods and thought. He had experimented with varying approaches to reach the high ground near Vicksburg. Once he had slipped below the city, he cut loose from his supply base—a bold decision that Sherman opposed—to speed his march and enhance his maneuverability. He drew skillfully upon the resources at hand, particularly the navy. Unlike most army generals, Grant grasped the possibilities of joint operations. Selflessly committed to victory, and convinced that an army-navy team offered the only hope of success, he had no qualms about dealing with Porter as a peer, something few army officers would do. And Porter proved himself more than worthy of coequal status.

By contrast, Sherman and Porter established a much more personal relationship. Both quick-tongued, energetic, extremely intelligent, and wholly devoted to their profession of arms, these two liked each other immediately, and within a week were fast friends. Whether they were telling jokes, teasing, or damning the world of politics, they were at ease with each other.

Like Grant, Sherman appreciated the navy. But while Grant's interest was utilitarian, the maritime had a special attraction for Sherman. Since his travels to California in the 1840s, sailors and the sea had intrigued him. With his unquenchable curiosity, Sherman enjoyed poking around Porter's gunboats and talking naval matters. He entered the admiral's world with enthusiasm, setting himself apart from most army officers and winning new friends within the sister service.

Sherman's relentless pursuit of mastery of the art of war appealed to Porter. A naval officer who had spent years charting channels, he appreciated Sherman's passion for maps and geographic features. "The General himself," Porter wrote with but slight exaggeration, "had one peculiarity and that was a very correct knowledge of the topography of all places he had operated in or was about to operate in. He never forgot a house, a road or a bayou—in fact he seemed to possess all the crafts of a backwoodsman and never even forgot a 'blazed' tree." During active operations or in preparation for them, the general was almost a man possessed. "Sherman's whole mind was so absorbed in whatever work he had before him," Porter observed, "that he never thought of eating, sleeping or his dress." Instead, his "great delight was to pore over maps and he seemed to take in all the roads, fields and rivers, as if they were good to eat and drink, or he would spend the night in writing out general orders, which were always very full and explicit."

Throughout the Vicksburg campaign, Porter noticed that he and Sherman agreed with each other time after time. They conceived problems similarly and generated comparable solutions. That same consensus existed in their fundamental approach to war. As they communicated more and more, it occurred to both men that their thoughts on how the Union should conduct the war effort converged. After eighteen months of observation, contemplation, and analysis, Sherman had concluded that mere occupation of Confederate territory squandered resources and did little to subdue the rebellion. The Union needed to gain control of the Mississippi River and use it as a springboard for raids directed at the interior of the Confederacy. Federal troops would eat the food, take away the slaves, destroy the railroads, and make life so miserable for the inhabitants that they would realize secession and war were not proper solutions to their political complaints. "The possession of the river, with an army capable of disembarking and striking inland, would have a mighty influence," he insisted to Porter. War's devastations had already sapped many Confederates of their passion for secession, and his new troops, the men of 1862, "came with ideas of making vigorous war, which means universal destruction, and it requires hard handling to repress excesses."

Porter not only vowed, "Whatever control I have on the river shall be exerted to help the army," but also endorsed Sherman's approach to the war. "I am of the opinion that there is but one way to make war, and that is to harass your enemy all you can. I have tried to be as unpleasant to the rebels on the river as possible, and hope that the new armies now going into the field will give them [the rebels] a taste of devastation that may bring them to their senses." The army general and navy admiral thought as one.

In comparing Grant with Sherman, Porter marveled at their marked differences. "I don't suppose there ever was a greater contrast between any two men," he averred, "than between Grant and Sherman." He described Grant as unimposing physically. Still, he was a congenial-looking fellow with agreeable features, simple in taste, and calm in demeanor. Sherman, however, was "a hard weather beaten soldier, with naturally a corrugated face, a nervous, restless, active man." Grant resembled any private; Sherman looked "every much a general." Porter once doubted that he had ever held more than a twenty-minute conversation with Grant; Sherman gabbed almost incessantly. Grant chose good people and could delegate work, while Sherman "attended to all the details himself." In fact, Porter thought, "They were unlike in every thing except in their skill as soldiers, yet they agreed perfectly." What made the tandem so successful, Porter concluded, was that "Grant and Sherman together combine qualities possessed by no one general that ever lived; what one wants the other possesses."

Porter shared characteristics with both men. Temperamentally more akin to Sherman, he could act decisively, a quality that most observers regarded as one of Grant's strongest features. Intellectually, Porter fit more comfortably with Sherman, and he certainly found Sherman's company more enjoyable and intimate. But there was something reassuring about Grant, his quiet confidence and serenity soothing the more mercurial admiral. Like Grant and Sherman, Porter possessed a resourceful nature, and results, not methods, dominated his approach to military service in wartime. Once, after responding to a series of hypothetical questions from a young officer, Porter snarled back with his biting sarcasm, "All I have to say is that when the time comes to use your judgment you must use it; and if you do it right, you will hear from me damned quick; and if you do it wrong, you will hear from me a damned sight quicker!"

The Vicksburg juggernaut brought Grant, Sherman, and Porter together as only such an operation could. From their difficult experiences, they learned to depend on one another, and they developed mutual respect as individuals and as warriors. With each man possessing different talents and skills, they fed off one another, exchanging ideas, each increasing his knowledge of the other service, and evolving and maturing as joint commanders. The Vicksburg campaign tossed the three together; and from it they emerged with powerful professional and personal bonds. In the years to come, rich and lasting friendships blossomed among them, but the heart of the relationship stemmed from the demanding service along the Mississippi River.

✦

FIVE DAYS AFTER THE SURRENDER of Vicksburg, Port Hudson fell to Union control, and now the Mississippi River ran "unvexed to the sea." All three men received promotions for their invaluable services. Porter earned a commission with the permanent rank of rear admiral. Both Grant and Sherman had held the rank of major general of volunteers; now the War Department also elevated Grant from brigadier general to major general in the Regular Army and awarded Sherman a brigadier generalship in the Regular Army.

Although Sherman and Porter continued to communicate and cooperate, they never again joined forces for a large-scale operation. As Sherman commented in mid-October, "You have almost finished your job and can and will, doubtless with infinite pleasure, help us who must live whilst we penetrate the very bowels of this land." The intimacy between them never waned. When personal tragedy struck Sherman, he poured out his heart to the tough-minded admiral. "I lost, recently, my little boy by sickness incurred during his visit to my camp on Big Black," a heartbroken Sherman revealed. "He was my pride and hope of life, and his loss takes from me the great incentive to excel, and now I must work on purely and exclusively for love of country and professional pride." Sherman concluded by saying, "To you I can always unfold my thoughts as one worthy and capable of appreciating the feelings of a soldier and gentleman."

In Sherman's absence, Porter prepared chatty, informative letters of considerable length, which the admiral wittily justified by admitting that "sailors will spin long yarns—it is part of their nature." Porter continued the practice with periodic reports throughout the remainder of the war. The two friends could accomplish more through direct, personal communication, discussing ideas and solving problems as they had done at Vicksburg, than by working through official military channels.

After Grant was assigned to central Tennessee, his communication with Porter slowed to a trickle. Only terse, businesslike dispatches passed between them over telegraph lines. When trouble erupted back in the Mississippi River valley, though, Porter did not hesitate to bring the matter to Grant's attention, using a belated congratulatory message to write his friend a lengthy letter. "If I have not sooner congratulated you on your splendid victory at Chattanooga," explained the admiral, "it was not because I did not share in the joy of your triumph, for you have no greater well-wisher than myself. I congratulate you now with all my heart, and now that you have finished that business so well, I must tell you that the guerrillas are kicking up the mischief on the river." Grant replied that Sherman was returning there to quash the partisans and launch his raiding strategy along the river. Porter was delighted. "I was glad to receive yours of the 20th instant, and to hear that I was soon to see my old friend Sherman, whom I esteem as you do. Indeed," joked the whiskered admiral, "we have been so much together and in so many hard places that we look upon him as the property of the navy."

Time permitted Sherman to organize a march on Meridian, Mississippi, living off the land and demolishing the railroad as he traveled. But other pressing matters precluded his intended raid up the Red River in Louisiana. The president had elevated Grant to lieutenant general, and Sherman would direct one of the two major Union thrusts that spring, with his target the Confederate army in northern Georgia. The campaign up the Red River lapsed to Porter and, by default, to Nathaniel P. Banks.

Porter was worried. He feared the consequences of a volunteer commander directing a joint operation. Sherman allayed the admiral's uneasiness by assigning 10,000 of his own troops under a trusted subordinate, Brigadier General Andrew Jackson Smith, to assist in the endeavor. As it turned out, the Porter-Smith combination could not secure victory, only stave off a disastrous defeat. Three converging columns—one under Banks, another under Major General Frederick Steele that never materialized, and the third under Porter and Smith—were to link up at Alexandria, Louisiana, and then advance as far upriver as Shreveport, breaking up Confederate opposition and gathering valuable supplies of cotton. Alexandria fell to Porter and Smith on March 19; despite promises, however, Banks started late and arrived after the fight. At that point, low water nearly terminated the campaign. Sherman had authorized Porter to cancel operations if the gunboats could not pass up the rapids. They barely did. Banks then led the column on, but a Confederate command routed his forces at Sabine Cross Roads on April 8. Smith's two divisions, along with some other Union troops, abruptly halted the Rebel pursuit at Pleasant Hill the next day. Nevertheless, Banks had had enough, and his troops continued their precipitous retreat. Rebel batteries and dropping water levels made the withdrawal a living hell for Porter. Only the imaginative labors of a Wisconsin officer, who erected a dam to raise the water level and float Porter's fleet over the rapids by mid-May, saved the admiral from an utter catastrophe.

Porter laid full blame on Banks's doorstep. "You know my opinion of political generals," the admiral fumed to Sherman after the two battles. "It is a crying sin to put the lives of thousands in the hands of such men, and the time has come when there should be a stop put to it." Two days later, he approached the failure more philosophically, but his attitude toward Banks and officers of his ilk had not budged:

> You know I have always said that Providence was fighting this great battle its own way, and brings these reverses to teach us, a proud, stiff-necked, and unthankful people, how to be contented under a good Government if peaceful times come again. I hope it will teach us not to place the destinies of a great nation in the hands of political generals and volunteer admirals.

Porter survived the Red River expedition with his reputation largely intact, perhaps not with the public but certainly with the Navy Department. And as Grant locked up with Lee around Petersburg, and Sherman battled his way to the outskirts of Atlanta and eventually captured the city, Porter returned east. The secretary of the navy wanted Porter to head a flying squadron in the Atlantic that would chase blockade-runners. Porter respectfully begged off. Such mundane duties offered no appeal; he best served the nation as a combat commander. Some days later, the secretary proposed a joint army-navy operation to North Carolina to seize Fort Fisher, which controlled the blockade-runners' last haven, Wilmington. Porter leaped at the opportunity.

Immediately, he paid his old friend Grant a visit at his headquarters in City Point, Virginia. After lengthy discussions, Grant endorsed the concept and assigned Major General Godfrey Weitzel, a brainy engineer officer, to command the army. Soon, however, problems developed. Fort Fisher was part of Major General Benjamin Butler's department, and he proposed an idea that intrigued authorities in Washington: Butler suggested that they load an old vessel full of gunpowder and explode it near the fort, either demolishing the bastion or so stunning the garrison that an assault would carry the works swiftly. Porter, whose nature attracted him to fresh methods and bold ideas, thought it was worth a try. Grant considered the project ridiculous, but he refused to expend capital to block it. Then Butler, another political general who had tussled with Porter during the campaign for New Orleans in 1862, decided to head the army contingent personally.

Not until mid-December 1864 did the expedition get under way. Incompetence ruled the army operation. Poor preparations, inexcusable delays, and a lack of aggressiveness hounded Butler's command, and gale-force winds worsened its woes. The gunpowder ship explosion proved a pyrotechnic spectacle, but it did no damage to the fort, and Porter had to rely solely on his naval gunfire to soften the enemy positions and support the landing on Christmas Day. Butler's men were thirty hours late, and only 2,500 soldiers went ashore. Weitzel reconnoitered and found the defenses too strong. Much to Porter's mortification, he and Butler canceled the attack. By imputation and later accusation, the naval bombardment had failed to dislodge enough cannon in Fort Fisher for an assault to succeed.

Porter was livid. To the secretary of the navy, he bemoaned the incompetence of the army officers who headed the expedition and beseeched the secretary not to withdraw his fleet until they had conquered the fort. All the army needed, Porter insisted, was a skilled commander. That day, he dispatched his top subordinate, Captain K. Randolph Breese, with a letter for Sherman to come up and take control of the affair. "This," Porter enticed his comrade, "is merely on your way to Richmond. Take this place and you take the 'crème de la crème' of the rebellion." Sherman's masterful handling of the operation would "let our people see the folly of employing such generals as Butler and Banks. I have tried them both, and God save me from further connections with such generals."

Sherman declined Porter's invitation; instead, he intended to take Wilmington from the rear, after his march through South Carolina. It did not matter. The previous day, the secretary of the navy showed Grant the dispatches he had received from Porter. Butler had failed wretchedly, and the admiral insisted that a combination of army and navy forces under a good general officer could take the fort. Grant sided with his old friend. "I know Admiral Porter to be possessed of as fine judgment as any other officer and capable of taking as great risks," the lieutenant general informed the secretary of war. That day, Grant urged the admiral to hold fast. He would send the same troops, reinforced by a brigade. Brigadier General Alfred H. Terry would command.

With Grant's involvement, the new expedition functioned superbly. Grant had handed Terry seated orders; not until he and his force had lost sight of land did they know their destination. Terry's written instructions could not have been more explicit. "It is exceedingly desirable that the most complete understanding should exist between yourself and the naval commander," Grant explained. "I suggest, therefore, that you consult with Admiral Porter freely, and get from him the part to be performed by each branch of the public service, so that there may be unity of action." After directing Terry to prepare a written plan of attack, the lieutenant general ordered Terry to subordinate himself to Porter. "I have served with Admiral Porter, and know that you can rely on his judgment and his nerve to undertake what he proposes. I would, therefore, defer to him as much as is consistent with your own responsibilities." To avoid any misconceptions, the lieutenant general also prepared a letter to Porter, introducing Terry and informing the admiral that "General Terry will show you the instructions he is acting under." He went on to discuss reinforcements that he held on alert in Baltimore and proposed some options for an attack. Then Porter's old friend concluded with the statement, "General Terry will consult with you fully, and will be governed by your suggestions as far as his responsibility for the safety of his command will admit of." Grant had established a unified command.

Together, Porter and Terry conceived and executed a brilliant operation. Porter reworked his gunfire plan, and on January 13, 1865, after an extensive naval bombardment, Terry and his men, augmented by more than 1,000 marines and sailors under Captain Breese, landed and dug in on the beach. The innovative Porter had requested Terry to assign a signal corpsman to his flagship. Thus, when the landing and attack took place, Terry and Porter had ship-to-shore communications. As the amphibious force maneuvered its way up to the Confederate fortifications, Terry and Breese could direct close naval-gunfire support through the wig-wag system (signaling with flags). By mid-afternoon the following day, Terry gave the signal, and the ground troops stormed the walls. For nearly seven hours they battled, sometimes hand to hand. Finally, at 10:00 P.M., Terry lofted a signal flare into the sky. The Union had secured Fort Fisher.

For his role in the victory, Porter praised Terry effusively. "General Terry is entitled to the highest praise and the gratitude of his country for the manner in which he has conducted his part of the operations," the tough-minded admiral commented to Secretary Welles. "He is my beau ideal of a soldier and a general." Porter probably did not know that Terry, like Butler and Banks, was a citizen soldier.

Meanwhile, Butler had returned to Washington in failure. He placed the entire blame squarely on Porter's shoulders, and the politician-turned-general convinced some congressional friends to hold hearings on the matter; but the triumph at Fort Fisher with essentially the same resources pulled the rug out from beneath any damaging investigation. At Grant's request, Lincoln relieved Butler of command of the Department of North Carolina and Virginia and ordered him to return to Massachusetts and await orders. As Sherman crowed to Porter on January 17, "I am rejoiced that the current of events has carried Butler to Lowell, where he should have stayed and confined his belli-cose operations to the factory girls." Butler acted as a thorn in Porter's side for the remainder of the admiral's life, attacking him publicly and both resur-recting incidents and conjuring up fictitious tales that portrayed Porter in a bad light.

Although the campaign concluded well for the navy and the army alike, Porter was furious with Grant. Twice in a row on major operations, political generals had caused disasters and squandered the lives of many fine soldiers and sailors. Grant had known of Butler's incompetence before the first at-tempt, yet he had refused to intervene and replace him with someone of tal-ent, fearful of taking on a general with political clout. Porter and the men of the joint campaign had suffered as a consequence. Worse, Washington rumors falsely indicated that Grant and the army had assumed credit for initiating the expedition. In a war fought predominantly on the ground, army achieve-ments vastly overshadow navy heroics. This stung high-ranking officers and political heads of the Navy Department, and they were particularly tender about the army stealing the applause for navy valor and success. In a confidential letter to Welles, Porter foolishly blasted Grant with broadside after broadside. He accused Grant of being "always willing to take the credit when anything is done, and equally ready to lay the blame of the failure on the navy." Porter reminded the secretary, "I have served with the lieutenant-general before, where I never worked so hard in my life to make a man succeed as I did for him." Yet, he complained, Grant paid little more than lip service to the navy's efforts. "He wants magnanimity, like most officers of the army, and is so avaricious as regards fame that he will never, if he can help it, do justice to our department." Grant displayed "indifference" toward the operation "until he found his reputation at stake." Meanwhile, Porter had risked his own reputation with the likes of Butler. "His course proves to me that he would sacrifice his best friend rather than let any odium fall upon Lieutenant General Grant." Grant deserved blame, not credit.

As he had done earlier in the war when he disparaged McClellan and the Army of the Potomac, Porter let emotions rule reason. The invective acted therapeutically, releasing pent-up frustration and stress from the two ventures, and in a short time Porter felt as warmly as ever toward Grant. The letter, however, came back to haunt him. In 1870, after President Grant had issued a commission promoting Vice Admiral Porter to the rank of admiral, someone dug up the letter to influence the Senate confirmation vote. The harsh words stung the president. Since their days at Vicksburg, Grant had counted Porter among his closest friends. It was hard for the president to believe Porter had ever harbored such vicious thoughts toward him.

Porter reacted with honesty and speed. He immediately admitted authorship of the letter and publicly condemned himself for it. To demonstrate his true feelings, the admiral turned over his wartime journal to a newspaperman for publication. All of its passages regarding Grant indicated deep affection and admiration for the general and the man. Then, hat in hand, he went to the White House. Still too hurt to forgive, Grant declined to see him, so Porter wrote him a lengthy letter, explaining why he had acted and felt so foolishly after the battle for Fort Fisher and apologizing for his misdeed. Surely their deep friendship since the event, long before he had any hint that Grant would seek the presidency, indicated his genuine sentiments toward him, Porter contended. Nearly three weeks later, Porter received an invitation to visit the White House. The president and the admiral cloistered for an hour, and when they stepped from the room, all had been forgiven. Grant had accepted Porter's explanation, and the two friends put the letter behind them.

In the decades following the war, Porter retained a rich relationship with both Grant and Sherman. As president, Grant not only promoted Porter but even wanted him to serve as his secretary of the navy; however, Porter did not want a political job. Grant's fondness for the man and respect for his talents never diminished. Late in life, Grant wrote, "Among naval officers I have always placed Porter in the highest rank. I believe Porter to be as great an admiral as Lord Nelson." Grant was the first of the triumvirate to pass away, succumbing to cancer in 1885.

Sherman and Porter, the ranking officers of their respective services, led the drive toward professionalism in the armed forces. Their friendship, founded at the base of Haynes' Bluff, retained its strength throughout their declining years. "Lord High Admiral of the U.S. Navy" was Sherman's pet name for Porter. Sherman retired as commanding general of the army in 1884.

Porter, the eldest of the trio, outlasted his friends in service. A naval officer to the end, he sustained a massive heart attack in 1890. The tough old admiral hung on for some months, but his faculties degenerated, and on February 13, 1891, he expired at his Washington home—in an upright, seated position. Sherman, who had recently developed pneumonia, outlived his old friend by a single day.

GRANT AT VICKSBURG: A LESSON IN OPERATIONAL ART

JOSEPH T. GLATTHAAR

Can there be a better example of the value of surprise, a campaign that misled and mystified the enemy, than U. S. Grant's wide swing around the river port of Vicksburg, Mississippi, which ended with the penning of an entire Confederate army? "Grant broke free from his own communications," the military historian Russell F. Weigley writes, "to confound those enemies who tried to break his supply lines. He marched rapidly, shifted direction deftly, hit hard when fighting became necessary, but achieved his objectives less through battle with its casualties than by deceptive maneuver." It was the Western theater's version of Stonewall Jackson's Shenandoah Valley campaign, with consequences that were more devastating to the other side.

Grant, whose career had so recently been sunk in shadow, now seemed to advance from triumph to triumph. He, surely, was the most unexpected leader that the Civil War created. The forty-seven-day siege of Vicksburg may not have been to his liking; but costly direct assaults, as he soon discovered, were useless. Starvation and a gradual tightening of the trench noose worked better. Marshal Vauban, the seventeenth-century French general, who was the master of siegecraft, would have approved. As Joseph T. Glatthaar points out, "For the second time—the first being at Fort Donelson in February 1862—Grant had captured a Confederate army." With the fall of Vicksburg, one day after the end of the battle of Gettysburg, the Union had all but accomplished another essential feature of the Anaconda Plan—the clearing of the Mississippi River and splitting in two of the Confederacy. At the very moment that Lee's badly mauled army was retreating in the rain back to Virginia, the Confederate commander John C. Pemberton met Grant under a flag of truce to arrange a surrender that would be the strategic turning point of the war.

Joseph T. Glatthaar is a professor of history at the University of Houston and the author of *Partners in Command: The Relationships Between Leaders in the Civil War.*

THE VICKSBURG CAMPAIGN WAS ULYSSES S. GRANT'S STER-
ling military feat of the Civil War. In it, he exhibited complete mastery of what modern soldiers call the operational art of war—the use of military forces in major campaigns to fulfill strategic goals in a particular theater.

In contrast to the Union situation in the West, the Confederate high command in 1863 was in utter disagreement and, consequently, disarray. In November 1862, Jefferson Davis had created a huge military region, extending from the Appalachian Mountains to the Mississippi River, and assigned General Joseph E. Johnston to head it. Johnston would formulate strategic and operational plans for Lieutenant General John C. Pemberton, commander of forces in Mississippi and eastern Louisiana, and General Braxton Bragg, commander of the Army of Tennessee. He would advise them on all matters and, whenever present, command the armies. Unfortunately, Johnston lacked strategic vision. He could not imagine how anyone could supervise forces hundreds of miles apart. Disillusioned with the command structure and incapable of rising to the demands of his assignment, he never truly took charge. As a result, Pemberton communicated with both Johnston and Davis, and during the critical aspects of the Vicksburg campaign, he received conflicting directives from his two superiors.

A West Point graduate with deep brown eyes and dark hair streaked with gray, Pemberton hailed from Pennsylvania but threw his support to the Confederacy because of his wife's strong Virginia ties. In the Mexican War he had earned an excellent reputation. With greater age and added responsibility, however, he had become indecisive and defensive-minded.

Fortunately for the Confederates, the watery topography around Vicksburg benefited them. The heights extended well up the Yazoo River, which emptied into the Mississippi seven or eight miles north of the city. The high ground also hugged the eastern bank of the Mississippi River for some miles to the south. Combined with the swamps, rivers, and bayous that cut up the entire region, the terrain features inhibited offensive operations and limited the number of viable routes into the environs.

By the beginning of April 1863, after three months of efforts to take Vicksburg from the north or west, it seemed that Grant had exhausted his options. Then he decided to shift his troops below Vicksburg along the western bank of the Mississippi, shuttle them across the river, and turn Pemberton's south flank instead of his north. Once across, Grant's army could sweep up the high ground to Vicksburg, strike northeast toward the Mississippi state capital of Jackson, and then drive directly on Vicksburg, or instead march south to link with Major General Nathaniel P. Banks at Port Hudson, as the War Department had urged him to do.

To confuse Pemberton during the troop transfer, Grant ordered Major General William T. Sherman to feign an attack on Haynes' Bluff, north of Vicksburg, and Colonel Benjamin Grierson, a Quaker by upbringing but a fighter by birth, to lead an extensive cavalry raid that would disrupt rail and telegraphic communications and frighten the Mississippi citizenry. By April 30, Commodore David Dixon Porter had begun crossing Major General John A. McClernand's corps to the east bank of the Mississippi at Bruinsburg.

On the Confederate side, all was chaos. Short of cavalry and baffled by the Federal ruses, Pemberton struggled to detect Grant's intentions and then reacted slowly. Only as Porter ferried McClernand's and Major General James B. McPherson's men across the river did Pemberton grasp the gravity of his predicament. Because he had stretched his command thin to protect Vicksburg well beyond the city's boundaries, Pemberton could not respond effectively. In fact, his command outnumbered Grant's, yet he could not concentrate his 40,000 troops rapidly enough to stop the Yankees. He funneled a meager 5,000 reinforcements to Brigadier General John S. Bowen, who received the assignment of blocking the Union advance inland. Although Bowen was an excellent soldier, his combined force of approximately 8,000 was no match for the 25,000 Federals marching cross-country.

Early on May 1, McClernand's troops began to press the Confederates near Port Gibson. The choppy terrain, dense canebrake, and a stout defense by Bowen's men held the Federals at bay throughout much of the day. By late afternoon, however, the battle tilted in the Union's favor. Major General John A. ("Black Jack") Logan's division of McPherson's corps hustled to the front and joined in the attack on the left. The added weight of Federal forces crushed the Confederates. Nevertheless, Bowen regained control and both his wings fell back in good order across Bayou Pierre, destroying the bridges behind them.

With the victory at Port Gibson, Grant faced the critical moment of the campaign. All along, he had intended to send McClernand's corps to Banks. But on May 3, he received a message indicating that it would be some time before Banks could employ those troops effectively. Rather than squander the manpower, Grant elected to push on with his own campaign, drawing on the momentum of his recent battlefield success. Once Sherman's corps crossed the river, Grant would strike to the northeast for Jackson, taking with him all the supplies his army could carry and confiscating other edibles from the countryside. For the time being, he would not sever his supply line completely, but he would try to keep the army as self-contained as possible.

As the Federal columns marched to the northeast, the perplexed Pemberton continued to make wrong decisions. Davis ordered him to hold Vicksburg at all hazards; Johnston, who was collecting reinforcements around Jackson in mid-May, insisted that he concentrate his forces and attack Grant. His own cautious nature told him to draw his troops together, dig in along the Big Black River, and wait for Grant to attack him. Again he misread the situation, this time assuming that Grant's movement toward Jackson was a trick. Brigadier General John Gregg and his brigade paid the price.

Guarding Raymond, about fifteen miles southwest of Jackson, Gregg had instructions to assail the Union right flank as it pivoted toward the Big Black River. But on May 12, McPherson's whole corps attacked him. In a chaotic fight amid dust, smoke, woods, and almost impenetrable thickets, Gregg masterfully blocked the Union advance for a time; but by mid-afternoon, the Rebel right buckled. The town fell to overwhelming Federal numbers.

With Raymond now under Union control, Grant had positioned his command between Pemberton's army at the Big Black River and Johnston's forces at Jackson. His next move was to isolate and defeat Johnston, before turning on Pemberton. Early the next morning, he sent Sherman's columns northeast to Jackson. McPherson directed a march north to Clinton, destroyed the railroad, and moved on Jackson from the west. A third component of Grant's army gathered around Raymond to check any movements by Pemberton toward Jackson.

On May 14, Sherman and McPherson converged on Jackson during a torrential rainstorm. Johnston, now commanding in person, lacked the necessary troops to oppose them. "I am too late," he absolved himself to Richmond authorities. The Confederate general made a show but, in the end, all he could do was evacuate the garrison's few thousand troops to the north. Jackson, the Mississippi state capital, fell after feeble resistance.

Late that afternoon, Grant, Sherman, and McPherson gathered in town to congratulate one another on their victory. The Yankee celebration did not last long. Some months earlier, the Federals had expelled a man from Memphis for uttering disloyal words in public. Actually, the civilian was a Union supporter, and the event was staged to win the confidence of Confederate officers. So well had he gained their trust that Johnston chose him as one of three couriers to attempt to deliver a vital message to Pemberton, urging him to advance on Clinton, where Johnston would attempt to join him. The spy handed the message personally to McPherson. With knowledge of Johnston's plans, Grant reacted swiftly. He directed Sherman to destroy anything of military value in Jackson, while the rest of the army marched west toward Bolton, between Vicksburg and Clinton, to block a Johnston-Pemberton combination.

As the Federal ranks converged on Pemberton's army, the Confederate commander finally decided to act. He held a council of war and emerged with a plan to disregard Johnston's order and strike southward at what he assumed was Grant's supply line. On May 15, he began the movement, but high waters and excessive dawdling delayed his progress. The following morning, a new directive from Johnston arrived, announcing the fall of Jackson and again calling for a combination at Clinton. This time, Pemberton obeyed, but it was too late.

Some 32,000 Federal troops approached Pemberton's army of 23,000 along three separate roads, and by midmorning, skirmishing had begun on the southern and middle routes. Pemberton promptly deployed his men on a ridge overlooking Jackson Creek and secured the high ground to the north, Champion Hill (mistakenly called Champion's Hill then and since). Here, the most vicious fighting took place.

The divisions of Logan and Brigadier General Alvin P. Hovey opened the Battle of Champion's Hill by slamming into the Confederate left. Logan's command slipped partially around the flank, while Hovey's men mauled the Confederates around the hill, pushing them back and capturing several cannon. By early afternoon, Pemberton's army was on the verge of catastrophe.

Because the Union troops to the south had not pressed the attack vigorously, Pemberton ordered Bowen's division to reinforce the graycoats around the hill. With his usual aggressiveness, Bowen slammed his brigades into Hovey's, catching the Yankees by surprise and driving them back off the hill. So vicious was the fighting that Hovey later referred to the area as "a hill of death." A counterattack against Logan's men also gained the advantage, and for a time it seemed as if Pemberton might check the Federals. But Grant was relentless. Support arrived to bolster Hovey, and McClernand's columns to the south finally rumbled forward. Just like Port Gibson and Raymond, the weight of the Union columns was too much, and Pemberton withdrew hastily to his Big Black River line.

At the Battle of Champion's Hill, Grant suffered 2,400 casualties but inflicted almost 4,300. He gave Pemberton no respite. McClernand's and McPherson's corps pursued directly, while Sherman's men, now up from Jackson, swung to the north in hopes of sneaking around the Confederate left.

The following day, May 17, Yankee forces encountered the Rebels behind strong works at the Big Black River. As McClernand's troops deployed, a brigade of Iowa and Wisconsin men under Brigadier General Michael K. Lawler secured the northernmost position. Lawler—a mammoth Irishman— led by physical threats and fought with unbridled ferocity. He boldly shifted his men across open ground to a naturally shielded area close to the Rebel line. From there, he decided to storm the works. With two Hoosier regiments in support, Lawler placed his men in compact formation and ordered them to fix bayonets. He then mounted his horse, climbed out of the hollow, and shouted, "Forward!" With a rush his men crossed the open ground and hit the Confederate works left of center. They brushed aside abatis and fired a single round. Then, without hesitating, they waded across a bayou and clambered through some felled timber. The Confederates, stunned by the assault and unnerved by its swift execution, broke after the Yankee volley. Within three minutes, Lawler's columns blasted through Pemberton's defenses and shattered his position. By nighttime, Grant's army had collected 1,751 Rebel soldiers, at a cost of 279 casualties.

At the works around Vicksburg, Pemberton reorganized his scattered command. He still had time to escape. Sherman closed rapidly from the north, but McClernand lacked the strength to secure all the escape routes to the south. Johnston commanded him to save the army and abandon Vicksburg. But Davis's order to hold the city at all costs weighed more heavily on his mind, and he doubted his army could endure another battle outside the breastworks. After yet another council of war, Pemberton chose to hunker down and await succor from Johnston. It would never arrive.

Encouraged by his previous successes, Grant sought to close the campaign by immediately assaulting the works at Vicksburg. On May 19, he ordered his men forward. But this time the Confederate numbers were more than enough to meet the challenge. At a cost of over 900 casualties, Grant was able to secure only some advance gun emplacements.

Despite the repulse, Grant opted to give it one more try. He hated to sacrifice the initiative to a siege, and he also knew that Johnston had returned to Jackson and accumulated a substantial force. The renewed prospect of fight-

ing front and rear provided enough incentive to attack one more time. Three
days after the first defeat, Grant opened an assault all along the Confederate
line. Sherman and McPherson soon bogged down. McClernand, however,
reached the Rebel works and called for help. Another concerted attack, he insisted, would break through. Grant, Sherman, and McPherson did not believe
him, but Grant felt they had no choice, and he ordered the other two corps
forward. With little enthusiasm, the Yankees advanced—and failed. Somewhat unfairly, Grant blamed McClernand for these unnecessary losses; he resolved to settle down for a siege.

Since the opening of the campaign, Grant had been uneasy about McClernand's ability to command a corps. By mid-June he had the excuse he needed
to dismiss the powerful political appointee: McClernand had issued an
overblown congratulatory order to his own corps, denigrating the two others,
and the order had found its way into newspapers, in violation of War Department regulations. Grant removed him and placed Major General E. O. C. Ord
in command of the XIII Corps. In the end, Grant's military successes prevented any real political fallout.

One late May day, as the army dug in around Vicksburg, Grant rode behind the lines. A soldier recognized the commanding general and voiced his
complaint: "Hardtack." Others joined in, and soon a chorus of troops good-
naturedly chanted, "Hardtack! Hardtack!" They had endured the necessary
sacrifices on the campaign, including an exclusive diet of the saltless hard
cracker and meat, but now that they had secured positions for the foreseeable
future, the men wanted to diversify their rations. Grant pulled up his horse
and announced to the protesters that he had taken steps to open supply lines,
and soon they would have coffee and fresh bread. The soldiers burst into
cheers and laughter.

Once the army gained control of the high ground around Vicksburg, Grant
reestablished contact with the outside world. Porter and his fleet dominated
the waters near the city. Not only would his gunboats cooperate in any Union
attack and aid the army in its stranglehold on the Rebel garrison, but Porter
would also help convey messages to and from Washington. Grant notified
General in Chief Henry W. Halleck of his situation, and within days Federal
reinforcements and supplies poured into the area. The choke hold was becoming airtight.

For six weeks the Federals conducted an active siege. From the river,
Porter's gunboats and mortars lobbed shells into the city, inflicting misery on
civilians as well as soldiers. On the ground, Federals peppered Confederate
trenches with rifle shot and artillery shells. Any head that popped above the

entrenchments attracted the attention of several sharpshooters. Each day, Yankee troops inched closer to the Confederate works and dug saps to mine enemy positions. Twice Grant exploded mines; neither time did the subsequent assaults succeed. They also prepared two-way trenches, both to prevent Pemberton's army from breaking out and to discourage Johnston's forces from attacking in the rear. Grant even detached Sherman and some troops to keep a watchful eye on Johnston's command.

Davis and Secretary of War James A. Seddon urged Johnston to strike quickly. Instead, he squandered priceless time grumbling about inadequate resources and squabbling with Davis over his duties and responsibilities as a departmental commander. An attack on Grant's army never materialized. No doubt, Pemberton had undone himself by holing up in Vicksburg, but Johnston's lackluster efforts sealed his fate.

The Confederates suffered badly under the strain of a prolonged siege. Because of manpower shortages, Pemberton had to deploy nearly all his troops in trenches, without rotation. The scorching June sun slowly roasted the men in their cramped positions. Then heavy rains followed, soaking them and converting the dried clay into glutinous Mississippi mud. Prior to the siege, Confederate troops had lived on a ration of one-third meat and two-thirds meal. Gradually, the quality and quantity of food declined. Meal and coffee ran out, and an unsavory mixture of ground peas made a poor substitute. Eventually, soldiers were reduced to a small amount of boiled peas and two ounces of bacon per day. Some famished troops supplemented their diet with dog. As June rolled into July, mule meat replaced bacon. According to one soldier, it was grainy and had a "'horsey' flavor. To starving men, however, it was very good." By late June, disgruntlement had spread through the ranks, and some soldiers even talked of mutiny.

Civilians, unaccustomed to the brutality of warfare, also suffered a great deal. To survive the massive shelling, they dug caves into hillsides, which served as bombproof shelters. Day and night, the unrelenting scream of mortar rounds and their thunderous concussion unnerved people. "I shall never forget my extreme fear during the night, and my utter hopelessness of ever seeing the morning light," wrote one woman. "Terror stricken, we remained crouched in the cave, while shell after shell followed each other in quick succession. I endeavored by constant prayer to prepare myself for the sudden death I was almost certain awaited me." Despite the thickness of the ground above these caves, direct hits shook the area, sometimes causing roofs to collapse on occupants. Although individuals stocked their subterranean homes with furniture and other creature comforts, the suffocating heat, measly diet, boredom, fear, overcrowding, and swarms of mosquitoes made life for cave dwellers almost unbearable. But at least these excavations offered some shelter and protection. Aboveground residences were riddled with shell chunks and shards. Had their inhabitants not sought refuge underground, many more surely would have lost their lives.

For forty-seven days the debilitating siege continued. By the beginning of July, it became apparent to Pemberton that his cause was lost. One more powerful Union rush and his army would collapse. The Fourth of July was just a day away, and he hoped to use the national holiday to extract better terms from Grant. That morning, he sent two officers under flag of truce to the Union lines, requesting terms for capitulation. Grant demanded unconditional and immediate surrender. In the afternoon, he, Pemberton, and some other officers gathered. Again, Grant and Pemberton could not reach an agreement, and only the intervention of subordinate officers prevented a break. That evening, after a conference of senior Union officers, Grant agreed to parole the Rebel garrison, rather than ship them north to prisons. Later, some military and government officials criticized this arrangement. Grant, however, had grounds to justify it. Porter lacked the necessary transports to carry the prisoners, and with Johnston's army regathering to the east, it was better to have the whole matter concluded. Once the belligerents signed the surrender on July 4, Grant unleashed Sherman, who within a few weeks had driven Johnston well to the east of Jackson, where the Confederate commander no longer posed a threat. The campaign for Vicksburg had ended. Almost 30,000 Rebels and 172 artillery pieces had fallen into Yankee hands.

For the second time—the first being at Fort Donelson in February 1862—Grant had captured a Confederate army. During the struggle for Vicksburg, he had relied on boldness, speed, maneuverability, deception, surprise, and concentration at the decisive point to defeat two Confederate armies. Prior to the siege, he had fought and won five battles. Despite a preponderance of Confederate forces in the region, he achieved manpower superiority on each battlefield. He split the Rebel forces, severed their communications, pushed one field command to the northwest, and then drove another one back into the defenses of Vicksburg. With the fall of Port Hudson a few days later, the triumph at Vicksburg cut the Confederacy in two and gave the Union complete control of the Mississippi River. Coupled with the repulse of the Confederates at Gettysburg, Union fortunes suddenly revived. The campaign's extraordinary success also secured Grant's place as Lincoln's premier combat commander and paved the way for his promotion to commanding general eight months later.

HAWK IN THE FOWLYARD: JEB STUART

JOHN M. TAYLOR

Civil War cavalry always had more promise than it delivered. Cavalry was expensive to feed and equip—unless, like so many Confederate aristocrats, you brought along your own thoroughbred horse. (A decent horse cost around $110, ten times the average monthly pay of a private soldier in the Union army.) Training, too, was a problem, and at the beginning of the war there were few men experienced in horse warfare. Nor was the rough and still heavily forested American landscape suited to cavalry operations. Whereas Napoleon had once thrown massed divisions of horse soldiers into battle, Civil War armies could rarely rely on more than a few hundred men at one time. In the first three years of the war, the tactical historian Paddy Griffith notes, the cavalry of the Union Army of the Potomac made only five mounted charges against infantry during major battles, all with negligible effect. That was "far fewer than Marshal Ney's cavalry had made in three hours at Waterloo." The Confederates did resort to something approximating mass cavalry tactics before the Union did, and with a certain amount of success. Their deep raids gave the Union fits, but besides tearing up railroad lines and exposing unexploitable vulnerabilities, they had little effect. Worse, the cavalry was often not around when it was most needed.

But the cavalry did produce some of the most notable characters of the war, especially on the Confederate side—John Singleton Mosby, John Hunt Morgan, and Nathan Bedford Forrest. (Why did they, like naturalists or Protestant clerics, always use their middle names?) None was more deliberately flamboyant than James Ewell Brown Stuart—or, as he was more familiarly known, Jeb. Yet another West Pointer, Stuart had spent time on the frontier fighting Indians. He was not, however, a person who benefited from egalitarian democracy: He would have been perfectly suited to the horsy "mink and manure" set of England. Stuart affected a hat with a black ostrich plume and a yellow sash. This was not a man who, Jackson-like, sucked lemons. War, to him, was a great game, and he played it to the hilt. His raids could be spectacular, though like most popular art forms, they were always a bit short on substance. In June 1862, at the start of the Peninsula battles, Stuart and 1,200 men rode around McClellan's entire army. Before Manassas, he swooped down on the headquarters of the Union commander, John Pope; though Pope was away, Stuart's men did find his dispatch book, which was probably more valuable than its owner. At Chancellorsville, his patrols discovered that the Union right flank was "in the air." But in the Gettysburg campaign, he went off on a goose chase and famously lost touch with Lee's army. The fatal lure of the caper was, as John M. Taylor points out, forever Jeb Stuart's downside.

John M. Taylor is the author of eight books of history and biography, most recently a reassessment of Robert E. Lee, *Duty Faithfully Performed: Robert E. Lee and His Critics,* and *Confederate Raider: Raphael Semmes of the* Alabama. Taylor lives in McLean, Virginia.

A YANKEE GENERAL, THE AVUNCULAR JOHN SEDGWICK, PROBably put it best. Jeb Stuart, he maintained, "was the greatest cavalryman ever foaled in America." Equally impressive is the judgment of another of Stuart's adversaries, Union cavalry leader James H. Wilson. In a report prepared when the war was nearly over, General Wilson wrote of Stuart's death in 1864, "From it may be dated the permanent superiority of the national cavalry over that of the rebels."

The subject of these accolades was a rollicking, outgoing cavalier whose flamboyance sometimes seemed out of place among the pious leadership of the Army of Northern Virginia. It was difficult to overlook the young officer who, to many of his contemporaries, epitomized the élan of the cavalry. Not that Stuart was physically dominating, for he was not. There were even rumors that his beard concealed a weak chin, though this canard is belied by a photograph of a handsome young West Point graduate. What impressed people most about Stuart was his presentation: the quick blue eye, the sharpwittedness, and not least, the splendid horsemanship.

James Ewell Brown (later known as "Jeb") Stuart was a product of rural Virginia, where horses were a way of life. His relationship with both parents was oddly remote, and his early childhood was spent mainly in the company of his many siblings, romping the woods and fields, where he developed his famously rambunctious, roughhouse spirit. His later childhood was spent at various schools away from home. Despite his obvious intelligence, exemplified by an aptitude for mathematics, schoolwork was a chore for young Stuart. He did graduate from West Point in the top third of his class, in 1854, but with more of a reputation for horsemanship and fellowship than for scholarship.

At age twenty-one, Stuart was commissioned as a second lieutenant in the Mounted Rifles and stationed in West Texas for a few months. Then he was reassigned to a newly created cavalry unit and transferred to Fort Leavenworth, Kansas Territory. Following a whirlwind courtship, he married Flora Cooke, the daughter of a senior officer of the Old Army, Philip St. George Cooke, who commanded a regiment at the fort. In mid-1857, while on patrol in northwest Kansas, Stuart was shot point-blank in the chest by a wounded Cheyenne. Miraculously, the bullet was deflected by his sternum. Ever robust, he recovered quickly and was on hand for the birth of his daughter, named for her mother, in September. Over the next few years, Stuart hunted Kiowas and invented a couple of useful cavalry accoutrements such as "Stuart's Lightning Horse Hitcher." A son, named for Cooke, was born in 1860.

When Virginia seceded in April 1861, Stuart quickly resigned his U.S. Army commission and took his family home. If the young officer agonized over his course, there is no evidence of it; he was a Virginian, and most of his friends were siding with the South. His father-in-law saw things differently, and the decision of Colonel Cooke to stay with the Union brought a bitter estrangement from Stuart, who insisted that his son's name be legally changed. It was.

Placed in command of a Confederate cavalry regiment, Stuart quickly caught the eye of commanders like Joseph E. Johnston and Stonewall Jackson, and by late September he had been promoted to brigadier general. Quite apart from his obvious professional competence, Stuart was not easily overlooked. He complemented his Confederate gray uniform with cavalry boots above the knee, a yellow silk sash, and a brown felt slouch hat bedecked with a black ostrich plume. It was hard to view Jeb Stuart, armed with pistol and saber, as other than he was—the vaunting cavalier.

If there was one branch of arms in which the South began the war with a distinct advantage, it was the cavalry. Like Stuart, most Southern recruits came from rural areas with long equestrian traditions, and many squadrons were mounted on thoroughbred animals that were infinitely better than the government-issue nags of the U.S. Army. Although the South had neither the population nor the industrial base to compete with the North, many Confederates hoped their superior cavalry would make the difference in what they believed would be a short war.

One problem was that, in the view of many thoughtful soldiers, opportunities for the use of cavalry were diminishing. The increased range and accuracy of infantry weapons had earlier obliged Napoleon to make a distinction between light cavalry—useful for reconnaissance, harassment, and pursuit of the enemy—and heavy cavalry, good only for shock. At West Point, Stuart had been schooled in tactics based on the massed saber charge. To his credit, not even his thirst for glory led him to such foolishness against repeating rifles. Early in the war, he would use his horsemen for reconnaissance and the screening of infantry movements. Later, he and Nathan Bedford Forrest would discover new and creative employment for the mounted arm.

Fortunately for Stuart, he was well and favorably known to the Army of Northern Virginia's new commander, Robert E. Lee. The general had been superintendent at West Point when Stuart was a cadet; later, Lieutenant Stuart had accompanied him to Harpers Ferry when Lee had commanded the government force sent to capture John Brown and his raiders. In Stuart, the ever-aggressive Lee found a kindred spirit; in Lee, Stuart found a sympathetic authority figure whose approval he craved. After taking command of the Army of Northern Virginia on June 1, 1862, Lee invited suggestions from his subordinates about how to deal with Major General George B. McClellan's drive against Richmond. Stuart did not hesitate. He believed that McClellan would not attack Richmond until he had fortified his lines south of the Chickahominy River, and that Lee should therefore attack to the south. "We have an army far better adapted to attack than defense," he wrote. "Let us fight at an advantage before we are forced to fight at a disadvantage."

Lee shared this sentiment, but he was inclined to attack McClellan to the north rather than the south. He also intended to bring Jackson from the Shenandoah Valley to participate in the campaign, but he needed first to find out the state of affairs on McClellan's right flank. On June 10, Lee directed Stuart to make a "scouting movement" toward the enemy right, one designed to seize supplies and disrupt communications but having the primary objective of gaining intelligence on McClellan's dispositions. Stuart apparently suggested he might ride around McClellan's entire army. Lee made it clear that Stuart was not to hazard his command unnecessarily, but otherwise gave the cavalryman broad discretion.

Two days later, Stuart, with 1,200 troopers, rode off on one of the most spectacular missions of the war. It was to be the first—and perhaps the most famous—of many deep raids into enemy territory. He first took his command twenty-two miles north to the South Anna River. From there he turned east, moving behind the Federal right flank and ascertaining that there were no entrenchments there to anchor Fitz John Porter's corps. Brushing aside small detachments of Yankee cavalry—the pursuit, directed by father-in-law Philip St. George Cooke, was disorganized and ineffective—Stuart rode completely around McClellan's army, crossing the Chickahominy southeast of Richmond and returning to the capital after three days behind enemy lines. He was thus able to provide Lee with intelligence crucial to his commander's forthcoming offensive; equally important, he provided the South with a tonic at a time when good news was in short supply and morale was low. A Richmond reporter asked one of Stuart's troopers what the mission had accomplished:

> We have been in the saddle from Thursday morning until Saturday noon, never breaking rein nor breaking fast; we have whipped the enemy wherever he dared to appear; . . . we have burned 200 wagons laden with valuable stores, sunk or fired three large transports, captured 300 horses and mules . . . and brought in 170 prisoners, four officers, and many negroes.

"As to myself," the soldier concluded, "I wouldn't have missed the trip for a thousand dollars."

Even before the ride around McClellan, Lee's cavalry chief had not lacked attention. Now Stuart and his entourage were the subject of scrutiny by soldiers and reporters alike. They were hard to overlook, for Stuart insisted that his entire headquarters should be well turned out and well mounted. Like a medieval baron, he surrounded himself with musicians. His staff included a full-time minstrel, Sam Sweeney, and soldiers with musical skills often found themselves detailed to the cavalry as couriers.

Personal relations were important to Stuart. He insisted on staffing his headquarters with congenial men with whom he could share an easy, informal friendship, but he appears to have achieved this without any sacrifice in the quality of his troopers. His most trusted subordinate was probably Fitzhugh Lee, who happened to be the nephew of the army commander, but Stuart had a gift for picking out promising talent. One day a slightly built enlisted man appeared at the camp in Centreville, Virginia. Stuart saw something in the unlikely young soldier—named John Mosby—and, discovering that he was intimately familiar with the surrounding countryside, insisted that he join the headquarters staff for dinner. With Stuart's backing, Mosby would go on to become one of the war's most effective leaders of partisan forces.

Stuart soon found himself caught up in Lee's campaign to maneuver McClellan's besieging army away from Richmond. His mandate, as Lee began what became known as the Seven Days' campaign, was to harass McClellan's rear and to keep Lee advised of enemy intentions. Moving southeast along the Pamunkey River, Stuart encountered little opposition. His approach to the main Federal base at White House on June 28 caused the enemy to put it to the torch; even so, the Confederates captured enough commissary supplies to provide a feast for the hungry troopers. From there, Stuart was able to confirm that McClellan was retreating toward the James River.

In July, Stuart was promoted to major general and given Lee's two cavalry brigades, one commanded by Fitz Lee, the other by South Carolinian Wade Hampton. While McClellan's army nursed its wounds at Harrison's Landing, Lee moved to meet a new foe—the army of John Pope, now threatening Richmond from the north.

Once again, Lee was looking for a fight. Specifically, he wanted to deal with Pope before the Union general could be reinforced by McClellan. To keep the enemy off balance, Lee approved Stuart's proposal for a raid against Pope's communications and supply base at Catlett's Station. On August 22, Stuart set out with 1,500 men. As they clattered out of Warrenton, the Confederates had a stroke of good fortune, encountering a black man who agreed to guide them to Pope's headquarters. There, the Yankees were taken completely by surprise. In a tent near Pope's headquarters, a group of officers relaxed at the end of a long day. "I hope Jeb Stuart won't disturb us tonight," one of them wisecracked. At that moment Stuart's bugler blew the charge, and the Rebels were on them.

The raid at Catlett's Station was one of Stuart's most spectacular capers. His troopers missed Pope himself—the general was at the front—but captured his personal baggage, more than $500,000 in currency, and, most important of all, his dispatch book. Stuart rushed this intelligence find to Lee, who gained from it exact information about Pope's strength and dispositions.

Lee ordered Jackson to take a circuitous route to the enemy's rear and to place himself between the Federal army and Washington. On August 29, Jackson pounced on the Yankees at Manassas Junction. When Pope turned to give battle, he was struck on the flank by the remainder of Lee's army, under

Major General James Longstreet, who was threatened in turn for a time by Porter's V Corps. But Stuart ordered some of his men to drag pine boughs along a dusty road to simulate the arrival of a large body of infantry. This demonstration, on top of Porter's conviction that he already faced a superior force, brought his advance to a halt. The two-day Second Battle of Bull Run (Manassas) was a decisive Confederate victory in which Stuart received a fair share of the laurels.

When Lee undertook to move the war into Maryland the following month, the work for the cavalry was less glamorous. Nevertheless, Stuart effectively screened Lee's army on its march north, keeping the Federal cavalry from those mountain passes that gave access to the Confederate infantry. The ensuing Battle of Antietam was largely an infantry bloodbath, but Stuart anchored the extreme left of the Confederate line, and his horse artillery, led by the youthful Major John Pelham, helped secure a drawn battle for the hard-pressed Confederates.

No one used horse artillery more effectively than Jeb Stuart. He delighted in occupying a hill—any ridge would do—on an enemy flank. From there, a single battery or less, often firing canister, could have a devastating effect on an attacking column of infantry. The field at Antietam presented no such opportunity, but, three months later, at Fredericksburg, Stuart's favorite artilleryman, "the gallant Pelham," would advance two of his cannon and single-handedly halt an advancing Federal column. Stuart was devoted to Pelham, and he wept when the artilleryman was later killed.

Lee's first invasion of the North had fallen short of his hopes, but the stalemate at Antietam had in no way diminished his determination to take the war to the enemy. On October 6, 1862, he called Stuart to his headquarters, where they discussed a raid deep into the enemy heartland. Lee wanted to know what McClellan was doing and where his forces were deployed. Formal orders came two days later:

> You will . . . form a detachment of from twelve to fifteen hundred well mounted men . . . to cross the Potomac . . . and proceed to the rear of Chambersburg [Pennsylvania], and endeavor to destroy the railroad bridge over the branch of the Conococheague. Any other damage that you can inflict upon the enemy . . . you will also execute.

Making use of the latitude that Lee now allowed him, Stuart designated three 600-man divisions for the excursion, plus four guns of Pelham's horse artillery. They were off in the small hours of October 9, on a course to the north that took them immediately to the west of McClellan's army. There was no resistance, and not until that afternoon did a barrage of rumors convince the Federals that something was afoot. By nightfall Stuart was in Chambersburg, where dumbfounded town fathers had no choice but to surrender the town.

One of the Confederate prisoners that night was Alexander McClure, a prominent Pennsylvania publisher and a friend of Lincoln's. Although Stuart had forbidden confiscation of private property, several officers went to McClure's home to ask for coffee and bread. It proved to be a remarkable night. Confederate officers, McClure recalled, "politely asked permission to enter, and behaved with entire propriety." By morning McClure's coffee was gone, but he had passed a pleasant night, chatting with his "guests" about the war, their generals, and the shortage of coffee in the South.

Reluctantly, Stuart gave up his attempts to destroy the bridge for which he had come so far. It had turned out to be an iron bridge, and the short period in which he had made his preparations had not permitted him to obtain enough information about it. Undaunted, Stuart confided to an aide that he was determined to make a full circuit around McClellan's army in returning to Virginia, much as he had done outside Richmond. He justified his route on the grounds that the terrain to the east was favorable to cavalry, whereas infantry was almost certainly converging on the route he had traversed to Chambersburg.

On October 11, Stuart turned east to Cashtown, then directly south. His column was some five miles long, for it included not only his own dragoons but some 1,200 captured horses. By now the North was thoroughly alarmed, but Stuart had cut the telegraph wires to Chambersburg and there was no accurate information concerning his movements. The greatest enemy was fatigue. While Federal cavalry clattered off in response to a variety of alarms, Stuart led his weary troopers across the Potomac at White's Ford and thence to Leesburg. He had not suffered a single casualty.

Even within the Confederacy, the flamboyant cavalryman had critics who deprecated his achievements and deplored his canine appetite for praise. Regarding his latest raid, they could point out that Stuart had failed to destroy the bridge that was his nominal objective. But a raid like the one against Chambersburg included certain intangibles. Not only had Stuart carried the war to the enemy, he had made fools of the Federal military establishment. Considering that Confederate hopes rested heavily on eventual recognition by either Britain or France, this point carried some weight. Abraham Lincoln did not take the Chambersburg affair lightly. He reportedly told friends that when he was a boy "we used to play a game—three times around, and out. Stuart has been around McClellan twice. If he goes around him once more, gentlemen, McClellan will be out." As it happened, Lincoln did not wait for a third embarrassment. Within weeks of the Chambersburg raid, McClellan was out.

✦

As 1862 TURNED into 1863, Jeb Stuart had no way of knowing that the South was approaching the limit of its resources. Ever the romantic, he viewed the way in terms of individual combat, not as a collision between unequal economies and resources. Stuart looked on with approval as the Confederate cavalry grew in numbers and efficiency until, by the end of 1862, his own corps numbered some 600 officers and 8,500 sabers. He could not foresee that his own strength had peaked relative to that of the enemy, but there were ominous signs. Joseph Hooker, who had succeeded Ambrose Burnside as commander of the Army of the Potomac, was determined to strengthen his own mounted arm, and was consolidating his troopers into units of brigade size and larger. Soon, better mounted and better led, they would be able to meet Stuart's veterans on something approaching parity.

Hooker, however, would not be around for the transformation. But another debacle awaited the Army of the Potomac, this time at Chancellorsville. The Confederate strategy there was all Lee and Jackson, but the three-day battle provided still another showcase for Stuart's energy and versatility. When Hooker made the error of sending his own cavalry south on a raid against Lee's railroads, the Federals yielded control of the roads around Chancellorsville. As a result, Stuart's patrols discovered that Hooker's right flank was "in the air" and vulnerable to an attack from the west. Acting on this good intelligence, Lee took his most daring gamble. He divided his army, sending Stonewall Jackson, screened by Stuart's cavalry, to roll up Hooker's right flank.

The rout of the Federals that followed was marred primarily by the fatal wounding of Jackson by his own men on the night of May 2. Stuart was attached to Jackson's wing on that fateful night, and command of Jackson's corps temporarily passed to him. If the thirty-year-old Stuart was intimidated by the responsibility, there is no evidence. He was everywhere, directing infantry attacks aimed at reuniting the two wings of Lee's army. (At one time he was overheard parodying a popular camp song with words that ran, "Old Joe Hooker, come out of the wilderness.") Jackson's officers, many of whom shared the army's patronizing attitude toward cavalry, considered Stuart's performance remarkable. Porter Alexander, who commanded Jackson's artillery, wrote:

I do not think there was a more brilliant thing done in the war than Stuart's extricating that command from [an] extremely critical position. . . . The hard marching and the night fighting had thinned our ranks to less than 20,000 . . . but Stuart never seemed to hesitate or to doubt for one moment that he could just crash his way wherever he chose to strike.

Justly proud of his performance at Chancellorsville, Stuart may have aspired for a time to the command of Jackson's corps. Lee seems never to have seriously contemplated such a move, but considering the sharp drop in effectiveness of Jackson's old corps under Lieutenant General Richard S. Ewell, Stuart might have been a better choice. Stuart, in any case, was never one to sulk. A month after Chancellorsville he mounted a grand cavalry review, with Lee himself taking the salute.

While Stuart paraded, the Federals seized the initiative, and the result, on June 9, was the Battle of Brandy Station, the greatest cavalry battle ever fought in America. The Rebels managed to drive off the aggressive Yankees, but the margin of victory was slim, and the criticism directed at Stuart for allowing himself to be caught by surprise was galling to the cavalry commander.

Not Brandy Station, however, but the Gettysburg campaign that followed would prove to be the most controversial chapter in Stuart's story. Lee's plan again called for the cavalry to control the Blue Ridge Mountain passes while his infantry moved north. Stuart was then to cross the Potomac, make contact in Pennsylvania with Ewell's advance corps, and there play the cavalry's usual role in reconnaissance. Lee's poorly worded order invited misinterpretation. The operative paragraph read in part,

If General Hooker's Army remains inactive you can leave two brigades to watch him, and withdraw the three others, but should he not appear to be moving northward, I think you had better withdraw this side of the mountains tomorrow night, cross at Shepherdstown next day, and move over to Fredericktown.

Employing the freedom that he had always enjoyed in implementing Lee's orders, Stuart proposed to lead half his cavalry along a route between the Army of the Potomac and Washington, thereby playing on Lincoln's concern for the safety of the U.S. capital. The problem was that the Federals refused to accommodate Stuart's plan. They were also moving north, and Stuart was obliged to take a circuitous route to emerge east of the enemy infantry. North of Washington he set to making mischief, cutting the telegraph line at

Rockville and seizing several hundred prisoners and more than a hundred wagons. The prisoners were paroled, but the wagon train further slowed the cavalry's movements.

Stuart continued north, crossing into Pennsylvania near Hanover on June 30, but he was no longer certain of Lee's movements, much less those of the enemy, under the command of George Gordon Meade since June 28. Stuart's three brigades reached Carlisle, Pennsylvania, on the evening of July 1, and soon word arrived of a great battle at Gettysburg, about thirty miles to the south. When he joined Lee the next afternoon, ahead of his weary men, there was a characteristically mild rebuke from the army commander. "Well, General Stuart," Lee said, "you are here at last."

On the climactic third day, Lee ordered Stuart to flank the enemy right. Lee's thought was that if his cavalry could break through, they might be able to wreak havoc in Meade's rear, much as Stuart had done at Second Manassas. But when Stuart took his weary troopers down the York Pike, he found Yankee cavalry waiting. While Pickett launched his historic charge, Stuart's cavalrymen fought a fierce but largely meaningless battle against three brigades of Federal cavalry. At dusk, Stuart withdrew up the York Pike to rejoin Lee's defeated army.

Stuart's failure to keep Lee informed of enemy movements during the Gettysburg campaign came in for heavy criticism even at the time. Colonel Charles Marshall, a senior member of Lee's staff, and others in the Army of Northern Virginia believed that Stuart had violated the spirit if not the letter of his orders. Lee himself, slow to criticize commanders who enjoyed his confidence, included in his report a statement that "the movements of the army preceding the battle of Gettysburg had been much embarrassed by the absence of cavalry."

Stuart was aware of the criticism but seemed unchastened. One officer noted that during the retreat, Lee, A. P. Hill, Ewell, and Longstreet had passed his post "with . . . not even a battleflag to mark their rank." Stuart, in contrast, had passed through Martinsburg "with a large cavalcade of staff and couriers and two bugles blowing furiously."

Instead of admitting fault for the failure of the Gettysburg campaign, Stuart claimed to have spread "terror and consternation to the very gates of the [enemy] capital," while leaving Lee with sufficient cavalry for reconnaissance. Neither Stuart's conduct in the Gettysburg campaign nor his defense of it showed him at his best. Biographer Emory Thomas comments perceptively that Stuart "dealt with failure by not dealing with it, by denying it."

As for the impact of Stuart's absence in the days before Gettysburg, the most accurate verdict may have been that of Stuart's aide and later biographer, Henry B. McClellan. "It was not the want of cavalry that General Lee bewailed," McClellan wrote, "for he had enough of it had it been properly used. It was the absence of Stuart himself that he felt so keenly; for . . . it seemed as if his cavalry were concentrated in [Stuart's] person, and from him alone could information be expected."

✦

THE LULL THAT FOLLOWED Gettysburg was a boon to the Confederacy, but the hard riding of 1863 had seriously eroded its cavalry. During the winter that followed, Stuart worked assiduously to restore its fighting edge in the face of growing desertions and difficulty in obtaining remounts. He may have suspected that his slashing raids were a thing of the past, but he overlooked nothing in keeping his force at maximum effectiveness. He wrote to Fitz Lee in March 1864:

> I am anxious to have your whole command in the field but, entre nous, it cannot possibly be subsisted till the grass grows. . . . Look well to your forage—it is the existence of the cavalry. . . .
>
> I want your men practiced charging in column, solid and compact so as to shock. They generally disperse too much. Also, practice rear squadrons to dismount quickly & deploy to right & left in a fight. Urge commanders to command their men in action from a corporal up to brigadier.

A few weeks later, General Phil Sheridan, with 10,000 Yankee troopers, took a leaf from Stuart's own book and launched a raid in the direction of Richmond. By then Stuart commanded no more than 7,000 cavalrymen, and few of these had the fine mounts that characterized the Confederate cavalry in 1861. Moreover, before he could attempt to deal with Sheridan, Stuart had to leave about 3,000 troopers with Lee, whose army was locked in a campaign of attrition against Grant in the Wilderness.

Gathering all the men he could muster, about 3,000, Stuart managed to place his command between Sheridan and the capital at a crossroads known as Yellow Tavern, six miles north of Richmond. Stuart arrived before the Yankees, and decided that he must make a stand there if the capital was to be protected. He deployed his dismounted troopers along the Mountain Road, hoping to attack Sheridan's flank. In the event, when Sheridan's advance guard encountered the Confederates on the morning of May 11, it was the Federals—enjoying a numerical advantage of more than two to one—who attacked.

The first Federal attack, in the late morning of an unseasonably hot day, was repulsed. Early afternoon brought a lull in the fighting, and Stuart moved from one of his battered companies to another, offering advice and encouragement. At about four in the afternoon the Federals attacked again, employing both mounted and dismounted troops. Stuart, riding alone, joined the men of Company K, 1st Virginia Cavalry, defending along a rail fence. "Bully for old K," he shouted. "Give it to them, boys!"

Stuart added to the defense with his heavy cavalry revolver, but some of the attackers broke through the Confederate line. In the chaos that followed, several Yankees attempted to make their way back to the Federal lines, and one of them, on the run, took a quick shot at the cinnamon-bearded officer at the fence. Stuart, struck in the abdomen, reeled in his saddle. As he was carried to an ambulance, he saw some of his troopers retreating from the field. "Go back! Go back!" he cried. "Do your duty, as I have done mine, and our country will be safe." The next day, after more than twenty-four hours of pain, Stuart joined Stonewall Jackson in the pantheon of the dying Confederacy. There were not enough soldiers for an honor guard at his funeral, but such was Stuart's hold on the people of the South that for years his grave in Richmond's Hollywood Cemetery was seldom without flowers. Lee himself said, "I can scarcely think of him without weeping."

What was it about Jeb Stuart that brought such accolades from friend and foe alike? There was nothing of the grand strategist to the young cavalryman. In Bruce Catton's term, he was "pure act." He thought in tactical terms, and viewed even a war of attrition in terms of gallantry and the heroic gesture. Not even the constricting Federal noose that so limited his own initiative in late 1863 and early 1864 could persuade him that the war was more than adventure. His relentless romanticism was unusual in the later years of the war, but it contributed to a certain mystique.

Stuart was also a very professional soldier whose troopers, for the first three years of the war, were the equal of any in the world. He was not a great innovator, though he probably employed horse artillery more effectively than any of his contemporaries. What Stuart did do was to adapt instinctively to a situation in which the Napoleonic cavalry charge was obsolete, and to elevate the deep cavalry raid to something approaching an art form. No one else on either side, not even Bedford Forrest, could wreak more havoc behind the enemy lines with a comparatively small number of troopers. A staunch supporter of the Union complained in print, "Wherever Stuart rides, he carries terror with him. . . . He is as resistless as a hawk in a fowlyard."

THE ROCK OF CHICKAMAUGA: GEORGE H. THOMAS

JOHN BOWERS

The historian Bruce Catton once pointed out that "just twice in all the war was a major Confederate army driven away from a prepared position in complete rout—at Chattanooga and at Nashville." Both times one man directed the routing blow: George H. Thomas. Catton touches on an irony, because Thomas was better known as a defensive general, most notably for his stand at Snodgrass Hill during the Battle of Chickamauga in September 1863. Thomas saved a disintegrating Union army and the city of Chattanooga as well, and earned one of the most recognizable nicknames in American military history: "The Rock of Chickamauga." (Thomas was equally a rock at Stones River nine months earlier, another battle that saw a Union army on the verge of disaster.) Whether on offense or defense, Thomas was a general whom men would fight for, and they called him affectionate names like "Old Tom," "Uncle George," or, simply, "Pap." When he ordered them to take a line of Confederate entrenchments at the foot of Missionary Ridge, near Chattanooga, less than three months after the Chickamauga debacle, they did—and then kept right on going all the way to the summit.

George H. Thomas was a remarkable commander, but we are just beginning to rediscover his worth. "Thomas exploited the technology that offered enormous potential for advancing weapons and resources," the historian Thomas B. Buell writes, "mastered the art of logistics, and understood and employed combined arms—infantry, cavalry, and artillery—as no other general on either side. In matters of command and control, transportation, communications, intelligence, and cartography, Thomas's imprint on military doctrine would carry well into the twentieth century." Still, he made things difficult for hagiographers. He had the misfortune to serve, largely out of view, in the Western theater, to be continually at odds with U. S. Grant, and to be a Virginian. In his own time, people treated this staunch Union supporter as a man without a country and, until Nashville proved otherwise, doubted his loyalty. Grant, who mistook Thomas's penchant for careful preparation for a McClellan-like failure of nerve, had actually given orders to relieve the Virginian of command of the Army of the Cumberland when the news of Nashville arrived. "Old Pap," as John Bowers writes, always did things his own way, and if there was method in his actions, there was never madness.

John Bowers, whose grandfather fought on the Confederate side at Chickamauga, is the author of *Stonewall Jackson: Portrait of a Soldier* and *The Battles for Chattanooga.*

GEORGE H. THOMAS WAS A TRIUMPHANT CIVIL WAR GENERAL who led his men to victory in some of the war's hottest battles. He was a true Southerner, a son of the Old Dominion—and he fought for the North.

He was born in Southampton County, Virginia, not far from the North Carolina border, on July 31, 1816. He was gentry and a West Pointer (class of 1840, which included William Tecumseh Sherman and Richard S. Ewell), someone whose family had owned slaves, someone who could claim Southern ancestry as far back as Robert E. Lee could. Never was there a question as to Thomas's bona fides—even his accent was pure Virginian, with broad vowels and soft placement. Never was there a question about the ties that should have bound him to his region. Yet the day after Fort Sumter was fired upon in April 1861, Thomas, then a major in the regular army, did not resign his commission as so many other Southerners did. At Carlisle Barracks in Pennsylvania, he reaffirmed his loyalty to the Union—and caused his family in Virginia to disown him. His maiden sisters turned his picture to the wall, burned all his letters, and wrote him later in life only to suggest he change his name.

Few, if any, of Thomas's Virginia brethren could understand a man going against his own people, particularly when the Federals "invaded" Virginia soon afterward—fighting at First Manassas (Bull Run) on July 21, 1861— and remained intent on her destruction until peace at Appomattox on April 9, 1865. Why, so many in the South wanted to know, did Thomas turn out to be such a dedicated and formidable foe? Why did he unrelentingly, whole-heartedly dedicate himself to keeping the Union preserved and putting the rebellion down? Why?

✦

NAT TURNER'S REBELLION, which began on the night of August 21, 1831, may have been a pivotal event in Thomas's youth. This volcanic uprising, led by a firebrand slave, had no antecedent save for Indian raids a generation or so before. Turner's wild, marauding band wove at random through isolated farms in Southampton County, raping, plundering, ripping society apart at the seams. Fifteen-year-old Thomas was called upon to ride to neighboring farms and warn the incredulous that they were in peril. His own family barely escaped with their lives.

Some survivors feared the whole black race after that and believed Southern whites should leave the Union and band together for safety's sake. Not Thomas. What he had learned after seeing this revolt was that there is nothing much worse than chaos and a center not holding. Secession and the threat of disorder were not for him. George H. Thomas was everlastingly conservative, never the romantic cavalier for a "cause." There was nothing Hamlet-like about him. As a man and as a soldier, he was straightforward, unswerving, sure of himself.

As a West Point cadet, Thomas was meticulous and hardworking. Cadet William Starke Rosecrans, who would later command him in Tennessee, said the blue-eyed, square-jawed Thomas bore a remarkable resemblance to Gilbert Stuart's portrait of Washington. West Pointers actually dubbed him "George Washington," for manner as well as facial resemblance. Nervous, fidgety, redheaded William Tecumseh Sherman shared a room in the Old South Barracks with Thomas. "Cump" Sherman, only sixteen at the time and talking a blue streak, was sloppy in dress then as later and led the corps in demerits—one of the all-time great "hash makers" in Point history. As a plebe he garnered 109 demerits; Thomas in his whole four-year career attained but 87.

Thomas caused little fuss but gave anyone pause who was out to give him trouble. An early trait, and one he kept, was never to back down or cringe in the face of a threat. Cadet Stewart Van Vliet, who also shared the room with Sherman and Thomas, told a story years later about hazing:

> One evening a cadet came into our room and commenced to give us orders.
> He had said but a few words when Old Tom stepped up to him and said, "Leave

this room immediately or I will throw you through the window." There were no more attempts to haze us.

Ulysses S. Grant spent a year with Thomas at West Point and later knew him in the Old Army. But he never fully appreciated Thomas, and possibly did not trust him. "Thomas's dispositions were deliberately made and always good," Grant wrote. "He could not be driven from a point he was given to hold. He was not as good, however, in pursuit as he was in action." During the all-important Nashville campaign in December 1864, Grant had urged Thomas in frequent dispatches to attack Confederate general John B. Hood at once so that Hood could not escape north into Kentucky (and later attack Grant in Virginia). In his memoirs Grant writes, "At last I had to say to General Thomas that I should be obliged to remove him unless he acted promptly. He replied that he was very sorry, but he would move as soon as he could."

What faced Thomas on the road to Nashville was not the enemy but frozen, slippery ground that would not permit the essential advance of his cavalry. He would not move precipitously, but stayed by his guns and waited for a thaw. Grant ordered General John A. Logan to go to Thomas and take command if Thomas had not advanced by the time he got there. Then Grant changed his mind and said he himself would go to Nashville and take command. Still Thomas waited. He wasn't budging. When the ice melted on December 14, he geared up his army, moved, and overwhelmed Hood in one of the Union's greatest victories. Grant himself wrote, "He did move, and was successful from the start."

The qualities that Thomas showed, time after time, were patience and calm. "He would never do to conduct one of your campaigns," Grant said to Sherman, Thomas's former roommate. Sherman was excitable, given to wild mood swings, and more than once was thought certifiably crazy. Grant and Sherman had much in common and complemented each other well through the war. Both were theatrical by nature, highly eccentric, and had known periods, in peace and in the early stages of the war, when they were held in quite low esteem. Americans always cheer for the underdog—and Grant and Sherman were certainly that. They were counted out early—and came back to be made into celebrities in their day. They liked each other enormously and supported each other's positions. Later, someone asked Sherman to try to change some of President Grant's reconstruction ideas. "No," replied Sherman, according to General Richard W. Johnson. "Grant stood by me when I was crazy and I stood by him when he was drunk, and now we stand by each other."

Characterologically, Thomas was the opposite of Grant and Sherman—a methodical, levelheaded tactician who never flew by the seat of his pants but just as impressively won battles. His men adored him. They called him "Old Reliable," "Old Slow Trot," "Old Pap," "Uncle George," and "The Rock"—a father figure to tie oneself to. He was incorruptible—indeed in his case the word seems an understatement. After the war Grant was given a $50,000 house in Philadelphia by a group of wealthy citizens, and Sherman received one in Washington for twice that amount. When Thomas was offered a reward for his war record, he turned it down flat, saying, "While fully apprehending the motives which induce these kind offers, I contend that I cannot accept them and be wholly independent."

When Thomas went to extremes, he went perhaps to the extremes of rectitude—which does not always make good copy. He was no George S. Patton. When Grant asked him to hold a surrounded and besieged Chattanooga, Thomas replied, "We will hold the town till we starve"—not flamboyant, like General Anthony McAuliffe's reply of "Nuts!" to the Germans at Bastogne, but dramatic in its own way, and to the point.

In all matters prudent, Thomas waited to marry until he was thirty-six and securely ensconced as an artillery and cavalry instructor at West Point. He had received his academic post through the recommendation of Rosy Rosecrans, who would figure as Thomas's superior officer at Chickamauga. The superintendent at the Point at that time was Robert E. Lee. Thomas was a distinguished veteran of the Mexican War—as were Lee and Rosecrans—and a position at West Point was a favored retreat for these veterans.

There is no record of Thomas having had any *affaire de coeur* before age thirty-six. Until then, he had apparently been as chaste as a monk. In the spring of '52, though, he began checking out romantic novels and volumes of poetry from the academy library, in addition to his usual requests for works on military matters. It was not long until he became engaged, then married, to Frances Kellogg, whose widowed mother had been in the habit of bringing her along on visits to her nephew, Cadet Lyman M. Kellogg, class of 1852.

Frances Kellogg was tall and stately and five years younger than her husband. Due to the Civil War and the military life Thomas never left, the couple was separated for long periods. They were devoted, but remained childless. The Kelloggs were Yankees from Troy, New York, and some have speculated that being married to a Northerner may have influenced Thomas in renouncing the Southern cause after Sumter. Influence him she undoubtedly did—but something fundamental and unswerving in his own nature caused him to fight for the Union.

Although Thomas usually presented a stone-faced exterior of total probity and solemnity, he was not without humor, passion, and deep feeling. He knew how to take a drink, and when he felt slighted and wronged, he did not simply put up with it. A Union general who knew how to win, a distinct rara avis through much of the war, he bridled at his slow promotions in rank. He surmised (in all likelihood correctly) that his Southern background stood in his way, a permanent black cloud over his full acceptance by the Northern high command led by Grant and General Henry Halleck.

As for the South, during the all-important battle for Chattanooga in November 1863, Sherman asked Thomas if he had had any communication with General Braxton Bragg, who commanded the rebel army that they faced. Suddenly Thomas's blue eyes flashed and emotion poured out. "Damn him, I'll be even with him yet."

"What's the matter now?" Sherman wanted to know.

Thomas explained that not long before, he had tried to send a letter through rebel lines, under a flag of truce, and that it had come back with a note: "Respectfully returned to General Thomas. General Bragg declines to have any intercourse with a man who has betrayed his State." In more pleasant antebellum days, Thomas, Sherman, and Bragg had served together at Fort Moultrie, South Carolina. Sherman recalled that Thomas uttered many threats as to what he was going to do to his former friend Bragg—and that he was quite heated about it.

Bragg certainly suffered the effects of Thomas's intelligence and capability. It is probable that Chattanooga, gateway to Sherman's March to the Sea, would have fallen to Bragg and his army if not for Thomas. At the Battle of Chickamauga on September 19–20, 1863, the bulk of the Union forces fled in near panic into the city. Alexander McCook and Thomas Crittenden and even the redoubtable Rosecrans fled, their armies thrown into disarray by Hood, who broke through a quarter-mile gap and poured unexpectedly over Rosecrans's right wing.

The only one who held was Thomas. He rallied his corps and some survivors of Crittenden's command and stood on a steep, horseshoe-shaped elevation called Snodgrass Hill that protruded eastward from Missionary Ridge. He kept this position into the growing dark and bought enough time for most of Rosecrans's retreating troops to reach Chattanooga. General James Longstreet and his veterans of the charges at Gettysburg scaled Horseshoe Ridge, and it seemed they would easily grapple Thomas into submission. But he held—with some last-minute help from General Gordon Granger's reserve corps—and Old Pete Longstreet's men had to retreat down the ridge. The

Confederates did win a massive tactical victory at Chickamauga—in 8,000 blue-clads captured, tons of their supplies taken, and a Union army bottled up in Chattanooga—but one thing they couldn't claim: subduing George H. Thomas of Virginia.

Actually, Chickamauga was not the only place where Thomas was a rock. The Battle of Stones River, fought around New Year's 1863, near Murfreesboro, Tennessee, had been a rehearsal for Chickamauga, as hapless Bragg tarried in his retreat from Nashville but suddenly stood to fight. Rosecrans, the Union commander, felt the sting of rebel fire and considered retreating to Nashville but feared the Confederates might be blocking his way. He also had Thomas as a general in his army. Thomas spread calm among his troops. He stood patiently and firmly, saying, "This army does not retreat." In the end, Bragg did. At Chickamauga it happened again; Thomas could not be moved when the chips were down.

On the Confederate side, Chickamauga cost General Hood his right leg in the battle (his left arm had already been shattered at Gettysburg)—but dismemberment did not soften his rash and truculent nature. A short time after the leg was amputated—so close to the trunk that at first the battlefield surgeon did not think it could be done—Hood was back in the saddle, where he had to be strapped every morning in order to remain upright. His long, bearded face looks extremely dour and stern in the few photographs we have of him.

Braxton Bragg also would win no prize for cheerfulness. His visage reflects a woefully depressed personality. Unlike Thomas's men, Bragg's did not adore him, and his fellow officers were nearly always in open revolt. On paper, before a battle, he was a great tactician, but once the cannon boomed and muskets rattled and the fight took unexpected turns, he did as Rosecrans did—made a getaway, both to regroup and to rethink. He had few intimates and brooded alone. After the Union finally prevailed at Chattanooga, Bragg was kicked upstairs to become chief of staff for the Confederacy. Ironically, today the U.S. flag flies over Fort Bragg in North Carolina and over Fort Hood in Texas—but Fort Thomas, a small city in Kentucky, is no longer even a military installation.

Although Thomas was highly popular with his men, he was not friendly with them. He once said, "I am naturally reserved and have found it difficult to be on familiar, easy terms with my men." But his dignity, his steadiness, and his air of assurance aroused the affections of those under his command—as shown in the nicknames they gave him. "Old Slow Trot," a nickname he came by while an instructor at West Point, may be misleading at first: It did

not denote a lack of alacrity in pressing for battle—as one might think after
reading Grant on Thomas. It came from the care he took never to labor his
mount unnecessarily. A fine equestrian since boyhood, he always showed the
utmost consideration for a horse's welfare. When he led West Point cadets in
cavalry exercises and they began to chafe in anticipation of a gallop, there inevitably came Thomas's deep, rolling Southern accent to cool them down:
"Slow trot, gentlemen. Slow trot!"

The cavalry is ceremonial today, but in Thomas's day it was a prestigious
and crucial branch of the army. Grant sat well in the saddle and enjoyed racing to and fro among his men in the field. When he reined in his horse, he sat
relaxed, from all accounts, leaning forward to talk, his white socks drooping
above his black shoes, a large cigar in his hand or jutting from his mouth. His
preferred comrade-in-arms, Sherman, rode impulsively, intuitively, a raw
exposed nerve. Thomas was another kind of rider, and this tells something of
his character and the type of commander he was. Captain Henry Stone of
Thomas's staff once noted:

> When under fire, his movements . . . were as deliberate as at any time. . . .
> He was never seen riding up and down his lines waving his sword, shouting, or
> going through ceremonies. . . . On the march nobody ever saw him, with an es-
> cort trailing, dashing past a moving column of troops, throwing up dust or
> mud and compelling them to leave the road. If any had the right of way, it was
> they. He would break through the woods or flounder across a swamp rather
> than force his men from the road and wear them out by needless fatigue.

Thomas was persevering and dogged in advancing himself and his troops,
but there was never a recorded incident when he puffed himself up and
showed unseemly ambition—as did McClellan ("Young Napoleon") in blue
and P. G. T. Beauregard in gray. He would not step over someone to advance
his career. When he was appointed to succeed Major General Don Carlos
Buell as commander of the Army of the Ohio, Thomas, who was second-in-
command, notified Buell that he was declining the promotion because he
considered it unfair. He felt that Buell didn't deserve such treatment—and besides, looking realistically at the situation, he concluded that he wasn't quite
ready for the assignment. (Buell soon lost his command anyway.) Thomas also
at first refused to succeed General Rosecrans after the Battle of Chickamauga,
but Old Rosy himself persuaded him to accept the appointment.

If Thomas could be said to resemble anyone, it was perhaps Robert E. Lee.
Both were deeply Southern in temperament, both inspired unquestioning

devotion in their followers, and, most striking, both were so modest that some thought it almost a weakness. There was never a hint of scandal in their personal lives, and both were exceptionally kind and courteous. Grant and Sherman could be brusque and sometimes brutal in personal dealings. Never Thomas; never Lee.

Yet some deep, dark force simmered low in both Lee's and Thomas's psyches, and this force came out unbridled in war. Both could be expert, devastating killers—no other word for it. When ammunition ran low at Chickamauga, Thomas didn't blink an eye about calling for the bayonet. He opted always to fight, to punish his foe, to win. It was Lee who said, at Fredericksburg, "It is well that war is so terrible. We should grow too fond of it." And at a war council in Tennessee, it was Thomas alone who voted to stand and fight. He rose by the firelight and said, "Gentlemen, I know of no better place to die than right here," and walked out of the room and into the night.

Lee, who fought against the Union, is universally honored today. Public buildings and avenues are named after him, and in Eisenhower's White House his portrait hung on the wall. Thomas, who fought to save the Union and was crucial to its preservation, is held in far less esteem—if, indeed, most people even know who he was. Lee's home on the rise above the Potomac in Arlington is a national tourist attraction. Thomas's commodious boyhood home near Newsoms, Virginia, is not marked; in fact, natives of the region are said to often shake their heads when the curious ask where it is. Could it be we collectively romanticize the Lost Cause and those who led it, while even today we distrust, if not dislike, those who supported the Union but had to fight their own people to do so?

Grant was only one of the many Northerners who never completely trusted the Virginian. Who could fight his own people? And this suspicion in the North was more than matched by Southern abhorrence for his actions in scything down their armies.

After Thomas's death, General Sherman spoke before a crowd of veterans at the unveiling of Thomas's equestrian statue in Washington, D.C. He prophesied that a day would come when Southerners would forgive Thomas, that they would make pilgrimages to this statue erected to his memory. As far as that prediction goes, it may be said that few have ever paid attention to the statue in the center of a busy traffic circle in the nation's capital. No Southern delegation, as far as we know, has ever laid a wreath there. Today cars whiz by it and through a tunnel beneath, and it is the unusual tourist or passerby who takes a moment to honor the hero of the Battle of Chickamauga.

Various libels have been directed against Thomas. Sherman—his West

Point classmate and allegedly his friend—at one point said that Thomas and his Army of the Cumberland were addicted to the defensive and that a fresh furrow would stop the whole column. Today, however, long after the firing has died and records have been sifted through, Thomas's stature has grown among Civil War scholars to an almost towering presence. Bruce Catton writes:

> What a general could do, Thomas did; no more dependable soldier for a moment of crisis existed on the North American continent, or ever did exist. . . .
>
> Thomas comes down in history as the Rock of Chickamauga, the great defensive fighter, the man who could never be driven away but who was not much on the offensive. That may be a correct appraisal. Yet it may also be worth making note that just twice in all the war was a major Confederate army driven away from a prepared position in complete rout—at Chattanooga and at Nashville. Each time the blow that routed it was launched by Thomas.

Thomas, a Southerner, led Northern troops, and they revered him. They fought for him because, most important, he never asked them to do anything he wouldn't do. He did not lead a battle from a headquarters in the rear. He liked to sit astride his horse, reins in hand, while canisters thumped and minié balls buzzed past. There was never a question as to his physical bravery. A short time before the war, on August 26, 1860, while on a military exploration of the Conchos and Colorado Rivers, his detail engaged in a sharp fight with some plundering Indians. Thomas was painfully wounded by an arrow that entered his chin and lodged in his chest. He pulled out the arrow himself and kept the fight going until he was sure the Indians had been vanquished.

While recuperating from his wound in November 1860, on leave in his native Virginia, he suffered a worse injury. Alighting from a railroad train in the dark near Lynchburg, Virginia, deceived by the shadows of the moonlight, he believed he was stepping onto firm earth and instead plummeted down a deep ravine, severely wrenching his back. He was in great pain, and at the time, fearing he could never return to full duty, he looked around for an alternative way of life. The first job he sought was as commandant of cadets at the Virginia Military Institute. By the time he applied, however, the position had been filled and he just missed serving at the same seat of learning as an obscure and eccentric professor named Thomas J. Jackson, soon to be known as "Stonewall." Thomas remained in the army and suffered from his back for the rest of his life.

In the closing months of 1863, the decisive military action at Chattanooga signaled the Union's grasp at last on victory. Of the commanders, Thomas was most essential in that victory, which broke the Confederate siege of the town and started Sherman on his way to the sea.

The taking of Missionary Ridge in the late afternoon of November 25 was one of the war's most curious assaults—unusual in that Thomas's men had been ordered only to take the row of Confederate rifle pits at the base of the ridge, not the ridge itself. However, the inspired blue-clads, 20,000 strong, fought through an inferno, sometimes by bayonet, captured the fortifications, and, when they could have stopped and rested, kept up the pursuit of the rebels until they had captured the ridge as well. They did all this without a direct order from Thomas or anyone. In fact, officers—from second lieutenant on up—tried to stay them. But they were Old Pap's troops and knew what to do.

For perhaps the first time in the war, common soldiers led a charge while officers took up the rear—finally yelling, inappropriately, out of habit, "Follow me! Follow me!" At his command post down below, Grant fumed. He said commands would be lost if the unauthorized charge failed—meaning the ax would fall on Thomas. But Thomas did not worry. Through field glasses he watched his troops scale the impossibly steep, fortified ridge. They screamed "Chickamauga, Chickamauga!" at the frightened, fleeing rebels—and almost captured Bragg himself before it was over. It was a costly victory, though. When Thomas was asked if the dead should be buried by state, he replied, "No, no, mix 'em up. I'm *tired* of states' rights."

Charles A. Dana, who was there as an observer, wrote this report immediately afterward:

> Glory to God. The day is decisively ours. Missionary Ridge has just been carried by a magnificent charge of Thomas's troops. . . . The heights which Thomas carried by assault are at least 500 feet above Chattanooga Valley, with an inclination of at least 45 degrees, and exceedingly rugged and difficult. . . . The storming of the ridge by our troops was one of the greatest miracles in military history.

Thomas's Army of the Cumberland fought under Sherman through the bloody battle of Kenesaw Mountain and through the fall of Atlanta; and it was the impetuous Sherman who started the rumor of Thomas's "slowness" in a dispatch to Grant during the march to Atlanta: "My chief source of trouble is with the Army of the Cumberland, which is dreadfully slow." Thomas was anything but slow. His troops bore the brunt of the fighting to Atlanta—and were essential in its capture. Then it was Thomas and the Army of the Cumberland who pursued Hood from Atlanta, defeating him at Nashville—thus protecting Sherman's rear and allowing Grant to battle Lee into submission in Virginia.

After the victory in Nashville, the Army of the Cumberland performed mainly garrison duties during the few months left in the war, and Thomas was rewarded by promotion to major general. He served in Tennessee during Reconstruction, fighting any vestige of Confederate resurgence—guarding the polls, putting down the Ku Klux Klan—as if he had been born in Massachusetts. On the other hand, he went as far as anyone in obtaining pardons for former Confederate officers and their kin. He remained in the army and served on the Pacific coast in the first years of Grant's presidency.

Thomas died of a stroke on March 28, 1870, at age fifty-three, while stationed in San Francisco. His body was transported east in a crepe-festooned railroad car. Guns echoed in salute at every nearby army post, and in Chicago there was a great demonstration of pomp. At the funeral in Troy, New York, there were the bowed heads of President Grant; Generals Sherman, Philip Sheridan, and George Meade; and a host of cabinet members, governors, and former soldiers under Thomas's command. Twenty-five railway cars, hauled by a couple of locomotives, brought New York's National Guard. "Never before in the history of Troy were so many strangers in the city," the local *Times* said.

It seemed everyone was there save Thomas's family from Virginia. Not one of them attended. "Our brother George died to us in 'sixty-one," his sisters told their neighbors. All presents that he had sent to them through the years had been returned unopened—but he kept sending them. Till the end he knew how to do the correct thing.

CONSIDERING LONGSTREET'S LEGACY

GLENN W. LaFANTASIE

With the death of Stonewall Jackson, James Longstreet became Lee's right-hand man. Some of "Marse Robert's" saintlike Karma should have rubbed off on him. The transferrence didn't take. As Glenn W. LaFantasie says, "Generals are supposed to win their reputations on the battlefield, but in Longstreet's case his public image was mostly shaped by his actions after Appomattox." His bravery was never the issue: Fellow officers even worried about his recklessness under fire. Longstreet did have mixed feelings about Lee, whose "headlong combativeness" disturbed him. They argued at Gettysburg—Longstreet's objections to Lee's plans would come back to haunt. ("The issue of loyalty runs like a dark river through Longstreet's life," LaFantasie writes. "His friends and enemies never seemed quite certain where he stood.") Lee, however, was unreserved in his admiration for the man he called "my old war horse." That anointment should have permanently elevated Longstreet to the Confederate pantheon. But after the war he made a fatal mistake. He criticized Lee's decision to attack the Union center at Gettysburg on the final day of the battle, the event that we now remember as Pickett's Charge. The wrath of the Lee Cult descended on him. Lesser generals like Jubal Early blamed Longstreet for losing not just Gettysburg but the whole war. Longstreet compounded his apostasy by becoming a Republican and—what was almost as damning in the South of that time—a Catholic. This huge gruff man "was a warrior who could only wield a sword; he had no ability with the pen." That, in the end, would prove his undoing. But it should not, as LaFantasie points out, obscure his exceptional record in battle.

Glenn W. LaFantasie, who has taught Civil War history at Gettysburg College, lives in the Blue Ridge Mountains of Virginia. He is working on a book about Little Round Top.

THERE WAS SOMETHING ABOUT JAMES LONGSTREET THAT made people question his constancy. In his autumn years Longstreet met one of his family's former slaves, his old nurse Daniel, on a visit to Mississippi. "Marse Jim," said Daniel, "do you belong to any church?" Longstreet replied matter-of-factly, "I try to be a good Christian." Old Daniel stopped laughing long enough to say, "Something must have scared you mighty bad to change you so from what you was when I had to care for you." What old Daniel found so remarkable was not that Longstreet had embraced religion as an adult but that his former master's convictions could have changed so radically over the years. Daniel was not alone. Others who knew Longstreet during his long life—as a soldier in the United States Army, a Confederate general, postwar politician, or even as a friend—reacted to him in similar ways. In a famous quote, a subordinate once said of Longstreet, "I consider him a humbug."

Generals are supposed to win their reputations on the battlefield, but in Longstreet's case his public image was mostly shaped by his actions after Appomattox. Following the Civil War, Longstreet embraced the Republican party and earned the enmity of a cadre of former Confederate officers who, while elevating their beloved General Robert E. Lee to Southern sainthood, blamed Longstreet for losing the Battle of Gettysburg, causing the Confederacy's defeat in the war, and betraying the so-called Lost Cause.

After Longstreet's death, when the furor over his actions might have otherwise subsided historians kept up the attacks on Longstreet and perpetuated the controversy surrounding him. Except for a handful of writers—including Michael Shaara in his historical novel *The Killer Angels,* Glen Tucker in two books written more than thirty years ago about Longstreet at Gettysburg, and Jeffry D. Wert, Longstreet's most recent biographer—the general has had few defenders. Some Civil War historians, like Robert K. Krick, mince no words about Longstreet and his faults. Says Krick, "The record shows that Longstreet operated at times during the war with an unwholesome and unlovely attitude."

There is good reason for such bristling criticism. Longstreet's inconstancy—the apostasy his former slave found so manifestly amusing—hampered his effectiveness as a general officer during the Civil War and tarnished his good name in the years afterward. In fact, the issue of loyalty runs like a dark river through Longstreet's life. His friends and his enemies never seemed quite certain where he stood. For all the controversy surrounding him, when it comes to assessing Longstreet's merits and shortcomings as a military man, the heart of the matter is to be found in trying to resolve his wavering loyalties—to his country's cause, to his superior officers, and to himself.

In an era when states' rights dominated the politics of the South, James Longstreet held no particular allegiance to any Southern state. Born on his grandparents' plantation in Edgefield District, South Carolina, on January 8, 1821, Longstreet spent his early years on a plantation in northeastern Georgia. His father was from New Jersey and his mother from Maryland. To prepare him for entry into West Point in 1830, Longstreet's father sent him to attend an academy in Augusta and live with his uncle, Augustus Baldwin Longstreet. Augustus was an accomplished attorney and judge who would later win attention for his collection of humorous frontier anecdotes, *Georgia Scenes,* and for his outspoken support of secession in 1860. When his father died in 1833, Longstreet remained in Augusta, and his mother moved to Alabama. It was from Alabama, in fact, that Longstreet received his 1838 appointment to the United States Military Academy.

At West Point, his fellow cadets called him "Old Pete," a variation of his family nickname, "Peter." Even as a young man Longstreet cut an imposing figure. He stood six feet two inches tall and carried more than 200 pounds on his large frame. Later in life he became barrel-chested and paunchy, but in his youth he was muscular and solid. Longstreet's deep-set blue eyes and his reserved manner lent him an air of coolness. Yet he enjoyed practical jokes, had a fine sense of humor, and liked playing poker with his comrades. "As a cadet," Longstreet admitted, "I had more interest in the school of the soldier, horsemanship, sword exercise, and the outside game of football than in the academic courses."

✦

NO ONE EVER DOUBTED his bravery in combat or his potential for leadership. During the Mexican War he distinguished himself in one engagement after another. As a result of his courage and skill as an officer during the Battle of Monterrey in September 1846, Longstreet was promoted first to adjutant of the Eighth Infantry and later to first lieutenant. A year later at the Battle of Churubusco, Longstreet and a fellow officer led a bold assault on Mexican fortifications, with Longstreet carrying the colors and urging his men forward. Longstreet also carried the flag in an attack on Chapultepec a few weeks later. Hit in the thigh by a Mexican bullet, he gave the colors over to a fellow lieutenant, George E. Pickett, before falling in pain.

During the Civil War, Longstreet maintained his reputation for bravery and nerve. Edward Pollard, a Richmond newspaper editor during the war and a historian of the conflict, said there was "a certain fierce aspect to the man."

His men adored him and admired the fact that he did not shrink from leading his troops into battle and putting himself in dangerous situations on the battlefield. They called him a bulldog, and they were willing to follow him anywhere. One of his aides, Major Thomas J. Goree, admired Longstreet's coolness and daring under fire. He described how the general, during one battle, rode among his men "amid a perfect shower of balls . . . with a cigar in his mouth, rallying them, encouraging, and inspiring confidence among them."

Yet Longstreet's enthusiasm for battle caused concern among many of his compatriots. While traveling with General Lee's Army of Northern Virginia during the summer of 1863, British Lieutenant Arthur J. L. Fremantle noted that Longstreet's fellow officers expected that he would behave on the battlefield in "a reckless manner." Reckless or not, Longstreet loved being in the middle of a fight. He sprang to life during combat. In the smoke and fire of battle, said Goree, Longstreet seemed to be "one of the happiest men in the world."

Given his tendency to throw himself into the fray, it is remarkable that Longstreet has earned such an undeserved reputation as a defensive fighter. This reputation can be traced to his adept handling of his troops at the Battle of Fredericksburg in December 1862. During the battle he positioned his men behind a sunken road below Marye's Heights and watched as wave upon wave of assaulting Union troops was mowed down under withering fire from his guns. Lee was fearful that Longstreet's line would break. Longstreet knew better. "General," he said, "if you put every man now on the other side of the Potomac on that field to approach me over the same line, and give me plenty of ammunition, I will kill them all before they reach my line."

The controversy surrounding his actions at Gettysburg have also made historians believe that he favored defensive, rather than offensive, actions. After the war, Longstreet openly criticized Lee for not assuming the defensive posture at Gettysburg that would have allowed the Confederates to choose their own ground and wait for the Army of the Potomac to attack them.

While it is true that Longstreet would have preferred defensive maneuvers in Pennsylvania during the summer of 1863, he never consistently argued for defensive tactics, as some historians have implied. As a general, Longstreet was a pragmatist, using whatever tactic best suited the situation. His battle plans were aggressive and demonstrated a tendency toward hard-hitting assaults, such as the ones he led during the Peninsula campaign and at the battles of Second Manassas and Chickamauga. His soldiers never considered him to be simply a defensive fighter. "Longstreet is a bulldog soldier and cares nothing about flank movements," wrote one Texan in his command. "He takes a dead set at the center, and can whip any army on earth if he has men enough to fight until he is tired of it." Although now mostly forgotten in the fog of controversy that has shrouded him, Longstreet actually possessed an uncanny ability as a general to size up a situation and determine, coolly and objectively, whether to strike the enemy or hold his ground. For good reason, Lee valued Longstreet and called him "the staff in my right hand" and "my old war horse."

But off the battlefield it was an entirely different story. Without the swirl of combat around him, Longstreet fumbled and faltered. Throughout his long career in the service of two armies, Longstreet revealed that he was a far better warrior than he was a soldier. Some writers have maintained that Longstreet was overly ambitious, and that his hopes for advancement frequently got him into trouble. The fact is that Longstreet never appeared to have clear goals in mind. Like most men, he wanted to get ahead in life, but unless he could direct his men to take a certain hill or break an enemy's line, he could not always define for himself where he wanted to go, what he wanted to be, or who he really was.

This tendency toward indecisiveness became apparent during Longstreet's years as a young officer in the United States Army. Although he found military life appealing, he seemed unsure of where he wanted his army career to go. After the Mexican War, Longstreet married Louise Garland and took several brief assignments before settling down in San Antonio, Texas. While in Texas he served as the adjutant of the Eighth Infantry Regiment and later as chief commissary for the Department of Texas.

In June 1850, he asked to be transferred to the cavalry, but his request was denied. He longed for promotion and hoped that the mounted arm might give him the advancement he sought. Having failed in his effort to join the cavalry, Longstreet looked for other alternatives. He resigned as chief commissary and returned to the Eighth Infantry. Once he was back in the infantry he began leading patrols into Comanche Indian territory, leaving his wife and their two small children in San Antonio.

The dusty forays into the desolate Texas countryside could not have encouraged Longstreet about his chances for promotion. He was personally ambitious, but he also wanted the extra pay that would come with higher rank so that he could better support his family and place his children in decent schools. He finally received a promotion to captain in December 1852, and two years later he moved to Fort Bliss, Texas, where he got a taste of Indian fighting against the Apaches and even assumed temporary command of the post on two separate occasions.

✦

LONGSTREET SPENT four years at Fort Bliss—his longest assignment in the army. In 1858, he requested to be removed from frontier duty and assigned to a staff job, probably hoping he would win a major's commission sooner by sitting behind a desk rather than walking in front of an infantry patrol. He was right. Longstreet was promoted to major in the paymaster department and ordered to Fort Leavenworth, Kansas, and later to Albuquerque, New Mexico Territory.

As the sectional conflict between North and South heated up in the East, threatening the dissolution of the country, Longstreet and his comrades watched the events from afar with anxiety and suspense. Although Longstreet left no explicit account of his actions during this period, it would appear that he interpreted Abraham Lincoln's presidential election as a dire threat to the welfare of the Southern states. He took great interest in the course of secession as it spread its way through the states of the Deep South. After South Carolina withdrew from the Union on December 20, 1860, Longstreet wrote a letter to a friend, Congressman J. L. M. Curry of Alabama, offering his services to the governor of that state should Alabama decide to follow South Carolina out of the Union. Meanwhile, if one postwar source can be believed, his mother begged him to remain in service to the United States. But Longstreet had set his own course.

Why he offered himself to Alabama, and not Georgia, is a mystery. He may have reasoned that his chances were better in Alabama for gaining higher rank than they would have been in either Georgia or South Carolina. Whatever his purpose, his letter to Curry was, technically speaking, a treasonous act, for Longstreet was still wearing the uniform of a United States Army officer. However, his oath to defend the Constitution and to protect the nation from all enemies did not appear to weigh heavily on Longstreet's mind or conscience. During the secession crisis his loyalties were at best ambivalent and at worst duplicitous.

Unlike other Southerners, who justified their Confederate allegiance by claiming a stronger loyalty to their native states than to the United States, Longstreet never declared any special attachment to a state or even a particular affinity for the South. Some historians have argued that he ardently embraced states' rights because of the influence of his Uncle Augustus. However, there is little evidence to show he knew much about the constitutional background of secession or that his actions in the winter of 1860–61 were the result of deep political convictions. What seems most likely is that he recognized a clear opportunity for advancement; it was a fair bet that Alabama would follow in South Carolina's wake sooner or later and their fledgling armed force would need experienced leaders.

After Alabama seceded, Longstreet wrote to Governor Andrew B. Moore in February 1861 and offered his services directly to the state, "should she need a soldier who has seen hard service." Moore forwarded Longstreet's letter to Confederate Secretary of War Leroy P. Walker. Longstreet also arranged to have several prominent men endorse his suitability for high rank in the Confederate Army with letters of support to President Jefferson Davis. Longstreet's brother William also wrote to Davis and offered his younger brother's services "in any capacity that is within the scope of his profession."

On March 16, 1861, Confederate officials in Montgomery appointed Longstreet a lieutenant colonel. Not yet knowing about his commission but sure that some place would be found for him in the Confederate Army, Longstreet planned to resign from the U.S. Army around the beginning of April. He delayed his resignation when two other paymasters resigned their commissions, and his superior officer ordered him to take over their duties. To do so, however, meant waiting until mid-April when the payrolls would arrive. By the end of the month, he heard news of the firing on Fort Sumter and announced to his friends that he would leave the Army. He also received word of his commission in the Confederate service. On May 1, he accepted the appointment.

Having not yet resigned his commission in the U.S. Army, Longstreet had entered the service of a foreign nation—or, at the very least, of states in rebellion—without ending his service to the United States. Eight days later, he did resign from the U.S. Army, but at some point he actually accepted pay for concurrent service in both armies. Unsurprisingly, Longstreet never mentions this in his memoirs. He intimates that Alabama called him to service, when in fact his call came from the Confederate States alone. As biographer Jeffry Wert concludes, "What motivated him or how he justified it to himself remains a mystery; what he did, however, was not the act of an honorable man and officer."

During the war, Longstreet's inconstancy continued to plague him. Although his officers and men described him as brimming over with self-confidence, Longstreet never seemed to know what he really wanted. Probably he was happiest as a brigadier general serving under General Pierre Gustave Toutant Beauregard at the First Battle of Manassas and as a major general under the command of General Joseph E. Johnston. He admired Johnston and considered him the most able general in the service of the Confederacy, but Johnston's severe wound at the Battle of Seven Pines on May 31, 1862, removed him from command and elevated General Robert E. Lee to take his place.

Longstreet had mixed feelings about Lee. He served his new commander well and faithfully, but he stuck to his belief that Johnston was the better general. Although Lee praised Longstreet for his accomplishments and for his good advice, Longstreet himself never felt quite comfortable dealing with Lee. For one thing, he thought Lee was too aggressive. "In defensive warfare," Longstreet said, "he was perfect. When the hunt was up, his combativeness was overruling." In the field, Longstreet said, Lee's "characteristic fault was headlong combativeness." Ultimately, Lee simply took "too many chances." As a result, Longstreet kept trying to free himself from Lee's control.

Longstreet never learned the lesson that one cannot be loyal and disloyal at the same time. After the Battle of Antietam in September 1862, he wrote Johnston to say that while the Army of Northern Virginia had won some great victories under Lee's command, "I feel that you have their hearts more decidedly than any other leader can ever have." He offered to turn over to Johnston his command of the First Corps if Johnston could arrange for Longstreet to win a command in the Western theater. Nothing came of Longstreet's offer, but it revealed that his loyalty to Lee was tenuous at best.

✦

BEHIND LONGSTREET'S MANEUVERING for a Western assignment was his burning ambition to obtain higher rank and an independent command. Although he never explicitly set forth his goals for higher rank, or came right out and said he wanted command of a particular Confederate army, Longstreet's tortuous ambition occasionally rose to the surface in his dealings with Lee and with the Confederate War Department.

Just about the time Longstreet was promoted to major general in October 1861, he had asked to be relieved from command of his brigade. He believed he had been passed over for promotion and that men junior in rank had been elevated to major general. General Beauregard had to assure Longstreet that no injustice had been committed against him and that his own promotion was on its way. Later, in October 1862, his promotion to lieutenant general— which flew through the Confederate Senate mostly on the weight of Lee's unqualified recommendation—occurred precisely at the time when Longstreet was privately offering the command of his First Corps to Joseph Johnston.

Although ambition moved him, it did not dominate him. He once wrote of himself: "I am not prompted by any desire to do, or to attempt to do, great things. I only wish to do what I regard as my duty." Nevertheless, Longstreet always hoped for more glory than he received and tended to think more highly of himself than circumstances warranted. He was an outstanding field general, to be sure, known for carefully sizing up a situation before committing his troops to battle and knowing where to hit the enemy hard with overpowering force. Although after the war critics accused him of slowness, Longstreet's wartime reputation was as a fast hard-driver. Goree, in a letter home, told his mother that Longstreet was "exceedingly punctual and industrious." Whatever Longstreet set out to do, said Goree, he did "well and quickly."

But what Goree failed to mention was that Longstreet frequently found it difficult to admit his mistakes. He blamed others for errors and thus masked his own deficiencies, and in later life he made incredible claims for achievements in which he played no part. A case in point was Longstreet's claim that he came up with the plan to have Major General Thomas J. "Stonewall" Jackson join forces with Lee for the series of battles on the Virginia Peninsula that later became known as the Seven Days. While Longstreet realized that Jackson's corps could be used to help keep Major General George B. McClellan's Army of the Potomac out of Richmond, the plan was Lee's, and Lee issued the orders to Jackson. Longstreet did help Lee revise the battle plan and suggested the placement of Jackson's troops in the impending assault. But he could not honestly claim, as he did later in a private letter, that the Confederate offensive "was planned by me."

At the same time, Longstreet deftly blamed his own mistakes during the Peninsula campaign—namely, his failure to understand and follow precise orders at the Battle of Seven Pines in May 1862—on the ineptitude of a fellow major general, Benjamin Huger. When he was not blowing his own horn, Longstreet spent a good deal of time pointing his finger at others.

Longstreet did not always perform up to his own grand expectations when given the opportunity to prove his talents and his value to the Confederate cause. When he finally did get a chance to exercise independent command he demonstrated rather conclusively that he lacked the necessary skills to command an army. During the late winter and early spring of 1863, Lee sent Longstreet with two of his divisions to southeastern Virginia, in the vicinity of Suffolk, where Confederate defenses needed strengthening and the surrounding farms offered a good opportunity for foraging. While his foraging parties collected meager supplies from the Virginia and neighboring North

Carolina countryside, Longstreet laid siege to Suffolk, which was held by a Union force commanded by Major General John J. Peck. When Major General Joseph Hooker's Army of the Potomac advanced on Lee's forces in the vicinity of Chancellorsville, Virginia, Lee ordered Longstreet to return with his divisions in haste. Despite Lee's request, Longstreet found he could not break off the siege and get his supply wagons back from foraging fast enough to move his men north in time to help Lee defeat Hooker.

✦

SOME CRITICS have accused Longstreet of tardiness in not responding to Lee's order with more alacrity, but the fact is that Longstreet moved as quickly as he could after receiving word of the crisis along the Rappahannock River. He did not mishandle the Suffolk campaign or fail to obey Lee's order to rejoin the Army of Northern Virginia, but the overall execution of his mission seemed uninspired. The Suffolk siege got the Confederates nowhere; Peck's Federal troops retained a firm grip on the town and the surrounding area, and the supplies foraged in southern Virginia failed to solve the short rations problem that had plagued Lee's army for several months. Longstreet had little to show for his eight weeks of independent command around Suffolk.

In the fall of 1863 Longstreet got another taste of independent command when Lee sent him and two of his divisions south to serve with General Braxton Bragg's army in Georgia. Longstreet and his divisions arrived just in time to bring about a Confederate victory at the Battle of Chickamauga on September 20, 1863. Technically, Longstreet's men were on detached service rather than under his individual command, for he was required to report to Bragg, whom he personally detested.

Then things began going wrong for Longstreet. When he failed to prevent the Federals from reopening their supply line from Chattanooga to Alabama, he blamed Brigadier General Evander Law, one of his most reliable subordinates, and Brigadier General Jerome Robertson. After complaining endlessly about Bragg's shortcomings, Longstreet managed to win a new assignment for his divisions in East Tennessee, where they were told to dislodge Union Major General Ambrose E. Burnside's forces in and around Knoxville. When an attempt on November 29, 1863, to capture Fort Sanders near the city was botched, Longstreet blamed Major General Lafayette McLaws, a childhood friend and West Point classmate.

Everyone seemed to have an axe to grind. Law believed he had been unfairly passed over for promotion; Robertson took Law's side and protested the unfair treatment. McLaws felt maligned and unjustly accused of mistakes that Longstreet himself had helped to put into motion. At a time when Longstreet should have been assuming responsibility for the failure of the East Tennessee campaign, he instead preferred charges against three of his subordinates.

Feeling the burden of the fiasco at Knoxville, Longstreet realized that his experience as an independent commander had gone badly. Others also saw that Longstreet did not measure up when he was left on his own. As the famous Southern diarist Mary Boykin Chesnut recorded in her journal, "Detached from General Lee, what a horrible failure, what a slow humbug is Longstreet."

Longstreet combined strategic thinking with his desire for an independent command in the West. Prior to his detachment to Suffolk in 1863, he had suggested to Lee that he could lead the First Corps of the Army of Northern Virginia to reinforce Bragg in Tennessee, while Stonewall Jackson's corps stood its ground along the Rappahannock. Days later, Longstreet made it clear to Confederate Senator Louis Wigfall that he would be willing to accept a command in the West. By concentrating its forces in Tennessee, reasoned Longstreet, the Confederacy could overwhelm Union Major General William S. Rosecrans's army and regain its losses in that state. Lee rejected Longstreet's suggestion by sending him with two divisions to Suffolk and not to Tennessee.

Longstreet, however, was determined to push his plan further. On May 6, he met in Richmond with James A. Seddon, the Confederate secretary of war, to discuss the military situation in the West, the precarious state of affairs at Vicksburg, and his own ideas about how these matters could be properly resolved. Lee disapproved of sending any of his divisions to reinforce Bragg in the hopes of diverting Union Major General Ulysses S. Grant's attention away from Vicksburg. Nevertheless, Longstreet proposed his concentration plan to Seddon. As he saw it, once Rosecrans was whipped in Tennessee, a combined Confederate force could then invade Kentucky, forcing Grant to lift the siege at Vicksburg. In the end, President Davis sided with Lee and ordered Longstreet's divisions back to the Army of Northern Virginia—hence Longstreet's presence as Lee led the army north into Pennsylvania in the summer of 1863.

The stage was thus set for the clash between Longstreet and Lee during the Gettysburg campaign. This clash, more than any other controversy involving Longstreet and his role in the Civil War, continues to mark the man and cast a gloomy pall over his actions on that battlefield. Having failed to convince Lee and the Confederate high command that the Western armies should be reinforced, Longstreet maintained that he extracted a promise from Lee that the Northern invasion of 1863 would be a campaign "of defensive tactics: that we should work so as to force the enemy to attack us, in such good position as we might find in his own country." If Lee did agree to such tactics, he probably did not consider it a promise.

The Army of Northern Virginia and the Army of the Potomac converged on Gettysburg during the first three days of July. During that time, Longstreet tried repeatedly to maneuver the Confederates either into a position where the enemy would be forced to attack them or where Lee's forces could sweep around the flank of the Union army. But Lee would hear none of it. "The enemy is here," said Lee, "and if we do not whip him, he will whip us." Lee's battle plan for the second day at Gettysburg particularly disturbed Longstreet, who argued strenuously with his commander to reconsider an attack that was meant to roll up the Union left flank. When Lee stood his ground, Longstreet knew he had no choice but to carry out his orders as faithfully as possible. The fighting on the second day resulted in some minimal Confederate gains along the Emmitsburg Road, but the lateness of Longstreet's attack made some Confederate officers argue long after the war that he had apathetically followed Lee's orders that day.

On the battle's third day, Lee decided to launch a bold frontal attack against the Union center, and once again Longstreet protested against such a risky assault. Longstreet confronted Lee with his objections to a massed attack through open ground, pointing out that "the conditions were different from those in the days of Napoleon, when field batteries had a range of six hundred yards and musketry about sixty yards." Finally, said Longstreet, Lee became "impatient of listening, and tired of talking, and nothing was left but to proceed." Pickett's Charge became the most famous charge in American history and one of the worst disasters ever experienced by the Army of Northern Virginia. The repulse of the Confederate onslaught on Cemetery Ridge in effect ended the Battle of Gettysburg and Lee's invasion of the North. "Never was I so depressed as upon that day," wrote Longstreet in a newspaper article published long after the battle.

But it was Lee who assumed full responsibility for his defeat at Gettysburg; it was Lee who consoled his men as they limped back to the Confederate lines from Cemetery Ridge by telling them, "It is all my fault." After the battle, Southerners did not blame Longstreet for the loss at Gettysburg. It might have remained that way, in fact, if Longstreet had not decided after the war to reveal the details of his debate with Lee concerning tactics during the Pennsylvania invasion and, more significantly, if he had not chosen to criticize Lee.

After the war, in an interview with Northern journalist William Swinton, Longstreet made public his claim of Lee's promise to fight on the defensive during the Gettysburg campaign and his own disapproval of Lee's decision to attack the Union center on July 3. Swinton incorporated Longstreet's comments in a history of the Army of the Potomac, published in 1866. While Lee remained alive, no Southerners raised objections to Longstreet's description of the battle. However, two years after Lee's death in 1870, former Confederates, among them Major General Jubal Early, Brigadier General William Pendleton, and Major Walter Taylor, began an all-out assault against Longstreet. They attacked him for his objections to Lee's conduct during the Gettysburg campaign and the role he had played in the Confederate defeat. This Lee Cult, as it has become known, sought to silence any criticism of Lee and elevate him to an untouchable pedestal of fame and glory—an everlastingly noble symbol of the Lost Cause. The Lee defenders found Longstreet a convenient scapegoat to explain the defeat at Gettysburg. The Lee Cult ensured that Lee, despite his own admission of responsibility to his men, would not be blamed for losing the battle that, in the estimation of many Southerners, had decided the outcome of the entire war.

Despite many attempts, Longstreet could never get across the idea that he and Lee had worked well together during the war, had enjoyed a close relationship, and had not regarded one another as adversaries. Wrote Longstreet of his dealings with Lee: "The relations existing between us were affectionate, confidential, and even tender, from first to last. There was never a harsh word between us." He proudly noted that throughout their campaigning together, Lee "usually had his headquarters near mine." Lee's fondness for Longstreet was genuine. While Longstreet was on detached service in the West, Lee wrote him: "I missed you dreadfully and your brave corps. Your cheerful face and strong arm would have been invaluable. I hope you will return to me." But few members of the Lee Cult believed that Longstreet had any sincere devotion to his commander.

Longstreet inadvertently played into the hands of his foes and gave them grist for their mill. His gruff ways and unpolished manners—holdovers from his boyhood days in frontier Georgia—contrasted sharply with the romantic image of a Southern cavalier promoted by the Lee Cult. His ambition as an officer, particularly in the service of the Confederacy, made his desire for independent command look like an expression of disloyalty to his commanding officer. His questioning of Lee's tactical decisions made Longstreet look foolish and moronic, for Southerners regarded Lee as a military genius, which Longstreet clearly was not.

His poor writing ability ensured that he was overmatched in the war of words. From time to time, Longstreet, realizing this shortcoming, hired ghostwriters and editors to help him put his arguments down on paper. As a result, numerous errors—either the work of careless hired hands or Longstreet's fallible memory—found their way into his writings and hurt his effort to parry his assailants. His exaggerated claims for himself and his arrogant opinions convinced many of his readers that he was simply a prevaricator or a blowhard.

Not only did Longstreet dare to criticize Lee, but his political inconstancy convinced his fellow Southerners that he was a traitor to their cause. When asked in 1867 by a New Orleans newspaper to comment on Reconstruction policy in the South, Longstreet surprised everyone by reminding his fellow Southerners that "we are a conquered people." Because the North had won the war "fairly and squarely," the South could only follow one course: Accept the terms "that are now offered by the conquerors."

So committed was he to this policy of reconciliation that he decided to join ranks with the Republicans, and he said so in a public letter printed first in a New Orleans newspaper in June 1867 and then in papers and journals published around the country. In the South, Longstreet immediately was vilified as a traitor and a scalawag; he even received several death threats. In his naiveté, he could not understand what he had done to provoke such animosity. To Thomas Goree, he explained that he had only wanted to keep "the South out of the troubles that she has passed through since, and that was about the extent of my interest in the affairs of state."

Compounding his sin, Longstreet accepted a political appointment as surveyor of customs for the port of New Orleans from his friend in the antebellum army, Ulysses S. Grant, who had been elected president in 1868. The Republican governor of Louisiana placed Longstreet in command of the New Orleans militia in 1873. During a riot between the White League and the city's police and black militia, Longstreet was wounded and taken prisoner by the rioters. Order was restored only when President Grant sent in Federal troops.

In the late 1870s, after moving back to Georgia, Longstreet won appointments from President Rutherford B. Hayes's administration as a deputy collector of internal revenue and as a postmaster. Longstreet's most important appointment came in 1880 when President Hayes named him minister to Turkey, a job the former Confederate did not enjoy. He spent most of his short sojourn abroad biding his time until he could return to Georgia. Back in America, he accepted an appointment from President James Garfield as U.S. marshal for Georgia. Tragedy struck twice in 1889: A fire destroyed Longstreet's farmhouse and its contents, including his Civil War relics and li-

brary, and later that year Louise Longstreet died. Longstreet returned to public life as commissioner of railroads in the late 1890s, when the Republicans
regained the White House.

His string of Republican positions through the years did not endear him to
white Southerners or, especially, to the Lee Cult. Although Longstreet remained a popular figure at Confederate reunions and other veterans' meetings,
he found himself being cheered the loudest by Union veterans and the Northern authors of Civil War histories. As if his Republicanism and his heretical
criticism of Lee were not enough, Longstreet had also managed to alienate
white Southern Protestants when, in 1877, he left the Episcopal Church and
joined the Roman Catholic Church. His second wife, Helen Dortsch, whom
he married in 1897, explained that Longstreet's conversion came about because many of his Episcopal associates refused to occupy the same pew with
him after he had taken up the Republican cause. He remained a devout
Catholic until his death in 1904.

In his later years, the Civil War continued to take its toll on Longstreet. He
had been severely wounded in the Wilderness on May 6, 1864, mistakenly
shot by a Virginia regiment. As a result, he lost most of the use of his right
arm. He also suffered from a throat wound that had never fully healed. As an
old man, he became deaf and lost some of his eyesight to cancer. In
Gainesville, Georgia, he ran a small hotel. Occasionally he could be seen tend-
ing the vineyards near his modest home, dressed in a white linen coverall,
hunched over as he pruned the vines, his white hair and ample white whiskers
glistening bright in the southern sun.

It was a strikingly different picture than the one painted years before by
Thomas Goree of the feisty general who, with lighted cigar in mouth, went
galloping into the heat of battle, swinging his sword above his head and urging his men onward. That image of Longstreet is the one that has been most
frequently forgotten since the Civil War, lost in the fog of postwar controversy
and Longstreet's own inconsistencies and apostasies. Even if Longstreet lacked
direction as a young officer in the United States Army, became carried away
with ambitions for promotion and independent command in the Confederate
Army, was involved in postwar political activities that defied the acceptable
norms set forth by the white Southern establishment, and dared to criticize
the military wisdom of Robert E. Lee, the fact remains that the thing
Longstreet did best in life was lead men into battle.

Some men seem born to war. An aide, Moxley Sorrel, once observed that
Longstreet was an "undismayed warrior." In the blaze of battle, when the
whole world seemed to be coming apart at its seams, Longstreet remained

cool and calm. "He was like a rock in steadiness," said Sorrel. Longstreet came alive on the battlefield. He was a true warrior, a beacon of courage and inspiration to his men. His record of heroism in the Mexican War and his victories in the Civil War cannot be denied.

All things considered, it was Longstreet's métier as a pure fighter, a warrior in the truest sense, that made him a great general. Every general makes mistakes, and Longstreet certainly made his share of them. But in battle after battle he proved how effective he could be as the staff in Lee's right hand. His gruff manners were not only a mark of his frontier upbringing; they revealed, perhaps too clearly for some of his comrades, that he was unable to perfect a gentle mask for his warrior self.

But, sadly, he was a warrior who could only wield a sword; he had no ability with the pen. When it came time to do battle with the Lee Cult, confronting fellow generals who had—to a man—proven themselves to be mediocre officers on the real battlefields of the war, Longstreet was outmaneuvered and outgunned. He was, quite frankly, out of his element. James Longstreet belonged on a battlefield. When there were no real wars to fight, when all the real battles were finished, Longstreet wandered about in life rather aimlessly, searching for himself and for his rightful place in the world.

There were some special places where he had shown his true warrior colors: Monterrey, Churubusco, Chapultepec, Manassas, the Peninsula, Fredericksburg, Chickamauga, and the Wilderness. It should come as no surprise that at Appomattox, it was Longstreet who asked Lee to delay, even for just a little while, before going over to see Grant.

With the end of the Civil War, Longstreet the warrior disappeared almost entirely from view. Without war, Longstreet became someone other than who he truly was.

Today it is the man of inconstancy, the man of controversy, who stands now on the historical stage, waiting for further scorn to be heaped on him by those who see him as a Judas in the passion play of the Lost Cause. In forgetting that Longstreet was actually a rare breed—a man who was a natural warrior, a man who experienced his finest moments in the brutality of combat, a man whose instincts were so finely honed that he seemed in the swirl of battle to behave with the steadiness and dependability of an old war horse—we have forgotten who Longstreet truly was.

PALADIN OF THE REPUBLIC: PHILIP H. SHERIDAN

PAUL ANDREW HUTTON

The Union army may have entered the war with inferior generals, but it left with great ones: Grant, Sherman, and the bantam Irishman, Philip H. Sheridan. (All were West Pointers: The Civil War was, like no other in American history, a West Point war.) You can argue endlessly about the merits of the three, but when it came to fierceness in battle, one of them—Sheridan—had no equal. He was as adept at defense as he was quick to seize an advantage in attack: At Stones River the joint stand of Sheridan and George H. Thomas (whose name should be added to that short list) saved the Army of the Tennessee. As Grant's commander of cavalry in the Army of the Potomac, Sheridan turned the Union horse soldiers into a potent weapon by the introduction of massed shock tactics—and as Paul Andrew Hutton points out, "by dismounting them in battle and supplying them with artillery support." He may have been nasty, a hater, and a grudge holder with a social chip on his shoulder, but he had that almost supernatural knack of motivating his men to extraordinary efforts. On his black mount Rienzi—surely the most famous military horse since Alexander the Great's Bucephalus—he led them in two of the most inspiring episodes of the war: the spontaneous charge of his division of Thomas's Army of the Cumberland up Missionary Ridge in November 1863, which destroyed an entire Confederate army, and the rallying ride at Cedar Creek the next fall, which drove the Confederates out of the Shenandoah Valley once and for all. As a practitioner of total war, Sheridan was a commander in the modern mode. Wars, he understood, are won not just by killing but by destroying a people's will to resist—an ultimate aim of military strategy. In 1870 Sheridan observed the Franco-Prussian War from the Prussian side. He told Count Otto von

Bismarck that his Prussians were altogether too lenient in their treatment of the French. As he said—and his words have become an essence of the military imperative: "The people must be left nothing but their eyes to weep with over the war."

Paul Andrew Hutton, a professor of history at the University of New Mexico, is the author of *Phil Sheridan and His Army,* and the editor of *Frontier and Region, Soldiers West,* and *The Custer Reader.*

ABRAHAM LINCOLN, UPON FIRST MEETING GENERAL PHILIP H. Sheridan, was decidedly unimpressed. To him, Sheridan was a "brown, chunky little chap, with a long body, short legs, not enough neck to hang him, and such long arms that if his ankles itch he can scratch them without stooping." To make matters worse, the general was blessed with a bullet-shaped head with two large bumps in back that made it nearly impossible for him to keep a hat on. This oversize head was crowned by coarse, short-cropped hair that one wag said resembled a "coat of black paint."

Sheridan's eyes, however, were the mark of the man. His friend and aide John Schuyler Crosby insisted that "one could tell from his eyes in a moment whether he was serious, sad, or humorous, without noticing another feature of his face." Another friend admitted that Sheridan might well be a "stumpy, quadrangular little man" with a "forehead of no promise" but said "his eye and his mouth" marked him as a fierce warrior. Sheridan's features betrayed his Irish origins, although his voice carried no trace of a brogue. Those dark eyes, long and narrow beneath arched eyebrows, sparkled with the fire that held the line at Stones River, sent a bruised army roaring up Missionary Ridge, turned defeat into victory at Cedar Creek, and crushed Robert E. Lee's last hope at Five Forks.

By war's end Lincoln had had a change of opinion. "General Sheridan," the president told the Union hero, "when this particular war began, I thought a cavalryman should be at least six feet four inches high, but I have changed my mind. Five feet four will do in a pinch."

Sheridan was a latecomer to the war, for by the time he assumed command of a desk at General Henry W. Halleck's Missouri headquarters, Ulysses S. Grant had already won victories at Forts Henry and Donelson and William Tecumseh Sherman was commanding a division. Yet within four years Sheridan would rise from captain to major general in the regular army (at age thirty-three) and stand with Grant and Sherman as one of the Union's trinity of great commanders.

His origins gave little hint of the military glory that awaited him. The exact place of his birth is unknown, and he confused the issue considerably by claiming both Albany, New York, and Somerset, Ohio, on various official documents. Almost certainly neither was true, although the March 6, 1831, birthdate he claimed can probably be trusted. Sheridan was most likely born in County Cavan, Ireland, where his parents were tenant farmers, or on the ship en route to the United States. He was an infant when John and Mary Sheridan settled in Somerset, Ohio. Considering the fierce anti-Irish prejudice of the time, the subterfuge about his birthplace is understandable.

Sheridan was educated in Somerset's one-room schoolhouse, and he came away deeply influenced by the experience. "The little white schoolhouse made us superior to the South," he later remarked. "Education is invincible." At fourteen, his schooling over, he secured a clerk's position in a local general store. He quickly rose to be the bookkeeper of Somerset's largest dry-goods shop. His attention was often distracted, however, by news of battles in distant Mexico. The war, and dreams of martial glory, captivated the youngster. When he heard that the 1848 appointee from his district to West Point had failed the entrance exam, he appealed to his congressman to be allowed to fill the vacancy. Congressman Thomas Ritchie promptly returned a warrant for the class of 1848.

Sheridan's experience at West Point was not a happy one. The traditional hazing frayed his volatile temper, the refined manners and aristocratic pretensions of the Southern clique irritated him, and his studies failed to prosper. These frustrations finally exploded on the drill field one September afternoon in 1851, when he assaulted his Southern drill instructor. Suspended for one year, he returned unrepentant after nine humiliating months back at his Somerset bookkeeping job. He now compounded his poor grades with a miserable attitude that left him just eleven demerits from expulsion when he graduated, thirty-fourth in a class of fifty-two, in July 1853.

Brevet Second Lieutenant Sheridan was assigned to the 1st Infantry and ordered to Fort Duncan, Texas, perhaps the most isolated post on the frontier. Although he found the fort a decided improvement over West Point, he was not there long. He was transferred to the 4th Infantry and posted to Fort Reading, California, where pressure from gold miners and squatters was driving the local Indians to war. Sheridan's best friend from West Point, Lieutenant George Crook, was also there, and he likened the situation to "the fable of the wolf and the lamb." It was cruel, Crook lamented, that the soldiers "had to fight when our sympathies were with the Indians."

Sheridan did not share Crook's liberal sensibilities, and he was happy to march north against the Yakimas in October 1855. He distinguished himself in a series of sharp campaigns, earning commendation in general orders by General Winfield Scott for his heroism in a battle on the Cascades of the Columbia River in March 1856.

After years of guard duty at an Indian reservation in Oregon, he was delighted when orders finally arrived in September 1861, ordering him to the East. Sheridan hurried eastward, fearful that the five-month-old Civil War might end before he could join his new regiment. If the conflict lasted long enough, he confided to a friend, he hoped to "have a chance to earn a major's commission." He took pride in the fact that he was "untainted by politics," and that his thoughts had never "been disturbed by any discussion of the questions out of which the war grew." That was to change dramatically.

After impressive service on the staffs of Generals Samuel Curtis and Henry W. Halleck, Captain Sheridan was appointed colonel of the 2nd Michigan Cavalry on May 25, 1862. The new colonel of volunteers was ordered to garrison Booneville, Mississippi, well in advance of the Union lines. On July 1, Brigadier General James R. Chalmers's Confederate division struck Sheridan's 827 men. Although outnumbered by as much as six to one, Sheridan's men were armed with Colt revolving rifles and pistols, so they could fire twelve rounds before reloading. Sheridan's boldness, combined with his heavy firepower and his clever use of favorable terrain, confused the Rebels and sent them into a panicky retreat. This prompted Major General William Rosecrans and four of his brigadiers to wire Halleck, the general in chief. "Brigadiers scarce; good ones scarcer. . . . The undersigned respectfully beg that you will obtain the promotion of Sheridan. He is worth his weight in gold."

Not wishing to tempt fate further, Rosecrans ordered Sheridan to retire to division headquarters at Rienzi. While at headquarters, Sheridan was given a horse by Captain Archibald P. Campbell of the 2nd Michigan. Campbell found the large gelding unmanageable, but "Rienzi," as Sheridan named him, quickly became the young colonel's favorite mount. Jet black except for three white feet, sixteen hands high, and with incredible endurance, Rienzi covered five miles in an hour in his normal walking gait. Before the war was over he would become one of the most famous horses in history.

Soon after, Sheridan rode Rienzi on an important scouting expedition southward that discovered considerable movement toward Chattanooga by General Braxton Bragg's Confederate forces. Sheridan reported this information to Major General U. S. Grant, only recently reinstated as commander of the Army of the Tennessee, his post until right after Shiloh. This news prompted the transfer of several regiments to reinforce Union troops in Kentucky. Sheridan, subsequently ordered north, was delighted at the prospect of action.

Promoted to brigadier general of volunteers (dated July 1, the day of the Battle of Booneville) and given command in September of the newly organized 11th Division of Major General Don Carlos Buell's Army of the Ohio, Sheridan proved his mettle holding the Union line against five Rebel assaults at Perryville, Kentucky, on October 8, 1862. The Northern press dubbed him the "paladin of Perryville."

Rosecrans replaced Buell as commander of the redesignated Army of the Cumberland, and Sheridan was given command of the 3rd Division of General Alexander McCook's right wing of that army. At Stones River, Tennessee, from December 31, 1862, to January 2, 1863, Sheridan tenaciously held on amidst incredible slaughter to form the anchor that allowed General George Thomas's line to hold, bringing the Union an important but grisly victory—Sheridan's division alone suffered 1,633 casualties out of 4,164 men.

Stones River confirmed the bantam brigadier's growing reputation for courage and tenacity. "I knew it was infernal in there before I got in," said General Lovell Rousseau about the battle, "but I was convinced of it when I saw Phil Sheridan, with hat in one hand and sword in the other, fighting as if he was the devil incarnate, and swearing as if he had a fresh indulgence from Father Tracy every five minutes."

Rosecrans disapproved of Sheridan's vivid language, which eventually became legendary in the army, and admonished him during the fighting at Stones River. "Watch your language," he lectured his young brigadier. "Remember, the first bullet may send you to eternity." But eternity did not much concern Sheridan during battle. His mind was consumed instead with how to destroy the enemy. "I have never in my life taken a command into battle," Sheridan told Brigadier General Horace Porter, "and had the slightest desire to come out alive unless I won."

Stones River won another star in the volunteer army for Sheridan, but it was his actions at Chattanooga in November 1863 that earned him Grant's esteem and secured his future. This came, however, only after Sheridan shared in the humiliation of the Army of the Cumberland: first defeated at Chickamauga on September 20, then besieged in Chattanooga. His 3rd Division had seen little action on the first day of Chickamauga, finally going into battle to reinforce General Thomas's right. "Make way for Sheridan!" demanded his staff officers as the general galloped onto the battlefield. The fresh Union troops surged forward, only to be driven back with heavy casualties. "Make way for Sheridan!" shouted the men of the other Union units as Sheridan's soldiers retreated. The next day was even worse, as his men were rolled up with the rest of the Union right. While Thomas gallantly fought on, earning himself the nickname the Rock of Chickamauga, Sheridan and his division retreated with most of Rosecrans's army to Chattanooga.

Sheridan and his men were anxious to redeem themselves in front of the reinforcements from the Army of the Potomac under Joseph Hooker and the Army of the Tennessee under Sherman. But Grant, now in overall command west of the Appalachians, instead held the Cumberlanders in reserve on November 24 while the troops under Hooker and Sherman assaulted the Confederate positions, which loomed over the city on Lookout Mountain and Missionary Ridge.

On November 25 Sheridan finally got his chance. Sherman's forces had been repulsed four times from the north slope of Missionary Ridge when Grant ordered the Cumberlanders forward to assault rifle pits at the base of the central ridge, hoping to take the pressure off Sherman. Sheridan's division, one of four in the assault, overran the rifle pits with ease but then faced a murderous fire from the crest of the ridge. Sheridan sent an aide off to his commander, General Gordon Granger, begging permission to assault the crest. His men, however, could not be restrained. Without orders, they began to clamber up the broken face of the ridge toward their Confederate tormentors, 400 feet above them.

General Grant, observing the action from his temporary headquarters on nearby Orchard Knob, was horrified. He turned to Thomas, now commanding the Army of the Cumberland, and demanded to know who had ordered the troops up the ridge. "I don't know, I did not," Thomas replied. Grant then angrily asked Granger, commanding IV Corps, if he had given the order. "No, they started up without orders," Granger replied. "When these fellows get started all hell can't stop them." Taciturn as usual, Grant responded: "It's all right if it turns out all right. If not, someone will suffer." Granger promptly sent Captain Robert Averey of his staff off to Sheridan, with orders to take the ridge if he felt he could.

Sheridan was delighted to see Averey. "I didn't order them up," he declared, "but we are going to take that ridge!" Borrowing Averey's pewter flask, Sheridan then toasted Bragg's headquarters, directly above him atop the ridge. As he gulped down the brandy, a Confederate battery answered his impertinence with a volley that sent dirt and rocks flying all around him. Cursing Rebel rudeness, Sheridan tossed the flask away, mounted Rienzi, and led the division roaring up the ridge along a path.

Newspapers later called it the miracle of Missionary Ridge. The Cumberlanders swept up the face of the ridge as one, each regiment struggling to plant its colors on the crest first. Unlike the other Union commanders, Sheridan did not halt on the summit but pushed on after the fleeing Rebels to Chickamauga Station.

"Sheridan showed his genius in that battle," declared a delighted Grant, "and to him I owe the capture of most of the prisoners that were taken. Although commanding a division only, he saw in the crisis of that engagement that it was necessary to advance beyond the point indicated by his orders . . . and with the instinct of military genius pushed ahead." Sheridan never quit, and Grant, who was much the same, prized him for that quality.

When Grant went east in March 1864 as general in chief, he gave Sheridan command of the cavalry of the Army of the Potomac. Someone at the War Department remarked, "The officer you brought on from the West is rather a little fellow to handle your cavalry." To which Grant responded, "You will find him big enough for the purpose before we get through with him."

Sheridan and Brigadier General George Gordon Meade, in command of the Army of the Potomac, developed an immediate dislike for each other. Meade believed the cavalry's only roles were escorting, picketing, and scouting. Sheridan wanted to concentrate his 10,000 troopers and engage J. E. B. Stuart's supposedly invincible horsemen. After one particularly heated argument, Meade went to Grant to complain about Sheridan; for his trouble, he was ordered by the general in chief to allow Sheridan to go out and whip Stuart. Sheridan's troopers proceeded to avenge three years of humiliation by brushing aside the Rebel cavalry at Yellow Tavern, Virginia, mortally wounding Stuart in the process, and then raiding all the way to the gates of Richmond before rejoining the Union army.

When Lee sent Jubal Early up the Shenandoah Valley to threaten Washington and relieve the pressure on Richmond, Grant countered by placing Sheridan in command of the Army of the Shenandoah. Lincoln objected because of Sheridan's youth, but Grant felt youthful audacity was needed to seal off the Shenandoah from the Rebels once and for all. The reputations of Generals John C. Frémont, Nathaniel Banks, Franz Sigel, and David Hunter had been shattered in the Shenandoah, but Sheridan was to fare much better. In

September 1864, he defeated Early at the Third Battle of Winchester and at Fisher's Hill. Lincoln rewarded him with a brigadier's star in the regulars.

At Cedar Creek, Virginia, on October 19, however, Early caught the Federals napping while Sheridan was returning from a conference in Washington and routed a portion of the army. Sheridan, then fourteen miles away in Winchester, raced to the sound of guns. "As he galloped on his features gradually grew set, as though carved in stone," recalled his aide, Major George A. Forsyth, "and the same dull red glint I had seen in his piercing black eyes when, on other occasions, the battle was going against us, was there now."

At first he came upon knots of stragglers, but soon the numbers increased so that the pike was blocked by scores of panic-stricken men and jumbled wagons and caissons. Sheridan hailed a regimental chaplain who was making for Winchester at top speed. "Everything is lost; but all will be right when you get there," the chaplain breathlessly declared. He then put spurs to his horse and continued toward the rear.

Near Newtown, Sheridan met Captain William McKinley, an aide to General George Crook and a future president, and learned the first details of the morning battle. Early's men had surprised the left flank of Sheridan's army at 5:00 A.M., rolling up Crook's command and forcing two other corps to retreat to a defensive line just north of Middletown. But instead of pressing on, Early let his jaded men loot the captured Union camp. It was to be his undoing.

All along the road to Winchester, the stragglers began to turn around. Cheer after cheer, first from but a few throats, then from hundreds, then from thousands, went up. "Here's Phil Sheridan," they roared. "We're going back!" What had moments before been a panicked mob once again became an army.

Nearing the front, Sheridan saw the colors of Crook's troops rising up from the ground to greet him. Colonel Rutherford B. Hayes, another future president, recalled Sheridan calling out as he galloped by: "Boys, turn back; face the other way. I am going to sleep in that camp tonight or in hell."

Sheridan finally halted amidst a group of officers that included his best friend, Crook. "What are you doing way back here?" he joshed Crook as they embraced. Another officer noticed tears in both men's eyes. Just then the XIX Corps commander, Brigadier General William Emory, rode up and reported that he had assembled a division to cover the army's retreat. Sheridan's eyes flashed. "Retreat, hell!" he exclaimed. "We'll be back in our camps tonight."

Sheridan sent his commanders scurrying to rebuild the Federal lines for a counterattack. It would be late afternoon before they were ready. To encourage the men, and to let them all know he had returned, Sheridan now galloped along the entire Union line. "Sheridan—Sheridan—Sheridan !" chanted the men of the Army of the Shenandoah. At last, red-hot with a mixture of humiliation and fierce pride, they received the order to advance. Major Forsyth pushed to the front, enthralled by the sight: "'Shoulder arms! Forward! *March!*' And with martial tread and floating flags the line of the battle is away."

The Confederates, protected by a stone wall and hasty breastworks, opened a terrific fire and the infantry line faltered. Now onto the field dashed the golden-haired George Custer and his cavalry division, roaring defiance and smashing into the Rebel flank. Panic ensued as Early's army broke before the combined assault and disintegrated. Custer and the other cavalry commanders hotly pursued the fleeing Confederates until after nightfall.

General Early had lost 1,860 men killed or wounded and another 1,100 taken prisoner, as well as most of his artillery and baggage and, most important, the Shenandoah Valley. Having turned defeat into victory, Sheridan calmly accepted the reports and plaudits of his subordinate commanders. It was nine that night before Custer, the twenty-four-year-old brigadier general who was fast becoming Sheridan's favorite, returned to headquarters. Sheridan rushed to greet him, literally pulling him from the saddle and exclaiming, "You have done it for me this time, Custer!" The Boy General responded in kind, laughing and crying as he picked up his commander and waltzed him around the campfire.

Coming on the very eve of the presidential election, the victory at Cedar Creek proved a tonic for Lincoln and the Republicans. "Sheridan's Ride" became one of the most storied events of the war, immortalized in a popular poem by T. Buchanan Read that was memorized by generations of schoolchildren. The poem made Sheridan's black charger Rienzi one of the most famous horses in history. Congress tendered its thanks to Sheridan, who also received a promotion to major general in the regular army. He now stood firmly with Grant and Sherman in the front rank of Union generals.

Sheridan had eliminated a Confederate army at Cedar Creek, but Grant wanted him to destroy Rebel resources in the valley as well. Sheridan's Robbers, as his army was thereafter known by their enemies, so effectively ravaged Virginia's most bountiful valley that Sheridan could boast, with but little exaggeration, that "a crow would be compelled to carry his own rations" when crossing the Shenandoah.

Sensing the war would soon end, and anxious to "be in at the death," Sheridan gave up his independent command and hurriedly rejoined Grant in March 1865. He soon scored a smashing victory at Five Forks, captured Lieutenant General Richard Ewell and the right wing of the Rebel army at Sayler's

Creek, and blocked Lee's retreat at Appomattox. The young soldier then triumphantly capped off one of the most remarkable ascensions in modern military history with a stroll to the McLean house with his commander in chief.

✦

SHERIDAN WAS NO ROMANTIC. A modern soldier, he shared his friend Sherman's vision of war as "power unrestrained by constitution or compact." This power was to be used to cripple the enemy populace as well as the enemy army. "I do not hold war to mean simply that lines of men shall engage each other in battle," Sheridan later wrote. "This is but a duel, in which one combatant seeks the other's life; war means much more, and is far worse than this." For him, the key to success in war was the destruction of the enemy homeland and the eradication of the people's will to resist. He understood that "the loss of property weighs heavy with the most of mankind; heavier often, than the sacrifices made on the field of battle."

In October 1870, while serving as an observer with the Prussian army during the Franco-Prussian War, Sheridan advised Count Otto von Bismarck that his troops were too mild in their handling of French guerrillas. "The proper strategy," he told the Prussian, "consists in the first place in inflicting as telling blows as possible upon the enemy's army, and then causing the inhabitants so much suffering that they must long for peace, and force their government to demand it. The people must be left nothing but their eyes to weep with over the war."

Sheridan's heartlessness toward the enemy contrasted sharply with the compassion he displayed toward his own soldiers. He not only selected their campsites, but also went to great pains to be certain they were well fed and clothed. He viewed the relationship between officers and men as a social contract with obligations on each side. An officer who failed in his obligations was worthless. According to Sheridan, "a General lacking the confidence of his men is not less helpless than a general without an Army."

Although often described as the embodiment of the reckless cavalryman, Sheridan actually rarely if ever exposed his men to needless danger. He respected the intelligence of the common soldier and understood that "none realized more quickly than they the blundering that often takes place on the field of battle." If soldiers were to be called on to die, they must have "some tangible indemnity for the loss of life." Sheridan's men responded to this concern with unqualified devotion.

But if an officer or soldier failed to perform his duty, or even failed to display Sheridan's zeal for combat, the general's wrath was formidable. For example, his treatment of General Gouverneur K. Warren, the Gettysburg hero who commanded V Corps at Five Forks, was unmerciful. On the very eve of victory and right after the triumph at Five Forks, Sheridan removed Warren from command. His sins were in moving his troops into position too slowly and displaying a quiet calm in the face of the enemy, which the excitable Sheridan regarded as apathy.

Warren remained in the army, reverting to his regular rank of major in the engineers, and diligently worked to clear his name. President Rutherford B. Hayes, who had served under Sheridan but was not a great admirer, finally granted Warren a court of inquiry in 1879. The 1882 published findings of the court exonerated Warren in connection with three of the four reasons Sheridan had given for the removal. The verdict was a hard blow to Sheridan's pride. He loudly complained that the findings were "more in the nature of apologies than annunciation of the facts shown in the evidence." It did not matter to Warren: That anguished officer had died three months before the court vindicated him.

Sheridan was a real hater. His contempt for Meade was notorious, but his persecution of General William B. Hazen was an even more repulsive display of cruel, vindictive pettiness. After Missionary Ridge, Sheridan and Hazen argued over whose troops had reached the crest first and captured eleven Rebel cannons. Grant sided with Sheridan but the argument continued, and Sheridan never forgave Hazen. Sheridan again clashed with him on the Indian frontier in 1868, and their inability to cooperate damaged the effectiveness of the former's campaign. Hazen's friendship with Sherman protected him to some extent, but Sheridan managed to transfer his rival's regiment to Fort Buford, North Dakota, the army's most desolate post, in 1872. The final victory went to Hazen, however, when his close friend James A. Garfield was elected president. Hazen was promptly promoted to brigadier general and appointed chief signal officer, finally escaping Sheridan's malevolent influence.

✦

SHERIDAN EMERGED from the Civil War as the Union's premier combat officer. Rarely innovative, he nevertheless developed the cavalry into a more powerful force by dismounting them in battle and supplying them with artillery support. He utilized intelligence gathering, scouting, and spying to a far greater extent than other generals and always had a reputation for being remarkably well informed. Although cautious and painstaking in preparation for battle, once on the field he was quick-thinking, bold, and decisive. "A persevering terrier dog" was how his friend Sherman characterized him, "honest, modest, plucky and smart enough."

Grant's affections were often expressed through biased assessments, and his remarks about Sheridan were hyperbolic. Yet this estimate, given to Senator George Hoar, has the ring of truth:

> I believe General Sheridan has no superior as a general, either living or dead, and perhaps not an equal. . . . He has judgment, prudence, foresight and power to deal with dispositions needed in a great war. I entertained this opinion of him before he became generally known in the late war.

With the war over, Grant immediately sent Sheridan to the Texas border. There he provided matériel and moral support to the forces of Benito Juárez in their struggle with Maximilian, the puppet emperor of Mexico installed by Louis-Napoléon of France. The French soon abandoned Maximilian to his fate.

Although preoccupied with border affairs, Sheridan kept a wary eye on civil affairs in Texas and Louisiana. He distributed his troops at critical points to suppress night-riding white terrorists who attacked freed blacks and white Unionists. The war had radicalized the general, so that by Appomattox he was one of the most stridently Republican and bitterly anti-Southern officers in the army. He was particularly enraged by the various vagrancy and apprentice laws—called Black Codes—that the Texans enacted. Sheridan angrily declared that the laws resulted in "a policy of gross injustice toward the colored people on the part of the courts, and a reign of lawlessness and disorder ensued."

Sheridan was hardly a crusader, and he clearly subscribed to the racial prejudices of his time, but he was determined to protect the emancipated blacks. He felt that black Americans had earned their freedom during the war, and "it was the plain duty of those in authority to make it secure" and to "see that they had a fair chance in the battle of life."

Because he kept his troops close to the Texas urban centers to protect the blacks, Sheridan was heavily criticized by Texans for not protecting the frontier from Comanches. The general refused to move his men, noting that "if a white man is killed by the Indians on an extensive Indian frontier, the greatest excitement will take place, but over the killing of many freedmen in the settlements, nothing is done." Sheridan further angered the Texans when, on being asked by a reporter what he thought of the Lone Star State, he replied: "If I owned hell and Texas, I would rent Texas out and live in hell."

Sheridan's determined defense of the blacks, his bitter disputes with local politicians, his forceful suppression of white terrorism, and his zealous application of the Reconstruction laws of the congressional Radical Republicans led President Andrew Johnson to dismiss him as commander of the Fifth Military District on July 31, 1867. Reassigned to command the Department of the Missouri, which included present-day Kansas, Oklahoma, New Mexico, and Colorado, Sheridan soon found the task of frontier defense equally difficult but far more congenial to his temperament.

Throughout late 1868 and into 1869, Sheridan conducted a masterful winter campaign against the Cheyennes and allied tribes. In sharp encounters at the Washita in November 1868, at Soldier Springs in December, and at Summit Springs in July 1869, Sheridan's troopers broke the power of the Cheyennes and forced them onto reservations in Indian Territory (Oklahoma). The campaign won Sheridan a new reputation as the nation's top Indian fighter.

Campaigning against Indians in winter was hardly a novel idea, but Sheridan's campaign was universally greeted as a bold, innovative plan. He was convinced that his well-fed and well-clothed troopers could challenge the severe climate long enough to strike a decisive blow. Winter limited the natives' mobility, which was their greatest advantage over the soldiers. With their ponies weakened by the scarcity of fodder, the Indians would seek the comfort of their traditional winter camps, lulled into a false sense of security by the season. Distance and climate had always protected them, but the westward advance of the railways had ended that advantage. Supplies now could be rapidly shipped to distant depots and stockpiled for prolonged campaigns.

Sheridan, well aware of the vital role the railroads would play in bringing order and peace to the frontier, was determined to remove the Indian barrier that impeded the rapid advance of the lines. Thus he concentrated his forces against the Cheyennes, Arapahos, and Sioux, who ranged near the Kansas Pacific and Union Pacific lines, and paid only passing attention to the Kiowas and Comanches, who traditionally raided south into Texas and New Mexico.

After Grant took office as president in March 1869, he appointed Sheridan lieutenant general and gave him direct command of the Division of the Missouri. This vast command extended from Sheridan's Chicago headquarters to the western borders of Montana, Wyoming, Utah, and New Mexico, and from the Canadian line to the Mexican border. Most of the Indian population of the United States was scattered around the million square miles of his command; Sioux, Northern and Southern Cheyennes, Kiowas, Arapahos, Comanches, Utes, Piegans, Kickapoos, and Apaches all battled Sheridan's troopers. He gave overall direction to the final, and greatest, Indian campaigns waged on this continent. Between 1867 and 1884, his troops fought 619 engagements with the Western tribes, finally completing the subjugation of America's native peoples that had been set in motion almost 400 years before.

In these campaigns Sheridan usually employed the same strategy that had worked so well in 1868–69. In the Red River War of 1874–75 on the southern plains and the Great Sioux War of 1876–77 on the northern plains, he again attempted to employ winter as an ally (although both campaigns also saw summer fighting) and to have converging columns trap the Indians. Recognizing the difficulties of distance and terrain, he never expected these columns to meet or to work in concert, but rather to keep the natives insecure, off-balance, and constantly on the move. In neither of these great campaigns did the Indians suffer much loss of life in battle (in fact, far more soldiers than Indians were killed on the battlefield), but they were defeated by starvation, exposure, stock, and property losses, and unrelenting insecurity.

Such campaigns reaffirmed the effectiveness of Sheridan's total-war philosophy, for it was concern over the suffering of their families that finally forced the warriors onto the reservations to surrender. If Indian women and children had been allowed to find sanctuary on the reservations, which they were not, or if the soldiers had been prohibited from attacking the Indian villages, then Sheridan's strategy would have failed. Only by making war on the entire tribe—men, women, and children—could Sheridan hope for quick and decisive results.

He—and many officers—tended to underestimate the tenacity, courage, and ability of the Indians. This could have disastrous consequences, as it did on the northern plains during the Great Sioux War, when the Sioux outgeneraled George Crook at the Rosebud and George Custer at the Little Bighorn. Only after Sheridan turned to occupation of the Sioux hunting grounds, to constant harassing tactics, and to military control over the reservations did the Indians capitulate.

The infamous quote that "the only good Indian is a dead Indian" became emblematic of Sheridan's dealings with the Indians. Although the sentiment certainly did not originate with him, it nevertheless has the ring of Sheridan rhetoric. Captain Charles Nordstrom of the 10th Cavalry claimed that Sheridan made the remark in his presence at Fort Cobb in January 1869. According to Nordstrom, a Comanche leader named Toch-a-way, striking his chest as he approached Sheridan, declared: "Me Toch-a-way; me good Injun." To which the general reportedly smiled and replied, "The only good Indians I ever saw were dead."

Nothing troubled Sheridan more than the lack of firm national consensus on the righteousness of his Indian campaigns. During the Civil War a grateful nation had applauded his every action, but now he found himself bitterly criticized for pursuing similar tactics against the Western Indians. The public condemnation of his direction of Custer's 1868 Washita fight and Major Eugene M. Baker's 1870 Piegan massacre on the Marias River deeply wounded Sheridan.

He once explained to Sherman, in defense of his methods, that

> I have to select that season when I can catch the fiends; and if a village is attacked and women and children are killed, the responsibility is not with the soldiers but with the people whose crimes necessitated the attack. During the war did any one hesitate to attack a village or town occupied by the enemy because women and children were within its limits? Did we cease to throw shells into Vicksburg or Atlanta because women and children were there?

Keeping peace on the Indian frontier remained Sheridan's primary duty throughout his years as commander of the Division of the Missouri, but even in times of Indian unrest, he and his troops were quickly pulled back from the frontier to meet various threats to national order. They were called east, for example, to help out during the 1871 Chicago fire crisis, the 1876 Louisiana election crisis, and the great national railroad strike of 1877. Indian wars were already anachronistic to Gilded Age Americans, and the needs of the Western frontier were usually subordinated to more pressing political, economic, or social needs in the East.

Sheridan's pragmatism and elastic ethics made him the perfect soldier for an expansionist republic. He ruthlessly carried out the dictates of his government, never faltering in his conviction that what he did was right. Knowing only the soldier's life, he tended to view every situation as an opportunity to exercise military power. Deeply affected by the chaos of the Civil War, he was quick to apply force against all those who opposed his government's wishes— be they unreconstructed Southerners, striking Northern laborers, or Western Indians.

On November 1, 1883, General Sherman retired from the army, and Sheridan moved to Washington to assume the position of commanding general. By law, however, Sherman's four stars retired with him, so Sheridan was denied this highest grade. Moreover, he found his new position frustrating, for the office was devoid of any real power in peacetime. The bureau chiefs actually administered the army, and they reported directly to the secretary of war.

There was considerable talk in the 1880s of running Sheridan for president, although his Catholicism made nomination unlikely. Sheridan had no desire to run for political office anyway, and the blandishments of the professional politicians did not sway him. He had seen what politics had done to "the old man," as he called Grant, and he had no wish to chance such a fate. "I have led forlorn hopes enough in the army," he declared in March 1888. "This being pulled and hauled by politicians does not suit a soldier."

Another reason to decline politics was the precarious state of his health, for despite his relative youth Sheridan suffered from severe heart disease. By 1883 his oddly shaped figure had grown increasingly portly, his face flushed and fleshy, and his hair snow white. He now withdrew from the public light to spend more time with his young wife, Irene Rucker Sheridan (they were married in 1875), and their four children.

He spent much of his time working on his memoirs in the study of his roomy Washington home. He had been writing for a year when, in November 1887, his physician diagnosed the heart disease that would soon kill him.

Six months later, on May 22, 1888, just after returning from an inspection of the site for Fort Sheridan, near Chicago, the fifty-seven-year-old general collapsed with a massive heart attack. This news prompted Congress to revive the grade of general of the army, and President Grover Cleveland immediately signed the commission. So it was that Sheridan joined Washington, Grant, and Sherman in holding the four-star rank. The promotion lifted his spirits, but his frail body had been wracked by more heart attacks. Soon thereafter he was moved to his seaside cottage at Nonquitt, Massachusetts, where he died on Sunday, August 5, 1888.

He was buried at Arlington National Cemetery, as he had requested. His impressive gravestone was placed on a high, green knoll directly in front of the Custis-Lee Mansion, the home of his old foe, looking eastward toward the city of Washington. There it stands today, still guarding the Union he did so much to save.

V

THE LAST ACT

THE ANDERSONVILLES
OF THE NORTH

PHILIP BURNHAM

Treatment (or, more usually, mistreatment) of prisoners of war is an issue as old as war itself. By the Civil War, we had come a long way from antiquity, when POWs were generally slaughtered or enslaved. The prison camp, though, was still a new phenomenon, its first widespread use coming in the Napoleonic Wars, its development going hand in hand with the introduction of conscription and the raising of mass armies. Andersonville in southwest Georgia was certainly the most notorious of the Civil War prisons, with 29 percent of the 33,000 men who were packed into its twenty-six open-air acres dying of disease, starvation, and exposure. Conditions in the prison camps of the North were also deplorable; but since Union authorities were better able to supply food, clothing, and shelter, far less excusable. Atrocity stories, many of them apocryphal, coming from Southern camps led Washington to retaliate by cutting rations in Federal camps by 20 percent. It is not surprising that some 26,000 Rebels died in northern prison camps, as compared to 30,000 Union POWs in the south, marks of almost equal shame. The worst of the Northern camps was probably the one in Elmira, New York—"Helmira"—where men were beaten and hung by their thumbs, dubiously edible rats went for four cents a head, and empty pine coffins were piled in full view of the inmates, of whom one out of four died. They were the least remembered of Confederate casualties. But unlike Henry Wirz of Andersonville, a Union camp commander would never mount the scaffold.

Philip Burnham is the author of *How the Other Half Lived: A People's Guide to American Historic Sites* and *Indian Country, God's Country: Native Americans and the National Parks.* He is at work on a book about the prison camps of the North. Burnham lives in Washington, D.C.

IN OCTOBER OF 1864 A BAND OF SICK AND WOUNDED CON-
federate soldiers prepared to make their exodus home in a prisoner exchange
from the Union prison camp in Elmira, New York. Eyewitness A. M. Keiley
described their struggle like a nightmare out of Dante: "On they came on
their crutches, on their cots, borne in the arms of their friends," he wrote,
"creeping, some of them, on hands and knees, pale, gaunt, emaciated, some
with the seal of death stamped on their wasted cheeks and shriveled limbs."
Keiley watched as men feigned battle wounds or bribed Yankee officers to be
among the select; those who stayed behind were condemned to spend the
war's duration in a camp where the death toll reached into the hundreds every
month. As one survivor grimly concluded, "If there was ever a hell on earth,
Elmira Prison was that hell."

New York's prisoner-of-war camp—nicknamed "Helmira"—was only the
most infamous of dozens of Northern prisons where hunger, exposure, brutality, and disease were everyday hazards. Yet Elmira remains something of a
military secret, while the 30,000 Union soldiers who perished in places like
Georgia's Andersonville Prison and Libby Prison in Richmond are the stuff of
national legend. The numbers belie such a discrepancy. Some 26,000 Rebels
died in what was called "Yankee captivity"—six times the number of Confederate dead listed for the battle of Gettysburg; twice that for the dead of
Antietam, Chickamauga, Chancellorsville, Seven Days, Shiloh, and Second
Manassas combined.

Confederates don't inspire the usual American fascination with captivity.
In fact, captive Johnny Reb has been three times cursed in memory: he was
captured in battle; he fought on the losing side of the war; he defended a slave
regime regarded as morally repugnant. Whatever stigma still attaches to him,
his experience in squalid camps from the Atlantic Ocean to Lake Erie to the
Mississippi River was no less horrific. "To go into a prison of war is in all respects to be born again," wrote Sidney Lanier, a prominent man of letters who
had spent a grueling stretch as a POW in the North and, while imprisoned,
probably contracted the tuberculosis that would kill him. "For of the men in
all prisons of the late war, it might be said, as of births in the ordinary
world—they came in and went out naked."

One could say of Anthony M. Keiley that he took the high road to Elmira.
A member of the 12th Virginia Infantry, he was captured by Federal cavalry
in a June 1864 attack on the outskirts of Petersburg, Virginia. Though his
captors couldn't have known it, Keiley was no ordinary prisoner. A newspaper

editor and lawyer before the war, he disdained all thoughts of escaping military service, interrupting a promising career as a state politician to volunteer for the local militia when Petersburg came under siege.

Born in New Jersey in 1832, Keiley had moved South with his family as a young boy. But his homecoming as a POW was none too pleasant. He and his comrades were force-marched twenty-six miles and prodded "like cattle" by saber-wielding cavalrymen. They were boarded on a riverboat and dumped at Maryland's Point Lookout prison, where they were strip-searched for money and valuables. Assigned to bunk in a tent called the "Lyon's Den" by its eighteen residents, Keiley was introduced to a life that had "all the stupidity of a tread-mill without its exercise"—a test of his ability to avoid, among other hazards, the dangers of homesickness and depression.

Point Lookout, located at the southern tip of Maryland, where the Potomac River empties into Chesapeake Bay, was a rude primer for Elmira. The drinking water was, he wrote, so black that "a scum rises on the top of a vessel if it is left standing during the night." Food rations included "a half-pint of watery slop, by courtesy called 'soup.'" After a few days in the pen, "men became reckless because hopeless," wrote Keiley, "brutalized, because broken-spirited." One day when he wandered close to the deadline—a marker in the prison interior that inmates crossed at their peril—Keiley narrowly avoided being shot at by a prison guard, who threatened him with his life. Fearing his will to survive was crumbling, he volunteered for camp labor. "Another month here and I become a candidate for one of the piled-up pine boxes," he wrote in his journal. The first week, he noted, passed like a year.

In early July, Keiley's prayers to escape Point Lookout were answered—if being transferred to Elmira could be considered the answer to a prayer. On July 9, he and 280 others were packed into a narrow shiphold and bound for New York harbor, given a ration of bread and two ounces of fat for the next forty-eight hours. After landing, the prisoners were crammed on a train headed northwest, arriving the next day at what Keiley called "a sort of fungus of the Erie Railroad," a town of 15,000 people along the Chemung River. Called Elmira, the town near the Pennsylvania border was also a prominent stop on the Underground Railroad.

A mile from the town center was the Confederate prison, a camp erected early in the war to billet Union soldiers. Keiley and his troop, among the first prisoners to arrive, found a plank stockade twelve feet high enclosing thirty acres, lined with an exterior catwalk where guards could tread between sentry boxes. A series of thirty-five barracks in parallel rows housed 10,000 prisoners by mid-August, many forced to live in tents until additional housing could be raised. Finding a top bunk in Barracks 21 with a few Petersburg cronies, Keiley began his stint as a "fresh fish" at a prison one inmate described as "nearer Hades than I thought any place could be made by human cruelty."

Keiley seemed, at first glance, a fresh fish out of water. A former schoolteacher, he could cite Byron, Horace, Shakespeare, and Congreve on every topic from patriotism to human destiny. Still, he was no educated fool. A seasoned veteran, he had been commissioned a lieutenant in 1861 and served at Chancellorsville and Gettysburg before obtaining a discharge to pursue his political career. Fluent in Latin and French, Keiley must have cut a gentleman's jib in the hellhole that would swallow up thousands of his Rebel companions in the months to come.

Hardly a good old boy, then, Keiley would have seemed ripe to become an Elmira statistic. In the early weeks, he watched helplessly as guards meted out camp "justice": Prisoners were hung by their thumbs; bound and gagged; beaten for minor infractions. An "innocuous" fellow from his ward was shot for disobeying a guard. Keiley watched, appalled, as men who entered the hospital "perished from actual starvation."

His own chances didn't look much better when he came down with dysentery. Soon Keiley spent his own time in the hospital, where "as soon as [the doctors] learned to distinguish between quinine and magnesia they were removed to another field of labor." The lack of contact with the outside, what he believed were dishonest reports by the Sanitary Commission, even the prisoners' habit of stealing one another's rations—a maneuver called "flanking"—left him in a bitter funk as to his own prospects of ever getting out alive.

Instead, Keiley carved another path to survival. Using his political know-how, he struck up a modest friendship with prison commandant Major Henry Colt, a man he came to admire as a just and compassionate administrator. Horrified by the neglect of prisoners ("the men are being deliberately murdered by the surgeon"), Keiley, the lawyer turned camp activist, helped authorities, including Colt, cashier Dr. E. L. Sanger, an ignorant surgeon by most accounts and roundly hated by the prisoners.

To waylay depression, Keiley applied for camp work and became the keeper of the "Dooms-day Book," earning ten cents a day entering the names of incoming prisoners. Next he was entrusted with recording the morning death report, becoming a reluctant expert on Elmira mortality. Keiley was soon awarded a "comfortable room" with a bunk and full rations to share with friends—no need to worry about the cost of rats anymore, the going price four cents a head. The Petersburg politician had earned the ear of his captors, doing what he could to help the men who lived around him.

Not all prisoners were so well-connected. One of the men Keiley likely enrolled as an incoming prisoner was John King of the 25th Virginia Infantry, a carpenter by trade. A resident of Upsher County, Virginia, a region with strong pro-Union sentiments, King took fire from Little Round Top at Gettysburg and survived the Wilderness campaign, where a close friend was killed at his side. Helping build the breastworks at Spotsylvania Court House's Bloody Angle, he was captured in May 1864 and, like Keiley, shipped to Point Lookout. Not one to indulge in war stories, King claimed the most inspired charge he ever made while a soldier was a hungry rush on a cornfield in northern Virginia.

King arrived at Elmira on August 1 and was assigned to a tent in Ward 39, the basic organizational unit of the camp, and roughly equivalent to a barrack. His barrack wasn't completed until December, by which time the weather had turned bitterly cold, even for a hill-country Reb. Twenty-two years old, he wasn't impressed with the new accommodations: The barrack lacked a ceiling; the Yankees forbade all bedding for fear of lice ("it mattered little to us for we were already well supplied"); and the quarters weren't sufficiently heated. Even in the dead of winter, men were forced to stand three feet away from the stoves or feel the wrath of stick-swinging guards.

Camp conditions soon rendered King, like most prisoners, a mere ghost of himself. He spent a month in the hospital with "stubborn diarrhea"—a condition he imputed to eating tainted crackers—and suffered from blindness due to vitamin deficiency. He contracted scurvy, his mouth and gums "so spongy and sore that portions could be removed with the fingers." The "healthy" men, he remembered, were marched to the mess hall daily and ordered to scoop out cups of piping-hot soup—if they could handle it without being scalded. King admitted gnawing on a soup bone for hours at a time. "Many men, once strong, would cry for something to eat," he remembered. "I know from experience." When a package of food arrived from his sister, he was too sick even to partake.

Like Keiley, he couldn't fathom why the well-provisioned North didn't provide better for its prisoners. "The pants I had when arriving at Elmira were in such a bad condition," he wrote, "that for a long time I wore nothing but my underwear." When his shoes wore out, he wrapped his feet in rags; not until February was he issued a new pair of boots, by which time he'd developed frostbite. Unlike Keiley, he refused to cooperate with the Yankees, turning down a carpenter's job—probably to build coffins—at ten cents a day. Defying regulations, he crossed a work area and was forced to wear a "barrel shirt" as punishment and made to promenade across the compound.

There were small victories along the way. Several men from his ward escaped by digging a twenty-five-foot tunnel below their tent, nonchalantly emptying dirt-filled haversacks in the backwash of the Chemung that ran through the center of camp and was used for a latrine. But prisoner politics mystified him. King professed amazement that some of his fellows were allowed obvious privileges, including a well-dressed inmate named Shocky who was given permission to go over the wall and return periodically. King suspected that Shocky was a Freemason, a guess that may well have been accurate.

✦

YANKEE INGENUITY at Elmira proved no more remarkable than its Southern counterpart. King saw prisoners fashion gutta-percha buttons and mount them on silver for sale to camp officers. Watch chains were made from horsehair, fans from white pine, toothpicks from bone. One enterprising fellow built an engine and charged King a cracker to see it work. The crafts were sold or swapped to guards and officers, the proceeds spent at the sutler's store for needed provisions. A market near the cookhouse was set up where prisoners could swap their wares, since "money was too scarce with which to make purchases."

King endured almost a year at Elmira. By springtime of 1865, "at roll call there was no answer to nearly a third of the names." "Old Buttons," a friend who sewed battle patches on his shirt for every skirmish he'd seen, died while King was in the hospital. The dead were buried outside camp by a prisoner detail under administration of an escaped slave, one John Jones, paid $2.50 per body. The company and regiment of each corpse were recorded on a slip of paper and placed in a bottle before interment.

Only one occasion interrupted the ritual. With snowmelt, the Chemung flooded in March, and guards had to row through the camp to get provisions to prisoners. One day King stumbled upon several corpses wrapped in blankets—the graveyard was inaccessible until "in a week or so our old prison was in its natural condition." Nine months after arrival, King knew he was among the luckiest of Elmira's prisoners, "born-again" in a place where death was at least as common as it was on the battle front.

Though Keiley bragged of having stayed in "the best two of the Federal pens," his love of irony made the claim suspect. Elmira was one of dozens of Northern camps—and perhaps not the worst of the lot. From the sprawling tent city at Point Lookout to barracks like Douglas and Johnson's Island to imposing masonry forts like Lafayette (New York City), Delaware (on Pea Patch Island, across from Delaware City), and McHenry (Baltimore), Northern prisons came in many shapes. But camp life everywhere was dominated by two depressing facts: the constant presence of death and the almost complete absence of women. In spite of such hardships—perhaps because of them— prison routine struggled to imitate life on the outside.

Prisoners confined to Johnson's Island, a facility for officers in Lake Erie located three miles north of Sandusky, Ohio, found a barber, jeweler, baker, shoemaker, and tailor working out of barracks. Debating groups, religious services, and a Rebel Thespian Society held sway for the more metaphysical-minded. Johnson's Island wasn't typical—officers, often culled from enlisted men to break down military organization, received better treatment as POWs. The men on the island could buy uncensored newspapers—a rarity in Northern camps—and inmates contributed to the local *Sandusky Register.* Since free time was abundant, sports were popular; the prison baseball championship drew a crowd of several thousand people in 1864. Despite its setting in the middle of Lake Erie resort country, however, Johnson's Island was no holiday. "When the weather got below zero, the scenery was scarcely compensation for the suffering," remembered one inmate. "We bury our own dead," remarked another, "and on such occasions, like our working parties, we are always attended by a sufficient guard."

Chicago's Camp Douglas, four miles south of downtown, was even better endowed. A prisoner-produced newspaper, *The Vidette,* advertised novelties from tobacco pipes and medicinal remedies to upcoming variety shows. A photo studio permitted inmates to send their portraits to worried relatives back home. The Prisoners' Masonic Association was quartered in its own barrack and given a Yankee Mason for a guard—something that wouldn't have surprised John King. There were hospital flush toilets, a sewer system connecting with Lake Michigan, a circulating library, a garrison police force, and a fire department (five engines strong) as large as Chicago's, though neither was staffed by prisoners. Prisoners fashioned violins, guitars, and banjos from discarded scraps. In 1863, black inmates, some who had followed their masters into captivity, staged a minstrel show (admission: twenty-five cents) but had to change locale due to a crushing run on seats. Although alcohol was forbidden, other vices flourished. One prisoner made $10,000 (Federal) dealing faro to comrades who had somehow amassed a disposable income.

Money went a long way toward making the camps bearable. Prisoners who had stitched currency to coat linings or stuffed it in boots (Confederate scrip was discounted to only a few pennies on the dollar) could buy provisions from the camp sutler. Some received cash from friends and relatives, which was confiscated by camp officials in exchange for sutler's checks redeemable for everything from fresh vegetables to combs and needle and thread. In most camps, tobacco (or hardtack) functioned as currency—five chaws bought a shave at Elmira, ten a haircut. "Money will enable you to live anywhere," boasted well-to-do Lawrence Sangston, a member of the Maryland legislature, imprisoned at New York's Fort Lafayette and Boston's Fort Warren, "especially where there is a Yankee near and he wants it, as he usually does."

But the mail didn't always go through. Currency was often pilfered from the post. Parceled clothing had to be gray—anything blue might be used for an escape. Packages were closely inspected for contraband. Henry Kyd Douglas, a Virginia officer who had fought with Jackson's Stonewall Brigade, recalled a bottle of brandy sent him at Johnson's Island that had been drained, filled with water, and recorked by a middleman before finding its rightful owner. "I hope the Yankee who played that practical joke lived to repent it and was shot before the war ended," he wrote, presumably with tongue in cheek. By 1864, a grim Washington directive had limited all incoming parcels to sick and wounded prisoners, in retaliation for horror stories gleaned from returning Union prisoners.

✦

BETTER THAN POW FARE in the South, food rations were still meager. Union regulations required prisoners to receive the same amount of food as their captors, though, like much in the camps, theory was kinder than fact. Inmate rations were often cut, sometimes siphoned off by contractors or hungry guards, sometimes resold to augment emergency funds for hospital patients or to purchase camp "luxuries" like barrack stoves. By 1864, prisoners received two spare meals a day, totaling a few ounces of meat (or fat), soup, a loaf of bread, and infrequent portions of beans, potatoes, and coffee.

Prisoners took to making "bone butter" at Camp Morton in Indianapolis, boiling meat shanks to produce an edible residue. One Texan at Elmira offered that "broiled rat was superb," and John King added "they smelt very good while frying." Though rations could be supplemented through the sutler, price-gouging was common. King complained of prison inflation: Tobacco was fifteen cents a plug; flour was five cents and onions fifteen cents a pound. "Our rations were just enough to keep us tolerably hungry all the time," remembered one Camp Douglas prisoner, a sentiment echoed throughout the Northern camps. As atrocity stories about POWs in the South spread in 1864 (newspapers played a prominent role in fanning war hysteria), Washington retaliated by cutting rations 20 percent.

Isolation was an added burden—the worst, according to Keiley. He could only remember a few familial visits permitted men during his months at Elmira. Curtis Burke, imprisoned at Camp Morton, recalled a prisoner being allowed a first glimpse of his infant child and later showing him off in the barracks. But these were rare exceptions. The command censored letters—coming and going—in any way critical of the North. Many was the envelope that never arrived home; Keiley received several letters stripped of everything but a signature. (As King put it, "The people at home never knew how we suffered in prison.") At Camp Morton, the growing volume of sweetheart mail led authorities to forbid letters to anyone but family. Inventive correspondents made other arrangements, as those at Camp Douglas who took to flying kites above Chicago in a novel attempt at airmail, an enterprising way to escape the censor's pen.

Though this is hard for us to fathom, the prisoners were considered high entertainment. A businessman erected a twenty-five-foot tower outside Camp Douglas and charged decent Chicago folk ten cents to ascend and ogle the rebels. At Elmira stood two towers, where mostly female visitors paid fifteen cents for the privilege—the towers said to be crowded "especially on Sundays." Why "Barnum has not taken the prisoners off the hands of Abe, divided them into companies, and carried them in caravans through the country" was the embittered lament of Keiley. In Sandusky, Ohio, operators advertised excursion boat tours that circled Johnson's Island in hopes of catching a glimpse of its tenants. The camp sutler (Mr. Johnson himself) refused to sell any provisions unless prisoners first purchased a souvenir lithograph of the island. At three dollars a picture, it was no wonder counterfeit sutler's checks abounded.

The most subtle enemy was boredom. Euchre, checkers, marbles, housecleaning, and letter-writing could only fill so much time. Louse races became popular. Prisoners at Camp Chase, just outside Columbus, Ohio, removed body lice and placed them above a stove on an inverted pan, cheering them to a heated finish—the lice taking the names of favorite Union generals. But empty hours were common. "I have seen groups of battle-worn, homesick Confederates, their thin blankets drawn tight around their shoulders, stand in the lee of a barracks for an hour without speaking to one another," remembered a guard at Elmira, stationed there with an artillery unit due to reports of unruly prisoners. "They stood motionless and gazed into one another's haggard faces with despairing eyes. There was no need to talk, as all topics of conversation had long since been exhausted." As the war continued and hopes for victory flagged, the routine grew more listless. Men like Keiley volunteered for work details simply to get exercise—or a wage of five or ten cents a day to buy a chaw of tobacco.

Prisoners were confined to barracks at nightfall, lights and talking forbidden by eight or nine P.M. At Camp Douglas, a lit candle (a common tunneling tool) would draw a sentry's gunfire at night. Cooking on barrack stoves was, in some camps, forbidden, presumably because it was a fire hazard. Three or more prisoners congregating on the streets might be subject to discipline. At Douglas, men going to the latrines ("sinks") at night could neither veer from their path nor wear any clothing—or face the consequences. (One inmate was killed by a guard for urinating in the street.) While plenty of guards were sympathetic, every camp had its share of bullies and sadists. The desperation of many prisoners was such that "a man will pick your pocket in a prison," said Keiley, "who would sooner cut his own throat at home."

Punishments were brutal. Some offenders were hung by their thumbs, an experience so excruciating that many would faint or vomit within minutes. Others were made to clamber aboard the "mule," a piece of sharpened wood on legs that wrongdoers "rode" for hours at a time, sometimes with weights tied to their ankles. They were whipped with belt buckles, forced to sit barebottomed in the snow, were gagged with a baton of wood that could split open the edges of a mouth. Others were given solitary confinement on bread and water, cramped in small holes or "sweat boxes" and clamped to a ball and chain. Any prisoner, like King, made to wear a barrel marked with his sin ("I Am a Thief" or "I Ate a Dog") seems comic in retrospect, though the weight of the contraption would have made for a miserable walk through camp.

✦

NOT ALL PRISONERS were rebel yeomen. Celebrities included General John Hunt Morgan, William Henry Fitzhugh Lee (son of Robert E.), and Henry Morton Stanley, the journalist who later found Dr. Livingstone in Africa. The "Immortal Six Hundred," Confederate officers used as hostages during the siege of Charleston, were long a championed cause in the South. After enduring the privations of captivity under guard by the black Massachusetts 54th, they settled on their ennobling name. Nor were all prisoners white males. Keiley encountered a female member of an artillery company imprisoned at Point Lookout. For that matter, Camp Douglas numbered five women among its inmates in 1862; they probably disguised themselves to follow husbands or brothers into confinement. It boasted as well an array of Mexican, Spanish, Cherokee, and "contraband" (black) males of all shades. Several of the last were the "property" of other prisoners and eventually signed up to fight with the Federals. But not all blacks were so inclined: Private Isaac Wood, a bona fide combatant, eventually agreed to be exchanged for a Yankee prisoner.

The presence of blacks sparked fierce emotions. Point Lookout (the largest camp in the North, processing over 50,000 prisoners) was one of several to employ a company of Negro guards that included former slaves. Keiley abhorred "the grinning Ethiops" with a passion, while King, more tolerant, noted that he was aware of only one Negro who served at Elmira, and he "behaved like a gentleman." Harsh were Southern complaints of insolence on the part of these overseers ("Was there ever such a thing in civilized warfare?" complained one), while the guards were delighted that roles had been turned topsy-turvy. Captured rebels were paraded before Negro troops to hear bitter shouts of "Bottom rail on top!"—a common refrain hurled by black soldiers. Not every black was vindictive, however. A Point Lookout prisoner was gratified to be given ten dollars by one of the Negro guards—the benefactor turning out to be his former slave.

The ranks of POWs were swelled by political detainees with alleged Confederate sympathies—confined without trial or habeas corpus, a practice the Supreme Court would rule illegal after the war. The above-mentioned Sangston was hectored from his home by police in 1861 and spent the next several months detailing Yankee abominations in his diary. A proud patriot (and no mean ironist), Sangston wryly recorded on September 13, while being held at Baltimore's Fort McHenry, that "this is the anniversary of the day on which the 'Star Spangled Banner' was written by the grandfather of one of the prisoners." A few months later Sangston was paroled from Boston's Fort Warren, the most humane prison in the North, with only twelve deaths recorded during the war.

Many prisoners didn't wait for formal permission to take their leave. They effected escapes by tunneling (the "go-fur business"), disguise, or similar ruses, even if their total numbers were small. The Rock Island, Illinois, POW camp saw forty-one successful escapes out of an aggregate population of 12,000; only seventeen successfully absconded from Elmira, out of a similar number. But the shrewdness of many escape artists was legend. One Elmira inmate pricked himself with a hot poker to imitate smallpox scars and was admitted to the camp hospital, whence he later escaped. A Georgia sergeant nicknamed "Buttons" had prisoners lay him in a coffin and lightly cover it. When the cemetery wagon halted outside camp, Buttons rose up from the pine case and sauntered off, the teamster too frightened to protest. Though escapees especially prized blue cloth for fashioning a guard disguise, money, as usual, was more efficient. Those with political clout in the North could hire a lawyer ($100 a case in Chicago) to petition Washington for release. One Kentucky law firm successfully arranged for the parole of twenty prisoners.

There were less honorable options. Rebel informers—called "razor backs"—earned extra rations for betraying escape attempts. Others went so far as to take the oath of loyalty to the Union, derisively called "the dog" or "swallowing the eagle" in camp jargon. Both King and Keiley were proud of the fact that they didn't stoop to such a remedy—though Keiley cut something of a middle course. Oathtakers were billeted in separate barracks while waiting approval of their applications, taking jobs like hospital orderly for their trouble. When requests were approved, some men were paroled with the provision they stay within Northern lines. Nearly 6,000 prisoners took the oath to become "galvanized Yankees," sent West to fight Indians on the frontier and free Union troops for service against the South.

Contempt for oathtakers was nearly universal, even among guards. "These fellows looked like they had stolen something and been caught with it," remembered prisoner John Copley of the "galvanized" Yanks at Camp Douglas. "The ground had a special attraction for their eyes." Some were beaten up and thrown out of barracks when their true colors were discovered. More of them, however, likely took the oath from hunger pangs than for any love of being what Copley called a "Tory," though the hatred they engendered was no less. The Confederate enlistment rate at Douglas, where galvanized troops were actively recruited, was 13 percent. At Elmira, more than 150 Rebels "swallowed the eagle" before Lee's surrender. The lure of collaboration must have been considerable: more than one prisoner in ten was destined never to leave the Northern camps alive.

Sadly, many casualties were the result of political, not military, maneuvering. In 1862, North and South negotiated a prisoner exchange for repatriating captives. Within a year, however, the South had decided not to return black prisoners, treating them as "contraband" (slaves) and declaring their white officers subject to execution. Indeed, there are cases where both were summarily executed. In response, the North refused further exchanges, a decision that would doom many a POW to death. Short of manpower, Richmond stood more to gain from exchanges than did Washington—a fact General Grant understood. Except for the severely wounded or sick, exchanges were abandoned from mid-1863 until the North, sensing victory, agreed to reinstate them two months before Lee surrendered. In the interval, thousands of Confederates (and Yankees) died in captivity. Meanwhile, as one scholar has reflected, "the bureaucrats in Richmond were going to church on

Sundays with their nicely starched families"—a judgment that might equally apply to their counterparts in Washington.

With inadequate rations and shelter, not to mention the toll of physical punishment, prisoners quickly succumbed to disease. Malaria, dysentery, anemia, consumption, scurvy, bronchitis, and pneumonia were common killers. At Rock Island alone, 1,960 prisoners fell to pathogens, mostly the dreaded smallpox. (At the same camp, nearly 200 guards died of disease and exposure.) Hospital "pest houses" were developed to quarantine the afflicted, though they filled so quickly that many sick prisoners had to remain in barracks. The "dead house" for corpses was a common, if macabre, sight. As the war continued and the South felt the burden of invasion and blockade, her soldiers, already subsisting on bare rations, were more vulnerable than ever to disease.

Topography and bad planning killed many a man—and boy—in the Northern camps. Poor drainage plagued many sites, creating full-blown epidemics that might have been otherwise avoided. The Elmira camp was unaccountably built on the swampy banks of the Chemung River, a breeding ground for pestilence as soon as Keiley and his fellows began arriving in mid-1864. (Some of them were detailed to dig necessary drainage ditches—and died from disease in the doing.) The simple removal of human waste proved an unforeseen logistical problem in such places. Such was the confident prognosis for a short war that the North had assumed, in 1861, that Johnson's Island alone would be sufficient to hold all rebel POWs by the time the war had run its course.

✦

NOT LEAST, Northern winters were anathema to men from the Deep South, many of whom had never experienced a run of subfreezing weather. The North was stingy with blankets; Keiley recalled extras (anything more than one) being confiscated from prisoners by the authorities at Point Lookout. Typically, only one was allotted per man, aside from what his family might send—even in coldest January. (Late in the war, the South was permitted to sell cotton in the North to obtain money for prisoner clothing.) Elmira, as King wrote, "was an excellent place for [prisoners] to find their graves in the winter." "Helmira," in fact, became the final resting place for nearly 3,000 Rebels—24 percent of its inmates, a higher mortality rate, some estimates suggest, than even the infamous Andersonville could claim.

Some people defended Elmira. The drought-ridden summer of 1864 was the worst in memory, they said, ruining many of the crops that went to feed the camp. The following winter was even more extreme—in January, the Chemung had ice more than a foot thick. Indeed, some prisoners later attested that, under the circumstances, they could not have expected better treatment. Keiley's prison supervisor, Stephen Hopkins, claimed that many rebels were "better housed, better clothed, better fed, than they had ever been before in their lives." But Hopkins left in the early fall to accept a regimental commission. The truth probably lies somewhere between the caustic observations of Keiley and the predictable excuses of bureaucratic whitewash. Elmira was no death camp by twentieth-century standards; but it symbolized an administrative callousness usually ignored in discussions of the war.

In October 1864, rumors stirred of a prisoner exchange for the sick and wounded. Anthony Keiley engaged his wiles to find a way out of Elmira no matter the obstacles. Well-fed by camp standards, he wasn't likely to be among the paroled. Too destitute—and perhaps too proud—to offer a bribe, Keiley volunteered his services as a nurse to accompany the troops southward. His friendship with Henry Colt paid off. To his relief, the Yankees accepted, and Keiley was on a southbound train by mid-October, throwing a wadded-up missive at the feet of a strange woman on the Baltimore train platform, a letter to a friend telling him he was finally safe. By Baltimore, seven exchanged prisoners had already died.

The journey continued. Keiley's pack full of camp "souvenirs" was stolen at Point Lookout, a place he remembered none too fondly. On October 28, awaiting passage from Maryland, he pleaded the last leg of his case by claiming to have a disease with a name "as long as a 'Nantucket sea sarpint.'" The ruse got him on a ship headed for Hampton Roads, and by early November he was sailing up the Savannah River, "tired, hungry, and unkempt, but profoundly grateful." In Savannah, Georgia, the prisoners were cheered, though barricades of cotton bales, the crack of rifle fire, and exploding artillery shells were the order of the day with the city under siege. "In leaving prison," mused Keiley, "I found I had not come to peace, but to the presence of and the centre of the war."

He made his way back to Petersburg, anxious to write his memoirs; the first edition would burn in storage when the city was torched by Northern troops. In July of 1865, he was imprisoned for editing a newspaper that insulted the Military Commission at Richmond. But Keiley was nothing if not resourceful. Six years later, the man who said of prison life that it was "certain to make [men] hogs, and very likely to make them devils," was elected the mayor of Richmond, Virginia. He went on to a successful career in the diplomatic service, fathering three children and dying after an automobile accident in 1905 on the Place de la Concorde in Paris.

John King stayed on at Elmira many months after Keiley. With the news of Appomattox in the air, King, with only ten cents to his name, marched to the barracks tailor and bartered down his usual twenty-five-cent fee for turning a blanket into a proper pair of trousers. ("Wanamaker would have made a better fit.") In June, King was among a contingent of 300 men administered the oath of allegiance to the Union—an indignity he suffered since Lee had already surrendered. Given two days' rations and fare home, they were marched out of camp to board a train for Baltimore. King had devoured all of his food before they even walked through the front gate.

At Baltimore's Camden Street Station, some women saw him tearfully gnawing on an onion and took pity on him. "I concluded I would eat more onions," decided King, "as it was comforting for some one to look at me kindly." He took the train to Grafton, West Virginia, then walked the last thirty-six miles to what became the happiest reunion in his life.

By the time the last prisoner left Elmira on September 27, King was a long way from Ward 39. It took years for the frostbite to go away—and he regretted the lack of a pension. But in 1916 his grandchildren, he tells us, were "tall big men." John King was finishing his account of prison life while awaiting the arrival of his seventy-fourth birthday—"hale and hearty," as he finally put it down on paper, "and I thank our good master for it all."

"KILL THE LAST DAMN ONE OF THEM": THE FORT PILLOW MASSACRE

NOAH ANDRE TRUDEAU

Nathan Bedford Forrest was something of a redneck genius, a Snopes—why not say it?—who rose from the humblest of beginnings (he had no more than six months of elementary education) to become, by the beginning of the war, a successful planter and slave trader. He enlisted as a private in 1861; a year later he was a brigadier general. As a cavalry leader he had few equals, and his double envelopment of a Union column at Brice's Crossroads in June 1864 bore the stamp of a backwoods Hannibal. But just two months earlier, the man who once said, "War means fightin' and fightin' means killin'," had just presided over one of the most controversial episodes of the war. It involved the capture of a Federal outpost called Fort Pillow and the massacre—there is really no other word for it—of close to 300 Union soldiers, blacks who had joined the Northern army and, just as despised by the Confederates, Southern Unionists. The place wasn't even supposed to be a fort any longer. William T. Sherman had ordered that Fort Pillow be abandoned "absolutely." It was—only to be reoccupied. The man entrusted to carry out Sherman's orders, Major General Stephen A. Hurlbut, did a lucrative trade in confiscated cotton and needed the fort for the conduct of his illegal dealings. Did Forrest, the former slave trader, look the other way when his troops began to slaughter the largely black garrison, most of which had surrendered? Shortly there would be well-publicized military and congressional inquiries, full of gory details. Fort Pillow was a savage low point of the war, and Forrest would never live down its opprobrium. Perhaps the person who would go on to be a founder of the Ku Klux

Klan didn't care. But Fort Pillow was also, as Noah Andre Trudeau writes, "a military disaster waiting to happen," where greed and prejudice would collide head-on.

Noah Andre Trudeau is a director in the cultural-programs division of National Public Radio and the author of several books on the Civil War.

ON APRIL 12, 1864, TWO CONFEDERATE CAVALRY BRIGADES (about 1,500 men) commanded by Major General Nathan Bedford Forrest overran a Union post at Fort Pillow, Tennessee, fifty miles above Memphis on the eastern bank of the Mississippi River. Fort Pillow's garrison consisted of approximately 600 soldiers, almost equally divided between black and white. (The precise number will never be known; the two regiments involved were actively recruiting, and their muster rolls were incomplete.) Roughly half the fort's defenders died in the final Confederate assault or in the period immediately following it. As stories of what happened began to circulate, newspapers throughout the North quickly tagged this military action a "massacre." While this designation might be initially dismissed as part of the propaganda of the times, subsequent evaluations by historians have accepted and validated that the events on that April day broke the accepted rules of warfare. Of the killed or missing, some 195 came from the 6th U.S. Heavy Artillery (Colored) and the 2nd U.S. Light Artillery (Colored), while between 82 and 102 belonged to the white 13th Tennessee Cavalry (Union).

Forrest proclaimed it an object lesson to an enemy that had begun to arm black men. "The victory was complete . . . ," he said three days afterward. "The river was dyed with the blood of the slaughtered for 200 yards. . . . It is hoped that these facts will demonstrate to the Northern people that negro soldiers cannot cope with Southerners."

The specter of slaves with guns had haunted the Southern mind since well before the Civil War. "We have to rely more and more on the power of fear," observed a writer for the influential Southern publication *De Bow's Review* in 1849. "We are determined to continue masters, and to do so we have to draw the reign [*sic*] tighter and tighter day by day to be assured that we hold them in complete check."

This history of reactionary violence had tragic implications for the slaves who fled to join the Union army. Well into 1864, official Confederate policy refused to accord captured black soldiers the rights extended to military prisoners. Those who survived and reached Confederate rear-echelon areas were sorted according to their status as runaways or free men. Most of the former were returned into servitude, while those who had been free faced an open-ended incarceration with almost no hope of exchange. But a number of captured black soldiers never even made it that far, for the odds of them being killed once they had surrendered were much greater than for their white counterparts.

On August 3, 1863, for example, a detachment of twenty-one men and one black officer belonging to the 1st Regiment Louisiana Native Guards was captured near Jackson, Louisiana. The next day the prisoners were sent rearward in the custody of Arkansas mounted infantry. The captives never reached their objective. According to the commander of the Arkansas detachment, when four of the blacks tried to escape he "ordered the guard to shoot them down. In the confusion, the other negroes attempted to escape likewise." The officer then had the entire POW contingent killed, bragging in his official report that he had used his six-shooter to assist in the "execution of the order." Clearly there were few if any guarantees that a black soldier could expect to survive capture.

In one of those turnabouts that inevitably follows an ill-considered policy, the Union's assignment of most newly organized black units to rear-echelon duty put many in greater danger than if they had served with frontline commands. Ironically, it was the very document that freed these slaves and authorized their military enlistment that also determined most would serve in secondary capacities. In the words of Abraham Lincoln's Emancipation Proclamation of January 1, 1863, liberated slaves were to be "received into the armed services of the United States to garrison forts, positions, stations, and other places. . . ."

The practical result of this in Tennessee was that most units raised there wound up guarding the rail lines, supply posts, and other such points, which were generally isolated and vulnerable to enemy raiders. Union successes in 1863 served to put many of these garrison regiments directly in harm's way. By pushing down the Mississippi River and moving on an axis extending southward from Chattanooga, the Union left much of middle and west Tennessee wide open to enemy raiding operations. It was the kind of fluid, unpredictable arena that was tailor-made for Nathan Bedford Forrest, a military officer with a genius for improvisation. An archetype of the self-made man, Forrest—a planter and slave trader before the war—joined the Confederacy as a private and was soon commanding a mounted battalion. His aggressive and unorthodox cavalry tactics made him the bane of his Union opponents, while his outspoken bluntness and fierce pride kept him at odds with his Confederate superiors.

Mounted raids were Forrest's stock-in-trade. Early in December 1863, he led a small force from Mississippi to the town of Jackson, in south-central Tennessee, and for the rest of the month he gathered recruits and supplies. By the time converging Union columns finally forced him back across the state border, he had enlisted enough men to form two slim divisions. These he organized in early March 1864, and within two weeks he was on his way north again. With Major General William Tecumseh Sherman gathering Union strength outside Chattanooga, the prospect of ripping into the Tennessee transportation network held the promise for Forrest of inflicting some discomfort on that methodical buildup. On a more practical level, the reorganization of Forrest's command had added three Kentucky regiments badly in need of horseflesh. A raid through Tennessee into the Bluegrass State would give these troopers an opportunity to replenish their stock.

Forrest was also targeting the white population of Tennessee. The increasing number of west Tennesseans who had first joined and then dropped out of the Confederate service was a growing problem. Some had simply gone home to help their families survive in a devastated region; others had actually changed sides, becoming "homemade Yankees" or "Tennessee Tories." They joined with native Unionists intent on inflicting what Forrest termed "outrages" against those who were not on their side. One who caught Forrest's attention was Major William F. Bradford. In a book ghostwritten for Forrest after the war, he noted the "brutal, infamous conduct on the part of Bradford's Battalion toward the non-combatant people of West-Tennessee. . . ." Although recruited in towns that lay directly in Forrest's Path, Bradford's regiment had been moved out of harm's way—to Fort Pillow.

Forrest's lead brigade began filtering northward in mid-March and was soon established at Jackson. When he reached that point on March 21, Forrest learned that soon after his previous departure, a force of Tennessee Unionists had threatened to torch the town, relenting only when a ransom was paid. On March 22, Forrest proclaimed that the "officers and men" involved were "outlaws, and not entitled to be treated as prisoners of war falling into the hands of the forces of the Confederate States."

That same day, Forrest moved his headquarters several miles north to Trenton, from which he sent a 500-man strike force to capture Union City, near the Kentucky border. This was accomplished on March 24, with 475 Yankees surrendering. Forrest and most of the Confederate raiders bypassed Union City, striking northward and reaching Paducah, Kentucky, on March 25. A quick rush by his lead elements sent the Yankees tumbling back into a strong earthwork on the western side of the town known as Fort Anderson. For about an hour Forrest played a war of nerves, showing just enough of his units to convince the Union commander that there was a much greater force behind them. Then a rider with a white flag delivered to the enemy what one of Forrest's biographers has aptly termed "a typical surrender-or-else ultimatum." It usually praised the noble defense that had been offered to that point, declared that an overwhelming force stood poised to annihilate the garrison, and promised no mercy if unconditional terms were not immediately accepted. This particular one concluded: "If you surrender, you shall be treated as prisoners of war, but if I have to storm your works, you may expect no quarter."

This Federal commander chose to stand his ground and successfully repulsed an assault made by some Kentucky troops, apparently without Forrest's authority. Part of the Fort Anderson defense consisted of 274 men belonging to the 1st Kentucky Heavy Artillery (Colored), and the Union commander reported that "they fought as bravely as any troops in the fort." Although Forrest's men had previously come across small parties of black soldiers, this was the first time they had faced a significant number of them.

After failing to take the Paducah garrison, Forrest slowly retired to Jackson. There, on April 4, he sent a status report to his department commander. He was supremely confident of his "ability to whip any cavalry they can send against me, and can, if necessary, avoid their infantry." Almost as an afterthought, Forrest added, "There is a Federal force of 500 or 600 at Fort Pillow, which I shall attend to in a day or two. . . ."

Some four months earlier, as Sherman began the buildup for his Atlanta campaign, he had moved to clean up the clutter of small forts and outposts established during earlier phases of the Federal advance but no longer considered necessary. On January 11 he sent instructions to the officer commanding at Memphis to begin organization of the XVI Army Corps, which would take part in his march on Atlanta. Sherman wanted everything bent to this single task. "To enable you to effect this combination," he wrote the officer, "I hereby direct the force at Paducah to be reduced to three companies, Cairo to seven, Columbus to one white and one negro regiment, Memphis to two black and two white regiments. . . . Abandon Corinth and Fort Pillow absolutely, removing all public property to Cairo or Memphis. . . ."

The man entrusted to carry out these orders, Major General Stephen A. Hurlbut, already had a singular reputation for simultaneously advancing his personal wealth and his military career. His appointment to Memphis set the fox to watch the chickens. Cotton was still king for the hungry textile mills of the North, and the Mississippi Valley remained a prime source for this commodity. Successful Union military operations had spread U.S. controls over a vast region of cotton plantations, whose product was then selling for up to 80 cents a pound. It was all supposed to be managed by the Treasury Department, but the tangled army and navy jurisdictions, coupled with the normal chaos of war, guaranteed that there would be ample room for corruption.

Later that year, Hurlbut at first told a congressional committee that he had never received instructions to abandon Fort Pillow. This testimony was contradicted by another officer who had heard that Pillow had been first abandoned per Sherman's order and then, about a month later, quietly reoccupied. There is no plausible explanation for the reoccupation, though at least one writer has surmised that Hurlbut needed to change his illegal cotton operations from Memphis to a quieter spot and Fort Pillow fit the bill. Caught in this and other contradictions in his testimony, Hurlbut had to acknowledge that Fort Pillow was only "temporarily abandoned," citing as the reason for his action his concern that Confederate cannon placed on its bluff would disrupt Federal river traffic.

The first unit to reoccupy Fort Pillow after Sherman's abandonment order was a battalion of the 13th Tennessee Cavalry (Union) under the command of Major Bradford. His 285 men consisted of either loyal Tennessee Unionists or recent Confederate deserters—the two groups specifically targeted by Forrest for special attention. On March 28, Major Lionel F. Booth received orders from Hurlbut to transfer his battalion of the 6th U.S. Heavy Artillery (Colored) from Memphis to Fort Pillow and, once there, to assume overall command. Also assigned to the garrison was one section of Company D, 2nd U.S. Light Artillery (Colored), under Lieutenant Alexander M. Hunter.

It is difficult to gauge either the morale or the nature of race relations within the 6th U.S. Heavy Artillery (Colored). Conditions in west Tennessee at that time almost guaranteed that the army would not get the best runaway slaves. Since capture in uniform by Confederate raiders meant death or a return to slavery, most blacks wanted nothing to do with the army. At the same time, the increased Union activity meant ready work for willing laborers, and a black man could earn much more this way than the $10 per month being paid to black soldiers. As a result, many who filled these ranks were fresh runaways rounded up, as one Federal officer put it, "before their minds have been corrupted by life at private service, or in cities." The 6th Regiment, originally designated the 1st Regiment Alabama Siege Artillery (African Descent), was organized in mid-1863; most of its men were field hands from the Mississippi Valley cotton plantations.

When Major Booth arrived in late March, he quickly determined that he had far too few men to hold the existing defensive lines. Fort Pillow had been built by the Confederates in 1861 and named for Major General Gideon Pillow of the Provisional Army of Tennessee. Its three miles of trenches had been designed for a small army of 10,000 men. This perimeter was subsequently shortened to a mile so that about half that number could defend it. Combining Booth's four companies with Bradford's battalion created a force of only about 600 men, so Booth decided to construct a redoubt on a thirty-acre promontory at the north end of the mile-long line.

Working quickly, Booth's blacks built an earthen redan shaped like a W, with an enclosure of about an acre. The earthworks were six feet high and six feet thick (tapering to four feet across the top), fronted by a six-foot-deep ditch that was twelve feet wide. Six cannon were placed inside the redoubt, while additional rifle pits were dug some 30 to 300 yards on either flank. Directly behind the fort was the bluff itself, an extremely steep slope leading 100 feet down to the river. Just north of the redoubt was a small stream, known as both Cold Creek and Coal Creek, feeding into the river from the east.

Booth's redoubt left much to be desired. The river side was wide open; there were no walls or guns to cover any approach from that quarter. There Booth counted on fire support from the U.S. Navy river patrols. He also permitted a number of buildings close to his redoubt to remain intact. Although they served him as a post hospital and quartermaster offices, they could also provide close cover for enemy troops. Compounding the error, the lay of the land was such that the redoubt's cannon could not be depressed sufficiently to target this area. Further, a number of gullies broke up the terrain near the redoubt and the ground was littered with debris left from the land clearing; these offered ample hiding places for attackers. Most serious was the fact that Booth's redoubt was not on the highest point in the area; there were several knolls within rifle range that overlooked its interior.

It took Forrest more than the day or two he had predicted to organize his strike on Fort Pillow. Not until April 10 did Brigadier General James R. Chalmers's division of 1,500 men set off from Jackson "to some place we knew not where," related Sergeant Achilles V. Clark, a member of the 20th Tennessee Cavalry (Confederate). At the same time, two diversionary forces moved out, one back toward Paducah, the other to draw off any Federal relief coming out from Memphis. Two days later, at dawn, Chalmers drew up his men before

Fort Pillow. Colonel Tyree H. Bell's brigade was assigned to close on the northern and eastern sides of the fort, while the brigade commanded by Colonel Robert McCulloch targeted it from the south.

The first contact, as Chalmers later reported, "surprised the enemy's pickets and captured 4 of them." For perhaps two hours, the white Federals holding the intermediate line of breastworks held off the Confederate probes. Throughout this phase, Fort Pillow's six cannon fired furiously, and they were supported by the navy gunboat *New Era,* which was assisted by a spotter inside the defenses. However, the Confederates took full advantage of the topography: Bell's men, moving in from the north and east, used the labyrinth of small hills and interlacing narrow ravines to shield themselves effectively from the Yankee fusillade.

By 8:00 A.M., Chalmers's men had completely invested Fort Pillow's intermediate line. Confederate sharpshooters, positioned on the high ground, began to pick off some of the defenders. Sometime before 10:00 A.M., one of them shot and killed Major Booth. Responsibility for Fort Pillow's defense now passed to Major Bradford. About this time, a decision was made to send away as many of the civilians as possible. According to the log of the *New Era,* "@8.15 Took in tow an empty Coal Barge containing Females and non combat[ants;] towed it above Coal Creek out of danger. . . ."

When Forrest arrived at 10:00 A.M. to take charge (having ridden seventy-two miles in twenty-seven hours), he made a personal reconnaissance of the enemy's position. During this ride, two horses were killed under him, and he was badly bruised as a result. A cavalryman he passed during this reconnaissance remembered hearing him say, "There are not many—we must take them." Forrest realized that the buildings south of the fort offered a sheltered position he could use to stage troops for an assault. He ordered Chalmers to take those buildings and to move in along the Coal Creek gully. "The troops responded with alacrity and enthusiasm," reported Chalmers, "and in a short time took possession of all the rifle-pits around the fort, and closed up on all sides within 25 or 30 yards of the outer ditch." The defenders of Fort Pillow, white and black, were now squeezed together into Major Booth's ill-sited redoubt.

By 11:00 A.M., Forrest's men were in control of the area. His marksmen made it almost certain death for the Yankee artillerymen to show themselves at their guns. Forrest also had two cannon placed on a bluff south of the fort; they opened on the *New Era* at midday, forcing her to shift to a less advantageous firing position.

Forrest's men spent the next few hours sniping at the Union defenders, who could do very little against them. Forrest's adjutant, Captain Charles W. Anderson, reported, "The width or thickness of the works across the top prevented the garrison from firing down on us, as it could only be done by mounting and exposing themselves to the unerring fire of our sharpshooters. . . ." Then, at 3:30 P.M., Forrest sent forward a flag of truce with a message addressed to the fort's commander, who he believed was still Major Booth. It was classic surrender-or-die language:

> The conduct of the officers and men garrisoning Fort Pillow has been such as to entitle them to being treated as prisoners of war. I demand the unconditional surrender of the garrison, promising you that you shall be treated as prisoners of war. My men have received a fresh supply of ammunition, and from their present position can easily assault and capture the fort. Should my demand be refused, I cannot be responsible for the fate of your command.

"Up to this time," recorded the post's surgeon, "we had not lost in killed and wounded over 25 to 30 men. . . ." When the Union reply came back, it was a request for an hour's respite to think things over. In one of the many mysteries of this whole affair, Bradford signed the note (and all subsequent ones) using Major Booth's name. Even as these negotiations were taking place, Confederate scouts reported that three Federal steamers were approaching, one of which seemed to be "crowded with troops." Forrest promptly rejected the request for a sixty-minute grace period, instead allowing the commander twenty minutes to decide. While these negotiations were taking place, according to eyewitness testimony, "the white men of both sides were bantering each other from their respective positions, while some of the Negroes indulged in provoking, impudent jeers."

The scouting reports that moved Forrest to action were partially correct. Two Union steamers drew near the fort (a third turned back). One was the *Olive Branch*—carrying two batteries of artillerymen bound for Cairo, Illinois, but otherwise "being entirely defenseless"—and the other was either the *Hope* or the *M.R. Cheek,* running empty. A Union officer aboard the *Olive Branch* spotted the truce flag at the same time its captain was told by the commander of the *New Era* to pass without stopping, which both steamers did. Under a then-accepted rule of war, neither side was supposed to use the truce period to improve its position or bring up reinforcements.

Responding to this perceived threat, however, Forrest sent flanking detachments along the riverbank to forestall any landing attempt. These actions later became the basis for bitter accusations against the officer. Forrest's defenders argue that the readjustments that took place were legitimate responses to Union threats from the river, while his detractors maintain that the repositioning was not justified during a truce and that it exceeded what might be reasonably expected under the conditions. Nevertheless, given the overall weakness of the redoubt and the dominating position enjoyed by Forrest's men prior to the truce, the movements made while it was in effect provided no additional advantage to the attackers.

Bradford's final response, still using Booth's signature, to Forrest's ultimatum was terse and to the point: "I will not surrender." Forrest now prepared his men for the assault. It has been suggested that his failure at Paducah compelled him to attack Fort Pillow, lest his threats lose their credibility. Forrest left no testimony supporting or refuting this point, but his methodical preparations certainly suggest a firm resolve to take the fort by storm. When all was ready, Forrest—whose command post was uncharacteristically located about 400 yards behind his front line—ordered his bugler to sound the charge.

The Confederates leaped up from their concealed positions and rushed the fort. According to an officer in the garrison, they appeared "as if rising from out of the very earth" and "received our first fire, wavered, rallied again and finally succeeded in breaking our lines, and in thus gaining possession of the fort." Now Forrest's men were atop the parapet, firing down into the masses of bluecoated figures below.

Panic spread among the Federal troops, and afterward whites and blacks blamed each other for breaking first. What is clear is that a few Federals stood their ground, while most threw down their guns—some to run for the presumed safety of the bluff, others to raise their hands in surrender. But no one had lowered the U.S. flag, and few of the attackers had any intention of taking prisoners. According to one account, Bradford's entire contribution to the final Union defense of Fort Pillow was to shout, "Boys, save your lives!" after which he fled "down the creek"; at some point he was killed, under circumstances that are appropriately murky.

What happened next was a massacre, pure and simple. Corporal William A. Dickey, 13th Tennessee Cavalry (Union), ran from the wall when Forrest's Confederates breasted it. "The rebels followed closely," he recalled, "shooting down all who came in the way, white and black. . . . One rebel came to me and took my percussion caps, saying he had been killing Negroes so fast that his own had been exhausted; he added that he was going to shoot some more." According to Confederate sergeant Clark, the "slaughter was awful. Words cannot describe the scene. The poor deluded Negroes would run up to our men fall upon their knees and with uplifted hands scream for mercy but they were ordered to their feet and then shot down. The whitte [*sic*] men fared but little better." Wilbur H. Gaylord, a white sergeant in the 6th U.S. Heavy Artillery (Colored), was wounded when the final assault began and could not leave the wall. "I should think that 200 rebels passed over the works and passed by me while I lay there. When one rebel noticed that I was alive [he] shot . . . and missed me. . . . Just at this time I saw them shoot down 3 black men who were begging for their lives; and who had surrendered." George Shaw, a black private in the 6th, was wounded when he tried to surrender. As the Confederate raised his rifle, Shaw recalled him saying, "Damn you, you are fighting against your master."

Forrest and his officers appear to have exercised little positive control over their men during the half hour that followed the successful assault. A Southern newspaper correspondent, writing under the nom de plume Memphis, related that "Gen. Forrest expected a surrender after entering the fort, and anxiously looked for it, as he witnessed the carnage; but no token was given. . . ." Union cavalryman Daniel Stamps was captured after trying to escape down the bluff to the river. "While I was standing at the bottom of the hill," he later testified, "I heard a rebel officer shout out an order of some kind to the men who had taken us, and saw a rebel soldier standing by me. I asked him what the officer had said. . . . It was 'kill the last damn one of them.' The soldier replied to his officer that we had surrendered, that we were prisoners and must not be shot. The officer again replied, seeming crazy with rage that he had not been obeyed, 'I tell you to kill the last God damned one of them.' He then turned and galloped off." Achilles V. Clark swore that he "with several others tried to stop the butchery and at one time had partially succeeded, but Gen. Forrest ordered them shot down like dogs. . . ."

If Forrest did let his famous temper overcome his control, the lapse was momentary, for another Confederate soldier, Samuel H. Caldwell, wrote his wife on April 15 that "if General Forrest had not run between our men & the Yanks with his pistol and sabre drawn not a man would have been spared." On April 13, during a truce to remove the wounded, General Chalmers told a Federal officer that he and Forrest "stopped the massacre as soon as they were able to do so." He also explained that their men "had such a hatred toward the armed Negro that they could not be restrained from killing the negroes after they had captured them."

Even after the killing frenzy had spent itself, the ordeal was far from over. At least two of the Tennessee Union soldiers reported seeing wounded blacks killed as late as the next day. One of the two, James N. Taylor, related that

Confederate troops made "2 of the wounded Negroes stand upon their feet that they might see them fall again when shot; and shot they were." There were other reports, from both sides, of wounded men who were buried alive.

The cost to Forrest in taking Fort Pillow was 14 killed and 86 wounded. Perhaps the most careful accounting of Union losses was completed in 1989 by John Cimprich and Robert C. Mainfort Jr. Sifting through the military service records at the National Archives, supplemented by medical lists, pension files, muster rolls, military correspondence, and other contemporary sources, Cimprich and Mainfort determined that of the 585 to 605 men present that day, nearly half (between 277 and 297) were killed or mortally wounded. The mortality rate among the black troops was a staggering 64 percent, while the losses among the 13th Tennessee were between 31 and 34 percent. Some 226 members of the garrison were taken prisoner; of these, 58 were black and 168 white. The authors concluded: "This new quantitative and documentary evidence unequivocally demonstrates that a massacre occurred."

After Fort Pillow, Forrest returned to Jackson, where he would remain until May 2. Ahead lay the Battle of Brice's Cross Roads, perhaps his greatest military achievement. On the Union side, which began receiving reports about Fort Pillow on April 13, there was a military inquiry as well as a congressional investigation into the entire affair, but both seemed interested only in validating that a massacre had taken place. As to why Union troops were even there at all, the question was raised but not pursued. Perhaps not surprisingly, General Hurlbut managed to duck any culpability in the matter. On April 18 he was relieved of command of the XVI Corps and sent to the Department of the Gulf, where, Sherman believed, his administrative skills would be better employed. By war's end, a special military commission had recommended his arrest and trial for corrupt practices in the Department of the Gulf, but the issue was allowed to drop so that Hurlbut could be honorably discharged from the service. After the war, Hurlbut was a president of the Grand Army of the Republic and, drawing on personal friendships with two U.S. presidents, served as minister to Colombia and later to Peru. Charges of financial mismanagement were again leveled, but Hurlbut died before any investigation could begin.

"Remember Fort Pillow" became a battle cry for black troops from Resaca, Georgia, to Petersburg, Virginia. It does not appear to have been an entirely spontaneous action on their part; on a number of occasions, it was their white officers who initiated the cry. While it may have made the prospect of facing charging black troops more terrifying to the enemy, the effect could also boomerang as infuriated Confederates responded in kind. It also provided the white officers of black regiments an imagined justification for allowing their men to commit similar atrocities on captured Confederates. After watching his men gun down five Confederates attempting to surrender, a Federal officer in Virginia reflected, "Had it not been for Ft. Pillow, those 5 men might be alive now. . . ."

In many ways, Fort Pillow was a military disaster waiting to happen. The greed and incompetence of the area commander put troops into an exposed position that should have been abandoned. The very nature of Forrest's standard attack blueprint, with its pro forma surrender-or-die terms, on this occasion exacerbated the sectional and racial hatreds of his men. Whether he knowingly allowed his men to run riot, or simply lost control of them for thirty murderous minutes, will forever be an issue for debate. His failure to control his soldiers, and the collapse of all command authority within Fort Pillow, cleared the way for the killing that followed the breaching of the walls—which traditionally signaled the moment of victory.

The propaganda efforts by both sides after the fight added greatly to the clouding of history's final judgment. The report from the Congressional Committee on the Conduct of the War included all testimony without qualification, including fanciful accounts of women and children being shot down. Twenty thousand copies were printed and distributed. "Let Lincoln send a copy of this book to every home," declared a Northern diarist. "It is better than the draft or his greenbacks." Once the North's determination to play the race card was known to the South, the tenor of Confederate newspaper coverage changed; no longer was it a fearsome object lesson but a legitimate victory that had been blown out of all proportion. As for America's blacks, the victims of unchecked racial hatred in both the North and the South, word of what had happened at Fort Pillow came as no surprise. "I do not wonder at the conduct and disaster that transpired at Fort Pillow," a black soldier wrote from South Carolina. "I wonder that we have not had more New York riots and Fort Pillow massacres."

Because he commanded the Confederate forces at Fort Pillow, and because he was later a leader of the early Ku Klux Klan, to this day the name of Nathan Bedford Forrest is for many synonymous with racial oppression. For example, in 1979 black Tennesseans tried unsuccessfully to have his bust removed from the State Capitol; in another case a year later, Atlanta decided to change the name of its Forrest Avenue. Fort Pillow is a permanent stain on the career of a man who has also been widely described as "the foremost cavalry officer produced in America."

Military Institute; and *Two for the Summit,* a narrative of his experiences climbing mountains with his daughter, including Aconcagua in Argentina, the highest mountain in the world outside of Asia. Norman lives in Vermont and Alabama.

HISTORY GENERALLY REMEMBERS THOSE BATTLES WE CALL "decisive." Waterloo, Gettysburg, the Marne. But sometimes a small battle of minor consequence will, for some reason, escape the amnesia that blankets the past. We remember Balaklava, for example, though it was an indecisive engagement notable chiefly for the celebrated, suicidal British cavalry charge. The attention of a great poet can plainly count for a lot. The fight at the Alamo is better remembered by Americans than Chapultepec, though it was neither decisive nor, certainly, a victory. The legend is larger, surely, than the battle.

The affair at New Market, in western Virginia, on May 15, 1864, was a small action in a war that had grown large beyond anything anyone could have imagined when the fighting began, three years earlier; but it is better remembered than many larger battles whose outcomes had far more influence on the course of the war. And if the battle itself was small, it was the action of a tiny unit—some 250 soldiers who were more boys than men—that gave it a kind of mythic aura, a romantic hue in what the historian Shelby Foote has called "the last romantic and first modern war." The troops were unique in American history and their actions made the battle of New Market the most famous of many fought in the Shenandoah Valley.

The valley had been a vital theater in that war, the scene of Stonewall Jackson's remarkable 1862 campaign, and it would be fought over bitterly almost until the end. But in the spring of 1864, the decisive action was north of Richmond, between Robert E. Lee's Army of Northern Virginia and the Army of the Potomac under the command of yet another new general, Ulysses S. Grant. In early May 1864, those armies were grappling desperately in the dense, second-growth woods known as the Wilderness in the first of a long string of fierce battles that would go on for nearly a year and raise the savagery of the war to a new, almost intolerably bloody level. Grant had also sent General William Tecumseh Sherman against General Joseph E. Johnston in the Western theater of the war. Those two campaigns would both finish this war and change the nature of war itself.

THE BOYS OF NEW MARKET

GEOFFREY NORMAN

If history is the literature of what did happen, then the Civil War has to be the Great American Novel. For all its improbabilities, surprises, and unexpected twists, it could have been fiction, a sprawling Victorian epic, appropriately spun out in serial form. It wasn't fiction, of course, though the story had a certain symmetrical construction that almost smacked of an authorial hand. A well-built novel, Henry James once said, always puts its center in the middle; history obliged with two turning points halfway through the war, Gettysburg and Vicksburg. By the spring of 1864, the climactic passages of the epic were approaching. One of them was already taking place in the scrublands of tidewater Virginia, but that same May the robust Shenandoah Valley subplot was also reemerging. The Battle of New Market, in which cadets of the Virginia Military Institute took part, may have been unremarkable in terms of size, but, as Geoffrey Norman writes, "it was the action of a tiny unit—some 250 soldiers who were more boys than men—that gave it a kind of mythic aura." Take the moment when the cadets charged through a patch of low-lying marshy ground—much of the battle was fought in a thunderstorm—and some of them lost their boots to the sucking mud. In the lore of the South, that spot would forever after be known as "the field of lost shoes." Fifty-odd years later, at the Somme and Passchendaele, the same leather-consuming suction would be cited not as the stuff of legendary devotion to a cause but as a special horror of that almost plotless accretion that war had become.

Geoffrey Norman has written thirteen books and numerous magazine articles. His books include *Bouncing Back,* an account of the POW experience in Vietnam; *Alabama Showdown,* an examination of the football rivalry between Auburn University and the University of Alabama and the football culture in that state; *The Institute,* a history of the Virginia

In the Shenandoah Valley, meanwhile, the forces that faced each other were small and poorly organized; hardly armies at all. They were composed of just a few thousand men, not many of them first-line troops. Most of the units had not operated together before. Many were inadequately trained and had not seen action. Their commanders were also uncertain elements.

But the valley was crucial ground that neither side could afford to ignore. It was a vital agricultural asset for the hard-pressed South, which depended on its harvests—something General Philip Sheridan would demonstrate emphatically in the last months of the war. It was also an arrow pointed at the North's vitals. Jackson's Valley Campaign had frightened the Union into keeping troops around the capital to defend it against what was considered imminent attack. General Jubal Early would repeat this feat, in less convincing fashion, in the last year of the war. So the North could not afford to ignore the valley.

For the South, control of the valley could draw enemy forces away from the badly outnumbered Lee. A successful army in the valley, even a small one, could exert an influence much greater than the number of its muskets. It could also threaten the flank of an invading army as it moved on Richmond.

Both North and South, then, were mindful of the Shenandoah Valley in the spring of 1864, even if they could only afford to send small, ad hoc forces there.

To hold the valley, Grant, for his part, was obliged to depend on a general for whom he had little respect. The Union had been burdened by the services of a number of inadequate generals. Usually, they came by their stars through political influence, but Franz Sigel, Grant's commander in the valley, was something a little different—an affirmative action general. The Union Army included many immigrants, and a lot of them were Germans. The predominant feeling among them was that they should be commanded by one of their own. Other qualifications, including success in battle, were secondary.

Which was fortunate for Sigel, since he'd had very little success in battle, either in this war or as an officer in the German Republican army during the 1848 revolts—when he was beaten in at least three different battles before finally setting out for New York and a civilian job. But he was back in uniform when Americans went to war against each other in 1861. He quickly became a brigadier and went back to his old habits, contributing mightily to the Union defeat at Wilson's Creek, Missouri, in August 1861. In spite of his ineptitude, many German-speaking soldiers continued to believe in him. When he was relieved, they saw it as martyrdom. Failing ever upward, Sigel was promoted to major general and, in March 1862, actually turned in a credible per-

formance at the battle of Pea Ridge in northern Arkansas. But he was back in
form at the second battle of Bull Run a few months later. Along the way, he
had made enemies, but he had also increased his following and become a political force. That was, no doubt, why President Lincoln appointed him to
command the department that included the Shenandoah early in 1864, the
critical year of the war and, also, an election year. It was done because, one
cynic said, "the Dutch vote must be secured."

Sigel's German-speaking officers and troops were elated. His own commanders, however, were less enthusiastic. Grant's chief of staff, General Henry
Halleck, who'd had an earlier run-in with Sigel, wrote in a letter to General
Sherman, "It seems but little better than murder to give important commands to such men as Sigel." Grant, for his part, did not expect great things
from Sigel. In his original plan for operations in the valley, Grant envisioned
a supporting role for Sigel and hoped that he would be up to it. "If Sigel can't
skin himself," Grant said, borrowing one of President Lincoln's backwoods lo-
cutions, "he can hold a leg whilst someone else skins."

The Federals' spring 1864 campaign that Sigel was to have supported,
however, faltered after a promising start, leaving Sigel to skin on his own.

His opposite number was not inclined to be skinned in the first place, and
certainly not to stand still while Sigel held his leg. John C. Breckinridge was
not a professional soldier; he was, in fact, a politician, and a very successful
politician at that. He had been, at thirty-five, the youngest man ever elected
vice-president of the United States. This was in 1856, as running mate to the
unfortunate James Buchanan. After Lincoln was elected, Breckinridge served
his native Kentucky in the U.S. Senate and did what he could to prevent the
inevitable—the breakup of the Union. He remained stubbornly in the Senate,
opposing the war, as Kentucky chose the North—until finally, under threat of
arrest for treason, he reluctantly went with the South in September 1861.

He was commissioned a brigadier (his previous military experience was
limited to bloodless service in the Mexican War) and served capably from
Shiloh to Chickamauga. But like many other able men, he managed to antag-
onize the terrible-tempered General Baxton Bragg. So, in the spring of 1864,
when the South needed someone to command its limited and scattered forces
in the Shenandoah Valley, Breckinridge was available. Thanks to Bragg, he
was without a command.

But he was not without resources, not the least of which was the force of his
own personality. He was a tall man with striking features, and he had, not surprisingly, the orator's gift. In short, he inspired confidence.

He also had an eye for the facts of any situation, and he quickly realized that his troops were not merely few in number and widely dispersed; they were also woefully lacking in both training and experience. There had not been any fighting to speak of in the valley for some months. Even the troops who were veterans of earlier fighting had gotten soft.

Soon after he arrived in the valley, in early March, Breckinridge made a 400-mile horseback tour of his command and, along the way, put the men to work drilling and building defensive positions. The old, corrosive air of lassitude was soon replaced by a new sense of urgency.

Among his other advantages, Breckinridge had inherited some of the hardest-riding cavalrymen anywhere in the world. The valley was the domain of John Singleton Mosby, the guerrilla cavalryman, and several others who were cut from the same cloth. They were accustomed to riding literal circles around invading Union armies, and in the coming campaign they would screen Breckinridge, serve as his eyes, and harass enemy formations, especially the supply columns. In infantry and cannon, Breckinridge was outnumbered. In cavalry, however, he had the Union outclassed.

Still, Sigel outmanned him four to one, and by late April, it looked like he was on the move, coming up the valley (which runs south to north) from Martinsburg toward the vital New Market gap on the way to Staunton. If this advance went unchecked, Sigel would be in a position to destroy the crucial rail center and supply depots at Staunton, and also to threaten Lee's left—when Lee was already engaged by forces twice as large as his under the command of Grant. This was insupportable. Lee wired Breckinridge and ordered him to prevent such a move.

Ignoring the threat from the west—the one that was to do the actual skinning, in Grant's turn of phrase—Breckinridge moved north, down the valley, with alacrity to face Sigel, who was also on the move, coming north, up the valley. Ponderously.

Sigel left Martinsburg on April 29 and took three full days to reach Winchester, twenty-two miles away. He stopped there and drilled his troops for four days. On the fifth day, he ordered his men to wage a mock battle, which resulted in one regiment, the 34th Massachusetts, becoming separated and lost. Couriers had to be sent out at night to locate the unit and order it back to camp, where confidence was, understandably, not high. Meanwhile, as the drill sessions were being conducted and the mock battle was being fought, Sigel's wagon trains were being plundered by Mosby's men. The Confederates captured the general's personal supply train, which led to an order that such formations were to be guarded by 400 cavalry troopers.

Sigel moved, then stopped again at Strasburg. For the next week, the ac-

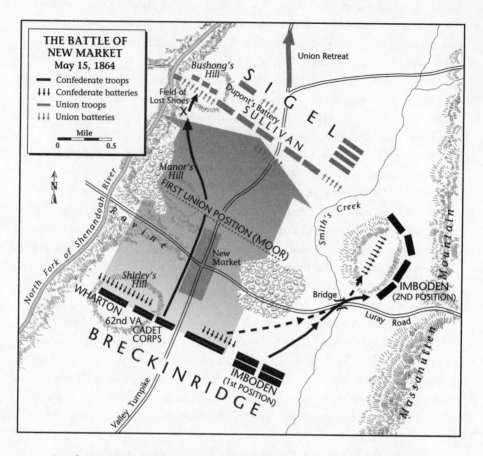

On the morning of May 15, 1864, Confederates commanded by John C. Breckinridge moved against the Federals at New Market, Virginia, in the Shenandoah Valley. By afternoon, with VMI cadets shoring up a critical weakness in the Confederate line, Moor's brigade had been defeated, and Sigel's forces were in full retreat. The map at right shows the position of the battlefield in the valley, just east of the north fork of the Shenandoah River.

tion was between the cavalry units of the two sides. The Confederates, under the command of General John Imboden, chased one Federal unit across the Potomac, then rode back up the valley to block Sigel's progress. They fought still another Union cavalry force outside the town of New Market and drove them. In three days, the Confederate horsemen had beaten two Union forces thirty miles apart and deprived General Sigel of his cavalry. In this and many other ways, the battle was a replay, in miniature, of the actions in eastern Virginia two years earlier.

Breckinridge, meanwhile, had asked for Lee's guidance. Should he engage Sigel, as Lee had originally ordered, or turn back to the southwest and face another threat as he was being encouraged to do by his old nemesis, Braxton Bragg, who was a military adviser in Richmond, operating, more or less, on his own? Breckinridge consulted Lee, who was heavily engaged near Spotsylvania, and who showed a characteristic (and, according to some, misplaced) trust in his subordinate. He wired back: "You must judge." Breckinridge decided to go for Sigel.

Breckinridge had been consolidating his forces at Staunton, which for one unit entailed marching sixty miles. It took three days. Breckinridge himself rode 145 miles from his headquarters to Staunton in three days. Another unit marched thirty-six miles in two days to join Breckinridge at Staunton and, eventually, fight for him at New Market. These last were the most improbable troops in this army of odds and ends, a reserve that Breckinridge hoped devoutly that he would never be forced to use, troops that the Confederate president, Jefferson Davis, had called "the seed corn of the Confederacy"—some 250 cadets from the Virginia Military Institute, or VMI.

VMI was the West Point of the South. More than 400 of its graduates had become Confederate officers, including twenty generals. Stonewall Jackson had taught at VMI and had been buried in Lexington, not far from the post. The cadets were scheduled to march in ceremonies to commemorate the anniversary of Jackson's death, May 10, but then, Breckinridge called for their services.

The mood at VMI was one of eager but frustrated anticipation. All around the war was going on, reaching a bloody climax, while at VMI, the boys were still drilling and going to class. That mood was described by John S. Wise in *The End of an Era,* one of the finest Confederate memoirs. Wise was one of the VMI cadets who fought at New Market. The title of the chapter describing the battle is "The Most Glorious Day of My Life."

> In the spring of 1864, I was still a cadet at the Virginia Military Institute. "Unrest" is the word to describe the feeling pervading the school. . . . Many cadets resigned. Good boys became bad boys for the express purpose of getting "shipped," parents and guardians having refused to permit them to resign.
>
> The stage-coaches for the railroad stations at Goshen and Staunton stopped at the Sallyport on nearly every trip to take on cadets departing for the front.
>
> Many a night, sauntering back and forth on the sentry-beat in front of the barracks, catching the sounds of loud talk and laughter from the officers' quarters, on pondering upon the last joyous squad of cadets who had scrambled to the top of the departing stage, my heart longed for the camp, and I wondered if my time would ever come. I was now over seventeen, and it did seem to me that I was old enough.
>
> The proverb saith, "All things come to him who waits."
>
> It was the 10th of May.

The superintendent of the institute had offered the services of his cadets in a letter to Breckinridge, who had expressed his thanks but declined the offer. A week later, when he saw the situation with more clarity, he changed his mind and sent for the cadets. They were to be his reserve in the coming battle with Sigel.

The cadets were called out by drum, and after the order had been read, they cheered wildly. They spent the rest of the night preparing, and in the morning, they marched down the valley, fifes and drummers playing "The Girl I

Left Behind Me." They wore their parade ground uniforms and, along the way, passed an Irish butcher who admired them, saying, "Begorra, an' it's no purtier drove av pigs hev passed this gate since this hog-killing began."

They made eighteen miles the first day, in good weather, and eighteen miles the second in rain that turned the road to slop. Occasionally they would march past resting veterans, who would cradle their muskets and sing "Rock-a-Bye Baby" at the young, nattily uniformed troops. The veterans offered to sell the cadets rosewood coffins lined with satin and to trim a lock to send back to their mothers after they'd been killed.

The cadets kept their discipline. Some did, however, slip out of camp to dance with the ladies in Staunton. They were young and it might have been three years earlier, before Manassas, when it was all still a glorious adventure.

On the morning of May 13, the two armies were separated by a distance of about seventy miles. If one vital objective existed anywhere between those armies, it would have to be New Market. Here, the valley was divided by Massanutten Mountain, which ran down its center. To the east was the Blue Ridge and a crucial gap that could allow a Union army to move on to Richmond.

Sigel was closer to New Market than Breckinridge and thus in a position to threaten Lee's flank, but he failed, typically, to take advantage of this opportunity. On May 13, he sent a small cavalry detachment of some 300 men forward. Imboden, with about 1,000 troopers, met and routed this force, giving Breckinridge the time he needed to bring up his army. On May 14, both he and Sigel moved on New Market in force.

Sigel, however, moved piecemeal, dividing his forces in the face of the enemy, a violation of the principles of war—but one that a general who seizes the initiative can get away with. Lee, of course, took this risk routinely, but he seldom lost the initiative. It was never Sigel's to lose.

Colonel Augustus Moor marched on New Market with 2,300 men from various commands, while the rest of Sigel's army was scattered along a twenty-mile route between New Market and Woodstock, Sigel's headquarters. Moor's troops engaged Imboden in a sharp action late in the day, with some of the fighting spilling into the town and terrifying the residents there. Imboden fell back, and Moor pushed as far as he dared. His troops held the village when night and the rain began to fall.

While the civilians in New Market passed the night in fear, their deliverers—Breckinridge's soldiers—were on the move. At 1:30 in the morning they marched out of Lacy Springs and down the Valley Turnpike. Their general had gone ahead, to find Imboden and to study the ground where he expected to fight. He found Imboden, sleeping in the open at 3:00 A.M., and told him the entire army would be in New Market by dawn.

Imboden later wrote about his meeting with Breckinridge, who had a quick eye for terrain. "The whole country for two or three miles lay before and below, like a map, and a few words of explanation from me as to roads, streams, etc., enabled General Breckinridge to grasp it all; and he remarked after five minutes study of the scene, 'We can attack and whip them here, and I'll do it.'"

At midnight, a courier from the general had arrived at the camp where the VMI boys were trying to sleep. Once again they were called out by the drum, and this time, before they marched, they gathered for a prayer that was delivered by one of their professors, Captain Frank Preston, who had lost an arm serving with Jackson at Winchester. According to one of the cadets, Preston spoke "of home, of father, of mother, of country, of victory and defeat, of life, of death, of eternity." It was a message that, in the dark and the gloom of that night, "sunk into the heart of every hearer."

The cadets formed up and marched through the mud, toward a distinct red glow on the horizon, and, along with the rest of Breckinridge's command, they were in position south of New Market shortly after dawn. The cadets were in reserve behind a line that had been designed to repulse an enemy attack. While he had moved decisively, Breckinridge wanted to fight a defensive battle from behind hastily erected breastworks that ran across the Valley Turnpike, with a hill on his left and low, swampy ground on his right. He was outnumbered and hoped to use Imboden's cavalry to provoke an attack by Sigel's troops.

Moor, however, held good ground of his own, north of town. He was also well aware of the situation. Outnumbered and not likely to be reinforced soon, he was not inclined to take Imboden's bait. By eleven o'clock, Breckinridge made up his mind to press him.

By now, Breckinridge's troops were on a piece of high ground called Shirley's Hill, facing the Federals on Manor's Hill, an opposing stretch of high ground. Breckinridge first softened up his enemy's position with cannon fire, then launched a two-stage infantry assault. A Federal gunner recalled the way he and his comrades felt when what they thought had been fence rails on the opposite ridge turned out to be bayonets and began moving toward them: "A cold chill ran down our backs."

Breckinridge's two brigades attacked, downhill, and routed Union skirmishers in the defile between the two hills. This was a rare case where the low ground was vital. Union cannons could not be depressed enough to fire on the Confederate troops there, resting and reforming for the next assault, up Manor's Hill.

The general who had led the assault, Gabriel Wharton—a VMI graduate from the class of 1847—realized that his men needed to reach the safety of the valley as quickly as possible. Good order was not essential; speed was. His men rushed down the slope and took almost no casualties. Once they had reached safety, it was the reserves' turn. This included the VMI cadets, who had been waiting for their moment under fire. Several cadets were so eager for battle that they had left their posts guarding the supply trains to join the assault.

Breckinridge had told the VMI commandant, Colonel Ship, that he had hoped it would not be necessary to expose the cadets, but "should the occasion require it," he would "use them very freely." Ship (who in 1888 changed his name to "Shipp" and is so listed in some Civil War reference books) no doubt spoke for all the ardent young men in his command when he asked the general not to deny the cadets their opportunity.

It was still 1861 in the minds of the boys and very young men of VMI— their average age was seventeen—when they formed up behind the school colors and began to march down Shirley's Hill into cannon range. They did not run; they marched quick time, which was what they believed their commanders expected of them. Wharton describes the cadets as proceeding, against the spirit of his own orders, which they had somehow not understood, "in beautiful order as tho' going to a dress parade."

Another officer wrote, "Nothing could have been handsomer than the perfect order in which they moved."

It was splendid, but there was a price. A shell tore a hole in the ranks and, for a moment, the advance faltered, not from fear but because the boys gave in to the instinct to stop and help the wounded—who included some of the boys who had left the safety of guard duty for action. Ship ordered the cadets to close up and move on. And the advance of the now bloodied cadets proceeded at achingly slow speed until they reached the valley and safety.

The cadets had taken casualties (several wounded, one of them seriously) and had still done their duty. They waited now in the valley, veterans among other veterans, for the order to advance up the hill.

Sigel had, meanwhile, arrived at the battlefield, with several of his regiments still strung out along the road behind him. (When he informed one of his officers that the troops were coming, the man said, simply, "Yes, General, but too late.")

Sigel's first instinct was to retreat, but Moor and others urged him to stay and fight. He gave in, saying, "We may as well fight them today as any day"— a remark that must have inspired great confidence in his men.

The Confederates attacked again, pushing the Union infantry back through New Market and onto a new position along yet another piece of high ground called Bushong's Hill. The VMI cadets marched, once more, as though they were back in Lexington, on parade.

It was now midday. Rain had turned the ground to thick, gluelike mud. The armies faced each other across a small valley along a half-mile line, with swollen streams on either flank. With the crisis at hand, both generals moved troops to straighten and improve their lines. Artillery kept up the fight.

Sigel formed his men into two lines, thinking that he could feed arriving troops into the second, much stronger, line while the first held up the inevitable Confederate advance. He had the larger army, but at the point of contact, he was outnumbered, and the two-line tactic served to emphasize the weakness. It was not possible for Sigel to bring the full weight of his numbers to bear against the enemy. His soldiers would have to fight piecemeal or risk firing into the backs of friendly troops. Furthermore, because Sigel's orders were vague at best, and because he had lost the confidence of some subordinates while others were incompetent (to the point of cowardice), the reinforcements he expected did not arrive in time.

When the Confederate assault came, the first line gave way. In the confusion, some Union troops in the second line fired into the backs of men in the first. One unit in the first line was utterly routed and did not stop to reform on the second line. The panicked men continued running, to the rear and safety.

It had been an ominously bad beginning for the men of Sigel's little army. By just after two in the afternoon, it would have been difficult to point to a single Union success. But Sigel's regiments still held a strong defensive position—in a way that was demonstrating, over and over, just how lethal modern arms could be in the defense.

Studying his enemy's position, Breckinridge said the time had come for an "ugly effort." He held the initiative, his army was fighting intact, not piecemeal, and he had pushed his enemy back all day. But the coming attack was, he knew, no sure thing.

The Confederate infantry advanced through a driving rain, and as the line closed with the Union troops, it began to take heavy fire from both muskets and cannon. One regiment lost seven of its company commanders. Another company lost forty of its sixty-two men. The advance staggered, then stopped, then began to give way, most critically at a junction between two units, the 51st and the 62nd Virginia. A gap opened here, in the center of Breckinridge's line. It was such a serious vulnerability that even Sigel could not fail to notice and exploit it.

An officer rode to Breckinridge with the news and pleaded, "General, why don't you put the cadets in line." The VMI boys were still in reserve, where Breckinridge wanted them.

Would they stand, he asked.

The officer assured him that they would.

Breckinridge had dreaded this moment and brooded over it for the rest of his life. Some of his staff officers said later that they saw tears in his eyes as he considered the decision.

"Put the boys in," he said, finally, "and may God forgive me for the order."

The cadets were in a position almost directly behind the gap in the Confederate lines. They moved forward, behind their flag. They had been under fire earlier, but it was nothing like this. A shell landed in the middle of one company, killing two of the cadets instantly and mortally wounding a third. The cadets closed up and continued their advance. Another cadet was killed by a musket ball a little farther on.

Ship, at the head of the formation, was hit. The wound initially looked serious, perhaps mortal. The advance stalled briefly, but another officer rallied the cadets. They moved forward through an orchard and then, at last, to the relative security of a rail fence.

They had filled the gap in Breckinridge's line. Schoolboys.

But they were not heroes yet. For now, they were merely part of a Confederate line that had been seriously weakened and was wavering, still in danger of collapsing under a Union counterattack.

The attack came and might have succeeded except that it was badly coordinated. A cavalry charge on the Union left was broken by Confederate infantry, one regiment of which, the 22nd Virginia, was under the command of George S. Patton, an 1852 VMI graduate, whose namesake would one day attend VMI and then go on to glory as commander of the 3rd U.S. Army.

Then, three Union infantry regiments attacked on the right, where the VMI cadets were holding their place in the line. One Union regiment, the 12th West Virginia, moved before the others were ready, then broke under heavy fire. The next regiment in line, the 1st West Virginia, also broke, leaving exposed the flanks of the last regiment, the 34th Massachusetts. Still, the

34th moved forward, taking 200 casualties—nearly half its strength—before it was ordered to retreat. In the terrible confusion, the order could not be heard, so the regimental commander was forced to grab the color-bearer and turn him to the rear to lead the retreat.

Sigel tried to reform his lines on the previous defensive position, but his moment had passed. The storm, which had covered the battlefield all day, reached a new level of fury, with lightning and thunder now added to the driving rain. The entire line of Confederate troops, including the VMI cadets, rose and attacked.

The Union line broke. Sigel, who was never accused of lacking courage, tried to rally his troops and even to help free a cannon that was stuck in the mud and to round up horses to help pull two other guns to safety.

The VMI cadets advanced through a section of low ground full of standing water and deep, clinging mud that sucked the shoes off some of their feet. This forlorn little depression became, in the lore, the "field of lost shoes." Their objective was a battery of Union guns, and the cadets bore remorselessly down on it. An officer in command of one of the units on their flank said, in admiration, that their charge "surpassed anything that I witnessed during the war."

A wounded Federal officer later wrote of their advance, "No one who saw it will ever forget it. No command but one most admirably drilled and disciplined could have done it."

The Union artillerymen abandoned on the field a twelve-pounder that the cheering, exhilarated cadets captured. It was the high-water moment of their war and, perhaps, their lives: the stuff of legend. The schoolboys had triumphed.

There was still a battle to finish. Sigel's troops were in full retreat, and his command might have been destroyed in detail had Imboden managed to demolish a bridge over the Shenandoah as Breckinridge had ordered. But Imboden had been uncharacteristically ineffective in this battle, and the bridge still stood. A resourceful Union artillery officer, Captain Henry Dupont, arrived on the battlefield and provided critical covering fire for Sigel's men, who managed to cross the river to safety. By then, Breckinridge had ordered the cadets out of the line, but not before one of them had taken twenty-three Union soldiers prisoner. The cadets had sustained almost 25 percent casualties, fifty-seven young men, ten of whom had been killed or would die of their wounds. An emotional Breckinridge rode to their position and spoke to them.

"Young gentlemen," he said, "I have you to thank for the result of today's operations."

Then, he added, "Well done, Virginians . . . well done, men."

The battle was a clear-cut Confederate victory and, as some later claimed, may have actually prolonged the war by a few months by protecting Lee's flank. Its effect on the outcome of the war, however, was far less than its influence on the young men from VMI who fought there, on the school itself (which was burned a few weeks later by another Union army), or on the literature of the "Lost Cause," which seized on the actions of the cadets as undeniable evidence of superior Southern valor. In time, some accounts of the battle made it seem as though only the cadets had fought there. The one abandoned cannon they captured became an entire battery. Their legend grew so far beyond the reality—which was impressive enough—that a reaction set in. As one historian of the battle later wrote, ". . . in the end, those who knew anything about the battle of New Market were divided into three classes: those who believed that the cadets had won the day; those who believed that the cadets had done some uncertain thing which had been greatly exaggerated; and those who believed that their part had been wholly without importance."

The cadets themselves, however, knew, and they kept the memory alive. There are several copies of an early history of the battle in the library at VMI, one of which is inscribed:

William P Upshur
Virginia Military Institute, Class 1902
From his father:
John Nottingham Upshur
Co C New Market Battalion
Virginia Military Institute, Class 1864

Upshur senior was wounded so severely in the leg during the battle that he was unable to return to VMI. He later became a prominent physician. His son, who became a Marine officer after graduating from VMI, went on to receive the Congressional Medal of Honor.

The lives of all the New Market cadets are recorded in another volume, found in the VMI library, and one reads the entries and realizes that these young men were, in Oliver Wendell Holmes's phrase, truly "touched by fire."

One of the New Market cadets, Thomas Gordon Hayes, became mayor of Baltimore.

Charles James Faulkner, who took the twenty-three prisoners, became, among other things, a United States senator.

William Fountain Battie was killed while trying, as an Arkansas sheriff, to make an arrest.

William H. Kennedy, like several other New Market cadets, served with Mosby after New Market.

John Bransford took part in the battle of Santiago, in the Spanish-American War, as a U.S. Navy surgeon.

Thomas Staples Martin became minority leader in the United States Senate.

George Raum became an author and Egyptologist whose extraordinary post–New Market career included being saved from a Union firing squad by Mosby's Rangers, riding with Mosby, meeting Stanley, Rhodes, and Kitchener in Africa, participating in the discovery and excavation of the Great Sphinx, and otherwise anticipating in real life the character Indiana Jones.

Erskine Mayo Ross became a prominent rancher, lawyer, and legendary judge in Los Angeles.

Charles William Turner became adjutant general of Montana and was later assassinated in Seattle.

Franklin Graham Gibson, who had one leg shattered, took a ball through the other thigh, one through the hand (costing him two fingers), and another in the cheek—seven wounds in all—taught French and mathematics at Richmond College and became a lawyer and prosecuting attorney.

Moses Ezekiel organized the Red Cross in Italy during the First World War. He was also a sculptor of international renown and was entitled to call himself "Sir Moses Ezekiel." However, his stone in Arlington National Cemetery reads merely:

Moses J. Ezekiel
Sergeant of Company C, Battalion
of Cadets of the
Virginia Military Institute

In 1906, Ezekiel's monument "Virginia Mourning Her Dead" was dedicated on the grounds of VMI. Six of the ten cadets killed at New Market are now buried beneath it. On May 15, every year, the corps of cadets marches in full dress parade. When the report is taken, the cadet adjutant steps forward and calls the names of each of the New Market dead.

"Private Jefferson."

A voice from the ranks answers firmly, "Private Jefferson died on the field of honor, Sir."

"Private Stanard."

"Private Stanard died on the field of honor, Sir."

And so on, until all the names have been called. The regimental commander takes the report, then lays a wreath at the foot of Ezekiel's somber monument. An honor guard fires a salute. Taps is played from the roof of the barracks, and the notes seem to quiver on the air.

The corps of cadets then passes in review, and the small affair at New Market, the most famous of all the actions in the Shenandoah Valley, is remembered again.

THE WALLS OF 1864

NOAH ANDRE TRUDEAU

In "The Walls of 1864," Noah Andre Trudeau puts his finger on one of the key characteristics of modern war: "The search for glory battles—single engagements with, it was hoped, a decisive outcome—was replaced by extended campaigns in which battles were the means to a strategic end, not an end in themselves." The stand-up set-piece encounters of previous years had given way to ones of constant contact, in which the only victory that counted was the last one, the one that finally broke an opponent's will to fight. The overland campaign in eastern Virginia of U. S. Grant, the new Union supreme commander, during May and June of 1864 was, in a sense, an attritional paradigm, modern warfare's first. Battles (with the calamitous exception of Cold Harbor) may have ended in draws, or marginal victories for Lee's Army of Northern Virginia; but the Confederates increasingly could not afford the kind of losses that were bearable for the Union. Meanwhile Grant relentlessly edged closer to Richmond. For the moment, the spade and the axe would make up for the Union superiority in men and matériel. As one division commander of Grant's Army of the Potomac wrote, "It became a recognized fact amongst the men themselves that when the enemy had occupied a position six or eight hours ahead of us, it was useless to attempt to take it." Grant's attempt to turn Lee's right flank and the ever-extending trench line that seemed always just a step ahead of his advances was a preview of the 1914 "Race for the Sea" in France and Belgium. The difference was that eventually Lee had to run out of diggers, and when he did, the war would be over. But if, in the short run, trenches saved Lee's army and Richmond, they would save Grant's as well, and with it, his overland campaign.

Noah Andre Trudeau is a director in the cultural-programs division of National Public Radio and the author of several books on the Civil War.

IN THE WINTER OF 1863–64, SOLDIERS ON BOTH SIDES OF the American Civil War learned the value of temporary field entrenchments. It did not result from any articulated shift in tactical doctrine, but rather seems to have emerged out of a spontaneous recognition by veteran troops that to dig was to survive. This fit well with the precepts of the new military leadership that took control of Union operations in this period. The advent of Ulysses S. Grant to supreme command of the United States armies signaled a change in policy. The search for glory battles—single engagements with, it was hoped, a decisive outcome—was replaced by extended campaigns in which battles were the means to a strategic end, not an end in themselves.

This wider context mattered little to the common soldiers, whose principal concern was what John Keegan has described as "the issue of personal survival." Many veteran troops (and it was they who were first to reach for shovels) were nearing the end of their three-year enlistments; only about half of those serving in the Army of the Potomac would reenlist for the duration. Yet one cannot ignore the shared, if unspoken, understanding between the men in the ranks and their leaders that the war would continue for an indefinite period. While en route to Washington to accept command of the Federal armies, Grant paused in Baltimore long enough to proclaim, in the words of a newspaperman present, that "his business was with war, while it existed, and his duty was to crush the spirit of treason and save the nation from destruction." It is more than coincidence that the winter he put his broad strategic vision of lengthy campaigns into motion, the individual fighting men also began to fully appreciate the body-saving value of temporary rifle pits and breastworks.

Union officers viewed this phenomenon with both surprise and admiration. Grant, commenting afterward about the Overland Campaign of May–June 1864, observed of the Army of the Potomac that "in every change of position or halt for the night, whether confronting the enemy or not, the moment arms were stacked the men entrenched themselves. For this purpose they would build up piles of logs or rails if they could be found in their front, and dig a ditch, throwing the dirt forward on the timber. . . . It was wonderful how quickly they could in this way construct defenses of considerable strength."

This "discovery" of entrenching was not limited to Billy Yank. Confederate industry in this regard was noted by a Federal staff officer, Lieutenant Colonel Theodore Lyman, who remarked during the Overland Campaign, "It is a rule that, when the Rebels halt, the first day gives them a good rifle-pit;

the second, a regular infantry parapet with artillery in position; and the third a parapet with an abatis in front and entrenched batteries behind." Lyman's observation was seconded by a Johnny Reb, Alexander Hunter, who said, "No sooner would a line be formed when the enemy was near, than every man was busy throwing up a little mound for protection."

The benefits of scraping out defensive positions now seemed obvious to everyone. Grant confidant and aide John Rawlins wrote to his wife in May 1864 that a "few hours always suffice for an army acting purely on the defensive to fortify itself, and the fortifications make up greatly for inferiority of numbers."

Grant's goal, in the main eastern operation of his grand strategic plan of 1864, was to engage and destroy Robert E. Lee's Army of Northern Virginia. One of the principal reasons Grant failed to accomplish this, despite a marked superiority of arms and men, was the deadly skill with which his adversary could fortify a position. According to one Army of the Potomac division commander, "It became a recognized fact amongst the men themselves that when the enemy had occupied a position six or eight hours ahead of us, it was useless to attempt to take it." Ironically, it was a line of *Union* entrenchments that kept the Overland Campaign from an early, ignominious end.

That occurred on May 6, at a patch of wasteland ten miles west of Fredericksburg, Virginia, known as the Wilderness. "Imagine," wrote a North Carolina officer who fought there, "a great, dismal forest containing . . . the worst kind of thicket of second-growth trees . . . so thick with small pines and scrub oak, cedar, dogweed and other growth common to the country [that] . . . one could see barely ten paces." The fighting erupted here on May 5, when the Army of Northern Virginia and the Army of the Potomac stumbled into an engagement neither had anticipated. Lee began the battle with almost one-third of his infantry camped a day's march away. He had hoped to force a pause in the Union advance without sparking a major fight until he had united his army. Grant and the Army of the Potomac high command had wanted to avoid any large-scale military action in the Wilderness, where their material superiority would be nullified by the junglelike terrain. But events in the Wilderness took their own course.

Since cross-country movement was so slow and difficult, the road system became the critical factor defining the sectors of combat. Union plans called for the 118,000-man Army of the Potomac, advancing in two long columns, to have passed southward through the Wilderness by the end of May 5. Actual command of the Union force rested with the hero of Gettysburg, Major General George Gordon Meade; but he reported directly to Grant, and Grant

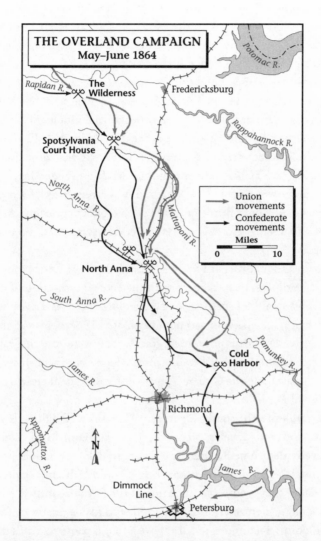

Both sides learned to appreciate fully the value of temporary field entrench-ments during the Overland Campaign. Grant's newly aggressive Army of the Potomac repeatedly failed to overcome Lee's Army of Northern Virginia as both armies maneuvered for advantage on their way toward Richmond. Grant had the advantage of numbers; Lee, of defending interior lines.

had placed his headquarters in the field with Meade's army. Lee's forces (approximately 60,000 total) lay to the west of the advance. His goal was to intercept the Federals using the two most important east-west arteries: the Orange Turnpike and the Orange Plank Road.

The morning of May 5 found the Union prongs separated. The head of one column (the V Corps, led by Major General Gouverneur K. Warren) was camped around Wilderness Tavern, near where the Orange Turnpike intersected the Germanna Ford Road. The other (the II Corps, led by Major General Winfield S. Hancock) was clustered at Todd's Tavern, almost seven miles farther south. The VI Corps, under Major General John Sedgwick, had crossed the Rapidan and was moving slowly to join Warren. The IX Corps, led by Major General Ambrose Burnside, had yet to cross after Sedgwick. The only direct link between these halves of the Federal army was the north-south Brock Road.

Lieutenant General Richard S. Ewell's Confederate II Corps, moving along the Orange Turnpike, made contact with the Federal army around dawn. The unexpected proximity of such a strong Rebel force came as a nasty surprise to the Union commanders, who had not anticipated Lee would react so quickly or aggressively. The marching orders for the day were canceled, and troops were concentrated to strike at Ewell's corps. Bloody but inconclusive fighting began at midday along the Orange Turnpike, across a small clearing known as Saunders Field.

Just two miles to the south, Lieutenant General A. P. Hill's III Corps was moving parallel with Ewell's, along the Orange Plank Road. Only a small Yankee cavalry detachment, fighting a stubborn delaying action, prevented it from reaching the Brock Road intersection. Should Hill's men gain control of that crossroads, they would cut the Army of the Potomac in two. The Federal high command recognized this danger in time to rush a reserve division to the threatened point. That force, in turn, gave enough pause to Hill's forward elements to allow Hancock's men to march from Todd's Tavern and link up with the rest of the army. Sharp but indecisive fighting followed until nightfall as Hill's soldiers met Hancock's in the forested thickets.

Almost as quickly as Hancock's men came into line along the Brock Road, they began to dig. According to a member of the Philadelphia Brigade, "The troops on the road commenced strengthening their position with logs, dead trees, and other *debris* of that character, of which there was an endless supply." Hancock later described the results of this effort as "a substantial line of breast-works . . . constructed of earth and logs the whole length of my line of battle. . . ."

Grant's plan for May 6 signaled a new Union aggressiveness in the east. He would strike the enemy on both its approach routes, with attacks along the Orange Turnpike and Orange Plank Road. Lee, for his part, was still awaiting his absent infantry—Lieutenant General James Longstreet's I Corps—before mounting his own offensive. Grant's attack began first. Union assaults by Warren's V Corps and Sedgwick's VI Corps along the Orange Turnpike stalled in the face of effective defenses by Ewell's troops. Farther south, however, on either side of the Orange Plank Road, Federal troops under Hancock enjoyed significant success. Just when it seemed that Lee's right flank would be destroyed, Longstreet's men arrived in time to launch a counterattack. Hancock's previously irresistible advance turned into a spiteful stalemate, with the main Union battle line a mile west of the Brock Road.

Once the situation stabilized, Lee looked for an opening and found one. His men, using an unfinished railroad bed to conceal their movements, swung around to strike the left flank of Hancock's advanced battle line, and sent it whirling back toward the Brock Road. Grant's own attempt to strike Lee's flank along the Orange Plank Road, using the IX Corps, came to naught thanks to slow marching and Burnside's tactical ineptness.

Lee's hopes for a quick follow-up thrust were dashed when Confederate soldiers, no less immune to the fog of war than their Yankee counterparts, mistook a mounted command party for enemy cavalry and fired upon it, seriously injuring Longstreet. (In a compound of ironies, Longstreet's wounding took place just four miles from the site in Chancellorsville where Stonewall Jackson had been fatally wounded by his own troops, almost exactly a year earlier.) Several vital hours passed while Lee personally worked to reorganize his troops for the final, crushing assault on the Union left. Success here would bar any further Federal movement to the south and likely force the enemy back across the Rapidan River.

Hancock and his officers used the unexpected respite to organize a defense along the Brock Road entrenchments. According to one of those present, "All the officers exerted themselves to rally the troops upon the rude and incomplete breastworks thrown up along the road the afternoon before." An officer who had tried in vain to halt his men west of the road recalled, "There suddenly loomed up a strong line of log breastworks . . . whereupon an old sailor in our ranks fitly expressed the feelings of all by shouting, 'Ship ahoy, land ahead, boys, land ahead!'"

By 4 P.M., when Lee's last great Wilderness offensive finally began rolling, Hancock's men were ready. The Confederate assault quickly ground to a standstill. For nearly thirty minutes the two sides exchanged volleys in a

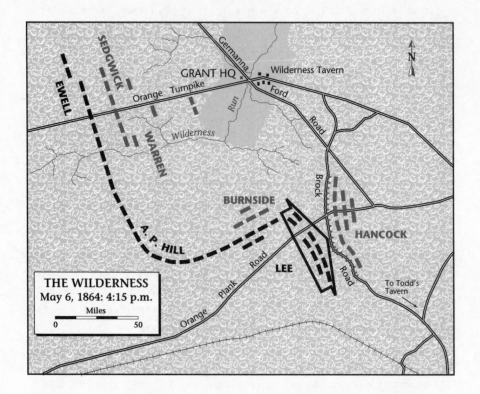

THE WILDERNESS
May 6, 1864: 4:15 p.m.

Miles

0   50

After a day and a half of bloody but indecisive fighting from the Orange Turnpike to the Orange Plank Road, the first battle of the Overland Campaign culminated in an unsuccessful Confederate assault, personally directed by Lee after Longstreet was wounded, against Hancock's entrenched Brock Road line.

thickening cloud formed from gunfire and smoldering brush ignited by powder embers. "The woods in front of Hancock had now taken fire," reported one of Grant's observers, "and the flames were communicated to his log breastworks. . . . The wind was . . . blowing in our direction, and the blinding smoke was driven in the faces of our men, while the fire itself swept down upon them. . . . At last . . . the breastworks became untenable, and some of the troops . . . now fell back in confusion."

At that moment, Lee sent his reserve brigade forward into the just-abandoned section of the Brock Road line. One stunned Yankee recalled, "On they came, like maddened demons, charging directly into the flames." But this thrust was not supported, and alert Union officers were able to pinch off the penetration from both sides. The Brock Road line had held. As one historian of the Wilderness, Edward Steere, later observed, "The last great charge that Lee was ever to launch with an expectation of destroying the Army of the Potomac had recoiled in defeat." The two days of fighting in the Wilderness had cost Grant more than 17,600 casualties, while Confederate losses totaled nearly 11,000.

The log-and-earthen walls along the Brock Road (remnants of which can still be seen) had saved the Union left and, most important, preserved Grant's possession of the strategic initiative. Had Lee broken that line and blocked the route south, Grant's options would have been far less appealing. Indeed, many Federal soldiers anticipated a withdrawal. In the 57th Pennsylvania they were saying, "We have had the usual three days' fighting on this side of the river, and by about night we will be back in our old camp." Grant, however, was firm in his resolve that there would be no turning back. On the night of May 7, the Union army began to slip out of its Wilderness trenches and move onto roads leading south to Spotsylvania Court House.

Lee initially misread the Federal movements to indicate a general retreat toward Fredericksburg, but he recovered once Grant's true direction was made known to him, marching hard to establish the Army of Northern Virginia in a blocking position across the Brock Road just north of Spotsylvania Court House before Grant arrived in the vicinity. After stiff combat at Laurel Hill on May 8 (where light fieldworks enabled a heavily outnumbered Confederate force to hold back one full corps and part of another), Lee's new defensive line began to take shape along an east-west axis. But he had already been forced to radically alter his corps command: Major General Richard H. Anderson replaced the wounded Longstreet, while Major General Jubal A. Early temporarily took over the III Corps because A. P. Hill reported himself too ill to command.

It was dark when Major General Edward Johnson's division of Ewell's corps moved to extend Lee's right. Johnson's men, disoriented in the darkness and confused by the thicketed terrain, took position along the brow of a ridge. When dawn arrived, Confederate engineers realized that the high ground Johnson had fortified did not follow the curve of the entrenchments to his left. Instead it jutted forward, creating a sizable salient, vulnerable to frontal and side attack.

After some discussion whether to pull Johnson's men back to tighten up the defensive perimeter, it was decided to leave the troops where they had entrenched, but to bolster the position with artillery. The salient measured about one-half mile at its neck and was nearly a mile from tip to base. A front line of logs and earth rose nearly four feet, and traverses were dug to defend against enfilading fire. Brigadier General James Walker, whose Stonewall Brigade held a position in the heart of the salient, pronounced it "one of the best lines of temporary field works I ever saw. It was apparently impregnable." The Southern farm boys were soon calling it the "Horse Shoe" or the "Mule Shoe."

An ambitious Union colonel named Emory Upton had been thinking about the enemy's ability to erect formidable field fortifications and how difficult it was to assault those positions using a standard line of battle. Musketry was almost useless against soldiers standing behind chest-high embankments, he reasoned, so the battle lines, which maximized the firepower of muzzle-loading weapons, were equally ineffective. Upton's cold-blooded solution was to group his men in a compact mass and to storm into the enemy works without pausing to shoot, accepting the certainty of front-rank casualties as inevitable. On May 10 he used a brigade, about 5,000 men whom he divided into four lines, to try out his theory, and he scored a local success against the western face of the salient. Upton's assault failed only for want of proper support. After reviewing the results of this effort, Grant said, "A brigade today—we'll try a corps tomorrow."

It took longer than anticipated to set up the attack Grant wanted. Not until dawn on May 12 was everything ready to go. Acting with his usual determination, Grant moved nearly all of Hancock's II Corps and portions of Major General Horatio Wright's VI Corps—nearly 28,000 men—to within three quarters of a mile from the tip of the "Mule Shoe." (Wright replaced Sedgwick, who had been killed by a sniper on May 9.)

Grant's actions were aided by drizzly weather, which muffled the sound of his plodding columns, and by another tactical miscalculation on Lee's part. After receiving various reports of Federal movements on the murky night of May 11, Lee concluded that Grant was preparing to leave Spotsylvania. So as to be able to pursue the Federals quickly, Lee issued orders pulling his artillery out of the salient—a difficult, time-consuming procedure. So when Hancock's assault troops came screaming out of the mist, there were no cannon ready to shatter the tightly packed formations with canister or case shot. Like a human tidal wave, Hancock's men broke over the timbered walls of the salient apex and spread into the trench system leading to the flanks and rear. Brief hand-to-hand combat erupted in the recesses formed by traverses, but these actions did not slow the Union advance.

Employing a concentrated force of this size to storm a fortified position was terra incognita for Federal tacticians, who failed to take into account the chaotic results of a successful assault by so many men. As one officer on the scene bitterly noted afterward, "The occasion for charging, for rush and confusion, was past and troops ought to have been soberly and deliberately put in position, and ordered to sweep down the rebel line. . . ." But instead more men piled into the breach, creating a leaderless mob that milled in fatal confusion, even as Lee and his subordinates were launching counterattack after counterattack against the blue mass. Despite an intoxicating initial success, the Federal high-water mark was reached within an hour of the breakthrough. From that point on, Confederate countermeasures began to eat away at the Federal incursion and squeeze it into a smaller and smaller pocket.

A deadlock was reached by midday. The series of violent Confederate counterattacks had been stopped, but Federal attempts to expand what was by now little more than a foothold were beaten back by blasts of rifle fire. Everyone went to ground, and for the rest of the day, and well into the night, the contest was among small groups struggling over a few feet of trenches. "Men fired into each other[']s faces, were shot through the crevices of the logs, [and] bayoneted over the top of the works," a Union survivor recalled. According to a Southerner, "Where the lines overlapped the men said they and the enemy both fired without showing their heads above the work, which was certain death. Guns were loaded, held up to the breastwork, depressed, and the trigger pulled with the thumb. One man . . . told me he several times took in his hand the barrel of a gun pointing down on him, held it up till it was fired and then let it go." The point along the west face of the salient, where combat was especially close-in and constant, became known as "the Bloody Angle."

Meanwhile, Lee was frantically erecting a new defensive line across the neck of the salient. This was completed in the dark, and after about 2 A.M. on May 13, his men were withdrawn from the caldron and put into the new earthworks. Union troops were too spent even to consider immediately assaulting this strong position. (Its design Lee entrusted to Confederate chief engineer M. L. Smith, whose work had confounded Grant a year earlier at Vicksburg. The efficacy of his engineering was proven on May 18 when an attempt to charge this line was beaten back almost entirely by artillery.) Confederate casualties on May 12 are estimated at between 5,000 and 6,000. Federal losses were tabulated at 6,820. The fighting for the trenches of the "Mule Shoe," which began with the Federal attack at 4:45 A.M. on May 12, did not fully end until 3:00 A.M. on May 13, making it at least one of the longest nonstop confrontations in the history of trench warfare.

Grant's all-out effort to mortally wound Lee's army had been dashed against the earthen bulwarks of the salient. Lee's new position at Spotsylvania

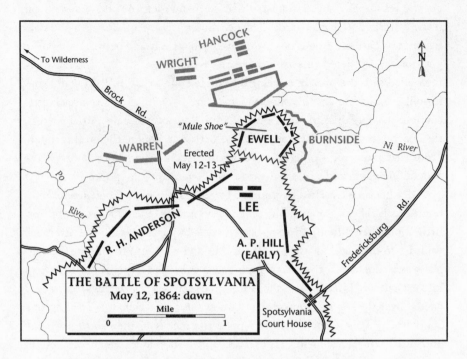

Charging through the mist at dawn, Hancock's men overwhelmed the apex of the "Mule Shoe" salient held by Ewell's men at Spotsylvania. But Lee's counterattacks checked and then pressed back the Federal advance. The bloody stalemate lasted into the night, with both sides clinging to sections of trench, while diversionary attacks by Warren and Burnside achieved nothing. Early on May 13, Lee withdrew behind a new line.

was stronger than ever. "[All] of our men . . . want Old Grant to fight us again so we can slauter the drunken scoundrels again," a Rebel gunner wrote to his family. "[T]here is hundreds and thousands of thir dead a laying in front of our breastworks yet unberried." The walls of Spotsylvania had saved Lee's army to fight again another day.

If the value of entrenchments wasn't yet clear, the point was made anew on May 19 at a little-known engagement that took place across the nearby fields of Harris Farm. The primary players, on the Union side, were the so-called Heavy Artillery regiments—made up of artillerymen recruited to handle the large-caliber cannon in the forts ringing Washington, but recently turned into infantry to meet Grant's manpower needs. The Army of the Potomac was

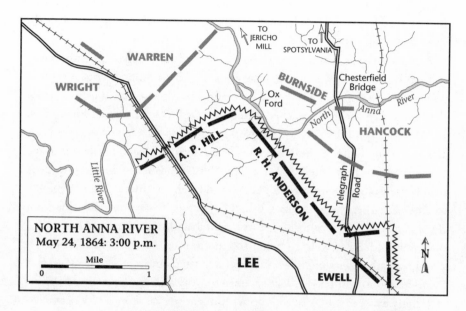

After the Federals left Spotsylvania, Lee dropped back to the south bank of the North Anna River. On May 23, Union forces made successful crossings against both of his flanks. Lee then improvised a V-shaped entrenched line anchored on the river, thus dividing the Union army into unsupported halves, which he hoped to attack. But Lee's sudden illness and the defensive entrenchments that the Federals dug turned a potential victory into a stalemate.

beginning the process of once more slipping to the south when Lee, suspecting something was in the wind, dispatched Ewell on a reconnaissance in force of the Union right flank. Ewell's veterans slammed into the green Heavies, who fought back in a stand-up style reminiscent of 1862. The Heavy Artillery regiments prevailed through sheer weight of numbers and prideful courage, but paid a terrible price in losses. As one officer later admitted, "We had not yet fully learned the habit of the old troops in digging themselves into a hole."

On the night of May 20, Federal soldiers belonging to Hancock's II Corps—Grant's favorite strike force—began the southward flanking march away from Spotsylvania. The rest of the Union army followed the next night. Once Lee learned of the movements, he immediately began to drop back toward Richmond. He hoped to rest his army for a few days along the south side of the North Anna River, but Grant's pressure was unrelenting. Approaching the river on a broad front, Federal troops on May 23 forced crossings at the Chesterfield Bridge on the Telegraph Road and at Jericho Mill, three and a half miles west.

Faced with a successful enemy advance against both flanks, Lee improvised brilliantly. His troops abandoned the river line that night, except for a naturally strong position at Ox Ford. Extending southwest and southeast from that point, Lee's men entrenched a line that took the form of an inverted V. Once secure behind his new earthworks, Lee awaited Grant's expected advance. The more the Federals moved forward on either flank on the south side of the river, the more they would be split into two isolated wings with Lee's men concentrated between them. Lee would be able to mass his force quickly to strike at either enemy wing, while the Federals, to reinforce one side from the other, faced a twelve-to-fifteen-mile march and two river crossings.

Union leaders were elated when the morning of May 24 brought almost unopposed advances along the Telegraph Road and out from Jericho Mill. But by midday, optimism had turned to concern. Any attempt by either of the increasingly exposed wings to link up with the other was stopped by heavy enemy skirmish lines, which also screened the strong earthworks from view. The moment had arrived for Lee to spring his trap, to hold one face of the V with a minimum number of troops and hurl everything else against the Federals spreading along the other side. But the orders were never issued. The cumulative effects of extended exposure, fatigue, age, and pressures from the unprecedented duration of the campaign were just too much for Lee, who was also suddenly carrying a much heavier burden of command. A. P. Hill was back in charge of the III Corps but not at full strength, Richard Ewell had fallen ill after the fighting on May 19 (Lee would replace him with Jubal Early on May 29), Richard Anderson's leadership of Longstreet's I Corps had been generally lackluster, and worst of all was the news of the death on May 12 of Lee's cavalry chief, J. E. B. Stuart, who had been mortally wounded at Yellow Tavern, near Richmond. Now, when it was left to Lee and Lee alone to direct the decisive movement, his body failed him. His trusted aide Major Charles Venable remembered, "As he lay prostrated by his sickness, he would often repeat: 'We must strike them a blow—we must never let them pass us again—we must strike them a blow.'"

By 8:30 A.M. on May 25, Grant had enough information to recognize Lee's trap. "It now looks as if Lee's position were such that it would not be prudent to fight a battle in the narrow space between the [North and South Anna] rivers," he told an aide. Once more the Federals took full advantage of an unexpected reprieve to dig their own fieldworks. By midday they were sufficiently entrenched to be secure against any assault Lee might attempt. His golden opportunity to damage the Army of the Potomac seriously—an opportunity created by adroit use of rapidly erected earthworks—had been nullified in less than twelve hours by the enemy's equally proficient ability with spade and ax. The result was by now only too familiar to both sides—stalemate.

Grant withdrew his two wings to the north side of the river on the night of May 26, then began another flanking maneuver. According to his aide Horace Porter, "On the march the general in chief, as he rode by, was vociferously cheered, as usual, by the troops. . . . [The] rank and file . . . understood fully that he had saved them on the North Anna from the slaughter which would probably have occurred if they had been thrown against Lee's formidable entrenchments. . . ."

Now the Union army was moving to the southeast along the far side of the Pamunkey River, while advance elements turned west toward Richmond at Hanovertown. By the morning of May 28, the entire Army of the Potomac (except Burnside's IX Corps) had crossed to the west side of the river. Federal probing attacks toward Richmond were blocked in scattered fighting on May 29–30. The result was another confrontational standoff, the battle lines running along the course of Totopotomoy Creek.

A few miles south was a crossroads known as Cold Harbor (an English name for a "shelter without fire," according to Porter; veterans knew this area as the site of fighting around Gaines' Mill in 1862). Possession of that point, Grant realized, would place him around Lee's right flank with a straight run into Richmond. Lee perceived the threat at almost the same time, and both sides rushed troops to Cold Harbor. As a result of the fighting there on May 31 and June 1, the Confederates lost both the crossroads and the first line of earthworks they had hurriedly erected. Grant immediately planned a May 12–type assault (this time using three corps) to roll over Lee's men before they could erect sufficient defenses to block him.

But the month of almost constant combat had taken a terrible toll on the Federals. Grant's orders shifting the II Corps from the Union right to left were not carried out in time for a sunrise assault on June 2. The attack was rescheduled for dawn on June 3.

Lee's men dug frantically throughout June 2. Confederate engineers from Richmond used long cord marked with small strips of white cloth, expertly laying out the lines to maximize fields of fire and minimize any dangerous salients. Ironically, this time the Confederate earthworks were low-lying and did not look at all impressive. "The country being generally level, and only slightly undulating, the sharpest eye could perceive through the woods and fields, nothing but faint lines of rifle-trenches," a Union officer recollected. Yet they were no less deadly.

A little before 5 A.M. on June 3, after a brief bombardment, formations from Hancock's II Corps, Wright's VI Corps, and Major General William F. ("Baldy") Smith's XVIII Corps (temporarily transferred from the Army of the James) surged forward, while Warren and Burnside demonstrated with their corps on the Federal right. A Yankee artilleryman watched in horror as an endless row of Rebel slouch hats popped up along the enemy parapets and then "the works glowed brightly with musketry, a storm of lead and iron struck the blue line, cutting gaps in it."

This mass charge by perhaps 60,000 Union soldiers was shattered in less than an hour. "The bullets did not whistle, they came with a rush like lightning," a dazed Connecticut soldier recalled. Major General Andrew A. Humphreys, the Army of the Potomac's chief of staff, later tallied the Federal losses for this day at 4,517 wounded and "at least 1,100" killed. Writing after the war, Grant confessed, "I have always regretted that the last assault on Cold Harbor was ever made."

The Overland Campaign was over. As Charles Dana, Lincoln's man at Grant's headquarters, explained on June 4, "Before moving from Culpeper [into the Wilderness, Grant] . . . expected . . . he would have a chance to crush Lee's army by fair fighting. . . . This expectation has been foiled by Lee's success in avoiding battle upon any equal terms." Those forty days cost Grant 54,259 men killed, wounded, or missing. With an army only one-half the size, Lee had losses proportionately as severe, totaling more than 31,700. On June 5, Grant decided to undertake an entirely new campaign, against the vital rail center of Petersburg.

The memory of those terrible walls could not be forgotten. Baldy Smith, whose tentative June 15 assault on Petersburg's impressive-looking but grossly undermanned Dimmock line gave Confederates precious time to reinforce the city, said after Cold Harbor, "It had come to be an axiom among both officers and men that a well-defended rifle trench could not be carried by a direct attack without the most careful preparation nor even then without fearful loss." According to a division commander in the eviscerated II Corps, the men had developed tactics reflecting their hatred of charging earthworks. "This feeling became so marked that when troops . . . were ordered forward, they went a certain distance and then lay down and opened fire. It became a saying in the army that when the old troops got as far forward as they thought they ought to go 'they sat down and made coffee!'"

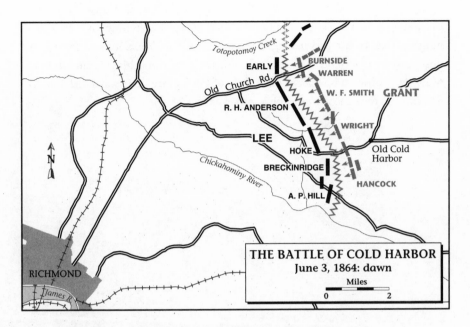

At Cold Harbor on June 3, some 60,000 Union troops were repulsed when they charged the quickly erected Confederate earthworks. Hancock's brief breakthrough was not supported, Wright and Smith made no headway, and Burnside and Warren contributed little. The slightest pause in the action saw Federals scraping out protective earthworks of their own.

There was one more try to storm an entrenched line using an elbow-to-elbow battle formation. On June 18 at Petersburg, nearly 900 men of the 1st Maine Heavy Artillery charged into withering fire near the Hare House. In ten minutes, 241 were killed and 371 wounded. After watching the survivors stumble back, the regiment's colonel confronted the general who had ordered the attack. "Here, you take my sword," the Maine officer declared. "I have no use for it now." Another regiment of Heavies was kept from following this bloody example by veterans who called out, "Lie down you damn fools, you can't take them forts!"

This message at last penetrated to the highest echelons of the Federal command. After June 18, and up until April 2, 1865, the mere sight of Confederate field entrenchments ahead terminated many an offensive operation at Petersburg.

The defensive works of the Wilderness, Spotsylvania, North Anna, and Cold Harbor had made impossible the kind of rapid marching and open-field fighting that Grant had managed so successfully at Vicksburg in 1863. The unsuccessful Overland Campaign led directly to something Grant did not want—the nine-and-a-half-month siege of Petersburg. The walls of 1864 had determined that there would be another winter of war.

THE FIERY TRAIL
OF THE *ALABAMA*

JOHN M. TAYLOR

The largely agrarian South had little to do with the sea, and the creation of a navy was something of an afterthought. The Union blockade rapidly sewed up the coast. But one part of the ad hoc Confederate Navy did score notable successes: the commerce raiders. A handful of roving cruisers, several of them surreptitiously built in England, destroyed more than 200 Union merchant vessels, with losses in the millions of dollars. The most famous of these raiders was the *Alabama,* a sail-and-steam hybrid that, on July 29, 1862—a month and a half before Antietam—slipped away from its Liverpool shipyard to begin two years of unchecked marauding. The protests of the U.S. minister to Great Britain, Charles Francis Adams, were unavailing: at this point, the cotton-starved British favored the Confederacy and were clearly looking for the excuse to intervene that never came about.

The captain of the *Alabama,* Raphael Semmes, was a genuine American hero—though not surprisingly he was vilified as a pirate in the Northern press. His men nicknamed him Old Beeswax for his carefully cultivated mustache and his strict but fair discipline. Ranging from Newfoundland to Singapore, the *Alabama* burned fifty-four Federal merchant ships, captured ten others, and sank one gunboat, destroying fully 5 percent of the U.S. merchant fleet. (In years to come, the German Kaiser, Wilhelm II, would make Semmes's postwar memoirs required reading for his admirals.) With the *Alabama* and an earlier ship, the *Sumter,* Semmes may have been the first commerce raider to operate in the age of steam; but when the *Alabama* finally encountered the Union cruiser *Kearsarge* off Cherbourg in June 1864, their meeting would establish not a first but a notable last—what John M. Taylor calls "the last one-on-one duel of the era of wooden ships." It would be a clash worthy of the novels of Patrick O'Brian (and was in fact immortalized on canvas by an eyewitness on the shore, the painter Manet).

After the war, Great Britain would pay the United States $15.5 million for losses inflicted by Confederate raiders built in English shipyards. Of that total, $6.75 million was charged to the *Alabama,* almost as much as the United States would, in 1867, pay the Russians for Alaska.

John M. Taylor is the author of eight books of history and biography, most recently a reassessment of Robert E. Lee, *Duty Faithfully Performed: Robert E. Lee and His Critics* and *Confederate Raider: Raphael Semmes of the* Alabama. Taylor lives in McLean, Virginia.

WORKERS IN THE JOHN LAIRD SHIPYARD AT BIRKENHEAD, near Liverpool, watched attentively on the morning of May 15, 1862, as a handsome steam bark slid into the waters of the Mersey River. The vessel was known to them as No. 290, for hers was the 290th keel laid at the Laird yards. Upon launching, she was named the *Enrica,* but the identity of her owners remained a subject of speculation, for she was being built to the specifications of a Royal Navy cruiser. As May turned into June, the new vessel sprouted three tall masts that would enable her to carry a broad spread of canvas, and took on two 300-horsepower engines for steam propulsion.

In the waterfront bars of Liverpool, it was said with a wink that the actual purchaser of the *Enrica* was the Southern Confederacy, then locked in a war to establish its independence from the United States. For once, the tipsters were right on the mark. The possibility that No. 290 was destined for the Confederacy had not been lost on the U.S. minister in London, Charles Francis Adams, who was bombarding the Foreign Office with demands that the ship be seized. By mid-July, James Bulloch, the adroit Confederate naval agent who had supervised construction of the *Enrica* for the government in Richmond, knew that time was growing short.

The ever-imaginative Bulloch arranged for the *Enrica*'s departure from England in the guise of a gala trial run. On the fine morning of July 29, the new bark sailed down the Mersey with local dignitaries on board. At dusk, however, Bulloch and his guests returned to Liverpool on a tugboat, leaving the *Enrica* off the coast of Wales at Moelfra Bay. British authorities had in fact been attempting to detain the *Enrica,* and Bulloch had thwarted them by the narrowest of margins.

On Sunday, August 10, the *Enrica* arrived at the island of Terceira in the Azores. Eight days later the *Agrippina,* a tender under charter to Bulloch, showed up with equipment for the Confederate cruiser, including a 100-pound Blakely rifle, an 8-inch smoothbore, six 32-pounders, and provisions. That afternoon a second vessel, the *Bahama,* arrived with officers and hands for the new vessel. Thanks to Bulloch, the complicated logistics of equipping and manning a cruiser outside British waters were carried out without a hitch. On Sunday, August 24, in the presence of the crews of the *Enrica* and the *Bahama,* the Union Jack fluttered down from the mainmast and was replaced by the naval ensign of the Confederacy. A band played "Dixie," and the mystery ship was officially christened the Confederate steamer *Alabama.*

The cruiser's designated commander was fifty-two-year-old Raphael Semmes, a Maryland native who had taken up residence in Alabama. Semmes had entered the U.S. Navy in 1832 and by 1861 had achieved the rank of commander. He was widely read in naval history and marine law and had written several books, including a lively narrative of his naval service during the Mexican War. A strong advocate of states' rights, Semmes had resigned his Federal commission even before the firing on Fort Sumter.

In April 1861, Confederate Secretary of the Navy Stephen Mallory gave Semmes command of one of the South's first warships, the 437-ton screw steamer *Sumter.* The *Sumter* and her more powerful successors were intended to tackle one of two missions that Mallory had established for the Confederate navy: to attack the North's merchant marine, so as to increase the cost of the war to the enemy and thus encourage Lincoln to acknowledge Southern independence. The navy's other mission—to construct a fleet of ironclads capable of breaking the Federal blockade—was beyond Confederate capabilities, but the first was not.

It had taken Semmes about two months to convert the *Sumter* into a warship, but he assembled a nucleus of able officers—no mean feat in the agrarian South, with its limited seafaring tradition. The *Sumter* broke the Federal blockade off New Orleans on June 30, 1861, and reached the open sea. Thereafter, during a six-month cruise, the little raider burned eight Northern ships and released ten others on bond—a procedure under which the owners of an American ship's neutral cargo were expected to reimburse the Confederacy for goods not destroyed.

Eventually, boiler problems and a need for coal obliged the *Sumter* to call at

Gibraltar. There she was blockaded by three Federal warships, with no prospect of escape. Having made the most of his ship's limited capabilities, Semmes directed that the *Sumter* be sold, and set out for Britain with most of his officers. There, to the disappointment of Bulloch, who had hoped for the command, Semmes was given the far more powerful *Alabama*.

Semmes's first challenge in the Azores was to persuade enough British sailors to sign aboard the *Alabama* so that he could take his new command to sea. He assured the hands of the *Alabama* and the *Bahama* that they were free to return to Britain if they chose, but he painted a glowing picture of life aboard the *Alabama*. He offered good pay—£4 10s. a month in gold for seamen, and £7 for firemen—plus grog twice a day and the prospect of prize money. He touched only briefly on the issues of the American war, but promised excitement and adventure. To his relief, he was able to sign on eighty British crewmen—enough to take the *Alabama* to sea. As time went on, he would supplement this nucleus with recruits from captured vessels.

Once Semmes had his officers and crew, he turned his attention to his ship. The *Alabama* represented the zenith of a hybrid marine form: ships powered by both sail and steam. She measured 220 feet in length, had a beam of 32 feet, and displaced 1,040 tons. She carried enough coal for eighteen days' steaming and had an innovation found on few ships of her day—a condenser that provided a gallon of fresh water per day for each man on board, enabling her to remain at sea for extended periods. Her two-bladed screw could be raised into a well when she was under sail, thus posing no drag in the water. She could make about twelve knots under sail alone, to which her engines could add another three knots. She came with a year's supply of spare gear. In the words of one of her officers, Lieutenant Arthur Sinclair, the *Alabama* "was at the same time a perfect steamer and a perfect sailing vessel, each entirely independent of the other." The ship's armament also was impressive: six 32-pounders and two pivot guns. A visitor to the *Alabama* would comment, "What strikes one most . . . is to see so small a vessel carrying such large metal."

Semmes was under orders to avoid engagements with enemy warships, for his was a special mission. The *Alabama,* as her commander wrote later, "was the first steamship in the history of the world—the defective little *Sumter* excepted—that was let loose against the commerce of a great commercial people." And Semmes set to his mission with a vengeance.

The *Alabama* had been at sea for only ten days when, on September 5, she sighted the first of the sixty-five victims she would claim over the next twenty-two months. The ship was a whaler—the *Ocmulgee,* of Edgartown,

Massachusetts—and the capture was easy, for the *Ocmulgee* had a whale lashed alongside when the *Alabama* approached. The raider had been flying the American flag—an accepted ruse in war—and in Semmes's recollection, nothing could exceed the Yankee skipper's "blank stare of astonishment" when the *Alabama* finally ran up the Confederate ensign.

The *Ocmulgee*'s crew was transferred to the *Alabama,* along with some provisions; officers were permitted to bring one trunk with them, others a single bag. Semmes prepared to burn the whaler, but with the guile that would become his trademark, he waited until daylight: Whalers operated in clusters, and he did not want to scatter them with an unexplained fire at night.

The *Alabama* spent two months in the Azores, burning eight vessels in all. The American whaling fleet—or what was left of it—returned to its home ports in New England, where shipowners filled the Northern press with tales of the "pirate" Semmes. The *Alabama,* too, worked her way westward. Semmes briefly considered throwing a few shells into New York City, but he thought better of it and instead seized several grain carriers off the New-foundland banks.

The *Alabama*'s captures followed a pattern. The raider would hail a ship on sight. If she did not heave to, Semmes would fire a blank cartridge. If she still failed to respond, he would send a shot from a thirty-two-pounder across her bow, and that would bring her to a halt. While the prize was boarded, Semmes stayed in his cabin; the skipper of his victim was taken to him there. Any ship whose papers showed her to be of neutral ownership was released. If she was U.S.-owned, Semmes transferred her crew to the *Alabama.*

For a commerce raider, the *Alabama* operated under an unusual handicap: Because of the Federal blockade, she had no home port to which Semmes might send prizes. He thus had to burn most of the ships he captured. After appropriating any usable provisions, a Rebel boarding party would pile up furniture and mattresses, douse them with lard or some other flammable substance, and fire the ship. Semmes's first officer was another veteran of the "Old Navy," John McIntosh Kell. The tough, red-bearded Kell later wrote:

> To watch the leaping flames on a burning ship gives an indescribable mental excitement that did not decrease with the frequency of the light, but it was always a relief to know the ships were tenantless as they disappeared in the lonely grandeur, specks of vanishing light in the "cradle of the deep."

Between captures, the crew had ample opportunity to take the measure of their skipper. Semmes had just turned fifty-three and was not physically im-

posing; some thought him past his prime for sea command. His one idiosyn-
crasy was a carefully cultivated mustache that led his sailors to call him "Old
Beeswax," but he was a tough disciplinarian; in his postwar memoir he outlined his command philosophy:

> On week days . . . about one fourth of the crew was exercised, either at the
> battery or with small arms. This not only gave them efficiency in the use of
> their weapons, but kept them employed—the constant employment of my men
> being a fundamental article of my philosophy. . . . My crew were never so
> happy as when they had plenty to do, and but little to think about.

Whatever the hands may have thought of Old Beeswax, Semmes appears to
have enjoyed the respect of virtually all his officers. First Officer Kell wor-
shiped his commander. And Lieutenant Sinclair later wrote that "Semmes
[understood] just how to keep himself near the hearts and in the confidence of
his men, without in the slightest degree descending from his dignity, or permitting direct approach." Semmes also impressed everyone with his professionalism. He was a student of every facet of seamanship—he digresses in his
memoir to discuss how variations in temperature affect the currents—and he
had a childlike wonder at the natural beauty of the sea.

Probably only Kell glimpsed the virulent hatred that Semmes nourished
for his enemy, the Yankees. Of them Semmes had written in his journal, "A
people so devoid of Christian charity, and wanting in so many of the essentials
of honesty, cannot be abandoned to their own folly by a just and benevolent
God." Yet not even his loathing for Northerners as a class could totally destroy his admiration for them as seamen, and as the war went on, the task of
burning their ships became less satisfying to him.

Semmes dealt with his prisoners as humanely as conditions permitted.
Captured crews were usually housed on deck but were afforded some protection from the elements. When the prisoners included women passengers,
Semmes's officers turned over the wardroom for their use. Prisoners received
full rations, and cooks among their number had access to the *Alabama*'s gal-
ley. Officers were occasionally placed in irons, generally after Semmes had
heard reports of mistreatment of Confederate prisoners. Because prisoners
were a nuisance, Semmes got rid of them as fast as possible. Sometimes he
landed them at a neutral port, but more often he transferred them to a captured ship whose cargo he had bonded.

From Newfoundland the raider worked her way south to Martinique,
where, on their first liberty, crewmen got so drunk that Semmes put some

twenty sailors in irons. The incident was a reminder that while the *Alabama*'s officers were reliable seamen, committed to the Confederate cause, most of the British crewmen were not. Much as the Duke of Wellington once called his army the scum of the earth, Semmes called his crew

> a precious set of rascals . . . faithless in . . . contracts, liars, thieves, and drunkards. There are . . . exceptions to this rule, but I am ashamed to say of the sailor class of the present day that I believe my crew to be a fair representation of it.

Kell, who supervised the boarding of every prize, had a firm rule that no member of the *Alabama*'s crew could board a captured vessel until any supply of spirits was thrown overboard. Even so, he and Semmes were constantly on the alert for smuggled liquor.

Semmes had passed up the temptation to show his flag off New York City the previous fall, but in the Caribbean he was inclined to stretch his orders and play a role in the ground campaign along the Texas coast. A Federal force under General Nathaniel P. Banks had captured Galveston in October 1862. Confederate forces had subsequently recaptured Galveston, but the city was blockaded by five Federal warships when the black-hulled *Alabama* arrived there on January 11, 1863.

Semmes considered his options. The city that he had contemplated bombarding was now in friendly hands, and he could hardly take on five enemy warships. While he deliberated, the Federals detached one of their fleet, the gunboat *Hatteras,* to check out the new arrival. It was a fatal error. Semmes set out toward open water, steaming slowly, luring his pursuer away from the other Federal warships.

Night had fallen by the time the *Hatteras* reached shouting distance of the *Alabama,* and Semmes, in reply to a hail from the Yankee, identified his ship as the HMS *Petrel.* While the Federal captain dispatched a boat to check out his story, Semmes ran up the Confederate ensign and loosed a broadside at point-blank range.

The *Hatteras* was an underpowered side-wheeler that had no business engaging the powerful *Alabama.* The U.S. gunboat struck her flag after an exchange that lasted only thirteen minutes; a few minutes later she sank in the shallow waters of the gulf. Two of her crew had been killed and three wounded. Semmes rescued the survivors and set course for the Atlantic.

The *Alabama* stopped at Jamaica, where Semmes paroled his prisoners and partook of the hospitality that he would encounter in British possessions throughout the *Alabama*'s two-year cruise. Then he turned his ship southeast around Brazil to work the heavily traveled trade routes of the South Atlantic. Four more ships were stopped and burned in the first weeks of 1863, raising the *Alabama*'s total to thirty.

However, coaling the raider was proving to be a problem. She still had the services of the *Agrippina* as a tender, but it was difficult for Semmes to anticipate every supply requirement, and he had little confidence in the master of the *Agrippina.* In southern latitudes, moreover, coal tended to be scarce as well as expensive. Fortunately for Semmes, he had a generous supply of gold for payment of ship's bills in remote corners of the world.

In June 1863, off the coast of South America, Semmes captured the U.S. clipper *Conrad,* bound for New York with wool from Argentina. He had been waiting for such a prize, and rather than burning her, he commissioned her as a Confederate cruiser, the *Tuscaloosa,* arming her with guns captured from another ship. This was one more example of Semmes's creative approach to commerce raiding; but the *Tuscaloosa* had little success as a raider.

From South America, Semmes set sail for the Cape of Good Hope. In August 1863 the *Alabama* reached Cape Town, where Semmes supervised some badly needed repairs on his ship. The Confederate commander found himself a celebrity in the British colony, in part because his latest seizure—the *Sea Bride,* from Boston—had been within sight of the cape. As in Jamaica, the *Alabama*'s officers were exhaustively entertained. Semmes held a shipboard "open house" that produced, in his view, "a generous outpouring of the better classes." He also came within a day of encountering a Federal warship that had been dogging his trail, a well-armed paddle wheeler, the *Vanderbilt.*

For all the outrage in the Northern press concerning the *Alabama*'s depredations, pursuit of the raider was disorganized and ineffectual. This was partly deliberate. The Confederacy never had more than a handful of commerce raiders at sea, and of these only the *Florida*—commissioned around the same time as the *Alabama* and destined to destroy thirty-eight ships—was in the *Alabama*'s class. The Lincoln administration regarded the maintenance and strengthening of the blockade of Southern ports as its first priority; it was not willing to weaken the blockade to track down the *Alabama,* the *Florida,* or one of their lesser consorts.

Even making allowances, however, Federal pursuit of the *Alabama* showed little imagination. The U.S. Navy dogged Semmes's trail as if convinced that the raider would remain in the area of its most recent capture. Semmes later wrote that had Navy Secretary Gideon Welles stationed a heavier and faster ship than the *Alabama* along two or three of the most traveled sea-lanes, "he must have driven me off, or greatly crippled me in my movements."

From Cape Town, the *Alabama* worked her way eastward across the Indian Ocean. There, most of the ships encountered proved to be neutral, and friendly captains warned Semmes that the Federals had a warship, the *Wyoming,* patrolling the Sunda Strait between Sumatra and Java. Nevertheless, Semmes seized and burned a New York clipper, the *Winged Racer,* off Java, and set off in pursuit of another, the *Contest,* the following morning.

The pursuit of the *Contest* proved to be an omen. For the first time, the *Alabama,* employing both sail and steam, was initially unable to overtake her prey. But the sun rose higher, the morning breeze died, and the Confederate raider eventually closed in. The *Contest* was burned—not without regret, for several of the *Alabama*'s officers vowed that they had never seen a more beautiful vessel. Only the failing wind had enabled the *Alabama* to make the capture, however, and Semmes realized that eighteen months at sea had taken a toll on his ship.

On December 21, 1863, the *Alabama* anchored at Singapore. There Semmes saw new evidence of the effectiveness of his campaign: Singapore harbor was filled with U.S. ships that had taken refuge there rather than chance an encounter with the *Alabama.* Within days of her arrival, about half of these were sold to neutral nations and flew new flags. The *Straits Times* estimated that Singapore was playing host to some seventeen American vessels aggregating 12,000 tons, some of which had "been lying there for upwards of three months and most of them for at least half that period."

On Christmas Eve 1863, the *Alabama* set course westward. Pickings were predictably slim, but the crew had their hands full with their own ship. The raider's boilers were operating at reduced efficiency, and some of her timbers were split beyond repair. First Officer Kell observed that the *Alabama* was "loose at every joint, her seams were open, and the copper on her bottom was in rolls." For all of Semmes's skill at improvisation, nothing but a month in dry dock could restore the raider to fighting trim.

By early March the *Alabama* was again off Cape Town, but because a belligerent vessel could provision at the same neutral port only once in a three-month period, she had to pass ten days offshore before docking. After coaling at Cape Town, Semmes turned northward. He intended to put his ship into dry dock in France, but he must have realized that the time necessary for repairs made it likely that the *Alabama* would be blockaded in port as the *Sumter* had been.

On April 22 the raider made the second of only three captures during 1864, the *Rockingham,* carrying a cargo of guano from Peru to Ireland. After the crew was taken off, Semmes directed that the prize be used for target practice—the raider's first live gun drill in many months. Sinclair later recalled that the sea was smooth and that the gun crews "amused themselves blithely" at point-blank range. Semmes thought his gun crews fired "to good effect," but Kell was less impressed: Of twenty-four rounds fired, only seven were seen to inflict damage. Ultimately, Semmes had to burn the *Rockingham.*

On April 27 the *Alabama* made her final capture, the *Tycoon,* out of New York with a mixed cargo. Semmes burned the Yankee vessel and resumed his northward course. He later wrote:

> The poor old *Alabama* was . . . like the wearied fox-hound, limping back after a long chase. . . . Her commander, like herself, was well-nigh worn down. Vigils by night and by day . . . had laid, in the three years of war he had been afloat, a load of a dozen years on his shoulders. The shadows of a sorrowful future, too, began to rest upon his spirit. The last batch of newspapers captured were full of disasters. Might it not be that, after all our trials and sacrifices, the cause for which we were struggling would be lost?

On June 11, 1864, the *Alabama* docked at the French port of Cherbourg. Word of her arrival was telegraphed all over Europe, and three days later the U.S. Navy ship *Kearsarge* appeared off the breakwater. Semmes had not yet received permission to make repairs at the French navy docks at Cherbourg, but he was allowed to disembark his prisoners and take on coal.

The Confederate commander faced a crucial decision. He knew his ship needed a refit, and he probably realized that the prudent course would be to do as he had with the *Sumter:* put her up for sale and fight another day. But his fighting blood was up, and he had no great respect for his enemies. Nor was he inclined to solicit recommendations from his officers; as skipper of the *Sumter* and then the *Alabama,* he was accustomed to making his own decisions. Shortly after the *Kearsarge* appeared, he called Kell to his cabin and explained his intentions.

"As you know, the arrival of the *Alabama* at this port has been telegraphed to all parts of Europe. Within a few days, Cherbourg will be effectively blockaded by Yankee cruisers. It is uncertain whether or not we shall be permitted to repair the *Alabama* here, and in the meantime, the delay is to our advantage. I think we may whip the *Kearsarge,* the two vessels being of wood and carrying about the same number of men and guns. Besides, Mr. Kell, although the Confederate States government has ordered me to avoid engagements with the enemy's cruisers, I am tired of running from that flaunting rag!"

Kell was not sure the decision to fight was wise. He reminded Semmes that in the *Rockingham* gun drill only one in three fuses had seemed effective. But Semmes was not to be deterred. He sent a message to Captain John A. Winslow of the *Kearsarge,* whom he had known in the Old Navy: He intended to fight.

Sunday, June 19, 1864, was a bright, cloudless day off Cherbourg. Aboard the *Alabama,* boilers were fired at daybreak, and Semmes inspected his crew at muster. Decks and brasswork were immaculate, and the crewmen were dressed in blue trousers and white tops. By 9:45 the cruiser was under way, cheered on by the crews of two French warships in the harbor.

The clash between the *Alabama* and the *Kearsarge* was, among other things, pure theater. It seemed that everyone in France wanted to watch what would prove to be the last one-on-one duel of the era of wooden ships. Excursion trains brought the curious, and throngs of small craft hovered outside the breakwater. Painter Edouard Manet, with brushes, paints, and easel, was on one of them.

The two ships were almost equal in size and armament. Both were hybrid steamers of about the same tonnage. The *Alabama* carried 149 crewmen and mounted eight guns; the *Kearsarge* had a crew of 163 and mounted seven guns. The outcome of the battle would depend largely on the skill of the gun crews and the condition of the ships, but the *Kearsarge* had an ace in the hole: The enterprising Winslow had made imaginative use of his ship's chains, draping them along vulnerable parts of the hull as impromptu armor and concealing them behind wood paneling. Semmes later denied knowledge of the chains, but there is evidence that he was warned about it.

After the *Alabama* entered the English Channel, Semmes steered directly for his antagonist, some four miles away. He rotated his two pivot guns to starboard and prepared to engage the enemy on that side. The *Alabama* opened fire at about 11 A.M., and soon both ships were exchanging shots from their starboard batteries. The *Kearsarge* sought to run under the *Alabama*'s stern, but Semmes parried this move by turning to starboard.

The two antagonists thus fought on a circular track, much of the time at a range of about 500 yards. They made seven complete circles during the course of the action, reminding one Northern sailor of "two flies crawling around on the rim of a saucer." Semmes may initially have wanted to put his ship alongside the *Kearsarge* for boarding, but the Yankee's greater speed ruled out this option.

From the first, the firing from the *Alabama* was rapid and wild. The Confederate cruiser fired more than 300 rounds, only 28 of which struck the *Kearsarge,* many of them in the rigging. In their excitement, the *Alabama*'s gunners fired some shot without removing the caps on their fuses—preventing them from exploding—and in other cases fired ramrods as well. It was not a disciplined performance. One of the *Alabama*'s crew conceded that the Confederate batteries were badly served: "The men all fought well, but the gunners did not know how to point and elevate the guns." In addition, the dark smoke emitted by the *Alabama*'s guns lent credence to Kell's fear that the raider's powder had deteriorated.

In contrast, Winslow and his crew fought with disciplined professionalism. Kell later conceded that the Yankee guns were "aimed with precision, and deliberate in fire."

"The firing now became very hot," Semmes related, "and . . . soon began to tell upon our hull, knocking down, killing and disabling a number of men . . . in different parts of the ship." Semmes ordered his gunners to use solid shot as well as shell, but to no effect. Meanwhile, the *Alabama*'s rudder was destroyed, forcing the Confederates to steer with tackles. In desperation, Semmes offered a reward to anyone who could put the *Kearsarge*'s forward pivot gun out of action.

Sinclair recalled how an eleven-inch shell from that weapon entered the *Alabama* at the waterline and exploded in the engine room, "in its passage throwing a volume of water on board, hiding for a moment the guns of [my] division." With his fires out, Semmes attempted to steer for land, only to have the *Kearsarge* station herself between the *Alabama* and the coast.

Shortly after noon, Semmes gave the order to abandon ship. The *Alabama* had suffered only nine killed in the battle, but some twenty others, including Semmes, had been wounded; twelve more would be drowned. Semmes and Kell, along with about forty others of the *Alabama*'s complement, had the good fortune to be rescued from the water by a British yacht, the *Deerhound,* which took them to England rather than turn them over to the *Kearsarge.* Seventy more were picked up by the *Kearsarge,* and another fifteen by excursion boats.

Semmes was lionized in England—British admirers replaced the sword that he had cast into the English Channel—but he was bitter over the loss of his ship, blaming the debacle on his defective powder and the *Kearsarge*'s protective chains. In point of fact, the battle off Cherbourg was the Civil War in microcosm: the gallant but outgunned South, ignoring its own shortcomings, heedlessly taking on a superior force.

During her twenty-two months at sea, the *Alabama* had burned fifty-four Federal merchant ships and had bonded ten others. When, after the war, British and U.S. negotiators determined that Britain owed the United States a total of $15.5 million for damage caused by ships sold to the Confederacy, the amount charged to the *Alabama*—$6.75 million—was much the highest. In addition to her remarkable toll in merchant shipping, the *Alabama* had sunk an enemy gunboat, the luckless *Hatteras,* and had brought untold embarrassment to the Federal navy. Semmes's record with the *Alabama* would not be approached by any raider in modern times.

Yet the raider's influence on the outcome of the Civil War was almost imperceptible. Its toll, however remarkable, represented only about 5 percent of U.S. shipping; the bulk of the U.S. merchant fleet stayed in port, transferred to neutral flags, or took their chances on the high seas. After all, the Confederacy's three or four commerce raiders could not be everywhere. Soaring rates for marine insurance added to the North's cost of waging war, but such economic damage was insignificant alongside the cost of the ground fighting in terms of either lives or matériel. The Northern states—economically self-sufficient—could ignore the depredations of Confederate raiders.

After the war, Semmes suggested that the North at first could not comprehend the threat posed by Confederate commerce destroyers. Yet when the threat materialized, he noted ruefully, the North was "too deeply engaged in the contest to heed it."

By the summer of 1864, there was no possibility of a replacement for the *Alabama,* and Semmes could have lived out the war comfortably in England. Instead, he made his way back to the Confederacy by way of Cuba and Mexico. In Richmond he was promoted to admiral and assigned to the command of the James River squadron in Virginia. Following the evacuation of Richmond, he burned his boats and formed his men into a naval brigade that served under General Joseph E. Johnston in the final weeks of the war. After the war Semmes was briefly under arrest, but he was never brought to trial and supported himself with a small law practice until his death in 1877.

Raphael Semmes was not the first commerce raider in the history of naval warfare, but he was the first to operate in the age of steam and he may have been the best of all time. Notwithstanding the unavailability of any home port, he managed to keep a wooden ship at sea for nearly two years without an overhaul and without losing either a crewman or a prisoner to disease. As a strategist, he demonstrated that a nation with a weak navy could nevertheless inflict great damage on any foe with a substantial merchant fleet. It is hardly surprising that Kaiser Wilhelm II made Semmes's postwar memoirs required reading for his admirals. In both world wars, German submarine and surface raiders would refine the qualities of speed, surprise, and endurance demonstrated by the *Alabama,* but with little of Semmes's regard for the lives of prisoners and crew.

In taking on the *Kearsarge,* however, Semmes had let his emotions control his judgment. His gun crews were insufficiently trained, he underestimated the enemy, and he committed a cardinal sin: He didn't keep his powder dry.

JUBAL EARLY'S RAID ON WASHINGTON

CHARLES C. OSBORNE

The most potentially dazzling gambit of the war was a last-ditch Lee conception: the Confederate raid on Washington in the summer of 1864. The plan was to send Jubal Early's corps, three infantry divisions 10,000 men strong, plus 4,000 cavalrymen, through the Shenandoah toward Maryland; they would then sweep down on Washington from the unexpected North. The key was to strike before Grant had time to release reinforcements from the trenches in front of Petersburg, where his offensive had stalled. It was one of those stratagems, the hook out of nowhere, that might have turned the war around. The nation's capital was, in the words of the historian Frank E. Vandiver, "the greatest prize ever offered to an American soldier."

There were, however, two immediate obstacles. The first was Early's lack not just of men but of first-class troops, increasingly a problem for the Confederates. The second was the ability—and personality—of Early himself. If he was a perfectly decent fighting general, "Old Jubal" was no Stonewall Jackson, and this was a moment that required a commander with his innovative drive. Careless about details such as reconnaissance, the abrasive Early, with his profane falsetto drawl, was not even a Longstreet (whose reputation he would savage after the war). Weather was also a determinant. Early's men marched straight into one of those energy-draining heat waves that are normal for a Potomac summer. In the end, the Confederates would get close enough to Washington to see, rising in the heat haze, the new iron dome of the Capitol. Would their frustration have increased had they known that they were being watched by Abraham Lincoln? He was, as Charles C. Osborne writes, "the only chief executive in office to brave bullets fired in battle."

Charles C. Osborne, a former editor for *Life,* is the author of *Jubal: The Life and Times of General Jubal A. Early.*

ON JUNE 24, 1864, A CONFEDERATE FORCE COMMANDED BY Lieutenant General Jubal A. Early, moving northward through the Shenandoah Valley, entered Lexington, Virginia—last resting place of Stonewall Jackson. The heart of this force was the II Corps, Army of Northern Virginia, commanded by Jackson before his death at Chancellorsville in 1863. One soldier described Jackson's old division "filing past his grave—arms reversed, flags dipped—in a bush as deep as midnight." General Early said nothing about this moment in his writings, but he must have been hoping that Stonewall's combative spirit would bless the corps's defiant endeavor in the days to come.

This enterprise was unprecedented—a Confederate advance directly against Washington, Abraham Lincoln's capital and the heart and soul of the Union. As Early's legion was paying tribute to Jackson in Lexington, only twelve days had passed since General Robert E. Lee had summoned Early to his headquarters near Gaines' Mill, Virginia, for a momentous conference.

Lee, leading the Army of Northern Virginia, was operating along the Chickahominy River near Richmond against Lieutenant General Ulysses S. Grant and the Army of the Potomac. The two sides had begun a furious digging of trenches around Petersburg. Grant was augmenting Union pressure on the Confederate capital with aggressive moves on other fronts—not least in the Shenandoah Valley. There, a Federal force was moving south with the aim of severing Confederate rail communications and destroying the valley's rich grain crops.

Lee ordered Early to march his corps as rapidly as possible to the valley. First, he was to frustrate Grant's plans; then he was to head north, cross the Potomac—and move on Washington. Lee hoped that maneuver might induce Grant to detach troops to defend the Northern capital, thus reducing the strain on Lee's defense of Richmond. Early was to accomplish this with only 10,000 infantry in three divisions, 4,000 cavalry, and 50 guns.

That Early would—or could—actually capture Washington may have seemed incredible, though if he were to occupy the city for even a short time the consequences could be far-reaching: The government might be forced to evacuate, leaving the United States Treasury to be sacked and the Union army's main supply depot destroyed. Such an outcome could slow the Union war effort to a crawl—maybe halt it, if only momentarily. Northern war-weariness, profound and growing as 1864 passed its midpoint, might be exacerbated. Lincoln, running for reelection, might lose irrecoverable ground with Northern voters. More remote—but dazzling—was the possibility that breaking into Washington might finally induce Britain and France to recognize Richmond and lend the active support to the Southern cause that they had so far withheld. For Lee, the possibility that even some of these things might happen justified the danger to his own capital that he courted in detaching Early's corps.

Early was hardly a perfect choice as leader of such an expedition. Forty-seven years old, the ambitious general was a West Pointer who had spent most of his life as a lawyer in his home county in southwest Virginia. His war record, so far, was mixed; he had performed well as a division commander under Stonewall Jackson at Cedar Mountain and Antietam, but had shown inertia and—possibly—poor judgment at Gettysburg and the Wilderness. In command of the II Corps only a couple of weeks, Early's ability to lead a formation of that size was far from proven.

The general's appearance and manner were strikingly idiosyncratic. Crippled by arthritis and the effects of an old wound, his back and shoulders were as stooped as those of a man far older. Piercing dark eyes flashed from his face, framed by thin hair and grizzled beard. A handsome sculpted nose, pursed lips, and thickset jaw communicated determination and an air of profound self-confidence. The general habitually wore a large white slouch hat, adorned with a black plume. In the field or in cool weather, Early complemented the flamboyance of the hat with a long white overcoat that fell to his heels.

In tones incongruously high and piping (one acquaintance likened its timbre to the sound of a "Chinese fiddle"), Early's voice expressed his opinions in terms that were often blunt, sarcastic, and disrespectful, and always, in the view of one acquaintance, "interestingly lurid and picturesque." Not least, Early was scathingly profane, spitting out oaths with streams of tobacco juice from a plug that was seldom absent from his jaw.

The general's personality was a legend in the Confederate States Army, where he had many enemies. But Lee knew Early was familiar with the valley, having campaigned there the previous winter with his own command, chasing Union cavalry raiders. Early's intellect was acute, his personal courage and imperturbability under pressure unquestioned. Finally, Lee knew him to be unmatched for boldness and intensity by anyone in the army since Stonewall himself. Many of Jackson's men and subordinate officers, with their own experience of his valley campaign of 1862, were now serving under Early, whose division commanders included such able, seasoned men as John Brown Gordon of Georgia, Stephen Dodson Ramseur of North Carolina, and Robert Rodes of Virginia. These veterans scarcely loved Early, but they respected him and would prove willing to follow him.

Leaving Lee's headquarters after their conference, Early hurried to issue the orders that would put the II Corps on the road by 3:00 A.M. the following day, June 13. He had just learned that a large Federal force was advancing along the valley toward Lynchburg, an essential center of transportation and a major supply depot. Pushing hard, Early marched his men into Charlottesville on June 17, having covered eighty miles in four days. From there, the troops could board trains on the Orange & Alexandria Railroad for the sixty-mile trip to Lynchburg.

The II Corps reached Lynchburg in time to combine with the garrison and a division of valley-based troops under Major General John C. Breckinridge (the former U.S. vice president) to thwart a Federal effort to seize the city. On June 18 the Confederate defenders of Lynchburg, though outnumbered two to one, drove off Union attackers under Major General David Hunter and chased them out of the valley. Retreating westward into the mountains of West Virginia, Hunter left the route to Washington wide open.

General Early ordered the advance. Moving swiftly northward, his force—augmented by Breckinridge's 2,000-man division and designated the Army of the Valley District—was in full control of the valley by July 4; the Federals had no idea of his intentions. Early's movement west was kept a secret until the raiders got closer to Washington; Lee had persuaded Jefferson Davis to withhold from the newspapers any information about the transfer of the II Corps—something the Confederate government had hitherto been unwilling to do. Grant, preoccupied with his Petersburg-Richmond campaign, knew about Hunter's failure at Lynchburg, but did not connect Early with it; the Union commander thought the II Corps was still facing him in eastern Virginia.

On July 5, Breckinridge crossed the Potomac at Shepherdstown with his contingent, and Early followed on the sixth with the rest of his force. The column marched north and then east through the passes in South and Catoctin Mountains en route to Washington via Frederick and Rockville.

Panicky word of rebel horsemen galloping loose all over Maryland and even Pennsylvania began circulating. Authorities in Washington puzzled over reports that Breckinridge and Major General George Pickett (who was actually still with Lee at Petersburg) were moving through the valley at the head of a column numbering between 10,000 and 30,000 men. President Lincoln intervened personally, as he seldom did now that Grant was his general in chief.

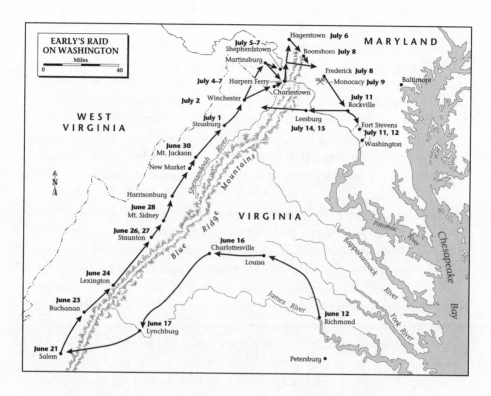

EARLY'S RAID
ON WASHINGTON
Miles
0   40

MARYLAND

Hagerstown July 6
July 5–7
Shepherdstown   Boonsboro July 8
Martinsburg
Frederick July 8
July 4–7 Harpers Ferry   Monocacy July 9   Baltimore
July 2 Winchester   Charlestown
July 11
July 1   Rockville
Strasburg   Leesburg
July 14, 15   Fort Stevens
June 30   July 11, 12
Mt. Jackson   Washington
New Market

WEST
VIRGINIA

Shenandoah River

Blue Ridge Mountains

Potomac River

Rappahannock River

Chesapeake Bay

Harrisonburg
June 28
Mt. Sidney   VIRGINIA
June 26, 27
Staunton   June 16
Charlottesville
Louisa
June 24
Lexington
June 23   James River
Buchanan   June 12
Richmond
June 17
Lynchburg
June 21
Salem   Petersburg

*Major General Lew Wallace, whose blundering at Shiloh nearly ended his
military career, redeemed himself with a rearguard action at Monocacy Junction that slowed Early's advance. The map above shows the raiders' route
through the Shenandoah, across the Potomac, and, after the critical delay at
Monocacy, to the outskirts of Washington. But the arrival of Federal reinforcements compelled Early to retreat west.*

The president ordered the army's chief of staff, Major General Henry W. Halleck, to have Hunter return to the valley immediately. Lincoln also asked the
governors of Massachusetts, New York, and Pennsylvania to send drafts of
100-day recruits to reinforce the defenses of Washington.

Grant, unpersuaded until now that Lee would detach any sizable force from
the defense of Richmond, began to take notice. Catching up with the unfolding reality, Union intelligence generated unmistakable evidence that Early
and a significant array of Confederates were operating in ever closer proximity
to Washington. Grant formally offered to send Halleck a corps from the Army

of the Potomac. Without firing a shot, Early was already beginning to achieve Lee's purpose in mounting the raid.

For the moment, no Union force stood between Early's invading column and its goal. But one man had already started acting on the threat: Major General Lew Wallace, later famous as the author of one of the best-selling novels of the late nineteenth century, *Ben-Hur.* At age thirty-seven, Wallace, an Indiana lawyer-politician who had served as a lieutenant in the Mexican War, found his career in abeyance. He was riding a desk as commander of the U.S. Army's Middle Department, with headquarters in Baltimore. Wallace had received this assignment as punishment for allegedly marching in the wrong direction at the Battle of Shiloh in 1862. Now, seeking to rehabilitate his career and alerted to the invasion by John Garrett, the energetic president of the Baltimore & Ohio Railroad, Wallace assumed that a possible goal for the Confederate thrust was Washington. In Baltimore, Wallace was close to the corridor that led from Harpers Ferry to the capital. Despite his gaunt, melancholy looks, Wallace was an optimist, but an astute and levelheaded one. Determined to try to deflect the invaders or at least delay them long enough to permit reinforcement of the capital, he studied a map and spotted a promising defensive position at Monocacy Junction, two miles southeast of Frederick.

Along the Monocacy River, a tributary of the Potomac, the junction not only joined spurs of the B&O running from Harpers Ferry and Frederick to Baltimore, but also lay between the Washington and Baltimore pikes leading east from Frederick. To defend the junction, Wallace could initially call on fewer than 3,000 men, including Maryland Home Guards and a small number of 100-day militiamen. Then, on July 7, Wallace fortuitously secured the services of a division of 3,350 veteran infantrymen, part of the Union VI Corps. Sent by Grant's order from eastern Virginia to reinforce Washington, they had traveled by water to Baltimore; from there, they had gone by train bound for Harpers Ferry, where they were ordered to intercept any invaders. When the division arrived at the junction, Wallace had their commander, Brigadier General James B. Ricketts, stay and help block Early—now identified as leader of the invaders, who were already well east of Harpers Ferry. Wallace's force at this point numbered about 5,800.

Approaching Frederick on July 8 with approximately 14,000 men, Early paused only long enough to demand $200,000 from the citizens of the town. The general was firm when the municipal fathers balked—but when they asked for time to find the money, he relented. Next morning, riding out in splendid, balmy summer weather, he deployed his command, whose forward elements had reported the enemy in position on the river. Sitting his horse, Early saw that the river, running from northeast to southwest, was really a stream here, less than twenty yards wide. The flat, open ground on the western bank was scored by the Washington and Baltimore pikes, which converged at Frederick; the two roads crossed the Monocacy roughly at right angles, forming a large letter A with the river as crossbar.

The Baltimore Pike spanned the Monocacy on a stone bridge almost two miles to Early's left; a little right of center, a covered wooden bridge carried the Washington Pike across the river. At the junction, the branches of the B&O joined and then crossed the river on an iron trestle. Early saw a ridge that dominated the east bank—where Union troops were forming up. He could only guess at Union strength—which he estimated at 8,000 to 10,000, about half his own force. But Early could see that the Federals had covered all three crossings in sufficient strength to make direct assault unacceptably costly. His remedy was to push across the river well downstream from the bridges and outflank the Union defense line on his right, with the aim of getting behind the bridges and gaining the Washington Pike.

The battle plan was uncomplicated. One of Early's divisions, under Rodes, was to demonstrate and skirmish with the defenders of the stone bridge; another division, under Ramseur, was to play the same part against men guarding the wooden bridge. Probably calculating that he was as yet opposed only by militia, Early decided to assign just one of his two remaining divisions to the flank attack that was to push the defenders out of his way.

An immediate problem was a means of crossing the river below the bridges. An anxious search for a ford by Early and his staff was unavailing, and by 11:00 A.M., Early's divisions were still on the wrong side of the river. Time, and his chances of reaching Washington before Grant sent reinforcements, were slipping away. From Monocacy Junction, the march to the capital, thirty miles away, could take the better part of two days. Heat, too, was beginning to play a part, as the late-morning temperature approached 90 degrees and was still climbing.

As the general watched, Brigadier General John McCausland's cavalry brigade trotted into view on the right—then crossed the river. The troopers had found the elusive ford. They dismounted and launched an impulsive attack on the rising ground in front of them, farmland that was thickly sown with bluecoats. Wallace had guessed that Early would try to flank the position, and he had placed his best troops—the men from the VI Corps—to frustrate such an attempt.

Winnowed by the deadly Union fire, McCausland's troopers recoiled. But they had shown Early how to get his assault division, under Gordon, across the river, where it was to outflank the Union line and smash through to the Washington Pike. Gordon led his men across and attacked. Intense musketry slowed the Confederates—and as they paused, Ricketts protected the Union flank by ordering a change of front, pivoting his line to defend the pike rather than the river crossing.

Against this new formation, Gordon's men needed two more assaults to dislodge Ricketts's veterans. In the second attack, the Virginians of Brigadier General William Terry's brigade swarmed up a knoll near the river anchoring the Union line. As Gordon remembered it, enthusiasm overwhelmed the Virginians with a "martial delirium," which called forth shouts of "At them, boys!" and "Charge them! Charge them!" Their ardor propelled the attackers up the hill and down on top of the Federals, who fled across a small stream. In its waters, Gordon remarked, "the dead and wounded of both sides mingled their blood . . . and when the struggle was ended a crimsoned current ran down toward the river."

The withdrawal of Ricketts's division ended the battle. The Union force made its escape up the Baltimore Pike. With 1,294 men killed or wounded, as well as 200 captured, Wallace had been driven out of Early's way. But Wallace, redeeming his disgrace at Shiloh, had accomplished his purpose: to slow the invaders down. The battle ended too late on July 9 for Early to resume his advance before nightfall. He had lost a whole day—and 900 irreplaceable men. Still, the city fathers of Frederick, giving Early the benefit of the doubt, now paid him his $200,000—in cash. (The Federal government later declined to come to the aid of the town, and the bank loans were not fully repaid—including about $400,000 in interest—until October 1951.)

In Maryland and northern Virginia, the weekend of July 9–10 was American summer at its most malevolent, setting records for heat and drought. No one who has suffered through the Potomac region's terrible July weather can doubt the weary discomfort of all the participants in Jubal Early's raid on Washington, raiders and defenders alike.

Early himself, contemplating the opportunity of his lifetime—reaching Washington before Federal reinforcements could arrive to block his triumphal entry into the city—was indifferent to the weather. Meanwhile the Union's leaders, though sweating in their wool suits and uniforms, seemed oddly detached in the face of the Confederate invasion. Margaret Leech summarized the prevailing atmosphere in *Reveille in Washington,* her matchless history of the capital at war: "Like a secret cult, the War Office was wrapped in impenetrable mystery. It had no information to give anyone about the invasion, and seemed to find the whole subject faintly distasteful."

Absence of solid information led, in time-honored fashion, to the spread of rumor and misstatement—which only increased as refugees poured into the city from the Maryland countryside. In the aftermath of the Monocacy fight, one Union soldier wrote, "pale-faced, anxious men solemnly asserted that certain information had been received at the War Department that at least 50,000 veteran soldiers were marching with Early." Late on the night of the battle, by the same account, a man in the bar at Willard's Hotel told the assembled drinkers that Wallace had been "disastrously defeated, and that our disordered troops were in full retreat." In the small hours, the story grew even more dire: Wallace's army had been annihilated, and government clerks were packing money, records, and books in boxes for evacuation to New York. There was more than rumor to that story. Lucius E. Chittenden, registrar of the Treasury, opened a door and discovered a group of Treasury officials bundling notes and certificates into mail sacks for loading aboard a government steamer bound for some haven to the north.

Skeptical voices decried such reports as exaggerated, claiming that the Confederate incursion, if there was one, involved "a light party"—no more, perhaps, than a few cavalry. But Secretary of War Edwin M. Stanton quietly arranged to have his personal hoard of gold ($5,000 of his own and $400 belonging to Mrs. Stanton) removed from his house and hidden in the residence of his clerk. Stanton and Halleck knew that without reinforcements from Grant there were only about 9,600 men available to man the thirty-seven miles of fortifications making up the defenses of Washington.

Meanwhile, at the Monocacy, badges and interrogation of prisoners—there were several hundred—had identified the VI Corps. But despite this evidence of growing Federal strength, Early sensed great opportunity. Anxious to seize the moment, he had his army depart from the junction at dawn on Sunday, July 10. Out front, McCausland led his troopers into the rising sun, followed by Breckinridge with his division and Gordon's. Rodes advanced next, with Ramseur in the rear.

On the march, along roads turned to suffocating corridors of dust, heat prostration felled hundreds of men and horses. By nightfall, the head of the column was entering Rockville, about twenty miles from the Monocacy— though most of the army halted in Gaithersburg, about five miles farther west. By this time, Early's expedition was more of a straggling procession than a coherent force prepared to capture a capital.

At reveille on Monday, July 11, the Confederate raiders were about fifteen miles—a day's march—from the capital. Early's plan was to arrive at the ramparts before nightfall and march into the city. Before sunrise he was mounted, riding after McCausland, who was still out ahead. Rodes led the infantry into another oven of a day, with Ramseur behind him and Breckinridge in the rear. McCausland was to take the Georgetown Pike to Tennallytown, just inside the District. The infantry (with cavalry brigades under Brigadier Generals John D. Imboden and William Jackson out ahead) would swing east, aiming for the vital entrance to the capital via the Seventh Street Road. Artillery was to march close behind the leading Confederate infantry regiments.

Grant and Halleck, aware by July 10 of the general direction of Early's advance, knew that they did not have to man the entire perimeter of fortifications. But Halleck urgently requested Grant to send him more troops. Grant duly dispatched the two other divisions of the VI Corps, as well as part of the XIX Corps, newly arrived in Virginia from Louisiana—about 11,000 men. Until they arrived—sometime on Monday, at the earliest—the forts standing in the invaders' path could be occupied only by two regiments of raw militia.

"I pushed on as rapidly as possible," Early later wrote, "hoping to get into the fortifications around Washington before they could be manned." Impatient, in heat that had already reached 94 degrees, the general pushed his horse into a gallop and overtook his cavalry, which was skirmishing with Federal troopers and shoving them back down the Seventh Street Road. Finally, the Union horsemen took refuge in a fort. Spying out the works with his binoculars from a distance of about half a mile, then checking a map, Early recognized Fort Stevens, a major bastion of the District's defenses. As he looked, his heart leaped: He could see that "the works were but feebly manned." The defenders looked like militia—some of them wearing linen dusters instead of the blue coats that Grant's troops generally wore.

For the moment, it appeared that Early had won the race. If Fort Stevens could be taken, his "foot cavalry" might march into Washington and seize what the historian Frank E. Vandiver called "the greatest prize ever offered to an American soldier." The prize was within reach: Early could see the new iron dome of the Capitol—completed only about seven months earlier—just six miles away, through the haze to the south.

But the dome might just as well have been a mirage. The Army of the Valley District's racing speed was certainly an illusion. The fact that it had not really won the race was all too plain. Of the perhaps 12,000 Southerners who had departed the Monocacy, no more than 3,000 were in any condition to fight, and few of those had caught up with their commander. As Early could clearly see, the force threatening Fort Stevens consisted of himself, a few staff officers, and a handful of cavalry.

The nearest infantry, with guns, was Rodes's division, moving down the Seventh Street Road from Silver Spring. But straggling had drained the division's available strength. It was easy enough for Early to order Rodes to attack Fort Stevens; but the division commander, unable to array enough men in line of battle, could only throw skirmishers out into the terrain before the fort—mainly farmland with houses and barns.

Priceless minutes crept by in the fierce heat as Early awaited the arrival of Rodes's lagging rear brigades. Glasses at his eyes, he watched the fort intently, as if its image, brought close by optical magnification, could similarly bring success closer. Then the image changed. At around 1:30 P.M., Early spied clouds of dust—and not long after, a substantial contingent of Federals marching into the fort. Dust veiled but did not conceal the deep blue of their uniforms.

So Grant, it seemed likely to Early, had reinforced the capital with his veterans. But maybe he had sent only enough men to stiffen the defenses at this one point; or perhaps these bluecoats were only well-outfitted militia. To find out, Early cantered down the line to his right in search of McCausland, who had been sent to probe the Tennallytown defenses on the Georgetown Pike. But the young cavalry general's news was no better: He reported far too much manpower in the line guarding the Pike to attack it with any promise of success.

Early returned to the Fort Stevens front to see how Rodes was doing. Once again the field glasses came out as he and Rodes reexamined the defenses. By now, it was plain to the generals that even fresh troops would have great difficulty in an assault.

After the hundreds of miles Early's army had marched and the casualties it had suffered at the Monocacy, was it now to slink away without even trying to grasp the prize? Early's wrathful soul rejected the very idea. But he also knew that Lee would scarcely thank him for losing his army by reckless action.

On the Union side, there was universal expectation that Early would attack. If he had, he might at least have created enormous confusion and dismay; the reinforcements, arriving exhausted after a hurried journey by water from eastern Virginia, were being allowed to rest while militia and convalescents held the forts. No one seemed immune from the heat. Sylvanus Cadwallader, a reporter from New York, watched Confederate troops arriving, stacking arms, and fixing dinner instead of deploying for a fight. It was Cadwallader's opinion, expressed later, that the Union positions could have been seized "with the loss of a few hundred men." The Confederates were encouraged to believe otherwise. The infantry on the line had been ordered to maintain rapid fire at will, whether or not they could see targets; some, drawn from units of dismounted cavalry, were shooting with breech-loading carbines, greatly augmenting their rate of fire and creating an impression of much greater numbers than were actually on hand.

For the Confederates, as night approached, it was time to reorganize, to see where matters stood. Early left Rodes's division watching Fort Stevens and made his way back toward Silver Spring. There, a couple of miles from the fort, stood the house of Francis Preston Blair, a man powerful in the affairs of Maryland and the Union. Oddly in this time of uncertainty and peril Blair had gone fishing in Pennsylvania, leaving his house empty. The mansion had been requisitioned as headquarters for the Army of the Valley District.

Early called his senior officers together for a council of war. Breckinridge, Gordon, Rodes, and Ramseur joined the general in the Blair dining room; wines from the Blair cellar were opened and sampled as the commanders discussed their situation. They made toasts hailing the imminent capture of Washington and the triumphant return of John Breckinridge to the vice president's chair in the Capitol.

Then Early brought the gathering back to business as he put the harsh dilemma to his lieutenants. The army had to do something immediately—or retreat. The danger of simply remaining in place was compounded by reliable knowledge—a report in a Northern newspaper—that Hunter was back in the Potomac region and could be expected to arrive at Harpers Ferry shortly. It would not be long before the passes through South and Catoctin Mountains and the fords across the Potomac would be sealed up in the Confederate army's rear. Nevertheless, Early asserted that failure to try an assault on the capital would be a terrible waste. He announced that the army would attack the next day.

In the small hours a courier arrived with the Confederates' first specific knowledge, gathered through intelligence sources in Baltimore, that two Union corps (the XIX as well as the VI) had been dispatched to Washington. Wispy though this information might be, Early could not ignore it. Hitting the Washington defenses head-on would be hard enough if they contained but one veteran corps; the presence of two corps could make the cost prohibitive. More facts were badly needed. Until he had them, Early decided to cancel the attack, pending a last look at sunup on Tuesday, July 12.

"As soon as it was light enough to see, I rode to the front and saw the parapet lined with troops," Early remembered later. It was no illusion. By dawn on July 12, the bulk of the Federal reinforcements were in position at and near Fort Stevens and other strongpoints. Even if the Confederates should break through the defenses facing them and into the city, how good were their chances of accomplishing much? Against unknown reserves that might outnumber the raiders, having to overcome house-to-house defenses would be costly. The whole Southern force might be tramped inside the city and annihilated.

Early made his final decision: He would remain in place during the day on July 12, then withdraw toward the Potomac fords under cover of darkness. He would abandon his greatest chance for glory, "after I had arrived in sight of the dome of the Capitol and given the Federal authorities a terrible fright."

During the twelfth, most of the Confederate troops outside Washington were able to stay quiet, resting in the shade. But Southern sharpshooters and skirmishers maintained their aggressiveness as the day wore on. Into this hostile atmosphere, with bullets buzzing around the parapet at Fort Stevens, stepped Abraham Lincoln, whose curiosity had drawn him out to the scene of combat. He was visible to the sharpshooters—though they may not have been able to recognize his tall figure and top hat—who poured fire into the fort. President Lincoln thus became the only chief executive in office to brave bullets fired in battle. The shooting was harrowingly effective; a man standing near Lincoln was wounded. According to one account, it was a VI Corps captain named Oliver Wendell Holmes who frantically ordered the president to take cover—shouting, "Get down, you damned fool, before you get shot!" Taken aback, the president obeyed.

Lincoln remained long enough to act in his capacity as commander in chief: He personally authorized the shelling of civilian houses where Confederate sharpshooters were sheltering. To flush the marksmen out of their positions and drive them off, the Union command called for a sortie by a brigade of the VI Corps under Colonel Daniel D. Bidwell. The brigade started forward around 6:00 P.M., braving fire from the Confederate skirmishers and sharpshooters. Then it encountered artillery and musket fire from Rodes's division. Calling for support, Bidwell pressed on, pushing the Confederates back. The affair looked, for a time, like a ripening battle—one that might not be easy for Early to break off. He knew how close his men were to the limit of their resources: A determined night assault on the Southerners might have had serious consequences. But darkness and heavy casualties in Bidwell's command—25 percent or more killed or wounded, including all six regimental commanders—brought a halt to the fighting.

The heavy Union losses may have stemmed in part from the desperate urgency of men who regarded themselves as defenders of their capital and their president. In any case, the end came none too soon for the exhausted Confederates, though their combat losses during the two days in front of Washington were only about 200 men.

Still presiding over Francis Preston Blair's house (where dirty dishes and empty bottles were left on the table, to be discovered later by the Federals), Early summoned Gordon and Breckinridge, who arrived after dark. They would lead the withdrawal, to be followed by Rodes and Ramseur. The route would be the Seventh Street Road back to Rockville, and from there via Poolesville to White's Ford. A selected rear guard of 200 officers and men would remain behind during the night to picket the Seventh Street Road.

Major Henry Kyd Douglas, a member of Early's staff, respected the general. But the major's mouth must have gone a bit dry when Early chose him to command the rear guard. The general, Douglas remembered, was "in a droll humor, perhaps one of relief, for he said to me in his falsetto drawl: 'Major, we haven't taken Washington, but we've scared Abe Lincoln like hell!'"

The major, unafraid of Early (who liked him for it), shot back: "Yes, general, but this afternoon when that Yankee line moved out against us, I think some other people were scared blue as hell's brimstone!"

Breckinridge, whose fate as a captive might have been most uncertain, found this exchange vastly amusing. Laughing, he asked, "How about that, general?"

"That's true," replied Early, "but it won't appear in history!" Douglas, of course, took care that it should appear. But the reason most narrators repeat the exchange is that Early had the aplomb not only to admit he was scared but to assert his control by making a joke of it. Early's final word was a cue, if ever there was one, for all present to laugh at the commanding general's witticism.

The retreat to the Potomac went smoothly, free of pursuit or even effective harassment. Grant and Lincoln had been most anxious that Early not escape across the river; but a muddled command structure and hesitancy at the highest military levels in the capital conspired to put a whole day's march between the raiders and Washington before any significant pursuit was organized. The Army of the Valley District was safely across the Potomac with its spoils on July 14.

"It would have been a queer finale of the campaign in Virginia," wrote Confederate War Department bureaucrat Robert Kean in a July 16 diary entry, "if while Grant is besieging Petersburg, Early was to capture Washington." Kean's sense of irony was deadly accurate. Still, Southerners had badly needed Early's raid to be a dramatic success. Hopes had run high, as even

Kean reflected in his declaration that "Early, Breckinridge, Rodes, Gordon and Ramseur are men to dare and do almost anything."

Southern newspapers had been sounding a similar inspiriting theme, a paean to the genius of Bobby Lee in sending what some called his most daring lieutenant back over the border to taunt and terrorize the North. Swelled by this publicity, expectations of a dramatic victory had briefly run so high that when the actual outcome was revealed, the letdown was severe. Some papers denounced what they trumpeted as Early's failure, which seemed the more abject because it had been such a close call. Other journals, while bemoaning the near miss, thanked Early for what he had accomplished—particularly in bringing back herds of horses and cattle from Maryland and ensuring the harvest of crops in the Shenandoah Valley.

If this had been all that Early's expedition had gained, it would—for a Confederacy facing mounting hunger—have been substantial. But it was not enough to dissipate a cloud of dissatisfaction that blinded many Southern eyes to some less tangible effects of Early's raid upon the North—particularly in the political realm. Early, just as he said, had shaken the nerves of Abe Lincoln—a candidate for reelection—and everyone else in authority in Washington; the incursion had brought the war to the people of Washington more vividly than ever before. Early had cleared the Shenandoah Valley of Federal troops and neutralized Hunter's army. The Confederates had approached Washington's inner defenses, something that Union siege forces had never done to Richmond. And the troops sent by Grant to relieve Washington did not return to help keep up the pressure on Lee. (Many of them remained in the Shenandoah Valley to serve under Sheridan in his autumn campaign.) Though Lee's hopes for foreign recognition were brought no closer by the operation, pro-Confederate voices in England, at least, were encouraged. According to the *Times* of London, the expedition demonstrated that "the Confederacy is more formidable . . . than ever."

In the wake of the raid, many Northerners were profoundly dejected. "I see no bright spot anywhere," a New Yorker wrote in his diary, "only humiliation and disaster." Others in the North, notably Lincoln's political opponents, were heartened; as one Democratic paper, looking ahead to the presidential election that fall, editorialized, "Lincoln is deader than dead."

But these marks of Early's raid would fade as the Confederate cause waned through the balance of 1864. Grant would tighten his hammerlock on Petersburg, Major General William T. Sherman would launch his March to the Sea from Atlanta, and Lincoln would be reelected. As for Jubal Early, a major military result of his raid—the diversion of two corps of Union infantry from the Petersburg front to Washington and the Shenandoah Valley—was eventually to produce the instrument of his destruction. Augmented to a total of 30,000 men by a cavalry corps and eighteen or more artillery batteries, these troops, commanded by Major General Philip Sheridan, would crush Early's army in three autumn battles in the valley.

But in mid-July 1864, it still seemed to many that, in Frank Vandiver's words, "the South, after four arduous years, with hostile armies near Richmond and knifing into Georgia, could still parry with one hand and thrust with the other."

Early's raid, with the events leading up to it and those that followed, may have helped to prolong the war many months. And if the Army of the Valley District had breached the gates of Washington, the war's end might have been incalculably different. But the effort—all along, perhaps, a forlorn hope—failed. Confederate arms would never strike so deep again.

THE CRATER

JOHN M. TAYLOR

The frustrations of a long war were growing, and as they did, leaders sought quick fixes and miracle expedients. Early's raid was one, but an even more glaring example was the incident of the Crater. By mid-June of 1864, Grant's offensive had stalled in front of the rail junction of Petersburg, southeast of Richmond, and the longest operation of the Civil War began. For the moment Lee still had the troops to counter Grant's flanking thrusts, and so the two sides dug in and settled down to a waiting game. It was trench warfare without the machine gun and long-range artillery, but even so, Petersburg offered a preview of things to come: In the next nine-plus months the combatants would lose a combined total of 70,000 men along lines that hardly budged. Like the generals of the Western Front, Grant and his lieutenants became obsessed with the problem of getting across no-man's-land (which wasn't yet called that). A former Pennsylvania engineer, Lieutenant Colonel Henry Pleasants, advanced a solution that would become commonplace for another military generation: to dig a tunnel under the opposing trenches, fill it with kegs of gunpowder, and then set off an explosion that would literally blow a hole in the Confederate line. As the Europeans would discover, mine warfare worked only if men could cross no-man's-land almost immediately, before the enemy had a chance to occupy the lip of the new crater—which provided an instant earthwork. Craters were also a magnet that lured men who sought protection from fire, only to find themselves trapped. Seconds counted. That was the rub at the Crater, where the Union attack did not go off for thirty minutes after the explosion, largely because of confusion and ineptitude behind the line. The corps commander in Pleasants' sector was none other than Ambrose E. Burnside, and the genial initiator of Fredericksburg was about to preside over another major fiasco. But Burnside wasn't the only person at blame. Commanders on both sides, from Grant and Lee down, seemed to be succumbing to fatigue, and were no longer paying attention to the small details that could make all the difference.

Another fact about the Battle of the Crater is worth remarking. Long after the Union attack had failed to achieve a breakthrough, Burnside sent in a division of black troops, mostly former slaves. Their slaughter was predictable, and was made worse by the refusal of the Confederates to take black prisoners. But the Crater and Fort Pillow were calamitous exceptions to the generally creditable performance of black troops, notably at Nashville in December 1864, where they made a memorable contribution to one of the greatest victories of the war.

John M. Taylor is the author of eight books of history and biography, most recently a reassessment of Robert E. Lee, *Duty Faithfully Performed: Robert E. Lee and His Critics,* and *Confederate Raider: Raphael Semmes of the* Alabama. Taylor lives in McLean, Virginia.

IF EVER THERE WAS A HARD-LUCK ARMY AMONG LINCOLN'S legions in the Civil War it was that most visible of units, the Army of the Potomac. Almost from the first it had faced the ablest of the Confederate commanders—men of the caliber of Lee, Jackson, and Stuart. It had confronted the most daunting of challenges: capture of the enemy's capital. And then there was the quality of its own commanders. Billy Yank had been led by the likes of Irwin McDowell, George McClellan, Joseph "Fighting Joe" Hooker, and Ambrose E. Burnside. Small wonder that the Army of the Potomac began its 1864 campaign against Richmond with some foreboding.

But there were positive signs as well. Recognizing that the defeat of Lee's army would effectively end the war, the North was sparing nothing to assure the success of the campaign. Although General George G. Meade retained nominal leadership of the Army of the Potomac, Ulysses S. Grant, the commanding general of all Union forces, traveled with Meade's army in this latest Virginia campaign. Beginning in April, the spring offensive took on the aspect of a continuous battle, with the 100,000-man Army of the Potomac moving inexorably south. Yet Robert E. Lee managed to keep his Army of Northern Virginia between Grant and the Confederate capital.

In one of his more skillful moves, Grant succeeded in stealing a march on Lee in mid-June, moving the bulk of his force from northeast of Richmond to positions south of the James River. But the Army of the Potomac's bad luck held. Grant's plan had called for an attack on the railroad junction at Petersburg, twenty-three miles south of Richmond, with a view to cutting off supplies to the capital. The movement went smoothly, and as dawn broke on June 16 the Federals had a good portion of General William Farrar "Baldy" Smith's corps within sight of Petersburg, where Confederate general P. G. T. Beauregard could muster only 3,000 defenders. But a combination of delays, bad maps, and imprecise orders on the Federal side enabled Beauregard to reinforce his lines until Lee could arrive with the main army. Grant, frustrated, returned to his cigars. Petersburg would have to be taken by siege.

The threat that Grant posed to Richmond and Petersburg was obvious, and Lee's army was in dire straits. At the same time, living conditions were almost as onerous for the Federals as for the Confederates. The summer dust lay inches deep—there had been no rain for weeks—and one New York soldier concluded that the combination of dust and heat was "killing more men than the Johnnies." An artilleryman quipped that one jumping grasshopper raised so much dust that the rebels thought Grant was moving again.

One of the regiments in General Ambrose E. Burnside's IX Corps, the 48th Pennsylvania Volunteers, included a large number of coal miners from Schuylkill County, Pennsylvania. Its commanding officer, Lieutenant Colonel Henry Pleasants, was an engineer who had worked for the Pennsylvania Railroad in the 1850s and had participated in the drilling of a 4,200-foot tunnel through the Alleghenies. One day late in June, the thirty-one-year-old Pleasants assembled his officers in an underground room near the front. "That goddamned fort is the only thing between us and Petersburg," he told them, adding, "I have an idea we can blow it up." Pleasants put his thoughts on paper and sent them up the chain of command. A few days later his division commander, Brigadier General Robert Potter, told Pleasants that the two of them had an appointment with the corps commander, General Burnside.

The forty-year-old Burnside was one of a number of senior generals on the Federal side who had graduated from West Point and then gone on to civil careers. After returning to service following the attack on Fort Sumter, he had led a successful operation against the North Carolina coast in 1862 and emerged as one of the army's more popular corps commanders. Burnside was modest and he took care of his troops. One soldier wrote that the men were always ready to cheer Burnside's "manly countenance, bald head and unmistakable whiskers"—muttonchop adornments that would enter the lexicon as sideburns and become a more permanent legacy than anything Burnside achieved on the battlefield.

In contrast to the soldiers of his IX Corps, many Federal officers did not hold Burnside in high esteem. In a brief stint as commander of the Army of the Potomac he had almost destroyed it in a frontal attack against Lee at Fredericksburg. Demoted to corps command, Burnside remained a soldier of modest capabilities, one who had to be kept under constant supervision.

Whatever his shortcomings, Burnside was open to innovation, as Potter and Pleasants discovered one evening in June. It was sweltering in Burnside's tent, but the corps commander put the two men at ease and listened to what Pleasants proposed: a tunnel under the rebel lines that could be filled with explosives and detonated to breach Lee's defenses. With such a breakthrough, the war could be brought to a speedy close! Burnside was impressed. He would have to take it up with Meade, but he told Pleasants to get his men to work on it. No great thought went into where the tunnel should best be dug; it was Pleasants's idea, and it would be done on his section of the line, which was only about 130 yards from the rebel defenses.

Burnside's immediate superior was the commander of the Army of the Potomac, Meade, whose usual irascibility was aggravated by the fact that he now had Grant looking over his shoulder. Meade indicated from the outset that he had no confidence in the mining scheme, but, perhaps influenced by Grant, he allowed the project to go forward. The idea of a protracted siege was no more appealing to Grant than it was to his soldiers, and the commanding general was attracted to a scheme that held out the promise of breaching Lee's defenses and ensuring the capture of Petersburg.

Digging began on June 25. The Confederate line ran roughly parallel to and east of the Jerusalem Plank Road. The land was gently rolling and relatively clear; no one worried too much about the fact that there was a distinct elevation behind the Confederate works that might assist rebel defenders.

Pleasants was beset with problems from the outset, and his later testimony before the congressional Joint Committee on the Conduct of the War only hints at what must have been daily frustrations. He had to dispose of the dirt removed from the mine, but no one was very helpful; ultimately, he was reduced to requisitioning old cracker boxes. His requests for special tools were ignored, even though the project had all the requisite approvals.

One problem particularly vexed Pleasants: he had to establish the depth and direction of the shaft to ensure that the eventual explosion would inflict serious damage. Once again, he was at the mercy of the army bureaucracy:

> I wanted an accurate instrument with which to make the necessary triangulations. I had to make them on the farthest front line, where the enemy's sharp-

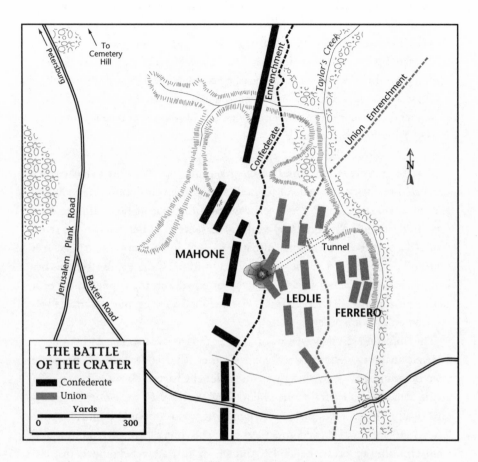

After a month of tunneling and laying explosives (see bar in the center of the map), on July 30, 1864, the Federals tried to break through to Petersburg, Virginia, by literally blowing a hole in rebel defenses. Despite slipshod planning, they might have succeeded, but for lamentable command by Ledlie and Ferrero, whose divisions were mauled in the Crater, and by Burnside, who kept sending men into the death trap.

shooters could reach me. I could not get the instrument I wanted, although
there was one at army headquarters, and General Burnside had to send to
Washington and get an old-fashioned theodolite, which was given to me. . . .
General Burnside told me that General Meade and Major Duane, chief engineer
of the Army of the Potomac, said the thing could not be done—that it was all
clap-trap and nonsense; that such a length of mine had never been excavated in
military operations, and could not be; that I would either get the men smoth-
ered, for want of air, or crushed by the failing of the earth.

A less determined man might have given up, but Pleasants persisted. An
air shaft just inside the Federal lines alleviated the ventilation problem, and
the cracker boxes proved effective in moving dirt out of the cramped, five-
foot-high tunnel. Within four weeks, Pleasants's soldier-miners had constructed a 510-foot shaft that terminated like a T in a gallery seventy-five feet
long and perpendicular to the main shaft. On July 23, the Pennsylvanians began placing 320 twenty-five-pound kegs of powder in the tunnel, most of it
in the horizontal gallery. Pleasants had asked for 560 kegs, but the charge was
reduced on Meade's order.

The Confederates, however, would not be caught by surprise. Although the
Federals maintained reasonably good security, the rebels learned, probably
from deserters, that something was up. Colonel Charles Wainwright, chief of
artillery in Major General Gouverneur K. Warren's V Corps, wrote in his diary on July 21 that rebel pickets were making good-humored inquiries about
"Burnside's mine." Their commanders took the threat seriously and initiated
countermining to locate the Yankee tunnel. By July 21, rebel sappers insisted
that they could hear the picks and shovels of their Federal counterparts. Confederate suspicions were well-founded, but the options were limited. Because
the Southerners could not simply abandon their lines, the initiative remained
with the Federals.

✦

ON JULY 26, Burnside submitted his plan of attack. He argued that although the rebels were aware of the tunneling, they did not know the location
of the tunnel or the scope of the proposed explosion. Time was of the essence,
however; the mine should be exploded and an attack launched within the next
two or three days. The assault should take place before dawn, with the lead division drawn up in formation before the mine was exploded. Each column
should include engineers to remove obstructions. In Burnside's judgment,
"our chances of success, in a plan of this kind, are more than even." Grant

agreed. In a feint to draw troops away from the Petersburg defenses, Grant ordered Major General Winfield Scott Hancock's II Corps, supported by cavalry, to make a diversionary thrust north of the James. Hancock began his move on July 26.

Meanwhile, Burnside was not idle. A recent addition to his corps was the 4th Division, made up of black troops—mostly former slaves—commanded by General Edward Ferrero and led by white officers. Burnside planned to use his entire corps in the attack, but he wanted Ferrero's division—which had seen little action, in contrast to his other depleted divisions—to lead. In the hot days of mid-July, Ferrero drilled his division in advancing along a narrow front and in deploying along both sides of what the Federals expected to be a very large crater.

It was here that things began to go wrong. On the afternoon before the attack, Meade told Burnside that Ferrero's division could not lead the advance. The entire operation was something of a gamble, and it should not be led by troops who had never been under fire. Burnside remonstrated, pointing out that Ferrero's division was his freshest and had been receiving special training. When Burnside appealed to Grant, the commanding general sided with Meade; the battle must be spearheaded by one of the white divisions, with Ferrero in support. Both Meade and Grant probably feared that if anything went wrong and Ferrero's division incurred heavy casualties, the generals would be vulnerable to charges of having callously sacrificed their black soldiers.

This crucial decision came on July 29, just twelve hours before the scheduled detonation of the mine. Burnside swallowed his annoyance and met that afternoon with the commanders of his three white divisions. General Robert B. Potter, under whom Pleasants served, was a capable commander with a good record. A second division was commanded by General Orlando B. Willcox, a solid professional who had been with the Army of the Potomac since Antietam. The third and most junior division commander was General James H. Ledlie, a civil engineer before the war, who had led a New York artillery regiment but who had only recently been promoted to division command. His division, composed largely of artillery and dismounted cavalry, was much the weakest in the IX Corps. Burnside himself had recently said of Ledlie's division, "They are worthless. They didn't enlist to fight."

As Bruce Catton has noted, the Army of the Potomac had a good many incompetent generals, but not many who were cowards. Ledlie was one of the few. In the attack before Petersburg on June 18, Ledlie had taken to the bottle, and at the climax of the battle he was far to the rear, heavily in his cups. This was embarrassing to the division, and Ledlie's staff appears to have kept this information from Burnside. Even so, the corps commander's behavior at this final conference before the battle bordered on the bizarre. Burnside had always liked to gamble; as a junior officer en route to a prewar posting, he had once gambled away his travel advance and had been obliged to borrow funds from a Louisville merchant. Now, in conference with Potter, Willcox, and Ledlie, Burnside declined to decide which unit should lead the advance, suggesting instead that his division commanders draw lots. The short straw, in vindication of Murphy's Law, went to Ledlie.

The final orders called for Ledlie's division to lead the advance through the enemy's works—or what remained of them—and thence to Cemetery Hill, about 400 yards behind the Confederate works. Ledlie was to be followed by Willcox and Potter in that order; Ferrero's would be the fourth and last division to advance. If all went well, Burnside's attack would be exploited by Ord's and Warren's corps. Earlier, Burnside had emphasized the importance of skirting the crater. Now, on the eve of the attack, the emphasis was on capturing Cemetery Hill, which was seen as the main objective. Hancock's diversionary attack had forced Lee to withdraw several divisions from the Petersburg front, and Federal prospects seemed bright.

✦

SHORTLY AFTER MIDNIGHT on July 30, Burnside's divisions were in position. Few of the Federal soldiers had slept, for word passed through the ranks that the long-rumored mine was about to go off. Three o'clock came and went, with much shuffling and glancing at watches. Pleasants had the fuse lit around 3:15 A.M., but a half hour passed without any explosion. At about 4:00 A.M., Pleasants directed Sergeant Henry Reese, a mine boss in civilian life, to investigate the delay. In one of the more nerve-racking episodes of the day, Reese, accompanied by Lieutenant Jacob Douty, entered the shaft, where they found that the fuse had died at the first splicing. The two men re-ignited the fuse and made a very rapid exit.

Lieutenant Joseph Scroggs, an officer in Ferrero's division, wrote in his diary that the suspense had become painful when, at 4:45 A.M., the mine finally detonated. Involving as it did 8,000 pounds of powder, it may have been the greatest man-made explosion up to that time. To men near the front, the blast seemed to occur in slow motion: first a long, deep rumble, then a swelling of the ground and a great rising. In Scroggs's words, "The earth shook and quivered under our feet . . . lifting the rebel fort with guns and garrison high in the air." Major William Powell of Ledlie's division remembered it as "a magnificent spectacle . . . as the mass of earth went up into the air, carrying with it men, guns, carriages, and timbers." Still another soldier felt it as "a heavy shaking of the earth, with a rumbling, muffled sound."

The men of Ledlie's division were struck dumb by what they had just seen; the Federals were almost as startled as the Confederates. A cloud of dust obscured what remained of the rebel entrenchments. Some of the attacking formations dissolved, and a few men headed for the rear. In the wake of the exploding mine, carefully placed Federal artillery—a total of 110 guns and 55 mortars—opened a thunderous barrage at Confederate defenses on either side of the Crater. Then Ledlie's advance brigade, commanded by Colonel E. G. Marshall, discovered a problem. Despite Burnside's orders, nothing had been done to remove defensive obstructions from in front of the Federals' own lines. The troops hacked out a narrow passage through the Union abatis—a maze of sharpened tree limbs—and clambered through and over the empty trenches that lay between the two lines. In the process, however, all semblance of formation was lost.

Some 130 yards ahead was the Crater—about 60 feet wide, 170 feet long, and 30 feet deep. The area was littered with guns, bodies, and timbers; a rebel artilleryman who had been completely buried except for his legs told his captors that he had been asleep at the time of the explosion and had awakened to find himself flying through the air. Twenty minutes after the explosion the men of Marshall's brigade were still staring in wonder at the smoldering crater, but they were soon pressed into it by the advance of those behind them.

Meanwhile, the Confederates were pulling themselves together. The timing of the blast had taken them by surprise, but they had known that something was brewing and were quick to respond. They had lost nearly 300 men in the explosion, and the Federal artillery barrage that ensued had driven Confederate defenders from the trenches adjacent to the Crater. But with the Federal attack slowed, Confederate artillery began to range on the Crater. From Cemetery Hill came the rattle of rebel musketry.

In the Crater, a handful of Union officers yelled themselves hoarse trying to get soldiers out of the hole and on with the attack. Ledlie, of course, was nowhere to be found; he was in a bombproof trench well within Federal lines, drinking rum supplied by a division surgeon. From time to time he would dispatch a messenger, ordering an advance toward the crest of the ridge. With the day's first light, Potter's and Willcox's divisions continued to use one narrow corridor to join the attack. Reinforcements were told to deploy into the deserted Confederate trenches on either side of the Crater, but the number of soldiers in "the hole" continued to increase.

+

MEADE HAD BELIEVED from the outset that if the attack was to succeed it
would have to do so in the first rush. But the period of about thirty minutes
when Cemetery Hill was there for the taking was now gone. Between the
Crater and Cemetery Hill was a small ravine, and Confederate commander
General William Malone put troops into it. By 6:00 A.M., fire from the ravine
was heavy. Rebel artillery also began to make itself felt. A four-gun Confederate battery north of the Crater directed canister into the Yankees who were
attempting to advance from the captured entrenchments. Federal artillery silenced several guns but could not put the battery out of action. The rebels also
had sixteen guns along the Jerusalem Plank Road, and as the July sun rose,
these began to do heavy execution.

By 6:30 it was clear that Cemetery Hill was not going to be taken easily
and might not be taken at all. But the attackers had no backup plan in case
their initial rush failed. Burnside, from his command post a quarter mile behind the Federal lines, continued to pour in his divisions; they pressed those
in front of them into the Crater, where the steep walls made any further advance difficult. General Edward Ord tried to advance his corps in support of
Burnside but found the way jammed. At 7:20 Burnside advised Meade by
field telegraph that he was doing all he could to move his men forward but
that the advance was difficult. When Meade asked angrily what was going on,
Burnside wired back that Meade's communication was "unofficer-like and un-
gentlemanly."

Ferrero's division had begun its advance at about 7:00 A.M. The division
commander was now doubtful about the enterprise, and he stopped by Burnside's command post to ask whether he was to continue the advance. Given
this chance to cut his losses, Burnside passed up the opportunity, telling Ferrero that Cemetery Hill remained his objective. Ferrero marched his black soldiers past the white troops of Ord's corps and in the direction of the Crater.
After ordering his division to advance, he stopped in Ledlie's dugout for a
drink.

Brigade and regimental commanders led the black soldiers into the fray,
moving around the southern lip of the Crater. "The fire upon them was incessant and severe," wrote Major Powell of Ledlie's staff, "and many acts of personal heroism were done here by officers and men." Powell related how one
black sergeant spotted one of his men attempting to take shelter in the Crater.
"None of your damn skulkin'!" the sergeant cried, and lifting the soldier by
the waistband of his trousers, he carried him to the crest of the Crater, threw
him over, and quickly followed.

Eventually, elements of three black regiments—perhaps 200 men— reached the little ravine from which the Confederates had been aiming such destructive fire. But the Rebels charged, and when the smoke had cleared, most bluecoats were running desperately for cover with enraged Southern infantry at their heels. To most Confederates, the North's employment of black troops was nothing short of infamous, and at the Crater no quarter was given.

At about 9:30 A.M. Meade ordered the withdrawal of all troops. This was easier said than done, for Confederate mortars by now were pouring a deadly fire into the Crater, where the Federals were packed so closely together that many could not use their weapons. As the sun rose higher, it beat down relentlessly on the wounded. Federal Lieutenant Freeman S. Bowley later recalled:

> With a dozen of my own company I went down the traverse to the Crater. . . . A full line around the crest of the Crater were loading and firing as fast as they could, and the men were dropping thick and fast, most of them shot through the head. . . . The day was fearfully hot; the wounded were crying for water, and the canteens were empty. . . . At 11 o'clock a determined charge was made by the enemy; we repulsed it, but when the fire slackened the ammunition was fearfully low.

Federal soldiers, in growing numbers, attempted to make their way back to their own lines but suffered heavy casualties. Shortly after noon, the Confederates of General William Mahone's division charged the Crater once again. Some bluecoats remembered cries of "Take the white man—kill the nigger." Black soldiers captured at the Crater were in some instances shot on the spot, and some captured white officers serving in black regiments lied about their units. This practice so angered one officer, Lieutenant Lemuel Dobbs of the 19th U.S. Colored Infantry, that when asked his unit he replied, "Nineteenth Niggers, by ——."

By one o'clock the battle was over. A Southern journalist who viewed the Crater later that day called it the most horrible sight he had ever seen. "The sides and bottom of the chasm were literally lined with Yankee dead," he informed his readers. "Some had evidently been killed with the butts of muskets as their crushed skulls and badly mashed faces too plainly indicated."

Grant was disgusted; he telegraphed General Henry Halleck in Washington that the debacle at the Crater was "the saddest affair I have witnessed in the war. . . . Such opportunity for carrying fortifications I have never seen and do not expect again to have." Two decades later, in his memoirs, Grant called the effort "a stupendous failure," one that had resulted from "inefficiency on the part of the corps commander [Burnside] and the incompetency of the division commander [Ledlie] who was sent to lead the assault."

Burnside had much to account for. Not only had he determined his order of battle by lot, but he had failed to assure that Federal defenses were cleared to facilitate the advance, and he had continued to move reinforcements into the battle after it was obvious that the Crater was a death trap. As General Ord later testified before a court of inquiry into the disaster, the soldiers in the Crater "were about as much use there as so many men at the bottom of a well."

But not all the onus belonged on Burnside. Grant and Meade made inexcusable errors. When Pleasants proposed the use of a mine, neither Grant nor Meade took any special interest, and Pleasants was left to pursue his plan in an area of the line where the topography would favor the defenders once the mine had exploded. Meade's arbitrary reduction in the size of the powder charge from 14,000 pounds to 8,000 pounds does not appear to have influenced the outcome, but it was nonetheless capricious. Then, of course, there was the question of which division should lead the advance. Although there may have been some justification for not putting a black division in the van, Meade was culpable for having altered his order of battle only hours before the mine was to explode.

Union casualties at the Crater approximated 3,800, with 504 killed, 1,881 wounded, and 1,413 missing—more than a third of the casualties came from Ferrero's division. Confederate losses totaled about 1,500, including 361 killed. The battle was not a major engagement in terms of the number of troops involved, but in strategic terms it represented Grant's last chance to gain Petersburg without a long and costly siege. The city would remain in Confederate hands until April 3, 1865, when Lee was at last compelled to abandon both Richmond and Petersburg.

There was no lack of recrimination among the Federal commanders. Horace Porter, an officer on Grant's staff, witnessed a shouting match between Meade and Burnside that, according to Porter, "went far toward confirming one's belief in the wealth and flexibility of the English language as a medium of personal dispute." The ax, however, fell selectively. Grant was held in such high esteem that Lincoln never considered replacing him. Others were less fortunate. Ledlie went home on sick leave; after returning to the army he was sent home once again, to await orders that never came. Ferrero was transferred to General Benjamin F. Butler's Army of the James. Meade wanted to court-martial Burnside, but Grant demurred; he ordered instead a court of inquiry, whose report was sufficiently damaging that Burnside requested a leave of absence from which he never returned to active service.

At the outset of the war, both armies had their share of incompetents like Ledlie, Burnside, and Ferrero. But most such officers were weeded out in the first year of fighting, and it is a reflection on the Federal high command that such bunglers remained in responsible positions in the fourth year of the war. The final word on the battle of the Crater may have been the judgment by Union colonel Charles Wainwright, who wrote of his superiors, "Surely such a lot of fools did not deserve to succeed."

THE BATTLE OF WESTPORT

NOAH ANDRE TRUDEAU

By the last half of 1864, time was running out for the Confederacy. Its greatest hope was somehow to derail the election campaign of Abraham Lincoln: Perhaps his Democratic opponent, George B. McClellan, would offer better terms if elected. That was certainly one of the principal reasons for Major General Sterling Price's invasion of Missouri in the fall—that, and the expectation of drawing troops from Sherman's drive into Georgia. Missouri was a tempting target. Its Union defenders were few and scattered, and their commanders were rejects who had been turfed out to a region where they could do the least harm. But they were fortunate in one respect: Price was their equal. A huge man, six feet two inches tall and weighing 300 pounds—he was forced to ride in a carriage—the former governor of Missouri had known little but defeat, but had never given up the dream of recapturing his home state. He was, unfortunately, the best of a bad lot in the Trans-Mississippi Department of the Confederacy, and so he was chosen to lead what became known as Price's Raid. This was not war as it was known east of the Mississippi, but a ragtag affair fought largely by cavalry, militia, and guerrilla irregulars who thought nothing of murdering prisoners. (Price had to ask one of the latter, "Bloody Bill" Anderson, to discard the scalps of Union victims fastened to his saddle.) Much of the Union force arrayed against Price was militia, some of whom the Republican governor of Kansas had hesitated to send because he was afraid of losing voters in a close election. The forces, 20,000 Union troops and 9,000 Confederates, would clash at the town of Westport, near Kansas City, Missouri, on October 23. The outcome of the largest battle west of the Mississippi may have hinged on Price's reluctance to abandon the huge wagon train he had brought to cart away the foodstuff and supplies—as well as the loot—he intended to confiscate along the way.

Noah Andre Trudeau is a director in the cultural-programs division of National Public Radio and the author of several books on the Civil War.

THE BATTLE OF WESTPORT, MISSOURI, FOUGHT WITHIN THE limits of today's greater Kansas City, was the largest Civil War land engagement west of the Mississippi. Little about it matched the traditional image of full-scale combat in that era. On the Union side, hastily mobilized militia units played a significant role in the fighting and selection of the battleground. The rebel force, the largest cavalry army ever within the Western Confederacy, had by the end of its campaign traveled an incredible 1,488 miles. The Confederates also employed ruthless guerrilla units as auxiliaries during this operation, and both sides slaughtered prisoners with routine indifference. It was a desperate last grab for glory for several Union officers who had notably failed elsewhere, and represented the pursuit of an impossible dream by a quixotic Confederate general.

That man was fifty-five-year-old Major General Sterling Price.

A certified hero of the Mexican War, a former congressman and governor of Missouri, the six-foot-two Price harbored a burning ambition to reclaim Missouri for the Confederacy. Ironically, it was Price, co-commanding at Wilson's Creek (1861) and Pea Ridge (1862), who played a major role in the engagements that dashed rebel hopes for the border state. These reverses took their toll; by 1864, the once trim Price weighed nearly 300 pounds and needed a carriage for any lengthy journey. Still, his men affectionately referred to him as "Old Pap." He had already directed so many forays into Missouri that residents there ruefully claimed five seasons for their state: spring, summer, fall, Price's Raid, and winter.

The operation that became known as Price's Raid was ordered by General Edmund Kirby Smith, responsible for the Confederate Department of the Trans-Mississippi—which encompassed the states of Missouri, Arkansas, Texas, the Indian Territory (modern Oklahoma), all of Louisiana west of the Mississippi, and a strip covering two-thirds of present-day Arizona and New Mexico. Viewed in far-off Richmond, the Trans-Mississippi was a bountiful source of supplies and manpower, but for the officers charged with its defense, the department was a nightmare. Roads were poor and the railroads few, almost all military goods were imported, and the number of men under arms seldom exceeded 50,000 at any time—this to defend 600,000 square miles.

The Western Confederacy's high-water mark came in May 1864, when two separate rebel forces defeated a Union effort to close on the vital Red River corridor from Louisiana and Arkansas. Having turned back Federal armies under Major Generals Nathaniel P. Banks and Frederick Steele, Kirby Smith believed it was time to reach again for Missouri. Price eagerly concurred; through contacts with underground sympathizers he believed that at least 30,000 Missouri volunteers were ready to join a Confederate army of liberation. His sources also indicated, quite accurately, that most regular Federal troops had been transferred out of the state. Besides Price's rosy assessment, there was pressure on Kirby Smith from the Confederate high command to do something in his department to divert U.S. troops from Sherman's drive on Atlanta.

After fending off an effort by Richmond to take 10,000 soldiers out of his department, Kirby Smith proceeded with plans for a large-scale mounted raid into Missouri. From the first, he wanted anybody but Price in command. He had a falling-out with the officer who was his first choice, and the next in line declined. This left Sterling Price, even though, in a fitness report he had written, Kirby Smith described Price as incapable of "organizing, disciplining . . . [or] operating an army." Nevertheless, at a Shreveport conference in early August, Price was put in charge, an infantry officer without cavalry experience.

Kirby Smith instructed Price to "make St. Louis the objective point." Capturing this city, he was told, "will do more toward rallying Missouri to your standard than the possession of any other point." Not surprisingly, Sterling Price saw possibilities beyond those narrowly envisioned by Kirby Smith. A Confederate success in Missouri, he felt, would weaken Lincoln in the 1864 election. Price also promised exiled Confederate governor Thomas C. Reynolds (accompanying the expedition) that he would seize Jefferson City. With a governor formally installed, the Confederate state would be a powerful symbol of the South's resurgence.

✦

ON AUGUST 28, after leaving Camden, Arkansas, Price rode to Princeton, where he took charge of the 4,000 cavalry assigned to the District of Arkansas. Also there was a sizable wagon train that contained forage for the march through devastated Arkansas and, once emptied, would be used to haul back confiscated foodstuffs and supplies. Worried that the Union garrison at Little Rock might try to intercept him, Price directed his columns to an uncontested crossing of the Arkansas River above the city at Dardanelle. He then proceeded northeasterly to the village of Pocahontas, where he connected with one of the best fighting divisions in the Trans-Mississippi, commanded by Brigadier General Joseph O. Shelby.

There Price formally organized what he called the "Army of Missouri." In addition to twelve cannon and the ponderous wagon train, there was Major General James F. Fagan's largely Arkansas division of 5,069 men, Major General John S. Marmaduke's division, predominantly of Missouri units totaling 3,756 men, and Shelby's Missouri division of 3,351. It was very much an army-in-progress. Whole regiments entered the rolls with only a small number of officers and men present for duty, the expectation being that the ranks would fill out once the Missouri volunteers began to flood in. On September 19, Price proudly reported that his three columns had entered southeastern Missouri "in fine health and spirits. We find the roads very rough and bad, but have not suffered much from that cause." There were weapons enough for only two-thirds of Price's army. The expectation was that captured Federal arsenals would supply the rest.

The U.S. commander in Missouri was Major General William S. Rosecrans, defeated at Chickamauga in 1863. Having known for some time that the Rebels were planning a raid, he refused to believe they could march unopposed into eastern Missouri because he expected that the Union forces at Little Rock under General Steele would prevent such a move. Steele, however, did nothing to stem the Rebel tide. Looking for news of Price in western or central Missouri, Rosecrans was unprepared when he learned that Shelby's men were approaching Pilot Knob, seventy-five miles south of St. Louis. Certain that this had to be a diversion for the real effort farther west, Rosecrans sent one of his subordinates, Brigadier General Thomas Ewing Jr., to assess Shelby's threat.

✦

EWING WAS MUCH HATED by Missouri Confederates. In early 1863, to destroy indigenous support for rebel guerrillas operating along the Kansas-Missouri border, Ewing issued his Order No. 11, which initiated the forcible deportation of thousands of "disloyal" families from large parts of four Missouri counties and mandated the confiscation or destruction of their property. Ewing reached Pilot Knob on September 26. There he immediately took command of a hexagonal earthwork known as Fort Davidson. By evening he had gathered enough intelligence to convince him that this was no diversion. Price, with an army Ewing overestimated at 19,000, was twenty-one miles away at Fredericktown. Following an inconclusive exchange of messages with Rosecrans in St. Louis, Ewing decided to stay and fight. For his part, Price was advised by General Shelby to bypass this outpost and to strike swiftly for St. Louis. However, Price felt that a quick victory over the hated Ewing would reap important propaganda benefits for the rebels, so he ordered Fagan's and Marmaduke's divisions to converge on Pilot Knob.

The fight that followed on September 27 was horribly mismanaged. Price's forces quickly gained possession of a dominating ring of hills, but the Confederate commander refrained from allowing a pre-assault artillery bombardment against Fort Davidson after learning there were innocent civilians inside. His sources also assured him that a portion of the garrison would not fire on the rebels, and his two principal subordinates were confident that the fort would fall before a show of force. Price ordered frontal assaults across wide-open fields. The different columns involved failed to coordinate, Ewing's men stuck to their guns, and the result was a slaughter. "I saw our boys pitching forward as we advanced every step, like wheat before a reaper," said a Confederate soldier.

As darkness ended the fighting, the rebels left more than 500 comrades lying wounded or dead. This repulse was bad enough, but that night Fort Davidson was rocked by several large explosions. When morning came, Price discovered that Ewing and the garrison had slipped away after lighting a slow fuse in the magazine. In addition, he learned from a spy that the Federals defending St. Louis had been reinforced so that they now outnumbered his own army. Out of frustration, Price allowed two of his divisions to waste the next four days fruitlessly chasing after Ewing while he proceeded with the rest toward Jefferson City to keep his promise to governor-in-exile Reynolds.

Until Pilot Knob, no one on the Union side knew for sure where Price was heading, because by crossing the Arkansas River above Little Rock, he maintained the illusion that central Missouri or even southern Kansas was his goal. The commander of the Federal Department of Kansas was the victor of Pea Ridge, Major General Samuel R. Curtis. That state, too, had been largely stripped of regular troops, so Curtis turned to the Kansas governor, Thomas Carney, to call out the militia. The problem was that Republican Carney was locked in a tough contest with a wing of his party led by the flamboyant and unscrupulous Senator James H. Lane. Carney, suspecting Curtis of pro-Lane leanings, doubted that Price's raiders posed any serious threat to Kansas. The governor allowed a few units to muster, but once the news from Pilot Knob put the rebels hundreds of miles away, he halted the mobilization. The last thing he wanted to see was his supporters tied up in militia service and kept away from their polling districts at election time.

While Carney was fretting, Rosecrans was getting help. On September 13, fourteen days before the fight at Pilot Knob, Major General Andrew J. Smith arrived in St. Louis heading 6,000 men originally slated for Sherman near Atlanta. On September 30, after feinting toward the Federal enclave, Price veered to the northwest. He moved his troopers at an average of ten miles a day, allowing them ample time to forage liberally from the countryside. Ever the politician, Price used the frequent pauses to make what one observer termed "eloquent speeches along the way." The lethargic rate of Price's advance allowed his opponents to get organized. By the time he drew near Jefferson City, the capital's defenses were fully manned by state militia units and regular troops hustled in from outlying garrisons.

The Confederates tested Jefferson City's defenses on October 7. The next day, over the choleric protestations of Governor Reynolds, Price decided to pass it by. Forty-eight hours later his columns bivouacked among the sympathetic farmers of Boonville. Price's decision not to attack Jefferson City signaled a change in Union posture from static to active defense. Already Smith's battle-tested infantry were heading west from St. Louis, while within Jefferson City, another Union officer under a cloud arrived to take charge. Major General Alfred Pleasonton, replaced as commander of the Army of the Potomac's cavalry for lackluster leadership during and after Gettysburg, now acted like a man possessed. He organized the approximately 4,100 cavalrymen available into a three-brigade division, which he placed under Brigadier General John B. Sanborn with orders to pursue Price. By the morning of October 9, Sanborn was snapping at the rebel rear guard.

The impasse between Carney and Curtis ended on October 9 when the Kansas governor sounded the tocsin. Most of the state's regular troops (about 4,000 in all) were grouped under the energetic leadership of Major General James G. Blunt, recalled from Indian fighting in western Kansas. By October 16, there were nearly 10,000 militiamen at assembly points along the Kansas-Missouri border. There was no time to issue uniforms to these civilians, so everyone wore a red badge for identification. The Kansas farm boys were soon calling themselves the "Sumach Millish," in deference to the crimson leaves they stuffed in their hat bands. Recalled one of these minutemen, "We were about as inefficient a force as could have been mobilized anywhere on earth to check the advance of a seasoned army." Curtis, titling his mixed command of militia and regulars the "Army of the Border," selected a defensive line in western Missouri along the Big Blue River. Work gangs of white volunteers and black soldiers began digging entrenchments along its west bank.

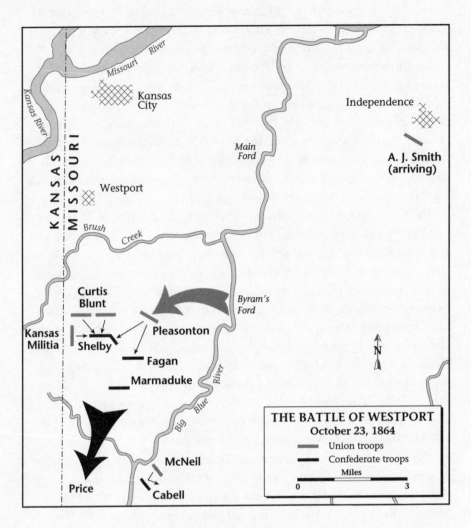

After successfully driving Blunt's vanguard out of Independence and flanking Curtis's line along the lower Big Blue River, Price attempted a knockout blow against Kansas City/Westport even as Pleasonton's cavalry closed on his rear. Fierce fighting on October 23 ended the dream of a Confederate Missouri.

✦

PRICE AND HIS MEN loitered for four days in Boonville. He picked up about 1,500 recruits (most unarmed), and met with some of the guerrilla leaders operating under the Stars and Bars. Among them was "Bloody Bill" Anderson, who rode into Price's camp fresh from a successful ambush near Centralia, Missouri, where his men had murdered 150 captured soldiers. Slung across Anderson's saddle was a collection of human scalps taken as trophies of his victories. Price, to his credit, refused to meet him until the ghastly souvenirs had been discarded. He then instructed the guerrilla chief to support the raid by destroying several bridges on the North Missouri Railroad. Anderson promptly rode off to continue his freebooting until he was killed on October 26.

There was an unwelcome reminder that the Federals would not long remain quiescent when, on October 11, several of Sanborn's units probed the Confederate outpost line east of Boonville. Two days after those clashes, Price resumed his westerly course. Despite growing evidence that the Federals were converging on him, Price continued to act as if he had all the time in the world. His cavalry army seldom moved more than 15 miles a day, a pace matched by A. J. Smith's hard-marching column, which now numbered nearly 9,000 men.

Governor Reynolds had nothing but scorn for the way Price was conducting the movement. Each morning, noted Reynolds, "the division which had marched and camped in the rear the day before passed to the front, the troops halting till it had done so." Also coming toward Price was General Blunt, moving out of Kansas with 2,000 horsemen and eight cannon. Late on October 18, after passing through Lexington and discovering Price's raiders nearby, Blunt asked General Curtis for immediate assistance.

Issues of jurisdiction regarding the use of the militia units seriously limited Curtis's tactical options. Most of the Kansas minutemen were unhappy having to cross the state border (some actually mutinied), and few would venture any great distance into Missouri. The best Curtis could do was to convince them to man the trenches along the Big Blue. The Kansas commander released 1,000 regulars to join Blunt, but no more.

Blunt's men challenged Price on October 19. The resulting firefight ended only when the outnumbered Federals withdrew through Lexington across the Little Blue River. Price knew now that enemy troops were massing in front and closing from behind. While increasing the pace somewhat, he still ordered his columns plus wagon train to continue toward Independence, Westport, and Kansas City. His orders from Kirby Smith had specified a return leg through Kansas and the Indian Territory, and it seems probable he was trying to adhere to that plan. Also on October 19, Blunt contacted some of Sanborn's men operating to the east. While there would never be regular communication between the two forces, enough messages did get through to allow each a reasonably accurate picture of the other.

To the west, Governor Carney again changed his mind. Convinced that Price was no longer approaching Kansas, and that the state of emergency could be lifted, he was preparing to disband the militia when news of Blunt's fight along the Little Blue provided hard proof that the danger was real.

After breasting a fierce defense mounted by Blunt's troopers along the Little Blue, the Confederates pushed across the river on October 21 and were soon chasing the last U.S. troopers out of Independence in actions constituting the first phase of the battle of Westport. A few miles farther west, General Curtis herded his militia into the earthworks stretching for fifteen miles along the Big Blue River. Among them was twenty-eight-year-old Private Samuel J. Reader of the 2nd Regiment, Kansas State Militia, who would later create a series of sketches and watercolors depicting the campaign. Curtis concentrated his strength where the principal road between Independence and Kansas City crossed the river. In a communication sent this day to General Rosecrans, he vowed that his army was "ready to make a stand at this place."

Only hard-fighting James Blunt was not so sanguine. He could not imagine why Price would butt against Curtis's formidable line when he could much more easily force a crossing at one of the river's upper fords. Blunt's assessment proved correct. After feinting toward the main position on the morning of October 22, Price threw the weight of his army against the Federals holding near Byram's Ford.

Price personally directed the successful attack, and the Confederates crossed in great numbers. The fighting was bitter, especially at Mockbee farm, where several hundred Kansas militiamen made a sacrificial last stand. "Down went the Federal infantry to a man," declared a Confederate, "rear rank and front rank, and a forest of bayonets seemed growing there and waving in the weird twilight." Among the captured was Private Reader, who, when cornered, decided that suicidal resistance was not for him. "Sudden Death has an ugly look, when he sternly and unexpectedly stares one in the face," reflected Reader in later years. Made a prisoner, he afterward escaped to make it home. Less lucky was Lieutenant Colonel Henry M. Greene of the 6th Kansas Volunteer Cavalry. Taken with the regimental surgeon, Greene was stripped of his boots and uniform, then shot three times. The surgeon escaped and, incredibly, Greene survived.

General Curtis, in imminent danger of being cut off, ordered everyone back to Westport and Kansas City. Hardly had Price savored this success when he learned that his rear guard, posted along the Little Blue, was retreating toward the main body under heavy pressure from the Federal cavalry. The troopers were now under direct command of General Pleasonton, who had an additional cavalry brigade with him from Smith's column. According to one of Price's officers, the Yankee riders displayed a "reckless fierceness" that he had "never seen equaled. . . ."

That night, at his headquarters in the Boston Adams house near Byram's Ford, Price pondered his two-front problem. The van of his column faced a badly shaken Union command on the outskirts of Westport, while its battered tail had finally halted on the west bank of the Big Blue at Byram's Ford. He was caught between two strong enemy wings. All that kept Price from using his cavalry's speed to elude this trap was the cumbersome train, now close to 600 wagons. Unwilling to give it up, Price had to fight to protect it. His only hope to cover its withdrawal would be to attack the Federals at Westport to pin them in Kansas City while, at the same time, fending off Pleasonton at Byram's Ford. Survival, not victory, was the goal. Accordingly, Marmaduke's division covered Byram's Ford, while Shelby and Fagan waited for dawn at Westport.

Just outside Westport, General Curtis also reviewed his options. The erratic performance of his Kansas militia had generally confirmed everyone's low expectations, and Blunt's regulars had failed to block Byram's Ford; not even the dull rumble of Pleasonton's guns could eliminate cause for serious concern. According to General Blunt, it took the forceful arguments of several people, including Jim Lane, to convince Curtis not to fall back into Kansas City. As it was, he placed most of the militia in the town's trenches as a reserve.

Pleasonton too was marshaling his forces for the coming fight. In what would prove to be the major tactical blunder of the campaign, he convinced Rosecrans to have Smith's infantry march north to support him near Independence. This was the second occasion that Smith had been redirected from an intercept course; this time it guaranteed that his men would be out of position to cut off Price south of Westport.

The stage was set for the largest Civil War battle west of the Mississippi River, with approximately 20,000 Union soldiers pitted against 9,000 Confederates. Among Federal commanders, there was a feeling that a last line had been drawn. A Kansas militiaman echoed his comrades when he declared that they waited for a fight "which we all knew would be decisive." As the long night wore on, wrote one of Curtis's officers, "we seemed encircled by the campfires of the rebels, which gleamed menacingly from the woods, as if mocking the anxiety which prevailed throughout our lines."

The cold sunrise of Sunday, October 23, saw Curtis's Federals drawn up along the north bank of Brush Creek, facing a parallel Confederate line to the south. Though shallow, the stream's precipitous banks were lined on both sides by a two-mile-thick belt of heavy timber that made troop movement difficult. Curtis had turned tactical control over to Blunt, who, characteristically, moved first by sending portions of three regular brigades across the ice-crusted creek. He did so without any immediate support, as many of the militiamen were only just arriving from Westport and Kansas City. Blunt's Federals ran into Shelby's men about a mile south of Brush Creek, also formed for a fight. After a mutual pounding that lasted about two hours (termed by one Confederate officer "the hardest battle of the campaign"), the Union troops struggled back across the stream. Both sides caught their breath and replenished empty cartridge boxes, while the artillery took up the challenge. Several Kansas militia regiments were positioned along the Brush Creek line at this time. With them was the only black unit to participate in the fighting, a section of the 2nd United States Colored Light Artillery.

When General Curtis reached the front around 11:00 A.M. he ordered the attack renewed. These assaults were driven back, but then Curtis learned from a local farmer of a narrow gulch that would provide enough concealment to allow a small column to penetrate the rebel line. Grabbing the nearest battery (the 9th Wisconsin), and an escort from the 11th Kansas Cavalry, Curtis moved into the defile.

To the east, General Pleasonton was also having a busy day. He arrived near Byram's Ford at daylight to find a brigade he had ordered to attack still getting organized. Pleasonton put its commander under arrest and replaced him with a subordinate. Soon after, his men began a series of attacks on Marmaduke's troopers, who held a rocky plateau about 900 yards west of the ford. Mounted Union cavalry tried a charge along the ford road only to be blasted back by rebel cannon. It took repeated rushes by parties of dismounted cavalry to at last engulf Marmaduke's line. A trooper in the 4th Iowa Cavalry never forgot how the men "scrambled through the gorges and clambered up the rocks, reformed hastily at the top, and dashed across the plateau with their biggest yell." As one Yankee battery hurriedly came up, deployed, and began to shoot at the retreating Rebels, Pleasonton urged them along, pointing and yelling, "Rebels, rebels, fire, fire, you damned asses!"

✦

EVEN AS MARMADUKE'S LINE GAVE WAY, Curtis and his farmer guide emerged from the gulch on the left and rear of Shelby's line. The Wisconsin gunners quickly brought their tubes to bear, pumping shells among the startled Confederates. This surprise appearance, coupled with a renewed push across Brush Creek led by General Blunt, began to force back Shelby and Pagan. The two sides repeatedly surged together for momentary positions of advantage in a fluid series of savage combats.

Along one section, a Colorado battery, setting up too far ahead of its support, was immediately charged by some Arkansas cavalry led by Colonel James H. McGehee. The Arkansans were hit on their flank by a company of the 15th Kansas Cavalry under Captain Curtis Johnson. As the charging lines meshed, Johnson and McGehee engaged in a personal combat with pistols. It ended with McGehee reported dead and Johnson wounded. Additional Federal troopers arrived to drive the Arkansas riders away from the guns. This later inspired the heroic painting of the battle N. C. Wyeth created for the Missouri capitol building, and the story was recounted in every postwar history of the engagement. However, reports of Colonel McGehee's death were much exaggerated. The hardy officer lived on to be wounded once more on October 25, and he surrendered at Shreveport on May 11, 1865.

It took a series of violent counterattacks by troops shifted over from Shelby's division to hold back Pleasonton long enough for the last of Price's men to extract themselves from the closing vise. It was about this time that most of the Kansas minutemen reached the scene. "Our militia continued to come swarming out of the forest," remarked General Curtis, "displaying a length and strength of numbers that surprised me." "It has ever been a marvel to me how any of Price's men escaped from those terrible environments," recollected one Rebel trooper. By the time the three days of fighting had ended, the battle of Westport had cost the Confederacy 492 casualties and the Union 500.

When the Federal linkup took place, Generals Pleasonton and Blunt met with General Curtis and his staff. Curtis wanted to push after Price with every soldier on hand. Pleasonton thought that his men were too worn-out and short of supplies to continue. The general himself, recorded a subordinate, "was quite sick and well-nigh exhausted." The militia commander also begged off so that his soldiers could return to Kansas in plenty of time for the election. It was finally agreed that Pleasonton's regulars and those under Blunt would go after Price. It took more time to get these troops organized, so that nearly twelve hours passed before the chase began.

This was not the only reprieve given Price this bloody day. Correctly gauging his opponent's Achilles' heel, General Pleasonton dispatched a full brigade to intercept the huge supply train. It was still morning when the Federals, under Brigadier General John McNeil, came upon the tail of the slow-moving procession. Only a prompt reaction by the troops of Brigadier General William L. Cabell's security force stopped McNeil from a quick victory. When Cabell appeared to be backed up by another brigade (actually unarmed Missouri recruits accompanying the wagons), McNeil concluded that he was facing "the entire force of the enemy." At this point he contented himself with harassing the rear guard.

Price's obstinate attachment to his supply wagons effectively squandered the precious gift of time he had received. The train, wrote one of the Southern cavalrymen, moved "as slowly as a gorged anaconda dragging its huge body over the prairie." The hard-riding Federals overtook the rebel column on October 25, at Mine Creek in Kansas. Here, an all-out charge swept the Union horsemen right into the Southern ranks, which in the words of an Iowa trooper, "fell away like a row of bricks." In about thirty minutes, 300 of Price's raiders were killed or wounded, and 900 captured. Private James Dunlevy of the 3rd Iowa secured bragging rights for countless postwar dinners when he snagged one dazed Confederate who turned out to be General Marmaduke. According to a Federal officer present, Rebel prisoners at Mine Creek found dressed in Union blue "in obedience to existing orders . . . were executed instanter."

General Price ordered a third of the wagon train destroyed after the Mine Creek disaster. On the Federal side, exhaustion, confusion, and contention among the senior officers first hobbled and then ended the pursuit, though Price's force continued to hemorrhage. Moving back through Arkansas, he furloughed whole brigades, allowing the soldiers to return to their homes with a promise (few kept) to reassemble in December. The rest slogged through the Indian Territory, where hunger, cold, and starvation became bitter companions. "This raid reminds me of the children of Israel marching through the Wilderness," wrote a rebel soldier. "But alas! We have no Moses to lead us." "Old Pap" was roundly cursed as "Goddamn Price!" Finally, on December 2, the remnants of Price's raid, some 3,500 in all, staggered into Laynesport, Arkansas.

There was little glory to pass around afterward. Generals Steele and Rosecrans were removed by U. S. Grant for their limpid response to the crisis, and Curtis was soon transferred out of Kansas to the Department of the Northwest. Pleasonton ended the war on a positive note, obtaining the brevet rank of major general in the U.S. Army. Sterling Price, forced to fend off attacks in the press that he branded "a tissue of falsehoods," asked for a court of inquiry to clear his name. It convened at Shreveport, but the war ended before any findings were issued. Price lived for a while in Mexico, then settled and died in St. Louis, finally achieving the objective point of his last campaign.

In later years, regional historians—partly to bolster their case for having the battlefield declared a national park—proclaimed Westport "the Western Gettysburg." This overstates its importance. A better comparison might be with Bentonville, North Carolina, a battle that finished off the offensive potential of a Rebel army. Despite losing nearly the entire force he had taken into Missouri and failing to realize any of his objectives, in his official report Price claimed positive results "of the most gratifying character" for the expedition. This blatant face-saving aside, the truth was that it effectively terminated organized Confederate resistance in the upper Trans-Mississippi and gave a new impetus to Federal counterinsurgency actions against guerrilla units. Through his consistent misreading of the strategic picture, his refusal to sensibly reduce the wagon train at any point in the operation, and by steadfastly applying infantry thinking to a cavalry army, Sterling Price wasted the last significant military asset of the Confederate Trans-Mississippi. As one staff officer concluded, Price had "the roar of a lion but the spring of a guinea pig." The war west of the Mississippi, begun at Wilson's Creek, was for all intents and purposes ended at Westport.

THE SECOND SURRENDER: BENNITT'S FARM, NORTH CAROLINA

JOHN M. TAYLOR

We usually assume that Lee's surrender to Grant at Appomattox on April 9, 1865, ended the Civil War. But weeks passed before forces scattered across the hundreds of former Confederate miles laid down their arms. The largest troop surrender was actually initiated eight days after Appomattox, near Durham, North Carolina, in the parlor of a farmer named James Bennitt. There, Joseph E. Johnston, commander of the only Confederate force of any size remaining in the East, some 30,000 men, met William T. Sherman and agreed on an armistice. "My small force is melting away like snow before the sun," he had told Jefferson Davis, who wanted the war to continue. But it was clear to Johnston that further resistance was not just futile but criminal. Even if Grant had not finally turned Lee's right flank at Five Forks on April 1—the only decisive battle, it has been said, is the last—Sherman and his 80,000-man Army of the Tennessee, by then the best fighting force in the world, would have been at his back by the beginning of May. Petersburg and Appomattox were only about 150 miles away, a week or so of hard marching through a demoralized land.

There would be backings and fillings in Washington, complaints about the supposed leniency of Sherman's terms, and an intervention in person by Grant: The final surrender agreement was not signed until April 26. At one point, John C. Breckinridge of Kentucky, the vice president under Buchanan, a Confederate general, and Davis's last secretary of war, accompanied Johnston to a meeting with Sherman. He saw Sherman absentmindedly take a swig of whiskey without offering any to the two Confederates. "No Kentucky gentleman would ever have taken that bottle away. He knew how much we needed it." Johnston refused to be upset—and, in fact, what developed in those tense days was one of the remarkable friendships in American history. By contrast, Lee and Grant saw each other one more time after Appomattox, on May 9, 1869, during Grant's first months in the White House. Their meeting lasted only a few chilly minutes.

John M. Taylor is the author of eight books of history and biography, most recently a reassessment of Robert E. Lee, *Duty Faithfully Performed: Robert E. Lee and His Critics,* and *Confederate Raider: Raphael Semmes of the* Alabama. Taylor lives in McLean, Virginia.

ON A SPRING DAY IN 1865, AN UNSCHEDULED TRAIN CHUFFED into the depot at Greensboro, North Carolina. The peaceful town of 2,000, all but ignored during four years of civil war, found itself a reluctant host to what remained of the government of the Confederacy. Aboard the train, which had left Danville, Virginia, twelve hours before, were President Jefferson Davis and most of his Cabinet. A second train carried a considerable cargo of Confederate gold.

Richmond had fallen on April 3. With Confederate currency now all but worthless, the ladies of the former capital were reduced to selling pastry to the Yankees in order to secure bread for their own tables. Six days later, on April 9, Robert E. Lee's Army of Northern Virginia had surrendered at Appomattox. Lee told a group of his soldiers, "I have done my best for you. My heart is too full to say more."

In the South as in the North, the fall of Richmond and the surrender by Lee were seen as signaling an end to a war that had killed more than 600,000 people and entailed total casualties of more than 1 million. Suggestions that the war might not be over were unpopular, and the reception accorded the Davis party at Greensboro was cool. One young Confederate soldier, eyeing the decrepit train that had brought Davis south from Richmond, characterized the president and his retinue as "a government on wheels . . . the marvelous and incongruous debris of the wreck of the Confederate capital."

Spring had come to North Carolina, but there was war-weariness everywhere. In Greensboro there was also fear—fear of economic collapse, fear of the embittered parolees from Lee's army who were filtering into the town, and, most of all, fear of Sherman. Sherman's Yankee army was approaching, and nothing the South could do seemed even to slow his advance.

One person for whom the war was not over was Jefferson Davis. Four years of war had left the Confederate president pale and wan, afflicted with insomnia and a variety of other ailments. But the fifty-six-year-old Mississippian was no less convinced of the justice of his cause in 1865 than he had been four years before. From Danville he had issued yet another call to arms. "We have now entered upon a new phase of the struggle," he proclaimed. "Relieved from the necessity of guarding particular points, our army will be free to move from point to point to strike the enemy. . . .

"Let us not despond then, my countrymen; but, relying on God, meet the foe with fresh defiance and . . . unconquerable hearts."

Defiance was in short supply in the Confederacy, but had Davis chosen to do so, he might have cited some numbers. Joseph E. Johnston, commanding the only Confederate force of any size in the East, still had some 30,000 men. In Mississippi and Alabama, General Richard Taylor had perhaps 20,000 more. And across the Mississippi lay Davis's main hope, a scattered force of 40,000, mostly in Texas, commanded by General Edmund Kirby Smith. Any wishful thinking based on these numbers, however, overlooked several pertinent facts. One was that Federal forces included a million men under arms with whom to confront the remaining Confederates. Another was that Sherman's army, totaling about 80,000 effectives, was close by, threatening to end all meaningful resistance east of the Mississippi.

No other name struck such fear into Southern hearts as that of William Tecumseh Sherman. The wiry, red-bearded Ohioan had begun the war in obscurity. Whereas prominent Confederates like Robert E. Lee and Joseph E. Johnston had risen to senior ranks in the Old Army, Sherman was the ex-superintendent of a little-known military academy in Louisiana. In 1861 something resembling a nervous breakdown had almost ended his Civil War career before it began. But Sherman was then assigned to serve under General Ulysses S. Grant in Kentucky. Teamed with Grant, he contributed to the series of Federal triumphs along the Mississippi that cut the Confederacy in two.

Sherman eventually was given an independent command, the Army of the Tennessee. After his augmented force had captured Atlanta in November 1864, he asked for and received permission to cut loose from his supply lines and "march to the sea." In devastating Georgia's economy en route to Savannah, Sherman set the pattern for total war.

"Cump" Sherman was an American original. He made a virtue of simple dress and simple life in the field. His men affectionately called him "Uncle Billy"; he in turn would sometimes stop and talk to groups of soldiers, bantering with them in his gruff, staccato manner. Like Davis, Sherman was something of an insomniac. He could be found in the small hours of the morning pacing his camp, poking a dying fire, visiting pickets.

Sherman hated war but liked soldiers and soldiering. Even though his brother John was a senator from Ohio, Sherman's greatest ire was reserved for politicians and newspaper reporters. He had no strong views on slavery, but had given a great deal of thought to how the war should be prosecuted. He saw the destruction of the Confederate economy as a means of hastening the end of the war, and he had no apology for the devastation his army wreaked. His march to the sea contributed only indirectly to the defeat of Lee's army, but it sapped the morale of the entire Confederacy.

Sherman had done little to control looting while his army was in South Carolina, for he shared his soldiers' animosity toward the state that had for so long been identified with secession. Discipline was tightened somewhat as the army crossed into North Carolina, and personal property was spared in some instances. Nonetheless, army foragers—or "bummers," as they were called—continued to roam the countryside in advance of the regular troops, "requisitioning" supplies. And entire pine forests, tapped for turpentine, were burned by soldiers for sport. The conflagrations were tremendous.

Sherman, at his headquarters near Smithfield, knew that organized Confederate resistance was near an end. But he was eager to see a formal surrender, lest Johnston's army disperse into guerrilla bands that might prolong the fighting indefinitely. In late March, Sherman had attended a conference aboard the gunboat *River Queen*—a meeting that had included President Abraham Lincoln, Grant, and Rear Admiral David Dixon Porter—at which Lincoln had stated his desire to get the rebel armies "back to their homes, at work on their farms and in their shops." Sherman thought he knew the kind of peace that the president had in mind. From Raleigh he wired Secretary of War Edwin Stanton, "I will accept the same terms as General Grant gave General Lee, and be careful not to complicate any points of civil policy."

✦

SHERMAN'S OUTNUMBERED OPPONENT was the makeshift Confederate army of General Joseph E. Johnston. Although Johnston had been unable to obstruct Sherman's march through the Carolinas, he had kept an army in the field and had fought tenacious delaying actions where circumstances permitted. On March 19 at Bentonville, North Carolina, he had thrown his little army against one wing of Sherman's command and had managed to come within an ace of victory.

Joe Johnston was one of the enigmas of the Civil War. The dapper, courtly Virginian made no attempt to mingle with his soldiers, as Sherman did, yet he was perhaps as respected by his men as Robert E. Lee had been by the Army of Northern Virginia. His superiors, however, had difficulties with Johnston. At the outset of the war, Davis had named three other generals, Lee among them, senior to Johnston, despite the fact that Johnston had outranked them in the Old Army. Johnston protested the slight and never forgave Jefferson Davis.

It was Johnston who had confronted Sherman in the campaign for Atlanta, and although the Virginian directed a skillful delaying action, Davis had relieved him in July 1864 for failing to halt the Yankee advance. When Johnston's successors had even worse luck against the rampaging Sherman, the wily Johnston—always formidable in defense—was restored to command. From the time of Lee's surrender, however, Johnston believed that his duty lay in making a decent peace.

At Greensboro, Davis was met by General P. G. T. Beauregard, another senior officer with whom Davis had crossed swords. Beauregard, now second in command to Johnston, had opened the war with the capture of Fort Sumter and a subsequent victory at the First Battle of Manassas. Since then his reputation had been in eclipse. At Greensboro, however, Beauregard greeted Davis cordially. He advised Davis that Johnston would be arriving the following day, April 12, and moved his headquarters, located in a baggage car, to a railroad siding within sight of Davis's train.

At the Cabinet meeting on April 12, Davis proposed re-forming the Army of Virginia, apparently ignoring the fact that the paroles granted to Lee's soldiers were conditioned on their not bearing arms against the Union. Johnston heard the president out in disdainful silence, and when he spoke it was in a tone of rebuke. In Johnston's view, the South now lacked both money and munitions, and to protract the war would be a crime. "The effect of our keeping [to] the field," he said, "would be, not to harm the enemy, but to complete the devastation of our country and the ruin of its people."

Johnston counterproposed that peace negotiations be initiated with Sherman at once. He was supported in this idea by all the Cabinet members in attendance except for Secretary of State Judah P. Benjamin. But Johnston reckoned without Jefferson Davis. Writing his memoirs two decades later, Davis recalled, "I had reason to believe that the spirit of the army in North Carolina was unbroken, for, though surrounded by circumstances well calcu-

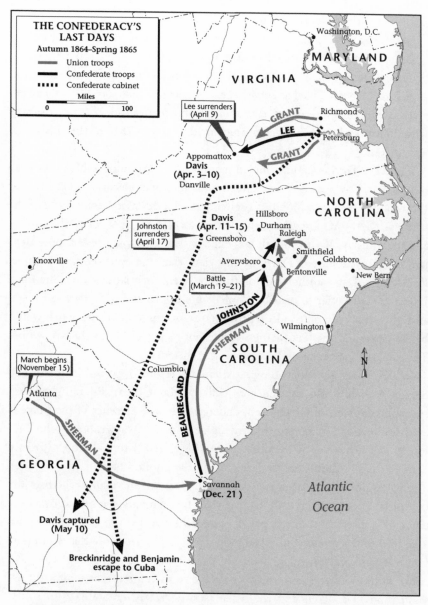

THE CONFEDERACY'S LAST DAYS
Autumn 1864–Spring 1865

— Union troops
— Confederate troops
····· Confederate cabinet

Miles
0 — 100

Confederate troops, first under Beauregard, then Johnston, fell back, fighting only rearguard actions, as Sherman marched through Georgia and South Carolina. In North Carolina they put up stiff resistance at Averysboro and Bentonville, but to no avail. Lee sued for peace at Appomattox on April 9, and Johnston at Durham on April 17. Davis was apprehended in southern Georgia in May.

lated to depress and discourage them, I had learned that they earnestly protested to their officers against . . . surrender."

That afternoon, Confederate secretary of war John C. Breckinridge arrived at Greensboro. Breckinridge had been vice president of the United States under James Buchanan, and an opponent of secession until nearly three months after First Manassas. He had served the Confederacy as a major general and enjoyed a wide measure of respect among Confederate leaders. After meeting with Johnston and Beauregard, Breckinridge agreed that further resistance was useless.

He joined Davis's Cabinet meeting on April 13. Around a table in the drab railroad car, Davis once again expressed confidence in victory, and then asked Johnston for his views. Johnston reiterated his pessimistic assessment of the previous day—"My small force is melting away like snow before the sun"—and stated flatly that the South was tired of war. Of those present, only Benjamin again supported Davis in his view that the war should continue. Reluctantly, Davis authorized Johnston to open negotiations with Sherman. Johnston could offer to disband Confederate troops and to recognize Federal authority, but only on condition that state governments in the South would be preserved and that Southerners would not be penalized for their rebellion. The status of former slaves was not even mentioned.

While Davis and his colleagues drafted a letter for Johnston to send to Sherman, their world continued to collapse about them. Pillaging soldiers roamed the streets of Greensboro, undeterred by the presence of the Confederate Cabinet and much of the army high command. Navy captain John Taylor Wood, who was a member of Davis's party, wrote, "Troops greatly demoralized, breaking into and destroying the public stores."

Because Johnston's letter was delayed in reaching Sherman—who had just established headquarters at Raleigh—their first meeting was set for April 17, eight days after Lee's surrender. Sherman had boarded the train that would take him to the rendezvous when a telegrapher ran up to say that an important telegram, in cipher, had just arrived. Sherman delayed his departure, and thirty minutes later was reading a message from Stanton that told of the assassination of Lincoln and the assault on Secretary of State William H. Seward. Swearing the telegrapher to secrecy, Sherman folded the telegram into his pocket and told the engineer to proceed.

At about 10 A.M. Sherman's train reached Durham, where a squadron of Union cavalry was waiting. Sherman and his entourage, under a white flag, rode for five miles along the Hillsboro road, where they met Johnston and his party. In Sherman's words:

We shook hands, and introduced our respective attendants. I asked if there was a place convenient where we could be private, and General Johnston said he had passed a small farmhouse a short distance back. . . . We rode back to it together side by side, our staff officers and escorts following.

Sherman and Johnston had never met, but in the course of the previous months they had developed a healthy professional respect for one another. Alone in the parlor of a farmer named James Bennitt, Sherman passed Johnston the telegram from Stanton and watched his antagonist closely.

The perspiration came out in large drops on his forehead, and he did not attempt to conceal his distress. He denounced the act as a disgrace to the age, and hoped I did not charge it to the Confederate Government. I told him I could not believe that he or General Lee, or the officers of the Confederate army, could possibly be privy to acts of assassination; but I would not say as much for Jeff. Davis.

The two soldiers quickly agreed that there should be no more fighting. But Sherman was bound by the terms that Grant had accorded Lee, and Johnston in theory was bound by the instructions that Davis had given him. The Virginian, prompted by his contempt for Jefferson Davis, had an idea: Why not "make one job of it" and settle the fate of all Confederates still under arms? Sherman was tempted, but he was also realistic. Could Johnston in fact deliver "all armies to the Rio Grande"? Johnston pointed out that Secretary of War Breckinridge was close at hand, and that Breckinridge's orders would be obeyed anywhere. It was sunset when the two generals parted, to meet the following day.

Sherman's immediate task, on returning to his headquarters, was to break the news of Lincoln's assassination. He first ordered all soldiers to camp, then issued a bulletin announcing the death of the president but exonerating the Confederate army from complicity in the assassination. Sherman and his generals watched their men closely. Many wept, and some demanded a final battle to avenge Lincoln, but Sherman's handling of the announcement prevented any serious breakdown in discipline.

On the morning of April 18, Sherman set off to meet with Johnston again, determined, in Sherman's own words, "to manifest real respect for [Lincoln's] memory by following after his death that policy which, if living, I felt certain he would have approved." At the Bennitt farmhouse, the two men resumed their talks. Johnston asked Sherman about the status of whites in the South.

Were they "the slaves of the people of the North"? Nonsense, Sherman replied; Southerners would be "equal to us in all respects" once they had submitted to Federal authority. Johnston was leading his conqueror into uncharted waters, but Sherman seemed oblivious to the danger. When Johnston suggested that they bring Breckinridge into their talks, Sherman at first refused, but when Johnston pointed out that Breckinridge might participate in his capacity as a Confederate general, Sherman assented.

Johnston and Breckinridge attempted to outline terms for Davis's personal surrender, but Sherman refused to deal on the basis of individuals. Then a courier arrived with surrender terms drafted by Confederate postmaster general John Reagan in Greensboro. Sherman looked them over, but set them aside as too general and verbose. He took pen in hand himself and began to write. At one point he rose, walked to his saddlebag, took out a bottle, and poured himself a long drink of whiskey. After sipping his drink at the window, he returned to his drafting. Shortly he passed a paper to Johnston with the remark "That's the best I can do."

Sherman's terms were sweeping. They called for all Confederate armies "now in existence" to be disbanded and all soldiers paroled. Existing state governments would continue, once their personnel had sworn allegiance to the Union. The inhabitants of all the Southern states were guaranteed their political rights, as defined by the Constitution. There was no mention of slavery, or of the status of former slaves. Sherman's only hedge was in the final paragraph, where the signatories pledged "to obtain the necessary authority . . . to carry out the above program."

Sherman and Johnston signed the document and parted on warm terms. As Johnston and Breckinridge rode away, Johnston asked what Breckinridge thought of their antagonist. "Oh, he's bright enough and a man of force, but Sherman is a hog," the Kentuckian responded. "Did you see him take that drink by himself?" asked Breckinridge—who was himself well known for his hard drinking. Johnston replied that Sherman had only been absentminded, but Breckinridge was unforgiving. "No Kentucky gentleman would ever have taken that bottle away. He knew how much we needed it."

President Andrew Johnson was meeting with his Cabinet when Grant, who was there by special invitation, outlined the terms agreed to by Sherman and Johnston. The Cabinet was shocked: The terms went far beyond those of Appomattox and constituted a virtual peace treaty. Particularly galling was the section that recognized the legality of the state governments of the Confederacy. When it became clear that the administration would not accept Sherman's agreement, Grant offered to go in person to Sherman and explain why his terms had been disapproved. The new president agreed to this suggestion and told Grant to order Sherman to annul the April 18 agreement and to draft new terms applicable only to Johnston's army.

Meanwhile, Sherman and Johnston awaited word from their respective superiors. Grant sent Sherman a telegram, then departed by oceangoing steamer to Beaufort, South Carolina. There he would have to find a train to take him north. He kept his mission a secret because he wanted to avoid publicly embarrassing Sherman. The Confederate Cabinet agreed to Sherman's terms on April 23, after Attorney General George Davis had noted cheerfully, "Taken as a whole the convention amounts to this: that the states of the Confederacy shall reenter the old Union upon the same footing on which they stood before seceding from it." Sherman received Grant's telegram that same day and took the rejection of his terms calmly. In the five days since the signing of the treaty, he may well have come to regret its scope, if not its spirit. He wrote Stanton on April 25 that "I admit my folly in embracing in a military convention any civil matters," but added that he had understood from Stanton that "the financial state of the country demanded military success and would warrant a little bending [as] to policy.

"I still believe that the General Government of the United States has made a mistake but that is none of my business."

Sherman called for a third meeting, and on April 26, seventeen days after Appomattox, he met Johnston again at Bennitt's farm; Grant, who had by then arrived in Raleigh, remained discreetly behind. Sherman explained the need for new terms of surrender, and he and Johnston quickly signed a five-point convention. It surrendered Johnston's army but took no account of other Confederate forces and avoided all political matters. As with Lee's army, officers and men were permitted to return to their homes. By establishing a rapport with Johnston, Sherman had effectively prevented any resort to guerrilla warfare on the part of Johnston's forces—the result that he had feared most.

Johnston, who may have anticipated a disavowal of Sherman's April 18 terms, issued a brief statement to his soldiers: Lee's surrender and the disintegration of the Confederacy's industrial base had "destroyed all hope of successful war." He had therefore surrendered, "to spare the blood of this gallant little army, [and] to prevent further sufferings."

So the war wound to a close. On May 4, at Mobile, Alabama, Confederate general Richard Taylor surrendered his Alabama-Mississippi command in accordance with the terms granted Lee and Johnston. Three weeks later, on May 26, the trans-Mississippi forces of General E. Kirby Smith—the last Confederate army of any size—stacked their arms. President Davis and his entourage had been captured in Georgia on May 10; the Confederate president would be incarcerated for two years before being released in 1867. Two important figures, however, broke off from the Davis group and set out on their own: Breckinridge and Benjamin eventually made it to Cuba. Breckinridge later returned with a presidential pardon; Benjamin lived out a prosperous life in England.

✦

AS THE CONFEDERACY COLLAPSED, Sherman became further involved in the surrender imbroglio. The way in which the administration repudiated his original terms soured relations between Sherman and Stanton, the acerbic secretary of war. In the course of informing the press of the terms that Sherman had offered Johnston, Stanton had suppressed a letter in which Grant had characterized Sherman as believing that he was acting in accordance with Lincoln's wishes. Rather, Stanton announced that Sherman had deliberately ignored Lincoln's instructions, as reiterated by President Johnson. Not content with these allegations of insubordination, Stanton charged Sherman with having made troop dispositions that would facilitate Davis's escape with his supposed hoard of Confederate gold, and virtually accused Sherman of disloyalty. The *New York Herald* declared that "Sherman's splendid military career is ended; he will retire under a cloud. . . . With a few unlucky strokes of his pen, he has blurred all the triumphs of his sword."

Sherman had not protested the overruling of his terms, but word of Stanton's charges infuriated him. He wrote to Grant, saying that he had never in his life disobeyed an order, "though many and many a time I have risked my life, health and reputation in obeying orders." Toward the end of May, Sherman appeared before the Committee on the Conduct of the War; he said that his April 18 terms, although not specifically authorized by Lincoln, would have been authorized by him had he lived.

In Washington, Sherman took his revenge in the most public way possible. The capital celebrated the end of the war with a two-day military review. Sherman's army paraded on the second day, May 24, and after passing President Johnson in the reviewing stand set up in front of the White House, Sherman dismounted and joined the reviewing party. He saluted the president and shook hands. But when Stanton, standing next to the president, started to extend his hand, Sherman, flushing deeply, ignored him; instead, the general shook hands with Grant and turned to watch the parade. Such was Sherman's prestige that his discourtesy went without rebuke.

Sherman never forgave Stanton. In contrast, the negotiations at Bennitt's farmhouse began a lasting friendship between Sherman and Johnston. The

Ohioan went on to become commanding general of the army, while Johnston served a term in Congress and was later appointed commissioner of railroads by President Grover Cleveland. When Sherman died in 1891—reviled in the South but widely admired in the North—one of the honorary pallbearers was Joseph E. Johnston. The day of the funeral was cold and rainy, and Johnston was by then eighty-two. "General, please put on your hat," a member of the party admonished. "You might get sick." Johnston replied, "If I were in his place, and he were standing here in mine, he would not put on his hat."

In ten days, Johnston, too, was dead.

REBEL WITHOUT A WAR:
THE *SHENANDOAH*

ROBERT F. JONES

There was no Manet to memorialize the most successful raider after the *Alabama,* the *Shenandoah,* and perhaps only the not-yet-invented moving picture could do justice to its exploits or the romantic settings of its passage around the world. A woman was even briefly involved. Like the *Alabama,* the *Shenandoah* was built in a Liverpool shipyard and was also a steam-and-sail hybrid. Commissioned after the *Alabama* went down, its mission was to damage and disperse the American whaling fleet, much of which was concentrated in the North Pacific. If the *Shenandoah*'s record of sinkings was not quite as exalted, the reason was that the end of the war cut it short. But there came the hitch. Captain James I. Waddell enjoyed his greatest successes *after* Appomattox—in fact, he did not get definite word of the end of the war until August 2, 1865. During a June rampage in the Bering Sea he took twenty-four whalers in a single week. The shot the *Shenandoah*'s thirty-two-pound Whitworth rifle fired across the bow of the *Sophia Thornton* on June 28—the day Waddell captured eleven whalers—was the last official shot of the Civil War.

Robert F. Jones is the author of seven novels and five works of nonfiction. He lives in Vermont.

THE MORNING OF OCTOBER 19, 1864, DAWNED FIERY RED over the little seaport of Funchal in the Madeira Islands, some 350 miles off the west coast of Africa. A brisk land breeze worked seaward, rattling the fronds of the palm trees and bellying the sails of small craft. On the deck of the British merchantman *Laurel,* a tall, somber, powerfully built man in civilian clothes paced impatiently, his eyes fixed on the harbor entrance to the south. The man walked with a slight limp, courtesy of a pistol ball received in a duel with a messmate some years earlier. He was James Iredell Waddell, forty years old, an Annapolis graduate, and late lieutenant in the United States Navy.

Stationed in China at the outbreak of the Civil War, the North Carolinian only learned of the hostilities toward the end of November 1861, when his returning ship, the sloop of war *John Adams,* reached the island of St. Helena in the South Atlantic. He promptly submitted his resignation to the Navy Department through his commanding officer. His letter to Secretary of the Navy Gideon Welles concluded: "In thus separating myself from associations which I have cherished for twenty years, I wish it to be understood that no doctrine of the right of secession, no wish for disunion of the States impel me, but simply because my home is the home of my people in the South, and I cannot bear arms against it or them."

When the *Adams* reached New York, Waddell made his way to Annapolis, where, after a brief reunion with his wife and child he proceeded alone by boat and wagon through Union lines to Richmond. There he soon assumed the same rank he had held, but now in the Confederate States Navy.

✦

BUMBOATS ALREADY SWARMED about the *Laurel,* offering all manner of delights to the merchantman's crew. A ship appeared at the harbor's mouth, and all eyes turned seaward. The three-masted vessel wore broad yards that could carry abundant canvas and was fitted with a tall red smokestack for those times when the winds turned fickle. She was slim and swift of line, with a low, sleek black hull. The glad banter of the bumboat crews quieted for a moment as they studied the approaching newcomer, which cruised back and forth across the harbor mouth, flying signal flags at her mastheads with a coded message intended for the *Laurel.*

Then a cry went up. *"Alabama! Outra Alabama!"* Waddell allowed himself a rare smile.

"Another *Alabama.*"

He certainly hoped so.

The black-hulled steam-sailer was the new merchant ship *Sea King* out of Liverpool, ostensibly built to carry British troops and supplies to India; but it was easy to see how the boatmen made their comparison. The *Alabama,* too, had been British-built and showed it in her design. Both ships were 220 feet long, displacing about 1,100 tons. They might have been twins when observed from above decks. But where the *Sea King* had only a single coal-fueled steam engine, generating 180 horsepower and capable of propelling her at

speeds up to ten knots, the *Alabama*'s two smaller engines combined to produce 300 horsepower, allowing her speeds up to fifteen knots under power.
The *Sea King* compensated somewhat with her greater spread of sail. She could
reel off sixteen knots with all canvas taut, where the *Alabama* could at best
turn fourteen.

Later that day, to maintain secrecy and avoid compromising Portuguese
neutrality, the *Sea King* rendezvoused with the *Laurel* off Madeira's northern
coast, where Waddell and a number of other suspiciously seaworthy "civilians" went aboard. There, after a transfer of ownership papers, flags, and
£45,000, the *Sea King* underwent a sea change. Suddenly she was the Confederate States Ship *Shenandoah,* the latest and what would prove to be the last of
the swift, evasive rebel raiders whose hit-burn-and-run tactics had plagued
the Union since the start of the Civil War.

Things were not going well for the Confederate navy in 1864. On June 19,
the *Alabama,* far and away the most successful Southern cruiser, had been
lured out of port in Cherbourg, France. Her skipper, Captain Raphael
Semmes, had accepted a challenge to engage in an "affair of honor" with the
USS *Kearsarge:* a duel to the death at sea. Southern pride could not resist. But
Semmes would have been wiser to stay safe in the neutral port. After a wild
close-range fight during which she was hulled numerous times by the Yankee's eleven-inch Dahlgren guns, the *Alabama* took her final plunge. During
nearly two years of raiding, though, she had captured sixty-five Union mer-
chantmen, fifty-five of which she had burned and sunk; another ten were released on bond. The total value of Yankee shipping put out of action:
$5,176,164.

Then, earlier in October, just as Waddell and his crew were sailing from
Liverpool aboard the *Laurel* for their rendezvous with the *Sea King,* the Confederate cruiser *Florida* had been trapped in the Brazilian port of Bahia by the
USS *Wachusetts,* sister ship of the *Kearsarge.* Since January 1863, the *Florida*
had taken thirty-seven Yankee prizes. With no escape possible, and refusing
an *Alabama*-style duel at sea, the *Florida* had instead been overwhelmed before
dawn by a sudden attack in the harbor by the Yankee vessel—a violation of
Brazilian neutrality that contravened all the rules of seagoing warfare, the
Confederates howled—and was presently being towed back to Norfolk, out of
the war for keeps.

The *Alabama* and the *Florida,* along with dozens of lesser Confederate warships and privateers, had wrought most of their havoc along Atlantic and
Caribbean shipping lanes. The *Shenandoah*'s mission, according to Waddell's
orders from James D. Bulloch, the South's canny secret agent in London who

had arranged for her purchase, would take her into hitherto unexploited waters. "You will proceed into the seas and among the islands frequented by the great American whaling fleet, a source of abundant wealth to our enemies and a nursery for their seamen," Bulloch wrote. "It is hoped that you may be able to greatly damage and disperse that fleet."

Waddell, a proud, stubborn man, was determined to do just that. While the *Laurel*'s secret cargo of Enfield rifles, revolvers, cutlasses, and eight heavy naval cannons was being manhandled onto the *Shenandoah*'s decks, the new skipper set out to recruit as many new hands as he could from the two ships' original companies. In addition to his twenty-three officers, Waddell had brought only a small cadre of ten Confederate Navy enlisted men with him. These were all seasoned veterans of the *Alabama,* survivors who had made their way to England from Cherbourg after her sinking, but he would need at least 150 hands to work and fight his ship effectively. Naively enough, his first recruiting appeals were to the sailorman's inborn sense of adventure. "I . . . pictured to them a brilliant, dashing cruise, and asked them to join the service of the Confederate States," he wrote later in his unpublished autobiography.

Only two hands at first responded—a fireman and a cabin boy. Sadder but wiser, Waddell produced a bucket of gold sovereigns. For hours he upped the ante, to as much as $35 a month for ordinary seamen, finally adding to that a substantial signing bonus of $85 for a six-month enlistment. Yet he could win over only seven more British crewmen. That brought the *Shenandoah*'s complement to a skeletal forty-two, of whom more than half were officers and petty officers—frighteningly close to the legendary peacetime military ratio of "all chiefs and no Indians." When Waddell's order "Take the ocean" was passed, the proud Southern officers had no choice but to remove their braided coats, roll up their sleeves, spit on their hands, and turn to at the anchor windlass along with the "deck apes." Otherwise they'd never have hoisted the hook.

"Thus the little adventurer entered upon her new career," Waddell wrote, "throwing out to the breeze the flag of the South. I was truly afloat."

✦

BUT PERHAPS NOT FOR LONG. In sorting through the mare's nest of gear and sea stores the *Laurel* had deposited on her decks, the *Shenandoah*'s crew could not find the gun tackles. Without them, the ship's battery—two rifled Whitworth thirty-two-pounders, two twelve-pound "chasers," and four eight-inch smoothbore carronades for her broadsides—would be only so much ballast. After a four-day search, the bolts were finally found—in a barrel of pickled beef—but the tackle blocks, which would serve as shock absorbers to prevent a gun from recoiling clean through the far side of the ship upon firing, could never be located. Until some reasonable substitutes could be liberated from a Yankee prize, the *Shenandoah* remained a toothless tiger. Relying on bluff alone, Waddell sailed south on his mission.

Ten days after dropping Madeira's green peaks below the horizon, the *Shenandoah* took her first prize. Waddell used an old privateering and naval ruse to effect the capture. On approaching the stranger, he broke out British colors at his masthead. She replied promptly with the Stars and Stripes. Then the *Shenandoah* revealed her true colors, replacing the Union Jack with the Stars and Bars of the Confederacy. A blank round from one of the twelve-pounders brought the Yankee merchantman luffing up into the wind. She proved to be a brand-new bark out of Searsport, Maine, the *Alena,* carrying $50,000 worth of railroad iron to Argentina. Her master, one Edward Staples, was brought aboard, put under oath by a prize board composed of Waddell's senior officers, his papers examined, then told: "Sir, your ship is condemned and we must sink her."

Staples said, "I've a daughter at home that that craft was named for, and it goes against me cursedly to see her destroyed. I know it's only the fortune of war, and I must take my chances with the rest. But it's damned hard, and I hope I shall have an opportunity of returning your polite attentions before this muss is over."

Boats began plying between the vessels, looting the *Alena* of every item of value the Confederates could use: books, dishes, pots and pans, basins, pitchers, and provisions. To Waddell's relief, enough tackle blocks were found to make his guns usable. The *Alena* had a crew of twelve men and three officers. Seven of the sailors decided to join the *Shenandoah*—perhaps the most valuable plunder of all.

Waddell, fearing that flames and smoke would bring down a Yankee cruiser or at least scare off other potential prizes, decided to scuttle the *Alena.* The ship's carpenter with a crew of five went aboard her and, after admiring her workmanship, bored holes below the waterline, then scurried back to the *Shenandoah.* All hands lined the rail to see her go. They watched the *Alena* settle, sails still set, until she sank stern first with a great groan of timbers and breaking masts. Huge, glassy bubbles welled up from her and broke on the surface, bearing spars and flotsam. Not one of the *Shenandoah*'s crew cheered. They, too, were sailors.

✦

THE *SHENANDOAH* WAS NOW in the "gut" of the Atlantic, the relatively tight, 1,800-mile-wide gap between the bulges of Africa and South America, through which all traffic heading for either the Cape of Good Hope or Cape Horn had to pass. Still, it would be six days before she raised her next prize, on November 5—a paltry, 150-ton schooner out of Boston, the *Charter Oak,* headed around the Horn to San Francisco with a cargo of dried fruit and canned vegetables. The skipper, Sam Gilman, was a practical Yankee. "Well, if you're going to burn her," he told the prize board, "for God's sake bring the preserved fruit aboard!"

They did.

Waddell found $200 in gold in the schooner's strongbox, but instead of appropriating it, as was his right under prize law, he turned it over to Gilman's wife—but only after extracting a promise from her that she would not give a cent to her husband.

"The promise of course was a mere pretense," he wrote in his journal that night. "The fact was I felt a compassion for the [woman] . . . the thought of inflicting unnecessary severity on a female made my heart shrink within."

Next came an elderly, wallowing bark out of Boston, the *De Godfrey,* worth only $10,000 herself but carrying $26,000 worth of beef and pork destined for Valparaiso, Chile. Unfortunately the meat was covered by a cargo of lumber that would have taken all day to shift if the edibles were to be salvaged. Waddell decided to burn it all.

"Darkness had settled when the rigging and sails took fire," wrote Lieutenant Cornelius Hunt, "but every rope could be seen as distinctly as upon a painted canvas, as the flames made their way from the deck and writhed upward like fiery serpents. Soon the yards came thundering down by the run as the lifts and halyards yielded to the devouring element, the standing rigging parted like blazing flax, and the spars simultaneously went by the board and left the hulk wrapped from stem to stern in one fierce blaze, like a floating, fiery furnace."

It didn't look quite that poetical to the *De Godfrey's* skipper. "That was a vessel which had done her duty well for forty years," he said. "She faced old Boreas in every part of the world . . . and after such a career to be destroyed by man on a calm night, on this tropic sea—too bad, too bad."

"War is a bad thing, there's no denying it," Waddell agreed.

The hundreds of prisoners he took from his prizes during the course of the cruise could only concur: Though most of the officers and (of course) any women found on board were granted free run of the ship after signing paroles, enlisted men and argumentative officers were usually confined in single leg-irons belowdecks on a diet of hardtack, bully beef, and water.

Three days after taking the *De Godfrey,* Waddell hailed a Danish brig, the

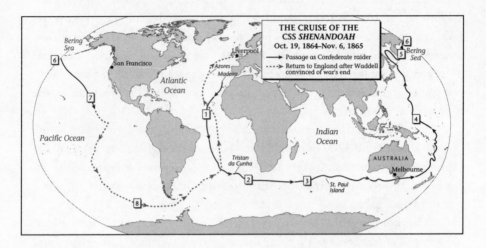

In Lieutenant Waddell's wake: (1) the Shenandoah's *first capture; (2) first New England whaler taken; (3) the* Delphine *and her tart-tongued mistress captured; (4) four Yankee whalers burned as Lee surrenders at Appomattox; (5) Waddell ignores news that the Civil War is over; (6)* Shenandoah's *biggest haul; (7) crew of British vessel finally convinces Waddell of war's end; (8) flight to England.*

Anna Jans. He arranged to have his prisoners taken to the neutral port of Rio de Janeiro. The brig's skipper agreed, "for the slight consideration of a chronometer, a barrel of beef, and one of biscuits."

Some of Waddell's officers questioned this decision. Once the prisoners were ashore, they would soon tell the American consul all about the *Shenandoah:* her last known location, course, speed, the size of her crew, condition of her armaments—all valuable intelligence to Yankee pursuers. Waddell went ahead with it anyway.

More prizes quickly followed. The slow old steam-brig *Susan,* bound from New York to Bahia with a load of coal: burned. The small, speedy schooner *Lizzie M. Stacey,* whose owner had planned to sell her in Hawaii: burned. And a spanking new Yankee clipper, the *Kate Prince* out of Portsmouth, New Hampshire: released by Waddell after her captain signed a $40,000 bond.

Waddell spared the clipper a fiery finish only because she was carrying a shipment of Cardiff coal. The British manifests were properly notarized, and to destroy the cargo would certainly harm the Confederate cause by alienating

Great Britain. The bond signed by the clipper's master was for the value of the ship alone, and since it would not come due until six months after the end of the war, which the South was clearly losing, he was delighted to affix his signature. Farther along on the cruise, Waddell would only release ships on bond when he needed them to house prisoners, who themselves would be freed only when they had signed paroles promising not to engage in further hostilities against the South.

Then, on December 3, the *Shenandoah* took the first New England whaler of the cruise. The *Edward,* out of New Bedford, Massachusetts, was processing slabs of blubber under a great plume of greasy smoke near the island of Tristan da Cunha when Waddell steamed up to take her captive. During the two days the *Shenandoah* lay alongside the whaling vessel, transferring rope, sailcloth, foul-weather gear that would come in handy at higher latitudes, nearly a ton of hardtack, and five excellent whaleboats, many curious Southerners went aboard the prize. "Blubber," reported the raider's surgeon, Dr. Charles Lining, "was much as I'd imagined it, but not so thick. It had a horrid smell and as the ship was greasy, I soon satisfied myself and came off."

After off-loading her captives at Falmouth Bay on Tristan da Cunha, where a small settlement of fifty castaways, deserters from whaling ships, and other lovers of loneliness somehow managed to eke out a living, the Confederate cruiser disappeared to the eastward. But the anxious Yankees did not have to wait long for rescue. On December 28, the USS *Iroquois* steamed into the harbor, hot on the trail of the *Shenandoah,* having learned of her presence in the South Atlantic from the *Anna Jans's* contingent of prisoners. But the Union vessel was an ancient, leaky hulk that could barely log seven knots under steam and bunkered only enough coal to cruise a few hundred miles at a crack. She posed no real threat to the rebel raider. Believing the *Shenandoah* headed for Cape Town at the tip of Africa, the *Iroquois* lumbered off in pursuit.

The *Shenandoah* was having troubles of her own. On the night of departure from Tristan, Waddell—whose worry about his ship's health was typical of commanding officers then and now—heard a barely discernible grating noise coming from the propeller shaft. Though the chief engineer could hear nothing, Waddell insisted. Next morning, after the *Shenandoah* shifted to sail, the screw was raised and, sure enough, a crack was found in the brass band coupling. There was nothing for it but to sail for Australia, where repairs could be made.

✦

FOR THREE WEEKS, making good time through the monstrous seas and strong, steady winds of the Roaring Forties, the *Shenandoah* took no prizes.

Gale after gale pummeled the ship. Everyone was cold and wet, all the time. The last goose in the poultry pen was offered up for Christmas dinner in the wardroom, stuffed with canned tomatoes, hardtack, and rum-soaked dried apples, but it was not a hit with the miserable mess. "The identical fowl that Commodore Noah took with him on his first and last cruise," joked a master's mate. Nobody laughed.

On December 29, with the weather at last abating, the *Shenandoah* raised the sails of the *Delphine,* a recently launched bark outward bound from Bangor, Maine, worth $25,000 and traveling in ballast to Burma to pick up a cargo of rice-polishing machinery. Taking her officers and crew aboard, along with the captain's young wife, Waddell burned the ship. Mrs. Lillias Nichols was a handsome woman, only twenty-six, but she had her husband totally cowed. "If I had been in command, you would never have taken the *Delphine,*" she told one officer. Noticing the stripes on Waddell's sleeve, she asked him: "Are you the pirate chief? What do you intend doing with us? I demand that we be put ashore immediately."

"The nearest land is St. Paul's Island," Waddell replied. "Would you care to be landed there?"

Lillias Nichols was seawoman enough to know that St. Paul, a dead volcanic cone well off the shipping lanes in the southern Indian Ocean, was one of the bleakest spots in the world. "No," she said, then stepped below and slammed the hatch.

As the cruise progressed, Mrs. Nichols loosened up a bit, even loaning one of the Confederate officers an illustrated magazine containing an article on the cruise of the *Alabama.* "She has tamed down somewhat," Waddell noted in his journal, "and I rather admire the discipline she has her husband under."

No more ships were taken en route to Melbourne, where the *Shenandoah* arrived on January 25, 1865—just in time to catch the monthly mail ship to London with Waddell's interim report to James Bulloch. Following maritime tradition, Waddell had kept the sextants and chronometers of the ships he had captured and burned, and the morning after arriving in Australia, he overheard Mrs. Nichols talking with her disconsolate husband in the next cabin.

"If those chronometers and sextants were mine," she said, "I guess I'd make him give them to me. I made him give me back all our books, didn't I?"

"All but one, dear," Nichols said. Inspecting the *Delphine*'s library before burning the ship, the *Shenandoah*'s executive officer, Lieutenant William Whittle, had found a copy of *Uncle Tom's Cabin.* It was quickly deep-sixed.

"I wish that steamer may be burned," Lillias Nichols said as she debarked the cruiser, feisty to the last.

There were plenty of people ashore who shared her incendiary sentiments. Even before the *Shenandoah* entered dry dock for repairs to the cracked shaft coupling, Waddell started receiving anonymous letters threatening her destruction. The American consul, William Blanchard, encouraged the raider's crew to desert, while at the same time raising Australian government concerns that Waddell was recruiting local seamen in violation of Britain's Foreign Enlistment Act. When a police inspector showed up with a warrant demanding a search of the vessel, Waddell said, "I will fight my ship rather than allow it." At one point, he wrote, "All the militia at Melbourne . . . turned out under arms, and artillery companies [were] sent to the beach to threaten the *Shenandoah*." It was a standoff. Though admiring crowds thronged the docks to view the "Rebel pirate," and her officers and crew were treated to many a dinner and drinking bash while ashore, several riots instigated by Union sympathizers also broke out in town. Fists, knives, and pistols were brandished, but no one was killed.

Though eight of his men had jumped ship during the Melbourne stay, forty-five new recruits had been smuggled aboard (unbeknownst to him, claimed Waddell). The *Shenandoah* finally sailed on February 18, 1865. The Pacific lay open before her. Word of her Melbourne appearance had not yet reached Washington, in those days before transoceanic cables, and the only Union warship in the western Pacific, the sailing sloop *Jamestown,* was laid up in a Shanghai shipyard for repairs.

Waddell had been three months without a prize when he stopped a Hawaiian-registered ship, the *Pelin,* and learned of four whalers anchored at Ascension Island (now Ponape) in the Caroline Islands. On April Fools' Day of 1865, he ghosted into the harbor and scooped them up. Their total value: $116,000. On April 9, even as his work parties were still transferring goods from the prizes prior to burning them, Robert E. Lee was surrendering at Appomattox. But Waddell did not hear the first rumor of the war's end until more than two months later.

Working northward during May toward the Kurile Islands and the Sea of Okhotsk, the *Shenandoah* found slim pickings prizewise, but ice floes up to thirty feet thick. She took a lone whaler on May 27, the *Abigail,* out of Cape Cod. Ten other whalers lay safe at anchor in open water behind an impassable fringing wall of sea ice. Waddell could see their masts, but there was no way he could approach them until wind or warming weather dispersed the fortuitously protective reef of ice. It was sheer good luck for the Yankees. But a Union turncoat named Thomas S. Manning, the *Abigail*'s second mate, was familiar with the richer whaling waters of the Aleutians and the Bering Sea, and at his urging, the *Shenandoah* turned her bows to the northeast. There, thanks to Manning, the cruiser took twenty-four vessels in a single week.

On June 22 she hit the first jackpot, capturing five New England whalers in the icy waters off Cape Navarin, Siberia. From the captain of the *Milo,* out of New Bedford, Waddell learned that the war was over. But the next day, in California newspapers taken from a different whaler, he read that Jefferson Davis had fled Richmond after Appomattox for Danville, Virginia, where he had vowed to pursue the conflict. Reason enough to continue.

The *Shenandoah* took a prize each day on June 23 and June 25, another six the next day, and—for a glorious finale—eleven vessels on June 28. One of them, the *Jireh Swift,* led her a merry chase through the ice floes before heaving to. The captain of one whaler stood by his harpoon cannon, defying capture, until Yankee common sense prevailed. Another ship, the *Sophia Thornton,* running for the sanctuary of Siberia's territorial waters, was finally stopped by a shot across her bow from the thirty-two-pound Whitworth rifle—the first time the gun had been fired in anger during the entire cruise, and, ironically, the last shot of the Civil War.

The scene provided a strange and eerily beautiful backdrop for the war's end: blue-black waters rank with the meat of flensed whales; wheeling gulls and screaming skuas; prizes laden with whale oil flaring against the hard northern skies; innocent seals and porpoises surfacing all around; flames reflected strangely on the glass-blue towers of icebergs tall as sailing ships.

Having cleaned out the Arctic and destroyed or bonded Yankee shipping worth $1,361,983 thus far, Waddell left his latest captives aboard two of the bonded captures—the *Milo* and the *General Pike*—and headed south. He had vague plans to steam into San Francisco and capture the city, or at least its shipping. But prudence won out and he continued down the coast. Then on August 2, off the tip of Baja California, Waddell hailed a British bark, the *Barracouta.* She was thirteen days out of San Francisco, and from her skipper he learned at last and incontrovertibly that the war had indeed ended. He ordered the guns stored below.

✦

THE *SHENANDOAH* WAS SUDDENLY A SHIP without a country. After long deliberation, Waddell decided to return her to Liverpool, whence she had departed ten months and some 45,000 miles earlier. Many of the officers and crew, fearing trial and imprisonment or even hanging for piracy by the vindictive Yankees, wanted to head either to Australia or South Africa. But Waddell prevailed. Still eluding any and all potential pursuers, the *Shenandoah* made her stormy way around Cape Horn and northward through the Atlantic. She raised the green coast of Ireland on November 5, and the next day steamed into the Mersey to strike the Stars and Bars for the last time.

In his final report to James Bulloch a few days later, Waddell summed up his ship's accomplishments: "The *Shenandoah* was actually cruising but eight months after the enemy's property, during which time she made thirty-eight captures, an average of a fraction over four per month. She released six on bond and destroyed thirty-two. She visited every ocean but the Antarctic. She was the only vessel that carried the flag around the world, and she flew it six months after the overthrow of the South. . . . The last gun in the defense of the South was fired from her deck on the 28th of June, Arctic Ocean. She ran a distance of 58,000 statute miles and met with no serious injury during a cruise of thirteen months. Her anchors were on her bows for eight months. She never lost a chase, and was second only to the celebrated *Alabama*. I claim for her officers and men a triumph over their enemies and over every obstacle, and for myself I claim to have done my duty."

Though the officers and crew of the *Shenandoah* were never charged with piracy, Waddell still feared reprisals against himself as her skipper. He lingered warily in Britain until 1875, when President Ulysses S. Grant personally assured him that he was welcome back home. For a while he lived in Annapolis, but the old camaraderie was gone. Finally hired by the Pacific Mail Lines to captain its new 4,000-ton liner, the *San Francisco,* Waddell found himself once more plying the waters between Melbourne and California. But he never completed his new ship's maiden voyage in 1877: On the way home from Australia, the *San Francisco* ran onto an uncharted reef off the Mexican coast. Exonerated of wrongdoing in the shipwreck, Waddell captained other vessels for the Pacific Mail Lines, until he was invited by the governor of Maryland to head the hunt for oyster pirates in Chesapeake Bay. This he did with great success. James Iredell Waddell was still at it in March 1886, when he died suddenly at the age of sixty-two.

As for the *Shenandoah,* the U.S. government—which had taken possession of the ship as soon as it reached Liverpool—sold her to the sultan of Zanzibar for $108,632.18. The sultan had planned to convert the cruiser to a luxury yacht, but when that proved too costly, the *Shenandoah,* now renamed the

Majidi, assumed duty as a lowly freighter. She lugged cargoes of coal, ivory, and gum arabic around the Indian Ocean until 1879, when on a routine trip to Bombay she tore out her bottom on an uncharted reef near the entrance to the Gulf of Aden. There she sank, swallowed by the deep like so many of her own sad victims.

ULYSSES S. GRANT'S FINAL VICTORY

JAMES M. McPHERSON

Twenty years after the Civil War, U. S. Grant's reputation and his fortunes were in tatters. Great men do not always make great presidents. Though personally honest, he had presided over notable scandals during his two terms. (Grant was probably a better chief executive than most historians have given him credit for being—or, on the glass-half-empty-half-full theory, not as bad.) Soured stock-market deals had left him deep in debt. Then, as he set out to write his memoirs, he learned that he was afflicted with incurable throat cancer. Grant soldiered on. In his introduction, he wrote that "I was reduced almost to the point of death, and it became impossible for me to attend to anything for weeks . . . I would have more hope of satisfying the expectation of the public if I could have allowed myself more time." James M. McPherson tells the story of his literary race with oblivion: In the months left to him, he wrote 300,000 words and created what may be his most enduring monument. It is a story, McPherson suggests, that may go far to explain why the Union won the war. "He knew what was in his mind. That was a rare quality in a writer or a general, but a necessary one for literary or military success."

At the archives in West Point a small piece of notepaper has been carefully preserved. The date is July 23, 1885, by which time Grant could no longer speak, and in pencil there is a four-word question to his doctor: "Is this the day?" It was.

James M. McPherson is one of the finest historians writing today. He is professor of history at Princeton University and the author of ten books, including *Battle Cry of Freedom,* which won the Pulitzer Prize in History.

When I put my pen to paper I did not know the first word that I should make
use of in writing the terms. I only knew what was in my mind, and I wished to
express it clearly, so that there could be no mistaking it.

SO WROTE ULYSSES S. GRANT IN THE SUMMER OF 1885, A FEW
weeks before he died of throat cancer. He was describing the scene in Wilmer
McLean's parlor at Appomattox Court House twenty years earlier, when he
had started to write the formal terms for the surrender of the Army of Northern Virginia. But he could have been describing his feelings in July 1884, as
he sat down to write the first of three articles for *Century* magazine's "Battles
and Leaders" series on the American Civil War.

These articles were subsequently incorporated into Grant's *Personal Memoirs,* two volumes totaling nearly 300,000 words written in a race against the
painful death that the author knew would soon overtake him. The result was
a military narrative that Mark Twain in 1885 and Edmund Wilson in 1962
judged to be the best work of its kind since Julius Caesar's *Commentaries,* and
that John Keegan in 1987 pronounced "the most revelatory autobiography of
high command to exist in any language."

Grant would have been astonished by this praise. He had resisted earlier
attempts to persuade him to write his memoirs, declaring that he had little
to say and less literary ability to say it. There is no reason to doubt his sincer-
ity in this conviction. Grant had always been loath to speak in public and
equally reluctant to consider writing for the public. As president of the
United States from 1869 to 1877, he had confined his communications to formal messages, proclamations, and executive orders drafted mainly by subordinates.

In 1880, after a post-presidential trip around the world, Grant bought a
brownstone in New York and settled down at age fifty-eight to a comfortable
retirement. He invested his life's savings in a brokerage partnership of his son
and Frederick Ward, a Wall Street high roller. Ward made a paper fortune in
speculative ventures, some of them illegal. In 1884 this house of cards collapsed with a crash that sent Ward to jail and left Grant with $180 in cash and
$150,000 in debts.

It was then that he overcame his literary shyness and accepted a commission to write three articles for the *Century.* They revealed a talent for lucid
prose, and although the $3,000 he earned for them would not begin to pay his
debts, it would at least pay the bills.

While working on the articles, however, Grant experienced growing pain in his throat. It was diagnosed in October 1884 as cancer, incurable and fatal. Grant accepted the verdict with the same outward calm and dignity that had marked his response to earlier misfortunes and triumphs alike. To earn more money for his family, he almost accepted an offer from the *Century* of the standard 10-percent royalty for his memoirs. But his friend Mark Twain, angry at being exploited by publishers, had formed his own publishing company, and he persuaded Grant to sign up with him for 70 percent of the net proceeds of sales by subscription. It was one of the few good financial decisions Grant ever made. The *Personal Memoirs* earned $450,000 for his family after his death, which came just days after he completed the final chapter.

Grant's indomitability in his battle against this grim deadline attracted almost as much attention and admiration as his victory over rebellion twenty years earlier. Both were triumphs of will and determination, of a clarity of conception and simplicity of execution that made a hard task look easy. To read Grant's memoirs with a knowledge of the circumstances in which he wrote them is to gain insight into the reasons for his military success.

In April 1885, when Grant had written a bit more than half the narrative—through the November 1863 battles of Chattanooga—he suffered a severe hemorrhage that left him apparently dying. But by an act of will, and with the help of cocaine for the pain, he recovered and returned to work. The chapters on the campaign from the Wilderness to Petersburg, written during periods of intense suffering and sleepless nights, bear witness to these conditions. The narrative becomes bogged down in details; digressions and repetition creep into the text. Just as the Union cause had reached a nadir in August 1864, with Grant blocked at Petersburg and Sherman seemingly stymied before Atlanta while war-weariness and defeatism in the North seemed sure to vanquish Lincoln in the presidential election, so did Grant's narrative flounder in these chapters.

As Grant's health temporarily improved in the late spring of 1885, so did the terse vigor of his prose. He led the reader through Sherman's capture of Atlanta and his marches through Georgia and the Carolinas, Sheridan's spectacular victories in the Shenandoah Valley, and the Army of the Potomac's campaign to Appomattox. These final chapters pulsate with the same energy that animated Union armies as they delivered their knockout blows in the winter and spring of 1864–65. Just as he had controlled the far-flung Union armies by telegraph during those final campaigns, Grant once again had the numerous threads of his narrative under control as he brought the story to its climax in Wilmer McLean's parlor.

Grant's strength of will, his determination to do the best he could with what he had, his refusal to give up or to complain about the cruelty of fate, help explain the success of both his generalship and his memoirs. These qualities were by no means common among Civil War generals. Many of them spent more time and energy clamoring for reinforcements or explaining why they could not do what they were ordered to do than they did in trying to carry out their orders. Their memoirs are full of self-serving excuses for failure, which was always somebody else's fault.

Early in his memoirs Grant described General Zachary Taylor, under whom he had served as a twenty-four-year-old lieutenant in the Mexican War. Taylor's little army won three battles against larger Mexican forces. Fearing that the general was becoming too popular and might win the Whig presidential nomination, Democratic president James Polk transferred most of Taylor's troops (including Grant's regiment) to General Winfield Scott's campaign against Mexico City. This left Taylor with only a handful of veterans and a few raw volunteer regiments. Nevertheless, he won the Battle of Buena Vista against an army three times larger than his own—and thereby ensured his election as the next president. Grant wrote nearly forty years later:

> General Taylor was not an officer to trouble the administration much with his demands, but was inclined to do the best he could with the means given him. . . . If he had thought that he was sent to perform an impossibility with the means given him, he would probably have informed the authorities of his opinion and . . . have gone on and done the best he could with the means at hand without parading his grievance before the public. No soldier could face either danger or responsibility more calmly than he. These are qualities more rarely found than genius or physical courage.

Whether subconsciously or not, with these words Grant described himself as much as he described Taylor. Old Zack became a role model for young Ulysses. "General Taylor never made any show or parade either of uniform or retinue." Neither did Grant when he was commanding general. "In dress he was possibly too plain, rarely wearing anything in the field to indicate his rank." Nor did Grant. "But he was known to every soldier in his army, and was respected by all." The same was true of Grant in the next war. "Taylor was not a conversationalist." Neither was Grant. "But on paper he could put his meaning so plainly that there could be no mistaking it. He knew how to express what he wanted to say in the fewest well-chosen words, but would not sacrifice meaning to the construction of high-sounding sentences." This describes Grant's prose perfectly, his memoirs as well as his wartime orders to subordinates.

This question of "plain meaning" is no small matter. There are many Civil War examples of vague, ambiguous, confusing orders that affected the outcome of a campaign or battle in unfortunate ways. Grant's orders, by contrast, were invariably clear and concise. Many of his wartime associates commented on this. George B. Meade's chief of staff wrote that

> there is one striking feature of Grant's orders; no matter how hurriedly he may write them on the field, no one ever has the slightest doubt as to their meaning, or even has to read them over a second time to understand them.

Unlike many other generals, Grant did not rely on staff officers to draft his orders and dispatches; he wrote them himself. Horace Porter of General George Thomas's staff first met Grant at Chattanooga in October 1863. After a daylong inspection of the besieged Army of the Cumberland, which was in dire condition, Grant returned to his headquarters and sat down to write. Porter was impressed

> by the manner in which he went to work at his correspondence. . . . His work was performed swiftly and uninterruptedly, but without any marked display of nervous energy. His thoughts flowed as freely from his mind as the ink from his , pen; he was never at a loss for an expression, and seldom interlined a word or made a material correction.

After a couple of hours, Grant gathered up the dispatches and had them sent by telegraph or courier to every point on the compass from Vicksburg to Washington, giving orders, Porter said, "for the taking of vigorous and comprehensive steps in every direction throughout his new and extensive command." These orders launched the movements that opened a new supply line into Chattanooga, brought in reinforcements, and prepared the Union armies for the campaigns that lifted the sieges of Chattanooga and Knoxville and drove Braxton Bragg's demoralized Army of Tennessee into Georgia after the assault on Missionary Ridge.

Porter, amazed by Grant's "singular mental powers and his rare military qualities," joined Grant's staff and served with him from the Wilderness to Appomattox. His own version of those events, entitled *Campaigning with Grant,* is next in value only to Grant's memoirs as a firsthand account of command decisions in that campaign.

Porter had particularly noticed how Grant never hesitated but wrote steadily, as if the thoughts flowed directly from his mind to the paper. How can this be reconciled with Grant's recollection that when he sat down to write out the surrender terms for Lee's army, he had no idea how to start? How can it be reconciled with his initial reluctance to write his memoirs because he thought he had no literary ability? The truth is, as he admitted in his account of writing the surrender terms, "I only knew what was in my mind."

There lies the explanation of Grant's ability as a writer: He knew what was in his mind. That is a rare quality in a writer or a general, but a necessary one for literary or military success. Once unlocked by an act of will, the mind poured out the words smoothly.

Grant had another and probably related talent, which might be described as a "topographical memory." He could remember every feature of the terrain over which he traveled, and find his way over it again; he could also look at a map and visualize the features of terrain he had never seen. Horace Porter noted that any map "seemed to become photographed indelibly on his brain, and he could follow its features without referring to it again."

Grant could see in his mind the disposition of troops over thousands of square miles, visualize their relationships to roads and terrain, and know how and where to move them to take advantage of topography. Most important, he could transpose this image into words that could be understood by others— though the modern reader of his memoirs would be well advised to have a set of Civil War maps on hand to match the maps in Grant's head.

During the last stages of his illness, unable to speak, Grant penned a note to his physician: "A verb is anything that signifies to be; to do; to suffer; I signify all three." It is not surprising that he would think of verbs at such a time; they are what give his writing its terse, muscular quality. As agents to translate thought into action, verbs offer a clue to the secret of Grant's military success, which also consisted of translating thought into action. Consider these orders to Sherman early in the Vicksburg campaign:

> You will proceed . . . to Memphis, taking with you one division of your present command. On your arrival at Memphis you will assume command of all the troops there . . . and organize them into brigades and divisions in your own army. As soon as possible move with them down the river to the vicinity of Vicksburg, and with the cooperation of the gunboat fleet . . . proceed to the reduction of that place.

In the manner of Caesar's *Veni, vidi, vici,* these sentences bristle with verbs of decision: "Proceed . . . take . . . assume command . . . organize . . . move . . . proceed to the reduction. . . ." Note also the virtual absence of adverbs and of all but essential adjectives. Grant used these modifiers only when necessary to his meaning. Take, for example, his famous reply to General Simon B. Buckner's request to negotiate terms for the surrender of Fort Donelson: "No terms except an unconditional and immediate surrender can be accepted. I propose to move immediately on your works." Not an excess word here; the adjectives and adverb strengthen and clarify the message; the words produce action— they become action.

The will to act, symbolized by the emphasis on active verbs in Grant's writing, illustrates another crucial facet of his generalship—what Grant himself called "moral courage." This was a quality different from and rarer than physical courage. Grant and many other men who became Civil War generals had demonstrated physical courage under fire in the Mexican War as junior officers carrying out the orders of their superiors. Moral courage involved a willingness to make decisions and initiate the orders. Some officers who were physically brave shrank from this responsibility, because decision risked error, and initiative risked failure.

This was George B. McClellan's defect as a commander: He was afraid to risk his army in an offensive because it might be defeated. He lacked the moral courage to act, to confront that terrible moment of truth, to decide and to risk. Grant, Lee, Jackson, Sheridan, and other victorious Civil War commanders had moral courage; they understood that without risking defeat they could never achieve victory.

Grant describes how he first confronted that moment of truth and learned the lesson of moral courage. His initial Civil War command was as colonel of the Twenty-first Illinois. In July 1861 the regiment was ordered to find Tom Harris's rebel guerrilla outfit in Missouri and attack it. Grant says:

> My sensations as we approached what I supposed might be "a field of battle" were anything but agreeable. I had been in all the engagements in Mexico that it was possible for one person to be in; but not in command. If some one else had been colonel and I had been lieutenant-colonel I do not think I would have felt any trepidation. . . . As we approached the brow of the hill from which it was expected we could see Harris' camp, and possibly find his men formed ready to meet us, my heart kept getting higher and higher until it felt to me as though it was in my throat.

But when the Twenty-first reached Harris's camp, they found it abandoned. Wrote Grant:

> My heart resumed its place. It occurred to me at once that Harris had been as much afraid of me as I had been of him. This was a view of the question I had never taken before; but it was one I never forgot afterwards. From that event to the close of the war, I never experienced trepidation upon confronting an enemy, though I always felt more or less anxiety. I never forgot that he had as much reason to fear my forces as I had his. The lesson was valuable.

Grant may have taken that lesson too much to heart; he forgot that there were times when he *should* fear the enemy's intentions. This lesson he learned the hard way, at both Fort Donelson and Shiloh. After the failure of the Union gunboats to subdue the Donelson batteries on February 14, 1862, Grant went downriver several miles to consult with Flag Officer Andrew Foote of the gunboat fleet. Grant was therefore absent on the morning of February 15 when the Confederate garrison launched its breakout attack. He confessed that "when I left the National line to visit Flag-officer Foote, I had no idea that there would be any engagement on land unless I brought it on myself."

It took one more such experience to drive this lesson home. This time it was the Confederate attack at Shiloh on April 6, 1862, when Grant was again absent at his headquarters seven miles downriver. "The fact is," he admits in the memoirs, "I regarded the campaign we were engaged in as an offensive one and had no idea that the enemy would leave strong entrenchments to take the initiative." Thereafter he had a healthier respect for the enemy's capabilities.

But this never paralyzed him or caused him to yield the initiative. At both Fort Donelson and Shiloh, Grant's recognition that the enemy still had as much reason to fear him as he to fear the enemy enabled him to wrest the initiative away and grasp victory. Upon returning to his troops at Donelson after a fast ride over icy roads, he calmly took charge and re-formed his broken lines. After hearing reports of the morning's fighting, he told a member of his staff, "Some of our men are pretty badly demoralized, but the enemy must be more so, for he has attempted to force his way out, but has fallen back: the one who attacks first now will be victorious and the enemy will have to be in a hurry if he gets ahead of me." Suiting action to words, he ordered a counterattack, drove back, and penned in the Confederate forces, and compelled their surrender.

At Shiloh, Grant conducted a fighting fallback until dusk stopped the

Confederate advance. His army was crippled, but he knew that the Confederates were just as badly hurt and that he would be reinforced during the night. Thus he replied to one subordinate who advised retreat: "Retreat? No. I propose to attack at daylight and whip them." And he did.

One of Grant's superstitions, described in the memoirs, was a dread of turning back or retracing his steps once he had set forth on a journey. If he took the wrong road or made a wrong turn, he would go across country or forward to the next turn rather than go back. This superstition reinforced his risk-taking inclination as a military commander. Crucial decisions in the Vicksburg and Wilderness campaigns illustrate this trait.

During the winter of 1862–63, Grant's river-based campaign against Vicksburg bogged down in the Louisiana and Mississippi swamps. While criticism mounted to an angry crescendo in the North, Grant remained calm and carefully worked out a daring plan: to run the gunboats past Vicksburg; cross his army to the east bank; cut loose from his base and communications; and live off the land while operating in Vicksburg's rear.

This was the highest-risk operation imaginable. Grant's staff and his most trusted subordinates, especially Sherman, opposed the plan. Sherman "expressed his alarm at the move I had ordered," wrote Grant, "saying that I was putting myself in a position voluntarily which an enemy would be glad to manoeuvre a year—or a long time—to get me in." Go back to Memphis, advised Sherman, establish a secure base of supplies, and move against Vicksburg overland, keeping open your communications—in other words, wage an orthodox campaign by the book.

But Grant threw away the book. He was confident his army could live off the land and substitute mobility for secure communications. "The country is already disheartened over the lack of success on the part of our armies," he told Sherman. He goes on to explain in the memoirs:

> If we went back as far as Memphis it would discourage the people so much that bases of supplies would be of no use: neither men to hold them nor supplies to put in them would be furnished. The problem for us was to move forward to a decisive victory, or our cause was lost. No progress was being made in any other field, and we had to go on.

Go on he did, to what military historians almost universally regard as the most brilliant and innovative campaign of the Civil War.

As Grant departed Washington a year later to set forth on what became the campaign from the Wilderness to Appomattox, he told President Lincoln that "whatever happens, there will be no turning back." What happened in the Wilderness, however, might have caused other Northern commanders to turn back; indeed, similar events in the same place had caused Joe Hooker to turn back exactly a year earlier.

On May 6, 1864, the second day of the Wilderness, Lee attacked and bent back both of Grant's flanks. That evening a distraught brigadier galloped up to Grant's headquarters to report disaster on the right. "I know Lee's methods well by past experience," panted the officer, in words recorded by Horace Porter. "He will throw his whole army between us and the Rapidan, and cut us off completely."

Grant slowly removed a cigar from his mouth and fixed the man with an icy stare. "Oh, I am heartily tired of hearing about what Lee is going to do. Some of you always seem to think he is suddenly going to turn a double somersault, and land in our rear and on both of our flanks at the same time. Go back to your command, and try to think what we are going to do ourselves, instead of what Lee is going to do."

Once again Grant suited action to words. He ordered preparations for a movement. Men in the ranks who had fought the Battle of Chancellorsville in these woods thought it was another retreat, but when they realized that this time they were moving south, the scales fell from their eyes. It was not "another Chancellorsville . . . another skedaddle" after all. "Our spirits rose," wrote a veteran who recalled this moment as a turning point of the war. "We marched free. The men began to sing." When Grant cantered by one corps, the soldiers recognized him and sent up a cheer. For the first time in a Virginia campaign, the Army of the Potomac was staying on the offensive after its initial battle. Nor did it turn back or retrace its steps until Appomattox eleven months later.

These incidents in the Wilderness do not come from the memoirs. Though Grant keeps himself at the center of the story, his memoirs exhibit less egotism than is typical of the genre. Grant is generous with praise of other officers (especially Sherman, Sheridan, and Meade) and sparing with criticism, carping, and backbiting. He is also willing to admit mistakes, most notably: "I have always regretted that the last assault at Cold Harbor was ever made. . . . No advantage whatever was gained to compensate for the heavy loss we sustained."

But Grant did not admit culpability for the heavy Union casualties in the whole campaign of May–June 1864. Nor should he have done so, despite the label of "butcher" and the subsequent analyses of his "campaign of attrition."